# INDUSTRIALIZING AFRICA

# INDUSTRIALIZING AFRICA:

## DEVELOPMENT OPTIONS AND CHALLENGES FOR THE 21ST CENTURY

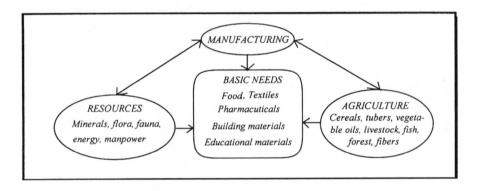

## MAKONNEN ALEMAYEHU

## Africa World Press, Inc.

P.O. Box 1892
Trenton, NJ 08607

P.O. Box 48
Asmara, ERITREA

# Africa World Press, Inc.

P.O. Box 1892    P.O. Box 48
Trenton, NJ 08607    Asmara, ERITREA

HC
800
.A695
2000

Book design: Wanjiku Ngugi
Cover design: Jonathan Gullery

**Library of Congress Cataloging-in-Publication Data**

Alemayehu, Makonnen.
   Industrializing Africa: development options and challenges for the 21st cnetury / Makonnen Alemayehu.
          p.   cm.
   Includes bibliographical references and index.
   ISBN 0-86543-652-5.
   ISBN 0-86543-653-3  (pbk)
      1. Industrialization--Africa.     I. Title.
   HC800.A695  1999
   338.96--dc21                                        99-14464
                                                        CIP

*Dedicated to*
*the Ethiopian People's Revolutionary Democratic Front*
*(EPRDF)*
*and the People of Ethiopia*

# CONTENTS

# ACKNOWLEDGMENTS

I am very grateful to the many people who helped me and facilitated my task of preparing this book. Their names are far too many to mention here. I am particularly indebted to Mr. Peter Lillie, a former official of the United Nations Industrial Development Organization. He edited the draft manuscript at a stage when it was about half complete and offered valuable comments. Many thanks are due to those who helped me acquire the skills needed to use a computer. My thanks also go to those who provided me with or assisted me in locating and obtaining reference materials, in particular, helpful sources at the Economic Commission for Africa (ECA), the Organization of African Unity (OAU), the United Nations Industrial Development Organization (UNIDO) Country Director in Ethiopia, Harvard University libraries (Lamont and the John Kennedy School of Government), the Library of Congress, and the Framingham Public Library.

# EXPLANATORY NOTES AND ABBREVIATIONS

## EXPLANATORY NOTES

| | |
|---|---|
| $ | United States dollars |
| - | Magnitude nil or negligible |
| … | Data not available |
| b | Billion (1,000 million) |
| bb | Billion barrels |
| cu m=m³ | Cubic meter |
| Gcal | Gigcalorie |
| Gw | Gigawatts |
| Ha | Hectares |
| K | Kilo=1000 grams |
| Kcal | Kilocalories |
| Kg | Kilograms |
| Kgce | Kilograms coal equivalent |
| Kwh | Kilowatt-hours |
| LPG | Liquefied Petroleum Gas |
| m | Million |
| mm | Millimeter |
| mt | Million tons |
| tcf/tcm | Trillion cubic feet/trillion cubic meters |
| tpe | Tons of petroleum equivalent |
| twh | Trillion watt hour |
| t/y | Tons per year |

| | |
|---|---|
| t or ton | Metric ton |
| w | Watt |

## ABBREVIATIONS

| | |
|---|---|
| ACP | African, Caribbean and Pacific (countries under the Lome convention) |
| ADB | African Development Bank |
| AEC | African Economic Community |
| AMU | Arab Maghreb Union |
| CEAO | Communaute Economique d'Afrique Orientale |
| CFA | Communaute Financiere Africaine |
| CILSS | Comite Permanent Ineretats de Lute contre la Secheresse dans la Sahel |
| ECA | Economic Commission for Africa |
| ECA/OAU/ UNIDO | Joint ECA/OAU/UNIDO Secretariat |
| ECCAS | Economic Community of Central African States |
| ECOWAS | Economic Community of West African States |
| ESCAP | Economic and Social Commission for Asia and the Pacific |
| EU | European Union |
| FADINAP | Fertilizer Advisory, Development and Information Network for Asia and the Pacific |
| FAO | Food and Agricultural Organization of the United Nations |
| GDP | Gross Domestic Product |
| GFCF | Gross Fixed Capital Formation |
| GNP | Gross National Product |
| GSP | General System of Preferences |

| | |
|---|---|
| IBRD | International Bank for Reconstruction and Development (World Bank) |
| ICSID | International Convention on Settlement of Investment Disputes |
| IDA | International Development Decade for Africa |
| IDDA | Industrial Development Decade |
| IFAD | International Food and Agriculture Development |
| IFC | International Finance Corporation |
| IGAD | Inter-Governmental Authority for Development (formerly IGADD) |
| ILO | International Labor Organization |
| IMF | International Monetary Fund |
| ISIC | International Standard Industrial Classification |
| ITC | International Trade Center |
| LDC | Least Developed Country |
| ITDG | Intermediate Technology Development Group |
| LPA | Lagos Plan of Action |
| LPDAIDC | Lima Declaration and Plan of Action on Industrial Development and Cooperation |
| MIGA | Multilateral Investment Guarantee Agency |
| MVA | Manufacturing Value added |
| NICs | Newly Industrialized Countries |
| OAU | Organization of African Unity |
| ODA | Official Development Assistance |
| OECD | Organization for Economic Cooperation and Development |
| OPEC | Organization of Petroleum Exporting Countries |
| PTA | Preferential Trade Area for Eastern and Southern Africa |

| | |
|---|---|
| SADC | Southern Africa Development Community (formerly SADCC) |
| SAP | Structural Adjustment Program |
| SID | Society for International development |
| ITDG | Intermediate Technology Development Group |
| SITC | Standard International Trade Classification |
| UDEAC | Union Duoiniere et Economique de l'Afrique Centrale |
| UN | United Nations |
| UNCTAD | United Nations Conference on Trade and development |
| UNCTC | United Nations Center on Transnational corporations |
| UNDP | United Nations Development Program |
| UNECE | United Nations Economic Commission for Europe |
| UNESCO | United Nations Educational, Scientific and Cultural Organization |
| UN-NADAF | United Nations New Agenda for the Development of Africa |
| UN-PAAERD | United Nations Program of Action for African Recovery and Development |
| UNTACDA | United Nations Transport and Communications Decade for Africa |
| UNIDO | United Nations Industrial Development Organization |
| UNIFEM | United Nations Development Fund for Women |
| USAID | United Nations Agency for International Development |
| WHO | World Health Organization |
| WTO | World Trade Organization |

For more abbreviations of institutions see annexes 4.9 and 15.3

## CHAPTER 1

# INTRODUCTION

The African continent is second only to Asia in size. It is characterized by diversity and comprises 53 states (excluding Western Sahara whose fate remains to be determined as well as Reunion, St. Helena, and the Canary Islands)—six islands, 15 landlocked states and 32 coastal nations at different stages of development. A number of these are mini-states in terms of population. Some are equally minor in terms of area. Some are richly endowed; others are not. They follow different administrative systems (mostly inherited from their former colonizers), practice various economic systems, and fall into different levels of industrial development.

It is now over three decades since the majority of African countries achieved independence. Despite the political, social and economic difficulties they had to contend with, practically all of them made significant progress until the early 1970s. With the advent of the oil crisis in 1973, that triggered a series of related crises, the outlook was less hopeful. In subsequent years, many countries went from bad to worse. Their economies and social conditions deteriorated. For many of them, per capita incomes and food production/availability have continued to fall. In short, many of them are now poorer than they were in the early 1970s and are importing increasing quantities of food that they cannot afford—imports that have to be supplemented by food aid.

Recognizing this stark reality, African countries, individually and collectively, have been trying to reverse the downward spiral of their economic and social conditions. They have given highest priority to agriculture and activities supporting agriculture so that they can feed their peoples.

Experience in the 1980s and early 1990s has shown that African countries have no hope of relief, if they continue with their traditional—now obsolete—ways of farming. Production structures need to be transformed fundamentally. Farming methods need to be modernized. More appropriate inputs, particularly, seeds, agricultural chemicals (fertilizers and pesticides), and agricultural equipment (tools, implements, machinery, and irrigation equipment) need to be used. These should increase production of food (and other basic needs) and reduce food losses. In view of the magnitude of the latter, a significant decrease in food losses alone could substantially reduce or wipe out the current food deficit plaguing Africa.

Most African countries import the agricultural equipment and chemicals they require. However, given their dwindling foreign exchange earnings following the 1973 and subsequent oil crises that drove up prices for industrial goods, their capacity to import has been severely and increasingly limited. Under the circumstances, they have no option but to produce a good part of their needs themselves if they are to break free of their perpetual dependency on the world community for food and other aid.

The above conclusion is the main premise for this book, the objective of which is to promote African industrialization through the development of industries that provide essential inputs to agriculture, process agricultural products, and facilitate the development of small-scale industries. The industries to be developed will have to be fully integrated, from the production and extraction of raw materials to local processing and fabrication, if sustained and meaningful industrial development is to take place. Industrial development based on imported basic metals (iron and steel, copper and aluminum) and basic chemicals (acids, bases, and intermediates) would merely mean dependency in a different form, which the African countries can ill afford.

Unless Africa is assisted in the development of the above industries, her peoples' survival will continue to be an increasingly onerous burden on the international community. The choice before that community is obvious. First and foremost, it has to pay fair prices to African export commodities and help Africa to build up the capacity to produce industrial inputs for agriculture locally, to process its agricultural commodities, and to establish small-scale industries. The end result of such assistance will be mutually beneficial since, ultimately, Africa will be able to purchase increasing quantities of goods and services from the countries providing assistance and thereby contribute to both increased international trade and the creation of employment in the same countries. It should be noted here that, with economies maturing over time in the other developing regions, Africa will eventually lead the world in economic growth rates. Assistance from the world community could enhance this process.

The term "industry" in its broader sense comprises manufacturing, mining, utilities, and construction. This book deals with the manufacturing component only. Manufacturing comprises the mechanical and chemical transformation of agricultural and mineral resources into basic, intermediate, and final products. Manufacturing and industry are used interchangeably in this restricted sense.

The book is divided into three parts, excluding Chapter 1 (Introduction). Part One: Political, Social, and Economic Conditions, comprises chapters 2 and 3. It is targeted at readers who may not have had adequate exposure to Africa, particularly potential investors unfamiliar with or less informed on investment opportunities in Africa.

Chapter 2 deals with the socio-political conditions of the continent. The political and social instabilities that characterize the continent are attributable in the main to the legacy of colonialism, the Cold War, and shortcomings in governance. Chapter 3 summarizes the economic conditions in as comprehensive a manner as possible. It reviews major economic indicators, past and current economic systems, and the attempts made to achieve economic cooperation and integration.

Part Two: Industrial Possibilities, consists of three chapters, one each on resources, industrial development, and industrial constraints. Chapter 4 describes the great potential wealth in resources and shows that Africa's natural and human (although unskilled) resources are abundant and awaiting orderly utilization. Chapter 5 reviews industrial development before and after independence. It describes attempts at and experiences in different industrialization strategies adopted by African countries. Its final section provides performance indicators of manufacturing. Chapter 6 has to do with factors constraining African industrial development. It reviews progress over the past 35 years following independence in most countries and concludes with a section on African countries' endeavors to improve the investment climate and to attract foreign investment.

Part Three: Prospects for Industrial Development, constitutes the core of the book and comprises Chapters 7 to 16. It gives indications of what can and should be done to industrialize Africa.

Chapter 7 identifies priority industries based on basic needs. It reviews the paths taken by other successful countries, particularly the newly industrializing countries (NICs), and focuses on the need to address the increasing dependency on foreign food aid. It emphasizes the basic needs and the agro-based approach and suggests various ways of implementing such an approach.

Chapter 8 focuses on the industrial branches oriented towards basic needs: food, pharmaceuticals, and textiles as well as building, educational, and packaging materials. In most cases, rough indications are given of supply/demand gaps; priority products are identified; stages of development are reviewed; and development strategies are suggested.

Chapters 9 to 13 deal with the implications of Chapter 8 in terms of the chemical, metallurgical, and engineering subsectors, i.e., the manufacture of chemicals, metals, and machinery and equipment required to produce the basic needs as defined in that chapter.

Chapter 14 discusses options for implementing the industrial priorities. The options considered are: industrialization based on (i) the import of industrial inputs and (ii) local production of industrial inputs. The second variant appears the logical choice as the first option is virtually impossible given the diminishing availability of foreign exchange. The chapter argues for the development of selected basic industries in the chemical, metal, and engineering subsectors that provide inputs to agriculture, process agricultural commodities, transport agricultural inputs and outputs, and enable the development of small-scale industries as well as industries producing other basic needs.

Chapter 15 deals with strategies for development. Integration is the key word in this chapter. It includes integration at the sectoral, inter-sectoral, country, and inter-country levels. Modalities of cooperation and implementation at the national, multinational, and international levels are suggested in this chapter. The chapter closes with a discussion on financial resources and suggestions for mobilizing such resources. The final chapter (16) deals with conclusions and recommendations on crucial constraints.

It is obviously very difficult, if not impossible, to write a book on African industry which, of necessity, involves generalizing about such a broad range of industrial experiences in so many countries. This book, nevertheless, attempts to do so. The shortcomings of the approach, in part, arise from having to treat such different countries as if they were homogenous—something they are not. Statistical figures on Africa[1] as a region which are sum totals of all or the majority of countries mask large disparities among countries, groups of countries and subregions. Quantities at the country level may and do range from nil in a small "least developed country" (LDC) to substantial amounts in a relatively large country. A similar situation pertains to the subregions[2] with North Africa dominating.

An attempt has been made to keep the book a manageable size. In order to do so, the following methods were adopted: frequent use of statistics as figures speak for themselves; maximum use of tabulated information (including combining in a single table data that are normally presented in separate tables); and minimum repetition, particularly on the subject of constraints, to which a whole chapter has been devoted. Detailed information is given in annexes so that those who want more information can access them, analyze them, and draw preliminary conclusions on the basis of computations. The tables in each chapter are, generally, limited to summaries followed, in many cases, by brief analytical presentations.

The accuracy of data and information, mainly arising from inadequate initial measurement and recording and a lacking in details, leaves much to be desired. It is not uncommon to find different figures for the same data in the same source of information. This holds true for this book as well. In part, this is due to updates and revisions as well as differences or changes in aggregation of products and countries. Furthermore, gaps in or inadequate availability of time series data has limited the use of an analytical approach. To counter this, some gaps in the data for certain years have been filled in with estimates by those who compiled the data, i.e., the sources from which the information was obtained. These shortcomings, attributable to delays in processing, some times result in the use of relatively old data and information that are inadequate to the task of aggregating inter-country and subregional comparisons and obtaining a regional picture. The explanatory notes in Annex 4.2 explain some of the discrepancies and incomparability in so far as agricultural products are concerned.

It is quite likely that many of these shortcomings will, ultimately, be overcome through microcomputing technology, which seems to be catching up in the region. It should be noted here that, in view of the above difficulties associated with information, alternative data and information are given when considered relevant and worthwhile. This has been, in part, done in order to help the reader associate different but related numerical information, generally for different periods or latest years available, and thus minimize the need of frequent searching for cross-references. This may give the impression of repetition. For the sake of simplicity, references have been limited to secondary sources when the information in the source used had been obtained from other sources.

## NOTES

1. In this book **"Continent"** refers to all 53 member countries of the continent, including its islands; **"Africa"** or **"region"**, or **"developing Africa"** (which are used interchangeably) generally refer to the continent less South Africa (which is classified as an "industrialized country); and **"Sub-Sharan Africa" (SSA)** generally refers to the continent less North Africa and South Africa.

2. According to ECA, the continent is divided into the following four subregions:**Central Africa**—Burundi, Cameroon, Central African Republic, Chad, Congo, and Congo K (former Zaire), Equatorial Guinea, Gabon, Rwanda, and Sao-Tome and Principe; **Eastern and Southern Africa**—Angola, Botswana, Comoros, Djibouti, Eritrea, Ethiopia, Kenya, Lesotho, Madagascar, Malawi, Mauritius, Mozambique, Namibia, Seychelles, Somalia, South Africa (rejoined in 1994), Swaziland, Tanzania, Ugand, Zambia, and Zimbabwe; **North Africa**—Algeria, Egypt, Libya, Morocco, Sudan, and Tunisia; **West Africa**—Benin, Burkina Faso, Cape Verde, Cote d'Ivoire, The Gambia, Ghana, Guinea, Guinea-Bissau, Liberia, Mali, Mauritania, Niger, Nigeria, Senegal, Sierra Leone, and Togo.

# PART ONE

# POLITICAL, SOCIAL, AND ECONOMIC CONDITIONS

## CHAPTER 2

# POLITICAL AND SOCIAL CONDITIONS

## BRIEF HISTORY

Not so long ago, Africa was still labeled the "dark continent". This archaic European notion was based on an inadequate knowledge of the continent, the denial that Africa had a history worthy of the name, and the assumption that African civilization and development started only with its colonization by Europe. Archaeological and historical evidences do not seem to bear out such a concept. In fact, some parts of Africa enjoyed higher civilization than many European countries during earlier times.

Except for north Africa and the region sough of Egypt (known as Ethiopia starting around mid of the last millennium B.C.), the continent was relatively unknown to the Europeans in ancient times. There are however, references to black Africans' presence in Europe toward the close of the Paleolithic Age, and to contacts with the Mediterranean area through the Phoenicians and the Carthaginians who traded on the West Coast of Africa in the 6th century B.C. The visit of an envoy of 30 Ethiopians to Avignon to offer the king of Spain *"aid against the infidels"* and Rome in 1306 A.D. was probably among the first official contact in Europe. Voyages of the Chinese Cheng Ho to the Red Sea and East Africa (1416-1424) was followed by the Portuguese sailors rounding the Cape of Good Hope starting in the 1430s with making contact with Prester John of Ethiopia[1] as one of the objectives. The Portuguese initiated the enslavement of West Africa in 1441 A.D. Slave trade in which Africans themselves participated was abolished by the Europeans outside Africa starting at the beginning of the 1800s (Reader 1998).

Archaeological findings in South Africa and the Great Rift Valley of East Africa (*National Geographic*, February 1997) in recent decades seem to support Darwin's theory that Africa was the cradle of mankind. The hominid remains of Australopithecus Afarensis, a female commonly known as Lucy, were found in 1974 and that of Ardipithecus Ramidus in 1994, both in the Afar region of Ethiopia. The former lived 3.18 million years ago, the latter, 4.4 million years ago. The latest (1998) find of human remains in the same region pushes the age of the oldest human ancestor found to date to the level of 5 million years. The species of human ancestor (Australopithecus Anamensis) found at Kanapoi in Kenya in 1995 has been dated at between 3.9 and 4.2 million years (Rachlin 1996). It is considered a cross between the two remains discovered in Ethiopia. That found in Buia region of Eritrea, in 1995, is between 2.5 and 4.0 million years old. The discovery in 1995 of a 3.0-3.5 million-year-old hominid (Australolpithecus Bahrelghazali) jawbone in Chad widens the area of the cradle of humanity.

The 2.5 million-year-old human jaw fossil of Homo Rudolffesis, discovered at Uraha in Malawi in 1991, was dubbed the oldest of the Genus Homo. The 1.6

million-year-old "Turkana Boy" found in northern Kenya in 1984 is said to resemble modern man (Tattersall 1997). These findings in Malawi and Kenya, the homo erectus that was supposed to have emergd in Africa over 1.7 million years ago, the one-million year old human skull discovered in 1995-1997 in Eritrea, the fossil finds at Klaisies River in South Africa, the skull of a 45,000-year-old child (modern man) discovered in Egypt in 1994 (BBC, October 17,1998), and others indicate that man not only originated but also evolved to Homo sapiens in Africa during the period 200,000-100,000 years or earlier before migrating to the other continents about 100,000 years ago.

Supporting evidences other than skeletons include: the 1978 find of the 3.6 million-year-old foot prints of hominids at Laetoli in Tanzania, and the 2.3 million-year-old stone tools discovered in 1996 in southern Ethiopia (*New York Times*, November 19, 1996). According to CNN Today (January 23, 1997), the tools (2.5 million years old) are the oldest to date.

As for history Africa, like other continents, had ancient civilizations as manifested by its many empires and kingdoms. The Egyptian civilization goes back to about 5000 B.C. by which time Egypt became the first nation-state of the world. By 3100 B.C., Upper and Lower Egypt were united under one ruler. Egypt boasts a recorded history going back to dates earlier than 3200 B.C.[2] The history of North Africa as a whole, starting with the establishment of Carthage toward the end of the 9th century B.C., was dominated and influenced by the Phoenicians, Greeks, Romans, Vandals (Germanic tribe), Arabs and the Ottoman Empire. During the 11th and 13th centuries A.D., Algerian rule extended beyond northwest Africa to southern Spain. The Moroccan Empire covered present day Algeria, Tunisia, Libya and parts of Spain and Portugal in the period 1147 - 1258 A.D.

The kingdom of Napata (800-300 B.C.), the empire of Meroe (300 B.C.-300 A.D.), the civilization of Ballana and Qustul (300 B.C.-300 A.D.) and the Christian kingdom (6th - 14th centuries A.D.) give indications of the high level of civilizations achieved by Nubia or Kush ( northern Sudan). Nubia ruled Egypt starting about 713 B.C. until it was ousted by the Assyrians in 654 B.C. (UNESCO, *A General History of Africa*). During a short time of this period, it was one of the most powerful empires in the world (Microsoft, *Encarta 96 Encyclopedia*). This is supported by Assyrian cuneiform inscriptions and Jewish records which equated it with Assyria, Babylon, Egypt, and Persia.

The empires of Axum (northern Ethiopia, Eritrea and eastern Sudan, 50 AD -1100 A.D.), preceded by pre-Axumite[3] in the last millennium B.C., Ghana (southeastern Mauritania and southwestern Mali 5th-11th centuries A.D.), and Songhai, centered around the largest bend of the Niger River, 1350-1560 A.D., were among the other civilizations that flourished in Africa. According to Manni (216-276 A.D.), a Persian writer, the Axumite, Chinese, Persian and Roman Empires were the four greatest empires of the world during the third century A.D. (UNESCO, *General History of Africa*). Another source confirms this by stating that *"the Arabs also considered the Aksumite state to be on par with the Islamic state, the Byzantine Empire, and China as one of the world's greatest kingdoms"* (Ofcansky 1993). The Axumite empire dominated Yemen (3rd and 6th century A.D.). The Songhai Empire, which was as large as Europe, was known for its well organized administration, roads, communication system, University of Sankore, and intellectual centers of Gao, Timbuktu and Jenne.

According to a number of sources, including Microsoft *(Encarta 96 and 97 Encyclopedia)* and Gordon et. al. (1996), other empires and kingdoms of later periods included those of:
• Kanem-Bornu, at its height including the region of Lake Chad and the Hausa States in Nigeria (8th-16thcenturies A.D.),
• Mali, at its zenith comprising a confederation of three independent states and 12 provinces and stretching from east of the Niger River to the Atlantic Ocean in the west, 1200-1500 A.D.,
• Kitwara, a great empire of which Uganda was a part, Middle-Ages 500-1450A.D.,
• Benin, part of southern Nigeria, 1500-1800 A.D.,
• Dahomey, southern part of Benin Republic, 1700-1900 A.D.,
• Bakongo, stretching from Angola to Gabon, 1400-1600 A.D.,
• Lunda, comprising parts of Angola, Zaire (Congo K)[4], and Zambia, 1450-1700 A.D.,
• Monomatapa (Mwene Mutapa), Zimbabwe, at its zenith stretching from the Indian Ocean to the Kalahari, 1400-1800 A.D.,
• Malawi, starting 16th century A.D.,
• Zulu, southern Africa, followed by the formation of new kingdoms, such as Basotho, Ndebele (Zimbabwe) and Gaza (Mozambique), 1800-1830 A.D., and
• Ashanti (Ghana), 1650-1900 A.D.
During the advent of colonialism, the Africans had a wide range of social and political structures, mostly decentralized, through which authority was exercised. The Ashanti of Ghana, the Obas of Benin, the Fulani Empire, the Mahdist State of the Sudan, Buganda (Uganda), Ethiopia, Merina (Madagascar), and Basuto in Southern Africa, to name a few, were among the territories under some forms of government (ADB, *African Development Report 1994*; and Stock 1995). The sophistication of the systems of the communal or political units varied from feudal to egalitarian, some of the latter based on elections. Examples of the latter include the "gada" system of the Oromo people in Ethiopia where power invested in persons were limited to eight years only; the peaceful, egalitarian and less-coercive political system that was practiced in Jenne-Jero, on the inland Niger delta in West Africa up to the 12th century A.D.; and elected village, district, provincial, and paramount councils which formed the basis of administration in British West Africa before colonization. In Ethiopia, where the former system prevailed, Emperor Tewodros II reunited the country which had suffered disintegration into provincial powers during the period 1769-1855.

Despite destruction by man and nature, some physical evidences supporting history do exist. The cave paintings (6500-1200 B.C.) in Algeria, the pyramids, the Sphinx, the Temple of Abu Simbel and many other archaeological relics and sites in Egypt are well known. Stone architecture (monuments and temples), irrigation systems and script of the Kush empire in the Sudan, and the university in Timbuktu, a commercial and religious center (10th -16th centuries A.D.) during the empire of Mali are some evidences of other African civilizations (Stock 1995). Others universities include Kurawain in Morocco and Al Azhar in Egypt, the latter founded in 970 A.D. The steles (largest monoliths in the world), the rock-hewn churches, palaces, castles, irrigation, dams, script (still in use in Ethiopia and Eritrea), musical notation, church schools (up to college equivalent level) and ancient currency (coins) in Ethiopia, the ruins of the Great Zimbabwe complex, the traditional fabric making in West Africa, and metalwork (including traditional bronze casts) in most countries are other indications of the level of African civilization and achievements before colonization.

The achievements referred to above give indications as to the level of science and technology attained in Africa generally predating contact with Europeans. This is despite the fact that, according to Reader (1998), the Africans, unlike their kins who emigrated, had to contend with more hostile environment (fragile soils, competition with animals, such as elephants, erratic weather, pests, parasites, diseases and predators) that had conditioned them for survival (minimize the risk of failure), not for development.[5] These constraints were compounded by the age-grade system with its respect for elders who were usually not for innovation and change.

Technology started with crude stone tools in Africa. Stone tool making and their applications to different uses were developed and refined with time and included blades, scrapers, hand axes, digging-sticks, adzes and projectile-points. Spears, arrows, bone needles, skin clothing and control of fire were other advances in technological innovation. In agriculture, the Africans domesticated plants, including the drought-resistant sorghum and millet. Reader cites archaeological evidences of deliberate plant productivity control at the Klasies River cave site in Southern Africa 70,000 years ago and indigenous terracing and irrigation canals in Sub-Saharan Africa. He claims that the 6,400-year old dugout canoe discovered in north-eastern Nigeria is the second oldest in the world. The drum was used as a means of communication. The Egyptians invented geometry and trigonometry and discovered the principles of astronomy. Smallpox vaccination was practiced in Africa long before it was invented elsewhere. It was administered by scratching a smallpox pustule from a smallpox patient using thorn and scratching a healthy person with the same thorn (Pappademos et. al. 1984).

With respect to modern technology, glassmaking, tool manufacture and textiles were cited as examples of indigenous technologies that were virtually eliminated by colonial policies (Emeagwali et. al. 1997). Iron smelting and the making of spears and agricultural tools were practiced in many countries before 2500 years ago (Gordon et. al. 1996). In fact, there is a theory that the process of reducing iron ore to iron is supposed to have been discovered by black Africans.

As for religion which was one of the major factors contributing to many cultures, parts of Africa, centuries before most other countries of the world, practiced the three religions that originated in the Middle East. Egypt was the first to adopt Christianity. It was followed by parts of present day Ethiopia, Eritrea and Sudan. In Ethiopia, Judaism was practiced before Christianity was introduced around 330 A.D. and Islam, during its inception (615 A.D.) during the Ethiopian King Armah's rule when the Prophet Muhammad himself advised his followers to emigrate to christian Ethiopia to escape Quraish persecution (Picdthall 1981). Despite a request by the Quraish leadership to extradiate the refugees, the latter were allowed to stay and practice their new religion, a manifestation of religious tolerance at the time.

In leadership and the literary and related fields, Africa has its great people. President Mandela of South Africa and Yared and Zera Yacob of Ethiopia are among such people. Yared (6th century A.D.) invented the Ethiopian musical notation and form of religious music also authoring five books (church poems, hymns and chants which continue to be used to this day by the Ethiopian and

Eritrean Orthodox  Churches). He was canonized. Zera Yacob (1599-1692), a contemporary of Rene Descartes, was a philosopher and authored the "Hateta" (an ethical and philosophical treatise). He rejected polygamy as men and women were in fairly equal proportion; objected the domination of women by men; condemned slavery *"because men came into the world equal;"* and married a servant (probably a slave). It has been said of him that *"he uttered thoughts which did not become current in Europe till the rationalist period in the eighteenth century"* (Pankhurst 1955). This evaluation is confirmed in a book titled *The Source of African Philosophy: the Ethiopian Philosophy of Man* by Professor Cluade Sumner, professor of philosophy at Addis Ababa University. The author stated that *"modern philosophy, in the sense of personal rationalistic critical investigation, began in Ethiopia with Zera Yacob at the same time as in England and France."*

Contributions to knowledge, politics, peace, etc., by people of African descent outside of Africa in the last few centuries have been minimized and deliberately omitted or suppressed. This is particularly the case in the Western Hemisphere. Thanks to time and increasingly conscientious generations some of the suppressed information have started to come out.

## POLITICAL CONDITIONS

The peoples inhabiting the African continent comprise hundreds of ethnic groups speaking over  800 languages (up to 1,995 according to another source). Accounting for about 10 percent of the world's population, the region is the most heterogeneous (in proportion to its population) continent in the world.

### Colonialism and Struggle for Independence
Except for Ethiopia and Liberia, the region was gradually colonized after Vasco da Gama rounded the Cape of Good Hope in 1497. Colonial subjugation in Africa under the pretext of civilizing and benefiting the natives (its worst exemplified by apartheid in South Africa), slavery (and the atrocities committed to enslave people and to facilitate slave trade) and forced labor destroyed the socio-economic fabric of the black race. The black man lost self-confidence and self-esteem and the productive force of the continent was depleted. The natural evolution of states was interrupted. There is no doubt that colonialism and slave trade have contributed to arresting and or slowing down the development of African civilization on its own. They will continue to contribute, for some time to come, the relatively slow progress of development—political, social and economic—in Africa compared to other developing regions.

The present political map (see Map 2.1) of the continent is essentially the outcome of the Congress of Berlin (1884-1885) (Chazan et al 1988). Great Britain, France, Belgium, Portugal, Spain, Germany and Italy constituted the major colonial powers. Germany lost its possessions following the First World War and Italy, the Second World War.

The result of the so-called Scramble for Africa was that the continent was balkanized into possessions whose boundaries ignored the ethnic, linguistic, cultural and religious makeup of the peoples concerned. To this day, it is common to find families on both sides of the border between countries accross the continent.

Those artificial boundaries, the division of the region into anglophone, francophone, lusophone, etc. countries, the different colonial systems and the legacies they left behind, compounded by ethnic and religious tensions, were potential sources of misunderstanding and conflict. Many of the sources and consequences of Africa's conflicts (wars between Libya and Chad, Somalia and Ethiopia, Morocco and POLISARIO, and internal conflicts in Nigeria, Somalia, Angola, Mozambique, Sudan, Rwanda, Burundi, etc.) have their roots in colonialism with its highly centralized administrative and economic systems, divide-and-rule strategy (setting ethnic or religious groups against one another, such as the Tutsis against the Hutus in Rwanda and Burundi) and the subsequent processes of decolonization and state formation. This was compounded by the support given to and propping up of certain African leaders during the Cold War era (by maintaining the status quo of governments, by usurping and maintaining power, by getting rid of political adversaries), no matter how corrupt and dictatorial the leadership, in order to keep communism from gaining a foothold in Africa and to prevent the access by communist countries to African resources and markets. This practice, particularly protection provided to certain leaders and groups, seems to continue after the closing of the Cold War as exemplified by France's intervention in Rwanda and in the Central African Republic in recent years. If it were not for the United States, intervention by a European power (s) would not have been ruled out in the case of Zaire in 1997. It appears that France is in the process of giving up its neocolonial policy, partly due to weakening support for France from the younger generation of elite Francophone Africans.

Although parts of the African territories were occupied relatively peacefully (some even at the request of the local leadership themselves) with the help of hunters, slave traders/raiders, explorers, missionaries, trading companies, scientific expeditons, etc., as well as using the "divide, conquer and rule" tactics, deception, ruses and treachery, there were armed resistance in many parts of the continent. Such was the case in northern Niger and western Uganda. In Southern Africa, The Khoisans (Hottentots) attacked the Dutch settlers' farms in 1659; the Xhosa waged the 'Frontier Wars' against the Dutch in 1779; and the Nama people lost after a year of guerrilla fighting against the Germans in 1905. In 1904, the Maji Maji rebellion against the Germans in Tanganyika was quelled using measures aimed at creating conditions leading to famine (Reader 1998). There were revolts in Algeria (1870), Ashantiland (1893-1900), Sierra Leone (1897), Tanganyika (Tanzania, 1905-1907), as well as the Sokoto (1906) and Matebeleand Shona (1896) (Microsoft, *Encarta 1996 Encyclopedia*).

In battles fought between the European colonizers, equipped with the most advanced weaponry of the time, and the indigenous people, the latter did win some battles. The Sotho (Lesotho) were, for instance, successful in resisting British attacks in the 1880s (Reader 1998). At the battle at Isandlawana in Natal in 1879 the Zulus defeated the British. The former were finally subdued after half a year of war. In the Sudan, the Mahdist uprising scored victories against the British/ Egyptian forces in 1883-1885, resulting in the evacuation of the forces from the Sudan. This was followed by the first defeat the Italian colonizers suffered at Dogali (Eritrea) in 1887[6] at the hands of the Ethiopians led by Ras Alula[7] under Emperor Yohannes IV, culminating in their defeat in the battle of Adwa led by Emperor Menilik II in 1896. Many of the above and other resistances were carried out during the 1889 to early 1900s outbreak of the rinderpest (probabaly inadvertently

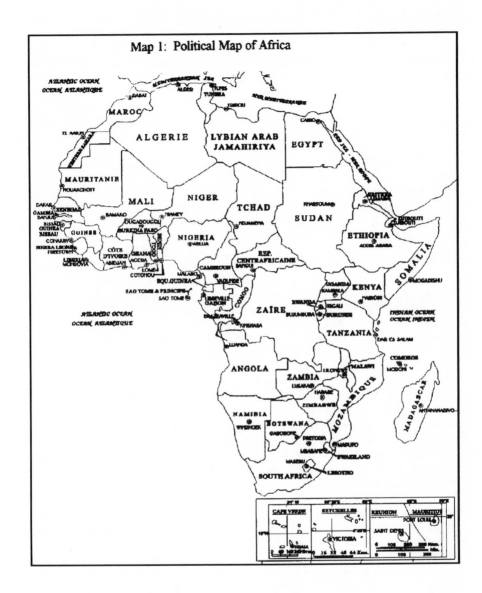

Map 1: Political Map of Africa

introduced by the Italians) epidemic which decimated 90-95 per cent of Ethiopia's cattle and resulted in devastating famine and diseases, thereby weakening the capacity of the people to resist. It was in the aftermath of the 1889-92 Great Ethiopian Famine which started with rinderpest epidemic that the battle of Adwa was fought.

The defeat at Dogali of one of the European powers reputed to be invincible was dubbed the Dogali crisis, disaster or disgrace (Doresse 1987). It was the first shock experienced by European colonizers who were poised to complete the balkanization of Africa. It was a victory shared by all Africa and a turning back of the tide of European colonialism. In the words of Petrides (1988), it was *"That pan African victory which spelled the end of the partitioning of Africa and debunked the myth of the invincibility of the foreign invader."*

Towards the end of the 1800s, Africans in Africa and in the diaspora started to react against the humiliation and inhumane treatment that their ancestors had suffered and they themselves were experiencing. There was even the idea of repatriation advocated by an African American, Henry McNeal Turner. At about the same time, labor movements were emerging in South Africa. In 1915 the "Africa for Africans" movement, headed by the Malawian John Ghilembwe, led the Nyasaland Rising. Outside Africa, in the West Indies and North America, the concept of Pan-Africanism, a concerted political movement against the dehumanization of the African and the colonial system, was born. The proponents of Pan-Africanism (W.E.B. Du Bois, Marcus Garvey, Henry Sylvester Williams, etc.) held a series of congresses, the first in 1900 in London and the second in Paris in 1919. The second and subsequent congresses brought the new world activists (the diaspora) together with African activists studying in the West, many of whom (Kwame Nkrumah, Jomo Kenyatta, Nnamdi Azikiwe, Leopold Senghor, etc.) later led their respective countries to independence. The 6th Congress, All-African People's Conference was held in Africa (Accra, Ghana) in 1958. The preceding African activists together with other African leaders such as Emperor Haile Selassie of Ethiopia and President Gamal Abdel Nasser of Egypt, crowned Pan-Africanism by establishing the Organization of African Unity (OAU) in 1963. This was achieved despite the political rifts between the Monrovia, Casablanca and Brazzaville groups at the time.

The last attempt at completing the balkanization of Africa and the second and last attempt at colonizing Ethiopia by fascist Italy, this time using fighter planes and chemical weapons, was made during the period 1936-1941. After five years of continued fighting, the country was liberated with the help of Great Britain, following Fascist Italy alliance with Nazi Germany during the Second World War. The anticolonial and liberation movements that followed the Pan-African movement intensified following the end of the Second World War. Various political parties sprung up in a number of African countries, many of them led by Pan-Africanist returnees who until then had been active mostly in the metropolitan countries.

Libya and Egypt won their independence in 1951 and 1954 (when the British army occupation ended in Egypt), respectively. They were followed by the Sudan, Morocco, and Tunisia in 1956, Ghana in 1957, Guinea in 1958, and most of the remaining countries in the 1960's. The first meeting of the heads of independent African states and governments was held in Accra, Ghana, in 1958. It was followed by one convened in Addis Ababa, Ethiopia, in 1960. Both were the precursors to the establishment of the OAU in 1963 with its headquarters in Addis Ababa. The OAU, a manifest of Pan-Africanism, played a leading role in emancipating those countries that later gained their independence in the process of decolonization.

Most African colonies achieved independence smoothly and peacefully, thanks to the doctrine of self-determination of nations adopted at the Paris Peace Conference in 1919 (whose application to African colonies was, unfortunately, delayed), the United Nations' Declaration on Granting of Independence to Colonial Countries and Peoples, and subsequent contributions made by the United Nations and the OAU. Some (Algeria, the Portuguese colonies, Kenya, Zimbabwe, etc.) had, however, to resort to armed struggles. In 1993, Eritrea became independent from Ethiopia. Elections in South Africa in April 1994 led to the demise of apartheid and the establishment of a government of national unity in South Africa in May 1994, with Nelson Mandela at the helm, 342 years after the white man arrived in South Africa. Now, with 53 sovereign states, Africa accounts for 28.6 percent of the 185 country membership of the United Nations. South Africa rejoined the OAU in June 1995 from which it had been previously expelled because of its apartheid policy .The status of Reunion (overseas department of France), St. Helena (British dependency), Canary Islands (provinces of Spain) and the former Spanish Sahara (Saharawi Republic) remains to be determined, the last awaiting the carrying out of a referendum.

## Independence and its Ramifications

Upon independence, African countries faced many constraints as they had little experience to equip them to administer, leave alone undertake, development tasks. The scarcity of educated, skilled and experienced Africans was the most serious. This was most apparent in the Portuguese and Belgian colonies where education of Africans was practically nil at advanced level. Although some changes were made on the eve of independence in some countries (home rule during the transition period), the administrative machinery inherited was designed to facilitate control of the peoples and perpetuate the exploitation of their resources for industries in the metropolitan countries. This, together with conditions imposed to take account of specific colonial interests, was unsuited to governance of the newly independent states.

In the 1960s, African governments became preoccupied with consolidating their political independence. Many of them started to introduce changes to the governmental systems they had inherited. Many of the changes were justified as they were intended to minimize these and other constraints. Other adjustments were of an authoritarian nature, made to consolidate and perpetuate the leaders' grip over the people. The strategies adopted included reorganizing public institutions, centralizing power, personalizing decision-making by heads of state and their henchmen, establishing one-party states, curtailing political opposition and competition, curbing freedom of the press and limiting the rights of associations and organizations. Idi Amin Dada of Uganda, Jean-Bedel Bokassa of the Central African Republic and Mengistu H. Mariam of Ethiopia were among the leaders notorious for their flagrant violations of the law and human rights in Africa.

In the absence of independent bodies, such as a free press, to expose malad-ministration, corruption, nepotism and embezzlement, these practices became increasingly contagious and rampant at the highest official levels and trickled down to the lowest level as nobody could be held accountable. Foreign suppliers of goods and services strengthened corruption by paying bribes to obtain busi-ness, thereby giving the local businesses and people the impression that corrup-tion was not, after all, a bad thing because the white man does it. These factors along with the dynamics of the Cold War aggravated political instability which was rooted in the colonial legacy.

Many of the civil and interstate wars in Africa were proxy wars between the superpowers of the time. The civil war in Angola and the Ethio-Somali war are good examples. In the case of the latter the United States, a supporter of Ethio-pia, and the former Soviet Union, a supporter of Somalia, swapped allegiances in 1977. This was followed by Somalia invading Ethiopia in 1977-1978. Intent upon preventing the spread of communism in Africa, the West, as noted earlier, sup-ported and encouraged any African leader, as long as he served the interest of the West or seemed to share their ideological loyalties. In short, it is apparent that foreign governments and companies have contributed significantly to making Africa what it is today. From recent events in Congo K, the conflict appeared to have an element of proxy between the American and the French governments. It should be noted that France, until recently, continued to influence most of its former colonies through its African policy, which included the protection of Afri-can regimes from internal opposition, including maintaining French military bases or presence in selected countries.

Until recent years, mainly as a consequence of the above described political conflicts, the continent was, and in part is, characterized by a proliferation of imposed civilian and military regimes. Many of these regimes were motivated by selfish objectives and usurped power through manipulating elections (the 1998 election in Togo, for example) and coups and counter coups. A number of their leaders (notable exceptions being ex-Presidents Mwalimu J. Nyerere of Tanza-nia, General Olusegun Obasanjo of Nigeria, and Leopold Sedar Senghor of Senegal, among the few genuine leaders who voluntarily resigned, that Africa has seen since independence through the 1980s) were repressive and corrupt. Some of them squandered a large part of their countries' human and meagre financial resources to keep their mostly inept leadership in power, no matter how rich or poor the country. At least one of them—ruling one of the richest countries in Africa, namely Congo K—was reported to be a billionnaire while his people were enduring poverty and suffering from internal conflict, of his own making.

Political unrest (internal conflicts, civil wars and wars between nations) con-tinue to affect some of the countries to this day. In recent years, countries experi-encing political problems include: Burundi, Liberia, Nigeria, Somalia, Sudan, Niger, Guinea, Central African Republic, Rwanda, Angola, Sierra Leone, the Congo, Comoros and Congo K. Nigeria and Cameroon clashed in February 1994 and in August 1995 over the Bakassi peninsula, while Sudan's relationship with its neighbors (Egypt, Eritrea, Ethiopia and Uganda) deteriorated in 1995. Niger witnessed the January 1996 military cout d'etat against the democratically elected government. It was followed in February 1996 by the failed coup d'etat in Guinea and in May 1996 by an army mutiny which was foiled with the help of French troops in the Central African Republic and eventually came to an end in July 1997. Regional leaders imposed economic sanctions on Burundi following the July 1996 take-over of power by former President Pierre Buyoya. The instability in Rwanda and Burundi spread to eastern Congo K toward the end of 1996 and the eastern Congolese K rebels extended their control in all directions during the first quarter of 1997 despite the use of white mercenaries by the Kinshasa government. The democratically elected president in the Congo (Brazzaville) was ousted by the former leader in 1997. Fighting between Eritrea and Ethiopia broke out in May 1998 and resumed in February 1999. This was immediately followed by a civil war in Guinea-Bissau.

While these conflicts were continuing, with some of them abating, many of the new and old and more serious conflicts were finding solutions. Examples of solutions of conflict, include: Mozambique where, following the 1992 peace accord, an election was held in October 1994; South Africa where apartheid ended and a multiracial and multiparty system is in operation; Lesotho where an internal conflict was averted in 1995 thanks to an intervention by certain African leaders; Angola where peace was achieved and a government of national unity was inaugurated in April 1997, but fighting resumed in 1997 and 1998; Sierra Leone where an elected civilian government that was set up with military intervention by the Nigerian and other West African governments in 1998 came under pressure from the rebel alliance; Liberia where, following the Abuja meeting of ECOWAS Heads of State with Liberian rebel leaders, a new interim government was formed in 1996 and election was held in July 1997; Rwanda where, following the end of the civil war in 1995, most Hutu refugees who fled the country fearing retribution returned from neighboring countries in 1996 and 1997; Congo K where, in May 1997, a transitional government of national salvation of the renamed Democratic Republic of the Congo was formed, but civil war errupted in 1998; and Somalia where, in 1998, an agreement among the factions was reached to form a transitional government which had not materialized up to the end of that year.

Until recent years, the OAU and subregional organizations have enjoyed little success in the difficult task of peace keeping operations and solving major conflicts in Africa. They have, however, began to achieve successes since 1995, following the establishment of the OAU Mechanism for Conflict Prevention, Management and Resolution (MCPMR) at the OAU's 20th summit in 1993. In 1997 the member nations were contemplating creating an emergency military force. They have started to take political and military actions against those who usurp power from legitimate governments. The conflict resolutions achieved in Lesotho, and Liberia are to their credit. ECOWAS's sanction and embargo and deployment of forces against the military regime in Sierra Leone to restore power to the elected government, the Central Organ of the MCPMR's support for ECOWAS's actions, and the declaration as null and void the referendum for self determination in Anjouan, Comoros, are good precedents which are likely to deter future cout d'etats on legitimate governments.

The Mechanism is also gaining support from African women. At the First Summit of Africa's First Ladies on Peace and Humanitarian Issues (May 1997), the First Ladies produced a program of activities in support of the Mechanism (OAU, *AEC Newsletter*, August-October 1997).

The Mechanism may eventually have ready contingents on stand-by in each OAU member state to be used where and when the need arises, such as in the case of the genocide of 500,000 to one million people in Rwanda in 1994. The "OAU Peace Fund," that was subsequently created will be used to finance activities related to conflict anticipation and prevention, peace-making, conflict resolution and peace-building.

The 1994 return to democratic rule in Haiti made possible with the pressure and support of the international community is a good example of the trend toward democratization outside the continent. Lessons from the Haitian and Bosnian experiences including subsequent events, can and should be applied to conflict areas in Africa. This could be achieved by support from developed countries for the OAU's efforts in the implementation of the latter's Mechanism. The Mechanism could benefit from a United Nations peace force, if and when established, the need for which has been gaining support in recent years, with the number of member states willing to participate having increased from 67 in 1997 to 81 in 1999. An agreement on creating a "Stand-by Forces High-Readiness Brigade" was signed in 1996 by Austria, Canada, Denmark, the Netherlands, Norway, Poland and Sweden. The Stand-by Forces would be deployed on orders of the Security Council (United Nations Association of the USA, *The Interdependent*). This initiative could, hopefully, serve as a nucleus for a larger rapid-deployment force comprising representatives of all United Nations member states.

The approval given by the Security Council to replace French troops by African soldiers in the Central African Republic in 1998 could be a harbinger of such a force which is likely to deter or minimize the outbreak of conflicts in the first instance. It should be noted that the force could be more effective and less expensive to operate than the current ad-hoc system of intervention, that also seems to give lower priority to African conflicts in comparison with other areas. The United States' initiative, "African crisis response force," was advanced by the United States' Secretary of State during his visit to some African countries in 1996 and appears to meet the need for a pan-African peace-keeping force, if and when created. This approach had started to materialize following the acceptance by seven African countries (Ethiopia, Ghana, Malawi, Mali, Senegal, Tunisia and Uganda) of American advisers to help set up in each country *"one battalion for rapid intervention anywhere in the continent"* (*Foreign Reporter*, September 4, 1997). During President Clinton's visit to Africa in 1998, US Special Forces were already training a Senegalese battalion following the one in Uganda.

## Towards Democratization

With the end of the Cold War and associated ideological conflicts in the second half of the 1980s, which led to the marginalization of the strategic importance of Africa, it is, with the passage of time, possible that there will be fewer and less conflicts. This, coupled with increasing linkage of foreign aid to the institution of democratic governance, a respect for human rights and adoption of market economy principles, if applied with flexibility which sould take account of conditions prevailing in each individual country, seems to augur well for the stability and democratization of Africa. Notwithstanding the policies already initiated by some African governments themselves in the wake of global trends towards democracy, before the new aid-related conditions were announced, political pluralism and economic reforms seem to be paying dividends in some African governments.

Having experimented with various political forms and directions and having recognized the changes that have taken place in the world in recent years (many of which are not in the interest of African countries) an increasing number of African leaders are maturing and boldly facing up to reality. They have come to recognize that a country cannot be immune from the political and social consequences of a declining economy. More and more countries are becoming sensitive to human rights issues; they are attempting to find peaceful solutions to their internal and external conflicts; and they are in the process of democratizing their governments. About half of the African countries are practicing or heading towards some form of multiparty political system and are in the process of introducing checks and balances into their governance. Countries that fall under this category include Benin, Botswana, Ethiopia, Malawi, Mali, Mozambique, Namibia, Senegal, South Africa, Zambia and Zimbabwe. Mali, for example, has been cited as a model of democracy following the overthrow of the Marxist regime in 1991. The successful implementataion of policies instituted and measures taken by the Nigerian governement in 1998, provided it leads to the formation of a democratically functioning elected government in 1999, is likely to boost the trend towards democratization in the continent. These and other achievements of the 1990s are, unfortunately, overshadowed by negative sensationalism in the media about famines and civil strifes.

Ethiopia is a good example of positive political and economic development in Africa. Following the end of the civil war in 1991, the Transitional Government of Ethiopia led the country through four years of a democratization process. It transformed the Marxist system into a multiparty federal system of democratic government in a country where democratic culture had been unheard of. The system comprised nine states based on major ethnic groups in a nation populated by over 80 ethnic entities. This is in contrast to the one-party system adopted in Uganda for fear that a multiparty system would divide the country along ethnic, regional or religious lines, reversing the Ethiopian logic. In 1998, measures were being taken leading to the establishment of an ombudsman and a human rights commission responsible to the Federal Parliament of Ethiopia.

The emergence of a new leadership and the transition to democratic regimes in Africa have been observed by different writers and commentators. For example, by 1988, Chazan et. al. had already noted positive trends toward such changes.They observed that, among other things, *"the severity of the crisis of the early part of the decade [1980s] evoked certain adjustments: more responsible financial management, cutbacks in the public sector, a relaxation of repression, decentralization and the last decade [1980s] has seen a new realism among many African leaders, a willingness to be self-critical and to accept responsibility for their policy decisions."* When addressing the White House conference on Africa, Mr. Brian Atwood, USAID Administrator, commended some 13 African leaders, most of whom had come to power in the last decade, for taking initiatives to enable Africa to realize its potential (*The Ethiopian Herald*, July 30, 1994). On another occasion in the same year, he mentioned the leaders of South Africa, Benin, Uganda, Senegal, Zambia and Ethiopia as a new generation of African leaders who *"remain the hopes of the continent in its struggle for political freedom and economic independence." (The Ethiopian Herald,* July 29, 1994) At about the same time, Mr. Wighard Hardtl, State Secretary, Federal Ministry for

Economic Cooperation and Development of the Federal Republic of Germany, pointed to positive factors, including the path to democracy being pursued by the majority of African governments (*The Ethiopian Herald*, August 2, 1994)[8].

Madagascar and Kenya are among the latest countries heading towards democracy. Following his victory in the election of February 1997, the president of the former seems to be on the right track in instituting changes. The Kenyan parliament amended the constitution of the country to accommodate multiparty democracy in November 1997. In May 1997, four African heads of governments and two vice-presidents were honored by the American Corporate Council for Africa for the initiative they took in development in their respective countries. In calling for a change of current inernational thinking about Africa, Dr. Salim Ahmed Salim, the Secretary-General of the OAU, stressed that " *not all African countries are a mirror image of Liberia, Somalia and Rwanda ... the process of democratization have taken root in more than 27 African countries ... thirty-seven African countries are implementing adjustment programmes" (The Ethiopian Herald,* March 1, 1995).

In his foreword to *Adjustment in Africa* published in 1994, Mr. Edward V. K. Jaycox, Vice-President, Africa Region, The World Bank, had this to say *"The path to economic progress and revival is now much better understood in Africa than at any time before, but managing this change has proved difficult."*

From the above, it appears that Africa has started to go through a process of improving political stability, something similar to that in Latin America not so long ago. It should be noted here that it took Western Europe centuries of bloodshed to achieve the relative peace and stability that it has enjoyed over the past 50 years before crisis started in the former Yugoslavia. The Irish problem in Great Britain, the ETA guerrillas struggling to separate the Basque region from Spain and the separatist movement in Italy are among the conflicts that continue to haunt parts of Western Europe. Given the end of the Cold War and subsequent encouraging developments, it is likely that stability, a precondition for development, will improve with time in Africa. The process has already begun. This does and will naturally create an enabling environment that will facilitate development, divert resources from destructive uses to development purposes and consequently improve the standard of living of Africa's peoples that is so badly needed. Indications of this trend are given in an ECA document (E/ECA/CM.20/3): *"Politically, Africa underwent considerable changes and the region as a whole experienced a significant overall improvement in human rights, political liberalization and freedom of organization and, to some extent, democratization.... 37 African countries have taken steps towards political liberalization as from the early 1990's; out of 18 presidential elections held during 1990-1993, eight could be classified as ' free and fair' and the number of countries as 'most free' increased from two in 1988 to nine in 1992."* Elections were expected in almost half of the African countries in 1996.

Attempts at political liberalization have faltered in some countries. Algeria and Libya are examples of such failures. The former's attempt at reforming domestic institutions and the latter's at reforming foreign policy were frustrated by hard-liners (Anderson 1995). It should be noted that the interests of the majority are enhanced by the degree of their participation in elections. For example, the low-voter turnout endemic in the United States of America, where ballots of higher-income Americans predominate, means that government decisions and actions are determined by and for the benefit of the few.

In multiethnic countries, such as most African countries, the democratization movement sweeping the region may lead to ethnic-based movements which could make governance and administration difficult, if not impossible. The Ethiopian experience to which we referred seems to be working and may prove to be one of the options that countries facing problems related to multiethnicism could consider and adopt.

The introduction and practice of democracy in developing countries requires a long process of political development and learning from experience. It is unrealistic to expect fledgling democracies, with the concomitant implementation of economic liberalization and all that it entails, to perform at par with those of the United States or Great Britain, although some critics do. Such critics, knowingly or unknowingly, have contributed and continue to contribute to the political instabilities of the very countries that should be encouraged and supported for adopting and struggling to adapt democratic principles to their respective conditions. Experience has shown that certain elements in the fledgling democracies oppose and create obstacles to implementing socio-economic policies and strategies beneficial to the people. Some even sabotage government activities and abuse the political and social freedoms gained through the introduction of democracy. As the saying goes, Rome was not built in a day and in the words of President Clinton *"there is no single blueprint for successful democracy."* It should be pointed out here that even in the United States, democracy cannot be said to be fully practiced. Narrow special interests, including corporations, with financial clout, for example, have significant influence over presidential and Congressional elections. As a consequence they advance their own causes or derive benefits through those elected to power through their influence. It is not uncommon to observe unequal penalties being imposed for the same or similar crimes.

## SOCIAL CONDITIONS [9]

As already referred to, the social system in many parts of Sub-Saharan Africa before colonization was basically egalitarian in that there was no coercive centralized control on the communities. In many areas societies functioned through the age-grade system whereby the duties of individuals changed with age, thereby avoiding permanent power holding by rulers. Compromise was the basis for collective authority (Reader 1998).

Although the above system was weakened and eventually done away with, little was done to improve the lot of the African during the colonial era. With the development of mining and urbanization, men left the rural areas, many of them forced at the beginning, to work in mines and towns. This inevitably disrupted family life, with men exposed to inhumane living conditions and women left behind carrying the full burden of labor that should have been shared.

Following independence, African countries found themselves financing social services and economic development to correct the imbalances created under colonialism. To do this most of them had to borrow funds from abroad. In the 1980s, economic and social conditions showed a marked downward trend. Infrastructure related to education and health deteriorated. For want of maintenance, schools and hospitals became dilapidated. Most of their equipment gradually fell into disuse for lack of spare parts and replacements. In short, using social and economic meters, the average African's standard of living was worse than it has been in the 1960s and 1970s. In his address to the Twenty-ninth Session of the Commission in 1994, the Executive Secretary of the ECA told the Conference that there was massive unemployment and that close to 60 percent of the African population was under the poverty line.

The *"UNDP Human Development Report 1997"* ranks countries using a new measurement, the Human Poverty Index (HPI). The three variables constituting the index are: vulnerability to death at an early age, the prevalence of illiteracy, and access to health services, safe water and adequate food. As in UNDP's Human Development Index (*HDI*, chapter 3), most African countries lag behind other developing countries. African countries constitute nine out of the bottom ten.

With the worsening economic conditions in the 1980s and increased poverty becoming endemic, partly due to policy mistakes by African leaders, about 29 African countries embarked upon structural adjustment programs in the mid-1980s. The adjustments were imposed mainly by the Bretton Woods institutions as conditions for loans or aid. Most of the programs, apparently, did not bring significant positive changes, possibly because of the inconsistency in and short time available for implementing such programs (see chapter 3). In the short run, some of them may well have contributed to worsening social conditions (cuts in public spending and therefore increased unemployment, etc.) with basic social services suffering the most.

The social conditions in developing countries, in general, leave much to be desired. This is particularly true in Africa, as evidenced by some of the social indicators (Annex 3.2). The situation is so pathetic and becomes the root cause of so many conflicts that there is an urgent need to redirect social policy worldwide. Social conditions will deteriorate as global competiton increases and the economic activities of developing countries become increasingly restricted. Aware of these real possibilities, the United Nations Secretary General at that time B. Boutros-Ghali, argued at the annual conference of the ILO in 1994 for a global social pact to distribute the world's wealth fairly (wealth sharing) and end the scourge of unemployment. It is apparent that there can be no genuine economic development without the realization of social justice and development on a global basis.

In recognition of the acute social problems facing the world poor, poverty, unemployment and social deprivation and disintegration among them, the United Nations World Summit on Social Development was held in Copenhagen, Denmark, in March 1995. The world community at the Summit which was attended by 120 Heads of State and Government and 182 nations, issued a declaration and a plan of action in which the world leaders declared *"We commit ourselves to the goal of eradicating poverty in the world .. to promote social development and social justice..."* The plan of action was approved by consensus, but is not legally binding, and the likelihood of its implementation to the extent required is therefore questionable. The cut in foreign aid that was being debated by the United States Congress at the time of the above declaration did not augur well.

In most African countries, a very small minority of the people, primarily those working for government and some major private companies, are entitled to pensions or provident funds. The rest have no access to any form of social security or welfare. In their old age, those who do not have access to family support have no alternative but to beg in order to survive or die in poverty. Legislation reported in

1997 in Zimbabwe pending enactment by parliament is, among others, expected to provide tax rebates for people supporting their elderly. This, if successful, could be emulated by other African countries and minimize destitution.

Wars between countries, internal conflicts, population pressures, unreliable rainfall, overgrazing and over-use of the soil and the erosion of the land base have exacerbated living conditions. As a consequence, serious damage has been done (and continues unabated) to the social fabric of rural communities. Although rich in natural resources, Africa is nowadays known for its inability to feed its peoples. In 1995, because of human rights abuses and the proliferation of ethnic conflicts, Africa had the highest number of refugees: 8 million, out of a world total of 27 million, in addition to 15 million displaced persons in 1994. With peace prevailing in a number of countries, such as Mozambique, and until 1998, Eritrea and Ethiopia, refugees have been and continue to be repatriated to their respective countries. There has, unfortunately, been a recent outflow of refugees from Rwanda, Burundi, Somalia and Sudan.

## Population
African demographic dynamics are characterized by exceptionally high fertility, a decreasing infant mortality rate (from 16.7 per 1,000 live births in 1960 to 96 per 1,000 live births in 1992), and an increasing life expectancy from 40.5 to 52.3 years over the same period (ECA, E/ECA/CM.21/8). According to other sources, during the period 1950-1990, the infant mortality rate fell steadily from 186 in 1950-1955 to 101 in 1985-1990 and 93 in 1990-1995. The corresponding figures for life expectancy during the last two decades were 37.8 and 51 years. By 2020, infant mortality rate is expected to fall further to 54 and life expectancy to increase to 70.4 (UN, *World Population Prospects*). These are among the factors explaining the high rates of population growth rates. For more recent years, see Annex 3.2.

Africa's total population of 224 million in 1950 rose to 633 million in 1990, with women accounting for approximately 52 percent around mid-1995. Its rate of growth during the period 1950-1990, significantly above the world average, increased steadily from 2.23 percent in 1950-1955 to 2.86 percent in 1980-1985 and declined marginally to 2.84 percent in 1985-1990. Based on a medium variant projection, which envisages a steady fall in the growth rate to 2.33 percent by 2020, the region's total population is expected to increase to 832 million by the year 2000 and to 1,348 million in 2020 (see Annex 2.2). Recognizing that such high rates result in stagnant or even worsening living standards and therefore are detrimental to social and economic development, most African countries have adopted national population policies and are in the process of implementing family planning programs.

Figure 2.1 is a diagrammatic presentation of the total and urban populations of the whole continent given in Annex 2.2.

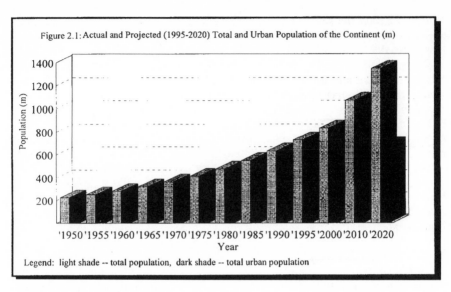

Figure 2.1: Actual and Projected (1995-2020) Total and Urban Population of the Continent (m)

Legend: light shade -- total population, dark shade -- total urban population

Mainly as a result of the falling infant mortality rate, the age structure is such that youth under the age of 15 constitute about 45 per cent of the total population. The proportion that consists of elderly people continues to increase due to the rising life expectancy. Both factors mean that an increasing financial burden will fall on the working population. The dependency ratio,[10] which was 84.2 in 1950, steadily rose to 91.7 in 1975 and declined to 90.6 in 1990. Therefore, economic conditions and social services will continue to deteriorate as long as job opportunities are limited for the working population.

The majority of people in Africa live in rural areas. The proportion of urban dwellers to total population varies from country to country. For Africa as a whole, as shown in Annex 2.2 and Figure 2.1 above, the urban population overall increased from 14.5 percent of total population in 1950 to 32.0 percent in 1990 (UN, *World Urbanization Prospects*). This is projected to increase further to 37.6 percent by the year 2000 and to 50.9 percent in 2020. The annual rate of change declined marginally from 4.55 percent in 1950-1955 to 4.51 percent from 1985-1990. It is projected to fall further to 3.68 per cent in 2015-2020. The corresponding figures for average annual rates of change in urbanization are: 2.32, 1.56 and 1.35. Rural to urban migration is the main factor contributing to the high rate of urbanization, matched by a growing negative trend in ruralization. In recent years, refugee movements have contributed to this state of affairs in many countries.

Based on FAO statistics (*FAO Production Yearbook 1994*), the total agricultural population in the region accounted for 65.3 percent of the total population in 1980. This dropped steadily to reach 43.4 percent in 1994. The corresponding figures for the economically active population in agriculture as a percentage of the total economically active population were 68.6 percent and 60.7 percent. The world averages for the latter were 50.8 percent and 44.7 percent respectively, with Africa surpassing them by more than 16 percentage points. The 1992 figures for the economically active population in agriculture by country are given in Annex 3.1.

Table 2.1 on the sectoral distribution of the economically active population confirms that the majority of people are engaged in agriculture. During the period 1970-1993, the share of agriculture decreased from 74.0 percent in 1970 to 61.1 percent in 1993. The corresponding figures for industry were 9.9 percent and 14.6 percent and for services, 16.1 percent and 24.3 percent. It is apparent that industry and services are recording gains at the expense of agriculture.

TABLE 2.1
PERCENTAGE DISTRIBUTION OF ECONOMICALLY ACTIVE POPULATION BY
SECTOR IN THE CONTINENT

| | Agriculture | | | | Industries | | | |
|---|---|---|---|---|---|---|---|---|
| | 1970 | 1980 | 1990 | 1993 | 1970 | 1980 | 1990 | 1993 |
| Africa, total | 74.0 | 68.2 | 63 | 61.1 | 9.9 | 12.1 | 14 | 14.6 |
| North Africa | 56.5 | 47.5 | 39.2 | 36.6 | 15.7 | 20.7 | 24.1 | 24.9 |
| West Africa | 75.5 | 71.4 | 67 | 65.5 | 8.7 | 10 | 11.6 | 11.9 |
| Central Africa | 83.3 | 76.4 | 70.8 | 68.7 | 7 | 9 | 11.4 | 12.2 |
| Eastern and Southern Africa | 77 | 71.8 | 67.2 | 65.5 | 9.2 | 11.1 | 12.4 | 12.8 |

Source: ECA, 1993, *African Socio-economic Indicators*, Addis Ababa.

The world community is aware of problems related to population in developing countries. The International Conference on Population and Development, held in Cairo in September 1995, was the most recent world forum to address such issues as population growth, poverty, unemployment and social disintegration: all of which are particularly relevant to Africa.

**Family Base**
The concept of family in Africa is that of an extended family system which includes parents, grand-parents, uncles, aunts, nephews, etc. Extended family is the basic social unit of most of the peoples. This social foundation underwent major changes with the advent of colonialism. People were employed as servants, guards, messengers and miners, the last often far away from home, including outside their home countries. Prevalent relationships were thus changed. Particularly damaging was the hardship that miners were exposed to and the separation from their families for extended periods. With time, it is likely that extended family tradition and fabric will be further weakened in the urban areas and later in the rural areas.

An interesting feature of African family life is the division of labor between the sexes. In the subsistence sector, women carry out 78- 90 percent of the activities related to food production, food processing, fuel and water supplies, brewing and 50 percent of animal husbandry in most parts of the continent; they contribute 60-80 per cent of field hands and 50 percent of cattle tenders in Sub-Saharan Africa, as well as 60 per cent of the internal trade in Africa (Chazan et. al. 1988).

Most womenfolk in Africa suffer from this gender bias. Culture and religions accord them a subordinate role, exposing them to harmful traditional practices and denying them the freedom of opinion. As a result, many suffer from illiteracy, malnutrition and health problems and the majority of the women are deprived of opportunities to own property, receive education and take up employment. Yet, they work harder and for longer hours than men, mainly at home but also outside the home in agriculture and trade. Yet their contribution is not reflected in national accounts.

Many countries are taking measures to correct such injustices by formulating and implementing specific policies and strategies and including provisions for women in population, health, education and business policies. At the international level, women's problems were addressed at the 1995 World Conference on Women in Beijing, China, the fourth such conference to be held. Other international fora where women's problems figured prominently include: the International Conference on Population and Development held in Cairo in 1994, and the World Summit for Social Development convened in Copenhagen, Denmark, in 1995. As for the industrial sector, promotion of the role of women in industrial development is a permanent feature in the work program of UNIDO.

## Education

At the dawn of independence, many African countries had an insignificant number of university graduates among their people. In the 1960s, for example, the United States media reported that Ethiopia had one chemical engineer who happened to be the author of this book. It was still worse in many other countries. This situation arose because of colonial policies which, generally, limited education to levels that would just enable Africans to perform clerical chores. A good part of this education was provided by missionaries.

Recognizing the serious constraints posed by illiteracy, African governments gave priority to education. In Sub-Saharan Africa, for instance, the share of expenditure on education in GNP rose from 5.1 percent in 1980 to 5.7 percent in 1992 (UNDP, *Human Resource Development 1996*). Africa achieved impressive gains in this arena in the 1960s and 1970s. Total enrollment rose on average by 5.6 percent from 1965-1970 and 8 percent from 1970-1980. Such progress, unfortunately, decelerated drastically in the 1980s. Enrollment rates fell to 2.8 percent in the 1980s and a gross enrollment ratio of school-age children at the primary level declined to almost 71 percent by the mid-1990s compared to about 81 percent in the mid-1980s.

Annex 2.3 shows some indicators of the state of education in Africa. An increasing trend is discernible in both enrollment and teaching staff at each and every level of education during the three decades leading up to 1990, excluding the peak in 1980 for the primary schooling. Despite this development, the region trails the other developing regions in both enrollment and teaching staff.

In terms of tertiary education, as in other levels, Africa lags behind all other world regions. Table 2.2 compares enrollments in tertiary technical subjects in 50 African countries with those of South Korea. It is evident from the table that total Korean technical enrollment is five times that of North Africa with the highest enrollment in developing Africa (excluding South Africa). That notwithstanding, it is not nowadays uncommon for university graduates unable to find employment in many countries, mainly because of stagnating economies.

TABLE 2.2
AFRICAN ENROLLMENTS IN TERTIARY TECHNICAL SUBJECTS
COMPARED WITH THOSE OF SOUTH KOREA (% of population)

| Countries | Natural sciences | Math & computers | Engineer-ing only | Total technical |
|---|---|---|---|---|
| Policy improving (15) | 0.02 | 0 | 0.01 | 0.03 |
| Policy deteriorating (14) | 0.02 | 0 | 0.01 | 0.03 |
| North Africa (5) | 0.01 | 0.01 | 0.09 | 0.21 |
| Low-income non-adjusting (16) | 0.01 | 0 | 0.01 | 0.02 |
| South Korea | ... | ... | 0.58 | 0.96 |

Source: ADB, 1995, *African Development Report 1995*, Abidjan.
( ) Number of countries, the first two groups being adjusting countries.

As for literacy, literacy rates have increased substantially since independence in many countries. The unweighted continental average literacy rate which was 38 percent in 1981 rose to 45 percent in 1984 and to 52 percent in 1991 (see Aannex 3.2). This progress is, however, marred by the increase in the absolute number of illiterates. In Sub-Saharan Africa, the number is projected to increase from 132 million in 1980 to 147 million in 2000 (ECA, E/ECA/CM.21/8). Ethiopia, which used to be one of the countries with the highest illiteracy rates (93 percent), is among the countries that has achieved significant progress. The rate fell to about 60 pecrent and the country qualified for the 1980 UNESCO Literacy award.

In spite of the impressive achievements made in the education sector, the region continues, albeit to a decreasing extent, to rely on foreign expertise. This would have been drastically reduced, had it not been for the "brain drain" phenomenon. Particularly true for persons with high-level technical skills, the exodus to western nations has adversely affected technical development and research and development (R&D) activities in the region. Attempts have been made in some countries to remedy some of the anomalies. In Ethiopia, for example, on the Scientific Revival Day of Africa (June 30 every year), the Science and Technology Commission awards funds to individuals on a competitive basis for R&D purposes. This along with the national science and technology policy and the invention, innovation and industrial design patent act have, it seems, encouraged the establishment of the Ethiopian Investors Association in 1995 as well as an increasing number of professional associations, not to speak of science and technology journals.

Although the strength of scientific and technical manpower started from a low base, its increase has been substantial. Africa's stock of scientists and engineers numbered 3,451 per million inhabitants compared with 8,263 for developing countries as a whole (ECA, E/ECA/CM.20/6). Its share in the world distribution of research and development scientists and engineers increased from a meagre 0.3 percent in 1970 to 0.4 percent in 1980 and 1990. The corresponding figures for expenditure on research and development were 0.2 and 0.3 percent, in a number of countries accounting for 0.1 to 0.3 percent of GNP during the

1970s and 1980s (UNIDO, *Industry and Development: Global Report 1991/92*). Even at these low levels in terms of world shares substantial R&D achievements were made in certain areas.

Progress in respect of the remaining indicators, except radio and TV, seem to be decelerating. Both expenditures on R&D and number of books published appear to have been stagnating at levels below those attained in 1980.

The world community views education as a fundamental right of all people. It was this recognition that led to the World Conference on Education for All in Jomtien, Thailand in 1990. The Conference adopted a World Declaration on Education for All and a Framework for Action to Meet Basic Learning Needs. These were intended, among other things, to universalize access to and promote equity in basic education. From a review of achievements during a major part of the first half of the 1990s it appears that no progress has been made. This obviously implies that with the present population structure (persons aged 15 or less accounting for close to 50 percent ) and population growth averaging about 3 percent annually , the goal of education for all will not be attained at the turn of the century or soon there after. In other words, it will be impossible to enroll all school age children as well as improve the quality of education by that date. It is, perhaps, the realization of this in 1996 that prompted the OAU to declare 1997-2006 the Education Decade for Africa.

## Health

Because most of the continent lies within the humid tropical and subtropical areas, vectors and tropical endemic diseases, such as malaria, river blindness and bilharzia, proliferate (see Annex 8.2). This means that the average African is exposed to these diseases in addition to those common in a temperate climate. In other words, more resources are needed in the health sector than in any other region in the world. It is apparent that Africa cannot afford this. It is unfortunate that campaigns that had reduced the prevalence of tropical diseases, such as those against malaria, have been interrupted in some countries for want of resources. Consequently, there is a resurgence of such diseases.

Despite the magnitude of the problem, many newly independent African countries registered significant successes in the health sector. In Sub-Saharan Africa, for instance, the public expenditure on health increased from 0.7 percent of GNP in 1960 to 2.4 percent of GDP in 1990 and the population/ doctor and population/ nurse ratios averaged 18,488 and 6,504 respectively [UNDP, "Human Development Report 1996"]. The population/physician ratio fell from 33,390 in 1965 to 23,610 in 1984 (World Bank, *Sub-Saharan Africa ...*). About 64 percent of the population had access to health services from 1985-1991 and 56 and 41 percent respectively to safe water and sanitation from 1988-1991. From 1985-1995, the percentage of rural and urban population with access to services were: 50 and 81 for health, 35 and 63 for safe water and 30 and 56 for sanitation. From 1990-1994, 64 percent and 51 percent of one-year olds were fully immunized against tuberculosis and measles respectively (UNDP, *Human Development Report 1996*). All these notwithstanding, statistics from another source (ECA, E/ECA/CM.21/ 8) indicate the precarious health situation in the continent. Sub-Saharan Africa accounts for 80 percent of the 110 million malaria (mainly P. falciparum) cases in the world (more than 90 percent of 300-500 million clinical cases each year, according to a more recent WHO document); 140 million people are affected by bilharzia; prenatal, infectious and parasitic illnesses account for 75 percent of infant deaths; and 2.5 percent of the adult population in Sub-Saharan Africa is infected with HIV.

The efforts made by the countries, however, suffered from drastic cuts in social welfare expenditures as a result of the economic crisis in the 1980s and the structural adjustment and related programs that followed. The difficulties facing the health sector were compounded by the proliferation of HIV infections. By the year 2000, 10 million children are expected to be orphaned as a result of AIDS. Because of this and the inordinate financial resources required to implement the Alma-Ata target of assuring "health for all by the year 2000", declared at the International Conference on Primary Health Care in 1978, achievement of that target is likely to be very difficult, if not impossible.

Mass immunization campaigns against measles, polio, whooping cough, diphtheria, tetanus and tuberculosis, as one of the means for achieving the target, are being conducted in many countries. The experience gained in eradicating small pox is being used to eradicate polio by the year 2000. The use of oral rehydration therapy is being  promoted and supported. Better nutrition and improved diets, hygiene and sanitation, safe water supplies, environmental sanitation and essential drug supplies are among the components of "health for all" that require attention  Because of the skyrocketing prices, many drugs are already out of the reach of people, excepting a diminishing minority.

Growing malnutrition is exacerbating the health problem in Africa where the average daily food consumption is only 85 percent of the internationally recommended requirement for healthy and active life. The daily intake of calories per capita increased to 2,337 in 1993 from 2,124 in 1970 (ADB, *African Development Report 1994*). This works out to a mere 10 percent change in 23 years. According to the World Bank, the calorie intake in Sub-Saharan Africa is expected to be 2,170 as against 3,470 in developed countries by 2010. In view of the disparity between the haves and have-nots (the latter by far the majority) and the likelihood of the increase having been absorbed by the few who were able to improve their standard of living, the per capita supply of calories for the majority is likely to have plummeted. Children who survive are exposed to the consequences of malnutrition during their critical growth period. These include vulnerability to diseases, inadequate development of their physical and intellectual capacities (mental retardation) and low productivity. It is quite apparent that poverty alleviation is the solution to this state of affairs.

## Employment

Human resources are plentiful in Africa, yet middle- and high-level personnel are not available in adequate numbers or quality. This is exacerbated by the unrelenting "brain drain" and the non-return of students studying abroad. According to ECA the (E/ECA/CM.20/6): *"It is estimated that 100,000 foreign technical advisors are working in Africa. Paradoxically, this is equivalent to the estimated number of African experts working in Europe and North America."* During the period 1985-1987 more than 30,000 Africans with middle and high level education emigrated to other parts of the world (ECA, *Africa in the 1990s and Beyond: ...*). Poor or inadequate working conditions, remuneration, status and promotion  (which is biased in favor of people in politics and administration) are among the reasons for this state of affairs.

Some 39 percent of the continent's population constituted the labor force in 1990-1992. Women accounted for 35 per cent of the total labor force. The 1990-1992 sectoral division in the total labor force was: agriculture (65%), industry (10%) and services (24%). The shares for industry and services in 1965 were 8 and 14 percent respectively (ECA, E/ECA/CM.21/8). According to another source, the share of agricultural labor in the total labor force fell from 76 percent in 1970 to 63 percent in 1993. Part of the loss in agriculture was taken up by industry and services, the former increasing from 8 to 15 percent and the latter, from 15 to 22 percent. Table 2.3 gives shares of sectoral employment in seven African countries together with their weighted averages in 1975 and 1985. The weighted average for services increased at the expense of the remaining sectors. The fall of the share of manufacturing was small relative to the others, from 14.63 per cent to 14.17 per cent.

TABLE 2.3
SECTORAL EMPLOYMENT SHARE IN SEVEN COUNTRIES IN 1975 AND 1985
(%)

| Country | Agriculture | | Services | | Manufacturing | | Other [a] | |
|---|---|---|---|---|---|---|---|---|
| | 1975 | 1985 | 1975 | 1985 | 1975 | 1985 | 1975 | 1985 |
| Burundi | 60.46 | 14.64 | 18.63 | 48.92 | 9.37 | 12.5 | 11.54 | 23.94 |
| Cote d'Ivoire | 21.66 | 17.29 | 39.19 | 61.6 | 21.46 | 15.86 | 17.69 | 5.25 |
| Ghana | 14.24 | 12.13 | 52.53 | 64.57 | 17.32 | 11.14 | 15.91 | 12.17 |
| Kenya | 29.37 | 20.51 | 52.01 | 59.8 | 12.29 | 13.52 | 6.32 | 6.16 |
| Sierra Leone | 8.04 | 8.57 | 59.23 | 54.36 | 9.53 | 11.73 | 23.2 | 25.34 |
| Zambia | 9.17 | 9.7 | 43.57 | 50.63 | 11.27 | 13.41 | 35.99 | 26.26 |
| Zimbabwe | 34.64 | 26.17 | 38.1 | 47.45 | 14.85 | 16.05 | 12.41 | 10.33 |
| Average [b] | 25.5 | 19.28 | 44.83 | 55.9 | 14.63 | 14.17 | 15.04 | 10.66 |

Source: UNIDO, 1993, *Industry and Development: Global Report 1992/93*, Vienna.
   a  Construction, mining and public utilities      b  Weighted group average

In 1985, the labor force in Africa totaled 79.6 million (ILO/JASPA, *African Employment Report*). The urban labor force accounted for 34.8 per cent and the informal sector employment for 20.6 percent. The corresponding figures for Nigeria, which accounted for 40.5 percent of Africa's total labor force, were 46.2 percent and 50.9 percent respectively. In Sub-Saharan Africa, total employment rose from 168 million in 1985 to 199 million in 1990, with corresponding employment rates of 85 percent and 87 percent. These figures are projected to increase to 279 million and 549 million and 88 percent and 90 percent in 2000 and 2020, respectively. The structure of employment in percent in 1965 and 1989-1991 was as follows: 79 and 67 for agriculture, 8 and 9 for industry and 13 and 24 for services (ILO, *Promoting Employment*). While the increase in the share of industry was marginal that of services nearly doubled, both at the expense of agriculture.

As do other parts of the world, Africa suffers from unemployment and under-employment. This is exacerbated by the migrations of rural people to urban areas seeking employment, which inflates the urban unemployment growth rate up to

10 percent per year. Unemployment increased from 7.7 per cent in 1978 to 22.8 percent in 1990. It has been reported that it is as high as 50 per cent in some countries. It may well rise to 30 per cent for the region as a whole in the year 2000, if the gap between population growth of over 3 percent and employment growth of 2.4 percent annually continues at current levels. School leavers and women are the hardest hit.

According to the ILO's 1994 World Labor Report, 6 million jobs should be created each year throughout the 1990s and 10 million at the beginning of the next century in order to accommodate all job seekers. It should be noted here that a number of countries implementing the World Bank structural adjustment programs or similar economic reform programs since the mid-1980s have compounded the unemployment crisis by retrenching civil servants. During the 1980s and 1990s, retrenchment affected between 10 percent and 30 percent of the total employment in the public sector in many African countries (ILO/JASPA, *African Development Report*). Similar retrenchments resulting from the privatization of state-owned enterprises are worsening the unemployment situation.

(For more details on this chapter refer to Annex 2.4 on the balance sheet of human development in Sub-Saharan Africa.)

## BIBLIOGRAPHY

ADB, 1994, *African Development Report 1994*, Abidjan.

Anderson, Lisa, 1995, "North Africa: The Limits of Liberalization," *Current History*," Vol. 94, No. 591, April 1995, Philadelphia.

BBC, 1998, October 17, 1998.

Chazan, Naomi, R. Mortimer, J. Ravenhill and D. Rothshild, 1988, *Politics and Society in Contemporary Afric*a, MacMillan Education Ltd., London.

CNN Today, 1997, January 1997.

Doresse, Jean, 1987, "Dogali: the Dimension of History," in *The Century of Dogali*, Proceedings of the International Symposium, edited by Taddesse Beyene, Taddesse Tamirat and Richard Pankhurst, 1987, Addis Ababa-Asmara.

ECA, 1994, *A Framework Agenda for Building and Utilizing Critical Capacities in Africa: Preliminary Report (E/ECA/CM.20/6)*, Addis Ababa.

ECA, 1994, *Report on the Implementation of the United Nations New Agenda for the Development of Africa in the 1990s (E/ECA/CM.20/3)*, Addis Ababa.

ECA, 1995, *Human Development in Africa, 1995 Report* (E/ECA/CM.21/8), Addis Ababa (extracted from UNDP's *Human Development Report 1994*).

ECA, 1996, *Africa in the 1990s and Beyond: ECA-Revised Long-Term Development Perspectives Study* (ECA/SERPD/TP/96/3), Addis Ababa.

Emeagwali, Gloria T. and Abubakar , Nurudeen, 1997, "Colonialism and African Indigenous Technology," *African Technology Forum*, Volume 7 No. 2.

FAO, 1994, *FAO Production Yearbook 1994*, Rome.

Foreign Reporter, 1997, "Helping Africa to Help America," No. 2462, September 4, 1997.

Gordon, April A. and Donald L. Gordon, eds., 1996, *Understanding Contemporary Africa*, Second edition, Lynne Reinner Publishers, Inc., Boulder.

ILO, 1996, *Promoting Employment*, Geneva.

ILO/JASPA, 1992, *African Employment Record,* ILO, Addis Ababa.

Microsoft, 1996, *Encarta 1996 Encyclopedia,* Redmond.

Microsoft, 1996, 1997, *Encarta 96 and 97 Encyclopedia,* Redmond.

National Geographic, 1997, *The Dawn of Humans,* February 1997.

OAU, 1997, "African First Ladies Strive for Peace," *AEC Newsletter*, August-October 1997.

Ofcansky, Thomas P. and La Verle Berry, eds. , 1993, *Ethiopia—A Country Study,* 4th edition, Federal Research Division, Library of Congress.

Pankhurst, Sylvia, 1955, *Ethiopia: A Cultural History*, Lalibela House, London.

Pappademos and Setima, Van, 1984, from "A Glimpse from the History of African Science," ESTC Newsletter, Ethiopian Science & Technology Commission, April 1995 and May 1996, Addis Ababa.

Petrides, S. Pierre, 1988, "Alula and Dogali, Their Place in Ethiopian History," *The Centenary of Dogali,* Institute of Ethiopian Studies, Addis Ababa University, Addis Ababa.

Pickthall, M., M., 1981, *Glorious Quran: Final Revelation from God* (Translated from its Original in Arabic), IQRA Book Center, Chicago.

Rachlin, Harvey, 1996, *Lucey's Bones, Sacred Stones, and Einstein's Brain*, Henry Holt and Company, Inc., New York (for part of the information).

Reader, John, 1998, *Africa: A Biography of the Continent,* Alfred A. Knopf, Inc. 1998, New York.

Stock, Robert, 1995, *Africa South of the Sahara: a Geographical Interpretation,* The Guilford Press, London.

Tattersall, Ian, 1997, Out of Africa Again ... and Again, *Scientific American*, April 1997.

The Ethiopian Herald, 1994, *Promotion of the Private Sector in Africa,* August 2, 1994, Addis Ababa.

The Ethiopian Herald, 1994, *SG Helps Boost Agricultural Productivity,* July 30, 1994, Addis Ababa.

The Ethiopian Herald, 1994, *US Invests 250 m. in Assistance to Rwanda Crisis,* July 29, 1994, Addis Ababa.

The Ethiopian Herald, 1995, *OAU Calls for Change in Global Thinking about Africa*, March 1, 1995, Addis Ababa.

The New York Times, 1996, November 19, 1996.

The United Nations Association of the USA, 1997, *The Interdependent,* Winter 1997, New York.

UN, 1993, *World Urbanization Prospects, the 1992 Revision,* New York.

UN, 1994, *World Population Prospects: The 1994 Revision* (Annex tables), New York.

UNDP, 1996, *Human Development Report 1996,* Oxford University Press, New York.

UNESCO, 1981, *General History of Africa II: Ancient Civilizations of Africa,* Heinemann, Berkeley.

UNIDO, 1991, *Industry and Development: Global Report 1991/92*, Vienna.

World Bank, 1989, *Sub-Saharan Africa: From Crisis to Sustainable Growth, a Long-term Perspective Study*, Washington, D.C.

## NOTES

1. As the reader will notice, there are more references in this book to Ethiopia than to any other country. This was done to illustrate happenings and trends in Africa. The reasons for the choice and a brief review of the political, social and economic situation in the country are given in Annex 2.1.
2. Because of space limitation and the fact that the Egyptian history is well known and well advertised suffice it here to say that Egypt occupies one of the highest places in world history.
3. D'mt kingdom with Yeha probably as its capital, in the eighth century B.C., according to UNESCO.
4. Zaire was renamed the Democratic Republic of Congo in May 1997. In this book, in order to avoid cofusing the two Congos, the former zaire is designated by Congo K, the K standing for the capital Kinshasa.
5. A chart on climatic conditions in the Sahara in the last 22,000 years which would have been expected to approximate conditions in other parts of Africa shows: humid, 20,000-15,000 B.C.; arid (glacial maximum), 15,000-10,000 B.C.; humid , 10,000-5,500 B.C.; arid, 5,500-4,500 B.C.; decreasing humidity, 4,500 B.C.-2,000 A.D..
6. The battle of Dogali was one of the many battles that Ethiopia fought during the last quarter of the 19th century against expansionists and inveders. Ethiopia engaged in many battles against the Mahdist forces of the Sudan and defeated the Ottoman Egyptian forces led by European and American mercenaries at Gundet (Eritrea) in 1875 and at Gura in 1876, both in Eritrea, and earlier in two battles by Emperor Tewodros.
7. Africa had had its share of renown generals and military strategists. Hannibal and Ras Alula were among such Africans. The former was famous for the greatest feats in military history, the Punic Wars during the third century B.C. The latter was dubbed "the Abyssinian generalissimo." According to professor Haggai Elrich, an Israeli Professor of history, at a public lecture he gave in July 1995 in Addis Ababa, Ethiopia, *"... during the third quarter of the nineteenth century, the individual structure of Ethiopian political system reached its peak ... and Ras Alula was the embodiment as his talent was mobilized to the talent of Ethiopian might. "* As attested by many writers he excelled as governor, administrator and diplomat and was a committed nationalist. He is given credit for his crucial contribution in intelligence gathering which was decisive in the victory of the battle of Adwa where he was dubbed the "chief of staff."
8. Other individuals who appreciated the new generation of African leaders and are optimistic about Africa's future include: General James L. Jamerson, Deputy Commander in Chief of the US. European Command, and Congressman Charles B. Rangel during their tours in Africa in 1997.
9. Some of the statistical information cited in this section and in Chapter 3 were drawn from ECA's Economic Report on Africa 1994 (E/ECA/CM.20/2) and Report on the Economic and Social Situation in Africa, 1995 (E/ECA/CM.21/3) which include data from other organizations (such as IMF, Word Bank, OECD, FAO, ILO, UNESCO and UNIDO).
10. Dependent population, ages less than 15 and over 65, as a percent of the potential labor force, ages 15 to 65 (World Bank, *World Resources: A Guide to the Global Environment*, 1997).

## CHAPTER 3

# ECONOMIC CONDITIONS

The first oil crisis in 1973 plunged the world into a recession featuring escalating inflation, slow economic growth, growing unemployment, declining productivity, and dwindling investment. This was manifested by sharply declining economic indicators in the majority of African countries. The declines were drastic and continuous and aggravated by subsequent sharp increases in oil prices. Since then more African countries have swelled the ranks of the least developed countries (LDCs) in the world. Whereas in 1994, Botswana graduated to the middle income group, Angola and Eritrea suffered relegation to lower ranks, increasing the number of African LDCs to 33 (out of 48 worldwide) compared to 21 in 1981.

## ECONOMIC INDICATORS

Annex 3.1 provides a general indication of population, area and GDP in 1992 by country, subregion and region. At the continental level, the agricultural population (total population in the rural area) can be seen to have accounted for almost 60 percent of the total population of 680 million. The economically active population in agriculture works out at 15.4 percent of the total agricultural population. This underscores the youth component in the African population.

Of the continent's total area of 2,937 million hectares, only 6.2 percent is arable and under permanent crops while 22.3 percent is forest area and woodland. An insignificant 0.4 percent of the total area is under irrigation. The Sahel, which stretches across Africa between the Sahara and the coastal and other countries to its south has 30 percent cultivable land of which only 35 percent is in use (Juo et. al. 1995).

### Gross Domestic Product

Following independence in the 1960s, the region did relatively well in the economic and social domains during the period 1961-1972. That performance was interrupted following the enormous increases in oil prices and consequently those of industrial goods prices in 1973. Over the past decade and a half, continental GDP at constant 1987 prices increased steadily but very slowly from $348.4 million in 1980 to $421.8 million in 1993 (Annex 3.2).

According to the United Nations Conference on Trade and Development (UNCTAD), Africa's annual real GDP rate of growth averaged about 4.1 percent in the period 1960-1980. The generally declining and fluctuating growth rates for the period 1980-1993 are shown in Annex 3.2. According to the IMF which observed *"marked improvements in Africa's economic performance in 1994-1995"*, Africa experienced significant improvement in economic performance in 1994 (2.9 percent) and 1995 (3.0 percent) compared with 0.8 percent and 0.9 percent in 1992 and 1993 respectively (IMF, *World Economic Outlook*). Sub-

Saharan African GDP grew by 4.7 percent in the period 1966-1973, then dipped to 0.7 percent in 1991-1994 and rose to an estimated 3.8 percent in 1995 (World Bank, *Global Economic Prospects & the Developing Countries*).

Higher rate of growth for the continent was expected in 1996 (UN, *World Economic and Social Survey 1996*). This expectation was met as, according to the ECA (*Report .... Planning, E/ECA/CM.23/12*), GDP grew at a rate of 4 percent in 1996 compared with the 2.7 percent achieved in 1995. Twenty four countries achieved growth rates exceeding 4 percent during 1995/96, 32 countries grew faster in that period than in1993/94, and fiscal and current deficits and inflation were reduced in many countries. According to the ADB, African GDP growth rate was 3.7 percent in 1997. It was expected by the United Nations to slow to an estimated 3.1 percent in 1997, compared to 4.4 percent in 1996, mainly due to a fall in oil prices (which affected oil exporting countries) and a decline in agricultural production resulting from drought and flooding attributable to the El Nino phenomenon. In its *World Economic Outlook* the IMF forecasted Africa's economy to increase by 3.7 percent in 1998 because of improvements in economic policies compared to 3.2 percent in 1997. In regard to Sub-Saharan Africa, the World Bank has predicted that the economy will grow by about 3.8 percent in Africa during the period 1995-2000 (FAO, *The State of Food and Agriculture 1995*). The economic reforms (discussed later in this chapter) that are being implemented are likely to contribute to the projected rate. This seems to be the case with African LDCs which, according to UNCTAD's *Trade and Development Report* 1997, registered an average GDP growth rate estimated at 4.6 percent in 1996 compared with 5.4 percent in 1995.

Figure 3.1 compares real GDP growth rates in Africa and Asia. It is apparent from the figure that Africa has been consistently lagging far behind developing Asia. After an upward trend in the 1993-1996 period its growth rate, according to the IMF, was expected to fall to 4.5 percent in 1996 from 5.3 percent the previous year, both figures being estimates.

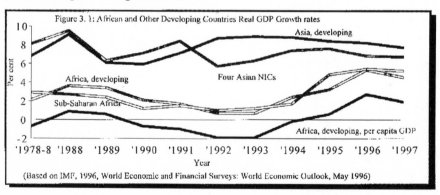

Figure 3. 1: African and Other Developing Countries Real GDP Growth rates

(Based on IMF, 1996, World Economic and Financial Surveys: World Economic Outlook, May 1996)

The economic performance of African subregions[1] during the period 1989-1993 (provisional for 1992 and preliminary estimates for 1993) in real GDP growth and at constant 1985 market prices is shown in Figure 3.2. Except for 1991, the performance of the Economic Community of the Central African States (ECCAS) was characterized by negative growth rates. All other subregions and groups (except net oil importers in 1992) registered positive rates, with the Economic

Community of West African States (ECOWAS) leading throughout the period. Based on 1992-1993 growth rates, Togo, Rwanda, Angola and Libya were among the worst performers and Equatorial Guinea, Malawi, Mauritania and Nigeria among the best.

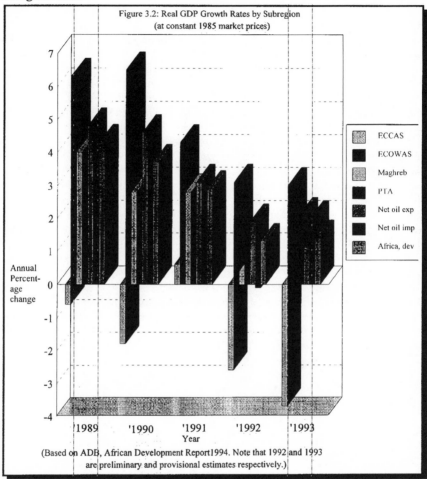

Figure 3.2: Real GDP Growth Rates by Subregion (at constant 1985 market prices)

(Based on ADB, African Development Report1994. Note that 1992 and 1993 are preliminary and provisional estimates respectively.)

Unlike total GDP which was characterized by positive but fluctuating rates of growth, the trend in regard to per capita GNP was downward (see Annex 3.2). GNP per capita at market prices (using the World Bank Atlas method of converting data in national currency to US dollars) for the continent as a whole declined steadily and dipped to $615 in 1993 from $860 in 1980, the corresponding figures for Sub-Saharan Africa being $520 and $720. During the 1980-1993 period the peak levels attained were $860 for Africa in 1980 and $770 for Sub-Saharan Africa in 1981. (Annex 3.3). Sub-Saharan figures for other years include: $250 in 1972, $400 in 1975, $600 in 1985 and $520 in 1990 (World Bank, *World Tables in Figures 1994*).

Between 1977 and 1985 the region's per capita GDP fell by 15 percent. GDP growth rates decelerated to 0.3 percent in 1993 from 3.8 percent in 1980 for the continent and to 0.8 percent form 2.4 percent fors Sub-Saharan Africa. Such trends were evident among other economic and social indicators, including gross domestic savings and gross domestic investment. These figures imply that most Africans were poorer in early 1990s than they were in the 1970s. The number of countries which attained per capita income of the early 1990s in earlier decades were: 11 in 1960 or earlier, eight in the 1960s, 14 in the 1970s and 9 in the 1980s. Only nine countries showed per capita incomes higher than ever before (UNDP, *Human Resource Development Report 1996*).

The above state of affairs is, in part, the result of the GDP growth rate failing to keep pace with the population growth rate and consequently leading to deteriorating socio-economic conditions in most African countries. Figure 3.3 on gross domestic savings and investment as percentage of GDP and perusal through Annex 3.3 show that this holds particularly true for Sub-Saharan African countries. From another source, gross investment as percentages of GDP in Sub-Saharan Africa were: 25.8, 19.3 and 16.3 in the periods 1970-1979, 1980-1989 and 1990-1994, respectively. Whereas public investment was marginally higher than private investment in the first period it was the opposite during the latter periods, with a 3.7 percentage margin during the last period (IFC, *Trends in Private Investment in Developing Countries 1990-94*). For the region as a whole, domestic savings were 29 percent, 17.6 percent and 17.6 percent in 1974-1981, 1982-1989 and 1990-1995, respectively, the corresponding figures for domestic investment being 31.9 percent, 22.4 percent and 20.7 percent (UNIDO, *Industrial Development: Global Report 1997*). Projections for the period 1998-2001, averaging 20.5 percent for savings and 23.3 percent for investment, given in the same source as Annex 3.9 are marginally higher than those achieved in 1995.

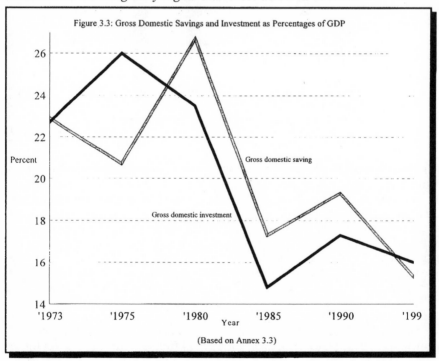

Figure 3.3: Gross Domestic Savings and Investment as Percentages of GDP

Percent

Gross domestic saving

Gross domestic investment

Year

(Based on Annex 3.3)

Table 3.1 compares the performance of the continent with those of developing countries. Most of the indicators showed a downward trend in Africa while they increased steadily in other developing countries. In Africa the real annual growth rate of GDP fell from 2.6 percent in 1975-82 to 1.6 percent in 1990-94, and in the developing countries it rose from 4.7 percent to 5.4 percent over the same period. The same applies to projections for the 1995-2000 period. Although the 1995-2000 GDP projection gap is substantial, it is much narrower than that of 1990-94. African GDP is expected to attain 72.6 percent of the rate of increase projected for developing countries in 1995-2000 in contrast to the 34.0 percent achieved in 1990-1994. It should be noted here that the rate of GDP growth (4.5 percent) used to project GDP during the period 1995-2000 is 75 percent of that assumed by the United Nations New Agenda for Development of Africa (UN-NADAF).

TABLE 3.1
COMPARISON OF THE PERFORMANCE OF SOME CONTINENTAL ECONOMIC INDICATORS WITH THOSE OF DEVELOPING COUNTRIES, INCLUDING PROJECTIONS FOR 1995-2000

|  | African continent | | | | Developing countries | | | |
|---|---|---|---|---|---|---|---|---|
|  | 1975-82 | 1983-89 | 1990-94 | 1995-2000 | 1975-82 | 1983-89 | 1990-94 | 1995-2000 |
| Real GDP (% per year) | 2.6 | 2.6 | 1.6 | 4.5 | 4.7 | 4.7 | 5.4 | 6.2 |
| Per capita GDP (% per year) | -0.2 | -0.3 | -11 | 1.9 | 2 | 2.5 | 3.5 | 4.2 |
| Consumer prices (% per year) | 16.1 | 16 | 26.1 | 8.5 | 21.7 | 38.4 | 44.1 | 8 |
| Savings (% of GDP) | 25.2 | 18.7 | 17.8 | 20.5 | 25.3 | 22.9 | 23.3 | 24.7 |
| Investment (% of GDP) | 29 | 20.8 | 21.1 | 22.3 | 25.9 | 23.9 | 25 | 25.6 |
| Current account balance (% of GDP) | -3.8 | -2.2 | -3.4 | -1.8 | -0.5 | -1 | -1.6 | -0.9 |
| Source: IMF, 1995, *World Economic Outlook*, Washington, D.C. | | | | | | | | |

During the years 1961-1987, 25 countries in the region registered positive growth rates and 10 showed negative rates. Mauritius and Botswana were among the exceptions that showed consistently high GDP growth rates throughout the 1980s. Mauritius achieved 10 percent and Botswana, 8.3 percent. Thanks to economic reform, Uganda's GDP growth, which had dipped to -2.5 percent in the 1980s (World Bank, *Sub-Saharan Africa ...*), registered 8 percent in 1994 with a 24.5 percent manufacturing growth rates (*Foreign Report*, May 4, 1995). It appears that there was a shift towards better frequency distribution of countries according to real GDP growth rates in the period 1992-1995. The number of countries with negative rates fell from 19 in 1993 to 11, 9 and 3 in 1994, 1995 and 1996, respectively. The corresponding numbers of countries with greater than 3 percent growth rates in these same years were 19, 27, 31 and 41 [ADB, *African Development Report* 1997).

According to *The Economist* (January 17, 1998), Angola, Uganda and Botswana were expected to be among the 20 fastest growing and one only (Libya) among the slowest growing countries in the world in 1998. Similar predictions for 1999 by the Economist Intellegence Unit show dramatic expansion of the number of African countries from three to eight (Uganda, Senegal, Cameroon, Cote d'Ivoire, Malawi, Tanzania, Ghana, and Egypt) in the 20 fastest growing emerging market economies, with Libya maintaining its previous position as the only African country in the 20 countries with negative rates of growth. This does not include countries, such as Ethiopia and Eritrea, which have been registering in recent year growth rates comparable to if not higher than above countries.

Table 3.2 presents the structure of Sub-Saharan Africa GDP at 1987 constant prices in 1965, 1987 and 1994. It is apparent that both industry (including mining, construction and utilities) and services have increased their shares at the expense of agriculture.

| TABLE 3.2 STRUCTURE OF SUB-SAHARAN AFRICA GDP (% at 1987 constant prices) | | | |
|---|---|---|---|
| | 1965 | 1987 | 1994 |
| Agriculture | 43 | 33 | 25 |
| Industry | 18 | 28 | 28 |
| Services | 39 | 39 | 47 |
| Source: ECA, 1996, *Measures to Consolidate Privatization in the African Industrial Sector with Special Emphasis on the program of the Second Industrial Development Decade for Africa.* | | | |

No significant changes seem to have taken place in the composition of the structure of GDP during the period 1975-1985. Figure 3.4 on sectoral shares of GDP in Sub-Saharan Africa confirms this. From the figure it is apparent that the share of agriculture which would have been expected to fall increased marginally in 1985 as did manufacturing. From more recent information, the 1995 structure of GDP was: 20 percent agriculture, 30 percent industry, 15 percent manufacturing and 48 percent services compared to 24, 36, 12 and 38 in 1980, respectively (World Bank, *The State in a Changing World*). The overall poor performance is partly due to inappropriate government policies and mismanagement of resources, continued recession in the industrialized countries, low levels and declines in domestic savings and investment, vagaries of weather, downward trends in and fluctuating prices of exports (Annex 3.4). These lead to lower export revenues and a lack of foreign currency to import agricultural and industrial inputs.

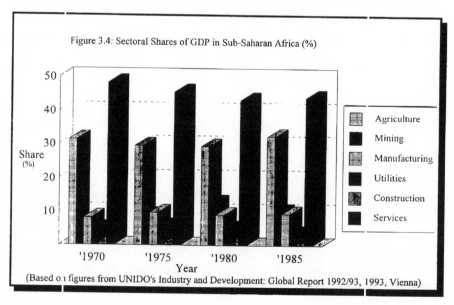

Figure 3.4: Sectoral Shares of GDP in Sub-Saharan Africa (%)

(Based on figures from UNIDO's Industry and Development: Global Report 1992/93, 1993, Vienna)

Gross domestic savings as a percent of GDP fell from 27.6 in 1980 to 16.2 in 1993. The figures for gross domestic investment were 25.0 and 18.7 respectively. Gross fixed capital formation dropped from $76.3 billion in 1980 to $58.9 billion in 1989 (ECA, E/ECA/CM.21/7). According to ADB gross domestic investment at constant market prices (1985) increased from $30.2 billion in 1970 to $71.8 billion in 1980 and seemed to have hovered around $54-55 billion during the late 1980s and early 1990s, including 1993 (ADB, *African Development Report 1994*).

The effect of economic performance of the developed economies on those of developing countries manifests itself in, among other things, purchasing power, savings and investment. It has been, for instance, estimated by the International Monetary Fund (IMF) that a one percent increase in the real GDP of the industrialized countries increases the purchasing power of developing countries by 3.4 percent.

As is well known, GDP per capita alone, as a socio-economic measure or as an indicator of living standards, is not satisfactory. Skewed distribution of incomes, different life styles based on traditional consumer goods and services and market exchange rates that do not reflect the real purchasing power of national currencies, among others, can make international comparisons meaningless. In recent years economists have come up with a number of new indicators. World Bank's wealth and genuine saving and UNDP's human development index (HDI) are among such indicators. At present, purchasing power parity (PPP) is used for making international comparisons. PPP measures the price of the same quantity of comparable goods and services in national currency that $1 would buy in an average country.

The HDI was introduced in 1990 (UNDP, *Human Development Report 1994*). This index (ranging between 0 and 1), which is considered a more adequate measure of social welfare, is based on three variables: longevity, education and income. Longevity is measured by life expectancy at birth; education is approximated by adult literacy rates and mean years of schooling; and income (purchasing power parity dollars) is represented by real per capita GDP adjusted for the local cost of living.[2] According to the index, the 1993 HDI for Sub-saharan Africa was 0.379 compared with 0.331 for all LDCs and 0.746 for the world as a whole (UNDP, *Human Development Report 1996*). The HDI for Sub-Saharan Africa rose progressively from about 0.201 in 1960 through 0.257 in 1970 to 0.312 in 1980. Of the 174 countries for which HDIs were given, Ethiopia, with the lowest adjusted real per capita GDP of $420 and HDI of 0.237, ranked higher in that indicator than six countries with higher adjusted real GDP per capita (ranging between $530 in Mali and $860 in Sierra Leone). In other words, Ethiopians with per capita GNP of $100 were, apparently, better off than their counterparts in these 6 countries.

For want of adequate information it is hazardous to venture into making projections, particularly at the continental level. Nevertheless, an attempt has been made below to project GDP and population growth up to the year 2000. Two methods, the historical trend and normative scenario, have been used.

(i). The historical trend is based on the following assumptions by the ECA:
- 3.1% GDP rate of growth and 1993 total GDP of $465.9 billion at 1990 constant prices, and
- 3.0% population rate of increase and 1993 total population of 699,840,000.

(ii). The normative scenario is based on the objective of the United Nations New Agenda for Africa's development:

- GDP growth rates of 6% (agriculture at 5%), considered a rate that could enable African countries to achieve sustained development) from 1995-2005 and 7% from 2005-2015 assuming 1993 total GDP of $465.9 billion at 1990 constant prices,
- 2.8% rate of population increase (medium variant) assuming 1993 total population of 699,840,000, and
- 3.2% annual average growth rate of income per capita.

Projections made on the basis of the above assumptions are presented in Table 3.3 below. It is apparent from the table that the historical trend method yields practically stagnant per capita GDP, a mere 25.6 percent increase by 2020, over a 27 year period. The normative scenario based projection, however, offers a relatively high increase, 163.3 percent. This indicates that if the continent is to develop, a combination of relatively high GDP and lower population growth rates will have to be achieved. Considering the low base of per capita GDP, the economic reforms adopted and being adopted by an increasing number of countries and the experiences in countries such as Morocco, Tunisia, Botswana, Mauritius and Uganda as well as other developing countries and regions, the normative scenario version appears implementable although it is quite likely that it will take some time before the 6 percent level of GDP growth is attained.

| | Actual | | Projection [b] | | | | | |
|---|---|---|---|---|---|---|---|---|
| | 1993 [a] | Rate of growth (%) [a] | 1995 | 2000 | 2005 | 2010 | 2015 | 2020 |
| Historical trend | | | | | | | | |
| Population (m) | 699.8 | 3 | 742.5 | 860.1 | 1020.9 | 1183.5 | 1372 | 1590.6 |
| Total GDP ($ b) | 465.9 | 3.1 | 523.5 | 700.5 | 841.3 | 980.1 | 1141.7 | 1330 |
| GDP per capita ($) | 665.76 | | 705.05 | 814.44 | 824.08 | 828.14 | 832.14 | 836.16 |
| Normative scenario | | | | | | | | |
| Population (m), medium variant | 699.8 | 2.8 | 719.5 | 849 | 974.9 | 1119.2 | 1284.9 | 1475.2 |
| Total GDP ($ b) | 465.9 | 6-7 | 523.5 | 700.5 | 937.4 | 1314.8 | 1844 | 2586.3 |
| GDP per capita ($) | 665.76 | | 727.59 | 825.09 | 961.53 | 1174.77 | 1435.13 | 1753.19 |

TABLE 3.3
ACTUAL AND PROJECTED POPULATION AND GDP IN AFRICA UNDER HISTORICAL TREND AND NORMATIVE SCENARIO

Source: a Economic Commission for Africa   b computed

Improved African economic performance, mainly resulting from temporary rises in prices of export agricultural commodities in recent years as observed by the World Bank and the IMF, seems to support the normative scenario. It should be noted that, despite the relatively low economic performance in recent years, GDP was expected to grow by 6 to 7 percent in 1997 in most East Asian countries, where the economic bases are very high compared to those in Africa.

ADB has made projections up to 2001. These are 5.3 percent in 1996 and an average of 4.6 percent during the period 1996-2001. According to ADB, " *Improvements in external factors affecting the African economies and the deepen-*

*ing of policy reforms"* are the basis for the 1996 projection (ADB, *African Development Report 1996*). Although more realistic, these projections, falling as they do between the historical trend and the normative scenario, will not likely achieve the level of economic development so badly needed.

## Agriculture

Agricultural development in Africa is hampered by many factors. These include: backward technologies, drought, deterioration of infrastructure, civil disturbances, lack of investment and unfavorable international prices. These have led to increasing dependency on food imports.

According to FAO figures (*FAO Production Yearbook*), the African continent covers a total area of about 3 billion hectares, of which 65.6 million hectares is under water. About 30 percent of the arable land (168 million hectares in 1990) is under rain-fed agriculture and therefore prone to fluctuations in production.

Both arable land and land under permanent crops have been increasing steadily; the former stood at 163.6 million hectares and the latter at 18.9 million hectares in 1992, including marginal land in some countries. This phenomenon also held true for land under irrigation which increased from just under one million hectares to 1.15 million hectares (mainly in Egypt, Sudan, Madagascar and Nigeria), out of a total of about 9 million hectares of irrigable land. By way of contrast, the fate of the area under forest and woodland (whether productive or not) was just the opposite, shrinking from 719.8 million hectares in 1977 to 656.4 million hectares in 1992 (see Annex 3.1 for details by country and subregion).

As can be observed in Annex 3.1 the majority of the population is engaged in agriculture. In 1980, the agricultural population accounted for 65.4 percent (computed) of the total population. This share has been declining slowly and stood at 59.3 percent in 1992 and 58.9 percent in 1993. A similar trend applies to the share of agriculturally active population in the total economically active population. In many countries, the large number of farmers have not been able to produce enough food to feed themselves let alone meet the requirements of the urban population. By contrast farmers in developed countries, who constitute about 2 to 3 percent of the population, produce food in excess of national needs to feed the hungry of the world.[3] Because of the steadily growing shortage of food since the 1970s, Africa's main preoccupation now and in the near future is improving its food self-sufficiency ratio by enhancing food productivity and production coupled with food security and early warning systems.

Agriculture accounts for about 19 percent of GDP (ranging from less than 5 percent in Seychelles to about 63 percent in Somalia in 1987-1993), the corresponding figure for Sub-Saharan Africa being about 30 percent (Annex 3.2). As shown in Annex 4.2, total African cereal production increased from 46.2 million tons in 1961 to 99.4 million in 1991 and dipped to 84 million in 1992 mainly due to the drought referred to earlier. The corresponding figures for roots and tubers were 48.1, 114 and 118.2. Not only were roots and tubers greater in magnitude but also seem to have exhibited more consistent and steady growth after 1980. From a recent source cereal output rose to 104.8 million tons, roots and tubers to 112.5 million tons and plantains to 21.2 million tons; and the population of livestock stood at 190 million cattle, 212 million sheep and one billion birds in 1995 (ADB, *African Development Report 1996*). The annex provides production figures for other agricultural commodities.

Agricultural output increased by an average of 2.7 percent in the 1960s (FAO, *Computer Files*). Figure 3.5 gives annual percentage change of agricultural production in Africa. Except for 1992, total production increased during the periods and years in the figure. The 1992 negative rate of growth is probably mainly due to the drought that hit Southern Africa in 1992. The 14.5 percent decline for cereals seems to support this assumption. Cereal production recovered in 1993 (up 13.2 percent) and in 1994 (up 9.0 percent) and declined to 2.5 percent in 1995, a rate that is lower than the population growth rate. In terms of indices (1979-1981=100), agricultural production at 5-year intervals during the period 1970-1990 and through 1994 a showed steady rising trend from 88 in 1970 to 139 in 1994 and 1995 (ADB, *African Development Report* 1996).

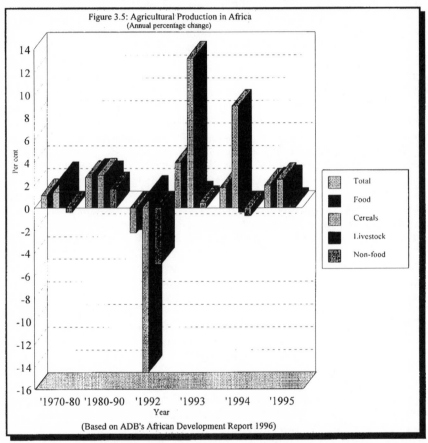

Figure 3.5: Agricultural Production in Africa
(Annual percentage change)

(Based on ADB's African Development Report 1996)

Table 3.4 presents 1993 actual quantities and 2008 perspectives of major foods in Africa. While the historical scenario is a continuation of past trends, the normative scenario assumes the attainment of a fair degree of food self-sufficiency with a population growth rate of 2.8 percent and per capita GDP growth of 3.1 percent. The projections under the normative scenario show that Africa will be self-sufficient in roots and tubers, pulses and meat but only 92.5 percent sufficient in cereals.

TABLE 3.4
THE PERSPECTIVES OF MAJOR FOODS IN AFRICA BY 2008 (1000 t)

| | Cereals | | | Roots and tubers | | | Pulses | | | Meat | | |
|---|---|---|---|---|---|---|---|---|---|---|---|---|
| | 1993 | 2008 | | 1993 | 2008 | | 1993 | 2008 | | 1993 | 2008 | |
| | | HS | NS | | HS | NS | | HS | NS | | HS | NS |
| Food | 104459 | 164260 | 209452 | 87910 | 144100 | 273150 | 6598 | 12760 | 13500 | 8494 | 14310 | 27700 |
| Industry | | | | 9600 | 9800 | 19900 | 768 | 1034 | 1789 | 8 | 9 | 17 |
| Waste and losses | | | | 17300 | 19900 | 2650 | 673 | 1359 | 981 | | | |
| Other uses | 2800 | 2000 | 4000 | | | | | | | | | |
| Total demand | 107259 | 166260 | 213452 | 114800 | 173820 | 295600 | 8039 | 15152 | 16270 | 8502 | 14319 | 27717 |
| Total production | 94686 | 109945 | 197366 | 120900 | 165125 | 295600 | 6881 | 13303 | 16270 | 7185 | 13230 | 27717 |
| Net trade | -12573 | -56315 | -16086 | -6100 | -8695 | - | -1158 | -849 | - | -1317 | -1089 | |
| Self-sufficiency ratio (%) | 88.2 | 66.2 | 92.5 | 95 | 95 | 100 | 85.6 | 87.8 | 100 | 84.5 | 92.4 | 100 |
| Per caput demand (kg) | 152.7 | 151.1 | 213.4 | | | | 11.4 | 15.9 | 16.6 | 12.2 | 13.1 | 27.8 |
| Per caput consumption (kg) | 148.8 | 149.3 | 209.4 | 174 | 131 | 273 | 9.4 | 11.6 | 13.5 | 12.1 | 13 | 27.7 |

Source: ECA, 1996, *Africa in the 1990s and Beyond: ECA-Revised Long-Term Development Perspectives Study* (ECA/SERPD/TP/96/3),Addis Ababa.     HS  Historical scenario     NS  Normal scenario

Information on per capita figures are more revealing. According to a statement by the FAO Director-General to the 1995 OAU Summit in Addis Ababa, per capita food production over the past 20 to 25 years has been falling. Production of staple foodstuff (wheat, rice, other cereals, cassava and tubers) in wheat equivalent fell from 210 kgs in 1970 to 204 kgs in 1975 and 179 kgs in 1980 (FAO, *African Agriculture: the Next 25 Years, Annex V*). As shown in Table 3.5 the per capita agricultural production index (1979-81=100) which stood at 97.3 in 1982 fluctuated in subsequent years and peaked at 98.2 in 1989 and 1991 and leveled off at about 93.3 during the three years thereafter. Except for livestock, although the peak and low years may vary, the food, crop and cereal production trends are similar to that of agriculture. In LDCs per capita food production dropped by 0.5 percent per year in 1970-1980, 0.8 percent in 1980-1989 and 1.3 percent in 1989-1993. Their average per capita daily dietary energy supplies of 2,050 kilocalories in 1988-1992 works out to 89.1 percent of the 2,300 required for normal body growth (UNCTAD, *The Least Developed Countries*, 1995 Report). It is apparent that the region suffered from the dwindling availability of locally produced foodstuffs.

TABLE 3.5
FAO INDICES OF AGRICULTURAL PRODUCTION IN THE CONTINENT( 1979-81=100)

| | 1970 | 1975 | 1980 | 1982 | 1983 | 1984 | 1985 | 1986 | 1987 | 1988 | 1989 | 1990 | 1991 | 1992 | 1993 | 1994 |
|---|---|---|---|---|---|---|---|---|---|---|---|---|---|---|---|---|
| | | | | | | Total production | | | | | | | | | | |
| Agriculture | 91.4 | 97.3 | 99.9 | 103.1 | 103.5 | 102.4 | 111 | 115.9 | 115.6 | 122.5 | 126.7 | 128.2 | 134.1 | 131.2 | 136.4 | 138.8 |
| Food | | | | 103.4 | 103.6 | 102.4 | 111.1 | 116.4 | 116.1 | 123.5 | 127.6 | 129.3 | 135.6 | 135 | 138.6 | 141.4 |
| Crops | | | | 102.5 | 103.2 | 111.4 | 118 | 116 | 124.6 | 128.9 | 128.9 | 129.7 | 136.9 | 132 | 138.9 | 142.6 |
| Cereals | | | | 101.4 | 89.7 | 90 | 115.4 | 121.9 | 112.4 | 128.8 | 135.5 | 125.1 | 141.5 | 121 | 137 | 149.2 |
| Livestock products | | | | 105.8 | 108.2 | 107.8 | 112.8 | 114.5 | 117.5 | 120.3 | 124.4 | 128 | 130.1 | 131.9 | 133.1 | 135.2 |
| | | | | | | Per caput production | | | | | | | | | | |
| Agriculture | | | | 97.3 | 93.3 | 91.5 | 96.4 | 97.8 | 94.8 | 97.6 | 98.2 | 96.5 | 98.2 | 93.3 | 94.2 | 93.1 |
| Food | | | | 97.6 | 93.3 | 91.5 | 96.5 | 98.2 | 95.2 | 98.4 | 98.9 | 97.4 | 99.2 | 94.6 | 95.8 | 95 |
| Crops | | | | 96.8 | 91.1 | 90.4 | 96.8 | 99.6 | 95.1 | 99.4 | 99.9 | 97.7 | 100.2 | 93.9 | 96 | 96 |
| Cereals | | | | 95.8 | 82.5 | 80.5 | 102.2 | 103.9 | 92.3 | 102.8 | 105 | 94.3 | 103.6 | 86.3 | 94.2 | 100.9 |
| Livestock | | | | 99.9 | 99.4 | 96.3 | 98 | 96.7 | 96.4 | 95.9 | 96.3 | 96.3 | 95.2 | 93.8 | 92 | 89 |

Source - FAO, 1993, 1994, F.40 Production Yearbook, Rome
- u  ADB, 1994, *African Development Report1994*, Abidjan for 1970, 1975 and 1980

45

The above downward trend in food production was recognized in the 1970s. As a result, and at the request of African member countries, the Regional Food Plan for Africa (not including South Africa) was prepared in 1978 by FAO in cooperation with ECA with a view to addressing the issue and proposing ways and means of increasing food self-sufficiency in Africa. Based on this Plan, a resolution of the FAO Regional Conference in 1979 invited the governments of African countries to *"prepare and implement appropriate policies and programs for improved food self-sufficiency, giving special attention to modernization of the subsistence and small farm sector..."*

In the 1960s, particularly during the second half, Africa was a net exporter of millet and sorghum, roots and tubers, pulses, vegetables, vegetable oils, fruits, mutton and lamb (FAO, *Regional Food Plan for Africa*). Most African countries experienced favorable terms of trade during the 1970s. The past two decades witnessed a decline in the food self-sufficiency ratio (%), averaging 75 from 1978-1982 after a drop from 98 in 1962-1964 and 90 in 1972-1974. Per capita food production declined by over 20 percent in Sub-Saharan Africa. During the period 1988-1993, food production lagged behind population growth in 33 out of 43 Sub-Saharan African countries. Crop and livestock production in 1993 increased by 3.4 percent following 1992, a year characterized by stagnation in production (FAO, *The State of Food and Agriculture 1994*). In 1969/1971, the food import dependency ratio ranged between 1.1 in Ethiopia and 90.9 in Djibouti. By 1988/1990, the situation had changed with Uganda registering the lowest dependency (1.4) and Mauritius, the highest (95.3).

Trade and aid in cereals, the most important food import item, is presented in Table 3.6. Net imports, which stood at 2.6 million tons in 1961, increased steadily and reached 17.2 million tons in 1980 and 31.1 million tons in 1993. Food aid ranged between 4.5 and 6.3 million tons during the beginning and end of the 1980/81-1991/92 period. In 1992/93, cereal import was 25 million tons of which 6 million tons was in the form of aid (FAO, *Food Crops and Shortage, Special Report*, No.1). Africa's share in total world food aid peaked at 61.2 percent in 1984/85. Since then it has shown a general downward trend until 1991/92. Because of the droughts in 1992 in Southern Africa and in 1994/95 in Eastern Africa it is likely to have increased substantially in subsequent years.

TABLE 3.6
AFRICAN TRADE IN CEREALS AND RECEIPTS OF CEREAL AID

Trade (Q=quantity in 1000 t and V= values in m $) [a]

| Year | 1961 | | 1965 | | 1970 | | 1975 | | 1980 | | 1985 | | 1990 | | 1993 | |
|---|---|---|---|---|---|---|---|---|---|---|---|---|---|---|---|---|
| | Q | V | Q | V | Q | V | Q | V | Q | V | Q | V | Q | V | Q | V |
| Import | 5038 | 371 | 5744 | 462 | 6624 | 514 | 12330 | 2570 | 21635 | 5120 | 30241 | 5539 | 28351 | 5168 | 34284 | 5518 |
| Export | 2435 | 155 | 1722 | 145 | 2996 | 222 | 4790 | 649 | 4356 | 771 | 1044 | 141 | 3785 | 534 | 3182 | 500 |
| Import - Export [c] | 2603 | 216 | 4022 | 317 | 3628 | 292 | 7540 | 192 | 17279 | 4349 | 20197 | 5398 | 24566 | 4634 | 31102 | 5018 |

AID (1000 t) [b]

| Year | 80/81 | 81/82 | 82/83 | 83/84 | 84/85 | 85/86 | 86/87 | 87/88 | 88/89 | 89/90 | 90/91 | 91/92 |
|---|---|---|---|---|---|---|---|---|---|---|---|---|
| Africa | 4512 | 4938 | 4658 | 5133 | 7655 | 5904 | 6320 | 6173 | 4704 | 4596 | 5747 | 6347 |
| World | 8673 | 8714 | 9155 | 9807 | 12511 | 10949 | 12599 | 13549 | 10215 | 11357 | 12322 | 13522 |
| African share in world aid (%) [b] | 52 | 56.7 | 50.9 | 52.3 | 61.2 | 53.9 | 50.2 | 45.7 | 45.9 | 40.6 | 46.5 | 46.9 |

Source - a FAO ,1994, FAOSTAT data, Statistics Division, Rome.
- b FAO , 1992, Food Aid in Figures, Vol. 10, Rome
- c Computed

During the period 1990-1993, the production of industrial/export crops fluctuated. Coffee fell from 1.28 million tons in 1990 to 1.1 million tons in 1993, the last figure accounting for 19 percent of world production. The corresponding figures for other crops were: 0.32 to 0.35 at 13.1 percent for tea; 1.4 to 1.29 at 53.33 percent for cocoa; 0.37 to 0.5 at 6 percent for tobacco; 1.27 to 1.39 at 8.30 percent for cotton lint (see Annex 4.2).

As can be observed from Annex 3.4, during the period 1982-1993, the price indices (1985=100) of commodities of interest to Africa peaked as follows: in 1990 for agricultural raw materials, 1988/89 for minerals, ores and metals, 1986 for tropical beverages and 1989 for food. The generally downward trend and fluctuating prices of specific African exports are shown in the same annex. As the figures are in current prices they, unfortunately, do not reflect the actual situation. A better perception of price trends based on price indices (1990=100) during the first half of the 1990s is given in the lower part of the annex. Some export commodities (cocoa, coffee, copper, hides, iron ore and newsprint) rose during 1994-1995, but so, unfortunately, did a number of African import items, including wheat and fertilizers (urea having peaked at 147.8 in March 1995). Declining and fluctuating export prices and increasing import prices have thus compounded the socio-economic difficulties of the region. According to the ADB, the fall in prices (except fuels) in the first half of 1995 was expected to negatively impact export prices in 1996.

From past history it is virtually impossible to predict how prices will behave in the future. Indications are, however, provided by the World Bank. During the second half of the 1990s, prices of all commodity groups, excluding fats and oils and other foods, were expected to increase in real terms, with minerals, metals and tropical timber showing significant increases. An opposite trend of declining prices in real terms was anticipated for the period 2000-2005, except for beverages, tropical timber and petroleum (World Bank, *Price Prospects for Major Primary Commodities*). As stated in a more recent document, the World Bank expects the following declining annual average price indices during the period 1996-2004: 2 percent for non-oil, 1 percent for metals and minerals, 2.5 percent for agricultural commodities and 5 to 6 percent for beverages (World Bank, *Global Economic Prospects and the Developing Countries*).

A multiple of factors contributed to the poor performance of African agriculture. These include declining soil fertility, recurring droughts, inadequate use of improved technology and deterioration of land resources (soil erosion) and the consequent increase of desertification, particularly in arid and semi-arid regions. The magnitude of decline in soil fertility can be illustrated by nutrient depletion during cropping in Sub-Saharan Africa. On the average, about 10 kg of N, 1.8 kg of P and 7.1 kg of K per hectare are lost annually under traditional farming practices. Overall annual depletion has been estimated at about 4 million tons of fertilizer nutrients which is not adequately compensated by fertilizer application (Ragland et. al. 1993).

About 40 percent of the land area is either too dry to support rain-fed agriculture (33%) or is characterized by variable rainfall (6%) (FAO, *Atlas of African Agriculture*), while a good part of Africa is prone to drought and desertification. According to the United Nations Environmental Program (UNEP), 73 percent of Africa's agriculturally used dry land has been degraded, resulting in declining land productivity. Other contributing factors include reduction or termination of subsidies (improved seeds, fertilizers, animal traction, distribution and sales, etc.) to farmers and a deterioration in rural infrastructure, partly as a result of structural adjustment programs which reduced public funding.

Despite its high contribution to GDP in many African countries, African agriculture leaves very much to be desired. For example, the performance of the Ghanaian economic recovery program (1983-1990) could have been still more successful, had it not been for the relatively poor performance of agriculture. According to government estimates, food crop yields are as low as 40 percent of their potential.

Various studies on African agricultural development agree that food production in Sub-Saharan Africa needs to grow by at least 4 percent per year in order to assure food security (availability, accessibility to the poor, acceptability and stability) and raise per capita incomes: 2.75 percent to feed the growing population; 1.00 percent to improve nutrition; and 0.25 percent to eliminate food imports progressively (World Bank, *Sub-Saharan Africa ...* ). The first component is evidently based on the assumption that the rate of population growth will average 2.75 percent during the period 1990-2020. The relatively high share assigned to improving nutrition is an indication of rampant malnutrition (deficiencies in specific nutrients) and undernutrition (inadequate calorie intake). It is in line with the International Conference on Nutrition organized by FAO and WHO in 1992 which agreed, among other things, to take measures needed to end famine and starvation in the world within the 1990s (FAO, *Dimension of Need*).

Given good weather conditions and the liberal agricultural policies implemented and being implemented in many African countries, agricultural output is likely to be boosted in the future and thereby reduce foreign handouts in the form of food aid. The policies encompass reform and investment in agriculture; water and soil conservation; intensification of land use and irrigation (only a small part of irrigable land is under irrigation, 10% in Eastern and Southern Africa); more and faster use of results from agricultural research and development centers; and better access to agricultural inputs, chemical and biological pest control, extension service and credit (such as the Birr 47 million revolving fund earmarked by the government of Ethiopia).

Those countries with areas favored by climatic conditions and with a potential for developing irrigation that would allow 2 to 3 crops per year should hasten the exploitation of these advantages. Food crop yields, which had been practically stagnant or even declining in most African countries since 1960, accounting for only 0.1 percentage points of the total 1.6 percent increase in food production (ECA, E/ECA/CM.21/10), can be two to four times the yields obtainable using traditional farming (Ragland et. al. 1993). Appropriate measures need to be taken to minimize the problems associated with the development of irrigation, specifically siltation, salinization and waterweed growth. With respect to salinization, measures should include the planting of salt-tolerant crops, if and when needed.

Significant increases in yield can be achieved through improving agronomic practices such as seedbed preparation; timely sowing; intercropping, including alley cropping (trees and crops); crop rotation; fallowing; natural fertilization, including mulching and using legumes and improved use of water. This and the two- to three-fold potential yield increases using appropriate combinations of technologies evidenced by thousands of field trials in many African countries, as well as multiple cropping from irrigation, constitute the bright feature of African agriculture. These possibilities are confirmed by the following examples showing ranges of average yields (output in Kilograms per hectare of cultivated area) during the period 1979-1983: 230-4,120 for maize in Botswana and Egypt, 145-3,790 for millet in Botswana and Egypt, 160-2,720 for sorghum in Botswana and Algeria and 520-4,340 for rice in Zimbabwe and Mauritius (FAO, *African Agriculture: the Next 25 years, Annex III*). The figures in Table 3.7 on irrigated land show how yields of rice, wheat and maize increased between 1961 and 1991 in Asia, China and Africa. The 1991 yields are considerably lower than those achieved by the best-performing countries. The 1991 maize yield in Africa was the same as that of Asia or China in 1961. The last two columns in the table, comparing overall average yields of cereals and roots/tubers in Africa with those of the world, give some indication of the potential for African food production.

| TABLE 3.7 COMPARISON OF YIELDS OF MAJOR CROPS DURING THE PERIOD 1961-1991 | | | | | |
|---|---|---|---|---|---|
| | Rice | Wheat | Maize | Cereals[a] | Roots/tubers[a] |
| Asia | ... | 0.7-2.6 | 1.2-3.4 | ... | ... |
| China | 2.3-5.7 | ... | 1.2-4.6 | ... | ... |
| Africa | ... | ... | 0.8-1.2 | 1.2 | 7.6 |
| World | ... | ... | ... | 2.8 | 12.3 |

Source: Compiled from World Bank, 1996, *World Resources 1996-97, Washington* D.C.
    a Overall average for 1992-1994 (rainfed and irrigated)

The real possibility for increasing yields is confirmed by recent developments in Ethiopia, where food self-sufficiency had been declining for over two decades. According to Sasakawa Global 2000 (SG 2000) Project Director in Ethiopia (*The Ethiopian Herald*, July 30, 1994), farmers with access to the services provided by the project, including selected seeds, almost quintupled their yield of sorghum from 1,700 kgs per hectare to 8,000 kgs per hectare in 1994. According to a later issue of *The Ethiopian Herald* (October 26, 1994), the Nazareth Agricultural Research Center has developed six new and better strains of sorghum that can withstand crop diseases and grow in arid and semi-arid areas. The new strains could raise yield  from 1,000 kgs per hectare to 3,000-6,000 kgs per hectare. Similar results were announced  for maize whose yield was increased from 1,800 kgs per hectare up to 6,000 kgs per hectare (*Addis Zemen*, September 2, 1994) and wheat whose yield can be raised from 1,200 kgs per hectare to 3,200 kgs per hectare, 5,000-8,000 kgs per hectare having been produced at demonstration centers (*The Ethiopian Herald*, December 30, 1994). Some of the improved seeds are resistant to drought, disease and weeds. Linseed whose yield per hectare was shown to increase from 400 kgs to 1,300-1,400 kgs is an example of a weed-resistant crop that was planned to be tested on farmers' plots in 1995/1996. Research recently carried out on wheat resulted in identifying three drought resistant and high yield species yielding 3,500-4,000 kgs per hectare compared to a traditional yield of 1,500 kgs per hectare. The discovery of maize yielding an average of 7,000 kgs per hectare was announced in the same source (*The Ethiopian Herald*, October 11, 1997).

The above examples and similar projects that were and are being carried out by FAO in many African countries, particularly those based on indigenous species, show the potential for increasing food production and therefore the viability and sustainability of agriculture in Africa. This seems to be confirmed by an FAO study conducted in 1984. Based on FAO's three scenarios, the population carrying capacity of Sub-Saharan Africa works out to many multiples of the 1975 population (1.1, 4.6 and 12.9 billions for low, intermediate and high levels of inputs, respectively). Other sources have shown that *"soil and water resources of Africa are adequate to support several times the present population"* (Ragland et. al. 1993). It is, however, unlikely that the high yield levels needed can be attained in the near future throughout the continent.

Better farming practices (both adaptive and innovative, designed with the concerned farmers playing substantial roles), including crop rotation, intercropping, use of organic fertilizers (compost, manure, green manure and humus) and selected seeds, a minimum to moderate but increasing rate of application of the right fertilizers (averaged only 11 kgs of nutrients per hectare on crop land in Sub-Saharan Africa in 1988-1990), judicious use of pesticides and herbicides, expansion of agricultural land, and support by adequate producer incentives could bring food production up to near self-sufficiency with minimum adverse impact on the environment. This could be reinforced by the exploitation of the potential advantages of the different ecological zones growing different crops that would enable member countries to specialize and therefore expand intra-African trade in an increasing number and quantity of agricultural commodities. In other words, it would not be difficult to substantially reduce food imports (34.3 million tons of cereals in 1993 according to Annex 4.3) within a reasonable period by using minimum agricultural inputs in many African countries.

In the long-run there is no reason why the continent cannot retain the status of net exporter of more agricultural products once its use of farming technology is on or nearly on a par with that of the rest of the world. It should be noted here that the Green Revolution (based on high yielding varieties and crop response to high inputs), which worked miracles in Asia and parts of Latin America, has hardly touched Africa. It trebled India's wheat production in 1967-1982 period and doubled Philippines' rice production from 1960-1980 (FAO, *Dimensions of Need*). Many Asian and Latin American countries which were in similar situation as Africa a few decades ago are currently significant food exporters.

Sooner or later Africa will have to experience some kind of green revolution, preferably one that would avoid or minimize the adverse effects on the environment the Asian green revolution produced. According to Marco Quinones, the SG 2000 director for Ethiopia, *"Within the next three to five years, Ethiopia could be the first country in Sub-Saharan Africa to achieve a broad-based green revolution"* (*The Ethiopian Herald*, October 18, 1997). It should be noted that the number of peasant farmers accommodated by extension packages (supprt, advice, agricultural inputs and credits) has dramatically increased from 35,000 in 1994/95 to about 600,000 in 1996/97 (*The Ethiopian Herald*, October 25, 1997) and 2.8 million in 1997/98 (Internet/Yahoo Search Results, *Ethiopian Agriculture*).

As implied above, achieving a measure of food self-sufficiency in Africa will, to a large extent, depend on agricultural research and development and the effective transfer of results to the farmer through extension services. More and more research in drought-resistant, low-risk and low-cost seed varieties and the optimum use of other agricultural inputs should be carried out in Africa. The importance of biotechnology and genetic engineering in manipulating plants to acquire desirable characteristics in a relatively short time, including drought-tolerance, disease-resistance and increased yield cannot be overemphasized; the same applies to animals.

Research which could optimize utilization of the natural resources could eventually bring about a green revolution, perhaps, better than that which occurred in Asia (particularly India, where growing conditions approximate those of Africa) in the 1960s and 1970s but possibly involving less environmental damage. Most of the genetic raw materials used to come from nearby areas where farmers live and work. It should be pointed out here that of the world's 20 major national plant gene banks only one (in Ethiopia) is in Africa, a region known for its biological diversity. Africa hosts four of the 16 international R&D centers that are coordinated by the Consultative Group on International Research (CGIAR). These are the International Center for Research in Agroforestry and the International Livestock Research Institute, both in Kenya, the International Institute of Tropical Agriculture in Nigeria and the West Africa Rice Development Association in Cote d'Ivoire (FAO, *Dimension of Need*).

Benefits accruing from research could be enhanced if the research into tropical agriculture being conducted in developed countries were to be redeployed to Africa, where conditions are more appropriate. The network of international agricultural research centers (IARCs), including the International Maize and Wheat Improvement Center (CIMMYT) in Mexico, the International Institute of Tropical Agriculture (IITA) in Nigeria, the West African Rice Development Association (WARDA) in Cote d'Ivoire, and the Special Program for African Agricultural Research (SPAAR) could play important roles in this regard. Other institutions that could play similar roles include the two recent European Union projects: Economics and Policy in Agricultural Research Systems, which is designed to support and strengthen national agricultural research systems and Wheat Breeding and Pathology Research, intended to benefit Ethiopia, Kenya, Tanzania and Uganda, which were likely to become operational in the 1990s.

Whatever strategies are adopted to increase the supply of food they require the formulation and implementation of agricultural policies, such as those summarized below in Table 3.8.

| TABLE 3.8<br>STRUCTURAL ADJUSTMENT POLICIES | | |
|---|---|---|
| Type of policy | Macroeconomic instruments | Sectoral (agricultural) instruments |
| 1. Pricing policy | Exchange rate, wage rate, interest rate | (Administered) output prices, wage rate, irrigation charges, agricultural interest rate |
| 2. Fiscal policy | Subsidies, tax rates, public expenditure (including public investment) | Subsidies, tax rates, public expenditure (including public investment) |
| 3. Monetary policy | Money supply targets, interest rate, credit allocation | Targets for agricultural credit, agricultural interest rate |
| 4. Trade policy | Tariffs and quotas, export subsidies | Tariffs and quotas, export subsidies |
| 5. Institutional reform | Monetary management rules, management of parastatals, divestiture of public enterprises | Marketing board reform, reduction of intermediation costs in agricultural banks, improved agricultural research |
| 6. Land policy [a] | Cadastral surveys, land taxes, zoning | Cadastral surveys, land taxes, land titling, sale policy on public land, consolidation of scattered parcels |

Source: ECA/FAO, 1992, *Food and Agriculture in Africa*, Staff Papers No. 2, Addis Ababa (adapted from Norton, 1987).
   a  As a prerequisite to land reform, emphasis is being given to broadening the legal framework applicable to (i) consolidation and prevention of land fragmentation, (ii) expropriation and land transfer, (iii) privatization of collective and included in consolidation schemes, land lease (duration, suspension, registration, etc.). For further details, see Seddon (1987).

The food situation and the dependence syndrome in many developing countries is a cause for great concern. In recognition of this, October 16th has been designated World Food Day by the world community. Its theme in 1996 was "Food for All." In its attempt to mitigate food deprivation in the world FAO has been organizing related conferences. The latest, the World Food Summit, convened in November 1996 at FAO's Headquarters in Rome, was preceded by regional conferences. It discussed the elimination of world hunger. In it's Rome Declaration, the participating nations pledged to work to cut the number undernourished people in the world in half by 2015. That worldwide figure is currently at 840 million and about one-third of the African population falls under the undernourished category. Unlike in other regions the absolute number of hungry people is expected to rise in Africa, according to FAO.

## Mining and Energy
The continent is richly endowed with minerals and energy resources. It occupies a leading position in terms of world reserves and production in many minerals and sources of energy.

Mining output, which contributes about 13 percent to Africa's GDP, continued to decline, dropping by 4.4 percent in 1991 compared to 1.3 percent the previous year and 0.8 percent in 1992. These contrast with an average increase of 1.7 percent in the 1960s. Production of non-fuel minerals suffered from internal production difficulties, lack of capital investment and increased exports from the former Soviet Union. Crude oil production fell marginally from 342 million tons in 1992 to 338 million tons (estimate) in 1993. This, coupled with weak prices, resulted in a sharp drop of oil revenues in oil producing countries.

Although there have been increases in reserves of some minerals after independence, much greater increase could have been expected. Foreign investors have diverted their attention to Latin America and Asia and more recently to the former socialist countries. As a result very little mineral exploration has been undertaken in Africa. Both African governments and foreign companies are apparently to blame: the former for increasing state control of mining operations and not providing enabling environment, the latter for lacking transparency and failing to train local staff and integrate their activities with the local economy. With the trend towards market economies throughout the continent there is no reason why both sides cannot come to terms and accommodate one another.

With respect to energy, hydrocarbons predominate in North Africa and West Africa, coal in Southern Africa, hydropower in Central and Eastern Africa and geothermal potential in Eastern Africa. A large part of the hydrocarbons (crude petroleum and natural gas) produced is exported. A relatively small part of the energy resources is currently utilized. For example, only about 4 percent of the hydropower potential has been tapped. Exploitation of these huge and varied forms of energy coupled with the adoption of technologies incorporating energy-efficient techniques and practices should give Africa a comparative advantage in manufacturing, particularly in energy-intensive industries, such as aluminum, copper, iron and steel, chlorine, ethylene, ammonia, pulp and paper and glass. This advantage could be further, reinforced if and when solar energy becomes competitive.

Production of energy is far from adequate in many countries. Obviously, there is an urgent need to expand the production and generation of energy substantially if agricultural and industrial developments are to be enhanced as they should. The World Bank projected an increase in total commercial energy supply in Sub-Saharan Africa from 34 million tons of oil equivalent in 1986 to 200 million tons of oil equivalent in 2020, the corresponding figures for woodfuels being 66 and 200 (World Bank, *Sub-Saharan Africa ...*). It is apparent from the projections that biomass (fuelwood, charcoal and agricultural residues) will continue to dominate (50% of total energy) in 2020. This bodes a disaster for African ecology unless large-scale afforestation and reforestation programs are introduced to counteract deforestation. As this is very unlikely in the near future, more efficient stoves and ovens and competitive alternatives to woodfuels will have to be found and used in the interim period. At the level of industry, wood-using establishments should improve their combustion efficiencies and/or switch to other forms of energy. More details on minerals and energy are provided in Chapter 4.

## Manufacturing Industry

With a 10-12 percent share in GDP over the period 1990-1993 (10.3% in 1986 and 10.5% in 1989), manufacturing ranked third after agriculture and mining in its contribution to GDP. This is relatively low compared to other developing regions and confirms that Africa is the least industrialized region in the world. Worse still, the gap between Africa and the other developing regions has widened as the annual rate of growth in manufacturing value added in percent show: Africa, 2 (1.9 in 1990, 0.3 in 1991, -0.8 in 1992 and 1.3 in 1993); Latin America, 3; and Asia 7.

The rate of growth in manufacturing value added dropped from more than 8 percent in the 1960s to 5.56 percent in the 1970s to 0.25 percent in the 1980s. A similar drastic fall occurred in regard to manufactured exports, and Africa's share in world exports declined from 1.12 percent in 1970 to 0.60 percent in 1975 (Sub-Saharan African market share fell to 0.3 percent in 1995 from 0.6 percent in 1970).

There are a number of reasons for this poor performance. These include: lack of adequate foreign exchange to import industrial inputs, difficulties with domestic supply of raw materials, rising cost of credit and political instability.

Following pressures from the donor community as well as on their own initiatives, many African countries have, in recent years, been trying to privatize public enterprises. Because of the complex nature of the process, however, it has not been an easy task.

After adopting the import substitution strategy for industrial development in the 1960s, African countries realized that they cannot industrialize in the real sense of the word by going it alone; they have since been working towards integrating their industrial development. One such mechanism was the Industrial Development Decade for Africa (IDDA). The first IDDA (1980-1990) which, unfortunately, did not accomplish much because of the competitive (production of the same or similar products) nature of African economies, the complexity of industrial integration and the deteriorating economic conditions in the 1980s, was followed by a second IDDA (1993-2002) the implementation of which is hampered by not only the same constraints but also by the need to rehabilitate existing facilities. Details on manufacturing are given in Chapter 6.

## Trade

The continent's trade by subregion and region during the period 1984-1992 is shown in Table 3.9. Whereas there were two negative trade balances for the region as a whole, there were five negative balances for Africa less South Africa. This indicates that, despite the trade embargo of that time on South Africa, that country played a key role in African trade. It should be noted that the trade balances mask the deteriorating terms of trade for the majority of African countries, especially those that do not export petroleum.

TABLE 3.9
IMPORTS AND EXPORTS OF THE AFRICAN CONTINENT (m $)

| | 1984 | 1985 | 1986 | 1987 | 1988 | 1989 | 1990 | 1991 | 1992 |
|---|---|---|---|---|---|---|---|---|---|
| North Africa | | | | | | | | | |
| -Imports | 35548 | 26245 | 29758 | 27528 | 31476 | 32860 | 37533 | 34214 | 37035 |
| -Exports | 31704 | 31152 | 22326 | 24830 | 23490 | 26782 | 35573 | 35224 | 33489 |
| West Africa | | | | | | | | | |
| -Imports | 11749 | 12723 | 11297 | 11768 | 11461 | 10696 | 10628 | 14797 | 17054 |
| -Exports | 18003 | 19461 | 12854 | 14524 | 13007 | 14988 | 20566 | 19630 | 19915 |
| Central Africa | | | | | | | | | |
| -Imports | 4028 | 4577 | 5071 | 4951 | 4583 | 4578 | 5215 | 5706 | 4387 |
| - Exports | 5600 | 4798 | 4423 | 4102 | 4468 | 5575 | 7019 | 7290 | 5998 |
| Eastern and Southern Africa | | | | | | | | | |
| - Imports | 22981 | 18598 | 20191 | 23414 | 27941 | 28728 | 30108 | 30777 | 31014 |
| - Exports | 24639 | 23489 | 25476 | 31442 | 30553 | 32082 | 35454 | 37397 | 39987 |
| South Africa | | | | | | | | | |
| - Imports | 12540 | 8510 | 9683 | 11424 | 15091 | 13573 | 12612 | 14268 | 14167 |
| - Exports | 15707 | 14751 | 16447 | 20593 | 19554 | 18899 | 21255 | 24936 | 26578 |
| - Balance of trade [a] | 3167 | 6241 | 6764 | 9169 | 4463 | 5326 | 8643 | 10668 | 12411 |
| Africa (incl. South Africa) | | | | | | | | | |
| - Imports | 74306 | 62143 | 66317 | 67661 | 75461 | 76862 | 83504 | 85494 | 89490 |
| - Exports | 79946 | 78900 | 65079 | 74898 | 71518 | 79427 | 98612 | 99541 | 99389 |
| - Balance of trade [a] | 5640 | 16757 | -1238 | 7237 | -3943 | 2565 | 15108 | 14047 | 9899 |
| Africa (encl.. South Africa) | | | | | | | | | |
| - Imports | 61766 | 53633 | 56634 | 56237 | 60370 | 63289 | 70892 | 71226 | 75323 |
| - Exports | 64239 | 64149 | 48632 | 54305 | 51964 | 60528 | 77357 | 74605 | 72811 |
| - Balance of trade [^] | 2473 | 10516 | -8002 | -1932 | -8406 | -2761 | 6465 | 3379 | -2512 |

Source: UN, 1994, *Foreign Trade Statistics for Africa*, E/ECA/STAT/Ser.A/36, New York.
a Computed

In general, Africa's low share in world trade has been steadily declining since 1980. It fell from 2.3 percent in 1990 to 2 percent in 1993 and increased to 2.2 percent in 1995. It averaged 3 percent in the 1960s. According to Annex 3.5, developing Africa's share of imports fell from 4.46 percent in 1975 to 2.01 percent in 1993. The same was true for exports (crude petroleum, precious stones, cocoa and coffee accounting for two-third of exports to industrialized countries) declining from 4.55 percent (1980) to 1.96 percent. This state of affairs is explained by the loss of markets of a number of products to other regions; the marginalization of Africa from the world economy following the end of the Cold-War era as Africa's traditional partners diverted their trade to other regions; and political instability, corruption, hostile domestic policies and nationalizations. Trade diversion is likely to worsen with the growing success of the European Union and similar regional organizations, especially as they develop cheaper substitutes for tropical products. This has already begun as intra-regional trade in North America, Asia and Latin America in the 1990-1994 period increased at faster rates than did extra-regional trade (UNIDO, *Industrial Development: Global Report 1996*). Africa's trade balance steadily dwindled from $0.16 billion in 1992 to -$7.18 billion in 1995 ($109.68 billion of exports and $116.86 billion of imports in 1995) (ADB, *African Development Report 1997*). In 1993, Africa's (excluding South Africa) exports stood at $71.4 billion and imports at $74.8 billion resulting in trade balance of -$3.4 billion. Africa is reported to have lost $65 billion worth of foreign currency earnings at 1990 prices during the period mid-1950s to 1990 (UNIDO, *The Globalization of Industry: Implications ...* ).

Official intra-African trade is small and stagnates at about 5 percent of total African trade. It steadily decreased from 10.3 percent in 1928 to 8.1 percent in 1958, 4.4 percent in 1983 but rose to 8.4 percent in 1993 (WTO, *Regionalism and the World Trading System*). The figures exclude significant informal trade which in ECOWAS, for instance, was estimated to be as large as 40 percent of recorded trade (UNIDO, *Industry and Development: Global Report 1993/94*). The structure of intra-African trade is heavily biased in favor of manufactured goods (14%) followed by foods, beverages and tobacco (5.3%) and crude materials and animal and vegetable oils (3.4%) which aggregate to about 6.0 percent of the total 1990 exports (ECA, *Africa in the 1990s and Beyond: ...* ).

Similar factor endowments, production of similar consumer goods, high production costs, inadequate and expensive transport connections, high cost and noncompetitive products, and lack of market information are some of the reasons for the low and stagnant intra-African trade. Although, in the longer run, similar consumer goods could find their way into markets beyond national boundaries, it is the production of intermediates and capital goods that could boost trade among African countries. Table 3.10 shows intra-trade of groups of countries, some of which correspond to subregions (ECOWAS, ECCAS, PTA - the Preferential Trade Area for Eastern and Southern Africa). As may be observed from the last four columns, ECOWAS and CEAO (comprising some of the member countries of ECOWAS) registered the highest intra-trade as a percentage of total exports in each group. The PTA came next. ECCAS and UDEAC (comprising some of the member countries of ECCAS) and Arab Maghreb Union (AMU) registered the lowest intra-trade.

| TABLE 3.10 INTRA-TRADE OF GROUPS OF AFRICAN COUNTRIES | | | | | | | | | | | |
| --- | --- | --- | --- | --- | --- | --- | --- | --- | --- | --- | --- |
| | Value of intra-trade ($m) | | | | Intra-trade of group as percentage of regional exports of each group | | | | Intra-trade of group as percentage of total exports of each group | | |
| | 1970 | 1980 | 1990 | 1992 | 1970 | 1980 | 1990 | 1992 | 1970 | 1980 | 1990 | 1992 |
| ECOWAS | 87 | 693 | 1470 | 1567 | 81.3 | 75.4 | 73.3 | 72.6 | 2.9 | 10.1 | 8.3 | 7.8 |
| AMU | 60 | 110 | 727 | 945 | 68.3 | 33.6 | 74.6 | 78.2 | 1.4 | 0.3 | 2.3 | 3 |
| PTA | 306 | 693 | 662 | 707 | 79.7 | 76.4 | 67.8 | 68.5 | 9.6 | 12.1 | 6.6 | 6.7 |
| CEAO | 52 | 438 | 479 | 534 | 63.9 | 55.8 | 41 | 42.4 | 6.6 | 9.8 | 9.9 | 10.5 |
| SADC | 100 | 107 | 360 | 333 | 62.7 | 32.9 | 71 | 65.3 | 5.2 | 5.1 | 5.2 | 4.4 |
| ECCAS | 30 | 98 | 171 | 158 | 13.4 | 51.6 | 40.2 | 36.5 | 2.4 | 1.6 | 2.3 | 2.1 |
| UDEAC | 22 | 84 | 139 | 120 | 52.2 | 70 | 45.4 | 31.3 | 4.9 | 1.8 | 2.4 | 2.1 |
| Source: UNCTAD, 1994, *UNCTAD Statistical Pocket Book*, Geneva. | | | | | | | | | | | |

As shown by Mercosur (Southern Latin American common market) intra-African trade can be increased through economic cooperation. Mercosur, comprising Argentina, Brazil, Paraguay and Uruguay (expanded to include Chile and Bolivia in 1996), which came into being in 1991, increased its intra-trade from $4 billion in 1990 to $14.5 billion in 1995 and $16.1 billion in 1996 (*The Economist*, October 21 and December 21, 1996). The increase was due to both trade-creation and trade-diversion, with more of the former. Significant improvement in intra-African trade, albeit between South Africa and other African countries, may be expected now that the embargo on South Africa has been lifted. That country's increase of 50 percent in its trade ($2.5 billion exports and $664 million imports) with the rest of Africa in 1994 over 1993 (Arnold 1995) gives an indication of what is to come. Huge trade balances in favor of South Africa and the havoc that South African exports are likely to cause to national industries (Zambian industries have become among the first casualties) will, unfortunately, hardly be in the long term interests of industrial development in many African countries. This apparent possibility could be minimized, if South Africa were to concentrate on investing in joint venture industries with local entrepreneurs in other African countries.

Africa's share in world trade by commodity classes is given in Annex 3.6. According to this annex, Africa's percentage share in world imports and exports drastically declined in 1992 compared to 1980, imports falling from 4.2 to 2.2 and exports from 4.7 to 1.9. While the percentage shares of chemical, machinery and transport equipment exports remained practically unchanged, these commodities shares in imports fell drastically: chemicals from 4.7 to 2.3 percent and machinery and transport equipment from 6.2 to 2.3 percent. The share in import of other manufactured goods showed a similar trend. These are a reflection of the multiple crises of the 1980s referred to elsewhere and underscore the fact that the economic and social development of the region was hampered by a lack of capital and intermediate goods and inputs.

Comparison of the rate of change of unit value of imports and exports shows that the unit value of the former was much more steady than that of the latter. In other words, while import prices were increasing, exports prices showed a persistent downward trend throughout the early 1990s. The ECA comprehensive commodity export price indices (1990=100) were 86.6 in 1991, 83.4 in 1992 and 78.4 in 1993, confirming the worsening terms of trade. The United Nations International Trade Statistics Yearbook export price index (1989=100) for machinery and transport equipment from developed countries increased to 153 in 1991. The opposite was true for export commodities from developing countries. The two indices for beverage crops and oilseeds, oils and fats, for instance, fell to 51 and 77 respectively.

Annex 3.7 compares contributions of African export commodities (both these including and excluding fuels), valued f.o.b., with those of developing countries and the world. Except for the world figures, two sets of figures are given, the second set excluding major petroleum and/or manufactured goods exporters. The annex reveals the role that petroleum plays in African exports. All primary commodities, including fuels, accounted for 92.9 percent of total exports in 1970. This very high share fell steadily to 83.3 percent in 1991, the corresponding figures for exports excluding fuels being 61.2 and 23.6, showing sharp decline in non-fuel exports.

A similar trend is observed with regard to Africa's share in global primary commodity exports. Whereas the share of all primary commodities declined from 10.4 percent in 1970 to 7.1 percent in 1991, that of non-fuel commodities dipped from 9.1 percent to 3.3 percent. Comparisons of these figures with those of other developing countries reveals Africa's rapidly declining capacity to earn foreign currency. Examples of commodities with falling trends in world percentage shares between 1970/71 and 1986/87 include: cocoa beans (80.6 to 62.2), coffee (27.6 to 20.4), groundnuts (52.2 to 29.3), palm oil (17.9 to 2.4), cotton (30.3 to 17.8), alumina (7.7 to 3.7), copper (28.6 to 19.4) and iron ore (12.5 to 5.4) (UNIDO, *Industry and Development : Global Report 1993/94*).

The UNCTAD Commodity Yearbook 1994 reveals that African countries are dependent on a limited number of export commodities as foreign exchange earners. The number of countries with three commodities accounting for over 50 percent of total exports was 46 out of 51 in 1975-1977. This figure changed significantly to 38 in 1989-1991. During the latter period, 21 countries had three commodities ranging between 80 and 99.7 percent of exports, four of which were at the 99 percent level. These figures show how vulnerable African countries could be to external shocks (recession, falling commodity prices, etc.) thanks to excessive reliance on a limited number of primary commodities to earn foreign exchange. The major export primary commodities accounting for over 30 percent of world exports in 1986/87 are: palm nuts (78.1%), cocoa beans (62.6%), bauxite (44.4%), phosphate (41.7%), manganese ore (38.7%), sisal (36.6%) and blister copper (35.5%). The share of manufactures in exports is less than 15 percent in most countries, yet Sub-Saharan countries registering over 20 percent during the period 1987-1990 include Mauritius (65.6%), Central African Republic (42.8%), Zimbabwe (30.9%), Comoros (26.5%), Senegal (25.9%), Cameroon (24.3%) and Sierra Leone (20.6%) (UNIDO, *Industry and Development: Global Report 1993/ 94*).

Annex 3.4 cites free market prices and price indices of selected African primary commodity exports for the period 1982-1993. In general, price trends during the period were downward and more pronounced and consistent during the second half. In 1992, prices for coffee, cocoa and crude petroleum were about half of those in 1982. In the case of the first commodity, this is confirmed by the beverage indices which dipped from 92 in 1982 to 52 in 1993.

The developed countries of Europe and North America are Africa's traditional trading partners. Trade with Japan has been expanding and other Asian countries are following suit. Africa should be aware of the booming economies in the latter countries and endeavor to expand trade with them, especially in view of the fact that some of those countries lack the resources that Africa has, thus presenting opportunities for a mutually advantageous relationships.

The limited intra-African trade referred to above is mainly due to the low degree of economic complementarity: states within the same economic grouping have similar production structures, produce high-cost products and have poor and inadequate infrastructure, resulting in high costs of transportation. Intra-community trade is at the very center of economic cooperation and integration in Africa. Measures, therefore, need to be taken immediately to create complementarity by, among other things, improving industrial productivity and competition, and by increasing and diversifying trade through the production of intermediates and capital goods for purposes of exchange. Initiatives taken and being taken by African countries in economic integration are discussed in the second part of this chapter.

## Debt and Resources Flows

African external debt in billions dollars increased from 276.7 in 1990 to 281.6 in 1991; it then fell to 278.8 in 1992, only to rise to 313 in 1994, 340 in 1996, and 344 in 1997. The seriousness of the debt burden to the region can be illustrated by the following 1992 percentage ratios: debt to GDP: 89.6; and debt repayment to exports of goods and services: 28.7. It is worth noting that because of the accumulation of unpaid interest both the London and Paris Club rescheduling have compounded these ratios. According to the ECA, *"...the African debt crisis can only be resolved by a dual strategy of removing constraints associated with the debt and simultaneously reviving growth in the African countries through the consolidation of internal processes of capital accumulation."* It is gratifying to note that the Paris Club had, already in 1995, started to reduce debt-servicing by up to 67 percent. External debt, debt services and some debt related ratios for developing Africa are given in Table 3.11.

| TABLE 3.11 DEVELOPING AFRICAN EXTERNAL DEBT | | | | | | | | | | |
|---|---|---|---|---|---|---|---|---|---|---|
| | Actual | | | | | | | | Estimate | |
| | 1988 | 1989 | 1990 | 1991 | 1992 | 1993 | 1994 | 1995 | 1996 | 1997 |
| External debt (b$) | 203.9 | 211.1 | 224.2 | 234 | 232.7 | 242.1 | 253.9 | 271.1 | 281.1 | 292.3 |
| External debt (% of exports of goods and services) | 256.7 | 248.4 | 228.3 | 243.8 | 241.5 | 259 | 266.7 | 252.4 | 241.3 | 236.2 |
| Debt-service payments (b$) | 140 | 143.5 | 149.7 | 159.9 | 182.5 | 193.8 | 214.8 | 267.5 | 248.5 | 255.6 |
| Debt-service payments (% of exports of goods and services) | 29.3 | 31 | 31.2 | 31.3 | 30.4 | 27.2 | 23.4 | 30.7 | 27.2 | 27.5 |
| Ratio of external debt to GDP (%) | 60.2 | 63.1 | 60.3 | 65.2 | 62 | 66.6 | 70.5 | 65.3 | 65.8 | 64.9 |
| Interest payments (% of exports of goods and services) | 12.5 | 13.3 | 12.4 | 12.5 | 10.7 | 10.5 | 10.5 | 10.9 | 12.2 | 12.5 |
| Amortization (% of exports of goods and services) | 16.7 | 17.7 | 18.8 | 18.8 | 19.7 | 16.7 | 12.9 | 19.8 | 15 | 15.1 |

Source: IMF, 1996, *World Economic and Financial Surveys: World Economic Outlook*, May 1996, Washington, D.C.

Total net resource flows (at 1991 prices and exchange rates) to Africa fell from $34.0 billion in 1985 to $23.3 billion in 1991. Of these the corresponding ODA receipts were $ 21.5 and $ 24.7 billion and total ODF, $ 25.5 and $ 24.6 billion (OECD, *1992 Survey*). The bilateral donor share has declined and private inflows have become outflows. The irony here is that Africa is suffering from a worsening deficit of net private transfers at a time when such transfer are badly needed.

Annex 3.8 provides debt related information on Sub-Saharan Africa (excluding South Africa). According to the annex, the debt stock of Sub-Saharan Africa, at current prices, rose steadily and more than doubled from $84 billion in 1980 to $200.4 billion in 1993 (projected at $210.7 billion in 1994). By contrast, the net debt transfer of $11.8 billion in 1980 turned negative ($-1.3 billion) in 1986; thereafter it continued to fluctuate and averaged -$2.0 billion in the yeats 1992-1993. It was projected to turn positive to $1.9 billion in 1994.

The net resource flows were $15.1and $15.7 billion in 1980 and 1993, respectively, indicating that growth of net resource flows lagged very much behind that of total debt. The grant component (excluding technical cooperation), however, increased overall, albeit at a slow rate, to $12.2 billion in 1993.

Debt ratio indicators, expressed in percentages, are revealing. The total debt stock/exports of goods and services ratio increased from 91.5 in 1980 to 253.1 in 1987 and hovered around the lower level of the later up to 1993 when it marginally surpassed the 1987 level. The same, more or less, applies to total debt stock/GNP ratios. As for the ratios of total debt service and interest payments to exports of goods and services, the trend is, generally, downward. Upward trends are only to be found for concessional/total debt stock and grant/GNP ratios. In general, most of these favorable ratios are indications of the special treatment extended by donors to 48 severely indebted low- and middle-income countries of which the African group numbered 30. The positive resource transfers were made possible through debt-relief and new concessional financing. To a varying degree, debt buybacks, debt exchanges, debt-for-equity swaps, capitalization of interest and outright debt forgiveness were used to achieve these positive resource transfers. It should, however, be noted that debt restructuring, i.e., repeated rescheduling and capitalization of interest, be it via the Paris Club or other mechanisms, increases the debt stock in the long run, and thereby limits the countries' capability to achieve progress in development.

In recent years, foreign direct investment (FDI) has become the largest single source of external finance for developing countries; yet Africa has benefited marginally. Its share of world total FDI fell from 3.4 percent in the years 1981-1985 to 1.4 percent in 1993 and 1.4 percent (estimate) in 1994. Its share in 1994 was 2.8 percent of the world total. The corresponding percentages for its share of developing countries were 12.2, 4.1, 3.6 and 10.9 (UNCTAD, *World Investment Report*). In the case of Sub-Saharan Africa, its share of the total FDI of all developing countries dipped from 18.8 percent in 1970 to nil in 1980, rose to 10.6 percent in 1989, and has to all intents and purposes been on the decline ever since (3.14 % in 1993). Worse still, most of the FDI goes to petroleum related projects in a limited number of countries.

It would be appropriate to close this section by referring to the ADB's assessment of the 1995 economic performance of the region. From their assessment it appears that Africa is on the verge of reversing its downward or stagnating economic trend. The ADB estimated that the African GDP at factor cost grew at 3 percent in 1995, at a rate slightly higher than that of the population (2.8%). Services and industry contributed 75 percent to this growth. In many countries inflation decreased; privatization and civil service restructuring continued; reha- bilitation and strengthening of institutions increased; and a number of stock exchanges were launched. Unfortunately, the external debt service increased to 27.3 percent compared to 25.8 percent in 1994 (ADB, *African Development Re- port 1996*).

## ECONOMIC SYSTEMS AND COOPERATION

### Economic Systems Practiced in Africa

African countries whose economies are characterized by export of crude materi- als and import of manufactures have experimented with a variety of economic systems. Some were based on capitalism or socialism or a mixture of the two, with, by far, the majority practicing the third variant, mixed economy. Practically all countries resorted to development planning which was encouraged and sup- ported by donors following independence. During the early years, expatriate ex- perts and consultants, mostly made available by donors, played the role of plan- ners. Many countries adopted the basic needs approach in the 1970s. This ap- proach was popularized by the International Labor Organization (ILO). Struc- tural adjustment in the 1980s and early 1990s and democratization (good gover- nance) and market reforms (mainly a consequence of the end of the Cold War) in the 1990s were imposed by donors.

Some countries have tried more than one of the systems. Botswana, Cameroon, Cote d'Ivoire and Mauritius were among the market-oriented groups. Angola, Benin, Egypt, Ethiopia, Ghana, Guinea, Madagascar, Mali, Mozambique, Soma- lia, Tanzania, Sudan, Uganda and Zambia were examples of countries that, at one time or another, joined the socialist camp. Quite a number of them (Egypt, Ethiopia, Madagascar, Mozambique, Somalia, Sudan, Tanzania, Uganda, Congo K, Zambia and Zimbabwe) resorted to nationalization as well as outright confis- cation of private manufacturing and other enterprises. In Ethiopia, government ownership of the means of production and provision of services attained an ab- surd level. The government operated retail shops and acted as a landlord, renting houses whose monthly rents were a fraction of one dollar. The consequence of all this was that from 1979-1980, the percentage share of the private sector in manu- facturing value added, for example, declined to 43.6 in Zambia, 47.3 in Ghana and 69 in Tanzania, the last two having substantially declined from 78.9 and 95, respectively in the early to mid-1960s (Meier et. al. 1989).

In many cases, the performance of the nationalized enterprises was such that output dropped substantially and in some cases ceased all together. Units were shut down owing to weaknesses in technical, managerial and entrepreneurial capabilities and politicization of management. This, for example, held true for Uganda where, by 1982, 15 out of 50 medium- and large-scale enterprises had stopped production (ECA, ECA/IHSD/IPPIS/033/93). Somecountries, such as Tan- zania, Uganda, Congo K and Zambia, had to invite former owners to return and take over enterprises that had been nationalized or confiscated. With the collapse of command socialism, the current shift is towards capitalism, although the mixed economy system is likely to persist for some time to come, mainly in the form of continuing public ownership of some infrastructure and services.

The move towards free market economies was boosted by pressure on the part of donors, bilateral and multilateral alike. Adoption of free market mechanism has become one of the conditions for obtaining aid. Many African countries found themselves reluctantly having to accept the mechanism. As weak as their economies are, it does not seem fair or even practical to force poor countries to open up their markets to world competition. It should be noted that the developed countries themselves, at one time or another, have used and benefited from a closed door policy to develop their economies at a time when competition was not as cut-throat as it is today.

The free market approach is not a panacea for all ills associated with industrial development under the conditions prevailing in most African countries. This has been demonstrated (Riddell 1990) by case studies in Zimbabwe, Kenya and Botswana, which concluded:

- *"that efficient manufacturing production can occur under a far from liberal trade regime;*
- *that a sheltered regional market can assist the drive to create efficient manufacturing units; and*
- *that factors other than price play a major role in determining the extreme variations in efficiency occurring within different industrial sub-sectors."*

In 1994, USAID was in the process of reviewing its conditions for giving aid (*The Economist*, May 7, 1994). The conditions that the receiving countries would have to meet were likely to include: building democracy, protecting the environment, fostering a sustainable economic environment and encouraging population control. Democratic principles, respect for human rights and the rule of law are the basis for cooperation between the EU and the ACP. Reform and privatization of state-owned enterprises are among the conditions that the World Bank and other financial institutions are increasingly imposing on their creditors. It seems that developing countries have to undertake the same changes that take place in industrialized countries. If the privatization of buildings and land used by central government departments in the United Kingdom, under consideration in 1996, would be implemented, it would not be unlikely that developing countries would be pressured to follow suit.

As referred to previously, economic performance in many African countries has been deteriorating since the second half of the 1970s, following the 1973 oil crisis and the slump in primary commodity prices. As a result 35 out of 53 Sub-Saharan African countries in 1997 (ECA, ECA/IHSD/IPPIS/003/96) were, engaged in implementing structural adjustment programs (SAPs) that date back to the mid-1980s, and which were introduced primarily under pressure from and with the assistance of the Bretton Woods institutions. SAP is an austerity program comprising two phases: short to medium term macroeconomic stabilization and reform of public sector enterprises. It aims at controlling and reducing public spending, curbing inflation, realigning exchange rates, rationalizing public investment, liberalizing trade, and reforming the civil service, public enterprises and the financial sector as well as boosting privatization.

Loans for different purposes were provided by the institutions. They were intended for structural adjustment (stabilizing the economies), economic recovery (including rehabilitation), sectoral adjustment (including industry and agriculture), trade policy and public management. Of the 81 loans approved during the period 1980-1988, 31 of them were for structural adjustment, 13 for agriculture, 9 each for economic recovery and industry and 5 for the public enterprise sector (Meier et, al. 1989).

The number of loans to public enterprises is an indication of the state of affairs in those enterprises. It is not unlikely that the loans had, among other things, directly or indirectly, contributed in rendering the public sector more efficient and improving the functioning of public enterprises, including via privatization. In fact, many of the privatization schemes that were and still are implemented seem to be the result of loan-funded activities. Despite many governments' efforts to privatize public enterprises, actual achievements to that end are not satisfactory, primarily due to administrative difficulties on the part of governments and the incapacity of the local business community to take over and manage the deregulated enterprises.

The Bretton Woods Institutions have been criticized for not addressing the fundamental issues, failing to account for the root causes of the particular economic malaise (focusing mainly on government failures) in individual countries, prescribing the same or similar medicine to all economic ills, rendering assistance too late, and neglecting long-term perspectives. SAPs were criticized for their inappropriateness, for being the means of ensuring loan repayment by African creditors, for not achieving visible improvements in economic performance, for not removing or minimizing structural constraints, for not bringing about significant structural transformation and growth, for deteriorating infrastructure, for weakening further the productive capacities, and for worsening the living conditions of the people (especially the low income group). In other words, their implementation resulted in stagnant economies (did not lead to sustained economic growth), thus entailing higher social costs and political risks for the regimes in power. It appears that they may have contributed to the de-industrialization process as they, among other things, did not provide adequate provision for industrial inputs needed to operate and maintain existing industries and services.

A ten-year program in Cote d'Ivoire which, together with Kenya, used to be cited as an economic model, is a good example of an, apparently, unsuccessful SAP. According to an assessment by the World Bank, *"The limited adjustment that was achieved was at a considerable cost. Negative real GDP growth characterized the decade [1981-1991], and poverty has risen steeply as a result"* (Husain et. al. 1994). The structural adjustment programs in Nigeria (1986-1990) and Zimbabwe (1990-1994) were considered failures (*New Africa*, March 1995). Following the need, expressed by critics led by the ECA, to introduce a social dimension into SAPs, the ADB, the World Bank and the UNDP jointly launched the Social Dimension of Adjustment (SDA) in 1987 to alleviate the adverse impact on the vulnerable segments of the population, especially the urban poor, adversely affected by the removal of subsidies on food, utilities and other essential services (World Bank, *Adjustment in Africa* ...). A social safety net program, the Social Fund for Development, was in operation in Egypt in the early 1990s following the adoption of its Economic Reform and Structural Adjustment Program. It provides financial grants and loans to the poor and the unemployed (ECA, ECA/IHSD/IPPIS/033/93).

Some of the countries implementing adjustment programs share the blame for the poor performance of the programs. They can be charged with some of the following: lack of commitment to and consistency in the implementation of stated policy changes (partly for fear of political instability, increased unemployment and poverty, etc.), lack of transparency and a slow pace of or incomplete implementation. Some of these constraints may have been relatively significant in countries that had previously followed socialist-oriented development strategies. Other factors that may have contributed to the unsatisfactory results are political instability (including in neighboring countries) and drought and other natural disasters. Another crucial factor is the short implementation period since instantaneous adjustment is not likely to be economically feasible or socially sustainable. This, in many cases resulted in the unlikely dismantling of state run institutions before adequate private sector replacement were made—thus disrupting and worsening social and economic activities.

Many countries have adopted and implemented, or are in the process of implementing, macroeconomic and structural reforms and adjustments. These include: Burkina Faso, the Gambia, Egypt, Ethiopia, Mauritius, Morocco, Nigeria, Tunisia, Kenya, Tanzania, Uganda, Zambia and Zimbabwe (UN, E/1995/50). In its *World Economic and Social Survey 1995*, the United Nations noted that the above countries and Ghana have made progress in macroeconomic and structural reforms. Mali is another, to be noted according to the World Bank and the IMF. It is possible that some of the economic gains were achieved as a result of the implementation of some of the SAPs, although how much of the gains are attributable to SAPs have not been determined. Mauritius successfully completed its adjustment program in the mid-1980s. Based on a study of 29 countries in Sub-Saharan Africa that implementd adjustment programs from 1987-1991, *"six ... had a large improvement in policies, nine a small improvement, and eleven a deterioration ... the six with the most improvement in macroeconomic policies between 1981-86 and 1987-91 enjoyed the strongest resurgence in economic performance. They experienced a median increase of almost 2 percentage points in the growth rate of gross domestic product (GDP) per capita..."* Per capita GDP increased by 1.5 percent for countries with small improvement and declined by 2.6 percent for those with deteriorating macroeconomic policies. Industry grew at 6 percent in countries with a large improvement and 1.7 percent in countries with deteriorating macroeconomic policies. Similar performances were observed in agriculture and exports (World Bank, *Adjustment in Africa: Lessons from Country Case Studies*). Many of the adjusting countries needed to focus on and intensify the sustained implementation of growth-oriented programs to restore economic growth in the context of a fundamental restructuring of their economies.

Table 3.12 gives indications of the effect of SAPs on the manufacturing industry in 29 adjusting and 21 non-adjusting African countries. It is apparent that the countries with policy deterioration did worse than the other groups in as far as MVA growth rates were concerned. In the case of growth rates of manufactured exports, the reverse was true during 1988-1992 as the policy deteriorating countries did better than the others, including the policy improving countries. It seems that, in general, SAPs have not brought about the significant changes in manufacturing that were expected. It should, however, be noted that the non-adjusting countries, particularly the low-income ones, showed the worst performance in manufactured exports, implying that SAPs had made overall positive contributions.

TABLE 3.12
TRENDS IN MANUFACTURING IN ADJUSTING AND NON-ADJUSTING AFRICAN COUNTRIES

| Countries | Mean annual real growth rate of MVA | | | | Real annual growth rates of manufactured exports | | | |
|---|---|---|---|---|---|---|---|---|
| | 1980-1993 | | 1990-1993 | | 1980-1992 | | 1988-1992 | |
| | Weighted | Simple | Weighted | Simple | Weighted | Simple | Weighted | Simple |
| Policy improving (15) | 2.7 | 3.59 | 4.41 | 3.09 | 2.75 | 3.41 | 9.35 | 4.77 |
| Policy deteriorating (14) | 1.64 | 1.91 | -1.67 | -3.35 | 4.66 | -0.82 | 10.03 | 8.25 |
| North Africa non-adjusting (5) | 3.75 | 2.2 | 0.33 | 1.43 | 11.18 | 11.23 | 6.15 | -5.54 |
| Low-income non-adjusting (16) | 2.12 | 3.17 | 0.05 | 1.87 | -8.25 | -3.7 | -15.77 | -9.63 |

Source: ADB, 1995, *African Development Report 1995*, Abidjan.    ( ) Number of countries in the group.

Ghana is one of the counties with a relatively good track record in reversing a declining economy by implementing SAPs. Its economy was characterized by a negative rate of growth before 1983. In its relatively diversified manufacturing industry, for instance, average capacity utilization plummeted to 21 percent and production declined 20 percent in 1982 (ADB, *African Development Report 1994*).

For over a decade of its history Ghana has implemented a series of economic recovery programs. Unlike some countries which abandoned or suspended their programs (because economic recovery did not work miracles after a few years of half-hearted implementation), Ghana displayed political will to accept a sustained process of reform long enough to achieve a turnaround in growth and continuing recovery. It started with stabilization and structural adjustment in 1983. Among the results achieved were: average GDP growth rate of about 4.7 percent during 1983-1991 (4% in 1992) compared to 1.5 percent during 1970-1983; percent changes in fiscal deficit from 2.7 percent of GDP in 1983 to positive 1.5 percent in 1992; and an increase in the share of capital spending in total government expenditures from 7.9 percent in 1983 to 20.1 percent in 1992 (FAO, *The State of Food and Agriculture*). Growth in manufacturing output reversed from -11.1 percent in 1983 to 12.8 and 22.2 percent in 1984 and 1985 respectively, mainly because of availability of imported inputs. The corresponding figures for consumer price indices were 122.8, 39.7 and 10.3 and for government budget deficit, 2.7, 1.8 and 2.0 (Meier et. al. 1989). Demonstrations against 17.5 percent value added tax flared up in May 1995, a manifestation of discontent with the hardships of the painful economic reforms exacerbated by a world recession and falling cocoa prices (*Foreign Report*, 8 June 1995). Although industry's share in GDP increased from 16 percent in 1975 to 21 percent in 1990 at the expense of services, that of agriculture remained stagnant at 48 percent (ADB, *African Development Report 1994*).

Ghana and Mauritius were among the adjusting economies that raised their investment/GDP ratios from 10.1 percent to 14.8 percent (Ghana) and from 21.4 percent to 29.6 percent (Mauritius) during 1980-1989 and 1990-1994 respectively (IFC, *Trends in Private Investment in Developing Countries 1990-94*). Whereas public investment was higher than private investment in Ghana it was the opposite in Mauritius. In the 1990s, development in Ghana was compromised following the 80 percent increase in wages of public employees and two years of drought (*The Economist*, December 7, 1996).

Tanzania is another country where SAPs seem to have shown some success. According to the Tanzanian delegation to an ECA meeting (ECA, ECA/IHSD/ IPPIS/033/93), *"Since the mid 1980s the performance of the Tanzania economy has improved due to subjection of structural adjustments by the IMF which resulted ito output growth and lowering of the inflation rate to an accomodatable position."* Examples of positive performance in certain parts of other programs can be cited from a World Bank publication (Husain et. al., 1994). In Kenya, the budget deficit (excluding grants) as a percentage of GDP improved from 5.8 in 1981-1984 to positive 4.5 in 1984-1991. In Nigeria, the following increases were observed: average real growth of GDP from -2.6 percent in 1980-1985 to 5.4 percent in 1986-1991, average manufacturing capacity utilization from 42.5 percent in 1986 to 50.6 percent in 1988 and manufacturing production index (1972=100) from 313.6 in 1984-1986 to 484.7 in 1987-1989. In Senegal, the inflation rate fell from 10 percent in the years 1982-1985 to 2.7 percent in 1986-1991, the fiscal deficit as a percentage of GDP improved from -8.0 in 1982 to 0.2 in 1991 and manufacturing value added as a percentage of GDP increased from 12 in 1980-1985 to 13.5 in 1986-1991. In Tanzania, the average annual GDP growth (percent) in real terms rose from 0.1 in 1981-1985 to 4.0 in 1986-1991 and gross domestic investment as a percentage of GDP from 14.3 to 31.6 for the same periods.

Ethiopia is a more recent example of an African country that has undergone a process of adjustment. Stabilization and structural measures were implemented during the first half of the 1990s. The former was meant to pave the way to economic recovery and growth and the latter, to a market-based economy. Substantial progress has been made in both cases during the four year transition (1991-1995) to a democratic government. For example, government revenue increased from 10.7 percent of GDP in1991/92 to 17.4 percent in 1994/95; government expenditure was rationalized with defense expenditure being drastically reduced from 48 percent of recurrent expenditure in 1990/91 to 12.3 percent in 1994/95; the local currency was devalued and a foreign exchange auction scheme instituted; inflation fell from 21 percent in 1990/91 to less than 10 percent in 1993/94; public enterprises were successfully put under autonomous management; and redundancy dealt with (*The Ethiopian Herald*, April 1, 1995) (see Annex 2.1 for more indicators of success in implementing SAP or its equivalent in Ethiopia).

In most African countries governments and public enterprises are characterized by a bloated workforce. Countries which went through SAPs tried to remedy this. In Ethiopia, for instance, retrenchment negatively affected only 3 percent of the civil service. Of the total 15,460 retrenched (civil servants and employees of public enterprises), 6.4 percent were redeployed, 25.6 percent were pensioned, 26.6 percent were compensated and 41.4 percent were made owners of four transport and one retail trade (*The Ethiopian Herald*, October 21 and 22, 1997).

SAPs pose a number of questions. What other options do most African countries, especially the increasingly marginalized least developed countries, have to escape their predicament? What would have been the lot of countries if they had not adopted and implemented SAPs ? Some of them, at least, usually go to the World Bank and the IMF, when their economies reach levels requiring tough prescriptions to halt and reverse the negative socio-economic trends. Is it not a fact that some of them (Ghana and Tanzania, for instance) went to the Bretton Woods institutions as a last resort because, apparently, they had no other option when their economic conditions hit rock bottom? Short of the bitter prescription pills, the option that such countries had was to continue with the downsliding economic trends; this would have meant worsening economic conditions for a growing number of their peoples. Would they have been better off without the programs? Generally, SAPs do halt or reverse falling economic trends.

Some belt tightening (although there is not much that can be done in some countries because of poverty) is needed and that is what SAPs are all about. African governments and their peoples should remind themselves under what conditions and sacrifices the industrialized countries developed themselves. In this regard, countries which have not adopted SAPs or have failed to benefit from SAPs would do well to assess the Ethiopian experience following the fall of the previous Ethiopian regime.

One of the solutions to reforming the public sector is to give the public enterprises autonomy to operate strictly on the same business basis as private enterprises, to be guided by the profit motive and subject to all rules and regulations governing private enterprises. This approach seems to have worked well in Ethiopia where each public enterprise is supervised by a board. In 1995, it was reported that 220 establishments had become profit making operations under the new system.

## Early Attempts at Economic Cooperation

During the colonial era and as an administrative measure, the metropolitan powers organized some of their territories into groups. The former British West Africa, the Federation of Rhodesia and Nysaland, the East African Community (EAC), the High Commission territories, French West Africa (AOF) and French Equatorial Africa (AEF) constituted such groupings.

Some of the groups were based on common services. The EAC, established in 1947/48, for instance, had common railways, ports and harbors, research institutions and a joint airline. It unfortunately collapsed in 1977. After renegotiations lasting many years, an agreement to restore cooperation was signed by the member states concerned in 1993. Following the setting up of a secretariat in March 1997, an action plan was launched; the three currencies were made convertible; and an agreement ending double taxation was signed (*Foreign Report*, May 15, 1997). In 1998, the member states were in the process of discussing a draft treaty for the establishment of a joint legislative assembly, a supreme court and a monetary union (*Pan African News Agency*, May 16, 1998).

Following independence, AOF and AEF continued to cooperate in certain areas. Use of common currency, the CFA franc which was pegged to the French franc, was one such area. This parity was, however, abrogated in January 1994 because of the strong value of the French franc, which had led to the appreciation of the CFA franc, thus bearing adverse consequences on the economies of the member states.

## Towards African Economic Community

After independence, most African countries in the 1960s showed positive growth in their economies. They could feed themselves while exporting food. They earned adequate foreign exchange enough to meet their relatively limited import requirements for basic needs and inputs for the import substituting industries they had established.

Because of their limited national economies and related inherent disadvantages and difficulties, African countries soon realized the need for cooperation. They realized that intra-African trade could be promoted when national markets were integrated and they had competitive goods with which to trade. They therefore opted for economic cooperation and integration with a view to benefiting collectively from the economies of scale through human, institutional and infrastructural capacity building. The West African Economic Community (CEAO), comprising the majority of French speaking countries in West Africa was among the first to be established and has probably been among the most successful economic groupings.

The Economic Commission for Africa (ECA), a United Nations regional office for Africa, was established in Addis Ababa, Ethiopia in 1958. It was instrumental in establishing about 30 ECA-sponsored institutions (subregional and regional inter-governmental organizations, see Annex 4.7) for research and development, science and technology, education and training, banking, cartography and remote sensing, among others, who carry out activities that would have otherwise been beyond the capacity of most individual countries. This approach was intended to achieve substantial cost effectiveness for all member states and to promote technical and economic cooperation. Examples of such institutions include the African Institute for Economic Development and Planning (IDEP), the African Development Bank (ADB), the Clearing House of the Preferential Trade Area for Eastern and Southern African States (PTA), the West African Clearing House of ECOWAS, the African Regional Center for Technology (ARCT), the African Regional Center for Engineering Design and Manufacturing (ARCEDEM), the African Regional Standards Organization (ARSO), the African Regional Industrial Property Organization (ARIPO), the African Organization for Intellectual Property ( AOIP), the Eastern and Southern Africa Mineral Resources Development Center (ESAMRDC), the African Organization for Cartography and Remote Sensing (AOCRS), the African Regional Center for Solar Energy (ARCSE), the Eastern and Southern Africa Management Institute (ESAMI) and the Pan African Telecommunications Network (PANAFTEL). ADB, ESAMI, ARSO and IDEP are among the successful ones.

Many of the institutions, however, suffer from insufficient financing, politicized appointments, inadequate managerial autonomy and functional duplication. ADB, ESAMI and ARCEDM, with the last two generating part of their financial needs, are among the exceptions. It was, for example, reported that by 1995 ARCEDEM was generating 50 percent of its budget through the sale of prototypes and the provision of training and consulting services (UNIDO, *Engineering Independence*). African countries are continuing their efforts to rationalize these institutions.

African countries formulated common African positions and promoted their common interests in international fora. As a result they have been able to extract some concessions from the international community, although not to the extent desired. Common African positions presented to global conferences and OAU Assembly of Heads of States and Government have related to such issues as environment and development, Africa's external indebtedness, population and development, natural disaster reduction and the status of women.

While the region was in the process of creating an enabling environment, the oil crisis in 1973 (followed later by the 1979 oil shock) reared its ugly head. The steady growth thitherto came to a halt in most countries, particularly in those that were not endowed with oil. Their foreign exchange earning capabilities declined because of very high oil prices and subsequent skyrocketing prices of industrial imports. Some countries had to use up to 80 percent of their foreign exchange earnings to purchase oil. In short, the economic and social conditions, even in the oil exporting countries themselves (because of subsequent fall of oil price), contnued to deteriorate until recently. It was under these circumstances that the number of the least developed countries in Africa increased to 32 (out of a world total of 48).

The oil crisis was exacerbated and followed by proliferating multiple crises and other difficulties: drought (1983/84, 1987, 1992, 1997) and famine, food crisis, debt crisis, collapse of prices of African export commodities, foreign exchange shortage, budget and balance of payments deficits and others.

Recognizing the quagmire that the continent was drifting into, African governments, individually and collectively, launched attempts to halt and reverse the trend. They took a series of initiatives, starting in the mid-1970s with the ECA's Revised Framework of Principles for the Implementation of the New International Economic Order in Africa. This lead to the Monrovia Declaration of Commitment of 1979 on *"guidelines and measures for national and collective self-reliance in economic and social development for the estabishment of a new international economic order"* and subsequently to the adoption of the OAU's Lagos Plan of Action (LPA) and the Final Act of Lagos (FAL) by African Heads of State and Government in 1980 (OAU, *Lagos Plan of Action*). According to the LPA, African regional integration culminating in an African Economic Community by the year 2000 was to be brought about by first achieving integration at the subregional level (North, West, Eastern, and Southern and Central). In the integration process aimed at the collective, accelerated, self-reliant and self-sustaining development of member states, each subregion was, generally, expected to pass successively through the stages of free trade area, customs union and economic community before merging into a regional economic community: the ultimate goal involving complete economic and political fusion. Among the African initiatives that followed the LPA, that became the corner stone for practically all subsequent measures and actions taken by the member states, the OAU, ECA and other African and non-African organizations, mention should be made of:

- ECA's Long-term Perspective Study on African Development of 1983,

- OAU's Africa's Priority Program for Economic Recovery (APPER) 1986-1990 of 1986,

- ECA's African Alternative Framework to Structural Adjustment Program for Socio-economic Recovery and Transformation (AAF-SAP) of 1989, and

- OAU's Abuja Treaty of 1991 which called for the economic integration of Africa and the establishment of an African Economic Community.

For its part, the international community came up with the United Nations Program of Action for African Economic Recovery and Development (UN-PAAERD) 1986-1990 of 1986, a North-South compact for Africa aimed at united action to assist Africa. Initiatives aimed at facilitating the implementation of the UN-PAAERD were undertaken by African countries. These included the Abuja International Conference on Africa: the Challenge of Economic Recovery and Accelerated Development in 1987, the Khartoum International Conference on the Human Dimension of Africa's Economic Recovery and Development in 1988 and the International Conference on Popular Participation in the Recovery and Development Process in Africa in 1990. Unfortunately, these and the other initiatives and blueprints (parallel and sometimes competing programs) did not result in any significant recovery, let alone development, partly because of the continuation of the world economic crisis into the early part of the 1990s and the lack of adequate support from the international community. In view of this and a further time lag, the above macro-economic figures will have to be revised upwards.

The UN-PAAERD was followed by the World Bank's *Long-term Perspective Study on Sub-Saharan Africa: from Crisis to Sustainable Growth of 1989*. The Paris Declaration and the Program of Action for the Least Developed Countries for the 1990s was designed to accelerate the growth and development of the least developed countries most of which are in Africa. More recently, the United Nations has drawn up the New Agenda for the Development of Africa in the 1990s (UN-NADAF) to succeed the UN-PAAERD. The Agenda is based on the principle of shared responsibility and full partnership between African countries and their partners in the sustained development of the region.

UN-NADAF envisages accelerated economic growth in Africa in the period 1995-2015. According to a quantitative macroeconomic model worked out by the ECA (E/ECA/CM.20/37/Rev.1), the African economy is expected to grow by 6 percent yearly during the period 1995-2005, rising to 7 percent over 2005-2015. To achieve the 6 percent growth rate, gross domestic investment will have to increase from 20 percent to 30-40 percent of GDP and gross domestic savings, from 18 percent to 30-35 percent of GNP. It should be noted that past savings-investment gaps have doubled from 1.8 percent in 1992 to 3.5 percent in 1996 (ADB, *African Development Report 1997*0). In Sub-Saharan Africa in 1980 and 1995, gross domestic savings and gross domestic investment as percent of GDP were 27 and 16 and 23 and 19, respectively (World Bank, *The State in a Changing World*). In view of these realities, the savings-investment gaps resulting from the above projections will have to come from external resources. The absolute magnitude has been estimated at US $ 433.8 billion or about $30 billion per year (in 1994 dollars) during the 1995-2005 period. The UN-NADAF mid-term review in 1996, unfortunately, showed that support from the international community was not satisfactory. The UN-NADAF was followed by the adoption of the United Nations System-Wide Special Initiative on Africa which was intended to reinforce the former.

Despite progress in economic performance in recent years referred to earlier, none of the policies, priorities, strategies and approaches adopted have significantly changed the lot of the African peoples. The world economy is shifting from industrial activities to services. The market mechanism, including privatization, that was and is still being imposed on developing countries, particularly those in Africa, does not seem justified at this stage of their development. It is no wonder that a new economic theory, based on a common heritage of mankind, is in the process of development.

Frustrations at the lack of progress with so many initiatives led the OAU Council of Ministers at their seventeenth Extra-ordinary Session in Cairo in March 1995 to adopt yet another initiative: "Re-launching Africa's Economic and Social Development: The Cairo Agenda for Action." The Agenda calls for serious commitment and action by the African countries themselves before resorting to assistance from their development partners. The issues dealt with included democracy, governance, peace, security, stability and sustainable development. High priority was given to food security, capacity building and human resource development along with issues related to industry, transport and communications, and regional economic cooperation and integration. The Agenda was expected to be adopted by the OAU summit in June 1996. At the international level, the Economic and Social Council (ECOSOC) of the United Nations was expected to focus on African economic recovery and development in 1995.

At the national level, development planning of the 1960s and 1970s gave way to crisis management and in the 1980s the tendency to replace such planning by short-term conventional SAPs with their inherent advers impact on the poor. This led to major adverse consequences requiring growth with equity. At the Maastricht meeting of the Global Coalition for Africa and the international community in the Netherlands in 1991, which set a growth rate for Africa of 4-5 percent, the meeting advised African countries to replace their earlier efforts by national long-term perspective studies and plans. This advice seems to have been heeded by a number of countries. At the international summit meeting of the Global Coalition for Africa held on June 2, 1994 in Harare, Zimbabwe, it was reported that Africa was undertaking economic structural adjustment programs, political reforms and regional integration and that the virtues of good governance and democracy were gaining ground in Africa. That progress has been made in these areas and more specifically in political pluralism, human rights, transparency and accountability, was noted at the thirtieth session of the Commission/Twenty-first Meeting of the Conference of Ministers, the highest organ of the ECA, in May 1995.

At the regional level, African countries have been devising ways and means of collectively solving common economic problems as well as those that they cannot handle at the national level. To this end , the Abuja Treaty establishing the African Economic Community (AEC) (OAU, *Treaty Establishing the African Economic Community*), which came into force on May 12, 1994 following ratification by 37 OAU member states, is expected to be fully operational by 2028 when the Regional[4] Economic Communities, its building blocks, will have become fully operational. Implementation of the Treaty will involve three stages: (a) strengthening the existing framework for cooperation and integration, (b) removal of tariff and non-tariff barriers and strengthening sectoral integration, and (c) establishing a Free Trade Area. At the First Summit of the AEC in June 1997, the OAU Heads of State and Government made a number of decisions, including: strengthening the regional economic communities and giving high priority to the harmonization and coordination of the communities' programs; and called upon member countries of each Community *"to adopt a dynamic program for rationalizing the communities"* (OAU, *AEC Newsletter*, August-October 1997).

The communities with the widest country coverage are: the Common market for Eastern and Southern Africa (COMESA), formerly PTA, the Southern Africa Development Community (SADC), ECCAS which in 1997 was reported to have virtually collapsed (apparently overshadowed by UDEAC), ECOWAS which seems to be facing duplication from the recently established Union Economique et Monetaire Ouest Africaine (UEMOA) with common currency, and starting in 1998, common tariff, and Arab Maghreb Union (AMU). They have started or are starting as subregional free trade areas leading to subregional common markets which are the prelude to subregional economic communities.[5]

The AEC is intended to enhance and facilitate economic cooperation and integration in the African region. Intra-African trade, currently a mere 5 percent of foreign trade, is expected to expand considerably resulting in real income gains. A four-dimensional integration process (infrastructure, trade liberalization and market expansion, production, and economic and monetary policy convergence) as well as sectoral (food and agriculture, industry, science and technology, energy, free movement of goods and services, etc.) harmonization and convergence in various fields constitute the main areas of focus in the process of creating the Community.

It should be noted here that the OAU Heads of State and Government established the OAU/Community Structure and mandated the establishment of the Community to the OAU Secretariat and the promotion, coordination and monitoring the implementation of the Abuja Treaty to the joint OAU/ECA/ADB Secretariat. In 1995 the Secretariat was engaged in activities related to establishing the necessary mechanisms for implementing the Treaty, including the strengthening of existing subregional economic communities, creating communities where they do not exist and drafting protocols, including one on industry. This is the first of the six stages envisaged for establishing the Community, the fifth being the establishment of the African Common Market by the year 2028. In line with this stage, a protocol on closer relations was signed in February 1998 between the AEC and four of the subregional groupings (COMESA, ECOWAS, IGAD and SADC). At the national level, national coordination committees are the mechanisms intended to coordinate activities within a country and serve as links with the subregional communities.

The Treaty incorporates specialized technical committees: the Committee on Industry, Science and Technology, Energy, Natural Resources and Environment being one of them. Industrial priorities include: basic (food and agro-based, metallurgical, mechanical and chemical) and small-scale industries. The creation of African multinational enterprises and the promotion of joint industrial development projects are among the strategies to be used.

The draft protocol on industry, inter alia, accorded priority to the establishment of basic and heavy, intermediate and agro- and agro-related industries, the promotion of industrial research and development, and the establishment and promotion of African multinational enterprises. Rehabilitation, regeneration and maintenance of existing industries, expansion and/or modernization of the industrial base, promotion and improvement of linkages among industries and increased involvement of small- and medium-scale industries are among the strategies envisaged to implement those priorities. The priorities and strategies seem to be in line with the 1991 Dakar Declaration on Industrialization and Economic Integration of the Conference of African Ministers of Industry which reaffirmed *"the critical roles of industry, economic integration and appropriate economic policies in the effort of Africa to achieve development and growth."*

The successful implementation and operation of the Community will yield free movement of goods, services, capital and people, eliminating customs checks, immigration control and other confining features of statehood. It would, to a large extent, depend on the development of trade among member states and the extent of the democratization process that has already begun. As log as inadequate infrastructures and lack of complementarity prevail and unless deliberate attempts are made to bring about comparative advantages in the form of specialization in production and services, it is unlikely that inter- and intra-African trade will improve. The remedy lies in a rational approach to the development of the production and services sectors, particularly industry.

The devaluation of the CFA franc (whose full convertibility has been guaranteed by the Bank of France) from 1FF=50 CFA francs to 1FF=100 CFA francs in January 1994 in 13 francophone and one Lusophone African countries may be a blessing in disguise. By minimizing exchange rate policy disparities which are detrimental to economic integration, it might facilitate the drawing up of genuine monetary cooperation agreements at the subregional level within the framework of ECOWAS and ECCAS. In this connection, it should be noted that French African policy has been a deterrent to economic cooperation between Francophone and Anglophone African countries.

The four subregional groups, the future subregional economic communities, are currently at different stages of development. COMESA (former PTA) comprising 25[6] member states (including some countries from the North and Central African subregions) and, unlike the PTA, vested with the power to impose sanctions on its member countries that default, has been the most successful so far. COMESA had instituted phased import tariff elimination by 1992, later changed to 2000 (Saasa 1991); by May 1997, it had already reduced tariffs between 60 percent and 80 percent on goods originating from member states (OAU, *Rapport* ... ). It has taken other measures to liberalize and facilitate trade, including the removal of non-tariff barriers. As a result, intra-COMESA trade rose to 8 percent compared to about 5 percent for intra-African trade (PTA, *PTA Banker*, Vol. 3, No. 9). Intra-COMESA trade doubled from $834 million in 1985 to $1.7 billion in 1994 and is expected to rise to $4 billion annually (OAU, *AEC Newsletter*, May-July 1997). By the end of 1995, recorded trade among COMESA member states was expected to surpass the $1 billion level. This would mean a 10.1 percent increase over that of 1994 (*The Ethiopian Herald*, 7 December 1994). Other successes up to 1992 when PTA celebrated its 10th anniversary included (*PTA Development Report*):

- The removal of non-physical barriers related to transport, including road customs transit documents, uniform tariff harmonizations in road transport and telecommunications and the introduction of expedited mail services;
- The development of programs on agricultural research and the prevention of post-harvest food losses;
- The provision of assistance to member states in the rehabilitation of

some industries (cement, metallurgical and pharmaceuticals) ;
• The introduction of the UAPTA travelers' cheques in 1988 to promote travel within the PTA area;
• The launching of the PTA Monetary Harmonization Program in 1990, a precursor to monetary union; and.
• The establishment of
  - COMESA Clearing House in Harare in 1984 for the settlement of payments for intra-COMESA transactions,
  -COMESA Trade and Development Bank in Bujumbura in 1985 to finance multinational projects and to promote trade among member states,
  - COMESA Re-insurance Company,
  - COMESA Commercial Arbitration Center,
  - COMESA Council of Bureaux on Third Party Motor Vehicle Insurance Scheme,
  - COMESA Metallurgical Technology Center in Harare,
  - Federation of Chambers of Commerce and Industry,
  - COMESA Leather and Leather Products Institute in Addis Ababa, and
  -African Joint Air Services.

The provision of information through its Trade Information Network (TINET) with terminals in practically all member states, the creation of COMESA Eastern and Southern Africa Business Organization, organizing trade fairs and technical fora, and removal of foreign exchange control by most member countries are among other successes. Recent additions to COMESA's enabling mechanisms include: the COMESA Court of Justice to arbitrate and impose sanctions related to contravening of agreements and the COMESA Carrier License to facilitate clearance of cargo vehicles transiting through member countries.

At the inaugural meeting of COMESA in Kampala, Uganda, in November 1993, COMESA superseded PTA. During that year, 12 out of 23 PTA member states had already ratified the treaty establishing COMESA.

In September 1984, the members of PTA had agreed to achieve zero tariffs by the year 2000. With COMESA becoming operational, goods, services, people and capital will move freely within and among the member states. A step towards this end was taken on 6 April 1995 when Ethiopia and Eritrea signed a free trade zone agreement. In other words, they opted for the continuation of the free movement of goods and people that prevailed before Eritrea became independent. Another agreement signed at the same time relates to efforts towards a comprehensive economic union. The introduction of the Nakfa (national currency) in Eritrea in 1997 and border dispute followed by clashes along the border, unfortunately, have adversely affected these exemplary cooperative relations.

On April 18, 1995, the Special Summit of the Inter-governmental Authority on Drought and Development (IGADD) whose initial objective was to fight desert encroachment, the Heads of State of IGADD declared more expanded cooperation in, among other things, the *"promotion of joint development strategy and harmonization of macro-economic policies and programs."* In keeping with that aim, the IGADD charter was amended at the 1996 summit and IGADD renamed the Inter-governmental Authority on Development (IGAD). Its objectives now include cooperation in the political, economic, security, human and environmental areas.

As in other subregions, there is a need to rationalize overlapping and competing subregional and regional economic integration institutions. COMESA favors a merger with the Southern Africa Development Community (SADC) which comprises 11 member states (all except Botswana being members of COMESA, as well) and was established in 1992 (formerly SADCC). Some members of the latter have expressed caution on the issue of merging. Some of the countries in the subregion (Botswana, South Africa and Zimbabwe) believe that COMESA is too large to be efficient. SADC wants each organization to be an autonomous yet complementary entity with distinct objectives and mandates. Another option is division into two separate communities, SADC for the southern countries and possibly IGAD for the northern countries. It appears that the 1996 revitalization and conversion of IGADD to IGAD may constitute such an option.

With respect to the other subregions, ECOWAS appears to have made some progress, including clarifying its position vis-a-vis other economic communities (MRU and CEAO) and through its ECOWAS Fund financing a number of infrastructural projects. In 1993, at the sixteenth conference of Heads of State and Government of ECOWAS, the member states signed a revised ECOWAS Treaty. That Treaty stipulates, among others, that ECOWAS is the only economic community in their subregion and that decisions made by ECOWAS are binding, dispensing with the earlier ratification requirement. These stipulations, obviously, have removed two of the major constraints to cooperation and integration that for years have blocked progress in the subregion. It should be pointed out here that ECOWAS has, so far, been the only community to have succeeded in putting into practice the free movement of persons. It had been reported recently that it has made progress in demolishing tariff barriers and launching travelers cheque to facilitate trade and tourism among memeber states, leading to the establishment of a single monetary zone by the year 2000. In regard to ECCAS whose member states already share a single currency, internal trade tariffs had been eliminated (*The Economist*, May 16, 1998).

Mainly due to the global sanctions imposed because of apartheid, and internal political instability, the economy of South Africa (whose GNP is close to five times that of SADC member states combined) was characterized by negative GDP growth rates, except in 1993 when it showed modest growth (ADB, *Economic Integration ...* ). Following the lifting of the embargo and the formation of a multiracial government, South Africa was readmitted as a member to the OAU and the ECA and joined SADC. Today, the country can adopt an export-led growth strategy aimed at African markets. It has already taken measures to establish trade relations with many countries in the region. It is possible that South African goods and services will compete with those imported from industrialized countries. African countries will, of course, expect reciprocity in that South Africa will draw its requirements from the region itself and its dominance will not compromise the development of neighboring economies. A positive relationship of this kind would augur well for the development of the region as a whole provided South Africa succeeds in playing the leadership role expected of it.

From indications thus far, the African economic conditions in the mid-1990s were better than those prevailing in the early 1990s. Africa may, however, become increasingly marginalized as competition within and protectionism by re-gionalized economic blocks grows. The European Union (EU) transited to an economic and monetary union with a single currency, the euro, in 1999. The North American Free Trade Agreement (NAFTA), the Latin American Associa-tion for Free Trade (LAAFT), Mercosur (southern Latin American common market), the Asia-Pacific Economic Cooperation (APEC), the Association of South East Asian Nations (ASEAN) and the Arab Free Trade Area (AFTA) will become still stronger. One of the agreements in APEC, which comprises 18 coun-tries, including the USA, Canada, China, Japan, and Australia, stipulates the removal of all trade barriers: by 2010 in the highly developed and by 2020 in developing member countries (Radin, *The Boston Sunday Globe*). The signing by 7 Central American countries of the Nicaragua Declaration II in September 1997 with the purpose of building a European-style union, is the latest initiative in trends toward regional cooperation (*The Wall Street Journal*, September 4, 1997).

As stated elsewhere, African governments are largely to blame for the deplor-able situation in which the region finds itself. In recent years, however, there seems to be a trend towards genuine economic and social reform and an intensi-fication of the democratization process. Many countries are following these trends and implementing sustained policy reforms. An article entitled "Emerging Af-rica" *The Economist* (June 14, 1997) attests such trends. In its own word, *"The idea that lasting prosperity demands stable government and the rule of law has taken hold almost everywhere ... most African governments ... have adopted prom-ising economic policies: sound money, fiscal rectitude and the encouragement of private business are their mantras ... inflation is being tamed and budget deficits are falling ... ."* During the period 1992-1995, the average rate of inflation fell to 27.3 percent while the budget deficit averaged 5.5 percent of GDP (ADB, *African Development Report 1997*).

According to another article in the same issue, entitled "An African Success Story," Southern Africa helped by good rains, showed a 6 percent rise in GDP in 1996 and is heading in the right direction. This is the brighter aspect of the continent's future. In other words, despite the marginalization referred to above, it is likely that many African countries will enjoy economic and social progress in the not too distant future. As for human rights, a draft protocol was to be considered for ratification at the annual summit of the OAU in June 1996, lead-ing to the creation of an African human rights court.

## BIBLIOGRPAPHY

ADB, 1993, *Economic Integration in Southern Africa,* Abidjan.

ADB, 1994, *African Development Report 1994,* Abidjan.

ADB, 1996, *African Development Report 1996,* Abidjan.

ADB, 1997, *African Development Report* 1997, Oxford University Press, New York.

Addis Zemen, 1994, September 22, 1994, Addis Ababa.

Arnold, Guy, 1995, "South Africa Strikes North," *African Business,* December 1995.

ECA, 1993, The Ad-Hoc Expert Group Meeting on Promotion of Investment in Industrial Projects in the Context of the Second Industrial Development Decade (IDDA II) (ECA/ IHSD/IPPIS/033/93), Addis Ababa.

ECA, 1994, *Report of the Fifteenth Meeting of the Technical Preparatory Committee of* the Whole (E/ECA/CM.20/37/Rev.1), Addis Ababa.

ECA, 1995, Food and Agriculture Production, Food Security and Food Self-sufficiency in Africa (E/ECA/CM.21/10), Addis Ababa.

ECA, 1995, Reviving Private Investment in Africa: Policies, Strategies and Programs (E/ECA/CM.21/7), Addis Ababa.

ECA, 1996, Africa in the 1990 and Beyond: ECA-Revised Long-Term Development Perspectives Study (ECA/SERPD/TP/96/3), Addis Ababa.

ECA, 1996, Measures to Consolidate Privatization in the African Industrial Sector with Special Emphasis on the Program of the Second Industrial Development Decade for Africa (ECA/IHSD/IPPIS/003/96), Addis Ababa.

ECA, 1997, Report of the Thirty-second Session of the Commission/Twenty-third Meeting of the Conference of African Ministers Responsible for Economic and Social Development and Planning (E/ECA/CM.23/12), Addis Ababa.

FAO, 1980, Regional Food Plan for Africa, Rome.

FAO, 1982, 1987, 1992, FAO Production Yearbook, Rome.

FAO, 1986, African Agriculture: the next 25 Years, Annex III, Raising Productivity, Rome.

FAO, 1986, African Agriculture: the next 25 Years, Annex V, Rome.

FAO, 1986, Atlas of African Agriculture: African agriculture: the next 25 years, Rome.

FAO, 1994, Computer Files, Statistics Division, February 1994, Rom.

FAO, 1994, Food Crops and Shortage, Special Report , No. 1, January-February, 1994, Rome.

FAO, 1994, The State of Food and Agriculture 1994, Rome.

FAO, 1995, Dimensions of Need, Rome.

FAO, 1995, The State of Food and Agriculture 1995, Rome.

Foreign Report, 1995, "The Gloom over Ghana," No. 2354, June 8, 1995

Foreign Report, 1995," Uganda Wakes Up," No. 2349, May 4, 1995.

Foreign Report, 1997, "East Africa Tries Again," No 2447, May 15, 1997.

Foreign Report, 1998, "East African Countries Move Closer to Integration," May 16, 1998.

Husain, Ishrat and Rashid Faruque, eds., 1994, Adjustment in Africa, Lessons from Country Case Studies, Regional and Sectoral Studis, The World Bank, Washington, D.C.

IFC, 1995, Trends in Privte Investment in Developing Countries 1990-94 (Discusson Paper No. 28), Washington, D.C.

IMF, 1996, World Eonomic Outlook, October 1996, Washington, D.C.

Internet (Yahoo Search Results), 1998, Ethiopian Agriculture: the Base for Overall Development, issued by the Office of the Government Spokesperson, September 2, 1998.

Juo, S.R. and Russell D Freed, editors, 1995, Agriculture and the Environment: Bridging Food Production and Environmental Protection in Developing Countries, ASA Special Publication Number 60, Madison.

Meier, Gerald M. and William F. Steel, eds., 1989, Industrial Adjustment in Sub-Saharan Africa, EDI Series in Economic Development, Published for The World Bank, Oxford University Press, New York.

Microsoft, 1996, Encarta 96 Encyclopedia, Redmond.

New Africa, 1995, "Sinister Side of SAP," No. 328, March 1995.

OAU, 1981, Lagos Plan of Action for the Development of Africa, International Institute for Labour Studies, Geneva.

OAU, 1991, Treaty Establishing the African Economic Community, Addis Ababa.

OAU, 1997, "COMESA: A Building Block for the African Economic Community," AEC Newsletter, May-July 1997.

OAU, 1997, Rapport: Mission Conjoint OUA-CEA Aupres des Communautés Economiques

Regionales CER) et Sous-regionales, Addis Ababa.

OAU, 1997, "The Main Conclusions and Decisions of the First Summit of the African Economic Community," *AEC Newsletter*, August-October 1997.

OECD, 1993, *Financing and External Debt of Developing Countries, 1992 Survey*, Paris.

PTA, 1995, *PTA Banker*, Newsletter of the COMESA Bankers' Association, Vol. 3, No. 9, June 1995, Lusaka, Zambia.

PTA, undated, *PTA Development Report: a Decade of Economic Integration 1982-1992*, Lusaka, Zambia.

Radin, Charles A., 1995, *The Boston Sunday Globe*, November 19, 1995, Boston.

Ragland, John and Lal, Rattan, editors, 1993, *Technologies for Sustainable Agriculture in the Tropics*, proceedings of two international symposia, ASA Special Publication Number 56, Madison.

Riddell, Roger C. et al, 1990, *Manufacturing Africa*, James Currey, London

Saasa, S. Oliver, ed., 1991, *Joining the Future: Economic Integration and Co-operation in Africa*, African Center for Technology Studies, Nairobi.

The Economist, 1994, "The Kindness of Strangers," May 7, 1994.

The Economist, 1996, "Ghana: A Referendum of the Boss," December 7, 1996.

The Economist, 1996, "Mercosur Survey," October 12, 1996 and "Mercosur: Now They Are Six," December 21, 1996.

The Economist, 1998, "France and Gabon: Black Emirate," May 16, 1998.

The Ethiopian Herald, 1994, "Comesa Trade Set to Rise," December 7, 1994, Addis Ababa.

The Ethiopian Herald, 1994, "Researchers Come up with Better Sorghum Species," October 26, 1994, Addis Ababa.

The Ethiopian Herald, 1994," SG Helps Boost Agricultural Productivity," July 30, 1994, Addis Ababa.

The Ethiopian Herald, 1994, "Wheat Yield per Hectare Can Rise to Three-fold," December 30, 1994, Addis Ababa.

The Ethiopian Herald, 1995, "Economic Stabilization," Recovery, April 1, 1995, Addis Ababa.

The Ethiopian Herald, 1997, "Agricultural Extension Aspects on Soil Fertility Maintenance," October 25, 1997.

The Ethiopian Herald, 1997, "Experts Discover Three High-yield Wheat Species," October 11, 1997, Addis Ababa.

The Ethiopian Herald, 1997, "Retrenchment Policy and its Implementation," October 21 and 22, 1997.

The Ethiopian Herald, 1997, "SG 2000 in Ethiopia," October 18, 1997, Addis Ababa.

The Wall Street Journal, 1997, "Central American Accord Signed," September 4, 1997.

UN, 1995, *World Economic and Social Survey 1995: Current Trends and Policies in the World Economy* (E/1995/50), New York.

UN, 1996, *World Economic and Social Survey 1996*, New York.

UNCTAD, 1995, *The Least Developed Countries, 1995 Report* (ID/B/41(2)/4), New York.

UNCTAD, 1995, *World Investment Report*, Geneva.

UNDP, 1994, *Human Development Report 1994*, Oxford University Press, New York.

UNDP, 1996, *Human Development Report 1996*, Oxford University Press, New York.

UNIDO, 1993, *Industry and Development: Global Report 1993/94*, Vienna.

UNIDO, 1995, *Engineering Independence* (Pilot program for the design, manufacture and testing of hydraulic maintenance presses (XA/RAF/94/X19), Vienna.

UNIDO, 1995, *The Globalization of Industry: Implications for Developing Countries beyond 2000*, Vienna.

UNIDO, 1996, *Industrial Development: Global Report 1996,* Vienna.

World Bank, 1989, *Sub-Saharan Africa: From Crisis to Sustainable Growth, a Long-term Perspective Study,* Washington, D. C.

World Bank, 1991, *Price Prospects for Major Primary Commodities, 1990-2005,* Volume I, Summary Energy, Metals and Minerals, Washington, D.C.

World Bank, 1994, *Adjustment in Africa: Lessons from Country Case Studies,* Washington, D.C.

World Bank, 1994, *World Tables 1994,* The Johns Hopkins University Press, Baltimore.

World Bank, 1995, *Global Economic Prospects and the Developing Countries.*

World Bank, 1996, *Global Economic Prospects & the Developing Countries,* Washington, D.C.

World Bank, 1996, *World Development Report 1996,* Oxford University Press, New York.

World Bank, 1997, *The State in a Changing World,* Oxford University Press, New York.

WTO, 1995, *Regionalism and the World Trading System,* Madrid.

# NOTES

1. The composition of some of the subregions here differs a little from that shown in Chapter 1. North Africa in Chapter 1 comprises Maghreb, Egypt and Sudan. Egypt does not figure in any of the subregions, except among the net oil exporters; Sudan is included in PTA and Mauritania in Maghreb.

2. The traditional measure of the cost of living is, at present, under scrutiny in the United States. The proponents for change claim that the cost price index is overestimated, currently by 1.1 percentage points. It does not take into account benefits accruing from improved and new products and changes from consumer spending patterns. Although the impact of these under present African conditions may not be that significant it may be so over time.

3. In the United States, for instance, about 1.8 percent of the population were farm residents in 1990 working on 51 million hectares in 1992 compared to 397 million hectares in 1935 (Microsoft, *Encarta 96 Encyclopedia*).

4. In the parlance of the OAU, the continent is divided into five regions which are equivalent to ECA's four subregions except that the latter's Eastern and Southern African subregion corresponds to the former's two regions: East Africa and Southern Africa. The final realization of the AEC will take 34 years, about the same duration that it took the European Economic Community to convert itself into a single market.

5. Implementing the community has been planned in six stages. The first stage as it applies to the draft protocol on industry includes (durations starting with the protocol entry into effect):

    -Harmonization of national and regional industrial policies and strategies,

    -Preparation of inventory of existing industries (within 3 years),

    -Preparation of indicative regional industrial development program (within 5 years), and

    -Preparation of inventory of key human resource development institutions and assessment of human resource capabilities (within 3 years).

6. COMESA member countries: Angola, Burundi, Comoros, Congo K, Djibouti, Egypt, Eritrea, Ethiopia, Kenya, Lesotho, Madagascar, Malawi, Mauritius, Mozambique, Namibia, Rwanda, Seychelles, Somalia, South Africa, Sudan, Swaziland, Tanzania, Uganda, Zambia and Zimbabwe.

# PART TWO

# INDUSTRIAL POSSIBILITIES

CHAPTER 4

# AVAILABILITY OF RESOURCES AND INFRASTRUCTURE FOR INDUSTRIAL DEVELOPMENT

With an area of about 3 billion hectares (FAO, *FAO Production Yearbook*) , Africa occupies about 23 percent of the world's total area. In size it is second to Asia; about 2 percent of its total area is covered by water.

The region is blessed with a variety of resources. An indication of African resources is given in Map 4.1. Exploitation of these resources started during the colonial era, with benefits going to the metropolitan countries. With the advent of independence, African governments gradually acquired part or total ownership of some of the resources and the means of exploitation thereof and involved themselves in their development and management. This transfer of ownership was not trouble-free; many of the production facilities suffered loses and even closure, due in part to falling world prices and mismanagement.

## AGRICULTURAL RESOURCES

The biodiversity of plants and animals in the world is huge. About 1.7 million species have already been identified. Estimates range between 3 million and 111 million (World Bank, *World Resources 1996-97*). Another source (ESCAP, *Agropesticides*) has this to say about flora: *"About 350,000 species of plants are known to man. Of these, less than 1 percent or about 3,000 species have economic value and less than 100 species are currently cultivated."* Africa's biodiversity is enormous, as evidenced by its innumerable flora and fauna. [1]

Of the total land area of Africa, of which 30 percent is potentially cultivable (FAO, *Atlas of African Agriculture*), only about 6 percent is arable land or land under permanent crops, in contrast to 11 percent for the world as a whole. Whereas land under permanent pasture increased slightly during the period 1976-1991, forest and woodland area shrank from 24 percent to 23 percent of the total area. Land under irrigation increased from 9.6 million hectares in 1976 to 11.4 million hectares in 1991 (*FAO Production Yearbook*). Egypt, Sudan, Morocco and South Africa together account for around 60 percent of the total irrigated area.

As mentioned earlier, the equator divides Africa into practically two equal parts. As one moves north or south of the equator (more pronounced for the north), one passes through the following bioclimatic regions in tropical and subtropical Africa (hillips 1967):

- Forest: highly humid, humid, humid-subhumid, tropical and subtropical covered by evergreen to mixed evergreen and deciduous vegetation;

- Wooded savana: subhumid, mild subarid, subarid, arid, subdesert, tropical, and subtropical covered by grass (depending on the availability of moisture) and evergreen in the moister seasons, deciduous in the drier seasons;

- Scrub: subhumid to subdesert covered by evergreen, deciduous and mixed woody growth, often closely intertwined, but may occur in the form of irregular groups or patches;

- Subdesert: wooded savana characterized by evergreen, deciduous, and mixed woody growth and shrubs, subshrubs, and brush; and

- Desert: vegetation, very, very spares to absent.

## Map 4.1: Natural Resources in Africa

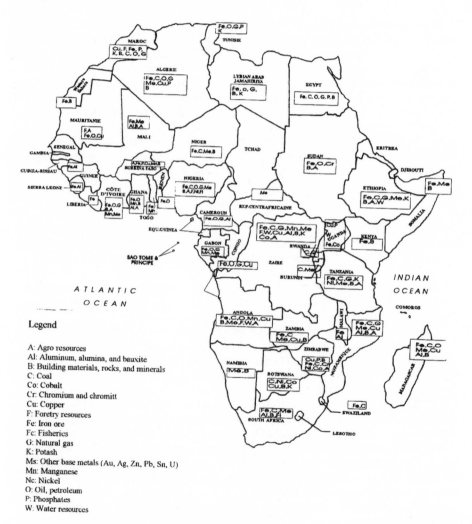

Legend

A: Agro resources
Al: Aluminum, alumina, and bauxite
B: Building materials, rocks, and minerals
C: Coal
Co: Cobalt
Cr: Chromium and chromitt
Cu: Copper
F: Foretry resources
Fe: Iron ore
Fc: Fisheries
G: Natural gas
K: Potash
Ms: Other base metals (Au, Ag, Zn, Pb, Sn, U)
Mn: Manganese
Nc: Nickel
O: Oil, petroleum
P: Phosphates
W: Water resources

The above, although locally modified by altitude, topography and soil, clearly shows the transition from tropical (hot and humid infested by disease and pests) to semi-tropical (part of which is characterized by inadequate and unpredictable rainfall) to desert (very high evaporation, typical of the northern part) and then to the Mediterranean. Acidic soil is widespread in the tropics and constitutes about 38 percent of the total land. The result of all these is a sensitive environment, susceptible to the vagaries of weather and ecosystems, exacerbated by low soil fertility said to be inadequate to sustain permanent agriculture—characteristics that distinguish Africa from the other continents. More than half of the region is uninhabitable. According to FAO, total cultivable land is 820 million hectares, half of which is marginal. Around 1985, only 27 percent of the total was cultivated.

According to a more recent source (FAO, *African Agriculture: the next 25 Years*, Annex IV), the continent is divided into the following six regions: Mediterranean and arid north Africa, Sudano-Sahelian Africa, humid and sub-humid west Africa, humid central Africa, sub-humid and mountainous east Africa, and sub-humid and semi-arid southern Africa. The countries comprising the regions and features related to cropping are compiled in Annex 4.1. The classification of the area into zones under each region (desert, arid, semi-arid, sub-humid, humid, etc.) and their respective proportions give some idea of the actual and potential areas for growing crops. In the Sudano-Sahelian region, for instance, the potential for tropical rainfed annual crops in the moist sub-humid areas is limited to only 7 percent. The situation regarding the sub-humid and mountainous east Africa is quite different in that a wide range of annual and perennial crops are and could be grown in the humid and moist sub-humid (41%) and dry sub-humid (11%) zones.

The positive aspect of the above are the diverse ecological zones and topography. Varying altitudes ranging from more than 100 meters below sea level to high plateau traversed by deep valleys and snow-capped mountains reaching a peak of 19,340 feet (Kilimanjaro) make Africa unique. In addition to being endowed with one of the most varied flora and fauna in the world, with maximum genetic diversity being in the tropical latitudes, Africa can boast a potential capacity to grow plants non-indegenous to Africa.

Plant growth days (pgd) and rainfall vary greatly from zone to zone. In the arid zone, pgd is less than 90 and rainfall ranges from nil to 500 mm. The corresponding figures for other zones are: semi-arid (90-180 and 500-1000), subhumid (180-270 and 1000-1500) and humid (greater than 270 and 1500) (ECA/FAO, *Adequate Feed and Feeding: ...* ).

Because of drought and desertification, coupled with erosion and the accompanying low fertility, the apparent advantages referred to above are being eroded and the region is experiencing a crisis in biodiversity, including genetic variation. In view of the potential in biotechnology and genetic engineering (development of foodstuffs, pharmaceuticals, fibers, gums, resins, dyes, and other industrial products based on existing flora and fauna), Africa stands to lose appreciably from the destruction and disappearance of its diversified flora and fauna. In recognition of this reality, attempts are being made by concerned African governments to introduce measures to conserve biological diversity as well as to prevent further deterioration. These include: conserving soils through terracing; conserving water by building dams (water basins, microbasins) and terraces; using ground water and aquifers judiciously; introducing reforestation and afforestation coupled with monitoring and controlling of tree-cutting; setting-up more and better planned irrigation systems; and eradicating diseases, such as trypanosomiasis and malaria. In this connection, aid provided in the form of food-for-work programs and other related assistance is crucial and therefore needs to be intensified, particularly for drought prone countries undertaking development activities related to soil and water conservation and reforestation and afforestation. UNEP through its Global Environment Facility was, starting in 1998, expected to provide funds to African countries to enable them implement the above attempts (including $20 million to Ethiopia, Kenya and Tanzania) (*PANA*, March16, 1998).

In addition to a loss of biodiversity through natural and indigenous man-made disasters, Africa is said to be experiencing "bio-piracy." According to a UNDP report in 1994, developing countries, including those in Africa, which account for 90 percent of the world's remaining biodiversity, are not recognized as owners of plants, fungus and bacteria that transnational corporations (agricultural and drug companies) use. The report advocates compensating the developing countries in the form of royalties.

## Flora

Agriculture in Africa is reported to have started more than 5,000 years ago. Many crops that now constitute African staple foodstuffs are indigenous to Africa. These are: sorghum, pearl millet, oil palm, teff, cowpea, and ensete (Dommen 1988). Other agricultural commodities originating in Africa include: shea butter, melon seed, niger seed, mango, coffee, kola, senna, and kenaf (McIlroy 1963). Finger millet, bulrush millet, African rice, yams, bambara groudnuts, castor oil, okra, garden eggs, watermelons, tamarind, and cotton are among plants domesticated in Africa (Stock 1995).

The potential for transplanting flora from other regions has been demonstrated, time and again, in the past. The introduction of maize, barley, rice, cassava, yam, potato, sweet potato, bean, tomato, chilli, orange, banana, pineapple, avocado pear, papaya, date palm, clove, vanilla fragran, sugar cane, coconut, cashew nut, sesame, sunflower, safflower, ground nut, soybean, tea, cacao, tobacco, sisal, rubber, cinchona tree, pyrethrum, and eucalyptus tree from other regions are examples of such success stories.

From the above, it is apparent that many of the agricultural commodities grown in Africa are exogenous. In view of this and despite the statement that *"The record of crop technology transfer to Sub-Saharan Africa from other continents in modern times has been one of failure"* (Dommen 1988), there is no doubt that this could be repeated with other plants with a view to mitigating the above crisis. The introduction of the eucalyptus and rubber trees into Ethiopia are recent examples of transplanting exogenous plants. Based on research work carried out using imported rubber trees which resulted in 17 hybrid species, a 20,000 hectare plantation will be developed (*The Ethiopian Herald*, November 8, 1994). What is required is the more rigorous selection of the areas intended to host the plants to be transplanted.

The major crops and agricultural products grown in Africa include the following:
- Cereals: maize, sorghum, millet, rice, wheat, and barley;
- Roots and tubers: cassava, yam, potato, and cocoyam;

- Legumes and oil-bearing crops: beans, peas, groundnuts, cottonseed, palm oil, coconuts, olives, sunflower, soybeans, sesame seed, cashew nuts, castor beans, and safflower;
- Vegetables: cassava leaves, lettuce;
- Fruits: bananas, oranges, grapes, pineapples, dates, mangos, papayas, and avocados;
- Stimulants: cocoa, coffee, tea, and tobacco;
- Vegetable fibers: cotton lint and sisal; and
- Others: sugar, vanilla fragrans, cloves, chillies and peppers, natural rubber, pyrethrum flowers, cinchona bark, senna, natural gums and resins, wattle bark, and mangrove bark. Production, import, export and net trade statistics for most of the above products are given in Annexes 4.2 and 4.3.

The above cereals and roots and tubers constitute the staple food of most of the peoples in the region. In terms of tonnage, the production of roots and tubers continue to lead cereals. The former steadily increased from 48.1 million tons in 1961 to 120.1 million tons in 1993. The corresponding figures for the latter were 46.2 and 94.7. Demand for cereals outstrips production. The gap between the consumption and production of cereals, roots, and tubers has been growing, amounting to close to 37 million tons in 1987. An indication of the production/demand gap is given under net exports in Annex 4.3. Although erratic, depending upon recurring drought, net imports of cereals steadily increased to 28.3 million tons in 1985 of which wheat accounted for about 70 percent, reached 31.1 million tons in 1993 and fell to 28.6 million tonnes in 1994. As a consequence, food self-sufficiency has been falling steadily, as indicated by food availability from local sources.

Other foodstuffs include legumes and oil-bearing crops and sugar. A good part of the stimulants and practically all of the rubber are exported. According to FAO projections made for the year 2000, production of major food crops in Sub-Saharan Africa will reach the level of 110 million tonnes per year. With consumption projected at 161 million tonnes there will be a deficit of 51 million tons (ECA, E/ECA/CM.21/10). About 56 percent of this deficit is expected to occur in West Africa.

Abysmally low yields (practically stagnant throughout the post-independence period), low labor productivity compounded by human disease (malaria, schistosomiasis, and trypanosmiasis) and rapid population growth (averaging 3 percent per year) are some of the main reasons for the above state of affairs. Agricultural research findings (including breakthroughs that could be achieved through biotechnology and genetic engineering), and field trials in the past three decades abound and can be expected to increase further in the future. The delivery system and the release of new and improved varieties of seeds to farmers, which was reported to have been very slow, need to be acceleratd. There is an urgent need for African governments to help put this accumulated wealth of knowledge into practice through the more efficient provision of advisory, technical, financial, and material (seeds, agricultural tools and implements, fertilizers, and pesticides, including biological control) inputs and services and incentives to farmers in a more effective manner than hitherto. Farmers should be involved right from the very outset so as to encourage better crop management systems. From agricultural policies adopted in recent years and being adopted by African governments, including family planning, it can be expected that farm yield and productivity will improve.

As noted above, wheat constitutes by far the largest single food-import item. This being the case, it is unfortunate that more and more Africans in the urban areas are acquiring a taste for wheat bread and wheat-related products. In view of the fact that the wheat-growing area in Africa is limited to some areas in North, East and Southern Africa, it is apparent that this changing pattern of consumption is very likely to have a still greater negative impact on the ever-declining food self-sufficiency ratio in Africa. Based on FAO indices (1979-1981=100), continental indices of per capita production of food were: 100.41 in 1980, 90.80 in 1984, 98.48 in 1986 and 93.95 in 1987. The fluctuations are mainly a reflection of changing weather conditions. According to FAO, Sub-Saharan Africa will have to supplement 25 percent of its food requirement with imports by the year 2000 unless urgent measures are implemented to boost regional capacity to improve food productivity and production significantly.

It is, of course, possible that modern farming will make it possible to increase substantially the production of foodstuffs in the long run, although, according to Dommen (1988) and Harris Harris (1987), the yield of traditional crops cannot be increased significantly. This, of course, implies the urgent need to adopt and adapt new, early-maturing and high-yielding varieties that are resistant to disease and pests and tolerant to drought, etc. The Zimbabwean hybrid maize, the Kenyan high-yielding maize, the high-yielding varieties of sorghum being used in Burkina Faso, Ethiopia, and Zambia, the IITA high-yielding cowpea varieties (one of which matures in only 60 days), and the improved (TMS 30572) cassava variety (Harris 1987) are examples of cereal varieties currently available and in use. Cassava possesses characteristics that suit African conditions. It is adaptable to rainfall ranging between 500 mm and 800 mm per year and to low fertility soils; can be grown on marginal land; and can be harvested within seven to 36 months.

Swaziland, Malawi, and Zimbabwe are countries that have shown a dramatic increase in per capita production of cereals through yield improvements resulting mainly from the use of fertilizers, while the Sudan and Cote d'Ivoire have achieved greater yields by expanding the cultivated area and Rwanda by intensifying farming (Harris 1987). In the case of Zimbabwe, maize yields of up to 10 tons per hectare, equivalent to the level attained by the top maize producers in the world, were achieved. The incentives provided by the government of Zimbabwe, which included "no surplus, no repayment" of credit for fertilizers and improved seeds, demonstrates the type of success that can be achieved with the right dose of incentives.

In 1986-1989, in Ghana, farmers who used high-yielding seeds, moderate amounts of chemical fertilizers, and improved agricultural practices based on assistance, including credit, provided by the Sasakawa-Global 2000 project, more than doubled their maize and sorghum production and more than tripled their profits (Dowswell 1989). In the Sudan, similar activities carried out with the assistance of the above project resulted in a three-fold increase in the sorghum yield on 1,200 hectares and a two-and-a-half-fold increase for wheat on 1,175 hectares (Dowswell 1989). These are some indications of the potential that awaits Africa, provided the right backing, including appropriate policies and incentives are adopted and properly implemented, coupled with faster and greater efforts to transfer agricultural research results to farmers.

The above and similar successes augur well for a green revolution in Africa. Because of the complexity of African agriculture, involving a variety of staple crops and soil and climatic conditions, however, the region's green revolution is bound to be quite different from that of India and Pakistan. In regard to one of the inputs, fertilizers, Harris had this to say *"Yet there is no way of dodging the need for fertilizers; as fallow periods decline, farmers cannot go on extracting crops from the same piece of land without putting something back in."* Given the low and declining fertility of the African soils, there does not seem to be an alternative to the increasing use of fertilizers. In view of advances in biotechnology it is possible that a green revolution suited to African conditions could be a combination of biotechnology and the classical green revolution.

## Forestry

The endowment in biodiversity referred to above also applies to the region's forest resources. In fact, tropical forests are characterized by extraordinary biological diversity and productivity. Forest lands are, however, limited to areas with adequate rainfall. In 1990, forest and other wooded land covered an area of 1,137 million hectares of which 545 million hectares comprised 541 million hectares of natural forest and the balance plantation forest. About half of the last is located in the tropical and the other half in the temperate areas (World Bank, *World Resources: A Guide to the Global Environment*). In recent decades, population pressures have resulted in an accelerated use of wood as firewood, and drought has added to the toll. As a result, the area covered by forests has been and still is dwindling; closed forests are estimated to have declined from 217 million hectares in 1980 to 207 million hectares in 1987 (ECA, Survey of Economic...). Africa lost about 18 percent of its tropical forest during the period 1960-1990. The loss continues unabated at 3.7 million hectares a year (ECA, *Africa in the 1990s and Beyond: ...* ).

The density of the forest decreases from dense rain forest around the equator to practically nil in the deserts north and south of the equator. Tropical hard woods (broad-leaved) predominate. In the 1940s, temperate hardwoods and conifers accounted for only 3.1 percent. Growth of conifers is limited to the Mediterranean area and the high mountains in East, Central, and Southern Africa (Hill 1952). Okoume and mohagany are among the major exportable species in the rain forests of West and Central Africa, the major exporting countries being Cote d'Ivoire, Gabon, Congo, and Cameroon.

Although annual roundwood production increased steadily from 333 million $m^3$ in 1977 to 430 million $m^3$ in 1986 (accounting for 13.2 percent of world production) and 540 million $m^3$ in 1991-1993, net exports fell from 12.1 million $m^3$ to 6.6 million $m^3$ over the 1977-1986 period. About 90 percent of the production is used as fuel. Africa is, however, a net importer of paper and paperboard (1.4 million $m^3$ in 1986) and wood-based panels.

About 20 percent of the closed tropical forest is selectively logged. Only 5 percent of the species are exploited (Harris 1987). Deforestation, mainly clearance for agriculture, is fastest in West Africa, followed by East and Southern Africa; it is accelerated by drought. Many African countries are undertaking afforestation and reforestation programs to mitigate and remedy this environmental degradation. Agroforestry, tree planting on and around farms, is expected to be an important aspect of the programs while improved stoves, which have been and are being developed to save up to and over 50 percent, is expected to reduce fuelwood requirements and thereby reduce deforestation.

The potential for increasing the local production of wood products (paper and paperboard and lumber-related products) is apparent from the above. Because the variety of species in natural forest makes it expensive to exploit, on a selective basis, the wood species suitable for pulping and since hard woods yield short fibers, it will be necessary to develop plantations. As for softwoods which yield long fibers, there are high elevation areas in many countries in Africa where such trees can be and are grown. Other non-wood sources for pulp making include bagasse, esparto grass, bamboo, stems of certain grains, and other grasses.

The benefits derived from natural forests is not limited to wood alone. Edible wild fruits and nuts, edible seeds and leaves, fibers and traditional medicine from leaves, roots, and pods are among the other useful products; their usefulness becomes more evident during period of drought.

## Fauna

With respect to fauna, the region is well endowed with domestic and wild life. Its shares in total world livestock are: cattle (13%), sheep (14%), goats (31%), and camels (75%). The livestock population (cattle, buffalo, sheep, goats, pigs, camels, horses, and chickens) was estimated at 222 million tropical livestock units (TLUs), a unit corresponding to an animal weighing 250 kg, in the mid-1980s (ECA, *survey of Economic...*). According to Annex 4.2, the stock of cattle was 122.1 million head in 1961. This increased steadily to 188.9 million in 1990 and stagnated at that level up to 1993. The combined sheep and goat stock was 378.3 million in 1993. The livestock population in terms of TLU by subregion is shown in Table 4.1. The quality of most livestock, including their low weight, leaves much to be desired.

TABLE 4.1
LIVESTOCK POPULATION (TLU) AND ANNUAL GROWTH RATE [a]

| Subregion | Tropical livestock unit (TLU) - m | | | | | Annual growth rate (%) | |
|---|---|---|---|---|---|---|---|
| | 1984 | 1992 | 1993 | 1994 [p] | 1995 [E] | 1992-1993 | 1993-1994 |
| North Africa | 33.13 | 37.95 | 39.14 | 40.37 | 41.63 | 3.13 | 3.14 |
| Central Africa | 8.63 | 11.31 | 11.17 | 11.38 | 12.08 | 2.3 | 2.24 |
| Great Lakes | 2.58 | 3.05 | 3.08 | 3.14 | 3.19 | 0.98 | 1.94 |
| East Africa | 83.62 | 81.28 | 78.14 | 75.23 | 74.61 | -3.86 | -3.72 |
| West Africa | 33.19 | 39.48 | 39.64 | 39.79 | 40.57 | 0.42 | 0.39 |
| Africa | 182.1 | 199.43 | 203.34 | 205.38 | 207.42 | 1.96 | 1 |

Source: ECA/FAO, ......, *Improving Food Security in Africa: The Ignored Contribution of Livestock*, Addis Ababa.
   a Calculations are done with Agrostat data (FAO, 1992)   p Projections   E Estimates

In 1983, the region boasted a permanent pasture of 778 million hectares (Dommen 1998). With close to 60 percent in the semi-arid and arid areas, the livestock population is said to be below potential, mainly because of livestock disease (trypanosomiasis) transmitted by the tse-tse fly. Some 50 million cattle are affected every year in some 37 countries in about one million hectares of tse-tse-fly-infested area, stretching mainly on either side of the equator. Control and eradication programs are currently being carried out in West and Southern Africa. Introduction of dwarf cattle such as ndama and muturu in West Africa tolerant to trypanosomiasis could help minimize the impact of the disease and enable farmers to use draught power, thereby raising the animals' productivity.

Rinderpest and bovine pleuropneumonia are other animal diseases common to the continent. The former is endemic in most countries in north-east Africa from Egypt to Tanzania. The latter is rampant (except in north Africa) in countries south of Kenya and Uganda, including South Africa, and in most of the countries in central Africa. Further information is provided in Annex 8.2.

Unlike in other regions, mixed farming, i.e., integration of animal husbandry with crop farming, has not been possible in the tse-tse fly infested area. Ethiopia (with the largest concentration), Kenya, Chad, Sudan, Somalia, Mali, and Mauritania are the major sources of livestock in Africa. Use of increasingly modern animal husbandry methods is likely to improve mixed farming as well as the hides and skins obtained from slaughtering. Control of tse-tse fly in the hot and humid parts of Africa is expected to contribute eventually to an increase in the livestock population.

A number of countries are trying to improve the low quality and productivity of their livestock. This is mainly done by cross-breeding native cattle (well adapted to African environment) with higher-producing breeds from outside and through artificial insemination. Sooner or later, genetic improvement will have to follow, as this will, hopefully, yield considerable improvements in the production of quality meat and milk in Africa.

The highlands of East Africa, the Sahel, as well as northern and southern Africa are considered suitable for livestock breeding. The countries in these areas could develop their animal husbandry and meet, in part at least, their neighbors demand for animal products. This is of special significance to the Sahelian countries, which are relatively less endowed with natural resources. It would be in the interest of economic cooperation and integration of the West African subregion if these countries were to be given the opportunity to specialize in all development related to livestock. These would include animal husbandry, processing of animal products, and eventually manufacturing machinery and equipment, such as those used in abattoirs, tanneries, and dairies, and units manufacturing leather products and processing slaughterhouse by-products.

Despite a large livestock population, most Africans suffer from inadequate protein intake. Meat self-sufficiency ratio fell from 94.7 percent in 1993 to 91.4 percent in 1994 (ECA, E/ECA/CM.21/10), and the situation in regard to dairy products is not likely to have been very different.

## AQUATIC RESOURCES

Fish is an important source of protein for many Africans, accounting for 21.1 percent of their intake of animal protein. This is significantly higher than the world average of 16.0 percent (World Bank, *World Resources 1996-97*) and (FAO, *Dimensions of Need*). It shows how important fishery is to Africa, where the diet is generally protein-deficient.

Surrounded by the Atlantic and Indian Oceans and the Mediterranean and Red Seas, Africa has a long coast line and therefore a high potential for marine resources. A good part of its coast line is in the tropics where marine life is more diversified (250,000 species in the world). Its coastline along the Atlantic Ocean is among the high-productivity areas in the world.

Left to the whims of individual countries and fishing companies, the oceans and seas could be overfished and eventually depleted. According to FAO, close to

70 percent of the world's marine fish stocks are adversely affected. In about 100 years, the world annual marine catch increased from 3 million tons to a stagnating 80 million tons. The 1982 Law of the Sea treaty was designed to prevent such inevitable depletion which, in recent years, has been aggravated by government subsidies to the tune of $54 billion a year and threatens the livelihood of millions of ordinary fishermen and their dependents all over the world (*The New York Times*, June 3, 1997). After many years of negotiations, the United Nations Convention on the Law of the Sea entered into force in November 1994 when the first meeting of the United Nations International Sea-bed Authority was held in Kingston, Jamaica. According to the Convention, African coastal states will be able to extend their maritime jurisdiction in an exclusive economic zone (EEZ) up to 320 kilometers (200 miles) as soon as the Authority delineates the zones. This offers Africa great potential for living and non-living resources in the form of food (flora and fauna), minerals, and energy. It is expected that the exploitation of Africa's rich marine resources will contribute markedly to improving its food balance and security.

At the moment, the benefits that African countries derive from the multipurpose use of the oceans and seas is limited to those related to fisheries. From information obtained at the Regional Leadership Seminar on Marine/Ocean Affairs in Africa in 1994, about 40 percent of Africa's fishery resources are exploited illegally accompanied by wastage caused by discarding unwanted species. Some areas are reported to have been over-fished. As a consequence, there is a danger of some fishstocks becoming extinct because of this overharvesting as well as pollution; local fishermen are finding it increasingly difficult to operate; and the price of fish continues to rise. This state of affairs is likely to worsen with increasing use of modern technologies, such as fish-finding sonars, trawl nets, use of satellites to spot fish, and the processing of catches on board.

The annual potential catch of fish in Africa is estimated at 10 million tons (ECA, *Survey...*). Annual catches averaged 3.6 million tons in the first half of 1980s; most of this was caught by foreign vessels and contributed less than 5 percent of world catch. According to the World Bank, the catch fell from 7.5 million tons in 1977 to 5.9 million tons in 1985 as a result of overfishing and climatic factors. It was 4.6 million tons in 1994 with 40 percent coming from inland waters and fish farms. West Africa accounted for 80 percent of the marine catches (ECA, E/ECA/CM.21/10). Overall, Africa is a net importer of fish. According to Annex 5.3, its net import of fresh, chilled, or frozen fish increased from a mere 30,000 tons in 1965 to 840,000 tons in 1990.

Fishing by indigenous people is characterized by lack of or inadequate modern means of fishing, preserving, and processing. About 20 to 40 percent of the catch is wasted due to spoilage. Many fishermen lose their lives and equipment when fishing off the coast using outdated boats and gears. Such risk limits their fishing capacity.

About 15.5 percent of the 1993 world fish harvest (101 million tons) came from aquaculture (World Bank, *World Resources 1996-97*). This method of fish production should be exploited to the maximum, particularly in land-locked countries and areas far from the coast. Some of the micro-dams and reservoirs being built in some African countries could be used for this purpose.

## MINERAL RESOURCES

Africa is well known for its land-based mineral wealth. What is currently known, however, is based on a relatively limited degree of exploration, mainly carried out during colonial times. Although exploratory activities have been undertaken since independence, much remains to be done. The weak demand for minerals in the world, exacerbated by high production levels (Blunden 1985) and recycling; strategic stockpiling in industrialized countries; and mismanagement by some African governments explain, in part, the slow progress made over the past three decades.

Potential for the further discovery of minerals is said to be bright. *"The ratio of known resources to the identified reserve base which lags in Africa at 8 to 1 for graphite, 5 to 1 for coal, 4 to 1 for the platinum group and tin; at 3 to 1 for chromite, lead and zinc, and for most other minerals at 1.5-2 to 1"* (de Kun 1987) gives some indications of that potential. Nonetheless, both investment and production have been decreasing in most mineral-producing African countries over the past two decades. According to the World Bank, 24 priority mineral locations with development possibilities have been identified in different countries in Sub-Saharan Africa, excluding West Africa, in recent years. In a study directed by de Kun for SADCC, 36 projects were identified in nine countries between Tanzania and Lesotho.

As for petroleum, the region's share is a mere 0.5 percent of the world's drilled wells. In view of this, *"as yet undiscovered oil (and gas) reserves might reach 47(50)% of estimated ultimate recoverable reserves in the whole Sahara, 47(56)% in the Gulf of Guinea and 58(66)% along the coast extending from Cameroon to Namibia"* (de Kun 1987). Recent activities seem to indicate that an interest in petroleum is reviving in Africa, as evidenced by the growing number of exploration licenses being granted to major international oil companies.

New oil fields were expected to be operational in Angola and Congo in 1995-1996 and possibly in Equatorial Guinea toward the end of the century. The fate of the relatively small oil fields in Chad, South Africa, and Sudan remains to be seen. Countries with prospects for new production include: Mozambique, Eritrea, South Africa, Madagascar, and Swaziland (Europa, *Africa South of the Sahara 1996*). In general, African crude oils have low sulfur content and are of high quality.

New gas fields were discovered in South Africa, Namibia, Ethiopia, Cote d'Ivoire, Ghana, Madagascar and Niger; yet most of them require further studies to establish whether they can be economically exploited (Spiegel 1995). Natural gas projects include the Kudu field in Namibia, the Pande field in Mozambique, the Songo Songo field in Tanzania, and the Galub field in Ethiopia. In regard to the last, it was reported that the government had signed in 1998 an agreement with investors for the exploitation of the gas.

The marine mineral potential of Africa is said to be vast. Manganese nodules containing copper, cobalt, and nickel are found in the South Atlantic and Indian Oceans. Other marine resources with potential are oil (which, according to a document presented at the Regional Leadership Seminar on Marine Ocean Affairs in Africa in 1994, may reach 6 to 10 percent of world offshore reserves) as well as salts and other products that can be extracted from sea water. The Red Sea hot brines are expected to be a significant source of such minerals as zinc, copper, and heavy metals.

Despite the region's mineral potential, investment in exploration, prospecting, and mining has, in the past two decades, been rather modest in Sub-Saharan Africa. In recent years, African governments have come to realize that their mining policies, including increasing state control, did not, in many cases, serve their interests. This came out clearly at the Fifth Regional Conference on the Development and Utilization of Mineral Resources in Africa held in Addis Ababa, Ethiopia, in 1993. Of the 14 African countries that made statements at or presented papers to the ministerial conference, 13 had adopted policies and promulgated (or were in the process of promulgating or revising) mining legislations and/or investment codes that involved and encouraged the private sector. As a result and because of the policy reforms, it was reported that investment in the mining sector was increasing, although, according to one of the participants, the African share in world development funds decreased from 25 percent in 1990 to 17 percent in 1992.

African governments were, in part, justified in adopting such policies and measures as nationalization, because of the attitude adopted and lack of transparency shown by foreign mining companies. Many such companies withheld information and failed to pay due shares to governments; they did not prepare nationals adequately nor promote them to senior positions.

The change that took place in Ethiopia in this respect, almost two years after the fall of the Marxist regime which monopolized all economic activities, including the mining sector, offers a good indication. The proclamations on mining and mining tax in June 1993 (negotiable royalties, exemption from custom duties and taxes on equipment and machinery, attractive foreign exchange control arrangements, maximum income tax of 45 percent, etc.), coupled with the new political and social stability reigning in the country, had yielded major dividends as the number of private companies seeking mineral licenses increased. This was a welcome in a country such as Ethiopia where the share of mining in GDP is a mere 0.3 percent.

For the sake of convenience, minerals are categorized in this book into ferrous metals, non-ferrous metals, precious metals and stones, and non-metals. The non-metals are in turn divided into industrial materials and building materials. From the outset, it should be noted that this section as well as that on energy resources draws heavily from *Mineral Economics of Africa* by N. de Kun. This holds particularly true for information on reserves at the country level and shares in world reserves in the 1980s. The word "reserve" here refers to an economically exploitable ore body and excludes mineral accumulation that has become uneconomical to operate. Figures for resources are, however, given whenever the quantities are considered significant. Reserve figures in individual country presentations were adopted in preference to those given for groups of countries whenever discrepancies arose between the two. The approach adopted here is intended to minimize inconsistencies that would otherwise arise from the use of reserve figures obtained from different sources. It should be noted here that some of the reserve figures will have changed as a result of exploratory activities carried out and revisions made in the ensuing period.

Analysis of information on reserves and production in the 1980s showed that, out of 103 minerals, the continent as a source of minerals in the world ranked as follows (share): first in 24 (23.3%), second in seven (6.8%), third in 21 (20.2%), and fourth in 12 (11.6%). Its share in world reserves ranged between 0.3 percent for diatomite through 50 to 85 percent for cobalt, gold, diamonds, vanadium, manganese, phosphate, platinum, palladium, ruthenium, and germanium and 90 percent each for chromium and iridium. In terms of production, the range was from practically nil in bismuth to 60 percent each for cobalt, gem diamonds, and iridium. A number of the minerals are produced as co-products and/or by-products of other metals. These include cobalt from copper, nickel, and zinc ores; germanium from zinc ores; nickel mainly from nickel-copper or iron sulfide ores; cadmium from zinc ores; indium from lead and zinc ores; and the platinum group (iridium, osmium, palladium, rhodium, and ruthenium) from nickel and copper ores.

Most of the minerals produced in Africa, up to 90 percent, are exported. Practically all the exports go to Western Europe and the United States of America. The balance is consumed mainly by the Republic of South Africa and the countries of North Africa.

The dependence of the industrialized countries on African minerals in the 1980s can be illustrated by the degree of dependence of the United States, particularly in the so-called strategic materials, some of which (the platinum group metals, vanadium, manganese ore, and chrome ore), according to Rae Weston (1984), are located overwhelmingly in South Africa and the former Soviet Union. In the steel industry, the United States' reliance on imports from Africa was 85 to 100 percent for ferromanganese, ferrochrome, cobalt, manganese ore and metal, chromite metallurgical and graphite. In electricity, electronics, photo and optics, it stood at 40 to 100 percent for germanium, selenium, indium, rhodium, cesium, iridium and phlogopite mica; in transport and aeronautics, 80 to 95 percent for rutile, platinum, and ruthenium; in chemical, medical, and packaging, 90 to 100 percent for palladium and chrome chemicals; and in gems, abrasives, and insulation, 100 percent for diamonds, corundum, amosite, and crocidolite. The end of the Cold War diminished the importance of some of the strategic minerals, while the potential supply from Siberia in Russia and from seabed mining as well as the increased supply from Latin America, coupled with the on-going process of substitution and recycling, means that Africa may well not maintain its leading position for some of the minerals in the future. In other words, Africa continues to lose its strategic value to the industrialized world as a result of marginalization.

Annex 4.4 shows production of metal-bearing ores and concentrates in Africa. Most of the ores and concentrates are given in terms of their metal content, indicated by "M." In view of the dominance of South Africa in minerals, it would be in order here to give some indication of the degree of that dominance. In the 1984 production of ores, South Africa's shares exceeding 30 percent were: iron (43.4), nickel (46.5), zinc (38.7), manganese (50.3), chromium (83.7), rutile (38.1), vanadium (100), antimony (85.4), silver (40.2), uranium (44.4), gold (96.1), magnesite (60.4,) and iron pyrites (52.1).

## Ferrous Metals

Africa ranks fourth with 10 percent (more than 6.7% according to another source) share of the world's iron-ore reserves. The iron-ore mines in Liberia, Guinea, and Mauritania are geared toward export. Because of internal strife production has virtually ceased in Liberia. Other countries in Africa exploit their iron ores mainly for captive use; these include South Africa, Egypt, Algeria, Zimbabwe, and Nigeria.

Africa is an important source of alloying materials. It accounts for 90, 80, 55, 50, 45, and 35 percent of world reserves of chromium, manganese, cobalt, vanadium, graphite flake (mainly in Madagascar) and fluorspar, respectively.

Total iron-ore reserves of the continent are about 34 billion tons (ONUDI, *Industrie Africaine de Fer et d'Acier*). The percentage subregional shares work out as follows: North Africa (20.4), West Africa (40.0), Central Africa (24.5), and Eastern and Southern Africa (15.1).

The following countries hold the major reserves of the main ferrous ores required by the steel industry:

- Iron ore (mt of Fe): Congo K (7,000, resource), South Africa (6,000), Guinea (1,400), Cote d'Ivoire (1,200, resource), Libya (1,200, resource), Gabon (700), Ghana (600, resource), Mauritania (500), Senegal (400), Guinea (400), Nigeria (380), Mali (380, resource), Tanzania (300), Liberia (230), Egypt (170), Morocco (140), Zimbabwe (100), Angola (80), Congo (60), Algeria (50), Sudan (50), Zambia (30) and Sierra Leone (30);
- Cobalt (kt): Congo K (1,200), Zambia (300), Burundi (300, resource), Morocco (40), South Africa (30), Burkina Faso (15, resource), Uganda (8), Zimbabwe (8), and Botswana (2.5);
- Manganese (mt): South Africa (13,000), Gabon (400), Burkina-Faso (8, resource), Ghana (5), Cote d'Ivoire (3, resource), Mali (3, resource), and Namibia (1.5);
- Vanadium (mt): South Africa (8), Namibia (4.5), Burkina Faso (0.5, resource), and Burundi (0.15, resource);
- Nickel (kt): South Africa (9,000), Burundi (1,200, resource), Botswana (450), Cote d'Ivoire (270, resource), Zimbabwe (220), Tanzania (200, resource), Swaziland (150), Madagascar (100), and Burkina Faso (100, resource);
- Chromite (mt): South Africa (3,200), Zimbabwe (750), and Madagascar (44);
- Molybdenum (kt): Niger (6); and
- Tungsten (kt): South Africa (20), Rwanda (12), Uganda (5), Namibia (2), Congo K (1.7), and Zimbabwe (1).

## Non-ferrous Metals

Although unevenly distributed, major non-ferrous minerals of economic significance abound in the region. These include copper, zinc, tin and lead ores, and bauxite. As pointed out elsewhere, most mineral ores were either shipped as mined or beneficiated to reduce the cost of transport, a seriously biased division of labor in favor of the industrialized countries. Some non-ferrous metals, such as copper, lead, and zinc, mainly because of their low concentration, were exceptions. These were smelted on the spot and exported as crude metal to Europe for refining during the colonial era.

In terms of tonnage use and relatively wide applications in developing countries, aluminum and copper play leading roles. Their ores, bauxite and copper ores, rank first and third in and account for 35 and 15 percent of world reserves, respectively, excluding copper that may be recovered from undersea manganese nodule mining. With reserves exceeding 11 billion tons, bauxite leads all non-ferrous metal ores. Guinea, the major source of bauxite, accounts for one-third (24 % according to another source) of the world reserves. As regards copper, the combined reserves in Zambia and Congo K work out to 13 percent of the world's reserves. Information on eight reserves in Zambia, each categorized into fully developed, partly developed, and undeveloped, works out to 467 million tonnes averaging 3.03 percent Cu (Smith 1987). Most recent estimates put the continental copper reserves at 17.6 percent of world reserves (ECA, *Africa in the 1990s and Beyond:* ... ).

According to another source (ECA/UNIDO, ECA/UNIDO/AFRICOP/TP/2/94), African reserves of copper metal are around 60 million tons and account for 17.6 percent of world reserves. Zambia and Congo K (the African copperbelt) between them account for 93.3 percent of those reserves. Total world reserves of bauxite are about 23 billion tons, with Guinea alone accounting for over 24 percent of this (ECA, ECA/UNIDO/AFRIALUM/TP/1/94).

The production facilities in the African copperbelt underwent difficulties following independence and nationalization. Production of copper, which accounted for 25 percent of world output in the 1960s, fell drastically to 6 percent in 1992 (*ADB, African Development Report 1994*). Gecamines of Congo K was the worse hit following the 1990 mine accident. Copper production plummeted from over 500,000 tons in the 1980s to about 30,000 tons in 1996. Just before the ousting of the Mobutu regime American Mineral Fields signed an agreement with the then rebels to engage in the processing of copper tailings (using leaching technology) and to build a 200,000 tonne per year zinc plant (*The Economist*, May 3, 1997).

As for the Zambia Consolidated Copper Mines Limited (ZCCM), production of copper reached its peak of 747,500 tons in 1969 and has been declining since (Smith 1987). Copper contributes about 90 percent of Zambia's export earnings and accounts for about 20 percent of GDP. In 1970, the Zambian government acquired 51 percent majority ownership in the copper mines which was subsequently increased to 60 percent in 1979. Currently, ZCCM is state-controlled. Up to the election in 1992, the chairman and chief executive of ZCCM was virtually responsible directly to the then president of the country (not to the Ministry of Mines). Declining grade of ore, working deeper deposits, low and fluctuating metal prices, shortage of spare parts and replacement equipment, and scarcity of skilled personnel were reported to be among the constraints facing the operation of the mines and processing. To mitigate these difficulties, ZCCM was supposed to have implemented a five-year plan designed to rehabilitate and rationalize the copper mining and processing industry. In early 1990s, plans and arrangements were being worked out for privatization.

The importance of other non-ferrous metals is shown by their ranking in world reserves. Platinum, hafnium, corundum, ruthenium, and iridium occupy first place in world reserves.

The following countries hold the major reserves of the main non-ferrous metal ores:

- Copper (mt): Congo K (25), Zambia (18), South Africa (6), Namibia (0.6), Botswana (0.4), Morocco (0.4), Mauritania (0.4), and Zimbabwe (0.2);
- Bauxite (mt): Guinea (7,000), Mali (600 and 1,500, resource), Cameroon (800), Ghana (500), Guinea Bissau (200), Madagascar (150, resource), Sierra Leone (100), and Malawi (60);
- Tin (kt): Namibia (60), Congo K (32), South Africa (25), Rwanda (20), Zimbabwe (20), Nigeria (10), Egypt (5), Uganda (2), and Namibia (0-60);
- Zinc (kt): South Africa (12,000), Congo K (1,100), Burkina Faso (1,000, resource), Namibia (300), Algeria (300), Tunisia (300), Zambia (100), Morocco (150), Sudan (150), Egypt (140), and Nigeria (80).
- Lead (kt): South Africa (5,000), Morocco (2,000), Namibia (350), Kenya (220, resource), Tunisia (200), Algeria (200), Nigeria (100), Zambia (50), and Egypt (20); and
- Cadmium (kt): South Africa (40), Congo K (15), Tunisia (1.5), Algeria (1), Namibia (1), and Morocco (0.6).

## Precious Metals and Stones

A number of countries in Africa are rich in precious metals. The following countries hold major reserves:

- Gold (t): South Africa (20,000), Zimbabwe (600), Congo K (150), Ghana (150), Mali(50), Tanzania (40), Cote d'Ivoire (30), Burkina Faso (30, resource), Senegal (18), Nigeria (6), Rwanda (10), and Botswana (6);
- Diamonds (million carats): South Africa (370), Congo K (230), Botswana (220), Ghana (75), Angola (30), Sierra Leone (25), Namibia (20), Tanzania (5), Central African Republic (5) and Guinea (5);
- Platinum group metals (kt): South Africa (50) and Zimbabwe (?, resource); and
- Silver (t): Zambia (750), Namibia (1,000), Tunisia (400), Zimbabwe (300), Sudan (260), Zambia (750), Mauritania (100), Burkina Faso (100, resource), Tanzania (35), Algeria (30), Ghana (10), and South Africa (10).

## Non-metallic Minerals
### Industrial Materials

This group comprises a wide range of materials, most of which are inputs for the chemical process industry. Some of these materials, such as sand, limestone, and shale, are also used as building materials. Practically all of the non-ferrous metals dealt with above are also used in the chemical process industry as raw materials and/or catalysts.

Phosphate rock, an important raw material for fertilizer making, constitutes one of the resources in this category. Africa accounts for 65 percent of world reserves and holds first place in this resource. About 90 percent of the African reserve is concentrated in one country, Morocco. According to a recent source (*Office Cherifien de Phosphates*) subsequent discoveries in Morocco have raised

Morocco's share in world reserves to 75 percent. Based on FAO statistics, African export of phosphate rock averaged 45.6 percent of those of the world during the period 1983-1988. The Moroccan share of this was 67.5 percent.

Potash is another fertilizer raw material which, unlike phosphate rock, is much less abundant. Economic reserves are found in a limited number of countries, including the Congo and Ethiopia. Although Botswana does not figure in the listing below, it has potassium-bearing brines from which potassium sulfate can be extracted.

The following countries hold major reserves of the main industrial materials:

- Phosphate (mt of $P_2 O_5$ ): Morocco (4,500), South Africa (180), Niger (150), Togo (80), Tunisia (80), Algeria (80), Egypt (70), Senegal (50), Zambia (50), Burkina Faso (20, resource), Uganda (10), Mali (10), Tanzania (5), Angola (2), Zimbabwe (2), Central African Republic (2, resource), Burundi (2, resource), Benin (1.5, resource), Malawi (1.3, resource);

- Potash (mt): Ethiopia (210, resource), Congo (20), Burundi (3), Libya (0.8, resource), and Uganda (0.7, sulfate);

- Limestone (mt): South Africa (2,000), Malawi (330, resource), Togo (205, resource), Burkina-Faso (56, resource), Tanzania (50), Niger (4, resource), and Burundi (4, resource);

- Salt (mt): Ethiopia (3,000, resource), Botswana (2,000, resource), Morocco (1,000), Algeria (900), and Mali (50);

- Sodium carbonate (mt): Botswana (400, resource), Tanzania (150, resource), Egypt (60), Kenya (55, resource), and Uganda (18);

- Sulfur (1000 $m^3$): Ethiopia (35); and

- Gypsum (mt): Libya (80,000, resource), Mauritania (4,000), Egypt (120), South Africa (90), and Sudan (30).

## Building Materials

Clays, sand, gravel, limestone, shale, and stone are the main building materials. They are, generally, found everywhere. Limestone is among the exceptions as it is not available in economic quantities in a number of countries in Africa, mainly West Africa.

As noted earlier most African minerals are either exported in raw state or after having undergone minimum processing, such as concentration. It is this recognition that prompted the First Regional Conference of Ministers responsible for the development and utilization of mineral resources in Africa, in their resolution on the promotion of mineral resources development and utilization in 1995, to urge African countries to encourage further processing of their minerals and to propose declaring a decade for the development of mineral industries in Africa (ECA, *Report of the First Regional Conference* ... ).

## ENERGY RESOURCES

The continent is endowed with a variety of energy resources which augur well for its future development. Most countries have one or more forms of energy. Petroleum and gas dominate in north Africa, coal in southern Africa, hydropower in central Africa, and geothermal in eastern Africa.

Biomass is, however, the most widely used. Use of biomass (wood, charcoal, organic residues, and dung) account for up to 80 to 90 percent (94% in Ethiopia) of energy consumption in some countries in the region. Increasing utilization of dung and organic residues as fuel is contributing to the deterioration of soil fertility and, therefore, to falling agricultural productivity. Fuelwood alone accounted for 67 percent of total continental consumption in 1970. This decreased to 56 percent and marginally rose to 58 percent in 1980 and 1990, respectively (FAO, *The State of Food and Agriculture 1994*).

Total estimates of reserves/potential of the main energy resources of the continent are as follows: petroleum (8.6 billion tons or 60.4 billion barrels), natural gas (8,600 billion m$^3$, proven), coal (60 billion tons, recoverable), and hydroelectric power (360 gigawatts) (ECA, ECA/NRD/AD-HOC). Over 90 percent of the coal is in South Africa. According to the World Bank, proved recoverable reserves as of 1993 were: petroleum (10.5 billion tons), natural gas (10,166 billion m$^3$), and coal (60.4 billion tons). Installed hydroelectric power stood at 20,689 Mw (World Bank, *World Resources 1996-97*).

Table 4.2 provides recoverable reserves of petroleum, natural gas, and coal in Africa. At the end of 1995, recoverable petroleum reserves increased to 73.1 billion barrels (7.2% of world total and reserve/production ratio of 29.2 years). The corresponding figures were: 9,400 billion m$^3$ (6.7% and over 100 years) for natural gas and 61.3 billion tonnes (6.0% and a range of 118- over 500 years) for coal. Over 90 percent of the coal is in South Africa. At the end of 1996, Africa accounted for 6 percent of the world's total proven reserves of petroleum (*The Economist*, August 2, 1997).

| | At end 1975 | At end 1985 | At end 1994 | At end 1995 | | | |
|---|---|---|---|---|---|---|---|
| | | | | TABLE 4.2 RESERVES OF PETROLEUM, NATURAL GAS AND COAL IN AFRICA | | | |
| | bb | bb | bb | bb | bt | % world share | R/P ratio year |
| Petroleum | 65.1 | 56.7 | 62.2 | 73.1 | 9.8 | 7.2 | 29.2 |
| | tcm | tcm | tcm | tcm | tcf | % world share | R/P ratio year |
| Natural gas | 5.9 | 5.6 | 9.7 | 9.4 | 334.6 | 6.7 | > 100 |
| Coal (bt) | | | | 61.3 | | 6 | up to 500 |
| | ... | ... | ... | ... | | | |

Source: BP *Statistical Review of World Energy 1996*, The British Petroleum Company p.l.c. 1996, Group Media and Publications.

New oil fields were expected to become operational in Angola and Congo in 1995-1996 and possibly Equatorial Guinea towards the end of the century. Additional production of 50,000 barrels per day in 1999 is expected to eventually rise to 400,000 barrels per day in Angola. In Chad, oil is expected to flow to a Cameroonian coast by the year 2000, with flow eventually rising to 250,000 barrels per day (*Africa Confidential*, March 28, 1997).

At the Sub-Saharan level, total primary energy supply projections are presented in Table 4.3. From the table it is apparent that the share of commercial energy is expected to increase to 50 percent while that of the traditional woodfuels to reduce to 50 percent in 2020. With 35 percentage points, petroleum will have the lion's share of the increase in commercial energy supply.

| TABLE 4.3<br>TOTAL PRIMARY ENERGY SUPPLY PROJECTIONS IN SUB-SAHARAN AFRICA | | | |
|---|---|---|---|
| Energy source | Actual<br>(% of primary energy supplies) | | Projected<br>(million tons<br>of energy<br>equivalent) |
| | 1960 | 1986 | 2020 |
| Commercial | | | |
| - Petroleum | 5.6 | 24 | 140 |
| - Natural gas | 0 | 3 | 30 |
| - Power (hydro and geothermal) | 0.5 | 3 | 20 |
| - Coal | 3.5 | 4 | 10 |
| Subtotal | 9.6 | 34 | 200 |
| Woodfuels | | 66 | 200 |
| Total | | 100 | 400 |
| Source: World Bank, 1989, *Sub-Saharan Africa: From Crisis to Sustainable Growth*,<br>Washington, D. C. (obtained from UNSO, Energy Statistics Yearbook). | | | |

Table 4.4 provides the likely situation in regard to petroleum production in Sub-Saharan Africa. According to the table, production is expected to rise close to 5 million barrels per day in the year 2000 compared with about 3.4 million barrels per day in 1966. Angola, Chad and Nigeria would account for the major part of the hefty 44 percent increase.

| TABLE 4.4<br>SAB-SAHARAN AFRICA OIL PRODUCTION FORECASTS<br>(1,000 barrels per day) | | | |
|---|---|---|---|
| | Actual, end 1996 | Forecast, end1997 | Forecast, 2000 |
| Angola | 710 | 780 | 1000 |
| Benin | 11 | 10 | 7 |
| Cameroon | 105 | 115 | 100 |
| Chad | - | - | 150 |
| Congo | 176 | 240 | 220 |
| Cote d'Ivoire | 16 | 16 | 20 |
| Equatorial Guinea | 38 | 70 | 70 |
| Gabon | 340 | 350 | 360 |
| Nigeria | 2013 | 2419 | 2980 |
| South Africa | 10 | 10 | 20 |
| Congo K | 22 | 22 | 28 |
| Total | 3441 | 4032 | 4955 |
| Source: Africa Confidential, 1997, "Oil and Gas - Going with the Flow,"<br>March 28, 1997. | | | |

Production and consumption of primary energy as well as refinery capacities are given for the period 1985-1995 in Annex 4.5. In 1995, Africa accounted for 10.3 percent and 3.2 percent of world production and consumption of petroleum respectively. The corresponding figures were 4.0 and 2.0 for natural gas and 5.1 and 3.9 for coal. From these and other figures in the table, it is apparent that Africa produces more energy than it consumes.

Annex 4.6 shows the primary energy balance by subregions (excluding South Africa). In all subregions where the structure of energy use is similar, except North Africa, traditional fuel accounts for about 65 percent of primary fuel used. Per capita consumption in Gcal in North Africa is 4.5 to 8 times those of other subregions.

Because of the low level of development in the region, the consumption of fuels is very low. Based on United Nations Energy Statistics Yearbooks (see Annex 4.7), in 1990, per capita apparent consumptions (including South Africa) were 157 Kg for solid fuels (coal equivalent) , excluding traditional fuel and 488 Kwh for electricity. These work out to 26.12 percent and 22.34 percent of world per capita apparent consumption. The corresponding percentages for other energy sources were: hard coal (35.05%), crude petroleum (30.82%) and coke (8.96%). These figures are very deceiving as South Africa accounts for a disproportionate portion of the total apparent consumptions, 89.63 percent of the solid fuels and 51.56 percent of the electricity. Table 4. 5 gives per capita consumption and projections for the major sources of energy in the continent.

| TABLE 4.5 PER CAPITA CONSUMPTION AND PROJECTIONS OF MAJOR ENERGY RESOURCES IN THE CONTINENT | | | |
|---|---|---|---|
| | 1992 | 1993 | 2008 |
| Crude petroleum (kg) | 164 | 167 | 1100 |
| Natural gas (megajoules) | 2298 | 2560 | 6223 |
| Coal (kg) | 210 | 203 | 362 |
| Electricity (kwh) | 476 | 447 | 535 |
| Source: ECA, 1996, *Africa in the 1990s and Beyond: ECA-Revised Long-Term Development Perspectives Study (ECA/SERPD/TP/96/3)*, Addis Ababa. | | | |

According to one source (UNIDO, *Appropriate ... Requirements*), total *"per capita consumption of 300 to 400 kgce [kg coal equivalent] would coincide with the minimum provision of food and shelter in a rural agricultural setting."* The same source suggests that 900 to 1,000 kgce would be needed to ensure a more socially acceptable human life.

As can be seen from Annex 4.8, Africa refines only a small part of its crude petroleum production. In 1990, its refining capacity, which accounted for 3.8

percent of world capacity, produced 3.47 percent of world output. Its share in natural gas liquid plant capacity of 5.43 percent was concentrated in Algeria, Egypt, Libya and Tunisia. Total production was 15 percent of world output.

Total proven reserves of natural gas, unevenly distributed in over 20 countries in Africa, estimated at over 10 trillion m$^3$ (ECA, ECA/IHSD/IDPS/CHM/002/94) as of 1990, are said to have increased in subsequent years (Ethiopian reserves have increased from 68 to 108 billion m$^3$). Algeria and Nigeria together account for about 80 percent of this.

Algeria, by far, is the largest producer of natural gas. Its liquefied natural gas (LNG) capacity increased from 2.8 million m$^3$ in 1969 to 30.5 million m$^3$ in 1984 (Khennas 1992). Its Maghreb-Europe gas pipeline with an annual capacity of 7.2 billion m$^3$ started operation in 1996, substantially increasing its natural gas export capability. Because of political instability in recent years, the implementation of the $3.6 billion natural gas liquefaction project in Nigeria has been delayed. It is expected to be operational by October 1999.

Currently, most of Africa's gas is exported. Domestic use is mainly in power generation and fertilizer making in Algeria, Libya, Egypt, and Nigeria. In 1988, production in some 19 countries with natural gas reserves stood at 155.8 billion m$^3$, of which Algeria accounted for over 70 percent. Of the total, 39.8 percent was marketed, 39.1 percent was reinjected, and 16.3 percent was flared. Consumption in practically the same countries was 24.1 million tons of petroleum equivalent (tpe) in 1987. This was forecast to increase to 47.5 and 110.7 million tpe in the year 2000 and 2020, respectively (Posh et. al., 1990).

The World Bank is in the process of assisting African countries with known reserves to utilize same, mainly for the purpose of power generation. There are, however, good cases for using gas in fertilizer making and in the form of compressed natural gas (CNG) as vehicle fuel, particularly in land-locked countries (Rwanda, Burundi and Eastern Congo K from Lake Kivu gas) far removed from sea ports.

In most petroleum-producing countries in Africa, associated gas continues to be flared and therefore has practically zero value. In Nigeria, the gas reinjection decree of 1979 was reported to have become effective by 1983. Projects are being developed or about to be implemented to make use of associated and non-associated gas, mainly for power generation to serve the needs of the country and, in some cases, neighboring countries (including in the form of LPG and condensates: gasoline, kerosene and diesel fuel) . These include Songo Songo in Tanzania, Galub in Ethiopia (agreement signed between a Chinese company and the Ethiopian government), Pande in Mozambique, Matanda in Cameroon, Alba in Equatorial Guinea, Lake Kivu in Rwanda /Congo K, Pointe-Indienne in the Congo, and Escravos in Nigeria (to also supply Ghana, Togo, and Benin). In this connection, it should be noted that, according to the World Bank forecast (*Overview of Prospects...*), petroleum prices in constant 1994 dollars will increase from $14.50 per barrel in 1994 to $19.37 in the year 2000 and $18.82 in 2005 and thereafter. It is not unlikely that the price of natural gas will be related to these forecasts, probably indirectly through the price of competing fuels such as fuel oil.

A non-traditional conversion of fossil fuels (natural gas and oxygen, hydrogen and oxygen, etc.) into electric power continues to be the subject of R&D in developed countries. More efficient and cost-effective fuel-cell technologies based on water electrolysis are expected to be commercialized at the turn of the century.

Because of their small size and modularity, fuel cells do not require extensive transmission and distribution lines (*Chemical Engineering Progress*, September 1996). They could prove to be practical under African conditions where, among other things, interconnections of grids are much to be desired and distribution and transmission lines are characterized by losses of up to 30 percent (ECA, *Africa in the 1990s and Beyond: ...* ).

Biomass and solar, wind, tidal, geothermal and waste-to-energy energy and hydropower constitute renewable sources of energy. The prospects for exploiting most of them in Africa are favorable.

As for electricity generated from major sources, Africa's share (2.59%), in world generating capacity was worse than that of hydrocarbons, despite the huge hydropower potential in the region. The corresponding figures by type were: thermal (2.87%), hydro (3.01%), nuclear (0.29%) and geothermal (0.85%). While the third was entirely accounted for by South Africa, the fourth was contributed wholly by Kenya. Production and other information is provided in Annex 4.7.

With respect to hydropower comprising a potential of over 360 gigawatts, the continent accounts for about 16 percent of this source of energy of the world (ECA/UNIDO, ECA/UNIDO/AFRIALUM/TP/1/94) of which less than 4 percent only is being exploited. Close to 30 percent of this potential is concentrated in one country, Congo K. Less than 5 percent of the continent's potential is currently being utilized. Other sources put Africa's share up to 35 to 40 percent of world hydropower potential.

The potential for geothermal energy is said to be large. Kenya has already started exploiting this source of energy. It generated 10 penta-joules of electricity in 1993. A 30 MW electric power plant was expected to start generating in 1997 in the Langano area in Ethiopia. It was reported in 1995 that another 30-MW-capacity plant was possible in the Tendaho area, where some of the geothermal fields are exceptionally close to the surface — a mere 250 meters below ground level — something considered unique by world standards (*The Ethiopian Herald*, June 10 and 16, 1995).

Because of its location straddling the equator, where the solar intensity is the highest, Africa is expected to benefit greatly from breakthroughs in solar energy technology based on a non-conventional and renewable source. Drying and preserving foodstuffs and water heating constitute relatively simple applications of solar energy. Generation of electricity from solar energy, a relatively sophisticated technology, has proved particularly useful in isolated rural areas that are not part of the conventional grid system. Currently, use of solar-based electricity is limited to pumping water from wells, to refrigerating medical supplies in hospitals and clinics, to providing lighting to schools, to powering educational television, and to recharging batteries. African countries have access to services provided by regional and international institutions which promote R&D in and the use of solar energy technology. These include the Solar Energy Research Center in Bamako, Niger, and the International Centre for Application of Solar Energy in Perth, Australia.

Wind is another renewable source of energy. In practically all countries there are likely to be areas where the power of wind could be harnessed to produce mechanical power and/or electricity. Some countries have already taken measures to exploit this inexhaustible source of energy.

The following countries hold the major reserves of the main sources of energy, many of which are also raw materials for the chemical process industry:

• Petroleum/oil (bb): Libya (20), Nigeria (17), Algeria (9), Egypt (4), Tunisia (2), Angola (1.8), Gabon (0.6), Congo (0.5), Cameroon (0.5), Sudan (0.3), Congo K (0.2), and Benin (0.1);

• Natural gas (tcf): Algeria (110), Nigeria (50), Libya (20), Egypt (10), Cameroon (5), Tunisia (4), Tanzania (4), Cote d'Ivoire (4), Mozambique (2.4, resource), Angola (2.2), Congo (2), Namibia (2), Ethiopia (1.3, resource), South Africa (>1), Rwanda and Congo K (1, methane), and Gabon (0.6) (many of these figures are considered conservative, as a number of them were revised up wards in subsequent years);

• Oil shale (bt): Morocco (40, resource) and Congo K (15);

• Other oil bearing resources: Madagascar (4.8 bb, heavy oil), Senegal (0.4 bb, heavy oil), and Madagascar (3 bt, tarsands);

• Coal (mt): South Africa (58,000), Botswana (3,500), Namibia (3,000), Swaziland (1,000), Malawi (800, resource), Madagascar (500), Mozambique (400), Zambia (300), Malawi (800, resource), Zimbabwe (250), Nigeria (90), Congo K (80), Algeria (50), Tanzania (30), Egypt (27), Cameroon (10), and Ethiopia (60);

• Lignite (mt): Madagascar (100), Mali (55, resource), Nigeria (50), Morocco (40, resource), Angola (30, resource), Ethiopia (10), and Sudan (2);

• Peat (mt): Rwanda (1,000, resource), Senegal (10), and Burundi (0.5, resource);

• Other carbonaceous resources (mt): Mali (800, bituminous shale), South Africa (1,000, anthracite), and Swaziland (0.15, anthracite);

• Hydropower (Gw): Congo K (130), Madagascar (64), Cameroon (23), Tanzania (21), Gabon (18), Sudan (14), Kenya (13, resource), Uganda (12), Mozambique (12), Burkina-Faso (12, resource), Central African Republic (11, resource), Nigeria (10), Angola (10), Congo (9), Ethiopia 9, resource), Guinea (6), Liberia (6, resource), Algeria (5), Zambia (5), Zimbabwe (4-5), Senegal (4), Egypt (4), Mali (3.5), Ghana (2), and Niger (2, resource);

• Uranium (kt): Morocco (3,000, very low grade resource), Niger (230), South Africa (190), Namibia (120), Egypt (100), Gabon (40), Algeria (33), and Central African Republic (17, resource);

• Geothermal: vast potential in the Great Rift-Valley of East Africa (from Eritrea in the north to Tanzania in the south); and

• Solar energy[2]: Vast potential in practically all African countries, provided technological/cost breakthroughs can be achieved.

## HUMAN RESOURCES

Following independence, African countries continued to depend on expatriates in both administrative and technical fields. They retained many former civil servants and hired advisors, experts and consultants to carry out even relatively simple activities. It appears that the on-the-job training of African nationals that was supposed to have been carried out by the expatriates was not, in many cases, as anticipated.

Because of the above situation and other constraints, labor productivity in Sub-Saharan Africa is low. This was once quite striking when the high cost of labor relative to its productivity was compared with that of South Asia, but this is no longer the case. The high cost of remuneration of government employees, a legacy of colonialism, has fallen in real terms and continues to fall in most countries because of inflation and devaluation of local currencies. In fact, in many countries real salaries and wages in the public sector have fallen below subsistence levels. This coupled with the learning process inherent in enterprises is likely to bring down the cost of labor, although not the morale of the employees. The cost of labor in South Asia is likely to increase faster as the Asian countries develop, *vide* Japan. It is therefore quite possible that the cost of labor will not be a serious constraining factor in African manufacturing.

As a result of the efforts made in the educational sector and professional training given to thousands of graduates of higher learning, both in Africa and abroad, coupled with the experience gained on the job, the serious skilled manpower constraints that prevailed at the threshold of independence are no longer serious. Professional associations, consulting firms and individuals, construction companies, etc., are available and growing in number as well as in capability and capacity. There is a growing pool of trainable graduates in most professions, including middle-level positions. The people-oriented strategies that an increasing number of countries have adopted and are adopting as well as measures that continue to be taken in regard to human resource development will ensure increasing availability of manpower in all categories. See Chapter 2 for further details on manpower.

## INFRASTRUCTURE

Africa lacks adequate and reliable infrastructure, both in physical (roads, railways, ports, airlines, telecommunications, water, energy) and institutional terms. Transport and communication links between countries are inadequate. During colonial times whatever transport network was put in place was designed to export agricultural and mineral resources to and import manufactured goods from the colonizing nations. Railways and roads thus radiated from the interior to ports on the sea coast. Modes of transport linking adjacent countries were thus non-existent or limited. Inadequacy or lack of services in transferring cargo from one mode of transport to another compounded the difficulties. With respect to air transport, passengers had to transit through European capitals in order to make flight connections to destinations in East or West Africa. Telecommunications services between African countries were routed through the capitals of the metropolitan powers. Institutions such as banks, mainly branches of those in the metropolitan countries, were established to facilitate trade between the colonies and the metropolitan countries.

Table 4.6 gives an indication of the road network system in Africa at the beginning of the 1990s. Half of the road network of the continent (excluding South Africa) was in poor to fair condition. Neglected maintenance, resulting mainly from the crisis in the 1980s, explains this state of affairs.

TABLE 4.6
NETWORK LENGTH AND CONDITION BY SUBREGION AT THE BEGINNING OF THE 1990S

| | Length (1000 km) | | | | Classified roads condition (%) | | | | | |
|---|---|---|---|---|---|---|---|---|---|---|
| | Total | Classified roads | | Rural roads | Paved | | | Unpaved | | |
| | | Paved | Unpaved | | Good | Fair | Poor | Good | Fair | Poor |
| North Africa | 240 | 109 | 64 | 67 | 44 | 39 | 17 | 10 | 17 | 73 |
| Eastern and Southern Africa | 561 | 62 | 192 | 307 | 49 | 36 | 15 | 38 | 31 | 31 |
| Central Africa | 284 | 9 | 118 | 157 | 37 | 25 | 38 | 35 | 33 | 32 |
| West Africa | 319 | 62 | 92 | 165 | 58 | 17 | 26 | 11 | 31 | 58 |
| Africa | 1404 | 242 | 466 | 696 | 50 | 30 | 20 | 20 | 25 | 55 |

Source: ECA, 1991, *Subsectoral Strategies: Roads and Road Transport* (DOC/UNTACDA/STRAT/91/04), Addis Ababa.

With respect to telecommunications, the actual number of telephone lines, teledensities and projected minimum teledensity targets at the end of the UNCATDA II are shown in Table 4.7. It is apparent from the last row that South Africa accounts for a third of the existing telephone lines.

TABLE 4.7
TELEPHONE LINES AND TELEDENSITIES IN AFRICA

| Subregion/ region | Actual | | | | | | | | Proj- ected |
|---|---|---|---|---|---|---|---|---|---|
| | 1989 | 1992 | | 1994 | | 1995 | | | 2000 |
| | Tele- density (per 1000) | Lines (1000) | Tele- density (per 1000) | Lines (1000) | Tele- density (per 1000) | Lines (1000) | Tele- density (per 1000) | | Tele- density (per 10000) |
| Eastern/South- ern Africa | 0.41 | 1071.9 | 0.52 | 1210 | 0.55 | 1315.5 | 0.55 | | 0.7 |
| West Africa | 0.24 | 644.4 | 0.34 | 758.6 | 0.37 | 864.6 | 0.41 | | 0.48 |
| Central Africa | 0.24 | 172 | 0.22 | 193.1 | 0.23 | 199.4 | 0.23 | | 0.52 |
| North Africa | 2.38 | 4464.4 | 3.03 | 5268.3 | 3.45 | 5965.2 | 3.82 | | 3.84 |
| Africa | | 6352.7 | 1.02 | 7430 | 1.13 | 8344.7 | 1.21 | | 1.72 |
| Africa * | | 9876.8 | 1.49 | 11274. 5 | 1.61 | 12263. 8 | 1.67 | | |

Source: Compiled from ECA's *Appraisal of Transport Sector Developments, Second Mid-term Assessment of UNCTAD II.*, Volume IV-B,(ECA/TPTCOM/EXP/97/2(iv)(B)), 1997, Cairo.
* Including South Africa

Road density (km/km²) and number of telephones per 1,000 inhabitants show how inadequate the road and telephone systems are in Africa. The former stood at 0.54 and the latter, 1.19, in 1992, both having increased from 0.05 and 0.8 in 1984, respectively (see Annex 3.2). The same applies to railways and shipping. Africa's share in the world's merchant fleet, for example, fell from 1.1 percent in 1980 to 1.0 percent in 1993 with corresponding figures for total tonnage (deadweight in million tonnes) of 7.1 and 6.9 (UNCTAD, *UNCTAD Statistical Pocket Book*). In regard to number of post offices, they average one per 30,000 inhabitants.

A measure of success has been registered in linking the road networks of neighboring countries following independence. This, unfortunately, has not been the case for the railways in 33 countries. Because of different gauges used, for example, it has not been possible to link neighboring railway systems and therefore neighboring countries. For this reason, and the flexibility that modern commercial vehicles offer, road systems have been developing much faster than the railway systems. As for maritime transport, few countries have managed to develop this mode of transport. Most of the maritime transport is handled by foreign vessels. Cataracts (which characterize many African rivers) impede riverine navigation. Inland water transport is, therefore, limited to lakes and some sections of such rivers.

Some measures were undertaken to improve the infrastructural situation in the past three decades at the national, subregional, and regional levels. The Tan-Zam Railway, many ports (Tema in Ghana, Port Harcourt in Nigeria, Matadi in Congo K, and Assab in Eritrea), and the Ethiopian Airlines, as well as the creation and successful operation of the Institute for Development and Economic Planning (IDEP) and the African Development Bank (ADB), are examples of successful infrastructures that were built after independence. A list of institutions sponsored and established by ECA, OAU and others is given in Annex 4.9.

The 1980s, unfortunately, saw a deterioration in the infrastructure built by the Africans themselves. Adequate maintenance was not carried out for want of foreign exchange needed to import spare parts and replacement equipment. Rehabilitation of old and establishment of new infrastructures are crucial to the successful development and operation of the African Economic Community — hence the urgency of measures to be taken in this regard. Both physical and institutional infrastructures are essential to the integration of the continent.

Telecommunications are, unfortunately, characterized by a diversity of equipment; yet Africa urgently needs to improve, expand, and modernize its telecommunications systems. An efficient telephone network is the basis for such means of electronic communication as facsimile and e-mail, the most convenient, cheapest, and swiftest means of sending and receiving messages and information. It is a prerequisite for modern business and access to global information networks. In an age of the informatics revolution, no country can afford to lag behind in this area. In countries experiencing communication difficulties cellular mobile telephone (cell phone) networks and satellite dishes could be partial answers, particularly for business and institutions. This approach was being considered in many African countries (Zimbabwe, Ethiopia, etc.) and, in some countries, such as Kenya and South Africa, have already been in use. Thanks to the latest advances in technology, mobile phone services are on the verge of becoming more relevant to African needs and conditions. Three international companies (Iridium, Globalstar and ICO) were, before the turn of the century, expected to launch their respective satellites that would enable customers to use mobile phones anywhere on earth (*The Economist*, June 13, 1998). In a vast region such as Africa where transport and communication are inadequate and expensive, video teleconferencing could prove useful at both government and business levels in developing and maintaining the badly needed economic integration and cooperation.

Aware of the crucial role that transport and communications services play in economic growth, the international community declared 1978-1988 as the United Nations Transport and Communications Decade in Africa (UNTACDA). UNTACDA was intended to focus attention on the special needs of transport and communications and bring about the physical integration in Africa. The trans-African highway network, including the Cairo-Gaborone (north-south), Mombasa-Lagos-Dakar (east-west) and feeder road links, is an example of physical integration. The highways traversing many countries were and are being implemented by upgrading existing national highways and completing missing connections between neighboring countries. Continental road network has been projected to increase from 2.23 million kilometers in 1993 to 3.22 million kilometers (historical scenario) and 3.60 million kilometers normative scenario) by 2008. The corresponding figures for railways (excluding South Africa) are 49,400, 61, 800 and 108,200 (ECA, *Africa in the 1990s and Beyond: ...* ).

Evaluation at the close of the decade showed that the transport and telecommunications systems were still far from adequate. The low level of the "decade program implementation" was mainly due to lack of resources. In view of the crucial importance of the sector, UNTACDA II (1991-2000) was declared, with the objective of establishing an efficient integrated transport and communications system in Africa. It comprised 708 projects of which 508 were on transport and 200, on telecommunications. Forty four of the former were abandoned during implementation. Development of manufacturing capacities for transport and communications equipment, components and spare parts constitutes one of the sub-objectives of the decade program. In view of the interdependence of infrastructure and industry, the ECA Conference of Ministers, in 1993, endorsed the harmonization of the implementation of IDDA II and UNTACDA II.

A mid-term evaluation of the performance of UNTACD II was conducted in 1994 (ECA, E/ECA/CM.21/6, Part II, Add.1). According to the evaluation, 294 out of 669 projects included in the first phase of the program were completed or being implemented or had been partially or fully financed. Inadequate mobilization of financial resources, partly due to the unsatisfactory operation of the implementation machinery, in particular the Resource Mobilization Committee, was the main reason for the low performance. It appears that no activities had been undertaken in regard to manufacturing. In resolution 804 (XXX), titled Implementation of Phase II of the Program for the Second United Nations Transport and Communications Decade in Africa (UNTACDA II), the twenty-first meeting of the Conference of Ministers Responsible for Economic and Social Development and Planning in 1995, among other things, urged the international community (all donors, international organizations, and financial institutions) to take part in, support, and contribute to the implementation of the decade program and activities.

The second mid-term assessment of UNCTADA II was carried out in 1997. Indications of the implementation of the Decade program are summarized in Table 4.8. From the table it is apparent that 16.2 percent of the projects have been completed, 25.3 percent were under execution and 37.0 percent were fully funded. Out of 70 regional transport projects 22 have been executed or were under execution, 20 were fully financed and 3 were partly financed. The corresponding figures for telecommunications were 12, 1, 3 and 2 (ECA, *Summary Second Mid-term Assessment of UNTACDA II*). In regard to manufacturing of transport equipment, components and spare parts, four existing national plants and workshops that could be developed as subregional plants have been identified. These are: the Zimbabwe Engineering Company Limited, the Chantier Naval et Industriel du Cameroun, the Ethiopian Akaki Spare Parts Plant and the Société Nationale de Chemins de Fer du Sénégal. The total funding of the Decade program at the time of assessment was a little over $4 billion (ECA, *Assessment of Summary Impact ...* ).

TABLE 4.8
IMPLEMENTATION OF UNCTADA II (1965-1997) - NUMBER OF PROJECTS

|  | Total aproved | Completed | Under execution | Fully financed |
|---|---|---|---|---|
| Road and road transport | 214 | 30 | 76 | 99 |
| Railways subsector | 89 | 26 | 11 | 31 |
| Maritime, port and multimodal transport | 104 | 13 | 16 | 23 |
| Inland water transport | 17 | 1 | 6 | 4 |
| Urban transport | 7 | 2 | 1 | 2 |
| Air transport | 77 | 14 | 16 | 30 |
| Telecommunications | 145 | 21 | 41 | 58 |
| Broadcasting | 29 | 3 | 6 | 6 |
| Postal services | 26 | 5 | 7 | 9 |
| Total | 708 | 115 | 180 | 262 |

Source: Compiled from ECA's *Appraisal of Transport Sector Developments, Second Mid-term Assessment of UNCTADA II* , Volumes IV-A and IV-B, (ECA/TPTCOM/EXP/97/2(iv)(A) and (B)), 1997, Cairo.

In the case of telecommunications, two projects, the Pan-African Telecommunications (PANAFTEL) and the Regional African Satellite Communications Organization (RASCOM) which will own a satellite that links with terrestrial networks in member states, are intended to help and facilitate the development of communications in the continent, particularly in rural and isolated areas. The work being carried out by these projects will be supplemented by the private sector, including two projects that were reported being promoted, one each by a Sudanese and an Ethiopian. At the workshop preceding the Third African-African American "root" Summit in May 1995 in Dakar, Senegal, for instance, it was disclosed that American telecommunication giants were planning to link Africa with the world information highway. Satellite links, radio phones, fiber optics links, and lines and cellular phones were the options being considered. AT&T was reported to be planning a $1.9-billion project (fiber-optic undersea loop around the continent) to be operational by 1999. According to US officials at the workshop, the telecommunications market in Africa, estimated at $1.5 billion, is likely to grow to $10-12 billion in 10 or more years time.

At the country level, the development of infrastructure is a priority area in many countries. In Ethiopia, for instance, 33 percent of the 1997/98 budget of about $430 million was allocated to road construction. In 1997 work was in progress to expand the existing 167,000 telephone lines to 767,000 and the service of mobile telephones was expected to start at the end of 1997 or soon thereafter.

Although efforts made during the two Decades have not achieved the desired results, the projects implemented, the activities carried out and the groundwork laid down are likely to facilitate and accelerate the development of transport and communications infrastructure in the future. It is obvious that much more remains to be done, starting with the rehabilitation of the deteriorating physical and institutional infrastructure, as well as the abolition of the nonphysical barriers to transit, such as customs procedures and coordination between different modes of transportation.

## BIBLIOGRPAHY

ADB, 1994, *African Development Report 1994*, Abidjan.

Africa Confidential, 1997, "Oil and Gas-Going with the Flow," March 28, 1997.

Blunden, John, 1985, *Mineral Resources and their Management*, Longman Group Limited, Harlow.

Chemical Engineering Progress, 1996, *Fuel Cells Poised to Provide Power*, September 1996.

de Kun, N., 1987, *Mineral Resources of Africa*, Elsevier Science Publishers B.V., Amsterdam.

Dommen, Arthur J., 1988, *Innovation in African Agriculture*, Westview Press, Boulder.

Dowswell, Christopher, 1989, *Feeding The Future: Agricultural Development Strategies for Africa*, Proceedings of Workshop 1989, organized by the Center for the Applied Studies in International Negotiations (CASIN/SAA/GLOBAL 2000).

ECA, 1988, *Survey of Economic and Social Conditions in Africa, 1986-1987* (E/ECA/CM.14/4), Addis Ababa.

ECA, 1994, *Production of Basic Chemicals from Natural Gas in Africa* (ECA/IHSD/IDPS/CHN/002/94), Addis Ababa.

ECA, 1994, *Prospects for the Increased Production of and Intra-African Trade in Aluminum Commodities and Metal Products* (ECA/UNIDO/AFRIALUM/TP/1/94), Addis Ababa.

ECA, 1995, *Food and Agricultural Production, Food Security and Food Self-sufficiency in Africa* (E/ECA/CM.21/10), Addis Ababa.

ECA, 1995, *Mid-term Evaluation of the Second United Nations Transport and Communications Decade in Africa (UNTACDA)* (E/ECA/CM.21/6), Part II, Add.1, Addis Ababa.

ECA, 1995, *Report of the First Regional Conference of African Ministers Responsible for the Development and Utilization of Mineral Resources and Energy* (ECA/NRD/RC/DUMRE/MIN/6), Accra.

ECA, 1996, *Africa in the 1990s and Beyond: ECA-Revised Long-Term Development Perspectives Study* (ECA/SERPD/TP/96/3), Addis Ababa.

ECA, 1997, *Assessment of Summary Impact: Second Mid-Term Evaluation of UNTACDA II*, Volume II (ECA/TPTCOM/EXP/97/2[vi]), Cairo.

ECA, 1997, *Summary Second Mid-Term Assessment of UNTACDA II*, Volume II (ECA/TPTCOM/EXP/97/A[2]), Cairo.

ECA/FAO, 1994, *Adequate Feed and Feeding: A Prerequisite for Sustainable Animal Agriculture Development in Tropical Africa*, Addis Ababa.

ECA/UNIDO, 1994, *Prospects for the Increased Production of and Intra-African Trade in Copper Metal and Copper Based Products* (ECA/UNIDO/AFRICOP/TP/2/94), Addis Ababa.

ESCAP, 1991, *Agro-pesticides: Properties and Functions Integrated Crop Protection*, Bangkok.

Europa, 1996, *Africa South of the Sahara 1996*, Twenty-fifth Edition, Europa Publications Limited, London.

FAO, 1986, *Atlas of African Agriculture* (African agriculture: the next 25 years), Rome.

FAO, 1992, *FAO Production Yearbook*, FAO, Rome.

FAO, 1994, *The State of Food and Agriculture 1994*, Rome.

FAO, 1995, *Dimensions of Need*, Rome.

FAO, 1986, *African Agriculture: the next 25 Years, Annex IV, Irrigation and Water Control*, Rome.

Harris, Paul, 1987, *The Greening of Africa*, Paladin, London.

Hill, Albert F., 1952, second edition, *Economic Botany*, McGraw-Hill Book Company, New York.

Khennas, Smail, ed., 1992, *Industrialization, Mineral Resources and Energy in Africa*, CODESRIA Book Series, Rowe, Oxford.

McIlroy, R.J., 1963, *An Introduction to Tropical Cash Crops*, Ibadan University Press, Ibadan, Nigeria.

Office Cherifien des Phosphates, 1992, *Communication Presentee par Monsieur Kendili Hadi, lors de l'Atelier Regional sur la Cooperation dans l'Utilisation des Engrais en Afrique*, Rabat.

ONUDI, 1990, *Industrie Africaine de Fer et d'Acier*, Vienna.

PANA, 1998, "UNEP Assists Ethiopia, Kenya and Tanzania on Biodiversity," *African News Online* (www.africanews.org), March 16, 1998.

Phillips, John, 1967, *The Development of Agriculture and Forestry in the Tropics*, revised edn, Frederick A. Praeger, New York.

Posh and Partners and Dorsh Consult, 1990, *Prefeasibility Study on Design of a Network of Gas Pipeline and an Integrated Communications Systems for Marketing African Natural Gas.*

Smith, Mike, 1987, "ZCCM on Course for Recovery," *Mining Magazine*, December, 1987.

Spiegel, Dominique, 1995, "New Scramble for African Fields," *African Business*, December 1995.

Stock, Robert, 1995, *Africa South of the Sahara: a Geographical Interpretation*, The Guilford Press, London.

The Economist, 1997, "Economic Indicators," August 2, 1997.

The Economist, 1997, "Zaire: Stored Wealth," May 3, 1997.

The Economist, 1998, "Staying in Touch," June 13, 1998.

The New York Times, 1997, "UN and Nature Group Oppose Fishing Subsidies," June 3,

1997.

The Ethiopian Herald, 1994, "Project to Plant Rubber Trees," November 8, 1994, Addis Ababa.

The Ethiopia Herald, 1995, "Promising Geothermal Exploration at Tendaho," June 10, 1995, and "When Energy Sparks in Afar Desert," June 16, 1995, Addis Ababa.

UNCTAD, 1994, *UNCTAD Statistical Pocket Book*, Geneva.

UNIDO, 1979, *Appropriate Industrial Technology for Energy for Rural Requirements*, New York.

Weston, Rae, 1984, *Strategic Materials, A World Survey*, Croom Helm Ltd., Kent.

World Bank, 1994, Overview of Prospects for Gas Development in Sub-Saharan countries (Draft Report), Washington, D.C.

World Bank, 1996, World Resources: A Guide to the Global Environment, Washington, D.C.

World Bank, 1996, World Resources 1996-97, Oxford University Press, New York.

World Bank, 1994, *Overview of Prospects for Gas Development in Sub-Saharan Countries* (Draft Report), Washington, D.C.

World Bank, 1996, *World Resources: A Guide to the Global Environment*, Washington, D.C.

World Bank, 1996, *World Resources 1996-97*, Oxford University Press, New York.

Yezarioyitu Ethiopia, 1994, Akababina Limal (Environment and Development), October 8, 1994, Addis Ababa.

Yezarioyitu Ethiopia, 1994, *Akababina Limat* (Environment and Development), October 8, 1994, Addis Ababa.

## NOTES

1. For instance, of the 7,000 plant species (out of 70,000 speciments) so far researched in Ethiopia and Eritrea, 12 percent are endemic. Of the fauna researched so far, 30 (11%) of the mammals are endemic. The corresponding figures for birds are 28 (3.3%) and 30 (43%) for other animals, including land and water animals (*Yezarioyitu Ethiopia*).

2. Two PV solar panel manufacturers in the USA, Evergreen Solar Inc. and SAE Americas Inc., are among companies worldwide that have recently announced substantial cost reduction in the making of solar panels (*The Boston Sunday Globe*, "Evergreen's Goal: Plugging in the Sun," January 18, 1998)

## CHAPTER 5

# INDUSTRIAL DEVELOPMENT[1]

In its broad sense and as defined in most African national accounts statistics, industry includes manufacturing, mining, construction, and utilities (electricity, water, and gas). This book focuses on manufacturing. The major concentrations of the manufacturing industry in Africa are shown in Map 5.1.

## PRE-INDEPENDENCE

During the colonial regime, manufacturing in the continent was generally at the handicraft and small-scale levels. In some countries this was supplemented by some relatively complex industries producing mainly for export. Production for local consumption focused on food, fiber and wood processing and metal working to supply some of the needs of the growing urban populations.

The supply of industrial goods from the metropolitan countries was reduced or cut off during World War II. This led to the establishment of more industries to meet some of the local demand, particularly in countries such as Zimbabwe and Kenya where the non-indigenous population was large.

### Agricultural Processing

The industrial processing of agricultural commodities was aimed mainly at primary processing, particularly for export. Further processing was carried out on products that needed to be preserved or were intended for local consumption. Examples of those agricultural commodities, their respective levels of processing (both pre- and post-independence, and their main growing areas, are presented in Annex 5.1.

From Annex 5.1, it is apparent that many of the local establishments produced intermediates that were processed into final products in the colonial countries. Several of these products were redirected to the African market at prices many times those of the intermediates themselves.

During the colonial period, practically all the food consumed by the African peoples was prepared at home by women. Traditional technologies, such as grating, grinding between two stones, pounding in mortar and pestle, and preserving were used, and the combination of technologies varied with the types of foods used.

## Map 5.1: Major Concentration of Industries in Africa

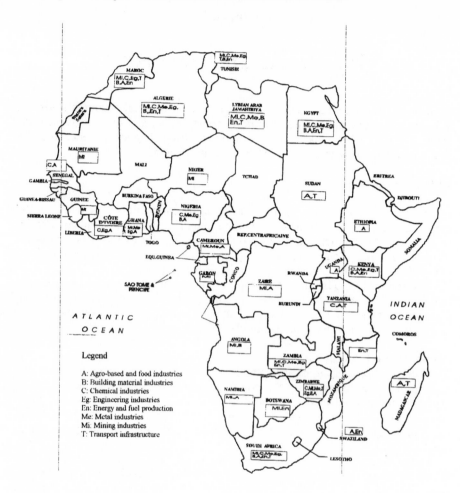

Legend

A: Agro-based and food industries
B: Building material industries
C: Chemical industries
Eg: Engineering industries
En: Energy and fuel production
Me: Metal industries
Mi: Mining industries
T: Transport infrastructure

## Mineral Processing

As detailed in Chapter 4, the African continent is endowed with a wide range of mineral resources. It is, in fact, a major supplier of many strategic minerals to the industrialized countries.

Extraction of minerals was practiced for centuries before the Europeans set foot on the continent. In the words of de Kun, *"When underdeveloped nomads still roamed Europe and North America, Africans already extensively used metals"* (de Kun 1987), a statement supported by even more recent research[2] refuting the view that African iron technology has been inferior to Western counterpart technology (Schmidt 1996).

About 30,000 years ago in Bomvu Ridge in Swaziland, the people recovered iron oxide. Ancient (400-500 B.C.) iron mines[3] in Akjoujt in Mauritania, in Nok in central Nigeria, and in the vicinity of Lake Victoria, and large Nubian slag heaps of iron ore smelting in Sudan, copper mines in In Gall in Niger, copper smelting in Tsumeb in Namibia, brass works in Nigeria and neighboring countries, metal ploughs and spear heads in many African countries, and coins (gold, silver, and brass), crowns and crosses in Ethiopia are examples of mining and smelting operations and metal workmanship that Africans achieved long before colonization.

During the colonial era, mines were selected and exploited with a view to meeting the needs of the colonial industries at home. To this end, infrastructure, particularly roads and railroads, were designed and built to facilitate the shipment of minerals and agricultural commodities to purpose-built ports. Services, such as banking and communications, were also developed with this in mind.

Transport cost seems to have been the main determinant factor in deciding the stage of processing of the minerals before they were shipped out of the country. Ores with relatively high metal content, such as iron ore, were given minimum treatment. Ores with very low metal concentration, such as copper ore, were processed up to the crude metal stage. Other ores, including tin, were subjected to processing between these two extremes.

Because of its very low concentration, copper ore processing (concentration, smelting and refining) comprised the most complex industry at the time. In fact, when it started operation around 1911 the Copperbelt in Zambia became the largest copper complex in the world. Finished copper output steadily increased from 250,000 tons in 1940 to 650,000 tons in 1960 in Zambia and from 150,000 tons to 270,000 tons in Congo K over the same period (de Kun 1987). So did the development and production of other industries and services catering to the mines.

The processing of minerals associated with copper did relatively well. Cobalt and nickel were recovered. Lead and zinc were other metals that were won from ores locally.

## POST-INDEPENDENCE

African industry is characterized by a traditional/modern dichotomy. The former covers production and service activities related to basic household and agricultural needs carried out at traditional handicraft level or by artisans (blacksmiths, potters, carpenters, weavers, etc.). It is practically based on human and animal power and uses mainly local resources, including metal scraps and waste materials. The latter generally involves imported technology, machinery and equipment, materials, and production systems. In general, it produces products that cater mainly to the acquired consumption patterns of urban dwellers. The larger enterprises are dominated by foreign capital and expertise.

On the eve of independence, the modern manufacturing base, except in Zimbabwe and some North African countries, was very low or non-existent. Manufacturing output and diversification increased rapidly during the first decade-and-a-half of independence, manufacturing accounting for about 10 percent of GDP. Some of the reasons for this were a very low initial industrial base; increase in total demand resulting from improved living standards; development of import substitution and building materials industries; some advances made in developing export industries; and the multiplier effect of all these and other factors. This rosy picture changed following the 1973 oil crisis. Since then, economic conditions in African countries have stagnated and in many cases deteriorated. By early 1980s, over 20 countries were experiencing a decline in manufacturing output and many plants were working at capacities well below 30 percent. Conditions for industrialization were therefore adversely affected and prospects of de-industrialization loomed large.

Local resource-based processes here are divided into two categories: those using indigenous technologies and those using imported technologies. The former, comprising food, beverage, textile, and garment making are mostly carried out at home by the womenfolk. The processes and operations used include cleaning, grinding or pounding, extracting (oil), spinning, and weaving.

Traditional grinding and pounding are tedious and time-consuming operations. In countries such as Ethiopia, they are being replaced by small flour mills scattered throughout the country. In other countries the mills are of medium and relatively large size producing more than one quality of flours. This is particularly true for relatively urbanized countries, such as Zambia.

Small to medium size expellers are the usual means of extracting oils from vegetable oils. In West Africa, pioneer mills established some 40 years ago were still in operation until quite recently. They have been replaced by more compact and efficient mills, some of which are equivalent in size to small flour mills.

As for textiles, the mills that had to be established were of necessity larger than food-processing plants. They are much more complex and use a larger number of imported inputs.

The other group of industries based on imported technologies include, sugar, beer, soft drink, footwear, cigarette, soap, detergent, cement, furniture, printing, and metal working, publishing industries. These are among the industrial activities that are traditionally introduced or adopted during the early stages of industrialization in developing countries; most of them are resource-based.

## Development Strategy

Many of the African countries experienced a number of development strategies. The duration and period of each strategy varied from country to country. The first was import substitution. This covered the period 1960s-1970s. It was followed by integrated rural development in the 1970s-1980s and structural adjustment in the 1980s-present (1998).

In the past 20 years (1975-1995), progress in manufacturing has been slow. Manufacturing has grown at only 0.6 percent per year, accounting on average for 11 percent of GDP and contributing about 1 percent to world manufacturing output in the first half of the 1990s (ECA/UNIDO, CAMI.12/6[a]). In most countries the structure of manufacturing hardly differed from what it had been in the 1970s, with food, beverages, cigarettes, and textiles and other import substitution industries dominating. Table 5.1 gives some idea of the evolution of manufacturing. Although the table was meant to apply to world LDCs with a long history of industrialization, it does, to a large extent, reflect the evolution of manufacturing in many African countries as well.

TABLE 5.1
EVOLUTION OF MANUFACTURING IN WORLD LDCS WITH A LONGER
HISTORY OF INDUSTRIALIZATION

| Period | Phase | Main characteristics |
|---|---|---|
| 1960s to early 1970s | Initiation of the manufacturing process | - Heavy government interventions through import protection and other subsidies in favor of investment in import substitution (and frequently large scale) manufacturing.<br>- Nationalization policies in many LDCs. |
| Mid-1970s to 1980s | Manufacturing crisis | - Stagnation and/or contraction in manufacturing output.<br>- Inefficient manufaturing parastatals rendering government budgets unsustainable. |
| 1980s to 1990s | Adjustment and reform | - Market-oriented macroeconomic and social reforms. |

Source: UNCTAD, 1995, *The Least Developed Countries*, 1995 Report, ID/B/4(2)/4, New York.

It is possible that some structural changes have taken place in a number of countries in recent years as happened in Ethiopia. In that country, the shares of basic iron and steel, fabricated metal products, machinery and equipment, motor vehicles (assembly) and non-metallic mineral products in MVA increased significantly during the period 1991/92-1995/96 (*Central Statistical Authority* 1997). Availability of inputs may partially explain such structural changes. The coming into operation of new production units, such as a rerolling mill in the case of the iron and steel, whose share surged from 1.46 percent in 1991/92 to an average of 3.47 percent in subsequent years, could be another factor.

In the 1970s, the prices of raw materials exported from the continent increased. Encouraged by this, many countries drew up and started to implement development plans, including industrial plans, some of them quite ambitious. This apparent success was short-lived as the multiple crises of the 1980s soon caught up. During the first half of the 1990s, only 30 to 50 percent of the industrial capacity was actually being utilized (ECA's Twenty-ninth Session of the Commission, May 1994). In Nigeria, for example, the Manufacturers Association of Nigeria estimated capacity utilization to be below 30 percent.

### •Import Substitution Strategy
The European life-style (and accompnying consumption patterns and tastes) were among the legacies that a segment of the urban people started to acquire during the colonial era. This process accelerated following independence, especially with those Africans in public service who took over the jobs and level of remuneration previously enjoyed by whites.

Except for part of their food and textile products, most African countries at the time of independence were completely dependent on imports of industrial consumer goods. It made sense then to produce locally some of the goods and services for which demand had been created through the acquired consumption patterns and tastes referred to above. Many countries, therefore, opted for the so called import-substitution strategy with a view to, among other things, reducing dependence on manufactured imports. Public enterprises played a substantial role in developing import-substitution industries focusing on consumer goods. That role received a boost through the nationalization of production and service companies by many governments following independence. Although starting from a low base, African countries made substantial progress in this area up to the early 1970s. This trend, unfortunately, went into reverse in the first half of the 1980s when the poor performance of public enterprises worsened. Since then, many of the World Bank loans have been given on conditions that included public enterprise reform and privatization.

Import-substitution can be accomplished in three phases. The first is done by locally producing the same previously imported goods, such as pharmaceuticals and agricultural equipment and machinery, from imported bulk finished materials and knocked-down fabricated parts and components. This involves the final stage of processing (formulation, mixing) or manufacturing (assembly) into consumer goods. The second, which could be considered a second stage of the first phase, progressively decreases the import content of domestic manufacture, i.e., upgrading the first approach to incorporate locally made materials, parts, and components. The third entails replacing the imported goods by the same or alternative goods made locally from basic indigenous raw materials, such as agricultural equipment and machinery made of metals extracted from local ores. All phases also depend to varying degrees on the import of non-material inputs.

The import-substitution strategy, an inward-looking approach, was regarded by some not only as an end in itself but also as a means to higher levels of industrial development. It was expected to facilitate industrial development by enabling the countries to acquire and familiarize themselves with technologies, thus providing their nationals with training opportunities. It was intended to lead progressively to backward integration from the final processing and manufacturing of consumer goods to raw material processing via intermediate making and the development of the capital goods industry. This dream did not come true for most countries. The oil crises in the 1970s and 1980s hit hard even those countries with relatively large economies capable of supporting a higher level of industrialization. Oil-importing African countries found themselves paying astronomical prices not only for oil but also for industrial goods and inputs so essential to their development. At one time some countries were using up to 80 percent of their foreign exchange earnings to import crude oil and petroleum products.

In the 1960s, African industries were completely dependent on foreign inputs, except for some local raw materials and unskilled labor. These inputs ranged from project identification to managing and operating industrial establishments and physical inputs. It was under these circumstances that import substitution industries were established and operated. Some of them catered solely to a tiny minority of the population, i.e., part of the urban segment whose demand for the goods produced had low potential for growth. This, coupled with the duplication of industrial establishments producing the same products in practically all countries in the region meant that African countries failed to trade or enter into industrial cooperation with each other.

Prior to the oil crises, most African countries had managed to earn enough foreign exchange to finance the inputs their import-substitution industries needed. These included the procurement of technical and management expertise; the purchase of machinery, equipment, spare parts, raw materials, and supplies; and the training of nationals. With dwindling foreign exchange earnings many industries were grossly underutilized and /or they were forced to shut down. This, together with the countries' reduced capability to establish new industries, led to what is known as "deindustrialization."

Import-substituting industries can be categorized into those based on either local or imported raw materials. The former include beverage, sugar, tobacco, textile, wood-products, brick, glass, and cement industries. The latter may include industries manufacturing paint, pharmaceuticals, pesticides, plastic products, rubber products, synthetic fibers textiles, perfumes, cosmetics, and metal products. Their import content is normally much higher and they generally involve the last stage of processing/manufacturing.

As would be expected, the local resources-based industries fared better during the oil crises. Since they were structurally linked with local resources, they did not have to import the major raw materials they used, thereby reducing their foreign exchange requirement.

As for the import-based industries, they suffered the most after the oil crises. The import component of their products normally accounted for a significant portion of the cost of production, so much so that many of them were characterized by very little value-added. They became liabilities as a result of their increasing foreign exchange requirements at a time of dwindling foreign exchange earnings.

### •Export-oriented Strategy

As noted in Chapter 3, most African primary commodities are exported in crude or semi-processed form. According to the twenty-ninth session of the Commission of ECA, held in May 1994, only about 10 percent of the minerals and fuels in the region are processed and used locally.

As reported by Bailey (1976), developing African countries exported five main types of goods in the 1970s. The categories were:

• Processed primary products (vegetable oils, foodstuffs, plywood and veneer, pulp and paper products, fabricated metals, etc.);

• Traditional labor-intensive goods (textiles, garments, footwear, simple engineering goods, etc.);

• Non-traditional labor-intensive goods (glassware, pottery, wigs, plastic and wooden items, simple furniture, etc.);

• Products and assemblies manufactured by multinational corporations (semiconductors, television tubes and valves, electronic components, etc.); and

• Manufactured goods which may have started off as import substitutes (car parts, electric wire and cables, bicycles, electric motors, simple machinery, etc.).

In general, only a limited number of African countries have benefited from the export of processed and manufactured goods (mainly in the first three categories). Success stories include pulp from Swaziland, furniture from Mauritius and Zimbabwe, sugar and clothing from Mauritius, and cocoa products from Cote d'Ivoire. In the last two categories, especially the so called "footloose" industries, African countries have achieved less. As late-comers they had to face stiff competition from Asian and Latin American exporters of processed and manufactured goods to the industrialized world, benefiting the least in the deployment of labor-intensive industries from industrialized to developing countries in the 1960s and 1970s.

Such being the case, it has been argued that African countries should have adopted export-led growth as a strategy instead of import substitution. The World Bank and IMF support this; in fact, they prescribe this strategy. With economies that were and still are characterized by low productivity and high cost, partly due to inappropriate macroeconomic policies, most African countries are still uncompetitive in the world market, except for certain products in some countries. A more realistic approach for most African countries would have been to start with import substitution industries and then move towards export, provided they could compete. An alternative would have been to combine import substitution and export-led growth, whenever practical. This was done by some countries. Such an approach across the board would have increased the producers' chances of competing in the world market, even using marginal costing, including charging higher prices on the domestic market. If the right macroeconomic policies had been adopted, more import substitution-industries would have integrated backwards to local raw material processing, thereby creating linkages with agriculture and mining that are often so sadly missing. Utilizing the operational experience gained by operating import-substitution industries, African producers could have achieved higher levels of productivity and competitiveness in export products.

The industrialized countries' practice of increasing import tariff rates as the degree of processing increased also acted as a serious deterrent to African exports. Non-tariff barriers were a second deterrent. Together they have contributed to the slow progress of industrialization in Africa. Coupled with the changing international division of labor (i.e., the slowing down and possible halt in the redeployment of labor-intensive industries from developed to developing countries as a result of innovative production methods in the former), these disincentives are very likely to make it virtually impossible for African countries to benefit from redeployment in the future.

### • Industrializing Industries Strategy

With the passage of time, the limitations of import-substitution strategy became apparent. Industry in the real sense of the word cannot and should not depend nearly exclusively on imported inputs. First, this would mean putting all one's eggs in one basket, an obviously impractical and unadvisable practice. Secondly, it calls for increased foreign exchange revenue at a time when it is rapidly dwindling. Thirdly, it would be tantamount to giving up exploiting one's own resources. The production structure clearly needed to be transformed by developing industrializing industries.

Industrializing industries are those industries that produce intermediate inputs for other industries. They comprise basic metal and chemical and engineering industries. They produce the metals and chemicals needed to make capital goods required by all industries and other economic and social activities. They provide the means for bringing about badly needed structural change.

120

Because of economies of scale and narrow and fragmented domestic markets, progress in developing these industries in Africa has been rather slow and limited to a small number of countries. Iron and steel industries have been established in Zimbabwe, Egypt, Algeria, Nigeria, and Libya; aluminum industries in Cameroon and Egypt; petrochemical industries in Algeria, Libya, Egypt, and Nigeria; and capital goods industries in Egypt, Algeria, Zimbabwe, etc.

## Production and Trade

Africa is the least industrialized continent. Annexes 5.2 through 5.6, which show regional production and trade statistics for selected processed/manufactured products at five-year intervals and for recent years, testify to this. The quantities of industrial goods produced are small when compared with those in a developed country. The same applies to trade statistics. As can be seen from the net trade figures, the continent is a net importer of many industrial products that could have been made locally using local natural resources. Some of the imports are made from the very same raw materials exported from the continent.

Annex 5.2 represents production of selected processed agricultural and related products in the region during the period 1961-1994. Products have been grouped into food and beverages, textiles, leather and leather goods, and forest and fishery products. In general, most food and beverage products showed an upward trend, although many of them have either stagnated or declined in recent years. Sugar, for instance, reached 8 million tons in 1992, yet fell in 1993 and 1994. The same trend can be observed in most other groups.

Trade in the above products is shown in Annex 5.3. From the net trade columns in the annex it is apparent that the terms of trade in regard to many products have been showing increasing deficits, most of which started before 1965. The products in this category include sugar, practically all oils (except groundnut oil), margarine, meat, dairy products, and beverages. A sugar deficit first appeared in 1975 and passed the one-million-ton level in 1990. Other products experiencing a similar fate include all wood products, except veneer sheets, wood pulp (including chemical and unbleached sulfate pulp), and crustaceans and molluscs (fresh, frozen, etc.).

The scope and diversity of agricultural processing varies from country to country. South Africa and Kenya are reported to be the only countries capable of processing more than 30 out of 42 products. The frequency distribution in regard to the other countries is as follows: 12 countries in 20-30 products, 21 countries in under 20 products and 18 countries in under 10 products (ECA/UNIDO, CAMI.12/6[a]).

Annexes 5.4, 5.5 and 5.6 give production figures for selected chemicals, metals, and engineering products, respectively. Sulfuric acid, phosphoric acid and ammonia are the intermediates with over one million tons of production. Details of phosphoric acid, ammonia, and fertilizer production are provided in Annexes 9.1 through 9.6. In 1993/94, total production of fertilizers was 5.1 million tons of nutrients, as compared with 3.5 million tons of consumption, resulting in excess overconsumption of more than 1.6 million tons and net export of about 1.3 million tons. The major producing countries are Morocco, Tunisia, Algeria, Egypt, South Africa, and Senegal.

Steel, copper, and aluminum are among the metals produced. In 1990, 12.6 million tons of crude steel ingots, 781,600 tons of copper (refined, unwrought), and 569,200 tons of aluminum (unwrought, primary) were produced. The corresponding figures for 1993 were 15.0 million, 662,000, and 614,000 tons, respectively. Whereas crude steel and aluminum reached the 1993 levels through a steady upward increase during 1970-1993, copper showed the opposite trend, with the highest output (980,600 tons) in 1975. Countries producing these metals are South Africa, Congo K, Zambia, Zimbabwe, Nigeria, Cameroon, Algeria,

Egypt, and Libya. More information on some metals is provided in Annexes 14.2 through 14.4.

As for engineering, metal works (including agricultural implements and equipment, albeit at different levels of sophistication) are ubiquitous in Africa. In 1992, production (excluding South Africa) included the following: 31.8 million pieces of agricultural hand tools, 1.1 million animal drawn implements, and 94,000 powered implements. Demand for these products were 60.1 million, 4.8 million, and 330,000, respectively. The assembly of motors, tractors, vehicles, and electronic equipment from imported parts and components constitutes the other major activity in this subsector. Further information on engineering products is given in Annexes 10.1, 11.1 and 14.1.

## Manufacturing Performance Indicators[4]
GDP, MVA and Trade Growth Rates

Although starting from a low base, African manufacturing performance in the 1960s and up to the oil crisis in 1973 was significant. During the 1963-1970 period, manufacturing value added (MVA) grew at an average annual rate of 8.3 percent, falling to 4.5 percent in 1979 and -0.5 percent in 1984. In contrast, the corresponding growth rate for GNP during the same period was 4.7 percent, averaging 2 percent during the 1950s (UNIDO, *Integrated Industrial... Subregion*). For the more recent period the rate of growth of manufacturing for the region (in percent) was as follows: 3.7 in the first half of the 1980s, 3.3 in 1989-1990, 2.8 in 1990-1991, 2 in 1989-1993, 0.4 in 1991-1992, and 1.5 in 1992-1993 (ECA/UNIDO, CAMI.12/5[b]/Rev.1). It surged to 4.6 percent in 1995 and plunged to 2.5 percent in 1996, apparently, due to *"sagging domestic demand and increased competition from cheap imports"* (UNIDO, *Industrial Africa, October 1997*). Average growth of manufacturing output in Sub-Saharan Africa in 1970 constant prices increased from 7.3 percent in 1960-65 to 9.3 in 1965-70 and fell to 4.4 in 1975-80. The corresponding ratios of manufacturing growth to GDP growth were 1.7, 2.1, and 1.2 (Meier et. al. 1989). MVA growth rates in Sub-Saharan Africa slowed down from 4.5 percent in 1996 to 4.1 percent in 1997 [UNIDO, *Industrial Africa*, September 1998]. A number of more recent manufacturing indicators in Sub-Saharan Africa are provided in Table 5.2.

TABLE 5.2
SELECTED MANUFACTURING INDICATORS IN SUB-SAHARAN AFRICA (%)

| | 1960 | 1970 | 1980 | 1990 | 1995 | |
|---|---|---|---|---|---|---|
| Regional share in global MVA | | 0.6 | 0.5 | 0.4 | 0.3 | |
| Share of MVA in GDP, current prices and $ exchange rates | 7 | 10.3 | 10.1 | 9.5 | | |
| Structure of MVA : | | | | | | |
| - Low technology (agro-industry, printing and publishing, petroleum refineries, coal products, china, glass, metals, etc.) | | 83.1 | 76.3 | 79.2 | 80.7 [a] | |
| - Machinery, excluding transport equipment | | 3.3 | 3.5 | 3.3 | 2.8 [a] | |
| - Transport equipment | | 2.7 | 7.9 | 4.8 | 4.1 [a] | |
| - Chemicals | | 9.1 | 11.1 | 11.5 | 11.2 [a] | |
| - Other manufacturing | | 1.9 | 1.2 | 1.2 | 1.2 [a] | |
| | | | 1970-1980 | 1980-1990 | 1990-1995 | |
| Growth rates of MVA, 1990 $ | | | 2 | 2.5 | 0.1 | |
| MVA share of GDP | | | 13.6 | 10.2 | 9.8 | |
| Labor productivity growth rate | | | -0.2 | 0.5 | -3 | |
| GDP growth rate | | | 3 | 2.2 | 1.2 | |
| | 1965-1970 | 1970-1975 | 1975-1980 | 1980-1985 | 1985-1990 | 1990-1995 |
| Manufacturing employment, growth per annum | 6 | 5.8 | 4.8 | -0.4 | -1.1 | 3 |

Source: UNIDO, 1996, *The Globalization of Industry: Implications for Developing Countries beyond 2000*, Vienna.
  a 1994

Annex 5.7 provides information on growth rates of GDP, MVA, and trade in manufactures during the periods 1975-1985 and 1985-1990. As can be observed from the annex, African growth in manufacturing at constant 1980 prices outpaced that of GDP during both periods, more than twice in 1975-1985 (5.1% against 2.5%). This was not the case with African LDCs in 1975-1985 and Sub-Saharan Africa in 1985-1990. On the basis of MVA/GDP ratios, Africa did better than the average for all developing countries in 1975-1985. However, the situation reversed sharply during the second half of the 1990s. More recent figures show that MVA growth rose from 0.4 percent in 1994 to 1.6 percent in 1995 in Sub-Saharan Africa; the corresponding figures for North Africa were 1.8 and 3.9. In terms of indices (1985=100), African manufacturing production (at 5-year interval) steadily increased from 47 in 1970 to 134 in 1991, dipped to 122 in 1993, and peaked at 144 in 1994. Table 5.3 provides another set of MVA indicators by subregion and by grouping.

TABLE 5.3
PERFORMANCE INDICATORS OF THE MANUFACTURING SECTOR BY
SUBREGION AND BY ECONOMICGROUPING

| Subregion/ economic grouping | % share of MVA in regional MVA | | | % share of MVA i n GDP | | | % MVA growth rate at 1990 prices | | |
|---|---|---|---|---|---|---|---|---|---|
| | 1992 | 1993 | 1994[1] | 1992 | 1993 | 1994 | 1992 | 1993 | 1994 |
| Developing Africa | 65.5 | 65.47 | 65.86 | 12.69 | 12.58 | 12.91 | 1.91 | -0.07 | 5.04 |
| South Africa | 34.5 | 34.53 | 34.14 | 24.29 | 24 | 24.28 | -3.28 | 0.04 | 3.28 |
| Africa | 100 | 100 | 100 | 15.19 | 15.05 | 15.36 | 0.06 | -0.04 | 4.43 |
| North Africa | 40.58 | 41.39 | 42.16 | 15.19 | 15.32 | 15.66 | 4.47 | 1.94 | 6.4 |
| West Africa | 9.34 | 9.22 | 9.56 | 8.05 | 7.64 | 8.11 | 1.4 | -1.3 | 8.35 |
| Eastern and Southern Africa | 44.9 | 44.67 | 44.14 | 19.9 | 19.71 | 19.99 | -2.76 | -0.55 | 3.2 |
| Central Africa | 5.18 | 4.73 | 4.13 | 10.48 | 10.04 | 9.64 | -9.41 | -8.76 | -8.79 |
| LDCs | 9.95 | 9.7 | 9.25 | 9.82 | 9.57 | 9.63 | 0.22 | -2.51 | -0.44 |
| Sub-Saharan Africa | 60.34 | 59.68 | 58.88 | 14.83 | 14.57 | 14.85 | -2.53 | -1.15 | 3.05 |

Source: UNIDO, 1997, *Restructuring Africa's Industrial Sector within the Context of the Abuja Treaty Establishing the African Economic Community and the Subregional and Regional Components of the Second United Nations Industrial Development Decade for Africa* (IDDA II), (CAMI 13/11), Accra.
  1  ECA preliminary estimates

Figure 5.1 compares growth rates of GDP and MVA in Sub-Saharan Africa. It is apparent that the growth of MVA relative to that of GDP was nowhere near that of the region referred to above. With respect to North Africa, the MVA growth rate (6.1%) which was at par with that of GDP in 1979-1980 more than doubled (5.6% against 2.6%) in 1980-1990 and plummeted to about half (1.1% against 2.1%) in 1990-1993, based on rates in the source for Figure 5.1.

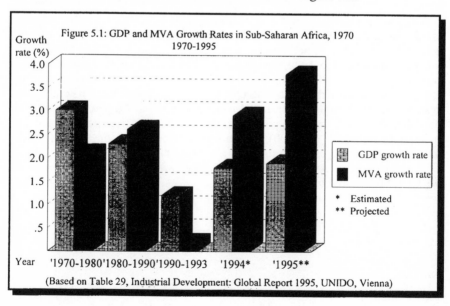

Figure 5.1: GDP and MVA Growth Rates in Sub-Saharan Africa, 1970
1970-1995

(Based on Table 29, Industrial Development: Global Report 1995, UNIDO, Vienna)

Annex 5.13 gives some indications of MVA growth rates at the country level in Sub-Saharan and North African countries. In the 1970s, 16 countries registered annual growth rates higher than 5 percent. Four of them, namely Libya, Nigeria, Tunisia, and Swaziland, surpassed the 10 percent level. By 1994, the number of countries with growth rates in excess of 5 percent marginally increased to 17. Mozambique, Gabon, Malawi, and Botswana exceeded the 10 percent level. The highest rates attained were 13.5 percent (Libya) in the 1970s and 27.3 percent (Mozambique) in 1994. Table 5.4 provides growth rates in selected countries in the second half of the 1980s and the first half of the 1990s.

TABLE 5.4
AVERAGE ANNUAL REAL GROWTH OF MVA IN SELECTED AFRICAN COUNTRIES (%)

| Country | 1985-1990 | 1990-1995 | Country | 1985-1990 | 1990-1995 | Country | 1985-1990 | 1990-1995 |
|---|---|---|---|---|---|---|---|---|
| Algeria | 1.1 | -3.5 | Ethiopia & Eritrea | 3 | 2.7 | Niger | 2.4 | 0.7 |
| Angola | -11.1 | -11.1 | Gabon | -7.2 | -0.2 | Nigeria | 5.2 | -0.3 |
| Benin | 6.2 | 2.9 | Gambia | 5.8 | 1.2 | Reunion | 3.6 | 2.3 |
| Botswana | 15.2 | 2.2 | Ghana | 6.3 | 1.4 | Rwanda | 0.2 | -16.4 |
| Burkina Faso | 0.4 | 2.8 | Guinea | 10.7 | 5.3 | Sao Tome Principe | -4.3 | 5 |
| Burundi | 6.4 | -7.4 | Guinea- Bissau | -7.4 | 0.5 | Senegal | 4.6 | 2.5 |
| Cameroon | 3 | -2.3 | Kenya | 5.8 | 2.3 | Seychelles | 11.2 | 0.2 |
| Cape Verde | 2.3 | 8.7 | Lesotho | 13.9 | 7 | Sierra Leone | -6.4 | 4.4 |
| Central Africa Republic | 3.9 | -0.2 | Liberia | 2.5 | 3.2 | Somalia | 5.2 | -0.5 |
| Chad | -2.2 | -0.9 | Libya | 3.5 | 8.7 | Sudan | -0.1 | 3.8 |
| Comoros | 0.1 | 3.9 | Madagascar | 1.5 | 0.7 | Swaziland | 8.4 | 3.7 |
| Congo | -3.3 | -5.2 | Malawi | 5 | -0.5 | Togo | 4.5 | -6.2 |
| Congo K | -2.5 | -10.7 | Mali | 4.7 | 4.5 | Tunisia | 4.9 | 5.7 |
| Cote d'Ivoire | -4.9 | 3.5 | Mauritania | 1.2 | 1.6 | Uganda | 8.7 | 12.9 |
| Djibouti | 4 | 2 | Mauritius | 10.4 | 5.2 | Tanzania | 3.6 | 3.6 |
| Egypt | 5 | 0.1 | Morocco | 3.9 | 1.6 | Zambia | 3.5 | -1 |
| Equatorial Guinea | -8.5 | 7.4 | Namibia | 5.8 | 8.2 | Zimbabwe | 5.2 | -3.4 |

Source: UNIDO, 1997, "Industrial Indicators," *Industrial Africa*, October 1997, Vienna.

The decline in manufacturing performance in the second half of the 1970s continued into the 1980s. Although indices (1980 =100) of total MVA at constant 1980 prices showed an upward trend for Africa and its LDCs with stagnation in Sub-Saharan Africa in 1981-1987 this was not the case with per capita MVA (see Annex 5.7). The latter was erratic for Africa and attained a maximum index of 110 in 1988. It was worse in African LDCs whose indices declined from 95 in 1981 to 90 in 1990 and contrasted with that of all LDCs which fared better.

There is a dearth of information on the ratio of value added to gross value of production, value added per person engaged, etc. The ratios for manufacturing in Ethiopia may give some indications of what the picture could look like in African countries with similar conditions and resource endowment. During the 1991/92-1995/96 period, the value addded/gross value ratio increased from 19.1 percent in 1991/92 to 29.6 percent in 1993/94 and fell to 27.5 percent in 1995/96. Wood and wood products, except furniture (48.2%), machinery and equipment (36.7%), paper and paper products and printing (36.3%), other non-metallic products (36.1%), tobacco products (31.5%), and food products and beverages (30.1%) were among the product groups registering ratios of over 30 percent in 1995/96. In regard to value added per person (labor productivity) it surged steadily from Birr 4,067 in 1991/92 to Birr 17,476 in 1995/96 (Central Statistical Authority, 1997).

As for trade, export growth rates of all commodities in Africa were considerably higher than imports (5.5% against 3.4%) in 1975-1985, but changed to 2 percent and 7 percent, respectively, during the second half of the 1990s. Increases in the export of manufactures, however, averaged 19.7 percent in 1985-1990, the highest average achieved (apparently because of low initial base).

African trade performance in the period 1970-1990 in a global development context confirms the above gloomy picture (Annex 5.18). At current prices, its share of world exports declined to 2.0 percent in 1990 from a peak of 4.7 percent in 1980. The fate of imports was similar, falling to 2.1 percent in 1990 from a peak of 4.2 percent in 1975. One of the major reasons for this state of affairs is obviously the inordinately low level of manufacturing, and therefore the low level of contribution of manufacturing to exports. This is reflected in the figures for Africa's share in the exports of manufactures for all developing countries; it fell drastically from 8.3 percent in 1970 to 2.5 percent in 1990.

### •Contribution of MVA to the Economy

Manufacturing value-added (MVA) in Africa rose steadily over the period 1970-1993. It grew by a factor of 2.6 to $42.8 billion at constant factor cost (1985). It apparently performed better than industry with a factor of 1.49 [ADB, African Development Report 1994].

The contributions of manufacturing to economic sectors and activities provides an indication of manufacturing performance. Annex 5.18 contains a number of ratios relating MVA to such sectors and activities, as well as shares by manufacturing branch and country group.

The contribution of MVA to GDP increased from 6.0 percent in 1960 to about 7.2 percent in 1972 and rose to about 8.0 percent at constant factor cost during 1975-1976 (UNIDO, *Integrated Industrial... Subregion*). According to annex 5.18, MVA at constant 1980 prices increased steadily from 7.5 percent in 1975 to 9.7 percent in 1990 (decreased from 9.4% to 8.7% for African LDCs). The corresponding figures for all developing countries were 16.9 and 20.2. These figures show that African MVA share in GDP was less than half that of all developing countries. A more recent source (UNIDO, *International Yearbook of Industrial Statistics* 1997) shows that at constant 1990 prices, it rose from 9.9 percent in 1980 to a peak of 11.6 percent in 1990 and remained stagnant at 11.4 percent up to 1994.

The share of MVA in GDP at constant 1980 prices in North Africa increased from 9.0 percent in 1975 to 11.7 percent in 1990. The corresponding figures for Sub-Saharan Africa were 6.9 and 8.3 and for African LDCs 9.4 and 8.7 (Annex 5.18). Four countries achieved over 20 percent MVA/GDP ratios in 1990: Zambia (26.2%), Zimbabwe (24.2%), Swaziland (23.5%), and Mauritius (23.5%). Eighteen countries had ratios ranging between 10 percent and 20 percent while 23 countries displayed negative rates (UNIDO, *African Industry in Figures 1993*). Table 5.5 compares share of industry and manufacturing by subregion and by leading countries in 1992.

| | | | TABLE 5.5 | | |
|---|---|---|---|---|---|
| SHARE OF INDUSTRY AND MANUFACTURING IN GDP, 1992 (percent) | | | | | |
| Subregion | Industry total | Manufactu r     -ing | Leading countries | Industry total | Manufactu r-ing |
| South Africa | 40 | 18 | South Africa | 34.5 | 24.9 |
| | | | Zimbabwe | 41.8 | 28.8 |
| | | | Zambia | 51.2 | 38.2 |
| North Africa | 35.4 | 12.6 | Algeria | 52.1 | 11.8 |
| | | | Egypt | 31.3 | 11.7 |
| | | | Morocco | 34.2 | 17.7 |
| East Africa | 19 | 9.9 | Mozambi-que | 42.8 | 24.7 |
| | | | Mauritius | 33.5 | 23.5 |
| | | | Kenya | 21.7 | 11.7 |
| West Africa | 22.3 | 8.9 | Nigeria | 29 | 10.2 |
| | | | Ghana | 16.6 | 11.2 |
| | | | Cote d'Ivoire | 21.6 | 13.6 |
| Central Africa | 24.6 | 8.3 | Cameroon | 33 | 13.8 |
| | | | Congo K | 313 | 1.4 |
| | | | Gabon | 50.3 | 7.4 |

Source: ECA/UNIDO, 1995, *Report on Regional Strategy for Rational Location of Industries in the Context of the Abuja Treaty*, Gaborone.

Table 5.6 supplements Table 5.5. Although there may  perhaps be some omissions, it nevertheless gives a general  idea about the concentration of industries at the subsector and national and subregional levels.

TABLE 5.6
SUBREGIONS AND COUNTRIES WITH MAJOR CONCENTRATION OF INDUSTRIES IN AFRICA

| Subregion/ industrial subsector | Mining industries | Chemical industries | Metal industries | Engineering industries | Building materials industries | Agro-based and food industries | Energy and fuel production | Transport infrastructure |
|---|---|---|---|---|---|---|---|---|
| North Africa | Algeria Egypt Libya Morocco Tunisia | Algeria Egypt Libya Morocco Tunisia | Algeria Egypt Libya Tunisia | Algeria Egypt Morocco Tunisia | Algeria Egypt Libya Morocco Tunisia | Egypt Morocco Sudan | Algeria Egypt Libya Morocco Tunisia | Algeria Egypt Libya Morocco Tunisia Sudan |
| Southern Africa | South Africa Botswana Namibia Zambia Zimbabwe | South Africa Zimbabwe Zambia | South Africa Zambia Zimbabwe | South Africa Zambia Zimbabwe | South Africa Zimbabwe | South Africa Zimbabwe Namibia Swaziland | South Africa Botswana Swaziland Zambia Zimbabwe | South Africa Zambia Zimbabwe |
| West Africa | Ghana Guinea Liberia Mauritania Niger | Nigeria Senegal Cote d'Ivoire | Nigeria Ghana | Nigeria Ghana Cote d'Ivoire | Nigeria | Nigeria Cote d' Ivoire Ghana Senegal | Nigeria Benin Cote d'Ivoire Ghana Niger Senegal | Nigeria Ghana |
| Central Africa | Angola Cameroon Gabon Congo K | - | Cameroon | - | Angola | Cameroon Congo K | Angola Congo Gabon Congo K | Angola Cameroon Congo K |
| East Africa | - | Mauritius Tanzania Kenya | Kenya | Kenya | Kenya | Kenya Uganda Tanzania Madagascar Malawi Mauritius | Kenya Malawi Mozambique | Kenya Tanzania Madagascar Mozambique |

Source: ECA/UNIDO, 1995, *Report on Regional Strategy for Rational Location of Industries in the Context of the Abuja Treaty*, Gaborone.

The share of industry groups in total MVA shows that consumer non-durables in the end-use group accounted for over 58 percent compared with a little over 40 percent in Latin America and South and East Asia in 1980 and 1987. In the factor intensity group, capital-intensive industries led the way, with 43.5 percent in 1980 and 42.2 percent in 1990. It is interesting to note here that the share of capital-intensive industries in the factor intensity group for the rest of the world, including the developed market economies, was practically the same as for Africa. This may be partly explained by the fact that, being dependent on technologies from developed countries, developing countries have no option but to use the same technologies as the developed countries. The contribution of resource-based industries grew from 26.9 percent in 1975 to 29.5 percent in 1990.

As for Africa's share in world manufacturing value added, it increased from 0.4 percent in the 1960s to about 0.5 percent in 1970 (*UNIDO, Integrated Industrial... Subregion*). It slowly rose to 1.0 percent in 1982 and hovered around 0.9-1.0 percent up to 1990 while that of the African LDCs declined from a meagre 0.2 percent to 0.1 percent during the 1970s and 1980s (Annex 5.18). Another source (ECA/UNIDO, CAMI.12/5(b)/Rev.1) shows that the regional share declined to 0.8 percent in 1994. A more recent source shows that Africa's share, at constant 1990 prices, stagnated at 0.9 percent in 1985 and during the first half of the 1990s. According to the targets set in IDDA I, Africa's share in world MVA was supposed to have attained 1.0 percent in 1990 (2 % in 2000). It should be noted here that the share of developing countries as a group increased steadily from 8.6 percent in the 1960s to 16 percent in 1990. The 1987 shares of the other developing regions were 6.1 percent for Latin America, 5.4 percent for South and East Asia and 1.8 percent for West Asia and Europe. The shares of the last two grew by 100 percent and 50 percent respectively during the 1970-1987 period

(UNIDO, *African Industry in Figures 1993*). African MVA shares in world MVA are compared with those of other developing countries in Figure 5.2.

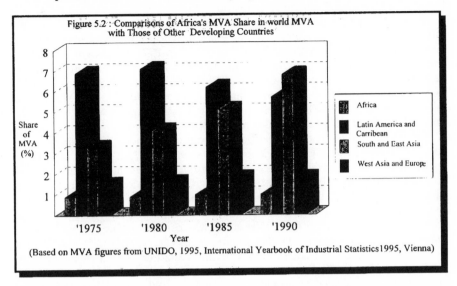

Figure 5.2 : Comparisons of Africa's MVA Share in world MVA with Those of Other Developing Countries

(Based on MVA figures from UNIDO, 1995, International Yearbook of Industrial Statistics 1995, Vienna)

With respect to Africa's share in the MVA of developing countries, it seems that, on the basis of latest information, it reached its peak of 6.7 percent in 1985 and steadily decreased to 5.6 percent in 1994, i.e., at constant 1990 prices.

Algeria, Egypt, Morocco, and Nigeria accounted for about 13.0 percent each of African MVA in 1990. Their combined share worked out to 53.9 percent. Tunisia, Zimbabwe, Libya, Cameroon, Kenya, and Cote d'Ivoire each displayed a share exceeding 3.0 percent. With a few exceptions, including Zimbabwe whose share was higher in 1975, the same countries were dominant in 1975. Algeria, Egypt and Nigeria increased their shares in 1990 (UNIDO, *African Industry in Figures 1993*).

### •Structure of MVA

The structure of MVA, share of Africa in world MVA, and share of selected country groups in MVA of Africa at branch level, at constant 1980 prices, are detailed in Annex 5.19. Food, textile, beverage, other chemicals, and petroleum refining constituted the major industries, each accounting for at least 5 percent of MVA. The same industries, with the exception of other chemicals, each contributed in excess of 2 percent to world MVA. Comparison of columns under "North Africa" and "African LDCs" clearly shows that the former accounts for disproportionate share in all branches except textiles. The leadership of North Africa in manufacturing is confirmed by its lion's share of total MVA which increased from 39.7 percent in 1970 to 50.1 percent in 1990. The opposite was the case in respect of Sub-Saharan Africa and African LDCs. Sub-Sahara African share in world MVA rose from 0.20 in 1970 to 0.30 percent in both 1980 and 1990 and grew at averages of 6.0 and 1.8 percent in 1970-1980 and 1980-1990, respectively (UNIDO, *Industry and Development: Global Report 1993/94*). From statistics for recent years (1985 and 1993) at constant 1990 prices, it appears that there has been some structural change: increase in the share of beverages, tobacco, wearing apparel, footwear, and petroleum refining industries, and reduction in food, textile, and other chemical industries.

In addition to growth rates, Annex 5.18 deals with trade-related shares and ratios. According to the annex African share in world imports of manufactured goods at current prices declined from 5.4 percent in 1975 to 2.1 percent in 1990, whereas exports stagnated at 0.4 percent. In terms of share in imports of all developing countries, Africa's share dwindled from a high of 19.7 percent in 1975 to 10.4 percent in 1990. The fate of import of manufactured goods was worse, falling from 22.1 to 9.9. The corresponding figures for exports were 16.7 and 9.2 for total exports and 5.2 and 2.5 for manufactured goods.

Manufactured goods dominate in the structure of imports. Their share in imports, at current prices, fell to 69.3 percent in 1990 from 73.0 percent in 1975. In regard to exports, mineral fuels accounted for over 60 percent and manufactured goods share tripled to 15.1 percent. Mauritius, Cote d'Ivoire and Zimbabwe contributed about half of the 1989 exports of manufactures of Sub-Saharan Africa. At current prices, export of African manufactures increased by an average of 16.34 percent per year in the 1970s and 9.82 percent in the 1980s (UNIDO, *Industry and Development : Global Report 1993/94*).

In terms of share of trade of all developing countries, Africa lags behind. Its 1975 import share of 21.1 percent of manufactured goods declined to 13.3 percent in 1985 and deteriorated further to 9.9 percent in 1990. Something similar happened to exports with 5.2, 2.6 and 2.5 as the corresponding figures.

It is not possible nor desirable to refer to all the indicators in the annexes. The figures cited above would suffice to give some indication of the performance of the manufacturing industry and related sectors under African conditions. What most of the indicators show is that the manufacturing industry did not perform satisfactorily during the 1980s for reasons given elsewhere. More details at branch, country, and group of country levels are provided in Annexes 5.8 through 5.12 and Annexes 5.14 through 5.17.

Information available on Eastern and Southern Africa (UNIDO, PPD.259 [SPEC]) gives some indication of the performance of the manufacturing industry at the subregional level. MVA accounted for about 30 percent of gross output during the 1980-1990 period. Burundi, Ethiopia, Zimbabwe, and Madagascar were the only countries that achieved over 40 percent and Kenya the lowest (12.9%) value added in 1990. In 1990, manufacturing value added averaged about 11.7 percent of GDP and ranged between 4 percent in Comoros and 26.4 percent in Zimbabwe. The low share is a manifestation of the very low level of industrialization of the subregion. The same conclusion applies in regard to rate of growth of manufacturing. It was 3.4 percent in 1980, 0.78 percent in 1985 and 3.5 percent in 1990. With respect to the structure of the manufacturing industry, food, beverages, and tobacco took the lead, contributing 48.9 percent of manufacturing value added. This was followed by textiles, wearing apparel, and leather (17.2%) and by chemicals, petroleum, rubber, and plastics (10.0%). From these it is apparent that agro-based industries, accounting for close to two-thirds of manufacturing value added, dominate the industry in the subregion. (Refer to annexes 5.8, 5.9, 5.11-5.17 and 5.19 for more analysis on the performance of the manufacturing industry.

## •Employment in Manufacturing

In regard to employment, the manufacturing sector has not been a big employer. Nor was its contribution to the growth of the labor force. Whereas in the 1980s total labor force increased by an average of 3 percent per year, that of manufacturing grew by only 1 percent per year (ECA/UNIDO, CAMI.12/9).

In 29 countries in tropical Africa, manufacturing employment increased from 1.55 million in 1980 to 1.76 million in 1990. Labor productivity ranged between $1,281 in Lesotho and $21,364 in Burundi and wage per worker between $774 in Somalia and $6,679 in Cote d'Ivoire in 1990 (UNIDO, *Industry and Development: Global Report 1992/93*). Labor productivity and wage per worker as percentage of North American level[5] for the 29 countries and North African and Western Asian countries in constant 1985 dollars are shown in Annex 5.20. From the total, it is apparent that both labor productivity and wage per worker were low and declining during the 1970s and 1980s. In 1990, a job done by one American required about 10 Africans, each earning a wage of 8.7 percent of that of an American. This is probably exaggerated, as in many countries public enterprises are usually overmanned. In any case, such gap in productivity and widening wage differential offer opportunities to be exploited by investors.

This chapter may be concluded with a positive note. If the performance of manufacturing in recent years is an indication of the future, Africa seems to be poised to make positive changes in industrial development. According to UNIDO's baseline scenario, world GDP growth rate will increase from 1.9 percent in 1990-1995 to 2.9 and 3.2 percent in 1995-2000 and 2000-2005, respectively. The scenario applying to tropical Africa and the manufacturing indicators expected to result thereof are shown in Table 5.7.

| TABLE 5.7 PROJECTED GDP AND MANUFACTURING INDICATORS IN TROPICAL AFRICA (%) | | | |
|---|---|---|---|
| | 1990-1995 | 1995-2000 | 2000-2005 |
| GDP growth rates | 3.1 | 2.9 | 3.1 |
| Shares in global GDP | 0.8 | 0.8 | 0.7 |
| Growth rates of MVA | 0.1 | 3.3 | 3.5 |
| Share in global MVA | 0.3 | 0.3 | 0.3 |
| Shares of MVA in GDP | 9.5 | 10.1 | 10.8 |
| Share in global manufactured exports | 0.3 | 0.3 | 0.3 |
| Source: UNIDO, 1996, The *Globalization of Industry: Implications for Developing Countries beyond 2000*, Vienna. | | | |

## BIBLIOGRAPHY

ADB, 1994, *African Development Report 1994*, Abidjan.

Bailey, Richard, 1976, *Africa's Industrial Future*, Davison Publishing Limited, Bland ford, U.K.

Central Statistical Authority (Ethiopia), 1997, "Report on Large and Medium Manufacturing and Electricity Industries Survey," *Statistical Bulletin 178,* October 1997, Addis Ababa.

de Kun, N., 1987, *Mineral Economics of Africa,* Elsevier Science Publisher B.V., Amsterdam.

ECA/UNIDO, 1995, *Development of Human Resources for Industrialization in Africa* (CAMI.12/9], Addis Ababa.

ECA/UNIDO, 1995, *Progress Report on the Implementation of the Program for the Second IDDA: (b) Joint Secretariat Report* (CAMI.12/5[b])/Rev.1), Addis Ababa.

ECA/UNIDO, 1995, *Report on Regional Strategy for Rational Location of Industries in the Context of the Abuja Treaty* ( CAMI.12/6[a]), Gaborone.

Meier, Gerald M., William F. Steel, eds., 1989, *Industrial Adjustment in Sub-Saharan Africa,* EDI Series in Economic Development, Published for The World Bank, Oxford University Press, New York.

Schmidt, Peter R., editor, 1996, *The Culture and Technology of African Iron Production,* University Press of Florida.

UNIDO, 1991, *Integrated Industrial Sector Program for the Eastern and Southern African Subregion,* prepared by the intergovernmental organizations in the subregion with the assistance of UNIDO, Nairobi.

UNIDO, 1993, *Industry and Development: Global Report 1992/93,* Vienna.

UNIDO, 1993, *Industry and Development: Global Report 1993/94,* Vienna.

UNIDO, 1993, *Implementation of the Subregional Program for the Second IDDA for Eastern and Southern Africa* (PPD.259 [SPEC]), Vienna.

UNIDO, 1994, *African Industry in Figures 1993,* Vienna.

UNIDO, 1997, *International Yearbook of Industrial Statistics 1997,* Vienna.

UNIDO, 1997, "Is Africa Ready for the Big Leap?," *Industrial Africa,* October 1997, Vienna.

UNIDO, 1998, "Sub-Saharan Africa: Encouraging Performance," *Industrial Africa,* No. 5, September 1998, Vienna.

# NOTES

1. Refer to Chapters 8 to13 for supplementary information on manufacturing.
2. A book titled "The Culture and Technology of African Iron Production."
3. Part of the information on iron is from  Robert Stock (1995), *Africa South of the Sahara: a Geographical Interpretation,* The Guilford Press, London.
4. This section is based mainly on Annexes 5.7 through 5.19.
5. According to an article "America's Power Plants," in *The Economist* (June 8, 1996), the United States of America leads the world in productivity in both capital and labor. This is contrary to those who think that Germany and Japan are ahead of the former.

CHAPTER 6

# PROGRESS IN LESSENING
# INDUSTRIAL CONSTRAINTS

The decision to implement an industrial project is taken after carefully analyzing the political, technical, financial, and commercial risks. In developed countries, the first and, to some extent, the second categories of risks are not that significant. Generally, all four risks could be crucial in developing countries, with varying degrees of significance, depending on the type of industrial project concerned.

In their efforts to industrialize and compress the time period required to follow the stages of industrializtion during the 19$^{th}$ and 20$^{th}$ centuries in developed countries, i.e., taking shortcuts towards development, African countries have had to face and still face innumerable constraints. Some of the constraints are internal, partly of their own making. Others are external, imposed on them by the outside world. This chapter tries to highlight the major constraints, many of which are due to the fragmentation of the continent into many mini-states. It also points out some of the attempts made to remedy them.

From the outset, an attempt has been made in this chapter to give a comprehensive picture of constraints at the time of independence in the 1960s and soon after, when capacities and capabilities were virtually non-existent. Different combinations of these constraints have impacted African countries at different points in time. Many of them still persist today at different levels of significance.

The relatively detailed presentation of factors inhibiting African industrialization is not intended to scare away the reader. On the contrary, it is meant to help the reader appreciate the multiple difficulties African countries have had to face in order to reach their present level of development. So much has changed in the interim period that most of the constraints are no longer as crucial as they were. Several of them would have even been less severe had it not been for the need to shift from long-term development to short-term stabilization because of political, economic, financial, and social crises that most of the countries have been confronting for over two decades.

The combination of major constraints and their impact varies from country to country. Whereas many African countries have managed and are managing to minimize many of the constraints, some constraints are worsening. Inadequate and decreasing investment flows and increasing competition among developing countries for foreign investment and markets are examples of the latter.

In this chapter, the first section identifies the major constraints. The second gives an indication of progress made to remove and minimize many of the constraints as well as trends towards better ways of doing things. The third focuses on measures being undertaken to attract foreign direct investment.

## CONSTRAINTS ON INDUSTRY

In the 1960s, following independence, many African countries rushed to set up import-substitution industries, mainly producing consumer goods. Given the condition at the time, this strategy, a relatively easy one to adopt, was probably the only feasible alternative. Both public and private production units were established. In the virtual absence of indigenous private industrial entrepreneurs, managers, and expertise, the former were meant to create capacities, including those considered strategic, and reduce increasing reliance on external inputs. The latter, mainly owned by foreign trading companies/suppliers of manufactures, were generally intended to protect their market shares. As a result, in Sub-Saharan Africa, industrial production grew at an average growth rate of 14.6 percent during 1965-1973 as compared with 6.6 percent for GDP. This high rate shrank to 1.4 percent in 1973-1983 while GDP fell to 2.1 (Meier et. al. 1989). Such drastic falls were interpreted as indicating the unsustainability of such a high rate of industrial growth and " the inability of African economies to adapt to changing conditions and external shocks." Although there is no denying this fact, it should be noted that owing to the very low industrial production base in mid-1960s, maintenance of the high rate could not have been expected; it was bound to decline with time. Unfortunately, the decline was precipitated, enhanced, and exacerbated by the 1973 and subsequent oil and many other crises, spiraling prices for manufactures, dwindling prices of African export commodities, and escalating tariff and nontariff barriers imposed by developed countries on African processed goods.

Low productivity and high costs, hence non-competitiveness, characterize African industry. Combinations of constraining factors, both internal and external, have contributed to Africa's predicament. A World Bank assessment that *"Africa's investment and operating costs are typically 50 to 100 percent above those in South Asia"* (World Bank, *Sub-Saharan Africa ...*) encapsulates the negative impact of the above constraints on African development. The high costs of investment and production are partly due to high transport cost, while additional investment is required to supplement other inadequate infrastructure, including utilities, and the high cost of labor arising from the use of expensive foreign experts and consultants. To be quite fair, one should note that the term "high cost" does not apply to all industries under all circumstances. In 1988-1989, the total production cost index (average=100) of aluminum in developing Africa, for example, was 97 compared with over 100 for Asian and most developed countries (UNIDO, *Industry and Development, Global Report 1992/93*). A similar conclusion can be drawn for the performance of the textile industry that is characterized by obsolete equipment in some African countries. Based on a 1.0 relative total factor productivity (RTFP) for textile mills with "best practices" in the United Kingdom, the RTFPs for spinning were 0.66 in Kenya in 1980 and 0.79 in Zimbabwe in 1985. Taking the time factor into account these figures are not likely to be very different from the 0.65 (India) and 0.60 (Pakistan) for spinning in 1967, (World Bank, *The Long-Term Perspective Study of Sub-Saharan Africa*).

High cost of production implies low profitability. This may not be the case under all circumstances. Take Lonrho, the transnational corporation in Africa, for example. *"Although Africa south of the Sahara accounted for only 18 percent of Lonrho's gross sales during 1985 to 1988, it provided half of its pretax profits"*

(Stock 1995). Despite the advantages it derives from its bigness and ubiquitous presence in Africa, such a high magnitude of profit margin is an indication that the alleged high cost of production may not be such a great deterrent after all.

The constraints dealt with in this chapter are grouped into four categories: adverse physical and climatic conditions, leadership crisis, inadequate industrial capacity, and industrial pollution. Most are internal, many of which can be and are controlled and improved by the host countries. Many are exogenous and are dependent on the vagaries of world economic conditions and market manipulations. Because of its underdevelopment and high dependency on the outside world, Africa is probably the most adversely affected continent in the world. The slightest economic crisis in developed countries bears repercussions that would not be felt in other developing regions. Thus, when the developed countires sneeze, African countries catch devastating cold. The opposite is the case in regard to good economic performance of developed market economies. When the developed countries' GDP growth rates tripled from 1.0 percent in 1993 to 2.9 percent in 1994, the rates for Sub-Saharan Africa and North Africa were 1.2 to 1.8 and 0.2 to 2.1, respectively. The corresponding figures for MVA were 4.4 to 5.3, -1.1 to 2.9 and -0.4 to 2.9 (UNIDO, *Industrial Development, Global Report 1995*).

**Adverse Physical and Climatic Conditions and Inadequate Infrastructure**
The physical features of the region vary significantly from area to area. Rugged (with steep slope exceeding 30 percent) areas are fragile and prone to degradation under population pressure, resulting in falling agricultural yield. Rough terrain means higher investment in plant and related support facilities. The same applies to the development of infrastructure which is compounded by low population density. Most African rivers are generally not navigable on part of their courses characterized as they are by rapids and falls. Road transport accounts for over 80 percent of freight and passenger movements. Given the lack of interconnections between the various railway systems, partly due to different gauges and their port-interior orientation, railways make a relatively low contribution to transport in Africa. In the northern part of the region, the Sahara desert effectively cuts off North Africa from the rest of the region.

The above constraints are compounded by disadvantages inherent in tropical climate (dense forests and swamps) characterized by pest and disease infestation on the one hand and dry and desert areas on the other. As if these were not enough, many countries suffer from very fixed dry and wet seasons characterized by erratic rainfall, and natural disasters. Recurrent drought, disruption of ecological balance, and fast growing desertification (due to felling of trees for fuel, overcropping, overgrazing, and deterioration of water resources) with destructive consequences on the rich African biodiversity are adversely affecting African industrial development. Many countries are in the process of addressing some of these problems.

Drought has become a permanent feature, a recurrent phenomenon of varying degree and frequency. More and more areas and countries are coming under its grip. In addition to the regional drought phenomena, Africa, as happened in 1997, suffers from the El Nino phenomenon which brought both drought and untimely rains and floods. In 1997, the United Nations established a task force to facilitate collaboration among countries in preventing and mitigating natural disasters related to El Nino and to coordinate follow-up actions. Under African conditions, poverty contributes the most to environmental degradation and therefore to drought from deforestation for fuelwood and farming, and overgrazing.

## Leadership Crisis

Although not generally given its due share, lack of good leadership is one, if not the most, crucial constraint. Thanks to dedicated and committed leadership with long-term vision, some relatively poor countries outside Africa, less endowed with natural resources, are now successfully competing with the developed world even though they used to be worse off than many African countries 3 or 4 decades ago. From World Bank (*The State in a Changing World*) information, policies, state size and capacity and unexplained factors, each accounted for about a third of the per capita GDP (more than five times those in Sub-Saharan Africa) increase of the East Asians in 1992 over 1964. The contribution of good governance is apparent.

A negligible number of the African leaders with good intentions emerged following independence in the 1960s. The majority of the leadership comprised incompetent and corrupt dictators. Many of them had an inadequate educational background. They seized power at gunpoint through coup d'etats and counter coups, made use of divide-and-rule tactics, and exposed their peoples to wars, ethnic and religious conflicts, and famines and condemned them to life on the run as refugees.

Practically everything they did revolved around consolidating their own power, no matter what it cost the nation and the people. Most of those countries' meagre resources were used to enrich their leaders and their cronies and surround them with costly security systems. They became millionaires overnight with accounts in foreign banks, while the taxpayers they ruled suffered from poverty and dictatorship. Resources from the national treasuries, which should have been invested in development to improve the standard of living, were squandered, leaving their subjects even poorer.

African leaders of the 1960s, for the most part, made decisions on the basis of their own whims. They did not want to relinquish power; they wanted to die as presidents, kings, and emperors. Many of them were toppled by others who in turn went through the same routine of consolidating power and enriching themselves and their cronies. They were, unfortunately, tolerated and even encouraged by the West, even to the extent of using foreign aid for personal purposes, in the attempt to prevent communism from taking hold in Africa.

With such people at the helm, it was inevitable that incompetency, inefficiency, corruption, bribery, embezzlement, and nepotism would run rampant, permeating the government all the way down to the lowest strata of the bureaucracy (messengers, doormen, and guards). Conforming to such a system of "corruption culture" was the best route to rising up the ladder of bureaucratic officialdom. This had a deleterious effect on many of the so-called "young educated Africans" who traded principles for political and economic gains and in the process degraded themselves. Most of them ended up comforming to the corrupt system, became bad models for their peoples, and exploited the very people, most of them illiterate, who paid the very taxes used for their education. As Prime Minister Meles of Ethiopia noted, many of the current owners (former government officials and private people) of wealth and businesses in the private sector owe their wealth to looting government treasuries, both directly and indirectly.

Economic and technical institutions were headed and staffed by political appointees. The bureaucrats, the so-called civil servants, were there to be served rather than to serve the people. It is apparent from this why Africa failed to develop and is in its present pathetic predicament of depending upon the generosity of those countries fortunate enough to have had good leadership.

Many countries in Africa, partly as a result of their colonial legacy and partly because of lack of good leadership, still suffer political instability. Whatever administrative and development policies and strategies the leadership formulated, they were usually inappropriate and inadequate. So were the objectives, which, by their very public nature, were multiple and therefore rather difficult to implement. Implementing projects and programs was exacerbated by conflicting objectives, mainly emanating from influential ethnic groups, politicians, and other interest groups.

Misguided policies and discriminatory practices which worked (and continue to work) against industrialization were not uncommon. For example, levying higher duties on intermediates than on finished imported products, the same as or similar to those locally made from the intermediates, obviously discourages the local manufacture of products using imported intermediates. In countries where those levies still exist, such anomalies need to be corrected immediately.

Obviously, the other constraints dealt with hereunder, as difficult as they are to manage on their own, become more so with bad leadership. Herein lies the critical role of bad leadership.

## Inadequate Industrial Capacity[1]

Rapid population growth, high rate of urbanization, and low and declining GDP per capita are among the factors characterizing the low level of economic development of Africa. By far, the small and fragmented national market resulting from small population and low and declining per capita GDP and therefore declining consumers' purchasing power is the single most important constraint in this category. It is exacerbated by grants and aid in kind (such as fertilizers in countries producing fertilizers).

The majority of countries in the region have populations of less than 10 million, most of them with very low purchasing power. In other words, the total national demand for many industrial products is small, usually equivalent to that of a single city or town in a developed country, and therefore insufficient to sustain modern viable industries characterized by economies of scale. This is compounded by the virtual absence or inadequate use or outlet for co- and/or by-products. When it comes to expanding existing capacity (since expansion in process industries can only be done in discrete stages), expansion becomes impractical, as the additional capacity results in excess capacity. The alternative to expansion (i.e., continuing with existing capacity) would mean supplementing demand through import and therefore raising the import bill until such a time as expansion is justified in terms of local market absorption.

For engineering products, the situation is even worse. Vehicles are a case in point. The proliferation of makes and models of vehicles in use in African countries, worsening with new imports from NICs, is staggering. In most countries it is virtually impossible to operate a vehicle assembly plant, let alone managing its manufacturing. Maintaining an inventory of spare parts for a myriad of makes and models is very expensive and ties up large amounts of capital, which African countries cannot afford.

Skilled manpower, albeit to a lesser extent, continues to be a limiting factor in industrial development. The term "manpower" here is used in an all-inclusive sense and includes skills in industrial planning, research and development, training, and all investment phases (pre-investment, investment, and operation), all essential for sustainable economic growth and development. In terms of professions, it means planners, analysts, engineers, technicians, managers, factory operators, entrepreneurs, etc. Insufficient modern indigenous entrepreneurs to undertake major investments, deficiencies in project identification and preparation, long delays (5 to 10 years in executing projects, resulting in higher investment costs), insufficient consulting services and construction companies, high downtime due to frequent breakdowns, low productivity, very low capacity utilization (25-40%), poor management, high cost of expatriate management and technicians, and relatively high cost of local labor (in the presence of a high and growing unemployment rate) relative to productivity compared with those in Asia—all these point up the inadequacy of skilled manpower. The relatively high salaries and wages, legacies of colonialism, have fallen and continue to fall in real terms because of high inflation and devaluation. In fact, remunerations in most countries nowadays fall far short in meeting the minimum financial needs of employees thereby contributing to rampant corruption. Other indicators include: weak or absent capabilities in product, equipment and process design and in standardization, selection, adoption, adaptation, and innovation of technology; as well as the brain drain occasioned by political instability, low salaries, and lack of local opportunities to use skills. Existing skilled manpower is further handicapped by limited access to technological, industrial, and commercial information. With the trend in the exponential growth of information and knowledge, access to and handling of information is likely to prove intractable.

Following independence, African countries were completely at the mercy of foreign advisors and expatriate vendors of machinery and equipment (usually second-hand) vendors. Some of the advisors were not adequately qualified to render advisory services; others lacked dedication and had their own agendas. As for the vendors, they went from country to country with some kind of model feasibility studies which they modified to reflect some of the local conditions but designed them to appear viable and profitable. In one of his missions to Eastern and Southern African countries in the 1960s, the author of this book saw a feasibility study on the desk of the Permanent Secretary for industry in one of the countries and suggested that he be allowed to take a look at it. The intention was to review it and provide the Permanent Secretary with a feedback on the study. He was told that the study was confidential. The project was implemented and subsequently proved difficult and costly to operate. Fertilizer projects in Kenya and Gabon provide further examples of vendor-promoted projects that, although machinery and equipment were brought to the sites, never took off.

During the colonial era in Africa, business in the modern sense was in the hands of non-Africans. Since independence, African entrepreneurs have been emerging, although not in the number and quality required. One of the reasons for the slow progress in the development of indigenous entrepreneurs is the fact that incentives, if given to local entrepreneurs, were much less than those given to foreign investors. This was even worse when it came to low-level entrepreneurs who by far constitute the largest majority of indigenous entrepreneurs.

Industry is relatively new to most indigenous entrepreneurs, who are active and relatively comfortable in trade, transportation, and real estate. They tend towards businesses that give quick-fix profits or get-rich quick speculative investment rather than productive investment. In recent years in Nigeria, for instance, pre-tax returns on investment were 30 percent for financing, 50 percent for construction, and up to 100 percent for trading (UNIDO, *Industry and Development: Global Report 1993/94*). It is apparent that African entrepreneurs need to be motivated to go into industry, particularly into joint ventures with foreign investors.

As is well known, development in industrialized countries was, until recently characterized by throw-away economy. African countries cannot afford such a system. Of necessity, factories have been using machinery and equipment for longer periods than in developed countries with the consequence that breakdowns are more frequent. Some establishments have been practicing intensive repair and re-use, two of the four Rs (repair, reconditioning, re-use, and recycling). As for the other two, a start has been made at reconditioning and recycling in some countries. Because of limited financial resources, it is possible that all four Rs will be a common practice in Africa in the long run. This may, however, prove difficult as machinery and equipment will contain more and more parts and components that have to be replaced rather than repaired.

Infant industries go through a learning process during which they need to be nurtured, until they develop and mature further. During this process, management and workers accumulate knowledge and working experience, and achieve progress in forms of productivity, consistent product quality, and reduction of loss due to rejects and waste of materials and marketing. All these developments and increases in production over time should progressively lead to lower costs per unit and, hopefully, to international competitiveness. This conclusion is likely to apply also to enterprises supplying inputs and marketing the products, if done through a second party.

Exports could ease national market constraints. However, partly due to inadequate market information and because of protectionism in the form of both tariff and non-tariff barriers, African countries have been finding it difficult to export their manufactured products. The system of "tariff escalation" adopted by developed countries means that import taxes increase as the degree of processing increases (expected to improve with the reduction of tariff escalation based on the Uruguay Round package of trade reforms). This is compounded by ocean freight rates that also escalate with the degree of processing making it more expensive to export African manufactures. Besides, African exports are burdened by higher freight rates, about 20 percent higher than those from other regions. Net freight and insurance payments were estimated to account for about 15 percent of Sub-Saharan Africa's export earnings in 1990/1991(UNIDO, *The Globalization of Industry: Implications ...* ). This situation is likely to worsen over time as more trading blocs become operational and expand their membership, as recently happened in regard to ASEAN which in 1997 admitted Burma, Cambodia, and Laos as members. The markets of the regional trading blocs will be gradually closed to outside suppliers as more specialized industries are developed to replace imports from outside the exclusive clubs and thus increasingly limit the number and quantities of products that African countries can export to the developed markets, including agricultural products as farm products are subsidized and protected in developed countries. All these constraints amount to telling developing countries, particularly African countries, not to industrialize.

Infrastructure, both physical and institutional, is one of the major industrial constraints. The state of roads, railroads, waterways, ports and harbors, air transport, multimodal transport, and communications and utilities leaves much to be desired. The same applies to institutions. Both types of infrastructure are inadequate and need rehabilitation, upgrading, and expansion. Inter-country and intra-subregional trade in raw materials and intermediate and final products is hampered by inadequate transport and telecommunications networks.

There is a dearth of institutions (inadequate or completely lacking), such as revenue departments, R&D institutions, engineering and design centers, consulting firms and contractors. In many countries, governments, for example, collect a fraction of the taxes. Some governments, such as those in Uganda and Ethiopia, are collecting increasingly higher taxes following the restructuring of their revenue departments. It is apparent that, because of economies of scale and the type and number required, no single country can establish and operate all the types of institutions it needs.

As technologies in the world market are designed for conditions and needs of industrialized countries they are generally inappropriate to the developing countries and consequently difficult and more costly to use. Many of them require adaptation. This coupled with inadequate capability to select technology and hardware and to negotiate their procurement, compounds the problems related to technology. African countries are still exposed to unscrupulous foreign engineering firms and equipment suppliers, many of whom manage to recommend and dump inappropriate, capital-intensive, and obsolete technologies and plants. They have, so far, made relatively limited progress in the sequence of technology development following the experience of other developing countries, particularly the NICs. This involves the adoption, assimilation, and adaptation of purchased technology followed by innovating new appropriate technology.

Technology-related and know-how-related constraints are many and crucial, including access, use, and development. The technological gap between Africa and the rest of the world continues to grow by leaps and bounds. This is likely to aggravate problems related to the acquisition of technology, including sourcing, negotiation, and cost. The skill requirement to acquire and utilize technology is now more complex and at a much higher level than it used to be.

Many technologies are not accessible. Those which are involve many restrictive conditions imposed by suppliers, such as market area restriction and deprivation from sharing the benefits accruing from adapting the technology to, say, new raw materials and climates and improving and updating the technology (including product design) as a result of R&D carried out in relation to a production facility in the host country. Generally, the continued association with the supplier of technology works more in favor of the supplier.

Like the rest of the world, African countries will benefit from the global development of emerging technologies. However, because of inadequate absorptive capacity, difficulties of access to the new technologies, and economies of scale, however, the advantages they derive will be minimal compared with other developing countries. In fact, some of the technologies (micro-electronics, informatics, new materials, and biotechnology), particularly those related to biotechnology and genetic engineering, may not be in the overall interest of Africa, although

Africa would be expected to benefit from them. Likely stagnating or decelerating demand for primary commodities in developed countries (because of substitute and new materials, more efficient processing of raw materials, recycling of used materials, changing patterns of consumption, etc.), advances in technology, and increasing automation as well as high rate of product and technology obsolescence are likely to further erode, directly and indirectly, further the so-called comparative advantage of African countries endowed with agrarian and mineral raw materials and relatively cheap labor. Labor-saving innovations and therefore increasingly capital-intensive machinery and equipment resulting from advances in automation and new technologies are reducing demand for the conventional type of workers (clerical and blue-collar) in developed countries. This does not augur well for developing countries. In fact, it is likely that this will contribute to halting and/or reversing the redeployment of labor-intensive (characterized by lowest-value-added) industries to developing countries, as is already the case with respect to textiles.

Natural resources alone do not explain the development and wealth attained by many relatively natural resource-poor countries, such as Switzerland, Japan, South Korea, Hong Kong, Taiwan, and Thailand. Table 6.1 illustrates that, in addition to the level of scientific and technological development, human and capital resources are becoming increasingly significant. Many natural resource-rich countries have tended to be wasteful (expanding government spending, high corruption, etc.). In short, they have the tendency to squander public financial resources accruing from the export of natural resources. Botswana could be cited as an exemplary exception; it avoided the temptation of expanding government expenditure and managed its financial resources wisely following the huge earning of foreign exchange from mineral exports, particularly during the diamond boom.

| TABLE 6.1 TOP 15 COUNTRIES , RANKED BY WEALTH PER HEAD, 1990 | | | | |
|---|---|---|---|---|
| Country | Wealth, $1000 per head | Source of wealth, % of total | | |
| | | People | Capital assets | Natural resources |
| Australia | 835 | 21 | 7 | 71 |
| Canada | 704 | 22 | 9 | 69 |
| Luxembourg | 658 | 83 | 12 | 4 |
| Switzerland | 647 | 78 | 19 | 3 |
| Japan | 565 | 81 | 18 | 2 |
| Sweden | 496 | 56 | 16 | 29 |
| Iceland | 486 | 23 | 16 | 61 |
| Quater | 473 | 51 | 11 | 39 |
| United Arab Emirates | 471 | 65 | 14 | 21 |
| Denmark | 463 | 76 | 17 | 7 |
| Norway | 424 | 48 | 22 | 30 |
| United States | 421 | 59 | 16 | 25 |
| France | 413 | 77 | 17 | 7 |
| Kuwait | 405 | 62 | 9 | 29 |
| Germany | 399 | 79 | 17 | 4 |

Source: The Economist, 1995, *The Natural Resources Myth*, 23 December - 5 January, 1995 (extracted from World Bank report on environmentally sustainable development).

A relatively high cost of factor inputs contribute to high investment and production cost. This was particularly true for imported inputs, such as expertise, know-how, technology, machinery, equipment, intermediates, and supplies. Capital investment is, for instance, reported to be 25 to 60 percent higher than international standards, and capital and operating costs 50 to 100 percent higher than in South Asia. This is explained, in part, by additional investment incurred in infrastructure. There is a need to delink infrastructure which does not form part of the battery limit of an industrial establishment.

Financing industrial projects is becoming increasingly crucial. This is true in regard to both internal and external sources of funds. In most African countries, domestic capital formation is low as a result of a low level of savings, an obvious consequence of poor living standards. There is a need for a more vigorous mobilization of traditional and informal financial systems: rotating funds, moneylenders, savings clubs, and the like.

The vagaries of world economic and market conditions play havoc with African development. African countries are dependent on export earnings with which they pay for their imports from a limited number of mineral and/or agricultural products. The fluctuating and falling trend in export prices resulting in losses of $5.6 billion in potential export earnings in 1990-1993 (ECA, E/ECA/CM.20/3) and spiraling prices of imports in the 1980s and early 1990s, were among the major external constraints. The generally stagnating world demand for raw materials and the decline in Africa's share of world trade was due partly to technologies using less raw materials (declining intensity of use) but also to more efficient substitutes and recycling. Such unfair international trading system manifested by huge and widening differences between prices of primary commodity exports from developing countries and imports from developed countries of capital, intermediate, and final consumer goods, particularly those made from the very raw materials originating from Africa, contribute to an outflow of surplus capital to industrialized countries. The raw material/intermediate product price gaps can be illustrated by the following examples (basic raw material as percent of intermediate product made from the raw material): 3% bauxite in semi-fabricated aluminum products, 21-30% iron ore and coal in rolled steel, 22-43% natural gas in ammonia, and 31% wood in plywood (Meier et. al. 1989).

The above inequitable and unstable international economic system, which obviously works in favor of the industrialized countries, was and is a bottleneck for development, particularly in the poor non-oil producing countries following the 1973 quadrupling of oil prices. A good part (up to 80 percent of their meagre export earnings in the 1980s) is used to purchase oil and oil products. Whatever is left goes for the purchase of basic necessities, such as pharmaceuticals and fertilizers. There is therefore practically very little left for importing the crucial industrial inputs for operating their industries, let alone for developing capital goods for strengthening and broadening their industrial base. A new world trade order is needed that rewards developing countries with fair prices for their exports and thus reduces their dependence on developed countries. In other words, fair trade—not aid—should eventually be the basis for African development.

Debt burden is another bottleneck. Most African countries are not in position to pay their debts, servicing of which continues to absorb about one-third of the region's total exports. Because of continuing devaluation, repayment of debt in terms of local currency is becoming increasingly difficult. Some of the debts were remissioned and/or rescheduled, yet despite these gestures from the lenders Africa's debt continued to rise and reached $ 344 billion in 1997. It is apparent that rescheduling postpones repayment and inflates the loan by accumulating interest.

Dwindling net capital inflow and worsening competition in attracting investment compound the situation created by falling/stagnating export prices and debt burden. Capital outflow is partly due to over invoicing (including intra-firm) of material inputs, machinery and consultancy and management services as well as underinvoicing of exports. With aid being diverted to Eastern Europe and other areas, Africa is being increasingly marginalized in international economic cooperation. Furthermore, industry has never been a priority area as far as donors are concerned.

Hitherto, aid has played an important role in economic development of many African countries. It is unfortunate that official assistance which is crucial to low-income countries is now declining in real terms or ceasing to grow at all. With this trend and more being directed towards relieving disasters (2 percent five years earlier to around 7 percent in 1994) (*The Economist*, May 7, 1994), it is practically impossible to boost investment through to a point at which growth could become self-sustaining, the ultimate objective of development. According to a study on American aid programs by the Overseas Development Council (ODC), less than $1 per person went to very low-income countries (most of which are in Africa). On the contrary, the corresponding figure for the relatively high-income countries was $ 250 (*The Economist*, May 7, 1994).

With these changing realities at the global level (globalization and liberalization of production and economic relations as well as the growth and expansion of economic blocks in the world), Africa has to come to terms with the emerging new world economic order. This new order came about after many years of hard negotiations and the "final act" of the Uruguay Round Agreement was signed in 1994. Unfortunately, it expects Africa, at the lowest level of development and the most vulnerable to external shocks, to compete on an equal footing with the rest of the world. This is tantamount to forcing a baby to run before crawling — in other words: deindustrialization. An equitable economic order is thus needed to address the predicament of developing countries, particularly African countries.

The World Trade Organization (WTO) which succeeded the General Agreement on Tariff and Trade (GATT) became operational at the beginning of 1995. Although world trade is now expected to increase by at least $ 200 billion annually, a preliminary analysis by ECA (E/ECA/CM.20/31) indicates that Africa will incur a loss of about $ 2.6 billion per year, primarily due to the losses of preferential margins under the Lome Convention (LC) and the General System of Preferences (GSP). Among the anticipated negative impacts of the Uruguay Round Agreement are:

• 50 percent and 80 percent reduced preferences for tropical products under the LC and the GSP, respectively;
• 16 percent and 60 percent fall in preferential margins for natural resource-based African exports under the LC and the GSP, respectively; and
• 5 to 10 percent increase in the prices of food products imported by African countries resulting from reduction of domestic support and export subsidies for agriculture in exporting countries.

The last may prove to be a blessing in disguise as it could stimulate African farmers to produce more.

The implementation of the agreement will be phased. The ten-year grace period granted to developing countries, particularly African countries, is far from adequate and will not enable African countries with very low industrial base to prepare themselves to compete in the world market. The current stiff competition in world market is expected to be aggravated by high compliance costs related to the enforcement of ISO-9000 on quality management system and ISO-14000 (draft) on international environmental management standards as well as eco-labelling. Eco-labelling which currently comprises voluntary individual national schemes in 20 countries is supposed to show that a product is more environmentally friendly than its equivalent. These, coupled with revolutionary technological developments, such as the information super-highway—where African communication (telephone) systems are inadequate—are likely to have adverse effects on African economic conditions and export capabilities. Africa will thus be forced to perpetuate its dependency on the world community. Furthermore, because of stricter enforcement of intellectual property rights, African countries will find it increasingly difficult to undergo the process of learning through copying technology in the same way as Japan and the NICs did in the earlier stages of their development. Imitating know-how and techniques in basic manufacturing is a crucial part of the learning process in technological development (absorption, adaptation, and development).

The inaugural ministerial conference of the WTO was held in Singapore in 1996. Thirty four countries accounting for over 90 percent of world trade in products related to information technology (semiconductors, computers, software, etc.) agreed to eliminate tariffs on these products during the period 1997-2000. The request for zero tariffs for exports from LDCs to industrialized countries put forward by African countries was watered down to a non-binding agreement ( OAU, *AEC Newsletter*, February-April 1997).

In the operation and maintenance of industrial establishments, African countries continue to experience problems and make use of expensive expatriates, the latter mainly during the construction and gestation periods. Preventive maintenance policies, systems, and practices are virtually unknown. Many fail to appreciate the contribution of proper maintenance in ensuring higher productivity and serviceability. In some situations, no provisions are made for repair and maintenance. Poor maintenance, characterized by frequent breakdowns, is exacerbated by inadequate or missing spare parts. Inventories are poor and foreign exchange rare. It is not unusual for production units to stand idle for weeks and months awaiting spare parts from abroad. The dwindling availability of foreign exchange continues to have a devastating effect on existing industries. Many industrial establishments, including those acquired second hand, are old and for want of foreign exchange their equipment and machinery have not been replaced. Many of them will close unless immediate measures are taken.

A combination of many of the constraints explain the abysmally low capacity utilization of many African plants or, worse still the closure of many of them, resulting in still greater shortages of industrial goods. Capacity utilization as low as 3 percent (Maluku steel plant in Congo K) was reported in the 1980s. In Tanzania, average capacity utilization plummeted to 24.8 percent in 1985 from 75 percent in 1975. In Nigeria, average capacity utilization in the petrochemical and iron and steel industries dropped to 25 percent in the mid-1980s (UNIDO, *Industry and Development: Global Report 1993/94*). The availability of industrial products can, be improved dramatically by raising capacity utilization. This was demonstrated in Ethiopia within two years following the end of the civil war in 1991. Industrial establishments that were closed and those operating at around 30 percent raised their capacity utilization to 70 percent (*The Ethiopian Herald*, November 1, 1994).

Other constraints include: growing dependence on imports; weak linkages between industry and other sectors; absence or inadequatcy of facilities for manufacturing critical parts and packaging materials; inadequate and untimely delivery of parts and components; long lead time for delivery of inputs; high cost, relatively poor quality, and lack or shortages of some local inputs; and difficulties in obtaining external investment funds. In Ethiopia, shortage of supply of raw materials and spare parts and absence of credit facilities were the major reasons given for industrial establishments not working at full capacity utilization in 1995/96 *(Central Statistical Authority* [Ethiopia 1997]).

In short, it is evident from the above constraints that African countries, particularly the low-income net food importing countries, are extremely vulnerable to the vagaries of the world economic situation. The slightest downward change in international demand and world prices, for instance, has a devastating effect on their economic and social development.

**Industrial Pollution**
Because of its worldwide impact, industrial pollution as a constraint on African industrialization deserves specific treatment here. Over the past few decades, the world has become increasingly conscious of the growing environmental crisis and the adverse changes in the global climatic and ecological systems. The changes are manifested through deforestation, soil erosion, desertification, drought, depletion of underground aquifers, pollution, and global warming. Deforestation in Africa is estimated at 5 million hectares annually and about 25 percent of all vegetated land is eroded (Juo et. al. 1995). This means substantial loss of biodiversity and therefore potentially valuable genetic information as most of the diversity occurs in forest areas. In regard to global warming, although there is a school of thought that disputes the theory of global warming, this century is reported to be warmer by 0.5 °C with 1998 as the warmest year so far. According to Britain's Meteorological Office, by the end of the next century, average temperatures might increase by 2.°C and sea-levels might rise by about 50 cm (*The Economist*, March 23, 1996). Global warming could aggravate drought in tropical and subtropical areas, thereby increasing the dependency of countries in such areas on imported food.

At this stage of development, industrial pollution as such is not of major concern to most African countries, especially considering the low stage of their development in polluting industries (such as leather tanning, textile dyeing, pulp and paper making and electroplating) and in gold and silver mining. They could, in due course, face difficulties in using conventional energy sources that pollute (such as coal and hydrocarbons) as well as nuclear energy. What is of serious concern for many at present and in the near future, however, is environmental degradation, including erosion, deforestation (1000 km² per year in Ethiopia alone, where the forest area has been reduced from 40% of the total surface at the beginning of the 1900s to 2% currently), soil erosion and desertification, the last costing Africa about $9 billion a year (UNDP, *Human Development Report 1996)*. In the words of the World Bank *"Eighty percent of the [Sub-Saharan African] soils are fragile, 47 percent of the land is too dry to support rainfed agriculture..."* (*Sub-Saharan Africa...* ). Population pressure arising from high population growth and abject poverty are the main causes for such a state of affairs. If the trend in environmental degradation continues unabated, it could produce irreversible damage to the ecosystem. It is hoped that the United Nations Convention to Combat Desertification, which was expected to be operational in 1997, will prove to be worthy of its name. It was reported that President Clinton's visit to Africa had brought home the urgency of controlling desertification in Africa.

Manufacturing is one of the economic activities that has contributed to the environmental crisis the world over. It does this both indirectly and directly. The former takes place during mining and when undertaking agriculture-related activities intended to provide industrial establishments with the raw materials, energy and water they need. It causes resource depletion and ecological disruption. The latter results from the generation of waste in solid, liquid and gas forms as well as heat and noise, the last impacting the production unit and immediate surroundings only. It is, generally, the waste that is normally ascribed to manufacturing activities.

Most of the industrial waste (excluding that utilized by the informal sector) has a negative impact on the environment and, therefore, needs to be controlled. It pollutes the air, soil, and water and both directly and indirectly affects living things adversely. A pollutant that cannot be converted into a useful product needs to be treated to make it, at least, less harmless before it is disposed of. Depending upon the type of pollutant, treatment and elimination could be very costly. Yet, generally, the cost of abating the bulk of pollutants could be relatively acceptable. It is, in some instances, the final traces that are difficult and costly to remove. Although the pollution caused at the moment is not significant because of the low level of development in most countries, industrial pollution is negatively impacting on industrial development in terms of cost. It becomes a major constraining factor as soon as and if pollution abatement equipment is incorporated in a production unit. This increases the cost of both investment and production, costs that industrialized countries did not (until recently) have to incur at the initial and subsequent stages of their industrialization. It is apparent that when deciding on implementing industrial projects African countries will have to make trade-offs between investment and pollution, including minimizing or eliminating the source of pollution to the greatest degree possible. As pollution has no boundary, a pollutant, particularly a gaseous pollutant, generated anywhere will impact the global ecosystem.

## MINIMIZING THE CONSTRAINTS ON INDUSTRY

In the 1960s and 1970s, the term "lack" applied to most of the constraints identified in the above section. Now terms like "inadequate" and "insufficient" are more appropriate. This indicates that some changes for the better have taken place. Many constraints, even those related to topography, climate, and natural calamities are, to some extent, amenable to improvement and changes with time.

The degree of severity and combination of constraints vary from country to country. In several countries, many constraints have eased considerably.

Up to the end of the 1980s, development programs and projects funded by the United Nations Development Program (UNDP) used to be executed by the United Nations specialized agencies, such as FAO, ILO, WHO, and UNIDO, using expertise from the world pool of experts. The decision made by the United Nations during the second half of the 1980s offered countries receiving United Nations aid the option to execute programs and projects themselves. This is a good indication of the progress made by developing countries, including African countries, in mitigating constraints and improving capacity building. Many countries are taking advantage of this opportunity and are making better use of the funds provided by drastically cutting the high cost of foreign experts. Furthermore, given their better knowledge of conditions in and needs of their respective countries as well as their apparent vested interest in developing their countries, local experts are likely to (and actually do) plan and execute programs and projects better than foreign experts. Eritrea is a good example of countries making intensive use of their nationals and institutions in areas related to capacity building.

Most of the internal constraints are of a temporary nature. African countries can and increasingly do exercise control over them thereby lessening their impact over time. This is, however, not the case with external constraints. African countries are at the mercy of world economic conditions manipulated and dictated by the major economies to their own advantage and at the expense of the small and weak African economies. Apparently, there is little that can be done about most external constraints at the individual country level.

The United Nations proclaimed the 1960s and 1970s the First and Second Development Decades, respectively. Both decades were a disappointment to developing countries, particularly African countries. At the regional level and in concert with other developing regions, attempts were made to impress upon the international community the need for a New International Economic Order (NIEO) in the 1980s in an attempt to (i) change the old order based on exchanging raw materials for manufactured goods between the developing and developed countries; and (ii) revoke import controls, such as the Common Agricultural Policy and the Multifiber Arrangement, the latter governed by a system of discriminatory quotas. The United States was in 1998 reported to be imposing 14.6 percent tariff on clothing imports, a rate *"five times higher than its average levy"* (*The Economist*, May 16, 1998). The third NIEO called for higher raw material prices with indexing (indexed to protect them against inflation), increased aid, easier transfer of technology, better access to markets in developed countries, and protection against worsening terms of trade. The NIEO was expected to give developing countries greater measure of control over their own resources. It did not materialize.

Some of the external constraints could be mitigated through a massive increase of foreign direct investment (FDI). This, however, has been shrinking since the 1980s, although this is no longer the case with the mining sector. Foreign companies which help countries to achieve the latter's development objectives are likely to gain greater acceptance by governments and the public in the countries in which they operate. They can enhance that acceptance by encouraging and helping indigenous entrepreneurs to carry out one or more of the following activities through subcontracting: production and supply of raw materials and goods and services needed by the foreign company (backward integration), production of intermediate and final products based on inputs produced by the foreign company (forward integration), and distribution and marketing of products produced by the foreign company. The tendency nowadays is for foreign companies to go into joint ventures with local individuals or companies. This is a precondition that foreign companies must meet if they wish to operate in certain countries.

The future of Africa is not, however, as gloomy as it may appear. With its trend towards democratic rule, its huge natural resources endowment, its cumulative learning experience acquired both in industry and in all socio-economic activities (including improving labor productivity and management), and its huge potential market, Africa has the potential to bring about the changes needed to reduce cost and achieve faster sustainable development. Low productivity (which is, in part, due to redundant workers in public enterprises) offers a potential to be exploited. The same applies to the low standard of living. The majority of the constraints are not insurmountable: their impact is lessening with time. Besides, one should take note of the adage "where there is a problem, there is an opportunity."

Following the decision of the United Nations General Assembly, each year November 20th is observed throughout the region as Africa Industrialization Day. The observance has as its objective the promotion of industrialization in Africa and shows the continuing international community's concern over Africa's poor progress towards industrialization. The theme for 1995 was "human resource development with special emphasis on support for industry." The theme for 1996 was "mobilization of financial resources for industry" and that for 1997, "the role of small and medium enterprises to develop industry ... ."

## Improving Leadership and Adopting an Appropriate Economic Development System

Partly due to the new situation following the end of the Cold War, better disciplined leaders are now emerging in Africa. The poor management of national economies described above and the bad image enjoyed by African leadership are changing for the better. This change was observed in 1997 by the US Secretary of State Madeleine K. Albright during her first visit to Africa when she spoke about Africa's best leaders sharing a *"common vision of empowerment—for all their citizens, for their nations, and for their continent."* Deficiencies associated with inadequate leadership have, in recent years, become less crucial. As noted in Chapter 2, an increasing number of countries are enjoying good and dedicated leadership. Political stability and liberal markets are budding, especially in countries such as Mozambique, Namibia, Uganda, Zimbabwe, Eritrea and Ethiopia (the last two until the start of border fighting between them in 1998) which have gone through devastating conflicts. Eritrea has become a prime example of a state capable of weeding out corruption. In Uganda, members of parliament who declared their assets toward the end of 1997 demanded that corrupt officials should be brought to heel.

The year 1996 witnessed the exposure and dismissal of corrupt cabinet ministers and high level government officials in Nigeria, Ethiopia, and Mali. In September 1998 the Nigerian government ordered all high level policy-making officials and state administrators to declare their assets and was in the process of recovering public money pilfered by some officials. The financial code promulgated in Ethiopia in 1998 carries 10-15 years imprisonment for corruption. A central body to "stamp out bribery and unethical practices" was expected to be operational in 1999.

During his visit to Ethiopia in October 1997, Mr. Robert S. McNamara, the former World Bank president and the 1997 co-chairman of the Global Coalition for Africa Forum of which the Ethiopian Prime Minister Meles Zenawi was also a co-chairman, said that Ethiopia's effort in the fight against corruption was *"exemplary to Africa."* At the Maputo summit of the Global Coalition for Africa, which focused on corruption, the Forum agreed on the need to carry out anti-corruption campaigns across Africa, including the use of independent watchdog bodies, the call made to the international community to implement anti-corruption legislation and address corruption related to procurement. According to Mr. McNamara, Benin, Ethiopia, Malawi, Mali, Tanzania, and Uganda are keen to combat corruption inside their respective governments. Transparency International (an anti-corruption pressure group based in Berlin), the 1997 OECD agreement to ban bribery of foreign officials and the anti-corruption mandate of the World Bank (*The Economist*, August 2, 1997) together with initiatives on the part of certain European countries, such as Germany, to end tax deductibility of bribes paid by their copmanies abroad are likely to contribute to reducing corruption in Africa. Return of funnds embezzled by Africans and stashed in banks and refusal to accept new funds by the banks in the West could help African countries reduce their debt and deter future corruption. It was gratifying to note that the Forum confirmed the need for such actions.

In their efforts to improve their worsening economic conditions, African countries experimented with a variety of economic management systems: capitalism, socialism/communism, and mixed economy, the last being the most widely practiced. In practically all systems and their variants, industrialization was among the priorities. In the capitalist and mixed economy systems, attempts were made to attract investment. These included incentives, such as tax and tariff concessions/duty free entry of industrial inputs (machinery, equipment, and intermediates), tax holidays, low tax rates and provision for the remittance of profits and repatriation of invested capital. Other incentives were provided to encourage export industries, some of which were established in export-processing zones. Multiple exchange rates, devaluation, direct subsidy, and tariff and tax remissions on imported material inputs were among the incentives given to export industries.

The rigid practice of ideologies that conditioned political as well economic relations among African countries has been one of the major factors that led to the failures of several attempts at integration. The East African Community is a case in point. Ideology is, fortunately, playing less of a negative role since the demise of Communism. Under the circumstances, it is to be expected that African countries will enhance their economic cooperation and integration, thereby facilitating the integrated development of industry.

One of the reservations regarding capitalism is the widening divergence in income among the social groups within a country, as is happening in some developed countries. In the United States, for instance, this trend is compounded by the *"shift of the tax burden from wealthier to poorer Americans, and the withdrawal of public funding"* from education and infrastructure which negatively impact on the low income group, including the lower four-fifths (Reich 1991). According to the same source, the top fifth of the American population in 1989 accounted for close to 51 percent of income net of tax. By 2020, the same group's earning is expected to reach the 60 percent level, compared with only 2 percent for the bottom fifth. The 15 percent flat tax rate being advocated by some members of Congress and Presidential aspirants, if implemented, is likely to worsen the plight of the majority of Americans.

Under a market economy, income gains favor the wealthy over the poor. In recent years, it seems that more and more people are experiencing hard times, partly due to technological change which is biased in favor of new skills. In the United States, for example, many people are worried about job security as demonstrated by the mass layoffs carried out in the guise of downsizing ostensibly to remain profitable (true for some which were failing), although some of the downsizers were, in 1996, already reported to be hiring again and others creating new jobs. An increasing number of people are working harder (more than one job) for compensations that would enable them to maintain their standard of living. The trend seems to be towards an increasingly highly-skewed income distribution,[2] growing income disparities, and social stratification, inevitably followed by worsening economic and spatial segregation according to income. Those with sub-collegiate educational levels are expected to continue to experience falling real wages and diminishing job opportunities. In Germany, where wages are the world's highest, unions have been forced to agree to lower their wages and raise productivity (*Business Week*, July 28, 1997). According to a poll conducted in 1997, worry about job insecurity jumped from 29 percent in 1991 to 42 percent in 1995 (Samuelson 1997).

In his essay titled "The Capitalist Threat," which appeared in the February 1997 issue of *The Atlantic Monthly*, Mr. George Soros, a wealthy American, expressed his misgivings on the excesses and *laissez faire* ideology of capitalism. He said that excessive individualism and incapability of cooperation between individuals and states will lead to instability and collapse. In the Letters to the Editor section of *The Economist* (February 15, 1997), all four letters from the USA, Italy, and the United Kingdom on Mr. Soros's view on capitalism were in support, indicating that 100 percent free market, an imperfect system, may not be the panacea that many believe or expect it to be.

As one of the letters referred to above put it, *"many nations are becoming appendages of world capitalism."* This could mean that, in the long run, something similar to the above phenomenon is likely to apply to developing countries characterized as they are by increasing poverty and growing unemployment, and therefore the possibility of excessive individualism dictating its terms for exploiting the workers. In the future, this situation could be further exacerbated when African countries would have reached the level of development in which routine production jobs are marginalized through automation and modern information technology. As buyers of technology, African countries will have no choice but to use many sophisticated technologies as technologies appropriate to their needs are likely to be less and less available over time. One way to minmize the increasing inequalities in developing countries is to facilitate and enable the workers and the people to share in the ownership of the business activities.

In view of the above, a sudden and wide opening of national markets to a highly competitive world market with globalized production and trade does not appear to be the right approach for most African countries. Such countries would be better off with a mixed economy, whereby public enterprises, particularly those related to infrastructure, continue to operate under government ownership but with autonomous management. Eventually, most, if not all, such enterprises could be passed on to the private sector as soon as it is ready to take them over.

## Market Expansion and Protection

Whatever measures are taken to develop industry, in the final analysis, markets (small partly because of suppressed demand) will, to a large extent, determine the success or failure of industrialization. The mainly imported input-based easy import-substitution industries whose products have now reached saturation level were generally set up to cater to a minority group, a small affluent group, in the urban area. Future industries will, of necessity, tend to be capital intensive and sensitive to economies of scale. At present, up to 80 percent of the population where the potential market is use very few manufactured products and services. Real sustainable industrial development could take place only, if these peoples' living standards were raised to a level where they could afford to purchase and appreciate industrial consumer goods and farm inputs and services. As farmers constitute the greatest majority. There is no other option but to raise their agricultural incomes through, among other things, increasing their agricultural productivity. Increased agricultural productivity means benefit accruing to the farmers, food becoming available to the urban population, and an enabling environment being created for industrial development through expanding markets and the provision of agricultural raw materials. In other words, development has to have its roots in farming.

One of the measures that African countries cannot neglect is the protection of their industries from unfair competition and dumping.[3] Such situations and practices hurt existing producers and discourage those who contemplate venturing into the industrial sector. This is very serious in regard to those who, because of lack or low level of industrial culture, require coaxing to venture into industry. The following are among the measures that can be used to mitigate the adverse impact of unfair competition: the judicious phasing-out of protection against imports through charging import duties and/or imposing quantitative restrictions on the same or competing products and/or their substitutes, exchange rate adjustments, subsidy, and public procurement. The period for and extent of protection for each existing industry (when needed) and project should be determined carefully, using such criteria as the degree of vulnerability to outside competition, the vagaries of the international market and the crucial nature of the industry to the country. The performance of protected industries should be monitored in order to ensure that the protection: (i) is applied according to schedule; (ii) does not exceed the prescribed time limit; and (iii) does not result in generating scarcity rents. Monitoring should include provision for quick and timely adjustment of protection—both positive and negative—when justified because of changes in market conditions, subsidies provided by exporting countries, dumping, and other unforeseen circumstances. An independent body with adequate resources should be established to determine the levels of phased protection and to review and monitor their implementation, including the maintenance of standard and quality. Membership of that body should include the private sector (chambers of commerce and industry, industry associations, engineering associations, labor unions, etc.) and relevant government and public institutions, such as science and technology commission and universities. While providing temporary protection from outside competition, governments may do well to provide support to producers (including technical assistance in improving quality and productivity) and stimulate domestic competition, which should benefit local customers and prepare manufacturers for the eventual exposure to foreign market forces.

As for export-oriented industrialization, one alternative would be to accord industries export incentives and facilities as was done in most East and South-East Asian countries. These included export processing zones, tax credits, subsidized credit, and provision of information.

Some people advocate the adoption of open economic policies and therefore object to such measures, while others argue that protection encourages inefficient and high-cost production. These kinds of arguments have been and continue to be used against establishing almost any type of industry in Africa, thereby deterring African industrialization. In reality, however, in the early stages of their industrialization, the industrialized countries themselves resorted to protecting their agricultural production and fledgling manufacturing industries—and they still do resort to protectionist practices. The textile industry is a case in point. Although they claim to practice free market *"each mixes government protection and market forces"* (Samuelson 1997). In an article titled "State Aid" in the Economist (November 22, 1998) Europe's competition commissioner expressed his worry about *"subsidies paid to industry by EU member states"*—which amounted to $52 billion dispensed to firms in 1994.

The Food Security Act of 1985 in the United States of America and its equivalent in the European Union (Common Agricultural Policy) support and subsidize agricultural production and exports resulting in unfair competition and discouraging farmers in developing countries.

According to Reich (1991), President Clinton's Labor Secretary, *"By the end of the 1980s, almost a third of the standard goods manufactured in the United States, by value, were protected against international competition."* The manufacture of Airbus passenger jets is subsidized by the European countries that own the company. Assistance to declining industries, such as shipbuilding and steel-making, and tariffs that escalate with the degree of processing of materials exported by developing countries, many of which depend on one or two commodities to earn foreign exchange, are other obvious examples. Tropical fruit may be used to illustrate tariff escalation. In 1986, while fresh fruit carried zero tariff under the African, Caribbean, and Pacific (ACP), the most favorable arrangement for African countries, preserved and prepared fruits (juices) were charged 0.9 and 4.6 percent, respectively. The equivalent tariffs were 4.0, 8.9, and 11.4 in Japan under the General System of Preferences and 8.7 (fresh) and 46.7 (prepared) in the USA under the most favored-nation principle (UN, A/45/581). Such tariffs obviously impede the development of industries in African countries.

Some developed countries (France, Italy, and Sweden) give budgetary compensation to their public enterprises for undertaking social objectives (Meier et. al. 1989). In 1996, the privatization committee in France suspended the sale of Thomson's Multimedia unit to Daewoo Elctronics of South Korea because this involved the transfer of French asset to a foreign company (*The Economist*, December 14, 1996). Since 1991, state aid to manufacturing in EU has been steadily rising and topped about ECU 44 billion in 1994 (*The Economist*, March 15, 1997).

Each ton of coal produced in Germany is subsidized 70 percent and yet it could be replaced by imported coal at 25 percent of the German coal price *(The Economist,* March 15, 1997).

Most of the newly industrialized countries, such as India and China, have resorted to protecting their infant industries and still do. Shipping conference freight rates that escalate with the degree of processing have a similar negative impact on African industrialization. Such being the reality and taking into account market imperfections, in general why are African countries with all the constraints and crises they continue to face being pressured to open wide their economies to the world market, characterized as it is by cut-throat competition? Does not rapid process of globalization of financial markets, production and services and exposure to import competition bring about negative impacts on traditional industries (resource-based and labor-intensive industries), as happened in Ghana where imports devastated many manufacturing establishments? Can poor African countries afford to bankrupt their meagre production and service activities, in other words, deindustrialize and destroy whatever related technological and managerial capabilities and capacities have been built, because of unfair competition from networks of internationally integrated financing, sourcing, production, marketing, R&D, etc. systems with capabilities to easily manipulate business activities, including dumping? Is not rapid trade liberalization likely to worsen Africa's dependency on imports, drastically increase disparities of wealth between the haves and the have-nots, and prevent new entry into the production and export activities involving relatively difficult and complex technologies requiring long learning and gestation period? What about the adverse effect on the already disadvantaged (*vis-a-vis* the TNCs with increasing merger mania and growing monopoly power of world economic activities and their affiliates in developing countries) indigenous industrial entrepreneurs who will certainly suffer and be discouraged to take risks because of globalization and liberalization?

With limitations of policy options that globalization, the new economic order entails, it would appear that African countries are being indirectly told not to industrialize but to continue their traditional role of providing the industrialized countries with inexpensive raw materials the later require. In view of the above and the need for the costly and time consuming learning process, the introduction of import liberalization in most African countries will have to be postponed for a longer time period than envisaged in the "final act" of the Uruguay Round Agreement until their industries are sufficiently developed to withstand a certain level of competition. The duration of the phasing out of trade restrictions will depend upon fair prices for African exports and the quality, appropriateness, timeliness, and magnitude of technical and economic assistance from the industrialized countries.

As recently as 1995, South Africa, the most advanced country on the African continent, was sheltering its manufacturing sector (characterized by a strategy of import substitution) from outside competition. In the words of Vice-President W. F. de Klerk, " *To survive we had to close up, to survive we had to build in a lot of unacceptable restrictions and rules and regulations and bureaucratic measures, if we did not do so we would have been economically dead"* (*The Monitor*, February 11-12, 1995).

There is no doubt that sooner or later African countries will have to adopt trade liberalization. The question is when and how. Many have already started the process. The rest are likely to follow suit in the not too distant future. The how depends, among other things, on the extent and pace of liberalization. The findings of UNCTAD could illustrate this. Comparison of change in African LDCs MVA/GDP ratios during 1980-1990 showed that low liberalizers averaged -0.2 percent, high liberalizers [4] 1.5 percent, and medium liberalizers [5] 4.25 percent (UNCTAD, *The Least Developed Countries, 1995 Report*). It is apparent that the medium liberalizers fared far better, with three times the rate of change in the MVA/GDP ratios in comparison with that of the high liberalizers. This indicates that fast liberalization seems neither desirable nor practical under current conditions in most African countries. In any case, it does not seem wise to implement liberalizing measures without first observing the performance of enterprises after the removal of distortions in financial markets, discrepancies in import duties (finished goods versus imported inputs), the high cost of local inputs, etc.

If developed countries justify resorting to protective measures, there is no reason why African countries cannot do the same, all the more so as global competition is more intense now than at the time the developed countries themselves were industrializing. It is difficult to comprehend how African countries, without government interventions as facilitator, regulator and investor, particularly in infrastructure, can liberalize their economies rapidly without adequate provision against market failures under imperfect market conditions manipulated by large corporations and their subsidiaries in the host countries.

Poor developing countries cannot afford to close down existing industries when the products they produce cannot compete with those imported from outside. The situation becomes unpalatable when foreign goods are smuggled or dumped in the local market. Worse still, the goods so smuggled or dumped are second-hand or out-of-season in the exporting countries. The smuggling is done by large informal sectors with the help of customs officials who enrich themselves by collecting rents. Imported ready-made clothes, including second-hand ("salvage") are a case in point in Ethiopia. This does not augur well for the relatively well developed textile industry in the country. The industry started to feel the pinch in 1995. By 1997 most of the 18 textile mills and garment industries were in the red because of competition with imported textiles and clothing, a consequence of old and outdated machinery and equipment, lack of capability to meet the changing demand, inadequate management and skills, and very high increase in the price of inputs, particularly cotton. The "Ethio Textile Week" exhibition and bazar was organized in 1997 with a view to identifying rectification measures. If measures are not taken to curb the trend, the consequences are likely to be serious in terms of large idle assets and unemployment not only in regard to the textile mills (about 30,000 workers) but also to cotton production and other downstream production units (including tailoring employing thousands of people) and services. The caustic soda plant is another example of a local industry risking closure because of competition from imported caustic soda as well as mismanagement.

In the event that closure of an industrial enterprise is justified, a study on an optimum use of the facility should be undertaken. Could it, for instance, be converted to produce some other products by modifying the set-up and adding machinery and equipment? Surely, some of the existing assets, particularly those related to utilities and other infrastructure, could, with modification, if necessary, be utilized by the new enterprise.

Another argument used against developing certain industries (specifically, import-substitution industries) is that such industries continue to require foreign exchange to operate. The only way to reduce or not use foreign exchange is to either reduce or avoid completely the consumption of goods: this is virtually impossible with most goods, particularly those that meet basic needs. Under the circumstances, the options are either to produce them locally or import them. Now, the option depends on the net benefit the country could reap from it. In general, local production is beneficial to a country because of its multiplier effect: it utilizes some local factor inputs, provides employment, transfers technical and managerial experience, and contributes to the economy in general. This being the case, foreign exchange seems to be the major factor in deciding which way to go. Of course, the logical thing to do is to look at the net annual foreign exchange the country will have to incur. Put simply, if the net foreign exchange (price of the imported good concerned less the cost of all inputs imported to make the same good locally) is negative, local production may not make sense, although other factors (such as employment) may tip the balance. On the contrary, if it is positive, which is usually the case, then local production makes sense because the country benefits by saving foreign exchange, no matter how small.

The Lome Convention, which associates the African, Caribbean, and Pacific (ACP) countries with the Eurpean Community (now the European Union) allows the former to export tariff-free and quota-free manufactured goods and 96 percent of their agricultural products to the latter (Bailey 1976). It provides financial aid and stabilizes export earnings in the event that commodity prices fall. Its Industrial Cooperation Committee and Centre for Industrial Development (CID) undertake industry-related activities. These arrangements do not appear to compensate African countries fully for the losses they incur through price distortions and manipulations. It would not be far from the truth to state that developed countries determine prices not only of their manufactures but also of export commodities (whether processed or not) from developing countries. Had this not been the case (i.e., had African exports been fairly priced in relation to the final product that African countries pay for the manufactures incorporating their exports), African countries would not be in the pathetic situation they find themselves in today. Under these circumstances, part of the aid they receive should be regarded as compensation for losses arising from such price manipulations.

## Progress in Capacity Building

The term "capacity building" covers capability (manpower) and capacity (institutions). The former comprises entrepreneurship, management, skills, and technology; the latter includes R&D institutions, engineering design centers and consulting firms, and construction companies as well as repair and maintenance facilities.

As both capability and capacity from project identification to factory operation were practically nil at the advent of independence, countries had to resort to acquiring all the technical, managerial, and material (except those available locally) inputs they needed from outside at very high cost. Reports, studies, proposals, etc. were accepted without questioning for lack of expertise to evaluate them, thereby contributing to the failure of many projects.[6] The use of foreign inputs, naturally, inflated not only the cost of production but also the foreign exchange component. As foreign exchange was available, industrial planners and industrialists were not concerned with the implications of foreign exchange. They did not, for instance, try hard enough to replace imported inputs by locally available materials. This apathy started to change following the 1973 oil crisis, when the scarcity of foreign exchange became manifest. This, coupled with the capability and capacity built and the experience and knowledge accumulated by African entrepreneurs and industrialists over the past three decades, enabled African countries to achieve a measure of self-reliance in planning, developing, and operating industries. As a result, conditions have changed in favor of better organized and relatively more efficiently operated industries (including continually improving productivity and declining use of high-cost expatriates) which are likely to reduce their foreign exchange needs with time.

During the colonial regime, business was in the hands of foreigners and Africans were virtually barred from acquiring a modern business culture in most countries. To a large extent, this situation persists in private manufacturing enterprises which are mostly controlled by expatriates or transnational corporations. Whatever Africans did was basically limited to petty trade (informal sector) in addition to farming. In the past three decades, despite competition from well-established foreign firms, many Africans have upgraded themselves from petty traders to higher level entrepreneurs (real estate, transport services, small hotels, etc.) while more modern entrepreneurs, including industrialists, are emerging. Based on field interviews with 36 African entrepreneurs in six countries, it has been recorded that *"Impressive growth records of the entrepreneurs interviewed ... do indicate an ability to meet local and foreign competition and satisfy market demand effectively"* (IFC, *African Entrepreneurs: Pioneers of Development*). Such success was partly achieved through a process of Africanization pursued by African governments, including reserving certain areas of economic activities to indigenous businessmen.

In 1974, the Nigerian Enterprises Promotion Decree (which contained a provision for compensating previous owners, for example) brought many private-sector enterprises under Nigerian control while the federal government acquired 55 percent equity share in the oil industry. Similar Government measures in favor of local entrepreneurs are changing the attitudes of people towards development, a very essential pre-condition for development in the region. More can be done to attract indigenous people with money to invest in industry through the "build-operate-transfer" arrangement. This would involve setting up public industries and transferring their ownership to the private sector once they have proved themselves viable. This approach minimizes the chances of failure and attracts the private sector; it was one of the reasons for the miraculous development of Japan. A UNIDO document titled "Guidelines for Infrastructure Development through Build-Operate-Trasfer (BOT) Projects" could serve as a starting point for those who wish to involve their nationals increasingly participate in the process of industrialization.

Exposure to industrial culture is a relatively new phenomenon to indigenous Africans. Most of them are very comfortable as traders, owners of relatively simple catering operations, and speculators in real estate, enjoying high profit margins mainly by buying and selling, higher than those accruing to producers. This is even worse with black-marketers, who, because of the scarcity of goods, earn windfall profits at the expense of both the customer and the country. The scarcity rents they enjoy are sometimes purposely created by the black-marketeers themselves through speculative stockpiling. There are those rent-seekers who make huge profits because of their connections with government officials. It should be noted here that the tendency to look for quick-fix profits applies to foreign investors as well. There is apparently no incentive for traders to shift from this lucrative trade to the more risky, less-rewarding and more difficult task of managing an industry, which requires a longer gestation period. In fact, local production enterprises in many countries are directly and/or indirectly discriminated against, as they have little or no access to the incentives accorded to foreign investors. Measures should therefore be taken to curb the appetite of rent-seekers on the one hand and to provide adequate incentives to local entrepreneurs so as to turn their attention to the productive sectors—industry and agriculture. This would mean shifting profits from traders and black-marketers to producers, as the latter usually have lower profit margins than the former.

Despite the above picture, thousands of entrepreneurs with initiative and drive have demonstrated their capabilities against all odds. A good example is the Suame Magazine in Kumasi, Ghana, which the author had the opportunity to visit in the 1980s. The workshops and garages owned and manned by hundreds of Ghanaians make and modify spare parts; repair, rehabilitate, and rebuild vehicles, equipment, and machinery; and make various goods from scrap materials. Even though not as concentrated as the Suame Magazine, similar entrepreneurs abound in practically all African countries. It is obvious that with proper incentives and support, such entrepreneurs can organize and upgrade themselves to medium- and large-scale enterprises in a relatively short time. Proper incentives would include those that could encourage and facilitate the dispersal of manufacturing capacities. This could help bring development to areas that, under normal circumstances, would not attract investors and make possible new divisions of labor and specialization. The recent success in dispersing investment in Ethiopia may be cited as an example. Appropriate Federal Government initiatives and State incentives in the last five years resulted in diverting investment from the capital to the states, thereby reducing the share of the former from 80.8 percent to 31 percent.

In view of the above and despite the trend toward privatization, governments and/or their institutions would be expected to continue to play a crucial but declining entrepreneurial role until their citizens are able to assume that role. As is well known, thanks to the colonial legacy, businesses, particularly those requiring high levels of investment, technology, expertise, and management as well as large market, are generally in the hands of expatriates. Continuing or increasing domination by and dependence on foreign investment (with malpractices such as transfer pricing and the resulting foreign exchange leakages) may not be in the long-term interest of foreign investment as it could, sooner or later, create resentment[7] on the part of the public in the host countries, and such popular resentment has been known to lead to political changes. The extent of transfer pricing can be illustrated by an example from Colombia involving pharmaceutical intermediates for local formulation. Parent companies in 1981 were, on average, charging their subsidiaries prices some 155 percent over world market prices. The overcharging was, in some cases, as outrageously high as 50 times the cost from other sources (Melrose 1983). According to Seidman (*African Development Perspectives Yearbook 1992/93*), transnational corporations *"reap growing profits through fees-for-services and transfer pricing which annually drains away 10-15 % of the value of the average third world country's foreign trade."*

In most African countries, foreign firms and expatriates still control a major part of the key sectors of the economy. The proportion of indigenous ownership in production and services should increase over time in order to achieve a healthy relationship and interaction between the indigenous and foreign components of the business community. Among the measures that governments can and should take to minimize resentment against foreign domination is the privatization and transfer of public ownership of the means of production and services to indigenous people as far as practical. They could even go further and solicit foreign loans to import machinery, equipment, and spare parts for rehabilitating, upgrading, expanding and diversifying the enterprises so acquired. Another is to encourage private joint indigenous/foreign ventures. One measure worth considering is establishing industries, including joint ventures with foreign investors, and transferring the public shares to the indigenous population once the industries become operational and viable. This approach seems particularly appropriate for viable investment opportunities for which private investment is not forthcoming. The money obtained from the sale of these industrial establishments could be used as a revolving fund to finance other industries for the same purpose. Another is to allow local partners to hold a higher proportion of shares during the expansion of joint enterprises. All these strategies require developing and strengthening capital markets which most countries lack.

Entrepreneurs, particularly local entrepreneurs, contemplating the setting-up of industrial establishments in Africa face a number of the constraints discussed above. In a liberalized wide-open economy characterized by market imperfections (including constantly rising prices of manufactures and persistently declining and fluctuating commodity prices), they find themselves competing with imported goods produced in large-scale industries which benefit from economies of scale and the diversification and integration of management and marketing. Many fall victims to unfair competition from local production facilities owned by branches or affiliates of transnational corporations with global cost minimization and profit maximization strategies. Some do not engage in production for fear of stiff competition from such companies. Some, because of real comparative advantages, mainly resource-based, succeed in their ventures. Most (both import-substituting and export-oriented industries), however, require some kind of support and protection and deserve to be treated as "infant industries." Here it should be noted that Africa continues to be the dumping ground for surplus goods from developed countries, a process that started during the colonial era. The need for nurturing infant industries has been recognized by practically all African countries. Protection of infant industries was, for instance, made part of the COMESA Treaty.

The constraints dealt with above reflect conditions at the time of independence. The critical nature of most, particularly internal constraints and those related to capacity, continue to diminish with time and with the cumulative impact of the learning process (learning-by-doing and learning-by-observing) and the acquisition of technical and managerial skills and industrial experience. There is no comparison between their impact during the advent of independence and their impct today. Constraints related to capacity (human and infrastructural) were the theme of ECA's Twentieth Meeting of the Conference of Ministers Responsible for Economic and Social Development and Planning, May 1994. The theme "Building Critical Capacities in Africa for Accelerated Growth and Sustainable Development" was meant to focus attention on improving the capacities of African countries in certain critical areas. The areas dealt with were:

(a) critical capacities in support of good governance, human rights, political stability, peace and security;

(b) critical capacities for effective socio-economic policy analysis and management;

(c) building, strengthening, and effectively utilizing human capacities for sustained development;

(d) developing entrepreneurial capacities for public and private sector enterprise;

(e) building and utilizing physical infrastructural capacities;

(f) capacity building for food production, food security, and self-sufficiency;

(g) capacities to exploit natural resources and diversify African economies into processing and manufacturing; and

(h) critical capacities for the mobilization and efficient allocation of domestic and external financial resources.

"Promoting accelerated growth and sustainable development in Africa through the building of critical capacities" was the theme at the Twenty-first Meeting of the Conference of Ministers in April 1995. The Conference hailed the theme as timely and very relevant. This shows the importance that African countries continue to attach to capacity building and therefore their resolve to tackle one of the causes, if not the major root cause, of underdevelopment. Full use of existing capabilities and capacities, including increased and better utilization of African indigenous expertise, was considered imperative while resorting to creating new capabilities and capacities. Regional cooperation in science and technology, including information and telematics, was stressed. The above-cited eight priority areas will be restructured to include economic integration, cooperation, and negotiating capabilities; management of the environment; and science and technology. The launching of the Framework Agenda for building and utilizing critical capacities in Africa was scheduled for January 1996.

As for infrastructure, practically all countries are in the process of implementing development activities. Inter-state transport links are much better now. Slowly but surely, missing road transport links between neighboring countries are being completed. Air transport which involved going via Europe for people traveling between East Africa and West Africa is becoming a thing of the past. The same applies to communications which used to be routed via Europe. The United Nations Transport and Communications Decade (UNTCD), currently in its second phase, is intended to help remedy constraints on transport and communications. Although varying in degree and intensity, improvements in other areas of physical infrastructure, such as electricity, are evident.

With respect to the lack and inadequacy of institutional infrastructure, African countries are trying to remedy such constraints through the establishment and operation of multinational, subregional and regional institutions. The thirty ECA-sponsored institutions referred to in Chapter 4 were designed and established to help minimize many of the above-cited critical capacities, particularly those relating to manpower and institutions, by taking advantage of economies of scale. These institutions, however, suffer from a lack of resources. Studies carried out to rationalize and harmonize them led to the proposal to consolidate eleven of them into three. Whatever institutions are finally retained will require that they be strengthened and made more effective, if they are to achieve the objectives they were intended for. The latest (1997) report on the rationalization and harmonization which the ECA Conference of Ministers endorsed for implementation categorized the institutions into the following groups: (a) cartography, mapping, and remote sensing; (b) engineering and industrial technology; (c) economic and social development; (d) finance and trade; and (e) minerals and transport.

Although the burden on industry to invest in infrastructure is likely to lessen over time with the development of infrastructure, governments may have to underwrite, at least, some of the costs related to infrastructure, particularly those having to do with strategic projects. This kind of incentive is provided in the Moroccan industrial investment code (UNCTC, ST/CTC/91).

It should be noted here that some of the constraints faced at the advent of independence, particularly the lack of manpower, but also the setbacks that surfaced in the 1980s (mainly due to an accumulation of crises precipitated by unfavorable developments in the international economy), are expected to continue hampering development. It is very unlikely, however, that they will be as crucial as they have been in the past. In fact, the rehabilitation, strengthening, and broadening of infrastructure that has taken and is taking place will significantly lessen the impact of these constraints. Skilled manpower, the basis for capacity building, which used to be a major constraint during the first two decades after independence is, for instance, no longer as crucial as it used to be. Gone are the days when Africans were completely dependent on foreign expertise. There are now trained and experienced Africans in most professions in the majority of African countries. Some of them, unfortunately, are underutilized, poorly motivated, and probably frustrated (due to nepotism, lack of or inadequate working facilities, etc.) and require some incentives to optimize their contributions.

Donors could and should optimize their assistance by maximizing the use of local institutions and experts available at the national, subregional and regional levels in areas in which African countries have built expertise and institutional capacity. Because of the very high cost of foreign inputs, particularly expertise and related administrative expenses accounting for a major part of most project costs, it is obvious that funds spent on a project using local inputs could be implemented at a fraction of that based on foreign inputs. In other words, there is a definite need for restructuring the type of assistance provided by donors, i.e., foreign technology, expertise, equipment and materials should only be used when such inputs or their substitutes are not available locally, both in the country and in the region. This will enhance self-sustained development, a condition required for real growth and development, and reduce the exodus of the educated to developed countries. It is an irony that poor developing countries with a paucity of skilled manpower are indirectly subsidizing the education of developed countries.

There is also a growing pool of trainable graduates from vocational and technical schools and universities, some of them already experiencing difficulties in finding employment.

Furthermore, the colonial education and training systems inherited did not address the needs for industrial education; in any case, those systems were not designed to meet the requirements of a modern productive industry. In view of these deficits, many African countries have taken and are taking measures to change the standard of education and training to suit their requirements. The new comprehensive education and training system in Ethiopia is a good example. According to this system, students who do not meet the requirements to continue or are unable to complete formal education at the secondary and tertiary levels are given opportunities to receive technical and vocational training in fields of their choice that will enable them to find employment or create employment for themselves, the level of training being commensurate with the level of education attained.

As for engineers, much more needs to be done. First, engineering students should be given opportunities to gain experience in enterprises and institutions in their respective fields during their long holidays. Secondly, their work experience should be evaluated and considered among the requirements for graduation. Thirdly, since the type of on-the-job training that is done in the industrialized countries is inadequate or virtually absent, graduates should be given six month's or a year's special training in the field in which they intend to work or specialize. This could be done in enterprises and institutions, both locally and abroad.

The process of building capabilities in many fields is a continuing process. Industrial consultancy and engineering organizations are among such capabilities. All Metal Founders in Zimbabwe, Public Finance and Management Consultancy Group in Nigeria, Ghana Regional Appropriate Technology Industrial Service in Ghana, Technical Design and Construction Office in Congo, African Consultancy Enterprise in Cameroon and Engineering Design Center in Ethiopia have been among those cited as highly competent organizations (ECA/UNIDO, CAMI.12/9). Such organizations are considered among the most important and in their absence the skills they impart are relatively difficult to master under African conditions.

Continuing training and exposure of entrepreneurs, management, and skilled labor to new techniques and innovations should be a permanent feature of every African country. Attaining a critical mass of skilled manpower, especially in so as far as new technologies are concerned, is a must if industries in African countries are to survive intensive international competition enhanced by global trade liberalization. This should be supplemented by continuous training as technical knowledge has been estimated to depreciate 10 to 15 percent per year (UNIDO, *Industrial Development: Global Report 1996*). At the Forum on the Future Competitiveness of African Economics held in Dakar, Senegal (February 1999), human resource development figured as the most crucial factor determining success in competition. Both the public and the private sectors should play their respective roles in training. The example set by the Ethiopian government—which, following the reorganization of public enterprises and the ongoing process of privatization, allocates funds to the chambers of commerce and industry to organize and conduct seminars, workshops, and training—seems to be worth emulating.

## Controlling Industrial Pollution

At present and in the near future, because of low level and slow growth of industrialization, industrial pollution is not likely to be of serious concern in most African countries. Consumption of industrial goods is minimal. Reuse and recycling of many industrial products in practically all countries, particularly household goods, is high. In Ethiopia, for instance, newspapers are used by shop owners to pack their sales; plastic and glass containers serve to hold and store food, beverages, and other things; tires are converted into sandals used by the poor; scrap metals are converted into numerous products for both household and other uses; sheet glass scraps and used cardboards are made into small mirrors; plastic sheets are used by the homeless as shelter; and returnable glass bottles and plastic pallets for beverages are widely used. In other words, many industrial products are optimally utilized in Africa, thereby effectively reducing demand for many products and minimizing the use of basic raw materials and energy and, obviously, pollution.

Aware of the global danger, the international community has been taking measures to minimize the crisis and hopefully to solve the problem eventually. Among the measures taken have been the establishment of the United Nations Environmental Programme (UNEP) in Nairobi, Kenya, and the organization of conferences on the environment and development, the first in the 1990s being the "Earth Summit" in Rio de Janeiro, Brazil, in 1992. The ensuing Rio Declaration of the Summit called for integrating the environment with economic development. The Earth Summit in New York in June 1997, organized to review progress after the Rio summit showed that not much has been done. The promises made by the rich countries to transfer more resources and technology to the poor countries to implement the Declaration have not materialized. Exceptions include UNIDO projects financed by the Montreal Protocol on Multilateral Fund for limiting the future use of ozone-depleting substances in some developing countries, including Algeria and Egypt. The Kyoto conference in Japan in December 1997 agreed on an average cut of 5.2 percent from 1990 gas emission levels in the next 15 years. It appears that, despite the fact that the United States is responsible for 20 percent of the global carbon dioxide emission, the government is not likely to have the agreement ratified by Congress within a short time. Consequently, it is possible that measures to implement the agreement may not be taken in the foreseeable future.

With their current and anticipated economic difficulties, African countries can hardly be expected to incur additional capital investments and operating costs to control pollution. They should not be penalized in the process of controlling pollution which was built up during the century-long industrialization process of the developed countries.

It is obviously incumbent upon the international community to prevent or minimize pollution and environmental degradation by helping African countries not only to integrate environmental considerations into their industrial policies and strategies but also to implement such policies and strategies aimed at controlling pollution and preventing and reversing environmental degradation. Making available environmentally-friendly technologies (clean and low-waste technologies), equipment, and other inputs at subsidized and affordable prices, and providing finance and training that could enable African countries to achieve ecologically sustainable industrial development are among the forms of assistance required. Assistance of this kind is essential in implementing an environmentally sound industrial development strategy in Africa, a preventive strategy for which there is no acceptable alternative. The alternative, if it is an alternative, would be for African countries to adopt less costly and less effective pollution control or completely ignore pollution control with serious global ecological and environmental consequences.

## Procurement of Inputs and Finance

In the broader sense, inputs here comprise material, human, technological, and financial resources. As most of these inputs are covered under other sections, material inputs (raw materials, intermediates, energy) and finance constitute the focus of this section.

Availability of raw materials in the quantity, quality, and time required is of crucial importance to the continuous and profitable operation of production units. This is particularly so in drought-prone areas where, because of inadequate rainfall, agriculture-based supplies are frequently disrupted.

In recent years, the availability and supply of inputs have improved in many countries because of measures taken by governments. The National Policy on Disaster Prevention and Management, which includes integrating relief aid with development activities in rehabilitating the environment, adopted in 1995 by the Transitional Government of Ethiopia, is a case in point. It will take some years before the country attains a higher and more sustainable degree of self-sufficiency in food. In the meantime those who need food aid will have access to it in the form of payment for work rendered in development activities related to projects intended to minimize the effects of drought and other natural calamities. Similar measures are being taken by other countries.

Many African countries continue their efforts to secure their raw material, intermediates, and energy resources locally. There are instances of resourcing done at the multinational level. Lack of access to imports arising from a paucity of foreign exchange could stimulate domestic production. In other words, it could be a blessing in disguise. This happened twice in the former Southern Rhodesia, now Zimbabwe. The first occasion was during the Second World War when access to manufactured goods from Europe was practically cut off; the second took place from mid-1960s to 1980, when the world community imposed sanctions on the country because of its unilateral declaration of independence. Zimbabwe owes, in good part, its present level of development to these two events which forced the country to develop import-substitution industries, including steel making. There is no doubt that, although not on the same scale as former Southern Rhodesia, similar developments took place in many African countries following the foreign exchange crunch. The Suwame Magazine in Ghana referred to earlier is a good example of such a development. African countries would be well advised to turn the foreign exchange disadvantage into an advantage following these examples.

Because of experience and better planning and project development, new imported input-oriented industries are likely to be based on more appropriate technologies adapted to local conditions. They are expected to use more and more local inputs and to be more efficiently operated thereby minimizing inputs that involve foreign exchange. Because of market saturation for import substitution consumer goods over time and the inevitable need for attaining some level of self-reliance in local inputs, a shift into intermediate goods production would constitute the next stage of import substitution. This includes the production of basic metals and chemicals characterized by economies of scale; unfortunately, this is beyond the reach of many countries. In other words, unless groups of countries pool their resources and markets, shifting to intermediate goods may remain a dream for a long time to come.

Diversification of agricultural products has been recommended as a panacea for all kinds of economic ills, including the crucial foreign exchange constraint. How realistic is this approach? What happens to coffee, for example, if an increasing number of countries grow coffee, as seems to be happening in countries, like Zambia. The world market for coffee will be flooded, thereby depressing coffee prices. This would, of course, benefit consumers in developed countries, but would eventually harm the producers and the exporting countries by aggravating their vulnerability to the vagaries of world market, falling prices. The additional foreign exchange earnings they hoped for may not be forthcoming. It is quite possible that the diversification process may end up calling for more foreign exchange. Countries contemplating agricultural diversification solely for the purpose of increasing foreign exchange earnings should remember this scenario when deciding on such diversification.

Increasing poverty in and marginalization by the globalization process of African countries could drive their people to diversify into growing drug-containing plants. Of all the developing regions, Africa has, so far, been relatively free form drug problems. Some farmers in a number of countries, however, have in recent years started growing cannabis. This could be a harbinger to growing all kinds of drug plants and the subsequent problems not only for Africa but also for the world.

With respect to finance, Africa is in the process of starvation. Foreign capital inflows have been declining, particularly following the end of the Cold War and increasing debt repayment. In recent years, this has deteriorated to net outflows. The measures and actions African countries are taking to attract foreign investment is dealt with in the last section of this chapter. Suffice it to say here that many countries will find it impossible to develop without the injection of massive foreign capital, particularly in view of the increasing external debt servicing.

There are many ways and means of alleviating the debt burden of African countries. Restructuring, rescheduling, and cancellation are among the schemes practiced. The latest event in regard to the last is the debt relief of up to $7.7 billion that the finance ministers of the Group of Seven agreed upon in September 1996 in Washington, D.C., to give to 20 of the world's most heavily indebted countries, many of them in Africa.

Innovative mechanisms identified by UNIDO comprise debt-equity swaps, venture capital companies and funds, country funds focused on developing-country stock markets, industrial leasing, and build-operate-transfer arrangements. The first involves acquiring equity in a domestic company; the second investing in new enterprises or corporate restructuring; the third identifying and acclaiming domestic companies; the fourth using equipment temporarily for a fee; and the fifth the public sector developing and operating infrastructure services for a given period. Under present conditions, the third and fifth alternatives may not be practical in some African countries for some time to come.

Another approach, known as direct expatriate nationals investment (DENT), could contribute to diminishing debt repayment in hard currency. It is based on expatriates of an African country securing a debt voucher for the total debt by paying in hard currency only a fraction of the total debt to the creditors and redeeming the whole debt in local currency of and from the debtor country. It is, of course, possible to envisage an arrangement between the indebted country and the expatriates concerned whereby redeeming would be less than 100 percent.

As for technological capability building, two suggestions have been put forward by institutions, one local and one external. The former, ADB, proposed an endowment fund starting with $500 million to provide 250 professional positions in Abidjan and other selected centers of excellence in Africa to carry out activities aimed at economic integration in Africa. The latter, the Independent Group on Financial Flows to Developing Countries, argued for the establishment of a $1 billion OECD endowment fund to be administered by the ADB to develop African leadership in policy-making, and professional, technological, and managerial areas (UNIDO, *Industry and Development, Global Report 1992/93*). If implemented these suggestions could make a difference.

## Industrial Cooperation as a Development Strategy
As far back as 1955 the developing countries recognized the need for a new order at the global level and organized the Asia-Africa Conference in Bandug, Indonesia. This conference was the precursor of the Non Aligned Nations (NAN), which in subsequent years served to articulate common developing countries positions in world affairs. It came out with a new perception of the world in which developing countries had a role to play.

As a result of efforts made by NAN and other organizations, the international community came out with the Lima Declaration and Plan of Action on Industrial Development and Cooperation in 1975. It unequivocally declared that the share of developing countries should be increased to at least 25 percent of total world industrial production by the year 2000. In 1980, because of the special situation of Africa, the world community declared the 1980s the Industrial Development Decade for Africa (IDDA). According to IDDA, the African share in world manufacturing value added (MVA) was to increase from 0.8 percent in 1970 to 1 percent in 1990 and 2 percent in the year 2000. Mainly because of the world economic crisis and the multiple crises in Africa, IDDA was doomed to failure. In view of the disappointing result of the first IDDA and the continuing deteriorating economic and social conditions of the continent, IDDA II for the 1990s decade was declared. From indications so far, IDDA II is not likely to be much different from IDDA I.

With respect to large industries and industries sensitive to economies of scale (thus requiring markets beyond national boundaries) and other related constraints, attempts were and continue to be made to pool and integrate the markets in a number of countries. The fertilizer factory in Senegal and the cement mill in Ghana both were examples of such, albeit unsuccessful, attempts.

At the subregional level, the United Nations Economic Commission for Africa (ECA), the United Nations Industrial Development Organization (UNIDO), and the Organization of African Unity (OAU), which jointly sponsor and organize the biennial African Conference of Ministers of Industry, continue to promote multinational industries following the Lima Declaration and Plan of Action, the Lagos Plan of Action, and the IDDA II program. The approach used is to identify industries and propose suitable locations. Once the proposals have been accepted by the member states concerned, decisions would ideally be made by member states at the different stages of project development until the project is ready for handing over to prospective investors which may include interested governments. The earlier the stage of handing-over, the better.

At present, success stories are hard to come by. Now that more and more economic blocs are being established, making it increasingly harder, if not impossible, for African countries to continue their traditional way of going it alone, and now that an increasing number of African countries are recognizing that there is no alternative to industrial cooperation, it is likely that they will take cooperation more seriously. With cooperation, many of the constraints, both internal and external, will be minimized.

## Conclusion

In summary, most of the constraints identified above are of a temporary nature. Except for some of the topographical, climatic, environmental, and external (debt, negative resource transfers, disinvestment, market fluctuation, etc.) constraints, all the rest have shown dramatic improvements since independence and are likely to improve further within the foreseeable future. From development activities (soil and water conservation, afforestation, etc.) being carried out in drought-prone countries, such as Burkina Faso, Eritrea, Ethiopia, and Kenya, the adverse impacts of climatic and environmental conditions will probably lessen over time.

There is a trend, following the end of the Cold War, towards better governance and pursuance of macro-economic reform. More and more governments are practicing the rule of law and respect for and observance of human rights, for which a protocol on the African Court on Human and Peoples' Rights was under preparation in 1997 for adoption by the OAU Heads of State and Government. The Mauritius Declaration which, among other things, urges African governments to create national human rights institutions and recognizes the role of NGO's therein was adopted by African governments in 1999. In this connection, we should note the existence of the African Commission on Human and Peoples' Rights based in Banjul, the Gambia.

An increasing number of public enterprises are functioning as commercial businesses with profit making as their major objective.

Current trends, the build up of capability and learning experience of three decades, and the effects of the measures and actions being taken by many African governments will increasingly minimize most constraints. Such optimistic conclusions are based on the following positive factors (some already referred to above) in support of faster and integrated socio-economic development in which industry will play a major role:

- In general, peace and stability are prevailing with the resolutions of conflicts (despite some recent setbacks whose effect on business ownership and operation is likely to be minimal);

- African leadership is maturing and becoming more transparent and accountable to society;

- There is a trend towards good governance and decentralization of governmental authority;

- There are signs of consistent and predictable application of laws and administrative regulations;

- Governments are introducing and implementing sound economic and social policies;
- Economies are being liberalized;
- Investment climate is improving;
- There is a trend towards better use of resources; and
- Economies of most African countries are growing at faster rates and substantially higher than those of population.

An IMF observation (*World Economic Outlook*) that "The *outlook for Africa has continued to improve with the recent implementation of structural reforms and stabilization programs in a number of countries,*" seems to confirm the above conclusions. The IMF had predicted that in countries implementing IMF's structural adjustment facility (SAF) or enhanced structural adjustment facility (ESAF), GDP would grow by 5.5 percent while inflation would fall to below 10 percent in 1995-96.

All these positive trends call for enormous amounts of resources if they are to materialize and exert a sustained significant impact on development. However, at a time when assistance should be increased to maintain the momentum of change, some donors are reducing their assistance. The apparent positive changes are likely to reverse or ground to a halt unless urgent drastic actions are taken by Africa's development partners. In some cases, sliding towards dictatorship cannot be ruled out. Payment of fair prices for African raw materials, writing off foreign debts, offering increased aid in the form of grants and concessional loans and increasing the flow of foreign direct investment (FDI) are called for. The increase in primary commodity prices that started in 1994 following the global economic recovery needs to be sustained.

## IMPROVING THE INVESTMENT CLIMATE

As noted in the preceding section, improving the investment climate figures among the factors being promoted and supported to enhance socio-economic development in African countries. This factor is particularly crucial for industrial development. This section, therefore, focuses on the investment climate as it relates to the industrial sector.

It is apparent that an array of constraints (political instability, economic and social difficulties, bureaucracies, corruption, excessive foreign debt, etc.) has contributed to he high cost of doing business in Africa as reported by some sources. This has, apparently, been one of the reasons for declining foreign investment. Countries such as Egypt and the oil-exporting countries, which account for a large share of foreign investment in Africa, have been exceptions in this regard. Foreign capital participation in Egypt's 1987/88-1991/92 plan, for instance, was 35 percent (18% Arab and 17% other investors) of total investment, part of which was for establishments located in free zones (ECA, ECA/IHSD/IPPIS/033/93).

According to an UNCTAD report titled "Foreign Direct Investment in Africa," Africa leads other developing regions in terms of rates of return on private investment. This was confirmed by the secretary general of the United Nations when addressing a meeting of the United Nations' Economic and Social Council in Geneva in July 1995. During the period 1980-1993, rates of return on United States FDI from developing Africa were significantly higher for 11 years than those for developing countries as a whole. The returns for 12 years were even higher than those of United States FDI in developed countries. The returns in the manufacturing sector, although generally lower, peaked at 48.9 percent in 1988 (UN, *Foreign Direct Investment in Africa*). In 1998 Susan Rice, the Assistant Secretary of State for African Affairs, further confirmed the high rate of return by stating that it was *"some three times higher than the average return elsewhere in the world."* President Clinton, while addressing the US-African Ministerial on Partnership for the 21st Century pointed out that return on American investments in Africa of 36 percent compared with 14 percent worldwide in 1997. All these show that, despite the high cost of doing business in Africa referred to above, the potential of the continent to attract investment is good. Risks associated with political and social instability (which, however, are lessening in many countries) seem to be among the main factors explaining the stagnating foreign investment flow into Africa.

Having realized the havoc that their past inhospitable policies have brought to their respective economies, most, if not all, African countries have shifted their attention to creating enabling environments for both the public and private sectors and to focusing on their roles of developing physical and institutional infrastructures. To this end, they are reducing the direct role of the state in production; they have formulated and are implementing macroeconomic policies, strategies, legislation, and incentives for the smoother development and operation of enterprises. An increasing number of them (Algeria, Burkina Faso, Cote d'Ivoire, Niger, Senegal, Tunisia, Kenya, Togo, Ethiopia, etc.) are operating through "one-stop" investment centers to provide supporting services and minimize bureaucratic and related time-consuming procedures (supply of information, facilitating formalities, expediting legal and other processes, etc.). If they are to discharge their duties effectively, the centers should enjoy a measure of autonomy under a board comprising high-ranking representatives of relevant ministries and other bodies (which impact on industrial enterprises) and institutions and the private sector.

The negative image (war, drought, poverty, famine, disease, and mismanagement) applies to a diminishing number of countries. Yet, unfortunately, the international media, instead of reporting a balanced view of things (i.e., one that includes success stories of political, social, and economic developments which abound nowadays, seem to have generalized the negative features and applied them to the whole continent. Following her visits to some African countries in 1997, the American first lady, Hillary R. Clinton, noted that success stories are ignored.

Particular importance should be attached to an independent transparent judiciary (as part of an enabling environment) as stressed by Regina C. Brown, the US Deputy Assistant Secretary of State for African Affairs, when giving testimony before the International Trade Commission in 1995. She cited South Africa, Cote d'Ivoire, Ghana, Uganda, and Botswana as successful examples for investment in Africa. Governments are becoming more mature, realistic, and pragmatic. As groups, governments are integrating their economies into subregional common markets which, eventually, will be expected to lead to a regional economic communities. This process is, among other things, expected to integrate the small and fragmented national markets into viable subregional and regional markets.

As noted earlier, celebrating Africa Industrialization Day, November 20th each year, has been adopted as one of the means of promoting industrial development in Africa. "The Transfer of Technology and Engineering" was the theme in 1993 and "The Role of the Private Sector in African Industrialization" in 1994 (ECA/UNIDO, CAMI.12/4). A film titled "Private Industry—Engine of Progress" and IDDA posters were among the materials used for the celebration. Celebrations at the country level include: organizing seminars, conferences, debates, exhibitions, press conferences, interviews; delivering addresses and messages on the media; and awarding industrialists. The following were among the topics of these activities in 1994: "Situation of Privatization and Perspectives on the Country's Industrialization" in Burkina Faso; "The Private Sector in the Twenty-first Century" in Ghana; "Private Sector and its Role in Industrialization" in Mali; and "Sound Science Foundation in Secondary Schools: The Role of the Private Sector" in Nigeria. The regional theme for 1995 was "Human Resource Development with Special Emphasis on Support Services for Industry." "Accelerating trade and investment in Africa" was the theme of ECA's Twenty-third Meeting of the Conference of African Ministers Responsible for Economic and Social Development and Planning (1997). All these and other themes testify to the efforts being made by African countries to facilitate economic development, particularly industrial development, to attract investment, and to render the private sector the engine of growth.

Changes have taken and are taking place in regard to African attitudes towards foreign investment. This has, among other things, to do with African countries' concern with dwindling foreign private capital flows. Annual flows of FDI into the continent which averaged $2.7 billion in the period 1985-1990, had declined to $2.5 billion in 1991 and apparently stagnated at this level in 1993 (ECA/UNIDO, CAMI.12/5[b]/REV.1). According to another source (ECA, E/ECA/CM.21/7), flows of FDI averaged $2 billion during the first half of the 1980s, $3 billion during the second, and $3 billion in 1991. The corresponding African shares (%) of total flows to developing economies were 4, 4 and 2 showing to what extent Africa has been marginalized in this respect. During the period 1992-1995, FDI peaked at $4.2 billion in 1994 having risen from $2.17 billion in the previous year. In this connection, it should be noted that most of the FDI went to oil-exporting countries.

African concerns arising from such a state of affairs were, among others, expressed in resolution 798 (XXX) titled "Promotion of Private Investment in Africa of the Twenty-first Meeting of the Conference of Ministers Responsible for Economic and Social Development and Planning of African Countries," held in Addis Ababa, Ethiopia, May 1995. The first operative paragraph of the resolution *"Calls upon African countries to intensify their efforts to create and maintain an enabling environment for private sector development and the growth of private capital flows, especially in productive activities through the institution of the necessary macroeconomic framework which would emphasize improving infrastrurcural and human development resources capacities."* As one of the follow-ups to this resolution, ECA with the support of other institutions, including stock markets and the media, was reported to be planning to organize an investment promotion conference on " Reviving Private Investment in Africa: Challenges and Opportunities." Among other things, the conference was expected to come up with an action plan for domestic and foreign investment in Africa.

The important role of the private sector was highlighted by holding the Private Sector Forum in Gaborone, Botswana, preceding the twelfth meeting of the

Conference of African Ministers of Industry convened at the same venue in mid-1995. The Forum organized by the African Business Round Table, among others, and attended by about 100 private sector operators was meant to initiate and strengthen the involvement of the private sector in the activities related to IDDA II. Enabling environment, implications of the Uruguay Round Agreement, mobilization of resources and regional cooperation, and the role of the private sector were among the topics discussed at the Forum.

The above Conference of African Ministers of Industry, whose theme was "Resource Mobilization," was jointly organized by ECA and UNIDO in cooperation with OAU. Many participants stressed the importance of involving the private sector in policy making, planning, and implementation of industrial programs. This was reflected in resolution 3 (XII) in which the Conference, *"cognizant of the need to ensure full participation of all agents of production, distribution and services in the industrialization process of African economies,"* called upon *"African countries to intensify their efforts to create and sustain an enabling environment for private sector development and the growth of private capital flows, especially in productive activities ... ."*

At the international community level, resolution GC.5/Res.12 on IDDA II of the 1993 General Conference of UNIDO requested the Director General of UNIDO *"to give high priority to the development of the African private sector ... ."* and urged the multilateral development finance and bilateral aid institutions *"to give high priority to increased investment in the industrial sector as a means of encouraging foreign private investment in the industrial sectors in Africa."* It is apparent that developed countries whose investors provide FDIs could facilitate the flow of investment by supporting and improving guarantee schemes and providing fiscal and other incentives for investing in African countries. This should be reinforced by the same countries improving access of LDCs to their markets.

In 1994, the General Assembly of the United Nations adopted resolution A/RES/49/107 reaffirming the importance of African industrialization and requesting UNIDO *"to give full assistance to improving the competitiveness of the industrial sector in Africa ... to mobilize resources and promote direct foreign investment to African countries."* The above resolutions have reinforced UNIDO's mandates of promoting industrial development in African countries. As in the past, UNIDO continues to organize investment promotion meetings at national, subregional, and regional levels, including preparation of integrated packages of investment and technical assistance projects for presentation at the meetings, as one of the means of fulfilling its mandates. Notable among the recent ones is the Round Table of African Investment Promotion Centers, which brought together representatives of African investment promotion centers and UNIDO Investment Promotion Service Offices in developed countries in 1992, and the Private Sector Expert Group Meeting on the Industrialization of Africa in Abidjan, Cote d'Ivoire, in 1995. The objective of the first was to establish an Investment Promotion Network aimed at mobilizing resources for investment in Africa. The second led to the holding of the Private Sector Forum in Botswana, referred to above.

UNIDO had planned to hold more investors' forums in 1995 in Morocco and Ghana and for COMESA member states. The last one to have been held in November/December 1995 in Kampala, Uganda, was aimed at generating international industrial cooperation in establishing joint ventures and wholly foreign-owned companies; transferring technology and technological, technical and managerial know-how; facilitating financing; and securing access to foreign markets (UNIDO, *COMESA Investors' Forum*). Other forums held in recent years include the Forum on Promotion of Financial Market Integration and Development in Africa (July 1997), the African Capital Markets Forum and the Addis Forum on Trade and Investment (March 1998) aimed at attracting global capital to Africa. Executive Summary of Investors' Guides to Selected Africa Countries, African Investment Promotion Agencies Directory, African Directory of Sources of Technical Information (Vol. One) and Industrial Development Review Series (country reports) are among UNIDO's reference materials that potential investors can access. Other sources that can be accessed include investment guides on Ethiopia, Madagsscar, Mali, Mozambique, and Uganda, to be prepared with the assistance of and in relation to a workshop organized by UNCTAD and the International Chamber of Commerce (ICC).

Trade fairs organized at the national, subregional and regional levels are other means of promoting trade, particularly intra-African trade, and therefore industry. The numerous fairs organized in Addis Ababa, Ethiopia, in recent years are examples of the first. The Third Addis Chamber International Trade Fair took place in November 1997. It was accompanied by a symposium on trade and investment ventures. The COMESA trade fairs and the 7th OAU/AEC All-Africa Trade and Tourism Fair (1997), at which market profiles of selected products were distributed and buyer/seller meetings held, are examples of the second and third.

The above resolution of the Conference of Ministers was, in fact, a reinstatement of what was already being done by the member states. Practically all African governments have taken measures to create an enabling environment and investment-conducive climate. They have formulated investment legislations and codes, many of which have been revised more than once and are still undergoing revisions. In Ethiopia, for instance, investment proclamations and Council of Ministers regulations to provide for investment incentives (revising a 1992 proclamation) were issued in 1996, resulting in a surge of investment[8]. There were 47 new approved foreign investment projects in mid-1996 to October 1997, compared with only 22 during the period 1992-mid-1996. The corresponding figures for manufacturing were 26 and 10. From these it is apparent that manufacturing accounted for about half of the projects. The manufacturing projects include: five assembly (one each for light vehicles, trucks, three-wheeled vehicles, diesel generator and computer), two construction materials, two pharmaceuticals plants and one organic fertilizer plant. Investors, over 40 percent of them in joint venture with local investors, come from over 20 countries. In terms of number of projects (at least three) per country of origin, Saudi Arabia leads, followed by the United States, South Korea, Italy, France, Kenya, Yemen, and Sudan. By 1998 the country had signed investment guarantee agreements with four countries and was in the process of doing the same with nine more, including China, Italy, Switzerland, Britain, the Netherlands, Germany, India and Algeria.

The Ministers Regulation in Ethiopia allows small-scale activities involving capital investment of less than Birr 250,000 (about $36,000) to benefit from the exemption of customs duty on machinery and equipment. This partially corrected the bias against small- and medium-sized enterprises referred to earlier. The latest revisions of the proclamation and regulation (June 1998) allow the private sector to own immovable property and to invest and participate in telecommunications, hydroelectric power generation, defense industry, distribution of petroleum products, etc. In regard to financial institutions, the control over bank lending rates by the National Bank of Ethiopia has been abolished and private banks have been authorized to deal with foreign currency transactions, including licensing foreign exchange for imports and issuing export permits. More proclamations related to the promotion of trade and investment were reported ready in draft form in 1998.

These measures in favor of the investor were being enhanced by a restructured customs authority instituted in 1997 (Proclamation No. 60/1997) aimed at reducing bureaucracy and corruption and facilitating the clearance of goods. In this connection, it would be opportune to note here that about 50 percent of the COMESA member countries are making use of the Automated System for Customs Data (ASYCUDA) for recording, storage, retrieval, etc. of imports and exports.

The degrees of comprehensives of investment codes may vary from country to country, depending upon the stage of development of the country, manpower development, resource endowment, priority sectors, etc. Generally, they include a combination of any of the following incentives and guarantees for enterprises meeting certain conditions:

• Ownership and local participation:
. Privatizaion/divestment—total or partial disengagement from government ownership,
. Minimal state equity participation, if any, in activities not reserved for state enterprises, and
. Joint venture/partnership with local investors, preferred by many governments.

• Tariff and fiscal provisions/concessions:
. Customs duties and taxes, partial or total exemption on capital goods, construction  materials and industrial inputs that are not locally available,
. Royalties, lower than in the past for mining,
. Accelerated depreciation,
. Investment tax credit,
. Tax holidays exempting enterprises from paying income tax for a given period (5-10 years),
. Loss carry forward to offset against future income,
. Exemption from withholding tax on profits and dividends,
. Exemption of expatriates from income tax,
. Currency retention for projects generating foreign exchange,
. Fiscal stability by freezing tax rates for a given period, and
. Incentives for reinvestment.

• Legal guarantees:
. Guarantees from nationalization and expropriation (adequate compensation, if expropriated),
. Repatriation of capital, capital gains,
. Transfer of profits, dividends, expatriate salaries,
. Right to holding foreign account, and
. International arbitration in case of disputes.

As stated above, these provisions should be taken as general indications of the guarantees and incentives that can be given by African governments. A summary of details of some of the common features of investment codes in six countries is provided in Annex 6.1. It should be noted here that in an effort to simplify and standardize the presentation and render the information comparable, some relevant details and references to exceptions had to be ignored. Although many of the codes incorporate amendments made since their promulgation, it is quite possible that more changes could have been made since. The improvement and simplification of investment procedure in Mozambique in 1995 is a case in point. One-stop investment procedure, replies to investment requests within 10 to 20 working days, and extension of the exceptional tax breaks granted to industrial free zones to any company exporting at least 85 percent of its production are among the changes introduced. A request would be presumed approved if a reply is not received within the stipulated time. In Ethiopia, an investment permit is given within 10 days after the applicant meets the required conditions at the federal level and within 30 days at the state level; land is allocated within 60 days following receipt of application from the investor.

In some countries, it is possible for investors to obtain more concessions not stipulated in the investment codes for projects of special economic and social interest to national development or because of the size and nature of the project, the location of the project in a lesser developed area, or the export orientation of the project. Some countries even offer land, infrastructure, and utilities at preferential rates. More liberal incentives are given to enterprises operating in export processing-zones, such as those in Mauritius, where textiles and garment production dominate, and in Tunisia.

On the basis of information in the above-cited annex, it is not possible to make generalizations. Some thing can be said, however, in regard to customs duties and corporate profit taxes. Duty and other tax-free concessions are generally given for imported equipment and material inputs not locally produced. Corporate and other taxes are partially or fully exempted, normally for 5 to 10 years. In the 1980s, corporate income tax rates were considered relatively high by international standards. According to more recent sources, it appears that the tax rates have been declining (35% in Ghana and Ethiopia and 15% in Botswana) and are not likely to exceed 45 percent. These compare with 57.4 percent in Germany and 38.2 percent in the EU (*The Economist*, July 27, 1996).

Generally, investment codes are biased in favor of foreign investment and large-scale industries. Until recently, small-scale enterprises and the informal sector (particularly the latter) had no access to incentives commensurate to their needs. Some countries have started to give more attention to catering to such needs, including channeling loans, one of the most difficult services to administer—even through peer groups. Some countries are likely to attempt a system similar to that of the Grameen Bank in Bangladesh, whose credit scheme has been highly successful in administering credits to the poor. The Microcredit Summit that was held in Washington D.C. in early 1997 had the objective of making credit available for self-development to 100 million of the world's poorest families. To this end, the UNDP has launched Microstart, a program that will contribute $41 million through micro-lending institutions (SID, *Development Connections, February, March* 1997).

All the countries in Annex 6.1 (except Mozambique) are members of one or more international organizations: the African Intellectual Property Organization (AIPO), the African Regional Industrial Property Organization (ARIPO), the Paris Convention for the Protection of Industrial Property (more than 30 countries), and the World Intellectual Property Organization (WIPO).

With respect to investment protection and resolving investment disputes, most African countries are signatories to treaties and arbitration mechanisms. About 230 bilateral investment treaties had been signed by African countries by the beginning of 1995 (UN, *Foreign Direct Investment in Africa*). By mid-1996, the number of bilateral investment treaties rose to 258; and 155 treaties for avoidance of double taxation were signed (UN, *World Investment Report 1996*). In 1994, African membership in organizations dealing with multilateral treaties and arbitration of investment disputes was as follows:

• 33 full members (plus 7 in the process of becoming full members) in the Multilateral Investment Guarantee Agency (MIGA) that provides insurance against political risks,

• 41 full members (plus 3 yet to enter into force) in the International Centre for Settlement of Investment Disputes (ICSID),

• 20 which ratified the New York Convention on the Recognition and Enforcement of Foreign Arbitral Awards, and

• 37 which are parties to the Paris Convention for the Protection of Industrial Property (ECA, *Foreign Direct Investment in Africa)*.

It would be reasonable to assume that the member countries have taken into account some of the concepts and rules and regulations governing the above organizations when revising or formulating their respective investment codes.

Most governments have established national bodies, generally known as investment centers, to promote investment and facilitate pre-investment activities. The centers are expected to drastically reduce redtape and corruption, including the unduly long time it takes to obtain government approval and investment concessions. Many governments have instituted systems whose objectives are to simplify investment procedures. It is intended to cater to all the needs of the investor, including government approval within a pre-determined time (8 weeks in Tunisia), thus avoiding the trouble of dealing with so many government institutions and bureaucrats. In some countries the centers are intended to operate as autonomous bodies. The investment center in Zambia is an example of such a center. It was established as a corporate body that can sue and be sued (ECA, ECA/IHSD/IPPIS/033/93).

Because of the competition to attract investment, the above incentives (many of which seem excessive) could inhibit the development of local initiatives and deprive developing countries of the badly needed revenues from customs duties, taxes, etc. For many of them in Sub-Sahara Africa, especially the poorer and less developed countries, revenues collected from taxation of international trade constitute a major part of government income. The average tax-on-international-trade to total-tax-revenue ratio was 0.43 in 1980 (0.48 in 1970) for 35 countries. In 1980, the ratio ranged between 0.07 in Zimbabwe and 0.77 in the Gambia. In 21 countries more than 80 percent of tax revenues on trade came from import tariffs (Meier et. al. 1989); reducing that revenue would worsen budget deficits.

Investors would, naturally, want to maximize benefits accruing from liberal investment codes. Under the circumstances, the host countries should obtain performance guarantees from investors in return for their generous terms and conditions. Given the poor economic and social conditions of the host countries and the long-term interest of the investors, it would be prudent if the investors could limit their profits to appropriate levels. As for management services, remuneration should be linked to performance, i.e., rewards for good performance, including training of nationals and replacement of expatriate management by trained nationals within a given period, and penalties for incompetency or malpractice.

In the past, incentives, particularly exemption of capital goods from customs duties and accelerated depreciation coupled with overvalued local currencies and access to local low-interest loans, resulted in capital-intensive production units in countries starved of employment opportunities. There is a need to harmonize investment codes at the subregional and regional levels in order to minimize disparities between codes and costs to the host countries.

Incentives are by themselves of no use in a politically unstable environment where political risks, for obvious reasons, are considered high. Peace, political stability, and predictability of government actions are, therefore, the preconditions that dispose a potential investor towards considering the possibility of investing in a given country. This can be illustrated by a number of American, Canadian, South African, British, and Swedish companies which in 1995 won tenders to prospect and mine gold in Ethiopia. Similar happenings were witnessed with respect to Eritrea in 1996. These, plus the interest shown by others in Ethiopia, including France, Syria and Lebanon (food, beverage and detergent industries and transportation), Saudi Arabia (industry, construction and agriculture, including gum and incense ), Italy, and Kuwait, confirm the political stability prevailing in both countries (until the outbreak of conflict in 1998) following the fall of the previous regime and hence the growing confidence the countries had started to enjoy inernationally.

The improvement in investment climate so far achieved as well as the trend towards further improvement augur well for investors. Implementation of the incentives and facilitating the work of the investors, however, may not, in practice, be as rosy as they are on paper. Many of the constraints discussed in this chapter are still there, albeit in varying degrees. Fortunately, an increasing number of countries are making efforts at improving implementation.

Readers seeking more details on improving the investment climate would be advised to refer to "Annex 3.1: Summary of Major Policy Measure Undertaken by Selected African Countries in 1993" in ADB's *African Development Report 1994*, Abidjan, Cote d'Ivoire. The summary provides information (budget deficit cuts, inflation reduction, exchange rate devaluation, trade liberalization, price controls, interest rate rise, civil service reform, public enterprise restructuring/ privatization, review with ADB, and social sector budget allocation) on 35 African countries.

## BIBLIOGRAPHY

ADB, 1997, *African Development Report 1997,* Oxford University Press, Inc., New York.
Bailey, Richard, 1976, *Africa's Industrial Future,* Davidson Publishing Limited, Blandford.

Business Week, 1997, "The German Worker is Making Sacrifice," July 28, 1997.

Central Statistical Authority (Ethiopia), 1997, "Report on Large and Medium Scale Manufacturing and Electricity Industries Survey," *Statistical Bulletin 178*, October 1997, Addis Ababa.

ECA, 1993, *Report: The Ad Hoc Expert Group Meeting on Promotion of Investment in Industrial Projects in the Context of the Second Industrial Development Decade (IDDA II)* (ECA/IHSD/IPPIS/033/93), Addis Ababa.

ECA, 1994, *Anticipated Impact of the Uruguay Round Agreements on African Economies: A Preliminary Analysis (E/ECA/CM.20/31)*, Addis Ababa.

ECA, 1994, "Foreign Direct Investment in Africa," *Transnational Focus*, No. 11, December 1994, Addis Ababa.

ECA, 1994, *Report of the Implementation of the United Nations New Agenda for the Development of Africa in the 1990s (E/ECA/CM.20/3)*, Addis Ababa.

ECA, 1995, *Reviving Private Investments in Africa: Policies, Strategies and Programmes* (E/ECA/CM.21/7), Addis Ababa.

ECA/UNIDO, 1995, *Africa Industrialization Day - 20 November 1994* (CAMI.12/4), Addis Ababa.

ECA/UNIDO, 1995, *Development of Human Resources for Industrialization in Africa* (CAMI.12/9), Addis Ababa.

ECA/UNIDO, 1995, *Progress Report on the Implementation of the Programme for the Second IDDA: (b) Joint Secretariat Report* (CAMI.12/5[b]/Rev.1), Addis Ababa.

IFC, 1990, *African Entrepreneurs: Pioneers of Development*, Washington, D.C.

IMF, 1995, *World Economic Outlook*, Washington, D.C.

Juo, Anthony S.R. and Russell D. Freed, editors, 1995, *Agriculture and the Environment: Bridging Food Production and Environmental Protection in Developing Countries*, ASA Special Publication, Number 60, Madison.

Meier, Gerald M. and William F. Steel, eds., 1989, *Industrial Adjustment in Sub-Saharan Africa*, EDI Series in Economic Development, Published for the World Bank, Oxford University Press, London.

Melrose, Dianna, 1983 (reprinted), *Bitter Pills*, OXFAM, Oxfam Print Unit, Oxford.

OAU, 1997, "OAU/AEC General Secretariat at First WTO Ministerial Conference in Singapore," *AEC Newsletter*, February-April 1997.

Reich, B. Robert, 1991, *The Work of Nations*, Simon & Schuster Ltd., London.

Samuelson, R. J.,1997, "A New Start for Europe," *Newsweek*, August 25, 1997.

Seidman, Ann, 1994, "The Meaning of 'Sustainable Development' in Africa," *African Development Perspectives Yearbook 1992/93, Vol. III: Energy and Sustainable Development*, LIT VERLAG, Hamburg.

SID, 1997, Microcredit Summit Convenes, *Development Connections*, February - March 1997, Washington D.C.

Stock, Robert, 1995, *Africa South of the Sahara: a Geographical Interpretation*, The Guilford Press, London.

The Monitor, 1995, "Open Economy," February 11-12, 1995, Addis Ababa.

The Economist, 1994, May 7, 1994.

The Economist, 1996, "After Thomson," December 14, 1996.

The Economist, 1996, "Company Taxes," July 27, 1996.

The Economist, 1996, " Stormy Weather Ahead," March 23, 1996.

The Economist, 1997, "Germany's Mad Mountain Men," March 15, 1997.

The Economist, 1997, "Who Will Listen to Mr. Clean?," August 2, 1997.

The Economist, 1997, "Thatcherites in Brussels (really)," March 15, 1997.

The Economist, 1998, "Fifty Years on," May 16, 1998.

The Ethiopian Herald, 1994, "Gov't Cancels over Three Bln. Birr Debt Owed by Productive Enterprises," November 1, 1994, Addis Ababa.

UN, 1995, *Foreign Direct Investment in Africa,* New York.

UN, 1996, *World Investment Report 1996* (UNCTAD estimates based on UNCTAD-DTCI, 1996a).

UNCTAD, 1995, *The Least Developed Countries, 1995 Report,* (ID/B/41(2)/4), New York.

UNCTC, 1991, *National Legislation and Regulations Relating to Transnational Corporations,* Volume VII (ST/CTC/91).

UNDP, 1996, *Human Development Report 1996,* Oxford University Press, New York.

UNIDO, 1992, *Industry and Development, Global Report 1992/93,* Vienna.

UNIDO, 1993, *Industry and Development: Global Report 1993/94,* Vienna.

UNIDO, 1995, *COMESA Investors' Forum,* Internet.

UNIDO, 1995, *Industrial Development, Global Report 1995,* Oxford University Press, Oxford.

UNIDO, 1995, *The Globalization of Industry: Implications for Developing Countries beyond 2000,* Vienna.

UNIDO, 1996, *Industrial Development: Global Report 1996,* Vienna.

World Bank, 1989, *Sub-Saharan Africa: From Crisis to Sustainable Growth, a Long-term Perspective Study,* Washington, D.C.

World Bank, 1990, *The Long-Term Perspective Study of Sub-Saharan Africa,* Volume 2, Economic and Social Policy Issues, Washington, D.C.

World Bank, 1997, *The State in a Changing World,* Oxford University Press, inc., New York.

## NOTES

1. This section includes all other constraints not dealt with in the first and second sections and that on pollution..

2. In an article titled "The State of Greed" in *U.S.News & World Report* (June 17, 1996), the average compensations of chief executive officers of the 500 biggest firms was 197 times higher than the salary of the average American worker in 1995.

3. Developed countries do use anti-dumping measures. According to *USA Today* (August 22, 1997), the United States was, in 1997, threatening to impose anti-dumping duties ranging from 173% to 454% on Japanese supercomputers.

4. Botswana, Bburundi, Central African Republic, and Lesotho.

5. Benin, Burkina Faso, Chad, Gambia, Guinea, and Malawi.

6. The following may illustrate how far African countries have progressed in manpower development. In the second half of the 1960s, the ECA contracted a consulting firm in Frankfurt, Germany, to carry out a chemical industry development study in Eastern Africa. The study was full of errors, wrong assumptions, and incorrect calculations. It had to be revised drastically before it was issued as an ECA document. A year later, the director of the consulting firm on a visit to ECA Headquarters confessed to the then director of the Industry and Natural Resources Division that, with ECA's feedback, his firm's work in Africa was properly appraised and criticized for the first time.

7. During a demonstration supporting reform in constitution designed for a one-party state staged in Nairobi, Kenya, in May 1997, shops and cars owned by Indians were looted and set on fire, respectively (*The Boston Sunday Globe*, 1 June 1997).

8. Of the total 3,520 projects (involving capital investment of about $3.9 billion) issued investment certificates during 1992-mid-1997, 669 ($680 million) were operational and 492 ($500) were under implementation by June 1997

# PART THREE

# INDUSTRIAL DEVELOPMENT PROSPECTS

CHAPTER 7

# PRIORITIES FOR INDUSTRIAL DEVELOPMENT

Enhancing the welfare of the peoples, i.e., raising their living standards and quality of life to the highest practical level through sustainable development and growth with equity, is or should be the ultimate objective of all African countries. This implies, in the first instance, alleviating poverty and satisfying basic needs (basic necessities of life) of the population. In the words of the South Commission's Report, the strategy to be used is to *"satisfy basic needs and support a progressive increase in living standards."* In general, since most of the population is agrarian, this objective can be met by developing agriculture. This involves increasing areas under cultivation, where feasible, but mainly fundamentally transforming production structures, particularly increasing agricultural (food in particular) yields, productivity, and production and introducing the industrial production of basic goods and services while creating an enabling environment. The translation of this objective into targets would, of necessity, vary from country to country, depending upon a country's resource endowment and the size of that country's market. The correct balance between agriculture and industry, for instance, needs to be determined at the country level. Whatever balance is adopted, the crucial role of industry in agriculture and of industry itself is apparent. This was confirmed by the 1995 World Summit for Social Development held in Copenhagen, Denmark, which stressed that the fundamental solution to poverty was through the creation of productive employment, industry being one of the sectors providing employment opportunities.

African industry is characterized by dualism. Both the informal sector (traditional) and modern production systems operate side by side. Although the informal sector in Sub-Sahara Africa employs about 60 percent of the urban workforce (UNDP, *Human Development Report 1993*), the modern sector, which is normally concentrated in and around big cities, seems to receive most of governments' attentions.

In the three decades following independence, African countries have come to recognize the crucial role of industrial development (see Chapter 5) in diversifying and structurally transforming their economies as well as in bringing about self-sustained and self-reliant growth and development. This has been emphasized in many fora and government decisions. For example, in the Lagos Plan of Action (LPA) (OAU, *Lagos Plan of Action*), which is the basis for African initiatives in the socio-economic development of the region, *"African member states accord, in their development plans, a major role to industrialization, in view of its impact on meeting the basic needs of the population, ensuring the integration of the economy and the modernization of society"* and proclaimed the 1980s the Industrial Development Decade for Africa (IDDA).

It seems that the need for Africa to industrialize (i.e., to make the transition from an agrarian society to one based on industry), has been recognized by only a few non-African countries and institutions. The United Nations, particularly UNIDO, is among the exceptions as an international organization that has been involved in assisting and facilitating African industrialization. According to UNIDO accelerated and sustained economic development *"could be achieved only by accelerated industrialization and higher investment in the region."* Riddell (*Manufacturing Africa*) summarizes the apparent lack of support by donors. He points out that *"the role of industry has tended to be ignored or underplayed, at least by Western donors and the international institutions ... underplaying the role of industry has been a mistake ... its [industry's] virtual absence in policy debate emanating from outside Africa ... the place of industry - currently and in the future - is notable by its absence from discussion and policy prescription or by the minor role that it is given [by Western agencies]."* As confirmed by Riddell, the World Bank seems, in recent years, to have recognized the need for industrial development in Africa.

The fact that the term "industrialized countries" is used synonimously with the term "developed countries" implies that industry plays a major role in development and sustained economic diversification. As far as the African countries are concerned, it is apparent that African industrialization is no longer debatable. What is debatable are the strategies to be used.

Import-substitution and export-promotion strategies have been tried by many countries. Resource-based and basic-industries (producing intermediates, equipment, and machinery) strategies have, in recent years, been focused upon because of the priority status given them by the OAU and ECA (see Chapter 5). Both strategies, the first in particular, could enhance the diversification of the industrial sector and therefore the local input content and the economic structure by fostering the optimal utilization of domestic natural resources (increasing domestic value-added) as well as the integration of economic activities. In view of competition, an area in which most African countries are disadvantaged, import substitution, essentially based on basic needs, is likely to be the strategy that they will continue to adopt for some time to come.

The economic development of a country or a region is the sum total of developments in all sectors of economic and social activities. The priority sectors vary from country or region to country or region. Generally, a lead role is assigned to one sector, usually a production sector which is either agriculture or industry. In some instances, infrastructure, particularly those sectors crucial to the development of other sectors, takes the lead. Of course, sectoral priorities change with time and circumstances.

The theory of comparative advantages, according to which Africa would have been better off as supplier of low value raw materials, some of which are being rapidly exhausted, coupled with falling world demand and prices did not work in favor of Africa. Partly as a result of this African countries are depending increasingly on outside assistance to feed their people. Their financial capacity (arising in part from the unequal distribution of earnings in world trade) to import even basic needs is dwindling. They cannot import capital goods, including spare parts and replacement equipment and machinery, to maintain whatever industries (mainly imported-input-oriented industries), agriculture, transport, and communications they have. In short, the future of Africa seems bleak.

From the above, it is apparent that African countries have become poor buyers from the world, particularly industrialized countries. Because of this, traditional exporters to Africa have forgone potential exports to Africa. This means that the world community has lost a chance to increase production and thereby to create job opportunities. In other words, the potential loss in trade in the world could be significant if the world does not promote the economic growth of African countries. Continuing worsening of economic and social conditions in Africa means deterioration as evidenced by faster deforestation, overgrazing, desertification, destruction of biodiversity, and uncontrolled and increasing pollution, all of which will contribute to adverse changes in the global environment. It is apparent that helping Africa to develop is in the interest of the world at large. The consequence of not doing enough now may prove to be much more disastrous and costlier in the not too distant future. Here, it would be opportune to cite a dictum from one of the mandates of the International Labor Organization (ILO): *"poverty anywhere constitutes a danger to posterity everywhere."*

In view of this bleak picture, the world has two options: (i) continue to provide just enough assistance to enable the African people to continue to lead lives of sub-subsistence and mere subsistence (give them fish); or (ii) help them to develop their agriculture, infrastructure, and industry (teach and enable them how to fish). The first option means providing handouts for poverty alleviation and emergency aid in perpetuity, which is unlikely and, in the long run, more costly. Besides, the suffering among the growing poorest social strata is very likely to lead to more rampant social unrest and political instability worse than those currently being witnessed in certain parts of Africa. In this connection, it is regrettable to note that the policies of some food donors tend to perpetuate dependency. For example, the United States *"prefer[s] providing African countries direct food aid rather than aid designed to boost production"* (Gromyko, 1990).

The second option would be something similar to the Marshall Plan, the initiative that brought recovery and development to devastated Europe after the Second World War. In view of the wrongs committed in Africa under colonialism and its consequences (the psychological effect of demeaning Africa, exploiting and exhausting its resources, balkanizing the region), the adverse consequences of the Cold War that supported and encouraged dictatorial and corrupt regimes and capitalist/communist proxy wars fought in Africa among Africans, and the unfair treatment to African exports resulting in deteriorating terms of trade, the developed world has a moral obligation to help Africa emerge from the quagmire. The zero-sum approach (whereby developed countries continue to gain at the expense of developing countries which are relegated to the role of suppliers of raw materials whose prices have been stagnant or declining), advocated by some in the developed countries, is, in the final analysis, not in the long-term interest of the world community. The opposite tack as expressed by Reich (*The Work of Nations*) makes more sense. He advocates promoting indigenous development, *"shifting high-volume, standardized production to the Third World nations,"* and opening markets for them in advanced economies.

A start could be made with countries that are ready to receive a "Marshall Plan" type of assistance, countries that have proved capable and willing to carry out the drastic economic and social reforms needed to establish a threshold of development and use external assistance properly. These countries will serve as models and the experience gained could facilitate and enhance the implementation of the plan in other countries.

In the first option, because of the deteriorating economic and social conditions of African countries, donors would eventually get nothing in return; in the second, they would benefit from selling capital and consumer goods as the demand for imports increases thanks to the improved standard of living that would come about through development and productive employment. Agricultural development in particular will raise the purchasing power of the rural area (where up to 80 percent of the people live), thereby stimulating the faster growth of manufacturing and, consequently, an increased demand for imported intermediates capital, and consumer goods. As one source has pointed out, in East Asia *"a 1 percentage point increase in agricultural growth tended to generate a 1.5 percentage point increase in the growth rate of the non-agricultural sector"* (UNDP, *Human Development Report 1996*). It should be noted here that many Asian and Latin American countries, by developing their economies, have become major buyers from developed countries.

There is no reason why Africa with its huge and fast growing potential market (import growth of about 7 percent per year) cannot play the same or similar role—provided that the world community helps it achieve self-sustaining and environmentally sound development (environment being a global concern requiring a global solution), especially now that the continent is going through the process of democratization and economic liberalization. In fact, in view of the progress that the other developing regions have made and the inevitable slowing of their economies (including rising cost of labor; the increasing saturation of demand for consumer goods in the developed countries; the region's enormous resource endowment; its virtually untouched potential market; its virtually unutilized inter-industry and inter-sectoral linkages and consequently potentially high multiplier effects coupled with rapid development and mutual relationships with the world), Africa could be a potentially dynamic force for the growth of world economy. In other words, Africa, accounting for five (Botswana, Cote d'Ivoire, Uganda, Angola, and Zimbabwe) of the 20 fastest-growing countries and only one (Libya) of the 20 slowest-growing countries in early 1997 (*The Economist*, January 25, 1997) is the market of tomorrow. It is, therefore, likely to be the focus of world trade in the future.

Development would enable African countries to exploit their natural resources, including producing growing surplus of some export commodities, and thereby earn foreign currency to buy the goods and services they need from the rest of the world. It is quite apparent that the world would be better of with the second option, which amounts to something like a new manufacturing world order.

The world is in transition from the industrial age to the information economy. It is going through its third industrial revolution based on intellect and information. The first was based on coal and steel, the second on oil and chemicals. These have led to advanced technologies, such as advanced materials (ceramics, metals, polymers, and composites), semiconductors, automatic data-processing equipment, software and fiber optics. Industrial development in most African countries has, of necessity, to be a mix of the first and second industrial revolutions. African countries, however, should enter selected aspects of the third revolution, preferably jointly, particularly informatics, but also genetic and solar. As regards biotechnology and genetic engineering, the 21st century is expected to be the century of biology. Having missed the first and second revolutions, they should not be left out of the third.

Priorities for development vary from country to country. They have been changing over time. Within the industrial sector, the following or their combinations were, at one time or another, considered priorities by some countries: import substitution, export development, labor-intensive industry, and intermediate technology.

At the advent of independence, Africa counted on the comparative advantages that it could derive from its natural resource endowment. This is borne out by the revealed comparative advantages (RCA) of a number of agro-related products in 47 African countries shown in Table 7.1. In terms of both positive RCA and the number of countries involved, African countries continued to be competitive up to 1994 in processed foods, leather products, and wood products. While the maximum RCA for wearing apparel decreased in 1994 compared with that of 1980, the number of countries remained the same. Furniture and non-metallic minerals increased their maximum RCAs in 1994. Beverages, tobacco, and footwear lost their comparative advantages over the years. According to the competitiveness index of the World Economic Forum, the most competitive African countries in 1998 in descending order were Mauritius, Tunisia, Namibia, Morocco, Egypt, South Africa and Ghana (*The Economist*, March 21, 1998).

TABLE 7.1
RANGE OF POSITIVE REVEALED COMPARATIVE ADVANTAGE (RCA) [a] IN AFRICA, 1976, 1980 AND 1994

| | Range of positive RCA (percent) | | | | | | Number of countries with positive RCA | | |
| --- | --- | --- | --- | --- | --- | --- | --- | --- | --- |
| | 1976 | | 1980 | | 1994 | | 1976 | 1980 | 1994 |
| | Max | Min | Max | Min | Max | Min | | | |
| Food manufacturing | 625.1 | 14.7 | 693.7 | 38.8 | 754.1 | 1 | 27 | 24 | 24 |
| Beverages | 302 | 5 | 22.3 | 3.2 | 59.3 | 1.7 | 7 | 4 | 4 |
| Tobacco | 78.3 | 3.9 | 223.1 | 9.8 | 118.7 | 1.5 | 9 | 6 | 5 |
| Textile | 53.4 | 5 | 56.7 | 2.2 | 90.2 | 8.2 | 2 | 3 | 5 |
| Wearing g apparel | 205.7 | 34.7 | 719.9 | 1.7 | 594.1 | 24.7 | 5 | 7 | 7 |
| Leather | 337.9 | 5.1 | 490.1 | 1.5 | 585.5 | 12.9 | 10 | 14 | 15 |
| Footwear | 334.3 | 42.9 | 106.2 | 1.1 | 76.9 | 16.1 | 3 | 4 | 8 |
| Wood products | 481.4 | 10.7 | 569.2 | 8.7 | 897.6 | 0.6 | 11 | 12 | 18 |
| Furniture | 29.1 | 1.1 | 18.5 | 3.5 | 109.8 | 6.6 | 5 | 3 | 6 |
| Non-metallic minerals | 82.5 | 29.1 | 82.4 | 47.2 | 105.6 | 5 | 4 | 2 | 2 |
| Total | | | | | | | 83 | 79 | 94 |

Source: UNIDO, 1997, *Agro-related Industrial Development in Africa*, Thirteenth Meeting of the Conference of African Ministers of Industry in Africa, Accra.

      a RCA indices measure the relative excess of net exports from a particular country in a particular product group relative to the net exports of this product in world exports, 100 representing world net exports.

      Max = Maximum     Min = Minimum

Unfortunately, resource endowment alone is no longer adequate. It needs to be combined with other factor inputs, such as high productive labor and capital, which are scarce under present African conditions, as well as a readiness and capability to respond quickly to changing markets and circumstances. Besides, the concept of resource-based comparative advantage has been changing in favor of human skills (knowledge-intensive), market access, and technology. According to a survey by an international business and financial advisory group, large market potential, expected return, strategic business location, pre-empting competition, and labor quality are the major factors attracting foreign investment (UNIDO, *The Globalization of Industry: Implications ...*). The development of new and improved materials, including those emanating from biotechnology and genetic engineering, have reduced and continue to reduce the developed world's needs for many traditional African exports, such as pyrethrum and vanilla. Many of the new materials are better substitutes and can be tailor-made for specific uses. The proportion of the cost of information-based inputs in both manufacturing and services is rising. In other words, although Africa may benefit from some of the improved and new materials and services, overall, it may end up being a net loser. This state of affairs has been aggravated by increasing competition from other countries (particularly following the end of the Cold War), and less willingness on the part of researchers in developed countries to share with their counterparts in developing countries the biological products of their work. This is unfortunate as the use of environment-friendly biotechnology could reduce the need for fertilizers and pesticides and other polluting and destructive activities negatively impacting the ecological system.

In the past, labor-intensive industries, such as garment- and footwear-making and electronic assembly, were redeployed to developing countries. This is currently taking place in regard to data-processing technology. Raw data generated in the USA are, for example, transmitted to and processed in India and Ireland and transmitted back to the USA. Unfortunately, Africa, as was the case with labor-intensive industries, will miss the opportunity to benefit from rendering such software services.

Under the circumstances and in view of the low-demand elasticities for many of Africa's agricultural commodities and the trend towards the creation of economic communities that are meant to promote trade within each community, thereby likely reducing trade with countries outside the community, Africa is being marginalized in the emerging new international division of labor. With the resulting de-linking that is becoming rampant, it has no choice but to make use of its resources, first and foremost, to aim at satisfying the basic needs of its peoples, and to bring about structural transformation and trade complementarity, thereby substantially increasing intra-African trade through cooperation in the production and distribution of intermediate and capital goods and basic needs among its member states. In other words, more and more countries will be forced to continue with or adopt inward import-substitution-oriented development strategies[1] (instead of export-oriented strategies proposed by some international organizations) based on optimal local content for collective self-reliance and aimed at meeting their basic needs as much as possible.

Some countries may have the opportunity to participate in labor-intensive exports as productivity and real wages in the newly industrialized countries (NICs) increase, resulting in NICs becoming less competitive in such exports (i.e., shifting towards higher value-added manufacturing). The World Bank has projected that the real East Asian GDP will grow at 8 percent over the next 10 years (which is probably unlikely because of the financial crisis that many of the countries were experiencing in 1998). Some of the NICs have already relocated labor-intensive production units, such as garment making from Taiwan to other Asian countries. African countries with clear comparative advantages and niche areas with export potential should, of course, adopt export-led strategies whenever feasible. Cotton textiles and clothing, leather and leather goods, wood products and processed fruits, vegetables, cocoa, coffee, tea, and tobacco are among goods with export potentials.

A comparative assessment of potential for industrial development in 25 African countries is presented in Annex 7.1. The second column in the annex shows countries ranked by established industries. The last column does the same for combined potential industrial development. The assessment is based on economic, industrial, and natural resources indicators. The first six countries (South Africa, Algeria, Egypt, Nigeria, Libya, and Zimbabwe) and their rankings in the last column are the same as those in the second column. This indicates that these countries will be able to maintain their present position for some time to come.

## EXPERIENCE OF THE NEWLY INDUSTRIALIZING COUNTRIES

Many developing countries the world over have tried a number of approaches or strategies for industrial development. Some have been successful. Others have failed. Yugoslavia (former), Israel, Argentina, Brazil, Chile, Colombia, Mexico, Uruguay, India, Hong Kong, Singapore, South Korea, Taiwan, Malaysia, and Thailand are considered among the successful. They are known as newly industrialized countries (NICs). The strategies they adopted included import substitution, export development, labor-intensive industry, intermediate technology, and combinations of any of these. From among the three types of economy, raw material exporting, import substituting, and manufactured goods exporting, they (like Africa today) were confined to the first type. Import substitution industrialization and export-oriented industrialization are not mutually exclusive.

Because of their large internal markets and availability of resources, it is apparent that the strategies adopted by the bigger countries, would, of necessity, be different from those of the others (the so-called "the four tigers" of Eastern Asia). Hong Kong and Singapore are city-states while Taiwan and South Korea are relatively small countries with limited resources and relatively small national markets. The 1960 population of South Korea (25 million) was the same as that of Ethiopia while that of Taiwan (11 million) was nearly the same as that of Tanzania or Algeria. As most African countries are too small to support the development of industries that could benefit from economies of scale, it can be assumed that the experiences of the four, particularly South Korea and Taiwan, may be more relevant to several of them. Both South Korea and Taiwan were practically at the same level of development as most African countries in the 1950s. Yet South Korea joined the Organization of Economic Cooperation and Development (OECD), the exclusive club of the industrialized countries in 1996 while the IMF, starting May 1997, was to reclassify South Korea, Hong Kong, Singapore, Taiwan, and Israel to advanced economies which include the industrial countries. It should be noted here that the big countries had the advantage of

producing goods for both domestic and export markets, thereby achieving economies of scale. They therefore pursued mainly inward-looking strategies: they
adopted import-substitution industrialization strategy, later followed by export
promotion to earn the foreign exchange they needed to pay for their imports.

Put simply, the strategies adopted by most Asian NICs were import substitution in the 1950s and 1960s, followed by export-led industrialization in the 1970s
and 1980s, in contrast to the Latin American NICs which opted for a higher level
import substitution (capital goods) during the latter period. As import substitution is a continuing process, however, it has continued to play a role during the
past two decades in the Asian NICs, but at increasingly higher technological
levels, producing a growing variety of products with increasing complexities,
both for home consumption and export.

The four differed in some aspects and the extent of emphasis in others. For
example, in South Korea, industrialization preceded agricultural development
while it was the opposite in Taiwan. Whereas the share of agriculture in net
domestic product (NDP) decreased from 47 percent in the early 1950s to 16 percent in the early 1980s in South Korea and from 35 percent to 9 percent in Taiwan, the contribution of agriculture to NDP was, for obvious reasons, practically
nil in Hong Kong and Singapore. South Korean industry, which is largely based
on indigenous enterprises, is characterized by relatively large industries while
light industries dominate in Taiwan, which emphasized local sourcing and subcontracting. Hong Kong adopted laissez faire strategy, the exact opposite of
Singapore's very high interventionist strategy.

In addition to government participation in activities related to industrialization, "the four tigers" have some common features. Although in varying degrees,
they all showed very high increases in GNP, and manufacturing output and exports from the mid-1950s to the mid-1980s with almost no contraction in their
economies (Harris 1986). They all went through fast structural transformation.
*"Their exemplary records of macroeconomic management are regarded as a major
reason for the economic [and employment] successes of the East Asian 'miracle'
economies ... "* (ILO, *World Employment 1995*). They invest 1 to 2 percent of
their GDP in R&D.

In practically all the successful countries, including the big ones, governments had to play multiple roles, including state capitalism, mainly because of
their desire to achieve a strong economic base at the time when they lacked indigenous entrepreneurs with resources and experiences to innovate and assume
risks. In Africa, many governments believed that, under the conditions prevailing at the time, the state was in a better position to assume the entrepreneurial
role. The result was a relatively high government ownership of the means of
production and services. In Cameroon, for example, state ownership (excluding
petroleum) was over 50 percent of total production and services in 1982 (ECA,
ECA/IHSD/IPPIS/003/96).

Commitment to and persistent application of sound policy reforms and implementation of plans and programs and human capital formation were among the
ingredients for success. *"The ability to rapidly accommodate adjustment and
structural change and the speedy adaptation to both shocks and favorable trends
when they present themselves have been suggested as constituting a competitive
advantage of the East Asian developing economies"* (UN, E/1995/50). The state
in South Korea was, for example, the sole investor in many industries. In 1991,

the public enterprise sector accounted for about 10 percent of GDP. As most of the privatization was limited to a reduction of state ownership (ILO, *World Labour Report 1995*), government ownership would still be substantial. This was the case in many African countries following independence where, unlike the successful countries, all business was practically in the hands of foreigners. It was apparent that, under the circumstances, only governments could force the pace of growth by assuming the pioneering role in production, in addition to providing economic and social infrastructure, regulating the rules for development, facilitating development activities, including mobilization of resources, and breaking through bottlenecks. In the words of Harris, *"It has not been 'free enterprise' nor multinational capital which has lead the process [of accelerated economic growth] but the deliberate and persistent efforts of governments."* He added that, by the end of the 1970s, *" In the newly industrializing countries, state capitalism was apparently everywhere supreme."*

The role of government, like that in Japan, was crucial to the achievement of the economic miracles in South Korea and Taiwan. In general, the governments were regulators, facilitators, and investors. As regulators, they ensured that the market did not fail. As facilitators, the governments formulated and implemented appropriate policies; introduced programs for the development of industry; helped create comparative advantages; and provided private industrial investors with incentives on changing basis and opportunities (no tariffs on imported raw materials; tax reliefs; credit and pricing policies; forcing mergers, specialization, and monopolies; labor policy; exchange rates favoring exports; mobilizing resources; export credit; ban on import of products made locally; supporting and facilitating exports; even selling below the cost of production, etc.).

In South Korea, the government promoted export by relating all concessions to export performance. As investors, the governments invested in new and risky industries, resulting in state capitalism accounting for a significant proportion of public savings and investment. In other words, the states initiated, directed, and supervised as well as contributed to growth and structural changes through public sector spending in the productive sectors, particularly in basic and heavy industries. In addition, they invested heavily in education, manpower development, and R&D as well as encouraged firms in the last two activities. In the words of the World Bank, the government of South Korea *"played lead roles in targeting, establishing, and protecting key industries"* (*Sub-Saharan Africa*). According to another source, "For *years, South Korea's rapid growth has been marked by protection and government assistance for the family-owned conglomerates known as chaebols that drive the economy"* (Baker, *The Christian Science Monitor*, February 7, 1996). The chaebols, which were specifically identified by the government, were required to subcontract the manufacture of parts and components to small and medium enterprises. The government provided such enterprises financial and fiscal support, exempted them from stamp tax, and gave them some tax deductions on parts of their investments. This strategy resulted in a wider spread of technology than would otherwise have been possible.

South Korea achieved high national savings, up to about 40 percent of GDP in 1988. The share of manufacturing in gross national product (GNP) in the early 1950s to early 1980s increased from under 9 percent to 30 percent in South Korea and from 12 to 33 percent in Taiwan. Employment in manufacturing rose from 6 percent of the work force in 1960 to 20 percent in 1982 in South Korea and from

14 percent to 32 percent in Taiwan during early 1950s to early 1980s. During the period from the mid-1950s to the mid-1980s, GNP increased by over 10 percent per year in six years in South Korea and in nine years in Taiwan; annual growth rate in manufacturing output was above 20 percent in 10 years in South Korea and nine years in Taiwan; and exports grew by over 20 percent per year in most years in South Korea and for 19 years in Taiwan. Exports as a percentage of gross domestic product in 1980 were 27.1 and 51.5 for South Korea and Taiwan, respectively. Much of the growth in manufacturing was obviously export-led. The composition of manufacturing output changed from light (food and textiles) to heavy industries (chemicals, metals, and engineering).

South Korea and Taiwan have some things in common. Both are blessed with peoples characterized by deeply entrenched work ethic, part of what is known as "Asian values." Both benefited from massive American military and civil aid. The infrastructure (Korea) and agricultural development (Taiwan) inherited from the Japanese occupation are claimed to have contributed to development in both countries. With declining aid starting in the early 1960s and the exhaustion of the potential for import substitution, both countries put more focus on exports as a means of earning foreign exchange and the encouragement of foreign investment. Industrial diversification followed the change in demand in overseas market in the 1970s. The manufacturing structure changed from labor-intensive (garments and textiles, plastic sandals and flowers, electronic components, etc.) to more and more capital-intensive and heavy industries as industrialization deepened and other newcomers in other countries took over the lower-valued outputs. Ships, steel, machinery, and petrochemicals and more recently circuit boards and keyboards for personal computers as well as memory chips were among the products of the capital-intensive industries.

The success story of the South Korean ship-building industry is well known. In the first half of 1983, the country accounted for 23 percent of the world market. One of its steel companies, Posco, ranked third among world steel producers in 1991 and 1992. The miraculous development of "the four tigers" was definitely made possible through the export of manufactured goods, contrary to the postulates of development economics at the time based on traditional raw material exporting economy (traditional world division of labor). According to the World Economic Forum and the International Institute for Management Development, "the four tigers" were among the 25 countries ranked according to competitiveness in 1996. Singapore and Hong Kong ranked first to third depending on the source of ranking (*The Economist*, June 1, 1996).

The export-led growth successes of South Korea and Taiwan were achieved under global market conditions that practically no longer exist, so much has changed in the world since these countries ventured into the world of industrialization. The massive American aid that helped these countries to develop is not available to African countries. Unlike the labor shortages in industrialized countries in the late fifties and early sixties, unemployment is now afflicting those countries, thus blocking relocation of industries to developing countries. The possibility for relocation of labor-intensive industries is further diminished because of innovation in the application of new information technologies to the production of goods and services being made possible and therefore changing modes of production, thanks to microelectronics-based production, as well as the fast development of biotechnology and genetic engineering. In addition, because of new technologies and advances in management, the share of the cost of labor in the final product continues to decline in developed countries. All these indicate the possibility that locational advantages may well shift to developed countries. These could lead to further restriction of exports from developing to developed countries which is likely to worsen following the formation and operation of regional economic blocs (regional trading blocs). For these reasons and the emerging next generation of "tigers" (Czech Republic, Argentina, Chile, Vietnam, and Indonesia), and despite some new exporters' (Malaysia, Philippines, Thailand, etc.) successes in displacing some of the NICs in regard to light industries in recent years, coupled with the virtual impossibility for so many African late-starters to compete with the older-established ones, it is quite apparent that none of the above successful countries could serve as models for African countries.

Experiences of the second generation of NICs, such as Indonesia, Malaysia, and Thailand, may be more relevant. Outward orientation, high savings and investment rates, high rates of expenditure on education and skill promotion, and effective selective interventions were some of the factors leading to rapid industrialization in these countries (UNIDO, *The Globalization of Industry: Implications ...* ). With the rapid pace of technological change compounded by increased costs resulting from the Uruguay Round agreements related to intellectual property rights, the threshold of entry into competitive industries has become and is becoming increasingly difficult in terms of cost and skill requirement for most African countries. As for exports from export processing zones (EPZs), the limited successes registered by Botswana, Cameroon, Egypt, Ghana, Kenya, Liberia, Madagascar, Morocco, Senegal, Togo, and Congo K testify to this. In other words, the mainly export-oriented route used by South Korea and Taiwan (the option proposed for Africa by some) and the replication of the Mauritian EPZ success story are likely to be difficult for most African countries. Nevertheless, Benin, Comoros, Eritrea, Malawi, Namibia, and Zimbabwe are either establishing or contemplating such zones. In this connection, it should be noted that, because of rising labor costs (as is the case in some of the NICs) and the trend toward capital-intensive techniques in traditionally labor-intensive industries (such as textiles and clothing) Mauritius itself has in recent years been experiencing declining employment in its EPZs. Some of the labor-intensive companies in Mauritius, like their counterparts in Asia, are in the process of relocating their production facilities to low-labor-cost countries, such as Madagascar and southern Africa.

Despite the negative conclusion on replicating the experiences of Asian countries, there are lessons to be learned from the experiences of those four countries. These include: committed leadership; state intervention as facilitator and investor; industrial and trade policies and strategies quickly adjustable to changing circumstances; top priority given to education and training[2], heavy investment in technology and R&D[3]; disciplined and relatively cheap skilled work force; combination of rapid growth with low inequality and high human development resulting in relatively equitable distribution of wealth[4]; use of inter-industry linkages, such as subcontracting; and expanding the number of ISO 9000 certified manufacturing firms. Many of these relate to the constraints dealt with in Chapter 6. For export-oriented projects to succeed in penetrating export markets, they will have to be supported by adequate policies and incentives that can be promptly adjusted to changing external circumstances. Whenever practical, it would make sense to produce for export as well as for domestic consumption.

The on-going East Asian financial crisis (starting in 1997) characterized by very high debt/equity ratios (up to 5:1), and collapsing currencies (and therefore currency flight and inability to pay off foreign debts) should not lessen the relevance to Africa of some of the experiences of the Asian NICs. African countries should be alert not to repeat what went wrong there, including unreliable legal systems, lack of corporate transparency, overborrowing (indiscriminate bank lending to projects and companies, often at government insistence) and overbuilding as well as conducting business on the basis of personal relationship and with the right connections. Given the Asian crisis, it appears that it may be worthwhile for African countries to look into the experiences in some Latin American countries which were reported to have made dramatic progress.

Before closing this section, reference should be made to the support given to industry in the industrialized countries. Most if not all developed countries formulate and implement policies and strategies in support of their industries. Some of them were involved in restructuring, nationalizing, and denationalizing of industries not so long ago. Many of them subsidize their industries through R&D, financing, export promotion, etc. They protect them from outside competition, especially from competitors outside their economic blocs. The Japanese government, for example, was reported to be considering whether to *"provide special funds to help regional manufacturers hurt by foreign competition to renovate their factories and develop new products"* (*The Economist*, August 31, 1996). In short, the strategies used by the NICs were used and are still used, albeit in part, by the developed countries themselves, indicating that similar approaches adopted by African countries are not, after all, peculiar to the latter. In fact, because of the initial stage of industrialization and harsh circumstances that African countries find themselves in, they are justified in adopting measures that protect their infant industries from unfair competition with well established industries elsewhere.

## INDUSTRIAL DEVELOPMENT DECADE FOR AFRICA

Following the 1973 oil crisis and subsequent global economic crises as well as natural disasters, African countries found themselves increasingly unable to feed themselves, let alone develop their economies. In recognition of the fact that a country cannot make real progress in economic development without industrial development, many African countries, at the advent of independence, adopted policies that were meant to promote industrial development. This concept became more relevant during the 1980s when, because of their preponderant dependence on imports, African countries were increasingly unable to import industrial products—capital, intermediate, and consumer goods.

In order to mitigate the above and many other constraints facing them and enhance their economic development, African countries, as noted in Chapter 3, came out with the Lagos Plan of Action (LPA) and the Final Act of Lagos (FAL) in April 1980. According to the LPA, economic development was to be attained through regional cooperation and integration and the industrial sector was to play the role of the engine of growth by contributing to collective self-reliant and self-sustained development. Paragraph 58 of the LPA, which was adopted by the OAU Assembly of Heads of States and Government, contained a proposal to proclaim the 1980s as the Industrial Development Decade for Africa (IDDA). Based on this desire of the African countries, the United Nations General Assembly, by its resolution A/Res./35/66B of 5 December 1980, proclaimed the IDDA and called upon UNIDO, ECA, and the OAU *"to formulate proposals to implement the program for the IDDA and to monitor its progress."* IDDA was declared *"for the purpose of focusing greater attention and evoking greater political commitment and financial and technical support, at the national, regional and international levels for the industrialization of Africa,"* Among other things, it was intended to bring about a transformation of production structures from predominantly agrarian to industrial economies. In other words, it was meant to contribute to self-reliant and self-sustainable economic and social development through expanding and diversifying manufacture. This was in turn expected to stimulate trade among African countries, which then as now account for a mere 5-6 percent of total African trade.

Following the above General Assembly resolution proclaiming the IDDA, UNIDO, ECA, and the OAU established the Joint Committee of the OAU/ ECA/ UNIDO secretariats. The committee prepared a draft program which was reviewed at different fora and adopted by resolution 1(vi) of the Sixth Conference of African Ministers of Industry in 1981. The program under the title " A Program for the Industrial Development Decade for Africa" was printed in 1982 (UN, *A Program...*).

The declaration of IDDA was in line with the Lima Declaration and Plan of Action on Industrial Development and Cooperation which was adopted by the Second General Conference of the United Nations Industrial Development Organization in 1975 following United Nations General Assembly Resolution 3087 (XXVIII) of 1973. The Lima Declaration was intended to promote industrial development of developing countries within the framework of new forms of international cooperation. Its target was to raise the share of developing countries in total world industrial production to at least 25 percent by the year 2000 (UNIDO, *Lima Declaration ...*). Based on this target, it was envisaged in the IDDA program that African share would increase to 1 percent in 1990 and to 2 percent by the year 2000.

Modalities for implementation were spelled out in the program. At the national level, a national coordinating committee, supported by a national operational focal point which would serve as a secretariat, was to be responsible for providing *"over-all direction and guidance for the formulation, promotion, implementation and monitoring of the Decade Programme."* A similar role was to be played by a subregional coordinating committee and a focal point at the subregional level. As for the region, the Conference of African Ministers of Industry and its subsidiary, the Follow-up Committee on Industrialization, which meet biennially, were to provide over-all policy guidance. The Joint Committee of the OAU/ECA/UNIDO secretariats was to provide support at all levels.

The IDDA program, unfortunately, fell miserably short of expectations, of being the engine of growth and structural transformation of African economies, particularly at the subregional and regional levels. In the Central African subregion, for instance, three multinational manufacturing projects were completed and two were under implementation in the early 1990s out of 41 industrial projects. The North African Subregion was more successful, having 16 core projects implemented, practically all of which were at the bilateral level, and five under implementation out of 42 projects (UN, E/1992/14/Add.1 [Part II]). The institution building part of the program was relatively better. The African Regional Center for Engineering Design and Manufacturing (ARCEDEM) was, for example, established during the IDDA.

The constraints leading to such poor performance at the subregional and regional levels are dealt with in Chapter 6. They include inappropriate selection and inadequate preparation of projects, lack of commitment and coordination among member countries and subregional organizations, a series of crises during the 1980s, political instability, scarcity of financial resources and lack of effective follow-up. In this connection, it should be noted that, because of the declining economic conditions, most African countries lacked resources (probably the major constraint for the failure of the implementation of the IDDA) to operate their production units and institutions, let alone spare resources for subregional or regional cooperation and integration.

From the worsening economic conditions that followed the IDDA declaration it was apparent that the Decade was proclaimed at the wrong time and for the wrong decade and therefore doomed to failure. In view of this and the increasing realization of the need to industrialize, the United Nations, following the adoption of the second IDDA by the OAU, declared 1993-2002 as IDDA II (Resolution 47/177 of 22 December 1992). According to IDDA II, African manufacturing is to grow at 8 percent per year.

As the industrial situation at the end of the 1980s and the beginning of the 1990s when the IDDA II was prepared was not significantly different from 1979/1980 when IDDA I was formulated, the objectives of the former apply to the latter. This is shown by the IDDA II priorities which are practically identical to those of IDDA I. The difference is that the IDDA II program was based on national programs; priorities were expanded to include energy, transport and communication and bio-technology industries (see Table 7.2); and the role of the private sector was taken into account to some extent. List of projects, including support projects, by subregion are presented in Annexes 7.2 to 7.5. The number of projects for the region as a whole total 233. They comprise 16 metal, 41 engineering, 44 chemical, 19 building materials, 40 agro-based, and 73 support projects. Support projects are infrastructural and human resource development projects that promote and facilitate industrial development. They include institution building, laboratory scale and pilot plant experimentation, training, pre-investment studies, expertise, and equipment. The third column in Table 7.2 shows priority industries proposed in this book.

| TABLE 7..2 COMPARISON OF PRIORITY INDUSTRIES | | |
|---|---|---|
| IDDA I [a] | IDDA II | Proposed |
| - Food processing industry | - Food and agro-based industries | - Industries oriented toward basic needs (food, textiles, pharmaceuticals, building materials, educational materials) |
| - Textiles | - Building and consrtuction industries | |
| - Forest-based industries | - Metallurgical industries | - Basic metals (iron and steel, aluminum, copper) |
| - Building materials and construction | - Mechanical industries | - Engineering (agricultural equipment and machinery; equipment and machinery for storing, processing, and transporting agricultural inputs and outputs; spare parts; machine tools) |
| - Metallurgical industry | - Electrical and electronic industries | |
| - Chemical industry | - Chemical and petrochemical industries | - Chemicals (fertilizers, pesticides, basic chemicals) |
| - Engineering industry | - Forestry industries | - Packaging materials |
| - Small-scale industries | - Energy industries | |
| - Packaging industry | -Textile and leather industries | |
| | - Transport and communication industries | |
| | - Bio-technology industries | |
| | - Intermediate and small-scale industries | - Industries producing inputs for small-scale industries |

Source: [a] - United Nations, 1982, *A Program for the Industrial Development Decade for Africa*, New York
[b] - United Nations, 1992, *Regional Cooperation: Second Industrial Development Decade for Africa    Note by the Secretary General — Addendum— Program for the Second Industrial Development Decade for Africa (1991-2000)*. New York..

A more recent list of high priorities in the agro-industry area compiled by UNIDO is presented in Table 7.3. This list is a comprehensive version of the food and agro-based industries and mechanical and chemical  industries related to agro-industries in IDDA II shown in Table 7. 2 above.

| TABLE 7.3 PRIORITY BRANCHES IN AGRO-INDUSTRY | |
|---|---|
| Food processing | Agro-input industries |
| - Coarse grain processing (especially maize, sorghum and millet) | - Tools and implements |
| - Root crop processing | - Tillage equipment |
| - Fruit and vegetable processing | - Sowing equipment |
| - Fish processing | - Animal traction equipment |
| - Dairy products | - Harvesting and threshing equipment |
| - Meat products | - Water production (irrigation) equipment |
| - Rehabilitation of existing sugar mills | - Simple diesel engines |
| - Oil seed processing | - Mini tractors |
| - Utilization of byproducts for producing animal feed (especially cassava  based) | - Tractor accessories |
| - Packaging and canning branches | - Spare parts for repair and maintenance |
| Non-food agro industries | - Storage facilities |
| - Low and medium count yarn, fabric, and gray cloth for local consumption | - Phosphate fertilizers and mixed formulations |
| - Standardized clothing products of the type exported by Bangladesh and Sri Lanka | - Mini fertilizer mixing plants |
| - The Maghreb could concentrate on styled clothing products and on increasing the share of locally produced fabric for garment making | - Pesticides (especially bio-pesticides) |
| - Leather clothing and footwear | |
| - Wood products | |

Source: UNIDO, 1997, *Agro-related Industrial Development in Africa*, Thirteenth Meeting of the Conference of African Ministers of Industry (CAMI.13/13), Accra.

IDDA II, as IDDA I, is to be implemented at the national, subregional, and regional levels. Institutional mechanisms at the corresponding levels are, obviously, needed to do this. At the national level, sponsoring member states are expected to integrate projects in the subregional programs in their respective industrial development plans. Industry-related activities are to be coordinated by IDDA national coordinating committees, comprising representatives of relevant government institutions and the private sector.

At the subregional level, activities related to the IDDA II subregional programs, including coordinating the formulation and implementation and follow-up and monitoring the implementation of the programs, is the responsibility of an Industrial Promotion Coordinating Committee, which could be an already existing intergovernmental organization (IGO) to be designated to play such a role. It would be supported by Sub-sectoral Strategic Management Committees whose membership should include representatives of governments, public and private enterprises, manufacturers associations, financial institutions, and chambers of commerce and industry.

In respect of the region, monitoring the IDDA program is expected to be carried out by the Intergovernmental Committee of Experts of the Whole on Industrialization in Africa (ICEWIA), which is responsible to the Conference of African Ministers of Industry (CAMI). These mechanisms are cosponsored by the ECA, OAU, and UNIDO. They meet biennially to review progress made in industrial development in the preceding two years in Africa and approve activities to be undertaken in the subsequent two years in the subregions and the region as a whole.

In general, the subregional and regional projects figuring in the subregional programs (and included in Annexes 7.2 to 7.5 are those that are sensitive to economies of scale requiring markets beyond national demand as well as huge investment, and therefore call for cooperation among a number of countries (see criteria for selecting multinational/subregional regional projects in Annex 7.6). The location, that is, the host country for each project as well as the sponsor(s), other than the host country, if available, are shown. The same applies to the status (degree of priority or time frame) of the project. It should be noted here that, given the lack of consistency and uniformity in presentation, an attempt has been made to recompile the list, whenever necessary, in order to make the list comparable and less repetitive. In other words, the list may appear different when compared with the source.

Most of the subregional projects are at the conceptual stage. This means that pre-investment studies and activities will have to be carried out on each of them by those concerned (African governments through their public enterprises and the private sector, both local and foreign). Many of them may require support activities, such as ascertaining the adequacy and quality of raw materials and energy, which may include field work on deposits. Some may even involve pilot plant operations to determine the optimal technological processes to be used in processing the raw materials intended to be exploited.

It is apparent from the above that some, if not many, of the projects may not prove viable. It is likely that some may drop out following the completion of market research (which should be undertaken prior to carrying out pre-feasibility or feasibility studies). This approach would help eliminate unviable projects right from the start and thus save time and money. Some projects will be eliminated upon the completion and appraisal of pre-feasibility and feasibility studies. This process, coupled with periodic revision of projects (as well as programs) which includes addition of new projects, would make it possible to maintain up-to-date portfolios of projects for promotion to potential investors/partners.

Those projects on which investment decisions are taken will be implemented by the partners who contributed to the pre-investment phase as well as others who may have joined later. This would be done by establishing a multinational enterprise responsible for the investment phase and eventually for the operating phase. The enterprise should take over as soon as an investment decision is made on a project.

Evaluation of progress in the implementation of the IDDA II program was carried out in 1994. Missions fielded to 14 countries showed that few countries had established national mechanisms (national IDDA coordinating committees), no donors or potential investors had been identified, and very few country IDDA projects had been integrated into national industrial programs. Feasibility studies were carried out for three of ten projects selected for evaluation. There was apparently very little activity undertaken in regard to the other projects. In other words, most of the projects were still at the conceptual stage (ECA/UNIDO, CAMI.12/6[a]). The story in regard to progress in subregional programs was similar. Recent (1997) mid-term evaluation showed that IDDA II has not generated the expected impact for practically the same reasons as for the 1994 evaluation (UNIDO, *Report of the Mid-term Programme Evaluation*). Feasibility studies were undertaken for three out of 10 IDDA II projects evaluated. The program was not promoted to the public and the private sectors. Governments were, apparently, under the impression that external funds would be available to implement the programs. Precedence had to be given to implementing structural adjustment programs and rehabilitating existing enterprises. Governments were preoccupied with activities related to political transition and economic liberalization, the latter meant leaving entrepreneurial activities to the private sector, which, as stated above, was practically unaware of IDDA II. Other reasons for the failure of IDDA II include: civil wars and general instability in some areas, lack of policy continuity because of changes of governments and their officials, and an inequitable international environment, including increasing international competitiveness. As in IDDA I, the main culprit is lack of financial resources, as member countries do not have adequate funds for internal, let alone for subregional or regional use. It is, perhaps, the main factor hindering cooperation in the industrial sector.

As would be expected, IDDA II was the focus of the Thirteenth Meeting of the Conference of African Ministers of Industry (May 1997), whose theme was "Africa's Industrialization and the 21st Century." In addition to its Intergovernmental Committee of Experts, the Conference was preceded by meetings of the Private Sector Forum and the Second Round Table of African Investment Promotion Agencies. In its Resolution 2 (XIII), the Conference adopted the plan of Action for the Alliance for Africa's Industrialization (adopted by the OAU Council of Ministers in 1996) and approved the creation of a Patron Group for Africa's Industrialization (five heads of state and government) and a Steering Committee (which held its first meeting in September 1998) to support the Alliance. All these are indications of the improved facilitating role that governments and the increasingly implementing role that the private sector would be expected to play in the industrial development of the region. It should be noted here that, by the end of IDDA II, even if performance will have proved insufficient, as is likely, the measures and preparatory activities taken and experience accumulated in the two decades could prove valuable in the industrial takeoff during the first decade of the next century.

## AGRO-BASED AND BASIC-NEEDS APPROACH

### Agriculture-based Basic Needs

Air, water, food, domestic fuel, health, clothing, shelter, education, and transportation are among the basic needs of people. The first and, to some extent, the second are, generally, not included when discussing basic needs. The exclusion of the first is, probably, because it is free for all, although increasing expenditure is being incurred to keep it usable. The consumer pays for it indirectly. In regard to the second, access to clean water is a serious problem to most peoples in practically all developing countries. Domestic fuel and transportation seem to be rarely mentioned as basic necessities.

Several of the other basic needs, which are the subject matter of this book, are, in part at least, obtainable from agriculture. Food is one of them. The priority accorded to agriculture is apparent from the fact that Africa has been losing its capacity to feed itself (see Annex 7.7 on food security, agricultural productivity, and share of FDI in GNP). More food needs to be produced not only to fill the production/consumption gap but also to improve the standard of nutrition as the number of people subject to chronic undernutrition had increased from 94 million in the 1970s to 175 million in the 1980s. In this connection, it should be noted that, under the historical scenario, food imports is projected to rise to 65.1 million tons in 2008 (ECA, *Africa in the 1990s and Beyond: ...*). The crucial nature of the food problem was stressed at the third Presidential Forum on the Management of Science and Technology in Africa held in Kampala, Uganda, in July 1995. At the meeting, the heads of state and government of the Eastern and Southern African subregion asserted that *"basic food and nutritional security has become the priority of priorities in Africa"* and continuation with the current trend in food production would mean *"Africa will be producing less than 75 percent of its food requirements by the year 2000."* In view of this predicament they committed themselves to pursue a 10-year multisectoral program of action aimed at achieving food and nutritional security. The urgent need for increasing reliance on locally grown foodstuffs and the attainment of food security is apparent. Food security here includes availability and access by those who cannot afford to buy it, particularly those who produce food.

Clothing is another basic need. With most African countries producing cotton, and cotton being suitable for African weather conditions, it makes sense to maximize the use of cotton for apparel.

Many medicines, including veterinary products, are derived from medicinal plants and animals while paper is made from wood and other agricultural materials. The former is a priority in the health sector and the latter in the educational sector. Both are basic needs.

Shelter is a basic need. Although wood, an agricultural product, can play either a major or a minor role in building homes, it constitutes an important element in shelter building. Others include thatching materials, such as straw and palm leaves.

Table 7. 4 gives an indication of actual and projected production and consumption and resulting gaps of selected agricultural products in the continent. The main food items (excluding roots and tubers), wheat, rice, course grains, palm oil, sugar and groundnuts, both actual and projected figures, show growing excess of consumption over production. The wheat deficit is the most alarming, having grown from 6.5 million tons in 1969-1971 to 20.1 million tons in 1986, and it is projected to climb to 36.7 million tons in 2000. The picture is much more dismal as far as developing Africa is concerned. Some of the deficits might be more glaring if South Africa were left out. (The World Bank, the source of information, draws attention to the large degree of uncertainty associated with the projections.) Details on production and trade of agricultural products are given in Annexes 4.2 and 4.3. The net trade figures could serve as proxies to production/consumption gaps.

**TABLE 7.4**
**ACTUAL AND PROJECTED PRODUCTION, CONSUMPTION AND**
**PRODUCTION/CONSUMPTION GAPS OF SELECTED AGRICULTURAL PRODUCTS IN**

| | Consumption/ production gap | Actual | | | | Projected | | |
|---|---|---|---|---|---|---|---|---|
| | | 1969-1971 | 1979-1981 | 1986 | 1990 * | 1990 | 1995 | 2000 |
| Wheat | Production | ... | ... | ... | 13.7 | ... | ... | ... |
| | Consumption | 14.3 | 23.7 | 29.7 | | 34.7 | 41.7 | 48.4 |
| | Gap [b] | -6.5 | -14.5 | -20.1 | | -22.5 | -30.5 | -36.7 |
| Rice | Production | 7.3 | 8.3 | 8.8 | 12.5 | 9.9 | 10.8 | 11.9 |
| | Consumption | 5 | 7.9 | 8.5 | | 9.8 | 11.4 | 13 |
| | Gap | 2.3 | 0.4 | 0.3 | | 0.1 | -0.6 | -1.1 |
| Coarse grains | Production | 43.7 | 53 | 52.9 | 62 | 56.6 | 60.1 | 64.3 |
| | Consumption | 40.2 | 51.4 | 60.1 | | 63.3 | 69.3 | 76 |
| | Gap | 3.5 | 1.6 | -7.2 | | -6.7 | -9.2 | -11.7 |
| Palm oil (oil equiv.) | Production | 1.2 | 1.3 | 1.5 | | 0.9 | 1 | 1.1 |
| | Consumption (apparent) | 1 | 1.4 | 1.1 | | 0.5 | 0.9 | 1.1 |
| | Gap | 0.2 | -0.1 | 0.4 | | -0.4 | -0.1 | 0 |
| Groundnuts (oil equiv.) | Production | 1.4 | 1.1 | 1.1 | | 0.9 | 1 | 1 |
| | Consumption (appar cnt) | 0.9 | 0.8 | 0.9 | | 0.9 | 0.9 | 1 |
| | Gap | 0.5 | 0.3 | 0.2 | | 0 | 0.1 | 0 |
| Sugar (centrifugal, raw) | Production | 4.7 | 6.1 | 7.5 | 7.8 | 8.2 | 9.8 | 11.3 |
| | Consumption ( apparent) | 3.5 | 4.9 | 8.3 | | 8.8 | 9.8 | 12.2 |
| | Gap | 1.2 | 1.2 | -0.8 | | -0.6 | 0 | -0.9 |
| Citrus fruits (total) | Production | 3.9 | 4.6 | 5.2 | | 5.8 | 6.5 | 7.3 |
| | Consumption | 2.8 | 3.3 | 4 | | 4.5 | 5.2 | 5.8 |
| | Gap | 1.1 | 1.3 | 1.2 | | 1.3 | 1.3 | 1.5 |
| Coffee (m bags) | Production | 21.2 | 19.5 | 20.1 | 21.1 | 20.5 | 21.7 | 22.5 |
| | Consumption (apparent) | ... | ... | ... | | ... | ... | ... |
| | Gap ( net exports) | 16.5 | 15 | 18 | | 16.3 | 17.7 | 18.7 |
| Coca | Production (beans) | 1 | 1 | 1.1 | 1.4 | 1.2 | 1.3 | 1.3 |
| | Consumption (apparent) | ... | ... | ... | | ... | ... | ... |
| | Gap (net exports) | 1 | 1 | 1.1 | | 1.2 | 1.3 | 1.3 |
| Tea (black) | Production | 0.1 | 0.2 | 0.3 | 0.3 | 0.3 | 0.4 | 0.4 |
| | Consumption (apparent) | 0.1 | 0.1 | 0.2 | | 0.2 | 0.2 | 0.2 |
| | Gap | 0 | 0.1 | 0.1 | | 0.1 | 0.2 | 0.2 |
| Tobacco | Production | 0.2 | 0.2 | 0.2 | 0.4 | 0.3 | 0.3 | 0.4 |
| | Consumption (apparent) | 0.1 | 0.2 | 0.2 | | 0.2 | 0.2 | 0.3 |
| | Gap | 0.1 | 0 | 0 | | 0.1 | 0.1 | 0.1 |
| Cotton | Production | 1.3 | 1.1 | 1.3 | 1.4 | 1.4 | 1.5 | 1.5 |
| | Consumption (domestic availability) | 0.6 | 0.7 | 0.7 | | 0.7 | 0.8 | 0.8 |
| | Gap | 0.7 | 0.4 | 0.6 | | 0.7 | 0.7 | 0.7 |

199

Table 7.4 cont...

| Natural rubber | Production | 0.2 | 0.2 | 0.2 | 0.3 | 0.3 | 0.4 | 0.4 |
|---|---|---|---|---|---|---|---|---|
| | Consumption (apparent) | 0.1 | 0.1 | 0.1 | | 0.2 | 0.2 | 0.2 |
| | Gap | 0.1 | 0.1 | 0.1 | | 0.1 | 0.2 | 0.2 |
| Sawnlogs and veneer logs (non-conifer) 1000 m³ | Production | 15.5 | 17.8 | 17.4 | | 18.3 | 19.6 | 21 |
| | Consumption (apparent) | 8.7 | 12.5 | 13.9 | | 15.2 | 17.1 | 19.1 |
| | Gap | 6.8 | 5.3 | 3.5 | | 3.1 | 2.5 | 1.9 |
| Sawnwood (non-conifer) | Production | 2.8 | 5.2 | 5.8 | | 6.3 | 7.1 | 7.8 |
| | Consumption (apparent) | 2.5 | 5.1 | 5.5 | | 5.9 | 6.5 | 7.1 |
| | Gap | 0.3 | 0.1 | 0.3 | | 0.4 | 0.6 | 0.7 |

Source: Compiled from The World Bank, 1989, *Price Prospects for Major Primary Commodities,*
1988-2000, Volume II, Food Products,Fertilizers, Agricultural Raw Materials,
Washington, D.C.
ª FAO, 1994, *FAOSTATdata,* Statistics Division, Rome.
Notes: Gap = Consumption - production, ᵇ Net imports = gross imports - gross exports

In the majority of countries in the 1980s and early 1990s, agriculture is the number one priority, a status given to it by the Lagos Plan of Action (LPA), OAU's Africa's Priority Program for Economic Recovery 1986-1990 (APPER), and the United Nations Programme of Action for African Economic Recovery and Development 1986-1990 (UNPAAERD). Attaining food self-sufficiency by the year 2000 is the target of the Lagos Plan of Action in the agricultural sector. In this connection, there is a correlation between food self-sufficiency (improving nutrition) and improving health. Malnutrition is one of the major causes of ill-health.

Measures envisaged to increase agricultural productivity and production were elaborated in the programs. Those that relate to agricultural inputs and industry include the following:

• Development of mechanization and use of modern-farm processing machinery, increased use of fertilizers and pesticides, use of improved and hybrid seed varieties;

• Improving and expanding storage capacity, distribution, and the marketing system;

• Placing at the disposal of the small farmers the necessary inputs for increased yields, better utilization, and improvement in management of water resources and the establishment of low-cost irrigation schemes;

• Development of industries for the production of agricultural tools and equipment, small-scale irrigation equipment, and agricultural inputs;

• Rehabilitation and development of agro-related industries;

• Processing of raw materials and intermediate inputs;

• Rehabilitation and upgrading of existing plants; and

• Establishment of engineering capacity for the production of spare parts and components for the overhaul, repair, and maintenance of vehicles, machinery, and equipment.

The industry related measures are in support of agriculture. In this connection, it should be noted that industrial products constitute about 75 percent of inputs to agriculture.

## Needs for the Development of Small-scale Industries

There are as many concepts and definitions, mainly based on capital investment and employment, of small-scale industries as there are countries. No attempt is, therefore, made here to define small-scale industry as such an attempt would be futile, particularly at the regional level. According to one source (UNIDO, *Small-scale Industry*, No. 11), small-scale industries can be categorized into two groups based on those who own/operate them: (i) traditional crafts and artisans (the informal sector) and (ii) small manufacturing enterprises. The former include handicrafts (cobblers, carpenters, potters, weavers, blacksmiths, tailors, etc.) or cottage and household industries which, unfortunately, are being replaced by the latter, thereby displacing traditional crafts and skills.

For the purpose of gaining some idea of the significance of small-scale industries in Sub-Saharan Africa, resort is made to an arbitrary approach which defines small-scale industry as an establishment *"with fewer than 50 workers."* Based on this definition, indications are that small-scale industries dominate, accounting for close to 70 percent of industrial employment, with most of the employment concentrated in those enterprises with a small number of employees. Ninety five percent of the enterprises employ fewer than five persons in Nigeria, Sierra Leone, and Ghana. Many of them are one-person owned and operated enterprises and are located in rural areas in the majority of countries (95% in Sierra Leone). They are mostly engaged in the production of clothing, wood products, metal products, food, etc., and in the repair of goods (Meier e.t al. 1989).

In recent years, it appears that many African countries have given priority to small-scale industry within the industrial sector. This priority was adopted, it seems, based partly on advice emanating from outside the region. There is even a school of thought which favors an informal sector-based development strategy (Marsdon 1990). The informal sector, although declining in its contribution to the economy, will continue to contribute substantially to development and entrepreneurship. It is, however, difficult to visualize how the industry-related informal sector, generally using rudimentary equipment under poor working conditions and producing low-quality products, can serve as basis for real and reasonably fast growth and development. As for small-scale industry, the International Symposium on Industrial Development: Issues, Discussions and Recommendations, in 1967, had this to say: *"policy should be to develop small-scale industry side by side with large industry and not instead of, or in preference to, large-scale or medium-sized industry"* (UNIDO, *Small-scale Industry*, No. 11). This policy is probably more relevant now because of progress made in industrialization and is likely to lead to better balanced development with broad-based foundations and is therefore worth considering and adopting.

There is no doubt about the relevance and the crucial role of small-scale industries to developing countries. Small-scale industries contribute significantly not only to economic development but also to industrial development itself. Most of the industrial inputs in developed countries, particularly parts and components for assembling plants, are made in specialized small-scale and micro-industries which form mutually interdependent networks with the users of their outputs. Small-scale industries require low investment per worker, a fraction of that of the medium- and large-scale industries. Many of them use local raw materials, renewable and alternative sources of energy, and by-products and wastes of other industries; utilize indigenous technology; produce basic needs that the majority of the people can afford; and help diversify the industrial structure of a country. Many of them are amenable to greater geographical dispersal, particularly the so called "footloose" industries, generally characterized by labor-intensity and high value but low weight or volume of products and therefore facilitating industrial decentralization. Usually, they serve markets within a relatively short radius from the plant location, thereby minimizing transport cost and consequently benefitting the customer, especially in the rural area. Some of them can be operated as home-based industries or subcontracted to individuals. Last but not least, they help develop semi-skilled manpower and entrepreneurial capabilities.

The establishment of the World Assembly of Small and Medium Enterprises (WASME) is an indication of the importance of small-scale industry. WASME held the seventh International Conference of Small and Medium Enterprises and organized an international trade fair in 1994 in Addis Ababa, Ethiopia. The Conference, which was held in Africa for the first time, had "Challenges and Opportunities for Small and Medium Enterprises in the New Global Economic Environment" as its theme.

Given the need to develop small-scale industries, the question is: Where will the equipment, accessories, part of the material inputs, and supplies come from? Now, except local raw materials (including scrap) for resource-based industries, even the raw material inputs for many small-scale industries will have to be either imported or locally produced—hence industrialization at a higher level producing inputs for further processing and fabrication at the small-scale level is an important condition for the development of small-scale industries. The materials imported could be in the form of semi-finished materials (inputs for fertilizer mixing, pesticides for formulation, pharmaceuticals for formulation) or intermediates (metals for metal workshops to make parts and components). With the continuing devaluation and scarcity of foreign exchange, it is possible that small-scale entrepreneurs will find it increasingly difficult to operate existing production units, let alone develop new ones. In this connection, it should be noted that small-scale industries are, generally, not entitled to duty-free imports of industrial inputs to which large-scale units are entitled. This is just one example of the bias against small-scale industries. Others include lack of or inadequate access to capital because of perceived high risks and the high cost of administering small loans and no or inadequate protection from imports. To these must be added diseconomies of scale in procurement of inputs and marketing of products.

Besides, many of the import-substitution type of small-scale industries are already saturated, implying the need to diversify the industry. Diversification means more types of material inputs and therefore more variety of imports of such materials. In this connection it should be noted that small-scale businesses, including industry, are characterized by proliferation. The entrepreneurs who engage themselves in such businesses do not, generally, undertake market research before deciding to go into a particular business activity. The end result is that resources which could have been utilized in other areas are wasted for lack of information and guidance. African countries with penuries of financial resources cannot afford this kind of waste.

Annex 11.1 lists examples of agricultural material processing at small-scale level relevant to African needs and conditions. Annex 14.1 provides a sample of small-scale metal working industries for making machinery and equipment under African needs and conditions. Many of the metal working industries could have contractual arrangements among themselves and with other industrial establishments, especially with assembly units.

Because of his or her limited exposure to industrial experience or absence of such experience, the latter being the case in most instances, the African small-scale entrepreneur is constrained by many factors, in addition to those referred to above. He or she finds it difficult to diversify or upgrade his or her activities, including switching over from trade to industry, because of competition from subsidiaries of or companies supported by transnational corporations. In recognition of these constraints, many African governments have tried to minimize some, if not all, of these constraints through institutions specifically established to ease and facilitate the establishment and operation of small-scale industries. Unfortunately, many of the attempts do not appear to have been that successful.

The indigenous entrepreneur, unlike his or her counterpart in developed countries, has very little if any working relationship with medium- or large-scale enterprises. Subcontractual arrangements are virtually unknown. Industrial extension services are provided in only a limited number of countries.

In order to mitigate some of the factors that constrain the development of small-scale industries, many African countries have devised policies, strategies, and programs that could promote development. They include the following:

• Coordination and integration of services and institutions responsible for the promotion of small-scale industries, the single-window approach (Algeria, Senegal, Tunisia, Kenya, Togo, Ethiopia) to simplify legal, administrative, negotiation, and authorization procedures;
• Formulation of investment codes that do not discriminate against small-scale industries but also provide additional incentives;
• Creation of a network of small-scale industries at the national level;
• Establishment and strengthening of national and subregional funds for small-scale industries;
• Creation of industrial estates; and
• Creation of an enabling environment, including political stability.

Assistance and support provided and that should be provided by governments and donors include any one or a combination of the following: data bank and technical, economic, and financial information service; project development from inception to feasibility study; selection of appropriate technology; construction of industrial estates, including ancillary estates for units working as subcontractors to larger industries; negotiation of technology acquisition/transfer; equipment and machinery hire-purchase arrangement; access to financial resources with concessional terms and conditions; procurement of equipment and machinery on concessional financial terms; bulk purchase and storage of raw materials; buyback and subcontracting arrangements between and among the informal sector, small-scale, medium-scale, and large-scale enterprises, both local and abroad; marketing and distribution of products; entrepreneurial development; common service facilities, such as testing laboratory, heat treatment, and electroplating; joint maintenance arrangements; and training of skilled personnel and upgrading of skills. For the operation at the village level, it may be necessary to supply some of the raw materials in semi-finished form, such as blanks for making tools. The role of industrial extension services, similar to those in agriculture, supported by industrial research, is crucial to enhancing the development of small-scale industry. The services should include economic and technical services as well as management development and product improvement. These and other forms of support and assistance should be continued with more vigor and broaden their coverage for a long time to come. Some of these may be extended to medium- and large-scale industries, which, because of their peculiar nature or strategic importance, require or deserve more support.

In general, tradespeople own and operate the smaller enterprises in the small-scale sector and therefore need more comprehensive assistance that could and should be provided through extension programs. The programs should include measures to inculcate profit motivation in the owners of small-scale enterprises. According to surveys carried out in West Africa, profit, unlike in modern business, is not the sole motive. In Sierra Leone in 1974, for instance, 42 percent of 226 small entrepreneurs gave security, having a family enterprise, following father's occupation, and acquiring prestige as motives. The corresponding figure in Burkina Faso was 45 percent (Meier et. al. 1989).

The whole range of support and assistance referred to above is not necessarily given as a package. If it is, it would be the exception rather than the rule. Whatever combination of support and assistance is provided by governments varies from country to country and from region to region within a country. Société Nationale d'Etudes et de Promotion Industrielle in Senegal, Village Industry Service in Zambia, Small Enterprises Development Corporation in Zimbabwe, Centre National d'Assistance aux Petites et Moyennes Enterprises in Cameroon, Centre d'Assistance et de Promotion de l'Entreprise Nationale in Cote d'Ivoire, and Agence de Promotion de l'Industrie in Tunisia are examples of institutions with diverse objectives and functions, as the names imply. At the regional level, there is the African Project Development Facility (APDF), whose objective is to accelerate the development of productive enterprises managed by private African entrepreneurs (ECA, ECA/IHSD/SSI/009/90). It provides services in project identification, development, and implementation. It is sponsored by UNDP in cooperation with IFC and ADB.

While providing assistance to small-scale industries in general, the Facility could focus on selected entrepreneurs—one group with existing production units and another group with project ideas—and promote and support them systematically to the point where they are really on their own feet. In the case of the former, measures to be taken would comprise undertaking diagnostic studies and helping the entrepreneurs implement the recommendations of the study, including training. With respect to the latter, the measures would involve identifying entrepreneurs; deciding on investment projects; undertaking preinvestment activities and studies; providing technical assistance in training; arranging credit; procuring machinery and equipment; and evaluating performance. Both groups could serve as models and the experience gained could be utilized in more efficient delivery of assistance to other small-scale enterprises and projects.

Industries, generally, gravitate toward locations with infrastructure. This has taken place at the expense of the rural area. Small-scale industries and "footloose" industries offer possibilities for decentralizing industries to rural areas. Industries processing agricultural materials are among those with good possibilities. Perishable materials and materials that result in much reduced weight or volume are candidates for export from rural to urban areas. Perishable materials and materials that produce products of higher weight or volume or fragility and intended to meet the needs of the rural population are candidates for rural production.

## PRIORITY INDUSTRIES

Manufacturing is a vast industry covering the production of hundreds of thousands of products. There is probably no country in the world that produces all its needs within its own borders. Even the largest economy in the world, the United States, with a huge market, depends on other countries to supplement its needs. From this, it is apparent that Africa is not looking for industrialization that could satisfy all its material needs. It is not asking for high-tech industries or industries that produce high-value products, such as fine chemicals, special polymers, specially coated and finished fabrics, special steels, or semiconductor chips. It is asking for the development of high volume traditional manufacturing that could meet the basic needs of its peoples.

Africa's agricultural and industrial product needs are many and diversified. It cannot, obviously, meet all its needs internally. Under the circumstances, it should develop agriculture and selected industries to satisfy its needs as much as possible, particularly basic needs. Ideally, its needs should be determined through market studies. This, evidently, requires a great deal of financial resources and time, an impossible task for this book. In view of this, an approach that gives indications in the form of rough orders of magnitude has been adopted.

Trade statistics that are available in time series for numerous products of interest to Africa could be used as a starting point and exports could be taken as indications of comparative advantage. From net trade figures and production, if available, it is possible to arrive at preliminary conclusions as to whether a product is worth considering for local production/manufacture or expansion (if a production/manufacturing facility exists), provided some of the required factor inputs are available locally. Annexes 4.2 and 4.3 and 5.2 through 5.7 were compiled with this purpose in mind.

Annex 4.2 and 4.3 give production, imports, exports, and net trade of selected agricultural commodities in the continent at five year intervals for the period 1965-1990 as well as some years of the early 1990s. Under crops, Africa has been a net importer with the exception of maize during the early part of the period. Its net import of cereal soared from 4.0 million tons in 1965 to 31.1 million tons in 1993. The corresponding figures for wheat, the most important single crop imported, were 3.9 and 20.2 and for rice, 0.5 and 3.6. From these figures it is obvious that substantial increase in the production of cereals is a priority. Other agricultural commodities characterized by net imports include: maize, barley, malt, pulses, fresh milk, and eggs. Imports of food were supplemented by food aid for countries that could not afford to import food. Food (cereals) aid increased from 4.37 million tons in 1980-1982 to 6.08 million tons in 1990-1992 and stood at 205,935 and 47, 221 tons for oils and milk, respectively, in 1990-1992 (World Bank, *World Resources 1996-97*).

Comparisons of net imports with local production show that imports have been growing much faster relative to production. For cereals as a whole, the net import/production ratio of 0.08 in 1965 peaked at 0.35 in 1985 and marginally fell to 0.33 in 1990. In terms of self-sufficiency in cereals, these correspond to 92.8 percent and 75.3 percent.

With respect to processed agricultural products in general, the trend is not very different from those of agricultural commodities (see Annex 5.3). With the exception of groundnut oil, roundwood, veneer sheets, wood pulp, chemical wood pulp, chemical sulfate pulp, crustaceans, molluscs, and fish products and preparations, Africa has been a net importer of many agricultural, forestry, and fishery products in the past two decades. In the 1960s and early 1970s, its status changed from a net exporter to a net importer of food. Its net export of 610,000 tons of raw sugar in 1970, for instance, changed to a net import of over a million tons in 1990. Other products with similar fate included: palm oil, oil cake, meat (fresh and canned), oil and fats, meals and animal feedstuffs, wine, sawnwood, wood-based panels and plywood.

In general, production of many products showed rising trend during the 1965-1990 period. For example, production of sugar increased from 3.34 million tons in 1965 to 8.0 million tons in 1992 and fell to 6.58 million tons in 1994. Production figures for other products for the years 1970 and 1990 were: 23,800 tons and 67,700 tons for chocolate, 17.8 million hectoliters and 57.3 million hectoliters for beer, 282,200 tonnes and 448,000 tons for cotton yarn, 126.7 million pairs and 198.5 million pairs for footwear, 710,000 tonnes and 2.28 million tons for woodpulp, etc. Such increases were not, however, adequate to meet the growing African consumption for most of the products. For example, based on figures in Annexes 5.2 and 5.3, apparent consumption of sugar works out to 3.32 million tons in 1965 and 8.84 million tons in 1990. These translate into 100.6 percent and 88.0 percent self-sufficiency in sugar respectively. For most products, consumption figures do not reflect demand as potential demand is much higher than levels indicated by apparent consumption.

The deficits of food and other agricultural materials indicated by net imports in Annex 5.3 will increase tremendously over time. According to a statement of the FAO Director-General delivered at the OAU Summit in 1995 in Addis Ababa, cereal import in 1994/95 was expected to amount to 31.4 million tons; the cereal deficit could reach the 50-million-ton level by the year 2010; and prices of food from the temperate zone are expected to increase. Potential grain shortages due to farming policy changes, including reduction in export subsidies in developed countries, and climatic changes which manifested themselves in 1995 are the main reasons for price increases. Worldwatch Institute annual report disclosed that worsening global climate was the major cause for the smallest grain harvest in 1995 since 1988 resulting in an all-time low of grain reserves (*The Boston Globe*, May 19, 1996). The 1996 drought in the southwestern quadrant of the United States, coupled with policy restricting acreage cultivated (currently lifted), could worsen the shortages and further raise the prices of grains.

The following are among the alternatives that can be considered to deal with such mounting food deficit:

(i) continue to import food,

(ii) increase production using imported agricultural inputs, and

(iii) increase production using locally produced agricultural inputs.

Alternative (i) is impractical for lack of foreign currency. Nor is it advisable to continue to import food or to receive food aid for obvious reasons, including the consequence of reducing incentive to produce locally.

Obviously, the huge additional and growing food requirement cannot be produced using traditional methods of farming and inputs by farmers engaged in subsistence agriculture. Most farmers of that kind have not been able to feed themselves, let alone produce surplus for the fast rising urban population.

Improved agricultural practices and modern inputs, including selected seeds (improved and high-yielding varieties), irrigation, fertilizers, pesticides, and agricultural tools, implements, and machinery would be among the inputs needed to bring about the phenomenal increase in productivity and production required —hence alternatives (ii) and (iii). In most instances, such inputs may have to be introduced progressively, taking account of the stage of farming practices and the inputs in use in the area concerned: the hoe in place of the stick, the sickle in place of the knife, the plough (where animal traction is practical)[5] in place of the hoe, the tractor in place of animals, etc. In view of the relatively poor African soils and climate amenable to pest infestation, there is no doubt that fertilizers and pesticides need to be used in increasing quantities. In regard to pesticides, an integrated management system, including biological control, insect growth regulators, and crop rotation, should be adopted as much as possible in order to minimize adverse change in the ecology system. Other inputs include storage systems, vehicles (carts, three-wheelers, trucks, etc.) to transport agricultural inputs to farms, and agricultural outputs to storage as well as to consumption centers and equipment and machinery for processing agricultural products.

Technological innovations in biotechnology and genetic engineering have contributed and continue to contribute to new and improved products, processes, and techniques, increasing productivity (including increasing the growth rates of plants and animals), delaying ripening and rotting, rendering plants resistant to pests, fungi and drought, and imparting salt tolerance to plants, including trees. The sectors benefiting from such innovations include agriculture (particularly food, especially significant because of the food crisis), chemicals (particularly pharmaceuticals, using genetically engineered strains of *E. Coli* for example), environmental control, and mining. Genetically engineered food (tomato, maize [corn], potatoes, and soybeans), improved vaccines, vaccine against hepatitis, crops resistant to diseases or tolerant to herbicides and bacteria modified to degrade pollutants, such as PCBS and dioxins, are examples of such innovations. World-wide development in this field has direct bearing, both positive and negative (replacing African exports and/or lowering their prices), on African agriculture in particular and other sectors in general. Examples of the former include synthesized substitutes for cocoa butter from palm oil and arabic gum from polyevulan, a polymer. Measures need to be taken, therefore, to minimize the negative impact that could arise from better and cheaper substitutes and the production of African agricultural export commodities or their substitutes in the backyards of developed countries—thus bringing about structural changes in production in developed countries and erosion of the comparative advantage of African countries.

In view of the above, the fact that very little R&D, if any, into genetically-engineered crops (excepting wheat and maize) of interest to developing countries is being undertaken in developed countries and the increasing difficulty of accessing innovations in this field, R&D in biotechnology and genetic engineering should be part and parcel of the agricultural priority. According to one source, the potential loss of African countries' *"export earnings due to advances in biotechnology in medium term is more than $3 billion per year"* (ECA/FAO, *Biotechnology Revolution ...*) The earlier that African countries can venture into this potential field, therefore, the better their future. Fortunately, biotechnology, being highly research-intensive but relatively less capital-intensive, may prove to be more accessible compared with the other emerging industries characterized by high entry barriers.

African countries should seek support and take advantage of the International Centre for Genetic Engineering and Biotechnology in Trieste, Italy, and New Delhi, India, and FAO's GERMPLASM in planning, establishing, and operating R&D institutions related to biotechnology and genetic engineering. Other institutions that could lend support are: the Agricultural Biotechnology for Sustainable Productivity supported by USAID, the Rockerfeller Foundation for rice biotechnology, the Netherlands Directorate General for International Cooperation for cassava technology, the Intermediate Biotechnology Service functioning as a clearing house, the Center for the Application of Molecular Biology to International Agriculture aimed at benefiting farmers in developing countries and the International Service for the Acquisition of Agri-Biotechnological Applications providing brokering services between developing countries and institutions with proven biotechnologies (Juo et. al. 1995).

Similar argument applies to the other agriculture-based basic needs related to health, clothing, education, and shelter.

Where will the agricultural inputs aimed at raising agricultural productivity and production come from? Alternatives (ii) and (iii), referred to earlier, are the answer to this question. Alternative (ii), based on imports, is out of the question for the same reason as for food import: African countries cannot simply afford the huge and growing annual foreign exchange needed. In 1995, for instance, the average unsubsidized price of fertilizers (urea/DAP) increased by over 40 percent over that of 1994 in Ethiopia resulting in raising the planned subsidy of Birr 50 million to Birr 180 million. Besides, it is not in the long-term interest of the region to depend on imports of such vital agricultural inputs. In addition, aid donors cannot be expected to provide inputs on a permanent basis. There is, therefore, no practical alternative to local production of the inputs, alternative (iii). This alternative (which is in line with the priority accorded to agriculture and sectors supporting agriculture by the OAU and the United Nations referred to in Chapter 3) is the basic premise of this book.

The above argument in favor of local production of inputs for agriculture also applies to small-scale industries. As small-scale industries span a whole gamut of industries, it would not be practical to cater to so diversified a field. Criteria such as number of establishments and potential for development should be used to select small-scale industries for inclusion in the planning of industrial development, particularly the capital goods industry.

Based on the above realities, the following are among the industrial branches deserving priority treatment in the agriculture-led strategy of industrial development:

• Agricultural chemicals,
• Agricultural equipment and machinery,
• Equipment and machinery for preserving, storing, processing and transporting agricultural inputs and products,
• Industries oriented toward other basic needs, and
• Industries producing inputs for small-scale industries.

The first four practically coincide with those in the OAU Common African Agricultural Programme (CAAP). The above priorities were, explicitly or implicitly, confirmed by the Alliance for Africa's Industrialization for which UNIDO was reported to be acting as an interim secretariat. The Alliance, a private-led initiative, was created to help forge partnership between governments and the private sector and to accelerate the industrialization process in Africa, particularly in enhancing the attainment of the objectives of IDDA II. It is expected to address the industry-related issues in the United Nations System-wide Special Initiative for Africa. Specifically, it is expected to *"promote and attract investment in economic activities that created added value"* [6] (UNIDO/ECA, *Alliance for Africa's Industrialization*). Unlike in the past when the private sector was relatively ignored, the Alliance involves government decision makers, the private sector/ business community, and international institutions. The launching was preceded by a high level expert meeting which included officials of investment promotion services from 17 African countries.

All the above industrial priorities, in fact all industries, have common requirements, equipment and machinery that are products of the engineering subsector. This subsector embodies most technologies in the equipment and machinery it makes and uses. It utilizes machine tools in making capital goods, including the priority equipment and machinery. In view of foreign exchange constraint to import machine tools, the need to achieve a level of self-reliance in this strategic subsector through the local manufacture of machine tools is a precondition for the self-sustaining development not only of the engineering industry but also of industry in general. Capability in the manufacture and use of machine tools would also contribute to the repair and maintenance of equipment and machinery used in all socio-economic activities.

In addition to their wide applications in other uses, chemicals and metals are major inputs to the engineering subsector. Obviously, such inputs, particularly the basic ones needed in large volumes, will have to be produced locally if African countries are to achieve a degree of self-sustaining development and succeed in solving or minimizing the food problem. The following branches of the three subsectors which provide inputs not only to agriculture and industry itself but also to other socio-economic activities therefore constitute additional industrial priorities:

• Machine tools and equipment and machinery related to agriculture and transport, as well as other capital goods for small-scale and spare-parts industries from the engineering subsector;

• Basic chemicals (sulfuric, phosphoric, nitric and hydrochloric acids and chlorine, caustic soda, and sodium carbonate) from the chemical subsector; and

• Basic metals (iron and steel, aluminum and copper) from the metallurgical subsector.

These additional priorities, it should be noted, are of strategic significance. They provide leverage over the rest of the economy. At the level of intermediate production, basic chemicals and metals are characterized by economies of scale and capital- and skill-intensity. The manufacture of engineering goods can be labor-intensive and lends itself more to decentralized operation. Planning the development of all three basic subsectors should, of course, take into account demand in other economic activities.

All the above priority industrial branches are dealt with in subsequent chapters. It should be noted that some of the basic chemicals (sufuric, phosphoric and nitric acids) are and will be produced within the fertilizer complexes. They are therefore dealt together with fertilizers.

The priorities arrived at above should be taken as minimum basis for development within the priorities of the second Industrial Development Decade for Africa (IDDA II). Countries with comparative advantages and markets for products not falling under the agricultural-led priorities should go ahead and develop industries, particularly resource-based industries. Petrochemicals in hydrocarbon and metals (other than iron and steel, copper and aluminum) in mineral resource-rich countries are examples of products whose production can and should be considered when and if circumstances permit. In this connection, it should be noted that the development of the capital goods industry is crucial not only to industrial development, but also to economic development in general.

Another approach towards determining industrial priorities in Africa is to identify industrial products needed in developing countries. The following are such products and conform both to the list of high growth elasticities and high inter-industrial linkages (Harris 1986). They are ranked in descending order of importance of elasticities in non-industrialized countries with small populations.

  • Paper and paper products;
  • Metal products, with machinery (electrical and mechanical) and transport equipment;
  • Chemicals, with petroleum and coal products (including plastics);
  • Wood and cork manufactures with furniture and fixtures;
  • Basic metal industries (iron and steel, aluminum, etc.);
  • Printing and publishing;
  • Rubber products;
  • Clothing and footwear;
  • Non metallic mineral products (cement, glass, etc.);
  • Leather products;
  • Textiles; and
  • Food, beverages, and tobacco.

Comparison of the above list with the agriculture and basic needs related priorities arrived at earlier shows that over 50 percent of the former correspond with the later. According to the above list, relatively more paper and metal products will be consumed with increasing income. As for textiles and food, the increase will be relatively less.

## STRATEGIES FOR IMPLEMENTING PRIORITY INDUSTRIES

Most of the priority industries are large-scale, capital-intensive, and sensitive to economies of scale. They therefore require large markets and capital investment which individual countries can ill afford. In other words, the solution to smallness lies in cooperation among African countries and making optimum use of the market and resources of the region, thereby minimizing duplication of production and service facilities.

### Cooperation and Integration in Industrial Development

As noted earlier, the African Economic Community is intended to provide a basis for cooperation. Attempts at industrial cooperation at the subregional level have been and continue to be made. In the past, the approach has been to undertake studies, including feasibility studies, and present them to potential investors in promotional meetings organized for this purpose. Practically all the studies were based on national markets and consequently failed to attract potential investors, mainly because of the small national markets.

Agreement among the member states concerned on projects to be promoted is a pre-condition for attracting potential investors. From past experience, it is essential to involve the potential investor(s) right from the beginning, immediately following the decision by member states to go ahead with a specific project. Thereafter decisions should be made by the local investors (including public enterprises) and the potential foreign investor(s) at every stage of the project development. This would enable the investors to evaluate the project and decide whether it is worthwhile continuing after each stage.

The stages of project development and implementation are:
- Identification of industrial possibilities in the subregion,
- Undertaking pre-feasibility and support studies and activities,
- Undertaking feasibility study,
- Undertaking engineering study,
- Formation of a company,
- Mobilization of investment,
- Training,
- Construction, and
- Operation.

The priorities and strategies identified imply structural transformation of the national economies, currently characterized by the production of primary commodities, to the manufacture of intermediates and capital goods required for agriculture and selected small-scale industries. Such crucial transformation can only be achieved by establishing optimally sized industries (that can sustain relatively large-scale units) based on market integration.

From the above priorities, it is apparent that, under African conditions, giving priority to agriculture without involving industry and vice-versa cannot work. Development depends on both—hence the importance of agro-industry, the production of agricultural inputs and the processing of agricultural outputs as well as the development of the basic industries required to produce the inputs and process the outputs.

Whether the best approach to development is via agriculture or industry is debatable. Developing countries, particularly African countries, have been advised to go the agricultural route, that is, produce and export agricultural commodities. If all developing countries were to follow the advice and pressure imposed on them, the world market would be flooded with the same kind of agricultural commodities, with the result that prices would be drastically depressed. This is what happened in the last two decades and continues to happen. South Korea ignored the advice and opted for industrialization. As is well known, South Korea is now an industrial success story. So too are other relatively small countries which lack major resources, such as Taiwan, Singapore, and Hong Kong, This excludes large countries, such as India, Mexico, and Brazil. Yet in practically all these cases, industrial development started with imported technology. This was then followed by the assimilation and subsequent adaptation of the technology and the development of local technology.

Technology can be transferred from developed to developing countries in many ways. These include: (i) the purchase of new equipment, (ii) direct foreign investment, (iii) the use of nonproprietary technology, (iv) acquisition of knowledge from nationals returning from or residing abroad, and (v) domestic R&D and reverse engineering (World Bank, *Proceedings of the World Bank Annual Conference ...* ). Although African countries resort to all modes of transfer, the first and second are probably the most common in most countries.

It is difficult to imagine a country, in this fast changing world, developing itself solely on the basis of agriculture or, for that matter, through specialization in primary commodity production. Baker et. al. (1986) and others support this view. The former states that *"no country can be said to have started on the path of self reliant industrialization unless it has begun the manufacture of at least some of the machinery and equipment required by its industrial sector. Selfsustaining industrialization, whether socialist or otherwise, cannot begin unless a country has built up a certain capacity in the manufacture of equipment goods, especially machine tools and machinery."*

Another author supporting African industrialization is Khennas (1992) who opens the preface of his *Industrialization, Mineral Resources and Energy in Africa* as follows: *"In any society, the production of technology and that of capital goods constitutes the only guarantee of autonomous development, which means the ability to meet social claims and to ensure a dynamic, expanding reproduction process."*

One approach to industrialization is through relocation of industries from developed countries. The type of industries that can be relocated include:
• Industries which have become obsolete because of product or technology innovation;
• Labor-intensive industries; and
• Polluting industries.

Relocating industries which fall into the above categories could, in principle, be welcomed. Careful consideration and selection should, however, precede their acquisition. In the case of the first, as the alternative for the owners is to incur cost in getting rid of them, the price of the plant needs to be very attractive. The owners should guarantee the availability of parts and components required to operate the plant in the future. As noted elsewhere, because of developments in automation, the relocation of labor-intensive industries is questionable. As for polluting industries, those who sell the plant or relocate and operate the plant should take the responsibility of equipping the plant with, at least, the minimum pollution abating equipment, short of that required by the developed country whence the plant originated.

Whatever priorities are selected and strategies adapted, African countries, preferably jointly, should involve themselves in the development of new technologies, particularly those related to biotechnology, genetic engineering, and solar energy. They need to undertake research and development activities in new technologies with potential for maximum benefit.

It is apparent that African countries need massive assistance to achieve sustainable industrialization. This author has been, for many years, toying with the idea of a "Marshall Plan" for Africa, if African countries would be blessed with dedicated leadership. Interestingly, this idea, already referred to, was the subject of discussion at the OAU summit in Tunisia in 1994. The president of Tunisia, the 1994/1995 chairman of the OAU, was mandated to lobby rich nations for an African version of a "Marshall Plan." More recently, American Congressman Charles B. Rangel, leading a presidential mission to Africa in 1997, said *"what I would like to see in Africa is a Marshall Plan similar to what we did after Wolrd War II in Europe."*

For each project to be implemented, the roles of the host country, other member countries, and public and private investors (local and foreign) should be spelled out. These include: sources and arrangements for the supply of raw and intermediate materials and energy; access to national and export (outside member countries) markets for the products; financing and equity share-holding; subcontracting, if needed; management of the enterprise; and linkages of the enterprise with corresponding national companies or corporations. The last is a very important factor in industrial cooperation and integration. Multinational and subregional projects should be designed with a view to optimizing vertical and horizontal integration so as to distribute downstream production units fairly among the greatest number of countries, provided this does not adversely affect the economic viability of the project as a whole.

This book argues in favor of starting with the development of the processing and manufacturing of agricultural inputs and outputs. This, of course, does not mean that industrial development should be limited to these. It means that, given the limited resources, agriculture-related industrialization should be given the highest priority in the short and medium term. It means that the majority of African countries should strive to develop their industries with a view to attaining a measure of self-reliance in food and other agriculture-based products. Of course, developing such industries, particularly basic industries, should take into account non-agricultural outlets, i.e., demand for other intermediate and final products. Those countries or groups of countries which could mobilize resources beyond those needed for processing and manufacturing agricultural inputs and outputs and other basic needs could and should develop industries in which they enjoy real comparative advantages.

Although complementarity may appear to be limited within the same ecological zones, different ecological zones offer opportunities for multinational cooperation in industries based on agriculture. Examples of such possibilities include the development of cotton textiles, meat, dairy products, and leather goods in the Sahelian countries for markets in the countries along the West African coast. It would be mutually beneficial if the coastal countries could let the relatively less endowed Sahelian countries specialize in these industries. The same would, to a lesser extent, apply to meat, dairy products, and leather goods produced in East Africa *vis-a-vis* other African countries. Making products from cocoa, coffee, tea, and rubber is an area that could be reserved to those countries that produce the commodities.

## Adoption of Appropriate Products and Technologies

The ever widening technology gap between the developing and developed countries is obviously a disadvantage to the former. The so-called traditional (relatively simple) technologies and techniques are becoming sophisticated and complex—hence increasingly costly and so relatively unaffordable for many developing countries. The trend is away from batch processing towards continuous processing. As a result, an increasing number of spare parts and replacement equipment for industries existing in Africa are likely to be unavailable in the world market. There will come a time when industrial establishments will be scrapped for want of such inputs. In addition to optimizing the use of labor, a serious negative factor under African conditions and needs, technologies will further raise the entry cost and barrier for African countries wishing to develop manufacturing, including the manufacturing of machinery and equipment and thus constrain the transfer of technology. The import of capital goods, licensing, and FDI are among the means of acquiring technology.

Technology acquisition through the import of capital goods has been the most used channel in Africa. In this approach technology is embodied in physical capital (equipment and machinery) as well as in the skill of people. It is because of underdevelopment, including inadequate technical and negotiating capabilities, that the cost of technology is much higher in Africa than in any other region. Payments are made in foreign currency for patents, licenses, know-how, trademarks, copyrights, and related technical services which, of necessity, are imported. This high cost is inflated further through the high cost of equipment and machinery and the overpricing of intermediates. Worse still, acquiring technology involves a number of restrictive practices and conditions. These include transfer pricing, prohibition on sharing the technical knowledge gained or improved during plant operation with third parties, and selling products outside the country concerned and reimporting the same technology every time a repeated use is required. Joint purchases of technologies by a group of enterprises in a country or group of countries could minimize some of these problems.

In general, a range of products serving the same or related purposes and technological options involving different degrees of capital- or labor-intensities and scale factors for producing the products are available. In recent years, because of sophisticated processes and quality controls through increasing automation and computerization, the number of options have become wider and are likely to increase in the future. Decisions on a particular product to be produced and technology to be adopted should, therefore, be arrived at after careful identification and thorough evaluation of technology options have been made.

In addition to trends toward automation and miniaturization, the development of microtechnology and nanotechnology, although at an early stage of development, not only could enhance the obsolescence of technology in use in Africa but also worsen the technology gap as well as the availability of replacement equipment and spare parts for existing industries. According to W. A. Richard of Pacific Northwest National Laboratory, "*In the not-to-distant future it will be possible to fabricate complex chemical systems within the volume of a cubic centimeter*" (*Chemical Engineering Progress*, April 1996). The January 1997 issue (*Chemical Engineering Progress*) revealed the advent of miniaturizing/scaling-down operations, such as reactors for the manufacture of specialty chemicals, including pharmaceuticals, in the same equipment. If and when available, this technology may help solve the constraint arising from economies of scale and enable more African countries to produce some fine chemicals which they could not otherwise produce. From information available from the Second International Conference on Microreaction Technology held in New Orleans in March 1998 research being carried out in microtechnology seem to be progressing well and fast. One of the participants of the Conference confirmed the optimistic prediction referred to above by saying *"In the foreseeable future we can anticipate the assembly of compact chemical processing and energy conversion systems that range in size from smaller than a cubic centimeter to assemblies encompassing several cubic meters"* (*Chemical Engineering Progress*, April 1998).

African countries have been indiscriminately adopting products and technologies irrespective of their real usefulness, prices, and adaptability to local environment, not to speak of domestic factor endowment. Many of the products incorporate standards, functions, and qualities that are neither needed nor used. Products should be designed to meet basic requirements commensurate with the standard of living, i.e., they should be relatively simple, functional, and as low-cost as possible. Existing designs should be replaced by simpler versions. The machinery and equipment for making such products should, as much as possible, be easy to manufacture, operate, and maintain. If this is done, it is quite likely that appropriate products can be made cheaper and more people can afford them. The car industry in India until recently was, for example, producing the mechanically simple and paraphernalia-striped old model of Morris Oxfords of the United Kingdom. There is no doubt that the Indian consumer benefited by access to a relatively low-cost vehicle whose configuration, unlike other cars, practically remained the same for decades.

It took industrialized countries centuries to attain their current stage of technology and sophistication. Technological development has accelerated markedly during this century, particularly since the 1950s. In the past few decades, the focus has been on highly processed and packaged products, rising sizes of production units, and increasing automation and computerized process-control systems. Such developments have, of course, brought escalating costs (relative to conditions in developing countries), both of consumer and capital goods, thus denying most peoples in developing countries access to more appropriate and cheaper products and machinery. Worse still, the trend seems to be shifting from repair to replacement, i.e., replacing worn out parts and components instead of repairing and reconditioning them.

Because of the above situation, it has become abundantly clear that African countries have no choice but to use machinery and equipment most of which is becoming increasingly irrelevant to their needs and deteriorating economies. This state of affairs evidently continues to lead to the adoption of medium- and relatively large-scale, capital-intensive industries concentrated in a few urban areas with adequate infrastructure at the expense of the small towns, and semi-urban and rural areas. The countries need technologies that can produce relatively simple products, particularly basic needs, at a low cost which they can afford, and that can be economically operated at decentralized locations. In general, there is, at this stage of their development, no need for sophisticated products that incorporate non-essential functions (that cater to the minority) which inflate the cost of products. This implies appropriate technologies which combine factor inputs (capital, labor, and material) in proportions commensurate with their availabilities. Labor being the most abundant, this means a bias towards labor-intensive industries, including indirect labor resulting from backward and forward linkages.

Despite the apparent advantage of a labor-intensive approach, capital-intensive industries abound in the region. This is, in part, explained by government policies that make capital cheaper relative to labor. Investment incentives (customs duty and excise tax free entry of capital goods, tax holidays, etc.) and local low-interest rates are among such policies. Other explanations may include the tendency for engineers and foreign companies to adopt advanced technologies as they are.

The concept of appropriate technology may vary from individual to individual as well as from institution to institution. According to a report of a ministerial-level meeting, International Forum on Appropriate Industrial Technology in 1978, it *"was viewed as being the technology mix contributing most to economic, social and environmental objectives, in relation to resource endowments and conditions of application in each country"* (UNIDO, *Conceptual....Technology*). It is a dynamic and flexible concept that has to do with conserving scarce resources, attaining higher economic efficiency, permitting wide application, ensuring consistency with local resources and conditions, and responding to changing economic and social conditions, needs, and tastes in the country or area concerned. It is something intermediate between the modern and the informal sectors. It could be an improved or upgraded version of existing technology, be it traditional or modern. According to Singer (Singer 1977), *"The ultimate objective is to ensure that a technology chosen is both efficient and in accordance with the needs and resources of the country."*

It should be emphasized here that appropriate technology is not equated with traditional or conventional technology (implying old, outdated, and inefficient technology). It may not necessarily be the best as long as it serves the purpose. It does not rule out resorting to the use of the state-of-the-art of technology prevailing at the time nor the use of older processes or second-hand equipment so long as it is more suited to the production for local market and is in good and viable operating condition. It does not mean neglecting industries characterized by high technology, skilled labor and capital intensity. The Sinai Technology Valley (STV), one of the areas of the Technology Development Program to be established in Egypt, is an example of a high technology center that the relatively better off African countries, individually or as a group, should venture into. The STV aims, among other things, at the production of hi-tech parts and components.

Appropriate technology ideally combines low capital cost, labor-intensive operations, and (as much as possible) local materials and skills and is relatively affordable. It could be an adapted version of an older technology. It comprises existing, improved, or upgraded as well as advanced technology. It could, for instance, include mini-water treatment plants, vacuum toilets, ultrasound cleaning of clothes, solar panels as roofing material, and home wind generators—some of the current technologies that could make homes more environmentally friendly. These were among the 1997 survey results of predictions of homes of the future by American chemical engineers (AIChExtra, April 1997).

It involves careful selection of the best alternatives of product(s) (including those satisfying the latent needs of the population with limited resources) to be made; the material and energy resources to be used; and the technology for making the product(s) from a myriad of technologies available elsewhere but compatible with real needs and development, taking into account optimum use of labor. In short, it means improved designs of products and production units; better tools, equipment, and machinery; simpler technology and scaled-down plants; and a combination of traditional and modern technologies suited to prevailing needs and conditions. It even means re-using technologies rendered obsolete due to technological progress in developed countries as long as they meet the needs of developing countries. The $50 refrigerator developed in India (*News Week*, August 4, 1997) is a good example of a product and technology involving some of the above factors. It should be noted here that the information and management aspects should be taken into consideration as part and parcel of appropriate technology.

The use of appropriate technology should not be considered a permanent feature of African industrialization. It is a temporary measure until such a time as African countries achieve a level of technological development that moves towards closing the technology gap. Even then it does not mean that will be the end of appropriate technology, for there will always be need for it under varying circumstances.

Sugar production could be used as an illustration. Of the different processes producing different qualities of sugar, the open pan process based on an appropriate technology seems worth considering when planning the development of the sugar industry. The sugar it produces is considered an acceptable substitute for plantation white sugar consumed domestically and would, perhaps, be acceptable if properly promoted, especially in the rural area where use of sugar is not yet that popular. It is made by a small-scale open pan process using relatively simple equipment and machinery, a good part of which can be made locally. The open pan process is labor-intensive, requiring modest skills, and involves low capital cost per unit of output as well as employment. Because of the small size that contrasts with the increasing plant size associated with the conventional vacuum-pan process and the inherently higher risk of economic failure, it is amenable to dispersion. It is a means of bringing the sugar industry to areas where the potential availability of cane is inadequate to justify large sugar mills. It also means low transport and distribution cost as market for the sugar produced would generally be limited to the area within a reasonable distance from the mill. According to UNIDO (*Appropriate ... Sugar*), a comparison of a group of 20 open pan mills with one conventional vacuum-pan mill, both based on the production of 15,000 tons of sugar per year, in the late 1970s, showed that the open pan group required an investment of $5 million and 3,600 workers versus $7.5 million and 720 workers for the conventional mill. Overall, the advantages of the open pan process could outweigh the disadvantages of high fuel consumption and low sugar yield which may have been improved by now.

Although the number may vary, practically all processing and manufacturing activities have a broad spectrum of alternative technologies. In other words, a product can be made in more than one way, depending on the likely combination of factor inputs and other techno-economic variables. The number of alternatives is narrowed down with the determination of the raw material(s) base and energy to be used. At this stage, the technological options, based on specific material and energy inputs, could still be wide. This variance is compounded by competing variations of the same basic technology provided by different suppliers of technology, thus making choice of technology difficult. The complex process of selecting an appropriate technology is illustrated by the case of ammonia. This chemical intermediate for making fertilizers and a wide range of chemicals can be made from a variety of carbonacious materials (natural gas, petroleum products, coal, lignite, and wood) and water. Although part of the technology used is common to all of the raw materials, the technology becomes progressively more complex and costly as the carbonacious material to be used changes from natural gas to petroleum products, etc., to wood. The part of technology which is common to all is characterized by many variations available from many suppliers.

From the above illustration, it is apparent that making technological choices is difficult and requires a high level of expertise in the specific industry concerned. This problem is common to all countries, although much more serious in the case of developing countries with limited availability of expertise. The problem is compounded because most of technologies available in the market are made to suit the needs of and conditions in developed countries. This is one of the reasons why so many industries have failed to perform or achieve the performance levels prescribed by the suppliers of industrial machinery and equipment, thus underscoring the need for appropriate technology.

The relevance of the concept of appropriate technology as defined above is apparent. The ideal solution to problems arising from inappropriate technology is to devise techologies that are appropriate. Until this is done, the adaptation of imported technology to suit local conditions is essential. This could be done by desegregating the technology to see if part of the processes, such as material handling, can be redesigned to use more labor and if part of the equipment can be fabricated in the host country. Modifications that cannot be done in the host country could be left to the supplier. The supplier should, of course, provide guidance and assistance during the process of modification.

In view of the speed with which technology continues to change and incorporates increasingly higher levels of automation, rendering technologies inappropriate to African needs, access to traditional technology and machinery and, worse still, to spare parts and replacement equipment for existing industries will be a serious constraint. The conclusion is that developing countries should master and improve upon technologies in use before it is too late. This would involve operating, maintaining, and repairing the capital goods incorporating the technology, upgrading the technology to incorporate new developments, introducing changes in the design of the technology. This is a temporary solution. The long-term solution is to innovate new technology of on'es own.

There are and there will be cases where use of relatively sophisticated automation and even some advanced technology, including information technology[7] (semiconductors, computers, software, and telecommunications) are a must. For example, for certain industries, where very precise quality control or safety is critical, there is little room for compromise. In some cases productivity and competitiveness could dictate the adoption of industrial automation. In general, the new processing or fabrication techniques as well as services involving information technology are easier, faster, and less expensive in the long run. The application of information technology in business, in particular, is becoming imperative. It enables small business to perform tasks that were the domain of big business and to undertake cooperative operations or share machines and services. These possibilities are relevant to business in Africa, where economies of scale are a deterrent to development. In this connection, the services provided by the Internet and e-mail could help African countries to leapfrog some of the constraints dealt with in this chapter.

The very nature of some industries, particularly those based on continuous processes, is such that the possibilities for substituting labor for capital are relatively limited compared with, say, manufacturing many engineering goods. Because of the need to meet strict quality standards for goods for export, there may, in many cases, be no option but to adopt the most advanced capital-intensive technology to produce such goods. Besides, African countries should, whenever appropriate, take advantage of the rapid diffusion of knowledge, made possible thanks to information technology, to do some catching-up with the developed world.

It is possible to use technology at different levels of sophistication during the same period. It would, for instance, make sense to, and some industries do, produce two qualities of the same product: export quality and lower quality products for local consumption. White crystal sugar for export and brown sugar for local use are examples of such possibilities. Beer is another product produced in two qualities, one for home consumption and one for export.

Partial introduction of appropriate technology is possible in practically all industries. To do this the technology packages selected as well as the related buildings and structures should be desegregated and reviewed to find out which parts can be procured or manufactured locally. A case in point relates to the building and structures of a plant. It is possible that a good part of the building and structures, which can be relatively simpler and less costly because of less harsh climatic conditions  than those of the originating country, can be made locally. Others are materials handling and product packaging. In countries with abundant labor,  mechanical or automatic handling and packaging could be limited to materials that, by their very nature, need such handling or packaging or which are dangerous. Appropriate technology could be devised to maximize the use of manpower for most material handling (flat trolleys, simple bag elevators, etc.) and packaging processes. The same would apply to mechanization and  automation minimizing the use of expensive equipment and control  instrumentation (reducing them to absolute practical minimum), including remote control, that could be replaced by manpower. It is quite apparent that most of the automation and computer-controlled operations whose practicality under African conditions is questionable are not in the interest of African countries, at least at the current and foreseeable stages of development. In fact, they are marginalizing whatever potential comparative advantages African countries enjoyed not so long ago but never had the occasion to benefit from.

The technology desegregation approach can be illustrated by a successful example in Ethiopia. The Kassk Spices & Herbes Extraction Factory, which started operation in 1997, incorporates locally manufactured heat exchangers, vessels, boiling kettles, extraction columns, conveyers, hoppers, dryers, and gutters using imported materials. There was, apparently, no foreign expertise involved in the setting up of the plant with a capital investment of about $4 million instead of $8.5 had it been done on a turn-key basis as usually would have been the case with such type of a relatively complex plant (*Investment Review*,  October 1, 1997). This example clearly shows to what extent  parts and components of a plant can be substituted by locally made ones.

The multipurpose concept which is used in engineering plants and to some extent in the production of fine chemicals in developed countries would be worth looking into. In developing countries where markets for many products are small and fragmented and where capacity utilization is low, the multipurpose approach could solve or minimize constraints arising from economies of scale. It could contribute to the production  and diversification of locally produced products, particularly in the process industry, and therefore to achieving a measure of self-sufficiency in industrial products.

A multipurpose equipment or plant is designed in such a way as to produce similar or related products on a campaign basis. Its design incorporates features that would make it feasible to process materials based on the same or related technology. In the case of process industries, for instance, it should be designed to accommodate the highest and lowest levels of temperature, pressure, corrosion resistance, etc. [8]required for the range of products to be produced.

The features incorporated in a multipurpose plant make it possible to operate the plant throughout the year which would be impossible and unprofitable with a single-purpose system. The capital cost would, naturally, be high but the additional cost would be marginal compared to what it would cost if more than one single-purpose units were to be set up to produce products that can be produced in a multipurpose plant. The fixed cost part of the operational cost would be minimized. Frequent downtime between campaigns would, however, mean trade-off between operating flexibility and efficiency. The problem associated with economies of scale for ammonia production can, for instance, be minimized by designing the ammonia plant to produce methanol as well. In view of the likely overall advantages, attempts should be made to take account of the multipurpose approach when developing projects that may be amenable to such an approach.

The need to screen carefully and adopt foreign technology cannot be overemphasized at this stage of industrial development in Africa. In selecting a technology, a distinction should be made between whether the technology is to be used to produce products for export or local consumption. Particular emphasis should be placed on absorption and modification, i.e., learning-by-doing, particularly at the shop floor level, and adapting the technology to local materials and conditions. This should, over time, be followed by replication of the acquired technology and the development of innovative processes, manufacturing and techniques which, of course, imply the development of capital goods production. Transnational corporations can play important role in this process. They could, as some do in other developing regions, among other things, conduct R&D relevant to the conditions and needs of developing countries in the developing countries themselves, including innovating appropriate technology, down-scaling and simplifying plants as well as up-scaling traditional technologies. R&D should, of course, be undertaken by the developing countries themselves, alone or in collaboration with transnational corporations and other relevant firms and institutions.

Turnkey contracts, which put African countries at the complete mercy of the providers of technologies were the most popular way of acquiring technology in Africa until recently. This together with guaranties for product quality and output involving initial management responsibility was apparently the best means, given the lack of capability and capacity, for the complex process of identifying, selecting, adopting, and adapting technology as well as installing, starting up, and operating plants. Now, although African countries have a long way to go before they achieve a measure of self-sufficiency in this area, many of them have acquired experience in some methods of technology acquisition. They are now tending towards the increasing use of consulting services and licensing arrangements. With the greater role that direct foreign investment is expected to play, transfer of technology by foreign investors is likely to contribute more than in the past.

For many countries, the small ones in particular, appropriate technology may be adopted step by step. They could start at the end of processing/fabrication and follow reverse integration. In the case of fertilizers, for instance, they could mix fertilizers; then convert intermediates (ammonia and phosphoric acid) into fertilizers; and finally make the intermediates. The iron and steel industry provides another example of this approach. The steps to follow comprise: rerolling, rolling, pig iron making, and steel making. The learning process, adequate time for planning at different stages, and investment spread over time are among the advantages of this approach. This approach enables planners to incorporate, at each stage of development, the latest appropriate technology current at the time.

One important factor is integration. As is well known, African industries have developed in isolation; interdependence is minimal. There is very little or no subcontracting between the small-, medium- and large-scale industries and therefore virtually little guidance and assistance provided to small-scale enterprises in training, technology, quality control, procurement, etc. The same applies to sharing common facilities and equipment and exchanging engineers and technicians. As a consequence, the role of small-scale industries as ancillary industries providing inputs to medium- and large-scale industries is limited. Appropriate technology would be more meaningful with the development of greater interdependence among industries in which large industries encourage medium- and small-scale industries and provide and help them utilize appropriate technology. The same would apply to medium-scale industries *vis-a-vis* small-scale industries. Such an interrelationship would enhance and facilitate the introduction of appropriate technology. In Japan, where state intervention was the major reason for the successful evolution of small enterprises, about 65 percent of small and medium-sized manufacturing enterprises are engaged in subcontracting (Berman 1994).

The crucial importance of government assistance to industry in the form of industrial services, including R&D, cannot be overemphasized at the current stage of industrial development in Africa. R&D institutions whose functions are to adapt imported technology to factor endowments and innovate and develop new technology are virtually absent in Africa, partly for want of government support. It should be noted here that R&D institutions in developed countries are heavily subsidized by governments. African governments should assist, strengthen, and create institutional infrastructure to undertake industrial R&D, including in-plant R&D, in upgrading indigenous/traditional technologies, in adapting conventional products and technologies (use of natural gas in place of coal for iron and steel making, for instance), and innovating new products, technologies, and manufacturing techniques. They should also develop engineering design capabilities and capacities, including de-scaling and up-scaling of plants; facilitate the identification, acquisition, and dissemination of appropriate technologies; and provide industrial extension services. In this connection, under African conditions, R&D should aim at optimizing R&D and production linkages.

It is, in part, due to inadequate linkages that many inventions, innovations, and technological improvements gather dust for want of mechanisms, including industrial extension service agents, to disseminate them. For example, threshers, donkey-drawn carts, ploughs, and other improved farm tools were, according to the National Farm Tools Research Programme in Ethiopia, made available to a limited number of farmers for the very same reason. To repeat the obvious, it would be in the interest of a country to assess carefully the technologies already adapted and modified in other developing countries, particularly countries with conditions similar to those in Africa, before committing resources for R&D. One could even go further and make twinning arrangements with such institutions, whereby African institutions could benefit through sharing experiences and receiving assistance.

At the national level, institutions dealing with appropriate technology are limited in number in Africa. The following are among those few (Singer 1977):

- Appropriate Technology Centre in Botswana;
- Technology Consultancy Centre in Kumasi, Ghana;
- Federal Institute of Industrial Research in Nigeria; and
- Small Industry Development Organization in Tanzania.

Similar institutions outside the continent include: Program on the Application of Science and Technology for Rural Areas in India, Development Technology Centre in Indonesia, Instituto de Investigaciones Tecnologicas in Colombia, Intermediate Technology Development Group in the United Kingdom and Volunteers in Technical Assistance (VITA) in the United States. There are institutions similar to the last one in other developed countries, most of which have a wealth of information on appropriate technologies developed to suit the conditions in developing countries. VITA's contributions to appropriate technology, for instance, include the following (VITA, *Publications*):

-Publications: tools for agriculture, hydraulic ram, design manual for water wheels, small-scale maize milling;

-Understanding technology series: adobe (sun-dried brick), small-scale paper making, paper recycling;

-Food-cycle technology source books: oil, fruits and vegetables, fish, cereal and root crops processing; and

-Industry profile series: fish oil and fish meal, glucose from cassava starch, unrefined grape juice.

There is an apparent need for African governments to promote R&Ds. Recognition of this need among African heads of state was manifested by the Presidential Forum on the Management of Science and Technology in Africa, which held its third meeting focussing on food and nutritional security in July 1995. As is done in industrialized countries, governments should allot a certain percentage of their GDP to R&D. This was done in Ethiopia in 1993 when the government decided to allot up to 1.5 percent of the country's GDP for the advancement of science and technology through the Ethiopian Science and Technology Commission. Intellectual property rights are protected; research funds to institutions and individuals are provided; and special incentives were being worked out for those interested in establishing and running R&D and related institutions. These measures were being reinforced by mobilizing and encouraging Ethiopian expatriates to return. Incentives designed to attract returnees include provision of residential houses and transport facilities.

The Commission conducts workshops every year to evaluate research results and suggest solutions related to problems encountered while carrying out research funded by its small grant scheme, numbering 250 projects during the period 1992/

93-1996/97. Projects related to industry (which accounted for 17.2 percent) included-low cost construction materials, multi-crop thresher, vegetable oil refining, and extraction of essential oils from gum olibanum. In addition, the Commission conducts a weekly radio program on popularizing science and technology in five local languages; provides financial support to over 50 professional associations and 20 scientific journals; and awards school science clubs. In 1997, it gave awards and prizes to nine industries with excellent performance. It was reported in 1997 that preparations were underway for organizing an exhibition aimed at *"ntroducing new inventions, encouraging innovations and creating healthy competition"* in trade as well as popularizing locally made products (*The Ethiopian Herald*, December 20, 1997).

As implied above, African countries do not have adequate capacities and capabilities, both financial and human, to develop and operate the R&D institutions they require at the individual country level. The sensible option would be to pool their meagre resources and establish and operate multi-country institutions. In recognition of this stark reality, African countries have already set up such institutions, including the following which are directly related to industry: African Regional Centre for Technology (ARCT), African Regional Centre for Engineering Design and Manufacturing (ARCEDEM), African Regional Organization for Standardization (ARSO), and African Regional Industrial Property Organization (ARIPO) ( see Annex 4.7). The performance of these institutions, unfortunately, leaves much to be desired, mainly for want of resources.

Practically all the work carried out in R&D in the world is for the needs in developed countries. There is a dire need to conduct much more R&D under African conditions. Advantages that can accrue include the direct interaction (feedback) with those concerned with the problems to be investigated, the relevance of the ensuing result(s), the relative ease in applying or commercializing the result(s) and capacity and capability building in R&D and related activities. Redeployment to Africa of R&D institutions in developed countries engaged in activities related to tropical conditions and forming joint venture arrangements with R&D institutions outside Africa could synergize and expedite the results needed for development. Transnational corporations operating in African countries could subcontract research activities to local institutions. This could prove mutually beneficial, as the cost incurred is likely to be a fraction of the cost in industrialized countries.

Under African conditions, the coverage of industrial R&D needs to be broad and integrated. Inclusion of activities related to surveys and development of natural resources is essential since most of the activities of the R&Ds would have to relate to the processing and utilization of natural resources.

The indiscriminate acquisition of technology from different sources has proved to be a critical constraint upon African industrialization, as it fragments the national markets that are already too small to support the development of industries required for sustainable economic and social development. The parts and components of the equipment and machinery so acquired are not standardized, thus necessitating the holding of huge and expensive stock pile, consequently tying up capital. In view of this, attempts should be made to rationalize parts and components through standardization, so that the small market constraint can be minimized. Delaying action on rationalization makes cooperation more and more difficult because of the growing vested interest in maintaining the status quo, thus necessitating a larger investment which will be required at a later stage to implement standardization.

## BIBLIOGRAPHY

AIChExtra, 1997, "Engineers Predict the Homes of the Future," April 1997.

Baker, C.R., Bhagavan, M.R., Mitschoke-Collande, P.V. and Wield, D.V., 1986, *African Industrialization,* Gower Publishing Company Limited, Aldershot.

Baker, Michael, 1996, *South Korea Watches a Conglomerate Fold,* The Christian Science Monitor, Boston.

Berman, Bruce J., editor, 1994, *African Capitalists in African Development,* Lynne Reinner Publishers, London.

Chemical Engineering Progress, 1996, "ChEs Seek Big Gains from Process Miniaturization," April 1996.

Chemical E engineering Progress, 1997, "The Future: Benefiting from New Tools, Techniques, and Teaching," January 1997.

Chemical Engineering Progress, 1998, "Big Opening Seen for Microchannels," April 1998.

ECA, 1990, *Directory of Project Profiles on Institutional Support for Small-scale Industries, ECA/IHSD/SSI/009/90,* Addis Ababa.

ECA, 1996, *Africa in the 1990s and Beyond: ECA-Revised Long-Term Development Perspectives Study* (ECA/SERPD/TP/96/3), Addis Ababa.

ECA, 1996, *Measures to Consolidate Privatization in the African Industrial Sector with Special Emphasis on the Programme of the Second Industrial Development Decade for Africa* (ECA/IHSD/IPPIS/003/96), Addis Ababa..

ECA/FAO, 1992, *Biotechnology Revolution: a Panacea or Myth to African Agriculture and Food Crisis?,* Addis Ababa.

ECA/UNIDO, 1995, *Report on Regional Strategy for Rational Location of Industries in the Context of theAbuja Treaty* (CAMI.12/6[a]), Addis Ababa.

Gromyko, Anatoly A., editor, 1990, "Development of Food Production and Distribution in the Agrarian Sector," *Agenda for Action: African-Soviet- Cooperation,* Lynne Reinner Publishers, London.

Harris, Nigel, 1986, *The End of the Third World,* I.B. Tauris and Co. Ltd., Bungay, U.K.

ILO, 1995, *World Employment 1995,* Geneva.

ILO, 1995, *World Labour Report 1995,* Geneva.

Investment Review, 1997, "Kassk Spices & Herbes Extraction Factory," Quarterly Newsletter Published by Ethiopian Investment Authority, October 1997 1, Addis Ababa.

Juo, Anthony S. R. and Freed Russell D., editors, 1995, *Agriculture and the Environment: Bridging Food Production and Environmental Protection in Developing Countries,* ASA Special Publication Number 60, Madison.

Khennas, Smail, ed., 1992, *Industrialization, Mineral Resources and Energy in Africa,* CODESRIA ,CODESRIA Book Series, Rowe, Oxford.

Marsdon, Keith, 1990, *African Entrepreneurs: Pioneers of Development,* Discussion Paper Number 9, IFC, Washington, D.C.

Meier, Gerald M. and william F. Steel, eds., 1989, *Industrial Adjustment in Sub-Saharan Africa,* EDI series in Economic Development, Published for the World Bank, Oxford University Press, New York.

News Week, 1997, "Making Sense of India," August 4, 1997.

OAU, 1981, *Lagos Plan of Action for the Development of Africa,* International Institute for Labour Studies, Geneva.

Reich, Robert B., 1991, *The Work of Nations,* Simon & Schuster, London.

Riddell, Roger C., 1990, *Manufacturing Africa,* Heinmann Educational Books Inc., Portsmouth.

Singer, Hans, 1977, *Technologies for Basic Needs,* ILO, Geneva.

The Boston Globe, 1996, *Vital Signs 1996,* Worldwatch Institute annual report, May 19, 196, Boston.

The Economist, 1996, *An UnMITIgated Success,* August 31, 1996.

The Economist, 1996, "The C-word Strikes Back," June 1, 1996.

The Economist, 1997, "Emerging Market Indicators," January 25, 1997.

The Economist, 1998, March 21, 1998.

The Ethiopian Herald, 1997, "Administration to Organize Development Oriented Exhibition" December 20, 1997.

UN, 1982, *A Programme for the Industrial Development Decade for Africa,* New York.

UN, 1992, *Regional Cooperation: Second Industrial Development Decade for Africa — Note by the secretary-general—Addendum: Programme for the Second Industrial Development Decade for Africa (1991-2000),* E/1992/14/Add.1 (Part II)), New York.

UN, 1995, *World Economic and Social Survey 1995: Current Trends and Policies in the World Economy,* (E/1995/50), New York.

UNDP, 1996, *Human Development Report 1993,* Oxford University Press, New York.

UNDP, 1996, *Human Development Report 1996,* Oxford University Press, New York.

UNIDO, 1969, " Small-scale Industry," *Industrialization of Developing Countries: Problems and Prospects,* UNIDO Monographs on Industrial Development, No. 11, UN, New York.

UNIDO, 1975, *Lima Declaration and Plan of Action on Industrial Development and Cooperation,* Vienna.

UNIDO, 1979, *No. 1, Conceptual and Policy Framework for Appropriate Industrial Technology,* Monographs on Appropriate Industrial Technology, *UN,* New York.

UNIDO, 1980, *No. 8, Appropriate Industrial Technology for Sugar,* Monographs on Appropriate Industrial Technology, UN, New York.

UNIDO, *1987, Opportunities for the Manufacture of Pharmaceutical Chemicals in Developing Countries,* PPD.48, Vienna.

UNIDO, 1996, *The Globalization of Industry: Implications for Developing Countries beyond 2000,* Vienna.

UNIDO/ECA, 1997, *Alliance for Africa's Industrialization,* Thirteenth Meeting of the Conference of African Ministers of Industry (CAMI.13/5), Accra.

UNIDO, 1997, Report of the Mid-term Programme Evaluation, IDDA II (GM/R.11), Vienna.

VITA, 1995, *Publications: 1995 Catalog,* Arlington.

World Bank, 1989, *Sub-Saharan Africa: From Crisis to Sustainable Growth,* Washington, D.C.

World Bank, 1992, *Proceedings of the World Bank: Annual Conference on Development Economics 1992.*

World Bank, *1997, World Resources 1996-97,* Washington, D.C.

## NOTES

1. This is in line with the 1987 findings of the South Commission chaired by ex-President Mwalimu J. Nyerere. The findings included the need for people-centered development, maximum national self-reliance, collective self-reliance and sharing science and technology among the countries of the south (*Eritrean Profile*, March 29, 1997).

2. The education and training experience in Singapore is exemplary. The country has a high quality education system relevant to emerging technological needs. Training is provided by many public institutions as well as by firms many of which receive government support. It includes skill training and apprenticeship for school leavers, part-time skills courses, customized courses and advanced manufacturing skills courses. Both on-the-job and off-the-job training are provided (ADB, *African Development Report 1996*).

3. The Korea Technology Development Corporation was established in the 1980s to facilitate access to funds for technological development. Provision of information on technological trends, identifying priority areas for technological development, promoting close links between industry and R&D institutes and bringing together researchers and inventors with entrepreneurs were among its functions (ADB, *African Development Report 1996*).

4. Equitable distribution of wealth was an important factor in Japan's post war recovery. The share of national income of the poorest 20 percent increased from 5 percent to 10 percent during the early 1960s and the mid-1980s. This was brought about through government commitment to equity in opportunities. In Malaysia, poverty reduction programs contributed to lowering the number of poor households to 14 percent in 1993 from 49 percent in 1970. Poverty incidence in Indonesia declined from 29 percent to 17 percent during 1980-1990 (UNDP, *Human Development Report 1996*).

5. Usually oxen are used as animal draught. It is now possible, according to the International Livestock Research Institute in Ethiopia and Kenya, to harness cows crossed between Ethiopian and European breeds without reducing their abilities to calve and give milk.

6. The core components of the Alliance are: (i) building institutional capacity for competitiveness, (ii) linking industry with agriculture, (iii) stimulating growth in the informal sector and small- and medium-scale industries, and (iv) promoting industrial partnership and investment.

7. A case in point is the local multiple distribution service (LMDS) technology. This new technology which is being licensed by Cellular Vision Technology & Telecommunications LP combines wireless cable TV, phone service, Internet access and videoconferencing (two-way communication). According to "A Technology Grows in Brooklyn," an article in *Business Week* (April 14,1997), *"the low cost of the system is particularly attractive to developing nations."*

8. A multipurpose batch reactor *"usually has the form of a tank, is equipped with some means of agitation and provision for heat transfer to regulate temperature of the reaction mixture between -100 and 3000 C, is made of stainless steel and glass- or enamel-lined steel and is connected to steam (less than 5 bar) and vacuum (higher than 10 mbar pressure). Its nominal capacity varies between 0.5 m3 and 3 m3"* [UNIDO, 1987, PPD.48].

## CHAPTER 8

# INDUSTRIES ORIENTED
# TOWARDS BASIC NEEDS

## FOOD INDUSTRY

The drought, famine, and human suffering that millions of Africans in some countries have endured are well known to the world. Food production has been lagging behind demand. Some of the main reasons for this state of affairs are inadequate incentives and material inputs, declining agricultural productivity in some areas, and natural and man-made disasters. The Regional Food Plan for Africa gives a good idea of the precarious food situation in the continent. Although published in 1980, the observations, conclusions and recommendations are even more valid now than they were then. According to the Plan's normative scenario, gross agricultural production was envisaged to grow by 4.0 percent per annum during 1990s as against 2.7 percent based on trend (2.1 percent in 1961/65-1975) (FAO, *Regional Food Plan for Africa*). As things have worsened during the ensuing period, a higher rate and therefore massive input would be required to achieve the same level of per capita improvement as in the Plan by the year 2000 and beyond.

Inadequate food production is compounded by food losses that occur at different stages, from cultivation to actual consumption. Increasing the shelf-life through processing coupled with proper storage could substantially reduce losses and permit the carryover of food products between seasons, an important factor, especially in drought-prone areas.

Most of the food produced in Africa does not undergo processing before delivery for sale and consumption. In fact, only about 10 to 15 percent of total agricultural production is processed (UNIDO/ECA, *Agro-related Industrial Development in Africa*). In Ghana, for instance, the proportion not processed is reported to be 87 percent (FAO, *The State of Food and Agriculture 1994*). Despite the fact that most of the food consumed by the people, especially in rural areas, may not be recorded as processed in statistics, the food processing-industry (together with beverages and tobacco) is the largest manufacturing industry, accounting for about 60 percent of the manufacturing value-added as well as a high proportion of capital expenditure in most African countries.

Food processing comprises a number of stages, depending upon the type of product to be processed and the extent of processing. In the case of cereals, for instance, it starts with dehusking, goes through milling, and ends up with baking, producing bread as a final product ready-for-consumption. Preservation (drying and treatment with salt or vinegar; freeze-drying; canning) is an important process which extends the shelf-lives of products, especially seasonal and perishable products.

Under present African conditions, food processing is one of the (if not the) most important industries with extensive multiplier effects. Its backward linkages with agriculture are obvious. All its raw material and part of its energy inputs come from agriculture. The equipment it uses at traditional and small-scale manufacture is carried out locally by craftsmen and artisans. Processing and utilization of by-products and wastes, including those from slaughterhouses, as animal feed and as fuel (including biogas), are examples of forward linkages. The implication of all these in terms of employment in agriculture, industry, transport, etc., cannot be overemphasized. In short, in addition to making more food available, the development of the food processing industry stimulates the development of other sectors and provides employment opportunities, both directly and indirectly.

## Status of the industry

As is well known, a growing number of African countries have gradually lost the capacity to feed their people. High rates of population growth, archaic farming methods, high pre-harvest losses (up to 30 %) and high losses (up to 30 %) *"during commercial circuit due to low processing base and inadequate technology"* and up to 10 percent loss between processing and consumption (ECA, ECA/IHSD/AGR/010/91) are among the main reasons for this state of affairs. The growing consumption/production gap is likely to get worse before it gets better. These staggering losses are, however, potential gains that should be exploited through proper farming, preserving, processing, storing, transporting, and final preparation for consumption.

The extent of loss during traditional processing and therefore the potential gain can be illustrated by palm oil extraction. Traditional extraction yields less than 50 percent oil, while indusrial extraction can achieve levels as high as 97 percent. This evidently means that close to half of the oil in the palm is discarded.

Protein deficiency is rampant in many countries in Africa. This is particularly the case in the 10 million km$^2$ (1,000 million hectares) tsetse fly-infested area which mainly covers West and Central Africa. Statistics in Table 8.1 give some indications of the gravity of the situation in the first half of the post-independence period. Production of meat and dairy products have been marginally increasing or stagnating (see Annex 5.2) with the result that their per capita production have been declining and total imports have been rising. During the period 1979-1981, imports as percent of total consumption averaged 6 percent for meat, 33 percent for dairy products expressed in fresh milk equivalent and 36.7 percent for fish (supply). Per capita consumptions were 14, 29 and 8.4 (supply) kg, respectively.

TABLE 8.1
PRODUCTION, IMPORT AND CONSUMPTION OF MEAT, DAIRY PRODUCTS AND FISH IN AFRICA  (1961-1984)

| | Production, import and consumption (1000 t) | | | | | Growth rate (%) | | |
|---|---|---|---|---|---|---|---|---|
| | 1961 | 1970 | 1980 | 1984 | 1979-1981 | 1961-1970 | 1970-1980 | 1980-1984 |
| Meat | | | | | | | | |
| - Production per caput, kg | | 11.21 | 10.76 | 10.49 | | | -0.4 | -0.65 |
| - Imports, total | | | | | 359 | | | |
| - Consumption, total | | | | | 5684 | | | |
| Milk and dairy products | | | | | | | | |
| - Production per caput, kg | | 27.47 | 26.83 | 26.89 | | | -0.24 | 0.05 |
| - Imports, total | 729 | 1599 | 4407 | 5515 | 3776ᵃ | 7.58 | 12.01 | |
| - Consumption, total | | | | | 11413* | | | |
| Fish | | | | | | | | |
| - Production, total | | | | | 3142 | | | |
| - Consumption, total | | | | | 3828 | | | |

Source: Compiled from FAO, 1986, *African Agriculture: the next 25 Years*, Annex V, Input Supply and Incentive Policies, Rome
   a  Fresh milk equivalent

The meat and dairy products deficiencies in West Africa which are partly covered by imports from abroad, could be partly met by more procurement from the Sahelian countries where the development of animal husbandry offers a good potential. This applies to other animal products, such as leather and leather products.

The variety of food processed  industrially depends mainly on the ecological zone and climatic conditions. According to frequency distribution estimates by ECA, two countries (South Africa and Kenya) process more than 30 food and agro products; 12 countries, 20 to 30; 21 countries, less than 20; and 18 countries, less than 10. It is apparent that the majority of the countries process less than 20 products and therefore depend more on imports.

Most of the food consumed is processed at home, using traditional methods of processing. In general, cereals are pounded using pestle and mortar; and the resulting food, comprising all the components (e.g., maize meal), is of more nutritional value than that milled with sophisticated equipment. Improvements in traditional technologies have been and continue to be made.

Whatever is recorded in statistics refers mainly to processing at the industrial level. Production figures for which information is available are shown in Annex 5.2. Annex 4.3 gives trade figures for agricultural commodities. From the latter, it is apparent that Africa is increasingly dependent on imports in order to supplement its food requirement.

Africa is an important producer and net exporter of some foodstuffs, such as cocoa products and seafood. It increased its cocoa grindings from 186,900 tons in 1986 to 203,000 tons in 1991 (120,000 tonnes by Cote d'Ivoire in 1992). In 1992, 61.4 percent of its grinding capacity  (16.1% of world capacity) of 606,000 tons was utilized. In 1991, Cote d'Ivoire exported 31,373 tons of cocoa butter and 20,498 tons of cocoa powder and cake (UNIDO, *Industry and Development: Global Report 1993/94*).

Africa's production of seafood rose from 4.28 million tons in 1985 to 5.16 million tons in 1990, the last accounting for 5.3 percent of world  production. In 1990, it imported 886,400 tons of fish and shellfish and exported 1.65 million tons of fish and shellfish, the former accounting for 2.25 percent and the latter for 4.53 percent of world production (UNIDO, *Industry and Development: Global Report 1993/94*).

Industrial food processing in Africa is primarily flour milling, cassava processing, oil extraction, and sugar milling. Small flour mills are increasingly to be found in both rural and the urban areas. Medium sized flour mills are generally located in or near the major urban centers. Most of the industrially preserved and processed foods are targeted at the relatively better off urban dwellers.

The situation is similar for other foodstuffs. More and more cassava is being processed using better cassava graters and at the small-scale level. Small oil mills (expellers) are becoming popular. All the sugar is produced in medium and large sugar cane and beet mills. Africa was a net importer of sugar, averaging 2 million tons in 1984-1986. The processing of fruits and vegetables appears to be developing rather slowly, thus necessitating imports of juices, pastes, and sauces.

With respect to stimulants, a small part of the coffee, tea, cocoa, and tobacco is processed into intermediates and final products, mostly for local consumption. Coffee extracts, packaged and instant tea, cocoa powder, and butter and chocolate and chocolate products are the main products.

## Priority Products

Maize, sorghum, millet, rice, wheat, cassava (manioc), and yam constitute the main staple foods in Africa. Maize accounting for over a third of cereal production is the most important cereal used. In 1993, it was followed by sorghum, rice, wheat, millet, and barley (see Annex 4.2). In some countries in West and Central Africa cassava, mainly in the form of gari and flour, contributes up to 60 percent of the total caloric intake. In terms of tonnage, roots and tubers (cassava whose yield was reported to have doubled in the 1980s and yam) lead cereals, the former with a production of 121 million tons and the latter with 94.7 million tons in 1993. Oleaginous crops (oil-palms, olives, groundnuts, coconuts, soybeans, etc.), fish and meat constitute other food components. Partly because of ecological differences, the sheer size of the continent, and the hundreds of nations and nationalities inhabiting the continent, staple food and eating habits vary greatly from area to area. Roots and tubers and palm oil , for instance, dominate in the coastal countries of Central and West Africa. The corresponding staple foods outside the hot and humid areas are grains, oil seeds, and nuts. From among the pulses, faba bean is the poor man's staple food in Egypt. Teff, a tiny grain peculiar to Ethiopia, is the staple food in the Ethiopian highlands. There is no such thing as an African staple diet.

Wheat, which is popular in urban areas in practically all African countries, is increasing in importance. Its popularity has been enhanced by its availability at relatively low prices. Overvalued local currencies, food aid and subsidies by exporting countries are among the factors that contribute to this state of affairs. This is unfortunate because many areas in Africa do not and cannot produce wheat competitively and therefore most of the countries will have to continue importing wheat in increasing quantities. In order to reduce and possibly arrest this trend, attempts are being made in some countries to introduce composite flours. Composite flours comprise a mixture of wheat flour with flours of other local grains or roots and tubers. Bread, biscuits, and pasta products made from composite flours seem to have gained acceptance in the countries where they have been introduced. The level of non-wheat substitution (% on the weight of composite flour) are: sorghum (15-20), millet (15-20), maize (20-25), rice (25-30), dry-milled cassava flour (20) and wet-milled cassava starch (30) (ECA, *Tech-*

*nical Compendium on Composite Flours*). Oil seeds, milk products, and fish-protein concentrates are used as sources of protein.

The importance of roots and tubers in the diet of Africans cannot be over-stressed. Reference to Annex 4.2 reveals this. In 1993, roots and tubers production was 1.27 times that of cereals, cassava alone being 79.0 percent that of cereals.

Most African infants suffer from malnutrition, particularly from a lack of adequate protein. As reported by J. Ngo Som (*Improving the Nutritional Status of the African Child*) malnutrition and related diseases account for about 4 million deaths per year of African children below the age five. With increasing attention being given to the young, particularly infants, baby foods and weaning foods to supplement their diet are likely to gain in importance.

Meat, dairy products, and fish are among other foodstuffs that deserve to be considered as priorities. The region is a net importer of the first and the second, despite its large livestock potential. According to one source (Ristic 1981), *"most of the future increase in livestock production is expected to occur in the tropical and subtropical regions of the world,"* with Africa's tropical rainbelt having the capacity to accommodate 125 million head of cattle. That potential could be realized, provided problems related to animal diseases and husbandry are resolved. Generally, there is little stratification or specialization in tropical cattle production systems, and tropical dairy management is said to be very difficult as tropical breeds cannot yield high levels of milk. Low tropical livestock productivity, in terms of both carcass and milk yields, should be increased through better animal husbandry and crossbreeding.

## Strategies for Development

With fast growing urbanization (averaging 4.4 percent per year during 1975-1995, projected to 4.1 percent during 1995-2015), the urban/rural population ratio is undergoing a rapid change and is expected to reach 47.2 percent by 2015 (UN, *World Economic and Social Survey 1996*). A third of the population is expected to depend on processed food in the not too distant future (ECA, ECA/IHSD/AGR/010/91). This means that more and more food will have to be processed industrially. Examples of food-processing technologies in use in Africa are presented in Annex 5.1. In many cases processing reduces the nutrient value of foods, making it necessary to enrich processed foods. Degermed and sifted maize meals, for instance, lose substantial portions of their protein, fat, calcium, iron, and vitamins, requiring enrichment by adding soybean meal, groundnut flour, and vitamins (ILO, *Small-Scale Maize Milling*). In view of the trend toward processed food, governments should, at least, avoid encouraging the consumption of refined foods, particularly in rural areas. In this connection, it should be noted that the trend toward health food in developed countries generally means non-refined food, i.e., food that incorporates some of the nutrients that are lost during processing.

In view of the preponderance of the rural population for some time to come, it would make sense to take measures that would facilitate food processing in rural areas. This would involve improving traditional processing methods and access to food-processing facilities in rural areas so as to ease the drudgery of processing and preparing food at home.

In the meantime, attempts should be made to develop facilities to cut down on post-harvest losses, particularly at the food-processing stage. This could be done by installing preservation and processing facilities in strategic locations close to production areas, to lengthen the shelf-lives of foodstuffs and meet the growing demand among the urban population. This approach is of special significance to seasonal and perishable products. Fruits, vegetables, roots and tubers, milk, and fish fall under this category. In the last case, cold storage chains will be required. Food irradiation should, when practical and financially feasible, be promoted to reduce food losses by disinfecting stored products; inhibiting sprouting; and eliminating food-borne diseases in meat, poultry, and sea food. The safety and effectiveness of irradiation has been endorsed by many national and international institutions, including the American Medical Association and the World Health Organization (WHO).

As for the vegetable oil industry, most of which is characterized by poor recovery, the oil retained in the oil cake could be extracted in central solvent extraction units, wherever conditions permit. This approach would increase oil yield as well as improve the oil cake, making it fit for animal feed.

The development of weaning foods needs to be accorded high priority. Because of certain advantages inherent in extrusion production, the adoption of this process should be investigated.

Marine fishery resources in Africa continue to be depleted through overfishing by foreign fleets; this practice should be stopped. African countries should develop fisheries (including fish farming and fish-processing capacities on their own and jointly with foreign investors, particularly with those already operating in their territorial waters. As for freshwater and coastal aquaculture, the FAO Director-General expects Africa's share in the world fish supply from these sources to increase from the present 15 percent to 30 percent by the year 2010. African countries should devise ways and means of achieving this target.

Generally, the canning industry is labor-intensive. In view of this and other benefits, some African countries should make efforts to expand existing units and establish new ones.

The food-processing industry provides backward linkages with agriculture and forward linkages with consumers and other industries. The former uses cereals, roots and tubers, oil-bearing crops, fruits, vegetables, livestock, and fish as raw materials and salt, sugar, spices, and packaging materials as other inputs from agriculture and industry. The latter includes the further product processing and converting by-products and waste into useful products, such as animal feed, compost for use as fertilizer, biogas for heating and lighting, as well as glue, gelatin, soap, and ethyl alcohol. In general, the forward linkages are virtually non-existent in many cases. Optimization of these linkages could conserve resources and bring additional benefits to the producers and the consumers. For these reasons governments and those engaged in processing should take measures to maximize linkages in the food-processing industry.

Under African conditions, the conversion of by-products and wastes into useful products is barely exploited, because of the small quantities of by-products and wastes produced in small farms. Ways and means need to be found to optimize the use of those small quantities of by-products and wastes. Given the inadequate level of nutrition and poor livestock conditions, the development of the animal feed industry deserves special attention. Many of the ingredients for animal feed making (crop residues and byproducts and wastes from processing operations, such as milling, slaughtering, oil pressing, sugar making, brewing, and baking) are available in most of the countries, in varying quantities. Crop residues include: maize stover, sorghum stover, rice straw, sugar cane tops, ground-nut husk, cocoa pods, banana/plantain leaves and pseudo stems, and cassava tops (ECA/FAO, *Adequate Feed and Feeding: ...* ). The quantities of cereal crop residues generated annually are significant in many countries. For example, 6.3 million tons of cereal straws, stover, and pulse residues were generated in Ethiopia in 1978/80 and 2.3 million tons of cereal crop residues and one million tons of dried cocoa pods were produced annually in Ghana and Nigeria, respectively (ECA/FAO, *Adequate Feed and Feeding: ...*). Fishery is another source for animal feed making. According to FAO, because of lack of selectivity, about 25 percent of total marine fish catch is discarded. Although this is supposed to be lower in regard to subsistence fishing, it could nevertheless be worth looking into.

Many uses and processes for converting agricultural byproducts and wastes have been innovated in recent years. These include: soybean soapstock to reduce dust on gravel roads; peanut hulls in carriers for fertilizer and herbicide; cotton gin waste compost as soil conditioner; compressed bales as wall panels from wheat or rice straw or other agricultural wastes; paper pulp from corn stover or grain sorghum stalks (Gogerty 1996).

The multi-purpose plant concept applies to food processing. Most related food-stuffs can be processed in the same plant. Many cereals can be milled in the same flour mill; vegetable oils in the same oil mill; fruits and vegetables in the same canning plant, provided the plant is designed with the necessary provisions. Attempts should, therefore, be made to introduce this approach to existing plants, when feasible, and maximize the utilization of multipurpose plants in new projects. The multi-purpose concept can be applied differently by putting together technologies and machinery and equipment for processing different types of agricultural products under the same roof. A UNIDO project incorporating a dehuller, a grinding mill, an oil press, a generator, and a motor, all mounted on a trailer (UNIDO, XA/RAF/94/126) is a good example of this. The mobile nature of the project is a distinct advantage when processing foodstuffs which are seasonal and produced in quantities that cannot justify permanent processing locations.

One thing that should be taken into account when planning and developing the food-processing industry is the need to ensure the involvement of women in every aspect of the development. This is a field in which women can excel if given the opportunity. In fact, the development of the industry should be the domain of women. To this end, women entrepreneurs should be identified, trained, encouraged and assisted to establish and operate food-processing industries. One could go further and apply this principle to the informal sector in general and small-scale industries in particular.

The multi-purpose food-processing platform promoted by UNIDO and by the International Food and Agriculture Development (IFAD) seems to mitigate many of the problems referred to elsewhere facing women, particularly in the rural area. It is based on an integrated arrangement whereby a generator which provides electricity for light, pumping water, and food processing (de-hulling, milling, oil pressing, etc.) meets the needs of a community. From the successes achieved in village communities in Burkina Faso and Mali, it may be worth replicating them in other African countries.

Last but not least, biotechnology and genetic engineering should be used to increase productivity in food production. The potential in these fields is so enormous that, under African conditions and needs, it would be suicidal to ignore taking measures to exploit the benefits. Thanks to biotechnology and genetic engineering, it is now possible to manipulate, modify, and alter plants to suit local needs and conditions and increase productivity. This is done through microbial inoculation and plant cell and tissue culture and single-cell-proteins (SCP). Raw materials for the last are or can be made available in many African countries in the form of natural gas. Embryo technology makes it possible to produce more offsprings from the same female animal. However, there is a negative aspect to all this. Potential loss of export markets for African agricultural produce is a possibility that cannot be discounted. In any event, African countries should take measures to optimize benefits accruing from developments in biotechnology and genetic engineering, so as to increase agricultural production, particularly food.

The substantial increase of food production in the continent will, to a large extent, depend on agricultural R&D. While each country should undertake R&D geared to activities peculiar to that country, it would make sense to maximize the use of the services of and results from the global agricultural research network. The network which is coordinated by the Consultative Group on International Agricultural Research (CGIAR) comprises 16 international centers. The centers are specialized in areas related to food production and natural resource management. The areas include crops, farm animals, fisheries, forestry, irrigation, and dry land management (FAO, *Dimensions of Need*).

## PHARMACEUTICAL INDUSTRY

In addition to tropical diseases, the continent is afflicted by diseases that were common to the industrialized countries in the nineteenth century. The former include malaria, bilharzia (schistosomiasis), river blindness (onchocerciasis), sleeping sickness (trypanosomiasis) and elephantiasis (filariasis) The latter include water- and food-borne diseases compounded by poor sanitary living conditions (amoeba, diarrhoea, typhoid, polio, hepatitis, and cholera) and respiratory infections (bronchitis, pneumonia, and tuberculosis). This state of affairs is exacerbated by malnutrition, a manifestation of poverty, said to be the single most widespread cause of ill-health (Melrose 1983). Much remains to be done to raise the average daily caloric intake per capita, which was 2,124 in 1970 and averaged 2,333 during 1990-1995 (ADB, *African Development Report 1996*). Annexes 8.1 and 8.2 give some idea of the types of diseases (human and animal) afflicting Africa, their vectors of transmission, the major infested areas, main preventive and curative treatments, and current research and eradication programs. In addition to their debilitating effect on animals and their overall negative economic consequences, some of the animal diseases constrain use of animal draft and the expansion of African trade in animals and animal products. Animals and animal products that do not meet the strict health requirements of the importing countries do not find market outside the country of origin.

In recent years, the world has witnessed the resurgence and rampant spread of some infectious diseases (including new ones), viz., malaria and tuberculosis, mainly because of resistance to drugs and chemicals, mutations in pathogens, man increasingly becoming host to pathogens hitherto limited to animals (attributed to environmental change), and the weakening of the immune system caused by HIV/AIDS. Interruption in spraying malarial areas because of conflicts and lack of resources coupled with mosquitoes building resistance[1] to drugs explains the resurgence of malaria. Malaria alone kills more than one million young children in tropical Africa (International Federation..., *Health Horizons*, No. 22). The World Declaration on the Control of Malaria adopted by the WHO Ministerial Conference on Malaria seems to be the first step toward ameliorating the deteriorating situation. Global warming is likely to aggravate the incidence of infectious diseases by, among other things, extending the range of vectors, such as mosquitoes and tse-tse flies, to higher altitudes and latitudes and causing perdator/prey imbalances. In recognition of the seriousness of the malaria situation, the Multinational Initiative on Malaria (MIM) was established in 1997 by 13 funding bodies to facilitate collaboration in activities related to malaria in Africa (WHO, *TDR News*, February 1998). The WHO Roll Black Malaria (RBM) project of 1998 intended to coordinate the above and other initiatives, including the Malaria Control Strategy of 1992 and the Medicines for Malaria Venture, has given priority to Africa. The last initiative has the development of new drugs as its ultimate objective.

As may be expected, the leading causes of death in Africa are different from those in the developed world. According to WHO, infectious and parasitic diseases (41.5%), diseases of the circulatory system (10.7%), malignant neoplasms (8.9%), prenatal and neonatal causes (7.9%), and external causes of mortality (7.9%) constitute the major causes of death in developing countries (WHO, *The World Health Report 1995: Bridging the Gaps*). In Ethiopia, for instance, they include: malnutrition, tuberculosis, gastro-interitis, chronic hepatitis, and bronchopneumonia. Ebola is among the emerging diseases that Africa will have to contend with in the future.

As for AIDS,[2] Africa is the worst-hit continent. In 1996, about 10 million people were estimated to be carriers of HIV. Given the prevalence of poverty, poor living conditions, and inadequate public support, things are likely to get worse with devastating health, social, and economic consequences. The limited and overstretched capacities of African governments to provide public health services have been aggravated by the consequences of macro-economic stabilization and adjustment programs. AIDS patients in Africa will not, therefore, benefit from the triple-drug therapy (already in mid-1997 reported to have sharply reduced death rate due to AIDS in the United States) that was made public at the International Conference on AIDS in Vancouver, Canada, in 1996, because of unaffordable prices (about $15,000 per patient per year). This state of affairs will be aggravated by lack of vaccine to prevent the spread of AIDS, as research being undertaken in regard to AIDS in developed countries is focused on curative drugs. Finding vaccine is more relevant under the African condition.

Donors need to increase their assistance substantially if the spread of AIDS is to be checked effectively. There is also an urgent need for pharmaceutical firms to help to alleviate the suffering of AIDS patients by donating funds and lowering the cost of drugs for HIV/AIDS and related diseases. They can follow the example of the Belgian pharmaceutical company, Janssen Pharmaceutica, which, based on an agreement with the World Health Organization (WHO), is meeting about one-third of the requirements for two anti-fungal agents needed to treat AIDS patients (International Federation ..., *Health Horizons*, NO.21).

As for pharmaceuticals in general, the International Federation of Pharmaceutical Manufacturers Association (IFPMA) has *"offered to supply essential drugs for public health service use in poor countries under 'special' conditions"*

(Melrose 1983). What those conditions were and whether the offer has been put into practice are not known to the author. In 1996, the British pharmaceutical firm Glaxo offered WHO malarol, a combination of two known drugs, to use in an anti-malaria treatment program. In regard to leprosy, the Nippon Foundation (Japan) had, in 1994, pledged to donate $10 million worth of multidrugs annually as a contribution towards eliminating leprosy by the turn of the century (WHO, *Fact Sheet*, October 1996). Acquisition of unused surgical supplies through charitable donations is an option to which Africa does not seem to have resorted so far. REMEDY, Recovered Medical Equipment for the Developing World, in the United States (Rosenblatt 1997), or similar organizations could be approached to recover and make available extra supplies that are discarded at the end of surgery.

The international community, for its part, has come up with a global health strategy which was incorporated in the 1978 Declaration of Alma-Ata of the International Conference on Primary Health Care. According to the Declaration, attaining "health for all by the year 2000" and providing total health and medical care coverage for all peoples are the goal of the world community. In the case of Africa, the strategy should stress prevention, as this is likely to prove cheaper in the long run. This would involve improving nutrition and sanitation coupled with prophylaxis. The need for treatment is, of course, unavoidable.

Thanks to the world community, measures have been and are being taken to get rid of a number of diseases or minimize their incidence. Smallpox has been eradicated. Progress has been made towards eradicating polio in many countries. Attempts were to have been made by mid-1990s to achieve the following goals: *"elimination of neonatal tetanus, a 95 percent reduction in measles deaths, an oral rehydration therapy (ORT) use rate of 80%, the eradication of guinea worm diseases, the virtual elimination of vitamin A deficiency"* (International Federation ... *Health Horizons*, No.22). Immunization of children against the five diseases (diphtheria, measles, pertussis or whooping cough, poliomyelitis, and tetanus) is an on-going process in many countries. In its broadcast on March 16, 1997, the BBC announced that, according to WHO, four tropical diseases (measles, polio, leprosy, and Guinea worm) will be eliminated within 10 years. All these and similar measures and actions would mean cost savings at the global level, as both developed and developing countries will not have to incur expenses indefinitely for preventive and curative purposes in the future.

In developing countries, pharmaceuticals account for over 50 percent of healthcare expenditure (UNIDO, UNIDO/IO.569). This is high compared to other developing countries.

As is well known the prices of pharmaceuticals are skyrocketing. They are beyond the reach of most individuals. This situation is worsening, with more and more people being deprived of life-saving medicines. This trend, coupled with deteriorating health services and pandemic AIDS in many African countries (particularly the least developed countries), does not augur well for the implementation of the Alma-Ata Declaration. The role that pharmaceuticals (diagnostic, prophylactic and therapeutic), are expected to play is apparent. Availability of and access to essential drugs constitutes part of the local health service; it is one of the global indicators used to monitor the implementation of the global strategy (WHO, Implementation of the Global Strategy ...). The outcome of the acquisitions in the pharmaceutical industry in the developed countries that took place in recent years with a view to bringing down costs remains to be seen in so far as developing countries are concerned.

## Status of the Industry

According to a number of sources, up to 80 percent of the peoples in African, particularly those who live in rural areas, have no access to modern medicine. They resort to traditional medicine, as was practiced all over the world until the beginning of the nineteenth century (Bannerman 1983). Treatments are administered by traditional medicine healers who are socially and culturally acceptable to the local population. Whatever modern pharmaceuticals are produced and imported are consumed by the 20 percent of the population, for the most part urban dwellers.

Consumption of pharmaceuticals in Africa is the lowest in the world. According to WHO (*The World Drug Situation*), consumption per capita increased from $3.0 in 1976 to $4.9 in 1985. Since the figures were, apparently, at current prices a great part of the increase was probably due to inflation. The corresponding figures for developing countries were $3.4 and $5.4 and for the world as a whole, $10.3 and $19.4. In 1985, the Japanese registered the highest per capita consumption at $116.2. All these figures indicate the huge potential demand in Africa.

There are large consumption discrepancies at the individual country level. Egypt, Algeria, and Nigeria with a combined consumption of $2 billion consumed $22, $15 and $8 per head respectively in 1985 (UNIDO, *Opportunities for the Manufacture...*) while Ethiopia, a mere $0.80 in 1993.

With tens of thousands of pharmaceutical products in the market it is, under present African conditions, virtually impossible to have a good picture by group of products let alone by individual products. The press release (October 15, 1998, in London) that IMS HEALTH was going to expand its market research services on pharmaceuticals throughout Sub-Saharan Africa is a welcome news. If implemented, this initiative could substantially improve the availability of information on the consumption of pharmaceuticals in Africa.

Practically all the pharmaceuticals consumed in most African countries are imported in the form of ready-to-use products, bulk products for local formulation and intermediates for further processing and formulation. Table 8.2 gives some indication of the magnitude of imports, both actual and projected, in 35 African countries. According to the table, pharmaceutical imports into these countries (at 1980 constant prices) are expected to grow by a factor of 9 from $1.13 billion in 1970 to $10.2 billion by the year 2000.

TABLE 8. 2
PROJECTIONS OF VALUE OF IMPORTS OF PHARMACEUTICALS AND MEDICINAL PLANTS INTO THIRTY FIVE AFRICAN COUNTRIES BY SUBREGION (Millions of Dollars at 1980 constant prices)

| Subregion/region | Actual | | | Projection | | | |
|---|---|---|---|---|---|---|---|
| | 1970 | 1980 | Compounded growth rate (%) | 1985 | 1990 | 1995 | 2 000 |
| North Africa | 311 | 569 | 6.2 | 769 | 1038 | 1403 | 1895 |
| West Africa | 435 | 628 | 3.7 | 753 | 903 | 1083 | 1299 |
| Central Africa | 183 | 110 | 4.6[a] | 138 | 172 | 216 | 270 |
| Eastern and Southern Africa | 196 | 184 | 5.8[b] | 244 | 323 | 429 | 568 |
| Total at 1980 constant prices | 1125 | 1491 | | 1904 | 2436 | 3131 | 4032 |
| Total, including 5% annual inflation allowance after 1980 | | | | 2401 | 3879 | 6284 | 10206 |

Source: Based on data in UN, *International Trade Statistics Yearbook*, 1968-1985 issues, New York.
 [a] Growth rate for the period 1976-1980.
 [b] Growth rate for the period 1970-1975.

Production is, generally, limited to formulation using imported inputs. Practically all countries import not only active ingredients but also additives, exipients, packaging materials, and labels. Even then, local production was reported to satisfy only about 20 percent of consumption in late 1970s (UNIDO, UNIDO/IOD.347) and to account for only 0.5 percent of world production in early 1980s (UNIDO, UNIDO/IO.569).

Immunologicals are among the bulk drugs produced in some African countries. Others include sulfa drugs and some antibiotics in Egypt and Algeria, industrial enzymes and paracetamol in Egypt, and aspirin and chloroquinephosphate in Ghana.

Table 8.3 compares Africa's position in the production of pharmaceutical vis-a-vis other groups. Despite the relatively large increase during the period 1960-1975, African production was only about 10 percent of that of all Southern developing countries.

TABLE 8.3
COMPARISON OF AFRICAN ESTIMATED SHARE OF
PHARMACEUTICALS WITH OTHER ECONOMIC GROUPS (%)

|  | 1960 | 1975 | 1980 |
|---|---|---|---|
| Africa | 0.2 | 1.3 | ... |
| Southern developing countries | 8.4 | 12 | 14 [a] |
| Developed countries, incl. centrally planned economies | 91.6 | 88 | 86 |
| Total | 100 | 100 | 100 |
| Value ($ b) | 7.9 | 37.5 | ... |

Source: UNIDO, 1980, *Appropriate Industrial Technology for Drugs and Pharmaceuticals*, New York.
    [a] Indicative only

Some production units pack finished products. Others carry out formulations into dosage forms, using ingredients imported in bulk. The rest, limited to a small number of countries, are more integrated in the sense that they start from imported intermediates and their value-added is appreciable.

## Priority Products

An enormous number of drugs, tens of thousands, are marketed in the world today. A host of brand names compete for the same generic products (international nonproprietary products that can be adopted for manufacture following the expiry date of patents of their brand-name drugs) and combinations of drugs (many of them unnecessary) and their variants and new drugs with no additional or only marginal advantages over existing drugs, made from about 1,000 active ingredients. These and other reasons prompted the World Health Organization (WHO) to come up with the WHO Model List of Essential Drugs relevant to developing countries. The list comprises about 220 drugs and vaccines with proven quality, efficacy and safety organized according to therapeutic groupings. The fifth list (1988) is given in Annex 8.3. The presentation has been simplified by limiting subgrouping to the first level and not identifying substitutability or complementarity. Anti-infective drugs; gastrointestinal drugs; hormones, other endocrine drugs, and contraceptives; and immunologicals are the groups that contained subgroupings at the second level. The seventh list exists but was not accessible at the time of writing.

Following the WHO list, many developing countries drew up their own national lists of essential drugs based on the pattern and prevalence of diseases, including tropical and water-borne diseases, and arising from poor living conditions and a lack of or inadequate awareness of hygiene. These lists serve as a basis for importing and selecting drugs for local production. The priorities identified below refer only to those with possibilities for local processing.

Because of their potential for development in practically all African countries, phytochemicals (drugs derived from medicinal plants) and the trend in developed countries towards alternative medicine which includes natural remedies seem to deserve top priority status. For the sake of convenience, they are divided into three groups. The first group comprises those derived from medicinal plants that are already industrially processed worldwide. Nineteen of them were selected as high priorities for processing in Africa at the Ad-hoc Expert Group Meeting on the Application of Research Findings in the Development of Pharmaceutical Industries Based on Indigenous Raw Materials in 1988. These include: quinine (anti-malarial, which continues to be effective in Africa) from cinchona bark, reserpine (anti-hypertensive) from rawolfia roots, sennosides (laxative) from cassia leaves, digoxinisides (cardiotonic) from digitalis purpurea leaves, and emetine (amoebicide) from cephaelis roots.

The second group refers to phytochemicals based on medicinal plants ready for commercialization. The following are among the 12 identified by the above meeting as priority drugs: saponins (molluscide) from phytolacca dodecandra fruit, flavonoids (liver damage) from garcinia kola seeds, thymol (anti-fungal) from ocium gratis multiflora leaves, and bezoic acid derivatives (anti-sickling) from zanthoxylum zanthoxyloides roots, and nyasoside (uterine cancer) from hypoxis nyasica tuber. The last two have been patented.

The third group consists of medicinal plants with potential for commercialization. Among the most promising are: gum from albizia ferruginea, sennosides from cassia podocarpa, piperine from piper guineese, and polypeptide-P from momordica charanitia. African institutions are involved in R&D on some of this group.

Other priority products include those derived from slaughterhouse by-products (sera, vaccines, insulin, capsules, etc.). In Africa, where access to drugs is very limited, prevention (prophylaxis) is considered more beneficial than treatment (therapeutics)—hence the need to accord priority status to immunologicals (sera and vaccines). Antibiotics based on fermentation constitute the last but not the least priority pharmaceuticals. Unlike those derived from plant and slaughterhouse, however, their production involves a much higher level of technology and economies of scale. For these and other reasons their production will be possible in a limited number of countries only.

Consideration should be given to the local manufacture of certain non-drugs. Of particular importance are materials, such as syringes and surgical gloves. Because of AIDS, the practice of reusing these items, especially the former, is being abandoned. This will, obviously, substantially increase demand and therefore justify their local manufacture in some countries.

## Strategies for Development

As may be appreciated, economies of scale play a negative role in procuring and importing drugs in Africa, which is heavily dependent on the import of drugs. Prices of ready-to-use drugs, bulk drugs for formulations, and intermediates for further processing could be substantially lower if procured in large quantities. This can be done by having cost-effective central purchasing/procurement agencies serving groups of countries. Member countries would periodically request the agency to buy on their behalf certain types and quantities of generic products. The agency would then purchase on the basis of international competitive tendering; ensure that the qualities of the drugs meet international standards and are of long shelf-life; and arrange direct delivery to the member states in accordance with their respective requests. The center would have the option, perhaps at a latter stage, to handle the distribution (including storages and shipment) of the purchases to its member countries. To achieve its objective, the center would have to stay abreast of developments in the pharmaceutical industry and be aware of current prices. It could and should resort to assistance and facilities provided by the World Health Organization (WHO), including its Certification Scheme on the Quality of Pharmaceutical Products Moving in International Commerce.

Each and every pharmaceutical is a composite of an active ingredient and many and varied ancillary products, including diluents, binders, lubricants, preservatives, and emulsifying and suspending agents. Petrochemicals, chemicals from coal, carbohydrates, medicinal plants, and animal products are the basic raw materials for the active ingredients. Starch, soyflour, sodium chloride, carbon dioxide and vegetable oils that are or can be made locally available are among the many and varied ancillary products.

From the above array of inputs alone, the complexity of making pharmaceuticals can be appreciated. Making active ingredients from chemicals is highly complex, sophisticated, sensitive to economies of scale, and capital-intensive. It requires a well-developed and diversified chemical industry which is beyond the reach of individual countries. In other words, unless African countries develop their chemical industries at the multi-country or subregional level, the development of a chemical-based pharmaceutical industry will remain a dream for a long time to come. There are, however, better possibilities with respect to ancillary products, a number of which could be produced locally. In this connection, the development of formulation units based on basic imported active substances should be encouraged throughout the region in order to minimize the escalating and unaffordable prices of pharmaceuticals. Such units will import generic drugs in bulk which are relatively cheaper; use local ancillary inputs; and produce relatively cheaper products if manufactured under generic names. The pharmaceutical industry submits various counter-arguments. The main one relates to quality standards of generics. Use of different excipients and differences in bio-availability are cited as important factors in this regard. Even if one accepts the quality argument (which may be the exception rather the rule), what good is it to the hundreds of millions of people who cannot afford "quality" drugs? Would they not be better of with something they can afford rather than without them? What about the same product manufactured under contract and sold under different brand names by well-known pharmaceutical manufacturers? Another argument put forward against the use of generics is that research into diseases endemic to poor economies will be adversely affected. As research in the developed world is very much skewed to the needs of these countries this argument does not seem to hold.

The price advantage to be derived from local formulation units is clearly indicated in Table 8.4 below. The price ratio of imported/locally formulated pharmaceuticals in the examples in the table ranges between 1.1 and 11.0—hence the advisability of developing local formulation. The pharmaceuticals with the low ratio are those involving the least processing and therefore offering minimum value-added.

| TABLE 8.4. COMPARISON OF LOCALLY FORMULATED AND IMPORTED PRICES OF PHARMACEUTICALS IN ETHIOPIA | | | | |
|---|---|---|---|---|
| Product | Unit of issue | Unit price (Birr ) | | |
| | | Local (L) | Imported (I) | I/L ratio |
| Acetylsalicylic acid | 10 tablets | 0.4 | 4.4 | 11 |
| Paracetamol | 10 tablets | 0.7 | 4.3 | 6.1 |
| Ampicillin | 10 capsules of 250 mg | 3.5 | 4.4 | 1.3 |
| | 10 capsules of 500 mg | 7.1 | 9.2 | 1.3 |
| Dipyrone ampoule | 2ml | 0.45 | 3.85 | 8.6 |
| Piperazine syrup | 30 ml | 0.9 | 5.95 | 6.6 |
| Berantin syrup | 125 ml | 3.45 | 14.4 | 4.2 |
| Procaine penicillin | 4 x 10 IU | 3.5 | 4 | 1.1 |
| Source: Le-ake-Tsion G. Selassie, , pharmacist, Addis Ababa. | | | | |

Carbohydrates, medicinal plants, and animal products are other local resources that can and should be considered. Antibiotics from carbohydrates via fermentation, drugs from medicinal plants and sera, and vaccines from animal products are possibilities worth looking into under current African needs, conditions, and capabilities. The rest of this section focuses on medicinal plants which abound in Africa. At the Ethiopian Traditional Medicine Preparation and Research Society's annual meeting in October 1997, for example, the representative of the Ethiopian Biodiversity Institute disclosed that the country was a host to about 250 plant species used by traditional healers.

The premises for the strategies for the development of the pharmaceutical industry in Africa are the role medicinal plants play as raw materials in the pharmaceutical industry and the relevance of indigenous R&D institutions. Promotion of activities in these two areas is likely to result in significant changes in bringing certain pharmaceuticals within the reach of more people who would not otherwise have access to modern medicines. In this connection, it should be noted that medicinal plants exported to developed countries are processed into drugs and sold back to Africa at ten times value-added (UNIDO, ID/WG.393/1).

It is a well known fact that medicinal plants contribute significantly to the production of pharmaceuticals. In the early 1970s, plant-derived drugs accounted for 33 percent of the total drugs produced in the industrialized countries (UNCTAD/GATT, *Markets for....* ). According to other sources, this figure accounts for up to 40 percent of all prescriptions and could even rise to a higher level, given the trend towards phytotherapy in developed countries. Herbs, the so-called convenience drugs, i.e., painkillers and psychotropic agents (stimulants, sedatives, tranquilizers, etc.) are in the process of boosting the utilization of plant-derived drugs.

Despite the fact that the efficacy and safety of many of the herbs used have not been established, 1,500 of them are currently marketed in the United States ($3.24 billion market) where their use has been growing by 20 to 35 percent per year in recent years. Clinical studies and toxicological assessments of more than 300 herbs have been undertaken by Commission E of Germany's national health agency. Some of the findings are reproduced in Annex 8.4. The American Herbal Products Association was expected to come out in July 1997 with a handbook on the safety of 600 herbs (*The Boston Glob Magazine*, July 13, 1997).

The above-cited growing trend of contribution of medicinal plants to a global drugs production coupled with the fact that the development of the pharmaceutical industry proper is both complex and highly sensitive to economies of scale and that many of the products are characterized by a high rate of product obsolescence (partly due to micro-organisms building up resistance over time) argues for opting  for the easier part of development, manufacturing pharmaceuticals from medicinal plants using relatively simple technology and equipment. The strategy is to optimize the utilization of plant-derived medicines through local processing into preparations and forms relatively affordable by the majority of the people. This strategy makes sense as Africa is blessed with diversified flora and fauna. Furthermore, thanks to its diversified topography and climate, the region has the potential to transplant flora from other parts of the world. In other words, the region should seriously consider these comparative advantages in its effort to lower the exorbitant and soaring prices demanded for drugs.

The above idea of integrating traditional medicine into the health system is in conformity with WHO's approach of fusing modern and traditional health care (Ebey-Teesendorf 1997). It could facilitate and enhance the implementation of WHO's  recommendation to its member states to use their traditional systems of medicine.

Three levels of development of plant-derived medicines can be envisaged. The first level, which is based on minimum processing  and could use simplified methods of quality control requiring no sophisticated equipment (OAU/STRC, *African Pharmacopoeia*), is to use hygienically produced standardized extracts and ground materials as such. Extracts in powder form as well as ground raw materials could be tabulated or packed in tea bags. Liquid extracts can be used as tinctures or formulated into mixtures or suspensions or emulsions. Such preparations, which are likely to win consumer approval and would be relatively cheap, may prove to be within the means of the majority of peoples (about 80 percent of the population), who cannot afford modern medicine and who, currently, resort to traditional medicine. The hygienical dosage forms could prove a better alternative to traditional medicines. In planning projects based on total extraction, export of part of the extracts could and should be taken into consideration, especially in view of the trend in developed countries towards phytotherapy.

The second is to isolate the active ingredients and formulate them into dosage forms. The third is to isolate intermediates, convert them into active ingredients and formulate them into dosage forms.

The three-level approach has definite merit in that practically all countries could start with the first stage. Many could begin straightaway with the second stage while fewer countries could enter the third stage within the foreseeable future. In the long run, it is very likely that many of them could cover all three stages.

Essential oil extraction and ethyl alcohol production would be considered part of the development of pharmaceuticals from medicinal plants. Ethyl alcohol is used both for extracting active ingredients and in its pure form as medicinal alcohol.

Given the unreliable supply of agricultural inputs on the market, it would be advisable to integrate processing with plantation. Local farmers should be encouraged to meet part of the requirement. Their participation could be enhanced if they were to be provided with technical assistance in farm management. In the event that production expands, they would be given the first option to supply the additional requirement. The integrated plantation/processing approach could make use of mixed and rotational farming which would enable the extracting facility to operate optimally throughout most of the year.

Viability of the integrated system could be further optimized by using multi-purpose equipment. On a campaign basis, different kinds of medicinal plants could be extracted and isolated, provided all the necessary features are incorporated into the flow system. The additional investment incurred would be marginal in comparison with the cost of investment that would be required for separate units.

As for the other priority pharmaceuticals (sera, vaccines, insulin, capsules, etc., and antibiotics), suffice it to say that measures should be taken to enhance their development. The same applies to the production of non-active ingredients (diluents, binders, lubricants, flavoring, etc. materials ). There is also a need to develop the packaging industry to produce bottles, sachets, bags, tubes, vials, ampoules and other containers which should be simple but able to effectively retain the potency of the drugs.

With respect to R&D, it is a well-known fact that R&D related to tropical conditions is marginal, especially in industrialized countries. WHO has pointed out that *"97 percent of the world's biomedical research funds are spent on diseases primarily of interest to the developed countries."* The London School of Hygiene & Tropical Medicine, where about 50 percent of the academic staff is engaged in tropical research (UNDP/World Bank/WHO, *TDR News*, June 1996), is probably among the few exceptions. Worse still is the trend in cutting funds and activities related to R&D in developed countries. Malaria is an example of disease control that has already been adversely affected. This growing critical gap needs to be narrowed by setting up new R&D institutions[3] and strengthening existing units in Africa. The names and addresses of 12 African R&D institutions and the medicinal plants under investigation in the 1980s are given in ECA's (ECA/IND/CHM/003/89). The redeployment from developed to developing countries of part of the research into new drugs for tropical diseases exemplified by the Wellcome Trust is most welcome. This approach, including subcontracting R&D in other drugs, needs to be replicated in Africa by as many pharmaceutical manufacturers as possible. It could help to counter the reduction in R&D expenditure and the associated risks in developed countries associated with the increasing research-to-marketing time lag (from 3 years in early 1960s to 10-13 years in early 1990s).

The bias against tropical and other diseases that are considered low priority in developed countries is also manifest in the flows of external aid to the health sector. In 1990, for example, less than $15 million were allocated for tuberculosis, the biggest killer (1.9 million deaths), while leprosy with negligible number of deaths was funded to the tune of more than $75 million (*The Economist*, May 20, 1995). In this connection, it is gratifying to note that the multidrug (rifampicin, clofazimine, and dapsone) therapy approach is contributing to the elimination of leprosy by the year 2000.

Water, the most basic need after air, adversely affects people and animals in three ways: scarcity, unpotability, and medium for water-borne diseases. The first is chronic in the drier and drought-prone areas. The second, especially surface water, requires treatment to make it drinkable. The third is the source of diseases, such as malaria and bilharsiasis. Ethiopia has two interesting developments in this regard. The first is the discovery of controlling bilharzia using a molluscide, "endod" (phytolacca dodecandra), to destroy the vector snail. The chemical (DDBASA) extracted from the plant is an ingredient for making soaps and detergents. Other claimed uses of "endod" relate to birth control and curing skin diseases. The second is the powder of aleko tree seeds. Discovered in 1995, the powder has water-purifying qualities (by absorbing impurities) and the power to kill germs. These and other research findings in Africa and elsewhere give hope that someday many of the debilitating effects of these human and animal scourges will, at least, be minimized using indigenous therapeutic and prophylactic substances.

African biodiversity, the very basis for developing the pharmaceutical industry, however, is threatened. Owing to climatic changes and other adverse changes brought about by the population, the number of African flora and fauna are being reduced at an alarming rate. The fact that about 75 percent of the world genetic diversity of agricultural crops has been lost since the beginning of this century shows just how serious the problem is ( FAO, *Dimensions of Need*). This disastrous trend, if not halted in time, will deprive not only Africa but the whole world of thousands of flora and fauna whose curative and preventive potentials are still unkown. It is therefore incumbent upon each African country to take measures to protect its flora and fauna, in general, and endangered endemic species in particular, within its territory. In this connection, it should be noted that *"250,000 to 750,000 species of higher (flowering) plants exist on earth,"* of which only about 1 percent are acknowledged to have real therapeutic value (Bannerman 1983).

As is well known, livestock in Africa suffer from many diseases. Protecting livestock from diseases through vaccination is the best that can be done. In this regard, some countries with relatively large livestock would do well to consider the possibility of introducing vaccine production and expanding existing plants. It was reported that the 26 production units (22 existing and 4 under establishment during the second half of the 1980s) were not in a position to meet the demand for vaccines (FAO, *Atlas of African Agriculture*). Production of genetically-engineered vaccine against rinderpest developed by an Ethiopian (FAO, *Dimensions of Need*) is expected to start in Ethiopia within a few years.

Last but not least, some of the populous countries could venture into manufacturing other pharmaceuticals. In this connection, it should be noted that most of the essential drugs can now be produced freely under generic names as their patent periods (16 to 20 years) have expired. There are also non-patented drugs. This means that many of the inhibiting factors, such as restrictive business (market) practices and the high cost of patents, licenses, know-how, and trademarks, are no longer there to discourage the local development of the pharmaceutical industry.

The pharmaceutical development strategy suggested above should be supplemented by the application of biotechnology and genetic engineering. New developments in biotechnology offer advantages (better process control and product purity) in traditional extraction and fermentation techniques. A start could be made with traditional but improved fermentation. This is an area that African countries should explore as much as possible with a view to finding and making drugs.

## TEXTILE INDUSTRY

Textiles are made from a variety of raw materials. These consist of natural fibers and man-made fibers, the latter comprising cellulosics and synthetics. Man-made fibers have been gaining increased market acceptance against cotton and wool. World consumption of cotton in relation to all fibers, for instance, declined from 73.0 percent in 1952 to 52.4 percent in 1971. Over the same period, man-made fibers showed a sharp increase from 16.7 percent to 40.3 percent with synthetics accounting for 25.4 percentage points having grown on average at an annual rate of 21.5 percent (UN, *International Trade in Cotton Textiles and the Developing Countries* .... ). In 1990, the share of cotton further fell to 46.0 percent (UNIDO, *Industry and Development: Global Report 1991/92*) and stood at 44 percent in 1994 (UN, *The Chemical Industry in 1994*). In terms of contribution to the manufacturing industry, the textile industry comes second to food in most African countries.

### Status of the Industry
As cotton grows in large areas in Africa, the textile mills in Africa are mainly based on cotton. Many of them, however, do import and use man-made fibers alongside and in combination with cotton.

Cotton yarn, production of which increased from 329,000 tons in 1975 to 448,000 tons in 1990 (Annex 5.2) is the major textile fiber in Africa. In 1966, yarn production and fabric production and consumption were 277,000 tons, 261,000 tons and 371,000 tons, respectively. The corresponding figures for cellulosics, the next most important fibers used, were 14,000, 41,000, and 73,000, and they were mainly imported (UNIDO, *Textile Industry*). As with industry in general, capacity utilization in textile mills has been low. In Tanzania, for example, it stood at around 40 percent in the period 1989-1991 ([ECA, CAMI.11/4 Inf.). In most countries production is entirely consumed locally.

According to one source (*Focus on African Industry*, Volume VI, No.1), based on an estimated 1.3 kg per capita consumption of cotton fiber in the year 2000, the additional demand for cotton in Africa will be of the order of 1.2 million tonnes of cotton fiber. Another sources indicates that demand for all textile fibers will increase from 2.1 million tons in 1993 to 3.1 million tons (historical scenario) and 5.6 million tons (normative scenario) in the year 2008 (ECA, *Africa in the 1990s and Beyond: ...* ).

## Priority Products

As indicated above, diverse fibers are used to produce textiles for different purposes. The focus in this section is on textiles aimed at meeting basic clothing needs, bearing in mind that Africa is a net importer of textiles and clothing.

In Africa, cotton is by far the most important natural fiber used to make fabrics; cellulosics, wool, and linen trailing far behind. Although the majority of the African peoples nowadays wear clothes originating from modern textile mills, both local and abroad, there are and will continue, for some time to come, to be those who will continue to use traditional clothing made by traditional spinners and weavers.

Being a renewable source of fiber grown extensively in the region and having qualities suitable to Africa's climate, cotton is likely to continue to be the preferred fiber for textile making in the continent. There is, of course, the possibility of a trade-off, competing with food crops for growing. Vicose rayon and acetate made from wood, another renewable resource, are possibilities worth considering, especially if integrated with pulp and paper making or if adequate quantities of cotton lint are available. It appears that Algeria (accounting for the whole capacity of 30,000 tons per year in Table 8.7) is the only country in Africa that produces dissolving pulp for making viscose rayon and acetate fibers, i.e. excluding the 420,000 tons in South Africa.

Nowadays the trend is toward fabrics made from blended fibers. It is possible to have tailor-made fabrics with desirable qualities by blending different fibers. Cotton/polyester blends, for instance, combine the good qualities of cotton (absorbency, resistance to static, piling, and heat) and those of polyester (wrinkle recovery, press retention, strength, stability, and abrasion resistance) (Hollen 1979).

The textile industry is among the first industries to be established in developing countries. It is to be found in many countries in the region. Countries without cotton mills are the exception rather than the rule. Mills may vary in the degree of integration and their sophistication. In some countries, part of the textile output is produced in industrial free zones.

During the past 35 years, African countries, with very few exceptions, did not benefit from the international division of labor, when operations related to the textile and wearing apparel industries were redeployed from developed to developing countries. Mauritius, Sudan, Egypt, Morocco, Tunisia, Botswana, and Lesotho were among the exceptions. Significant achievements were made by some of them. Apparel and textile exports accounted for 16.9 percent and 39.0 percent of total exports of manufactured goods in Morocco and Tunisia in 1985 respectively (UNIDO, *Industry Africa*, No.4).

Very few Sub-Saharan countries ventured into the textile and clothing industry for export and therefore the majority failed to take advantage of exemptions from tariffs and quantitative restrictions in the OECD countries. Many of the latecomers found it relatively difficult to meet the conditions of importing countries, i.e., the rules of origin which require backward integration to local fabric-making. Unlike most goods and commodities, the integration of the textile trade into GATT, now WTO (the phasing-out of multi-fiber arrangement), will last the whole 10-year transition period (UN, *World Economic and Social Survey 1995*). This means that by 2005, Sub-Saharan countries will lose the above advantages *vis-à-vis* other countries. The multi-fiber arrangement which was originally created in 1973, on a temporary basis, was intended to assist the adjustment of the textile industry in developed countries.

## Strategies for Development

From the above it is apparent that the development of the textile industry will have to continue its emphasis on cotton textiles. This will involve the rehabilitation, expansion, and diversification of existing mills and the establishment of new ones. Integration (comprising spinning, weaving/knitting, and finishing) will have to be optimized, particularly in both old unintegrated mills and in new units. The optimal combination of labor and capital should be established before investment decisions are made.

The use of semi-automatic small-scale looms in the rural and semi-urban areas should be encouraged. Such looms could be based on cotton yarns produced in big mills. Governments should provide assistance to traditional textile weavers in the form of providing inputs and helping with marketing, including government purchase of their products

Africa accounts for less than 1 percent of the world apparel MVA (ADB, African Development Report 1997). Such a low share could mean potential for developing the textile industry. Unfortunately, the hope that some day more African countries might find it possible to develop textile export industries have been dashed by recent technological innovations that have rendered the region's potential comparative advantage (cheap labor) less relevant. This has been compounded by protection that escalates with the degree of processing and by the provision of adjustment assistance to textile mills in developed market economy countries. The automation and computerization of production process seem to be weakening the redeployment trend in the textile industry. In the future, the possibility of developed countries establishing textile industries in developing countries will, perhaps, be limited. Worse still, those countries which host redeployed textile industries may well suffer as the developed countries become increasingly self-sufficient.

Textile mills and garment making establishments in some African countries, such as Ethiopia, Kenya, and Zimbabwe, are finding it difficult to sell their products. Dumping, illegal imports, and aid shipments, especially of second hand garments, are the main reasons for this state of affairs. If the governments concerned do not take immediate measures, the consequences will be grave in terms of dwindling capacity utilization and the eventual closure of textile mills and garment manufacturing establishments. This would, naturally, lead to loss of a substantive part of the industrial labor force as the textile industry accounts for a high proportion of industrial employment in African countries.

Many of the countries outside the humid tropics are suited for cotton growing. This is particularly true of the Sahelian countries, as these countries have limited resources; yet industrial integration in West Africa could be greatly enhanced if the countries in the subregion were to specialize in all aspects related to cotton (cotton growing, textiles production, garment making, and eventually manufacturing textile machinery and equipment). Among the Sahelian countries, Chad is reported to have made some progress in the export of cotton yarn and textiles.

It may be worthwhile undertaking studies to establish the scope for providing man-made fibers in countries where tree plantations could be developed or where adequate quantities of cotton lint could be sourced. Integrated pulp/paper/viscose rayon complexes may be considered, especially in countries with forest resources. This approach could render a pulp mill viable, which it would not otherwise be, were it planned to cater to a paper mill only.

## BUILDING MATERIALS INDUSTRY

Although more acute in developing countries, urban-related problems are world-wide problems. Urbanization and homelessness were discussed at the second United Nations Conference on Human Settlements (Habitat II) in June, 1996, in Istanbul, Turkey. Its theme was "sustainable human settlements in an urbanizing world and adequate shelter for all." The Habitat II plan of action that was adopted at the Conference endorsed the view that everyone must have equal access to shelter and natural resources. It seems, however, that there was no commitment on the part of the international community, except the $15 billion World Bank pledge for water- and garbage-related projects, to assist developing countries in implementing the plan of action.

The acute and growing shortage of shelter in Africa is, in part, due to rapid urbanization, the fastest in the world. During the 1980s, urban populations grew on average by 5.6 percent per year in contrast to 2.1 percent for the rural population and 3.0 percent for the population as a whole (FAO, *African Agriculture: the next 25 Years*, Annex V). This, coupled with the lack of employment opportunities and the multitude of crises referred to elsewhere, led to substandard shelters and slums and squatter settlements that are the main characteristics of many African cities and towns. The urban population which numbered 129 million in 1980 (195 million in 1990) is expected to grow sixfold to over 765 million, accounting for 52 percent of the total population in 2020. The vegetative growth of the urban population between 1990 and 2020 will require 112 million new units simply to accommodate the additional population (ECA, *Focus on Africa Industry*, Volume V, No.2). The implications of this inordinate concentration of people in terms of shelter and other services requirement, such as utilities, sanitation, and public transport, are obvious. It is equally obvious that African cities and towns will not be able to meet all these needs. In other words, unless rural areas are developed swiftly to slow the massive influx of people to urban areas, many African cities and towns will become completely unfit to live in.

In Africa, the building and construction industry, comprising buildings and infrasructure (civil works), such as roads, bridges, harbors, railway lines, and airports, is generally labor-intensive. Depending on the country concerned, it contributes *"between 4 and 10 percent of GDP and between 40 and 60 percent of total capital [fixed capital] investment"* (UNIDO, *Industry Africa*, No.4). Building materials constitute a large proportion of the capital, up to 80 percent of the total value of construction and 5 to 8 percent of total imports (ECA, *Focus on African Industry*, Volume V, No.2). These factors and the labor-intensive nature of the building industry which entails contributions from a variety of craftsmen are additional reasons for including the building materials industries in this chapter. Furthermore, the sheer size of its contribution to the economy and the positive correlation between construction and GDP observed in countries whose

GDP per capita increased at a fast rate means that the development of the construction and building materials industry can enhance economic development in general. Based on 1965 data, per capita cement consumption increased faster than GDP up to per capita consumption of 148 kg or GDP per capita of $390 and the growth rate decreased beyond these values (UNIDO, *Appropriate Industrial ... Building Materials*).

For the sake of convenience, buildings (housing) are grouped into two categories: traditional and modern. Modern buildings use a variety of materials produced by basic industries: steel rods and other profiles from the iron and steel industry; aluminum sheets and profiles from the aluminum industry; plastic pipes and sheets from the petrochemical industry; and paints and varnishes from the chemical industry. Other inputs, such as cement and glass, come from industries whose economic level of outputs, by African standards, are high and in some countries considered large-scale. The development of the former group of materials is related to the development of the basic industries for which the construction and building industry is one of the outlets. The latter group of materials are produced mainly to cater to the construction and building industry.

Many countries have tried to provide shelters to their peoples. One of the strategies that was found practical relates to the poor. This strategy provides plots with basic infrastructure (water, sewerage, and electricity) and lets the family build the shelter it can afford. Considering the growing shortage of housing and the lack of resources, this approach may well be the best that can be done for the poor in many African countries.

## Status of the Industry

In the urban and semi-urban areas, modern building materials have become popular. The bulky and heavy resource-oriented materials (cement, bricks, tiles, lime, aggregates, etc.) are generally produced in or near the major consumption centers. As shown in Annex 5.4, production of cement in the continent almost tripled from 18.2 million tons in 1970 to 51.8 million tons in 1990 while that of quicklime soared from 222,000 tonnes to 3.3 million tons. Production of concrete products increased from 1.24 million tons in 1972 to 2.14 million tonnes in 1981. The corresponding figures for floor and wall tiles were 2.65 and 9.93 million m$^2$ (UNID, *The Building Materials Industry in ... , UNIDO/IS.512*). ECA demand cement estimates for the year 2008 give 205.6 million tons (historical scenario) and 287.6 million tons (normative scenario), the latter expected to result in a production/consumption gap of 26.6 million tons. The demand projections compare with 84.6 million tons of consumption in 1993 (ECA, *Africa in the 1990s and Beyond: ... ).

Most African countries possess industries manufacturing one or more of the basic building materials. Cement, bricks and to some extent lime and tiles are produced in many countries. A number of countries produce reinforcing rods from scrap metal supplemented by imported billets. Very few countries produce sheet glass, Nigeria and Tanzania being the late comers. From these it is apparent that the building material industry in Africa is at the first stage of development, except for the making of walling materials.

Some countries have gone beyond the first stage and are increasingly diversifying their building material industries. They produce roofing materials (corrugated metal sheets), flooring materials (wood, plastic tiles), joinery (doors, windows), services (plastic pipes and conduits), finishes (paint), and sanitary equipment (ceramics). Many of these products are, however, based on imported inputs, namely rolled metal sheets and sections, plastic granules, paint components, etc., and the many chemicals required to convert them into final products.

Production and trade of other building materials are given in Annexes 5.2, 5.3 and 5.5. Wood and timber are important building components, in both traditional and modern buildings. Their production is limited to those countries with forest resources. As a result, the continent is a net importer of sawn wood, wood-based panels and plywood. Others, such as structural steel, nails, aluminum, plastics, paints, and glass, are imported in most of the countries, particularly those countries that do not have production units. In 1960, iron and steel products, timber, and cement accounted for 62, 13, and 12 percent of building materials imports in Africa (UNIDO, *Building Materials Industry*).

In 1960, *"Africa had to import a total of 58 percent of its building materials."* including glass, paints and varnishes, bricks, tiles, ceramics, cement, sawn wood and wood products (UNIDO, *Appropriate Industrial ... Materials*). This was at the time when African countries were beginning their transition to independence. Since then, as many building and related material industries have been established, it is likely that the level of dependence has gone down significantly.

## Priority Products

Traditional houses, particularly in rural areas, are generally built using locally available materials. The design depends upon climatic conditions and the availability of materials. In the warm-humid climate, organic materials, such as wood, bamboo, reeds, straw, and grass, are used. Inorganic materials, such as stone, brick, lime, and clay as well as some of the organic materials constitute the building materials in hot-dry areas. Combinations of materials from organic and inorganic resources, depending upon their availability, are used in areas comprising both humid and dry climates. Given the perishable nature of many of these materials, the houses are not durable and require frequent repair and replacement. Corrugated iron sheets and, to some extent, cement are finding their way into rural areas.

Bricks (including stabilized clay bricks), cement, stone, sand, wood, and corrugated iron sheets (in some instances) constitute the basic building materials for ordinary quasi-modern houses. For large and high-rise buildings, materials used include cement, aggregates for concrete, structural steel, metal frames for doors and windows, timber, plastics, glass, ceramics, and paints. These may be expected to continue to play the roles they have been playing in the past as changes in building technology are not likely for some time to come to affect drastically the resource-based materials, particularly under African conditions.

From the above it is apparent that a wide range of building materials is required to meet the needs of the above two categories of buildings. Some of them, cement, aggregates, and structural steels are used in large quantities in the construction of roads, bridges, railways, ports, and airports.

## Strategies for Development

Most building materials are bulky with low value/weight ratio. Transport costs for such materials could be as high as, if not more, expensive than the cost of the materials themselves. Transport costs could, therefore, be reduced by selecting production sites that reflect market needs. In other words, it is possible that dispersed high-cost smaller units, rather than one low-cost large unit, could be justified by optimizing combined production and transport costs. This concept should be kept in mind when planning bulky building materials industries.

Existing national building materials industries need to be rehabilitated and expanded. Expanding existing plants to cover the needs of neighboring countries could be a feasible approach. Because of economies of scale, the development of some building materials, such as structural steel, sheet glass and paint (production of components) will require joint efforts among member states.

Building materials are amenable to interchangeability. This needs to be taken into account when developing the industry. Mud, timber, bricks, stones, and cement blocks for walls; timber, concrete, and steel for structural frames; straw, grass, slates, clay tiles, concrete tiles, cement-natural fibers composites, asphalt, and sheet metals (corrugated iron sheets) for roofing; and timber, concrete, concrete tiles, brick tiles, and plastic tiles for flooring are examples of such substitutions. The choice is a matter of suitability, availability, and affordability.

Modern building materials are not within the reach of the rural and most urban populations, especially in urban slums and shanty towns. Affordable building materials are therefore needed to meet these people's demand. Although some technologies are available for utilizing traditional materials for low-cost housing, successful R&D results, both within Africa and elsewhere, need to be identified so that they can be applied with or without adaptation to maximizing the use of local materials. The following are among recent technology innovations in local building materials in Africa worth considering (ECA, *Focus on African Industry*, Volume V, No.2):

- Stabilized soil: Botswana, Nigeria, and Uganda;
- Soil blocks: Ethiopia, Ghana, Kenya, Tanzania, Uganda, and Zambia;
- Pozzolana: Ethiopia and Kenya;
- concrete roofing: Ethiopia, Kenya, Tanzania, Uganda, and Zambia;
- concrete roofing machine fabrication: Botswana and Ghana; and
- Machinery fabrication: Nigeria and Zambia.

The objectives of local R&D should be to make inexpensive, durable building materials which can be processed using minimal energy as well as simple, inexpensive equipment that can be operated and maintained by local people. Cheaper and improved and/or new binders and soil stabilization techniques are needed. Roofing materials deserve special attention, as the roof provides general protection to the whole structure and there are no satisfactory or inexpensive alternatives to thatching that are relatively durable compared with the wall and binder materials used in traditional rural dwellings. In this connection, the cement-sisal composite which can be made manually (UNIDO, *Appropriate Industrial ... Materials*) seems to offer a solution to the lack of roofing materials in countries endowed with sisal resource. Sisal and other natural fibers, including waste textile fibers, will, it is hoped, prove to be good replacements since asbestos-cement composite have been found to be a health hazard.

Clay, volcanic ash soil, natural fibers, and agricultural and industrial waste (such as rice husk and lime sludge, press mud waste from sugar mills, and blastfurnace slag, cement dust, stone dust and chips, sawdust, fly ash, banana leaves ash, bagasse ash, mineral rejects and tailings) are among the building materials that require further research. There is a need to establish whether research has been carried out elsewhere into the materials listed below so that appropriate technologies can be applied in Africa with or without local modification:

- Binders:
  . cement: mini cement-plants, Potland-pozzolana cements;
  . lime: mortar, hydrated lime-pozzolana composite (used as mortar, block or brick); and
  . gypsum (calcined): plastering and producing panels and board.
- Wall materials:
  . stone: granite, basalt, sandstone, marble, volcanic tuffs, limestone, etc., including stone splitting techniques;
  . mud/clay: mortar, plastering and for brick making, preferably stabilized using lime, cement, straw, etc.;
  . sand-lime compacted and cured, concrete cement-blocks; and
  . others: wood and bamboo plastered with mud mixed with cow dung.
- Roofing materials:
  . wood trusses;
  . stone slabs, slates;
  . clay tiles; and
  . cement-natural fibers composites, particularly cement-sisal composite (also used as wall plastering, window gratings, etc.).
- Foundations:
  . boulders, burnt bricks, stabilized soil blocks, etc.; and
- Floors:
  . stone slab, burnt bricks, clay tiles, wood, etc.

Emphasis should be given to technologies requiring minimal and/or using inexpensive energy resources, since energy is a major cost item in the production of many building materials. Agricultural residues, husks, straw, and residual oils are examples of energy resources that can be used to fire lime and clay brick kilns. Other technological considerations include suitability, maintainability, and simplicity of operation of production units. Many wood-based operations (sawmilling and making cement fiber board, gypsum fiber board, cement particle board, particle board, and plywood), for example, fall under this category (UNIDO, *The Building Materials Industry...* ).

In the building sector, cost can be reduced through the utilization of prefabricated building components. Although this trend is currently applicable to high-rise buildings, it is likely that builders of houses and small buildings will, in the long run, resort to the use of prefabricated components, starting, perhaps, with doors and windows and, eventually, ending with complete factory-built homes. It is possible that low-cost houses could benefit from R&D in this area. Other materials requiring R&D include clay pipes.

Building materials based on appropriate technologies are intended first and foremost to serve the rural population. Their manufacture may require government assistance. This would apply particularly to mini cement-mills based on vertical kiln and lime kilns. The mini-mills may not be able to compete with large mills whose cement sales price is based on freight equalization that distorts the real price of cement—hence the need to annul price-build up systems of this kind or subsidize mini-mills. As the trend in the past has been to convert wet-process mills to dry-process because of reduced energy consumption, new mills are likely to be of the latter type.

Last but not least, it would be advisable to consult UNIDO on the experience accumulated by the joint UNIDO-CID (Centre for Industrial Development) program for the promotion of building materials in Africa. This program which became operational in 1988 was to have promoted three to five projects, mainly related to stabilized clay bricks, cement components, wood and stones in some selected countries (UNIDO, *Industry and Development: Global Report 1991/92*).

## EDUCATIONAL MATERIALS INDUSTRY

Students in Africa suffer from either a lack of or inadequate and increasingly expensive educational materials, such as books, paper, pencils, pens, rulers, and protractors. As a result of these and other constraints, the quality of education leaves much to be desired. This situation is likely to worsen as long as the source of supply does not shift from foreign to local sources with cheaper and relatively less escalating prices. As is the case with other international commitments, UNESCO's "1978 Education for All by the Year 2000" which was declared by the international community will not have achieved its target at the close of this century.

As paper appears to be the most crucial educational material, this section focuses on pulp and paper.

### Status of the Industry

The total area covered by tropical forest in the continent decreased from 568 million hectares in 1980 to 527 million hectares in 1990 (FAO, *The State of Food and Agriculture 1994*). The latter works out to about 23.6 percent of the total land area and 30 percent of the world total tropical forest area. Moist deciduous forest accounts for 47.6 percent of total forest area, followed by dry deciduous forest (17.5%) and rain forest (16.4%). The declining trend could affect the availability of wood for pulping in the future if timely appropriate measures are not taken.

Although information on production and availability of educational materials is hard to come by, there is no doubt that there is substantial gap between demand and local production. Many countries have some kind of facilities where they produce exercise books and text books. In some countries paper is produced using imported pulp. Production of the other educational materials is more limited.

According to one of the issues of UNIDO's *Industry in Africa*, in 1978, Africa produced 600,000 tons of pulp and consumed the same quantity. The corresponding figures for paper were 800,000 tons and 2.0 million tons, indicating a huge supply/demand gap. In 1991, production increased to 893,000 tons of pulp (UNIDO, *Industry and Development: Global Report 1993/94*). This accounted for about 2.6 percent of world production. Capacities were 0.85 to 1.1 million tons for pulp and 1.1 to 1.4 million tons for paper indicating a capacity utilization of 64.0 percent and 61.5 percent, respectively. With a capacity of 180,000 tons of pulp per year, Swaziland accounts for 0.42 percent of world capacity (UNIDO, *Industry and Development: Global Report 1993/94)*. More recent demand figures and projections for paper and paper board are 8.1 million tons in 1993 and 36.8 million tons (historical scenario) and 41.5 million tons (normative scenario) in 2008.

All show huge production/demand gaps, 7.3, million tons, 35.4 million tons and 18.8 million tons respectively (ECA, *Africa in the 1990s and Beyond: ...* ).

The subregional shares of pulp and paper capacity, production, and consumption in the 1980s are shown in Table 8.5. It is apparent that the North African subregion accounts for about half of the pulp-related figures while the Eastern and Southern African subregion leads in respect of paper.

TABLE 8.5
SUBREGIONAL SHARE OF PULP AND PAPER CAPACITY, PRODUCTION AND CONSUMPTION IN AFRICA IN THE 1980s (%)

| | Pulp | | | Paper | | |
|---|---|---|---|---|---|---|
| | Capacity | Production | Consumption | Capacity | Production | Consumption |
| North Africa | 42 | 53 | 52 | 37 | 40 | 47 |
| West Africa | 22 | 15 | 28 | 6 | 5 | 16 |
| Eastern and Southern Africa | 31 | 32 | 18 | 57 | 45 | 37 |
| Central Africa | ... | ... | 2 | - | - | ... |

Source: UNIDO, 1989, *Pulp and Paper Industry in Developing Africa*, Industry Africa, IDDA Journal of the Industrial Development Decade for Africa, No.2, December 1989, Vienna.

According to UNIDO (*Appropriate...Small Pulp Mill*), a per capita paper consumption level of 30 kg is a minimum requirement to *"achieve full literacy, adequate communication and educational levels."* Based on this and the projected population figures in Annex 2.2, the regional potential demand for paper works out at 25 million tons in 2000 and 40 million tons in 2020. According to another source, the paper deficit in Africa is expected to increase from 4.3 million tons in 1990 to more than 5 million tons in 2000 (ECA, *Focus on African Industry*, Volume VI, No.1).

Table 8.6 summarizes production, capacity, trade, and consumption of paper and paper-board in Africa in 1990. Self-sufficiency in 1990 works out at 42.6 percent. The per capita consumption for the major producing countries ranged between 3 kg in Nigeria and 11kg in Egypt. African shares in world production and consumption were 0.4 percent and 0.8 percent, respectively. All these indicate that much needs to be done to develop the pulp and paper industry in Africa.

TABLE 8. 6
PRODUCTION, CAPACITY, TRADE AND CONSUMPTION OF PAPER AND PAPER-BOARD IN AFRICA IN 1990 (1000t)

| | Production | | Export | Consumption | | | Capacity | |
|---|---|---|---|---|---|---|---|---|
| | Total | Share (%)[a] | | Total | Share (%)[b] | Per capita | Total | Rate (%)[d] |
| | 1986 | 1990 | 1990 | 1990 | 1990 | 1990 | 1990 | 1990 | 1990 |
| Africa | | 855 | 0.4 | | 2005 | 0.8 | | | |
| -Nigeria [e] | 77 | 70 | | - | 320 | | 3 | 230 | 30 |
| - Egypt [e] | 147 | 223 | | - | 581 | | 11 | 220 | 101 |
| - Morocco [e] | 109 | 119 | | 2 | 216 | | 8 | 130 | 92 |
| - Kenya [e] | 96 | 123 | | 3 | 145 | | 5 | 130 | 95 |
| - Algeria [e] | 88 | 87 | | - | 230 | | 9 | 128 | 68 |
| - Zimbabwe [e] | ... | 87 | | 5 | 97 | | 10 | 90 | ... |

Source: Compiled from UNIDO, 1992, *Industry and Development: Global Report 1992/93*, Vienna.
a In world production  b In world consumption  c Kg per capita  d Capacity utilization  e Estimates

Table 8.7 gives pulp and paper capacities in Africa. The African share of world total woodpulp (paper grades) capacity works out at a mere 0.56 percent. This increased to 0.66 percent in 1993 and is, on the basis of the FAO surveys, expected to increase marginally to 0.68 in 1998. The corresponding figures for total paper and paperboard are 0.46, 0.47, and 0.47. The major woodpulp producing countries (annual tonnage capacities in 1993 in parenthesis) are : Nigeria ( 313,000), Swaziland (180,000), Gabon (175,000), Tanzania (140,000), Kenya (109,000), Morocco (92,000), Zimbabwe (79,000), and Zambia (33,000). Excluding South Africa, Algeria is the only country producing dissolving pulp (30,000-ton capacity).

TABLE 8.7
PULP AND PAPER CAPACITIES IN AFRICA

| | Total capacity (1000 t) | | | | Annual average increase (%) | |
|---|---|---|---|---|---|---|
| | 1988 | 1993 | 1996 | 1998 | 88-93 | 93-98 |
| Total woodpulp, paper grades | 889 | 1170 | 1264 | 1264 | 5.6 | 1.6 |
| - Mechanical | 125 | 152 | 153 | 153 | 4 | 0.1 |
| - Thermo-mechanical | 8 | 33 | 33 | 33 | 32.8 | 0 |
| - Semi-chemical | 115 | 68 | 92 | 92 | -10 | 6.2 |
| - Chemical | 641 | 917 | 986 | 986 | 7.4 | 1.5 |
| Other pulp | 141 | 201 | 199 | 199 | 7.3 | -0.2 |
| Dissolving pulp | 30 | 30 | 30 | 30 | 0 | 0 |
| Total paper and paperboard | 1109 | 1361 | 1500 | 1510 | 4.2 | 2.1 |
| - Newsprint | 140 | 172 | 177 | 177 | 4.2 | 0.6 |
| - Printing and writing | 367 | 367 | 392 | 406 | 0 | 2 |
| - Other paper and paperboard | 592 | 812 | 921 | 917 | 6.5 | 2.5 |

Source: FAO, 1994, Pulp *and Paper Capacities, Survey 1993-1998*, Rome.

During the period 1988-1993, average capacity increases were 5.6 percent for pulp and 4.2 percent for paper. These are expected to stand at 1.6 percent and 2.1, respectively in 1993-1998.

According to FAO (*Projected Pulp and Paper Mills...*), at the beginning of the 1990s, 16 African countries had pulp and paper mill projects covering the period 1990-2000. In terms of numbers of project, Egypt led with 10, followed by Morocco (5), Kenya (4), Cote d'Ivoire (3), and Zimbabwe (3). Some of the projects were integrated based on bagasse in Cote d'Ivoire, Egypt, Ethiopia, Kenya, and the Sudan; rice straw in Egypt; eucalyptus in Morcco and Sudan; soft wood in Cote d'Ivoire, Malawi, and Mozambique; waste paper in Cote d'Ivoire, Egypt, Mali and Zimbabwe; agricultural residues in Mali, and Tunisia.

Annual capacities of pulp mill projects (in tons) range from 2,000 (based on eucalyptus) in Morocco to 100,000 (based on pine and mixed tropical hardwoods) in Nigeria and 100,000 (based on bagasse, kenaf and eucalyptus) in the Sudan for export. Some of the paper mills are pulp import-oriented. Paper mill capacities range between 1,000 tons per year in a number of countries and 85,000 tons per year in Zimbabwe.

## Priority Products

As stated earlier, books, paper, pencils, pens, rulers, and protractors are among the priority products under present African conditions and needs. Paper, obviously, occupies the highest priority. Besides its use in educational activities, including book making, it is an essential input to the functioning of government and business, the media, and packaging.

## Strategies for Development

With reduced availability due to growing supply/demand gap and escalating cost of wood and other inputs for pulp making, the availability of paper, the most important educational material, at affordable prices may prove to be difficult in the future. In 1995, pulp prices per ton almost doubled from $380 to about $750. It is therefore apparent that something has got to be done soon to develop the pulp industry in Africa.

Although the impact of dwindling wood resources may not be visible now, its adverse effect could manifest itself through opportunities foregone in countries with rapidly disappearing forests. Such countries may not be able to develop the pulp and paper industries for want of adequate wood supplies. A similar conclusion, but more so, applies to other African countries which are dependent on the import of pulp and paper and are not endowed with wood needed to develop conventional pulp mills. Worse still is the fact that the technology for pulping heterogeneous tropical hard woods, the most common in African forests, is not that developed. This, coupled with the highly polluting nature of pulp and paper making (pollution abatement increasing capital cost by up to 20%)[4], the complex chemical recovery system involved and increasing technological sophistication makes conventional pulp making from wood, particularly the sulfate (Kraft) route, impossible for many countries.

What alternatives do African countries have? The alternative, perhaps, lies in the utilization of fast growing trees, such as eucalyptus with seven-year-cycle cropping (five year cropping of eucalyptus camaldulensis in Thailand and three croppings before replanting in Brazil) (Guest 1995), and non-wood fibers. The utilization of eucalyptus is likely to give the competitive edge to some countries as bleached kraft hardwood pulp could prove to be relatively cheap to produce. Pulp from sisal provides an option in countries producing sisal. Non-wood materials for pulp making include: bagasse, bamboo, reeds, straw, grass, cotton lint, and waste from timber and agricultural industries. Unfortunately, most of these alternatives, like hard woods, produce short-pulp and therefore need to be supplemented by long-pulp imports. The range of products that can be made from these raw materials is limited. For example, bagasse whose end-use is considered versatile, is suitable for making newsprint, writing-and-printing papers, and boards, while straw can be used for writing-and printing-papers, liner board and other types of board. Kenaf, which comprises long-fibers could possibly substitute long-fiber imports in some countries.

In view of the basic nature of paper, developing countries have no option but to develop some kind of pulping to at least satisfy part of their demand, even if it has to be subsidized for some time. Fortunately, the pulp industry, like many process industries, is characterized by material and technological options. The material options have been referred to above. The technological options comprise the mechanical, semi-chemical, and chemical processes, increasing in complexity in that order, and their many variants. It is possible that some countries will find variants that suit their needs. Mechanical pulping may be the answer in small and poorer countries, semi-chemical in larger countries, and chemical (sulfate) in large countries (in terms of population). Being the cheapest grade, use of mechanical pulp is, unfortunately, limited to newsprint. Countries with suitable wood resources, available or that can be developed in plantations, could possibly combine production for local consumption and export. The successful export-oriented pulp industry in Swaziland can be cited as an example. In any case, experience accumulated in operating pulp and paper mills based on non-wood inputs in countries such as Egypt, India, and the Philippines, would be worth considering when developing pulp and paper projects. Experience in India and the Philippines in pulping tropical hardwoods should be assessed for adoption to African conditions.

Recycling (3 to 5 times) of paper, if available in adequate quantities and at a reasonable price, is an additional option that should be considered, particularly for newsprint and packaging materials. The capital cost for a recycled unit is about half that for a kraft unit (Null 1996). Standardized and modular mini paper mills (250 t/d, by European standards), based on recycled fibers and chemical and mechanical pulps, can be procured through ECO-S of Finland, which provides franchised packages. Their capital and operational costs are lower than those of equivalent mills because, among other things, they are compact and do not dispose of liquid effluent (Westergard 1995). This route—which accounts for about 30 percent (over 35 percent in 1989 according to another source) of paper consumption in developed countries (UNIDO, *Appropriate ... Small Pulp Mills*) —and about 50 and 52 percent in the EU and Japan, respectively, in 1990 (UN, *Potentials and Policy Implications of Energy...* ) may prove difficult to justify because of the inadequate generation and high cost of collection of waste paper in many countries. In four countries for which information is available for 1989, the ratio of waste-paper utilization to paper and board production were Egypt (30%), Zimbabwe (38%), Algeria (47%), and Morocco (59%). Recovery rates in percent were 7.1, 26.3, 15.4 and 18.7, respectively (UNIDO, *Industry and Development: Global Report 1991/92*). Newsprint, cardboard, tissue paper, carton board, flutings, and liners for case making can be made from waste paper. Under certain circumstances, there may be merit in resorting to the manufacture of handmade paper and board based on rags, provided rags can be collected at affordable prices.

From the above, it is clear that developing pulp-and-paper projects is a complex process. Besides, pulp-and-paper projects are very capital intensive. According to Null (1996), during the period 1973-1993, *"capital spending for paper and allied products averaged 9.7% of sales."* The corresponding figures were: 5.9 for chemicals, 6.4 for primary metals, and 5.2 for all manufacturing. It would be worth spending time and money on identifying up-to-date alternative processes and carefully analyzing their relevance to the resources of and conditions in the country concerned. With the R&D undertaken elsewhere in the past two decades, it is not unlikely that a suitable technology could be found. It would, for instance, be interesting to find out what happened to the so called "universal pulping." UNIDO might help in this regard.

The problem of economies of scale and the attendant high investment and operating costs inherent in pulp-and paper-making could be mitigated through integration, backward and forward. The former refers to domestic exploitation of natural forest-cum-reafforestation or plantation of wood or the supply of non-wood inputs, the latter to production of dissolving pulp and viscose rayon (referred to in the section on textiles) and the whole range of woodworking industry.

The benefits of integration could be augmented by minimizing transport costs and cutting down the number of processes involved. Supply of bagasse to an adjoining pulp mill and fresh pulp to an adjoining paper mill are examples of savings on production and transport costs that can accrue through physical integration of facilities.

Integration with other secondary wood-processing industries could render viable an otherwise not viable pulp-and-paper project. Any combination of the following: saw milling; making panel, veneer, plywood, fiberboard and particleboard; furniture making; and package-making (bags, sacks, cartoons, crates, boxes, and pallets) constitute secondary wood processing. In addition, the economical use of wood residues and wastes, including slabs and off-cuts, could enhance that viabilitity. The multiplier effect that could accrue is evident.

Integration could be broadened through the production of some local resource-based non-wood inputs. These include: sizing materials (glue, rosin), fillers (sulfate of lime, kaolin), and coloring materials.

The development of the production of some educational materials, particularly books, paper, and pencils, may need cooperation among countries. The production of books could offer member states an opportunity to specialize and exchange their outputs.

## PACKAGING MATERIALS INDUSTRY

The purpose of packaging is to protect products during warehousing and distribution and enable them to reach the users intact as well as to extend the shelf-life of products such as food and pharmaceuticals. This means that the manufacture of packing materials needs to be developed concomitantly with basic needs industries. Packing materials are made from a variety of raw materials. These include: wood, fabrics, paper and paper board, glass, plastics, and metals sheets.

### Status of the Industry

Because of the low living standard in developing countries, very little packaging is used. The people utilize traditional local materials and/or resort to scavenging and buying used packages. Even those who can relatively afford such items continue to make use of packages after they have consumed their contents. Some industries have introduced the practice of returnable containers. More and more beverage industries are adopting the practice of using returnable glass and plastic bottles and plastic crates.

Production of packaging materials in most African countries is generally limited to the final stage of making packages. Many of the countries import materials for making packages as well as ready-to-use packages.

Many of the packaging industries produce a limited range of packages, mostly from wood, paper, cardboard, plastic, glass, and metal sheet. Although glass is produced in some countries, the glass industry has not, unfortunately, ventured much into the making of small bottles and vials for the pharmaceutical and cosmetic industries.

### Priority Products

Many of the common types of packing materials required in Africa are not very different from those in use in developed countries. The most important (both flexible and rigid) are those used to pack food, beverages, and pharmaceuticals. They include paper and plastic (polyethylene and polypropylene) sheets, sachets, bags, sacks; paper boxes and cartons; plastic and glass bottles and jars; metal cans; and wooden boxes and crates. Plastic retail carryout bags are gaining popularity for food packaging in groceries and other food shops. Some of the packages, designed and made for conditions in developed countries, are, however, not suited to the hot and humid as well as dry area characteristics of most of the continent. Packaging materials for domestic use, including bags and sacks from natural fibers, as long as they serve the purpose, need not be as sophisticated and costly as those in developed countries.

## Strategies for Development

The potential for developing the packaging industry to meet both existing and future demand is great. It needs to diversify its product mix with a view to replacing, to the maximum extent possible, those materials that Africa continues to import in large quantities. For the short and medium term, conventional packages seem to be adequate, although relatively new innovations, such as shrink-packaging, could be adopted.

Manufacture of packages is generally limited to relatively large content units. Practically all small containers and bottles and vials for the pharmaceutical and cosmetics industries are imported. Production of such packages could start in existing production facilities, using existing infrastructure and experience gained in operating the facilities.

The crucial importance of packaging, particularly for goods destined for export, needs no emphasis. This is one of the weak links in developing manufactures for export. No matter how good the quality of the contents, if the package is not up to the standard of the countries in which it is marketed, it is unlikely to penetrate the market. The sooner R&D is conducted into packaging materials and making packages, the better the future of packaging. Exporters should follow changes in packaging regulations and new trends in packaging in importing countries and take quick measures to conform to the new requirements. They should keep track of the Council Directives of the European Community and the Fair Packaging and Labeling Act of the United States of America.

The culture of hygienic re-use of packages and returnable containers should be encouraged, as this conserves and optimizes the utilization of raw materials and energy that is required to make packages as well as saves the foreign exchange spent on importing plastic granules, paper, pulp, and metal sheets.

Inadequate distribution methods, poor handling, maximizing the use of local raw materials (sisal, kenaf, raffia) and reducing dependency on imported inputs need to be taken into account when selecting and developing packaging materials under African conditions. Exposure to experience in kenaf in Zambia and raffia in Angola (UNIDO, *Industry and Development, No. 30*) and sisal in Tanzania may prove useful in deciding between indigenous natural fibers and imported synthetic fibers for bags and sacks. Maximizing the recycling and utilization of waste paper and rags should be among measures taken when developing the packaging industry.

Many of the small food, beverage, etc. industries are too small to operate their own modern packaging units. Their packaging operations could be handled by specialized packaging facilities serving a group of related small-scale industries.

The industries themselves could partially or fully own or subcontract the packaging operations to the central packing units.

As in many of the industries dealt with in this book, the application of the multipurpose concept to packaging should be looked into. In other words, a packaging plant should, whenever feasible, be designed to accommodate the manufacture of different types of packaging containers from as many materials as possible. Of course, manual packing, when practical, may be worth resorting to, as this would contribute to absorbing more labor.

## BIBLIOGRAPHY

ADB, 1996, *African Development Report 1996*, Abidjan.

ADB, 1997, *African Development Report 1997*, Oxford University Press Inc., New York.

Bannerman, H. R./WHO, 1983, *Traditional Medicine and Health Care Coverage*, WHO, Geneva.

Ebey-Tessendorf, K.L. and Cunningham P.W., 1997, "Africa: in Search of Solutions," *World Health*, WHO, March-April 1997.

ECA, 1985, *Technical Compendium on Composite Flours*, Addis Ababa.

ECA, 1989, *Technical Publication on the Application of Research Findings in the Development of Pharmaceutical Industries on the Basis of Indigenous Raw Materials*, ECA/IND/CHM/003/89, Addis Ababa.

ECA, 1991, *Technical Publication: Compendium on Selected Technologies and Equipment for Processing Maize, Tubers and Palm Oil*, ECA/IHSD/AGR/010/91, Addis Ababa.

ECA, 1992, "Urbanization Trends in Africa, and Prospects for the Development of Local Building Materials for Low Cost Housing," *Focus on African Industry*, Volume V, No. 2, Addis Ababa.

ECA, 1993, *Background Information to the Report to the Eleventh meeting of the Conference of African Ministers of Industry on Assessment of Policies and Strategies for the Rehabilitation and Revitalization of African Industries in Selected Sub-sectors (case studies)*, CAMI.11/4/Inf., Addis Ababa.

ECA, 1993, *Focus on African Industry*, Volume VI, No. 1, Addis Ababa.

ECA/FAO, 1994, *Adequate Feed and Feeding: a Prerequisite for Sustainable Animal Agriculture Development in Tropical Africa*, Addis Ababa.

ECA, 1996, *Africa in the 1990s and Beyond: ECA-Revised Long-Term Development Perspectives Study* (ECA/SERPD/TP/96/3), Addis Ababa.

FAO, 1980, *Regional Food Plan for Africa*, Rome.

FAO, 1986, *African Agriculture: the next 25 Years, Annex V, Inputs Supply and Incentive Policies*, Rome.

FAO, 1986, *Atlas of African Agriculture (*African agriculture: the next 25 years), Rome.

FAO, 1991, *Projected Pulp and Paper Mills in the World 1990-2000*, Rome.

FAO, 1994, *The State of Food and Agriculture 1994*, Rome.

FAO, 1995, *Dimension of Need: An Atlas of Food and Agriculture*, Rome.

Gogerty, Rex, 1996, "Crop Leftovers: More Uses, More Value," *Resource: Engineering & Technology for a Sustainable World*, July 1996.

Guest, David, 1995, "The Thai Advance toward a State-of-the-art MIill," *Pulp and Paper International*, November 1995.

Hollen, Norma, Jane Saddler and Anna Langford L., 1979, *Textiles*, fifth edition, Macmillan Publishing Co., Inc., New York.

ILO, 1984, *Small-scale Maize Milling,* Technical Memorandum No.7, Geneva.

International Federation of Pharmaceutical Manufacturers Associations, 1993/94, "Pharmaceutical Industry/WHO Colaboration Yields Medicine to Help Treat AIDS in Afrca," *Health Horizons,* No. 21, Winter 1993/94.

International Federation of Pharmaceutical Manufacturers Associations, 1994, "Antimalarial Drugs, Protect Pregnant Women and Newborns," Health *Horizons,* No. 22, Spring 1994.

Melrose, Dianna, 1983 (reprinted), *Bitter Pills,* OXFAM, Oxfam Print Unit, Oxford.

Null, David, 1996, "Risks of Recycled Fiber Projects Make Virgin Fiber More Attractive," *Pulp & Paper*, July 1996.

OAU/STRC, 1985, *African Pharmacopoeia,* Vol. I, Lagos.

Ristic, Miodrag and McIntyre Ian, editors, 1981, *Diseases of Cattle in the Tropics*, Marinus Nijhoff Publishers, The Hague.

Rosenblatt, W.H., 1997, "Surplus Medical Supplies," *World Health,* WHO, March-April 1997.

Som, J. Ngo, 1997, "Improving the Nutritional Status of the African Child," *African Technology Forum.*

The Boston Globe, 1997, "Herbal Renewal," July 13, 1997.

The Economist, 1995, *Tuberculosis Join the DOTS*, No. 7915, May 20, 1995.

UN, 1974, *International Trade in Cotton Textiles and the Developing Countries: Problems and Prospects*, New York.

UN, 1995, *World Economic and Social Survey 1995*, New York.

UN, 1996, *The Chemical Industry in 1994: Annual Review,* Economic Commission for Europe, Geneva.

UN, 1996, *World Economic and Social Survey 1996*, New York.

UN, 1997, *Potentials and Policy Implications of Energy and Material Efficiency Improvement,* New York.

UNCTAD/GATT, 1974, *Markets for Selected Medicinal Plants and their Derivatives*, Geneva.

UNDP/World Bank/WHO, 1996, "In Sickness or in Health: TDR's Partners," *TDR News,* June 1996.

UNIDO, 1969, *Building Materials Industry,* Industrialization of Developing Countries: Problems and Prospects, Monographs on Industrial Development, No. 3, UN, New York.

UNIDO, 1969, *Textile Industry,* Industrialization of Developing Countries: Problems and Prospects, UNIDO Monographs on Industrial Development, No. 7, UN, New York

UNIDO, 1979, *Appropriate Industrial Technology for Paper Products and Small pulp Mills,* Monographs on Appropriate Industrial Technology, No. 3, New York.

UNIDO, 1979, *Integrational Economic and Technical Cooperation among Developing Countries in the Pharmaceutical Sector, UNIDO/IOD.347, Vienna.*

UNIDO, 1980, *Appropriate Industrial Technology for Construction and Building Materials*, Monographs on Appropriate Industrial Technology, No. 12, UN, New York.

UINDO, 1983, *The Development of Drugs Based on Medicinal Plants,* ID/WG.393/1, Vienna.

UNIDO, 1987, *Opportunities for the Manufacture of Pharmaceuticals in Developing Countries*, PPD.48, Vienna.

UNIDO, 1987, *The Building Materials Industry: Its Role in Low-cost Shelter Programmes*, PPD.62, Vienna.

UNIDO, 1991, *Industry and Development: Global Report 1991/92*, Vienna.

UNIDO, 1991, *Industry and Development*, No. 30, Vienna.

UNIDO, 1993, *Industry and Development: Global Report 1993/94*, Vienna.

UNIDO, 1995, *Lightening the Load* (XA/RAF/94/126), Vienna.

UNIDO, undated, "Building Materials Industry in Africa," *Industry Africa*, IDDA Journal of the Industrial Development Decade for Africa, No. 4, Vienna.

UNIDO, undated, "Prospects for the Textile and Wearing Apparel Industries in the Countries of North Africa," *Industry Africa*, IDDA Journal of the Industrial Development Decade for Africa, No. 4, Vienna.

UNIDO, ——, UNIDO/IO.569, Vienna.

UNIDO, ——, *The Building Materials Industry in Developing Countries: an Analytical Appraisal*, UNIDO/IS.512, Vienna.

UNIDO, ——, *Appropriate ... Small Pulp Mills*, Vienna.

UNIDO, ——, *Appropriate industrial...Materials*, Vienna.

UNIDO/ECA, 1997, *Agro-related Industrial Development in Africa*, Thirteenth Meeting of the Conference of African Ministers of Industry (CAMI. 13/12), Accra.

Westergard, Sivert, 1995, "The Mini Urban Mill—Newsprint, Tissue and Board," *Paper Technology*, October 1995.

WHO, 1988, *The World Drug Situation*, Geneva.

WHO, 1993, *Implementation of the Global Strategy for Health for All by the Year 2000*, Second Edition, Geneva.

WHO, 1995, *The World Health Report 1995: Bridging the Gaps*, Geneva.

WHO, 1996, "Leprosy," *Fact Sheet*, October 1996.

WHO, 1998, "Multilateral Perspective on Malaria Begins to Take Shape," *TDR News*, February 1998.

## NOTES

1. Control is an option. One such option is the use of insecticide-treated nets. The Net Gain for Africa Task Force includes wide availability and affordability of nets among its objectives (WHO, *TDR news*, June 1997).

2. A glimmer of hope from Kasisi Orphanage in Lusaka, Zambia, 23 children out of 130 who tested HIV positive three years earlier were reported to have tested negative after treatment with various antibiotics (*The Ethiopian Herald*, July 25, 1995). A discovery in Tanzania reported in August 1995 relates to reducing the incidence of AIDS by treating sexually transmitted diseases.

3. African countries could establish working relationship with the Thailand—Tropical Disease Research reported being established in 1997. Malaria, hook-worm, tuberculosis, leprosy, schistosomiasis, onchocerciasis, trypanosomiasis, and AIDS are among the targeted diseases. National scientists of developing countries can obtain grants for research in such diseases (WHO, *TDR news*, June 1997).

4. R&D being conducted in the world will, hopefully, come out with pulp technology that could mitigate the cost of pollution. An example of such technology is the use of heat-resistant microbes in treating air and water emissions at the temperature of the effluents devised by the Pulp and Paper Center in the University of Toronto, Canada (*Chemical Engineering Progress*, February 1998).

## CHAPTER 9

# AGRICULTURAL CHEMICALS

Continuous cropping for centuries without replacing plant nutrients has depleted the African soils of their plant nutrients. For this and other reasons, including mineral leaching caused by heavy rainfall and high temperatures, soil fertility continues to decline, as indicated by deteriorating crop yields which are already very low. Population pressure is in the process of further fragmenting the already small land holdings of African farmers and the bringing into cultivation of unsuitable, fragile soils. This, coupled with chronic and periodically recurring droughts, has rendered many African countries incapable of feeding themselves. Under these circumstances, sustainable food production will have to increase considerably by bringing more land under cultivation, where such land exists, as has been the case in the past. It appears, however, that the solution to narrowing the growing gap between production and consumption lies mainly in increasing yield through intensive cultivation and labor productivity. This is confirmed by FAO, which estimated the following percent contributions to growth in crop production in Sub-Saharan Africa from 1988-1990 to 2010: increased yield (53), expansion of arable land (30), and cropping intensity (17) (World Bank, *World Resources 1996-97)*. The solutions to food shortage, according to another source, "must *be found in technical means of raising output, such as high-yielding seeds,*[1] *irrigation and fertilizers"* (*The Economist*, November 16, 1996).

According to an FAO study, rain-fed crops can be grown on about 30 percent of the land in Sub-Saharan Africa. One-quarter of this is farmed while the balance is generally covered by primary forest. Based on past experience (0.7% annual expansion of cultivated land in the 1970s and 1980s) and the need, for obvious reasons, to retain the forest intact, there is no option but to adopt farming systems that focus on sustainable intensive cultivation and are backed by policies that enable the farmer to be competitive. In this connection, subsidies given to European and American farmers should be taken into account when formulating and adopting such policies.

Because of high productivity a very small percent of the population in developed countries is engaged in farming compared with about 80 percent in Africa. According to the Voice of America (November 18, 1995), for instance, American farm workers in 1995 totaled 3.4 million, a mere 1.4 percent of the total population. The phenomenal increase in agricultural productivity may be illustrated by what has happened in the United States in the last 50 years. Between 1945 and 1993 the number of American farms shrank from 5.9 million to 2.1 million (Samuelson 1995), thanks to the optimal application of science and technology.

In the short run, under current African conditions, agricultural chemicals are among the inputs that could significantly increase soil fertility and thereby agricultural productivity, thus enabling the African farmer to produce more from the same plot of land. The potential for raising productivity is high and practical in view of the fact that current applications of agricultural chemicals are nil or below agronomic requirements and do not require high capital investment.

Although there are many products that constitute agricultural chemicals, fertilizers and pesticides are the most important, both in terms of quantity used and usefulness. Among the modern agricultural inputs, both groups of chemicals have the advantage of showing immediate results within one cropping season. In other words, application of fertilizers and pesticides with improved farming practices could start immediately, pending the introduction of other inputs. Fertilizers are the single most efficient and cost-effective solution to the problem of low-fertility soils, considered the major constraint on crop production. It is undoubtedly the recognition of the crucial role that fertilizers play in increasing agricultural productivity and production that prompted the OAU to establish in Harare, Zimbabwe, the African Centre for Fertilizer Development (ACFD,) whose main objective is to *"stimulate the proper production and use of fertilizers in order to increase crop yields and farmers' incomes"* (ACFD, *Brochure...Development*). The International Fertilizer Development Centre in the USA (Muscle Shoals, Alabama) supports ACFD in fulfilling its objectives.

It is possible that the growing food deficit could be reduced significantly within a short time by adopting good farming practices and using selected and improved seeds and applying fertilizers and pesticides. Reduction of food losses through good farming practices and the use of pesticides could substantially increase availability of food. In subsequent stages, with further improvements in agricultural practices and inputs (mechanization, use of hybrid seeds, increased use of fertilizers, pesticides, and irrigation), food self-sufficiency could be maximized. The hope that Africa will feed itself is pinned on the exploitation of this potential. It is this hope that is the basis of this book.

It is unlikely, however, that a desirable level of food self-sufficiency can be attained as long as wheat consumption continues to grow and is not, at least in part, substituted by maize, sorghum, cassava, etc. Governments need to devise ways and means to curb the taste for wheat being increasingly acquired by Africans in view of the fact that the possibility for increasing the production of wheat in Africa is not that promising.

## FERTILIZERS

All straight, compound, and mixed fertilizers are in use in the region. Because of cheaper transport costs per unit of nutrient, where transport cost is a determinant cost factor under African conditions, and less labor requirement in their application, the trend is towards the use of mixed and compound fertilizers, particularly the latter. Diammonium phosphate and urea are among the fertilizers that deserve promotion. As African soils are generally richer in potash than in nitrogenous and phosphate fertilizers, consumption of potash fertilizers is relatively low at present.

Table 9.1 gives indications of yields of some crops grown in four African countries. The very low yields speak for themselves. Except for groundnut and cotton, Kenya registered the highest yields, reflecting the higher agricultural level attained by Kenya. Comparison of these low yields with those in developed countries and with yields achieved recently and being achieved in Ethiopia (see Chapter 3) offers an indication of the potential for increasing food productivity and production. Fertilizer applications in most African countries are below agronomic requirements.

| | Wheat | Barley | Rice | Maize | Sorghum | Potato | Cassva | Ground -nut | Cotton seed | Sugar cane (t) | Coffee | Tea | Cocoa | Tobacco |
|---|---|---|---|---|---|---|---|---|---|---|---|---|---|---|
| **TABLE 9.1** AVERAGE YIELD PER HECTARE OF SELECTED CROPS IN FOUR AFRICAN COUNTRIES IN LATE 1980s (kg/hectare) | | | | | | | | | | | | | | |
| Congo | ... | ... | 1000 | 55 | ... | | 6657 | 603 | ... | 52.9 | 509 | ... | ... | ... |
| Ethiopia | 908 | 802 | ... | 1034 | ... | 6182 | ... | 596 | 2143 | 103.9 | 273 | ... | | ... |
| Kenya | 1721 | 965 | 5714 | 1267 | 1048 | 7500 | 7888 | 573 | 272 | 111.7 | 731 | 1450 | - | 4000 |
| Congo K | ... | ... | 821 | 714 | 714 | ... | 6649 | 702 | 357 | 44.9 | 380 | 663 | 243 | ... |
| Ethiopia (1994/95) | 3200 | | | 6000 | 3000 | | | | | | | | | |

Source: Compiled from M. M. Suri & Associates Pvt.Ltd./ECA, 1982, *Model Prefeasibility Study on Pesticide Formulation Units*, Addis Ababa.

Notes: Sugar cane in tons/hectare.

## Status of the Industry

Despite its dire need for fertilizers, the continent is the smallest user of fertilizers in the world. It consumed 3.8 million tons of nutrients in 1992/93 compared to 125.9 million tons for the world as a whole (see Annex 9.1). This works out at a mere 3.0 percent of world consumption. This goes down to 2.4 percent for Africa (excluding South Africa) and 1.1 percent for Sub-Saharan Africa.

Annex 9.2 shows the continent's share in world consumption of fertilizers by nutrients during the period 1975/76-1988/89. Its share in world consumption in 1985/86 were: 1.2 percent of N, 2.0 percent of $P_2O_5$ and 1.2 percent of $K_2O$. The corresponding figures for Latin America were 4.9, 7.0, and 6.6 and for the Near East, 3.9, 4.4 and 0.5.

In terms of intensity of fertilizer application, the continent is at the bottom of the league. Total fertilizer application per hectare of arable land and permanent crops increased from 9.6 kg in 1970 to 20.1 kg in 1985 in contrast to 49.0 and 87.1, respectively, for the world as a whole (Annex 9.1). The rates for the continent work out at 19.6 percent and 23.1 percent of those of the world. These figures would be substantially lower if countries such as Egypt (with corresponding rates of 131.2 and 347.3) and South Africa (42.2 and 66.7) were excluded. This would mean that most fertilizer applications are too low to maintain soil fertility and hence raise production appreciably. At the continent level, average annual fertilizer use on cropland (in kg/hectare) increased from 19 in 1983 to 21 in 1993, while that of the world fell from 88 to 83 (World Bank, *World Resources 1996-97*).

From figures derived (Ahmed El- Deeb 1992), Egyptian demand for N is projected to increase from 660,000 tons in 1988/89 to 870,000 tons in 1999/2000 and for $P_2O_5$ from 190,000 tons to 240,000 tons.

Consumption ratio ($N:P_2O_5:K_2O$) in the continent, characterized by relatively high $P_2O_5$ content, is significantly different from that of the rest of the world. It changed almost steadily from 1.00:0.80:0.40 in 1983/84 to 1.00:0.71:0.35 in 1988/89. During the same period, the world ratio changed marginally from 1.00:0.49:0.38 to 1.00:0.48:0.35. It is likely that the continent's ratio will continue to gravitate towards that of the world.

During the period 1975/76-1985/86, the following trends seem to have prevailed with regard to all fertilizer nutrients: rising production, imports, exports, and consumption and fluctuating net exports and consumption/production gaps.

Between 1985/86 and 1992/93, exports appeared to show a steady growth, while others fluctuated or stagnated. Consumption hovered around 3.6 million tons. The droughts that occurred during the first half of the 1990s may partly explain the stagnant consumption.

The rising cost of fertilizers is likely to have adversely affected the use of fertilizers in the latter part of the first half of the 1990s. This is illustrated in Table 9.2. Prices for fertilizer intermediates and fertilizer materials, except potash fertilizers and ammonium sulfate, fell between December 3, 1990 and January 4, 1993. As may be observed from the table, the prices of all non-potash fertilizers increased substantially in May 2, 1995 over those of January 4, 1990. The increases were: 78.2 percent for urea, 48.9 percent for diammonium phosphate, 19.9 percent for triple superphosphate, and 13.8 percent for compound fertilizers. Fluctuating and such high increases in prices coupled with similar increases in freight rates are, naturally, not welcomed by the African farmers. Unless subsidized to steady and slow price increases, many of the small farmers who use fertilizers as well as potential users (particularly those engaged in rainfed agriculture in countries such as Ethiopia, where fertilizer consumption doubled to the level of 200, 000 tons since the begining of the decade) could be discouraged from applying fertilizers. In this connection, it should be noted that the fertilizer price/output ratios are said to be lower in Africa than in Asia. The same applies to yields, mainly because of inadequate adaptive research and extension services.

TABLE 9.2
INTERNATIONAL FERTILIZER PRICE INDICATIONS ($ / t)

| Intermediate/fertilizer | Origin | 3 December 1990 | 4 January 1993 | 3 February 1994 | 5 January 1995 | 2 May 1995 |
|---|---|---|---|---|---|---|
| Ammonia | FOB Middle East | 115-130 | 90-110 | 115-125 | 175-195 | 210-215 |
| Phosphoric acid (P2O5) | FOB US Gulf | 280-300 | 235-245 | 225-235 | 275-285 | 290-355 |
| Ammonium sulfate | FOB bgd West Europe | 40-45 | 55-62 | 55-62 | 55-62 | 70-78 |
| Urea | FOB bgd Middle East | 165-170 | 122-130 | 124-127 | 223-225 | 222-227 |
| Diammonium phosphate | FOB bulk US Gulf | 184-187 | 133-135 | 156-160 | 200-201 | 197-202 |
| Triple superphosphate | FOB bulk US Gulf | 153-154 | 122-124 | 125-127 | 138-140 | 145-150 |
| Muriate of potash, standard | FOB bulk Northwest Europe | 95-102 | 100-110 | 75-108 | 105-115 | 95-115 |
| Muriate of potash, coarse/granular | FOB bulk Northwest Europe | 109-111 | 120-125 | 105-115 [a] | 105-125 | 105-125 |
| Sulfate of potash | FOB bulk Northwest Europe | 180-190 | 185-195 | 175-185 | 170-188 | 170-188 |
| Compounds, 15-15-15 bgd | FOB West Europe (MOP based) | 160-180 | 140-150 | 140-150 | 140-150 | 160-170 |

Source :  Compiled from FADINAP, 1990, 1993-1995, *Fertilizer Trade Information*, (dates of publication correspond to those shown above).
a Bagged

Phosphate fertilizers account for most of the exports, 11.3 percent of world exports in 1985/86, (Annex 9.2). Morocco and Tunisia were the major exporters, accounting between them for about 90 percent of Africa's exports. As for potash fertilizers, Africa is completely dependent on imports since the closure following inundation of the Holle potash mine in the Congo in 1977. The mine had attained peak production of 475,279 tons of potassium chloride (60% $K_2O$) in 1974 (ECA, ECA/NRD/MRU/TP/3/94). More details are given in Annex 9.1.

The impression gained from the previous paragraphs as well as from Annex 9.1 may be misleading in as far as the applicability of some of the positive factors to developing Africa and individual countries is concerned. The production, trade, and consumption figures in the annex refer to the continent; the share of developing Africa is substantially less. In 1990/91, for instance, this share ranged between 41 percent for nitrogenous fertilizers (N) consumption and 94 percent for exports of phosphate fertilizers ($P_2O_5$). The balance was accounted for by South Africa.

The number of countries producing fertilizers are not only limited, but the major producers export most of their outputs outside the region. Those which produce intermediates are even more limited (Annexes 9.4, 9.5 and 9.6). They comprise Algeria, Egypt, Libya, Tunisia, Nigeria, Madagascar, Zambia, and Zimbabwe for ammonia and Algeria, Morocco, Tunisia, Senegal, Tanzania, and Zimbabwe for phosphoric acid.

As shown in Annex 9.3, Africa is a net importer of ammonia, but a net exporter of phosphoric acid. During the period 1980-1991, net imports of the former peaked at 642,500 tons of N in 1989. This is mainly due to Algerian exports, which tripled in 1990-1991, and Libyan exports which increased from 4,600 tons in 1989 to 104, 600 tons in 1991. As for phosphoric acid exported from Morocco, Tunisia, Senegal, and South Africa, in descending order of importance, the peak was attained at 2.29 million tons of $P_2O_5$ in 1991. Morocco is the leading exporter of phosphoric acid in the world.

It is apparent that the majority of African countries are importers of fertilizers; some of them also import intermediates (ammonia and phosphoric acid) for local processing. In view of this and the consumption/production gaps (approximated by net imports), as well as the fact that many of the plants are old and obsolete and may need to be replaced or closed down (see Annex 9.1), it is apparent that there is plenty of room for new capacities. What is more, as total consumption accounts for only a small fraction of potential demand, additional capacities will be required to meet demand if the region is to achieve a significant level of food self-sufficiency. According to ECA projections based on FAO estimates, continental demand will increase from 3.6 million tons in 1993 to 7.0 million tons (historical scenario) or 9.3 million tons (normative scenario) by 2008. The last figure is equivalent to 9.0, 7.2, and 6.6 million tons of nitrogenous, phosphate, and potash fertilizer materials respectively (ECA, *Africa in the 1990s and Beyond:* ....).

Demand for fertilizers in SADC was projected to rise to 1.36 million tons of all nutrients in 1995, versus consumption of 896,000 tons in 1987. The breakdown of this projection by nutrient and by former SADCC and South Africa is shown in Table 9.3. From the table, it is apparent that South Africa has the lion's share of 64 percent of all nutrients. Zimbabwe, the next in line, trails far behind with 13.2 percent, followed by Malawi (10.3 percent), Zambia (6.8 percent) and Tanzania (4.1 percent).

**TABLE 9.3**
ACTUAL 1987 FERTILIZER CONSUMPTION AND PROJECTED DEMAND IN SADC in 1995/96 (1000 t nutrients)

| | Consumption (1987) | | | | Projection (1995) | | | |
|---|---|---|---|---|---|---|---|---|
| | N | $P_2O_5$ | $K_2O$ | Total | N | $P_2O_5$ | $K_2O$ | Total |
| SADCC countries (former) | | | | 356.3 | 315.6 | 140.1 | 60.7 | 516.4 |
| South Africa | 329 | 120 | 91 | 540 | 410 | 290 | 145 | 845 |
| SADC (incl. South Africa) | | | | 896.3 | 725.6 | 430.1 | 205.7 | 1361.4 |
| Share of South Africa (%) | | | | 60.3 | 56.5 | 67.4 | 70.5 | 62.1 |

Source: The World Bank/SADC, 1991, *An Action Plan for the Development of the Fertilizer Industry* ( Main Report, working draft and Working Paper 1), Washington DC.

Table 9.4 gives some ideas in regard to the situation of the fertilizer industry in early 1980s (1983/1984). Total capacity utilization stood at 47.9 and 50.1 percent for phosphate and nitrogenous fertilizers, respectively. Planned capacities, if implemented, would nearly double the former's capacity and more than double that of the latter.

**TABLE 9.4**
FERTILIZER INDUSTRY IN AFRICA IN 1883/84
(1000 t of nutrients)

| | $P_2O_5$[a] Phosphatic fertilizer | | | | $P_2O_5$[a] planned capacity | N[b] Nitrogen fertilizer | | | | N[b] planned capacity |
|---|---|---|---|---|---|---|---|---|---|---|
| | In-stalled capac-ity | 1983/84 prod-uction | % of local con-sumption | Export as % of prod-uction | | In-stalled capac-ity | 1983/84 prod-uction | % of total con-sumption | Export as % of prod-uction | |
| Mediterranean and arid North Africa | 2587 | 1196 | 93 | 74 | 2265 | 2054 | 983 | 98 | 33 | 1183 |
| Sudao-Sahelian Africa | 23 | 30 | 96 | 70 | 230 | - | 4 | 0 | 75 | 42 |
| Humid and Sub-humid West Africa | 18 | 6 | 1 | 50 | - | - | 2 | 0 | 67 | 602 |
| Humid Central Africa | - | 0 | 0 | 0 | - | - | 0 | 0 | 0 | 54 |
| Sub-humid and mountain East Africa | - | 0 | 0 | 0 | - | - | 0.0 | 13 | 0 | 46 |
| Sub-humid and semi-arid Southern Africa | 45 | 48 | 48 | 0 | - | 132 | 97 | 51 | 0 | 584 |
| Total | 2673 | 1280 | 89 | 71 | 2495 | 2186 | 1095 | 73 | 0 | 2511 |

Source: *African Agriculture: the next 25 Years, Annex V, Inputs Supply and Incentive Policies*, Rome.
    a $P_2O_5$ as phosphoric acid    b N derived from ammonia
Mediterranean and arid North Africa: Algeria, Egypt, Libya, Morocco, Tunisia.
Sudano-Sahelian Africa : Burkina Faso, Cape Verde, Chad, Djibouti, Gambia, Mali, Mauritania, Niger, Senegal, Somalia, Sudan.
Humid and Sub- humid West Africa: Benin, Ghana, Guinea, Guinea Bissaw, Cote d'Ivoire, Liberia, Nigeria, Sierra Leone, Togo.
Humid Central Africa: Cameroon, Central African Republic, Congo, Equatorial Guinea, Gabon, Sao Tome and Principe, Congo K.
Sub-humid and mountain East Africa: Burundi, Comoros, Ethiopia, Kenya, Madagascar, Mauritius, Rwanda Seychelles, Uganda.
Sub-humid and semi-arid Southern Africa: Angola, Botswana, Lesotho, Malawi, Mozambique, Namibia, Swaziland, Tanzania, Zambia, Zimbabwe

As is evident from Annexes 9.5 and 9.7, Morocco dominates in phosphoric acid ($P_2O_5$) capacities. Its annual combined existing capacity increased from 320,000 tons in 1973 to 2.62 million tons at the beginning of the 1990s. This was expected to almost double to 4.54 million tons by 1995 (5.2 million tons according to another source). Its annual fertilizer capacities in tons comprised: 320,000 of single superphosphate, 396,000 of triple superphosphate, 148,500 of ammonium-sulphide phosphate, 396,000 of monoammonium phosphate, 907,500 of diammonium phosphate, and 145,000 of NPK (Khennas 1992). The sulfur for making sulfuric acid for acidulating phosphate rock and ammonia and potash are imported. Diversification into the manufacture of detergents and dicalcium compounds and uranium extraction from phosphoric acid are possibilities under consideration in Morocco.

Tunisia is another country whose fertilizer industry is both in ward and out ward oriented. Unlike Morocco, however, it exports fertilizers (512,000 tons of DAP, 140,000 tons of ammonium nitrate and 155,000 tons of NPK in 1991).

In Egypt, capacities (tons/day) of natural gas-based nitrogenous fertilizer plants comprise: ammonia 4,000; nitric acid 3,400; urea 3,500; and ammonium nitrate (33.5%) 4,000 (Abdel Monem Ahmed Akeel). In 1992/93, Egypt produced the following fertilizers (tons): 387,000 of urea, 447,000 of ammonium nitrate, 20,000 of ammonium sulfate and 21,000 of calcium ammonium nitrate, all in N, and 140,000 of single superphosphate and 35,000 of triple superphosphate. Nitrogenous fertilizer (N) production is expected to increase to 1.03 million tons by 2000 (Osama El Ganiny 1993). Annual capacities in tons in Algeria were: ammonia 990,000, ammonium nitrate 825,000, urea 130,000, and phosphate fertilizers 550,000 (Boudiaf S.).

Generally, African fertilizer plants, particularly those that are state-owned, are characterized by low capacity utilization. The rates of capacity utilization for Algeria shown in Annex 9.7 illustrate this. These rates are the best performance achieved by the fertilizer plants in Algeria (Boudiaf). Errors made during project development, bad maintenance, lack of qualified workers, and small markets are among the reasons given by the author for such poor performance. Nitrogen Chemicals of Zambia, which had gone through a similar experience (design deficiencies, design and construction mistakes, insufficient technical expertise, poor maintenance, and low quality coal), has since been rehabilitated. In Tanzania, the Tanga Fertilizer Company ceased operation in 1991 for lack of imported inputs, inadequate skills and maintenance, etc. According to the World Bank, the Sable Chemical Industries Limited in Zimbabwe is a candidate for closure because of the growing scarcity and high price of electricity. These experiences do not, however, seem to apply to some of the major producers. According to Aboulhassen (1992), for instance, fertilizer plants in Tunisia operate at their maximum capacities and optimal yield.

Fertilizer project ideas and projects abound in the region. They include extension and diversification of existing plants as well as new ones. Many of them, unfortunately, for lack of adequate markets, financial resources, etc., have not progressed beyond the project idea or pre-feasibility stages, and some of those which went beyond the decision-making stage failed to materialize. The last could be illustrated by the attempts made in Kenya. In 1976, Ken-Ren Chemicals and Fertilizers was created to established a fertilizer complex. Because of difficulties it wound up in 1978. A subsequent government attempt to revive the project, renamed National Agricultural Chemicals and Fertilizers Ltd., failed following disagreements with Stamicarbon, the consulting firm retained by the government (The British Sulfur Corporation Limited, *Fertilizer International*).

The Tebessa phosphate fertilizer project in Algeria, for which a feasibility study exists, was reported in 1992 to have been looking for joint-venture partners (Boudiaf S.). A Tanzanian ammonia/urea project has been under promotion for many years. In recent years, the World Bank has been assisting the SADC countries in identifying areas for cooperation in the development of the fertilizer industry. Because of natural gas reserves in Tanzania, Mozambique, and Angola, these countries were considered potential hosts for nitrogenous fertilizer industries for SADC.

## Priority Products

The use of low analysis straight fertilizers (ammonium nitrate, ammonium sulfate, single superphosphate, muriate of potash, and potassium sulfate) has been significant. This is in contrast with the trend in multi-nutrient (binary and ternary) formulations in the developed world (The British Sulfur Corporation Limited, *Phosphorous & Potassium*).

Although straight fertilizers are still required for agronomical reasons (specific applications) and some for their sulfur content (as African soils are, generally, sulfur-deficient), it is possible that future trends may be biased towards high analysis (concentrated and compound) fertilizers, particularly urea and diammonium phosphate. These types of fertilizers display lower costs per unit of nutrient; they are cheaper to transport; and they require less labor to apply. The first is an important factor in Africa, where transport costs are very high and generally involve long distances.

Finely ground phosphate rock could be used, particularly on acidic soils. Partially acidulated phosphate rock involving less sophisticated technology and less sulfuric acid would, of course, be preferred.

As for potash, potassium sulfate may be preferred to potassium chloride because of its sulfur content. As the price of the former is normally more than twice that of the latter, however, demand for it is likely to remain small relative to potassium chloride. Returning residues from cereal crops which *"contain as much as 80 % of the $K_2O$ that was taken up by the crop"* could reduce the need for potash fertilizers (Parish 1985).

## Strategies for Development

Fertilizer applications in many African countries are far from being optimal for lack of information on crop responses and optimal fertilization rates arising from absent or inadequate research and extension services. A few types of formulations are generally used for different soil conditions, crops, farming practices, and rainfall, resulting in imbalanced applications. In other words, the compositions used may be inappropriate in the sense that they are either under- or over-formulated. This would mean inadequate nutrients in the case of the former and waste in the latter. With time it is possible that correct fertilization practices will be used, based on knowledge of specific soil and climatic conditions and crop requirement.

Fertilizers are high-volume, low-value materials. Their transport cost figures prominently in the prices that the farmers pay. In view of this and for strategic reasons it would be preferable and advisable if fertilizers could be produced in locations that would minimize the overall cost (production as well as transport) to the farmer.

For the above reasons, fertilizer projects should be based as much as possible on an integrated approach, producing fertilizers from basic raw materials. This may not be possible in many countries because of small national markets and lack of resources. Under such circumstances, member states should resort to cooperation. The approach suggested is based on the stages of fertilizer processing. According to this approach, fertilizer intermediates would be produced in countries enjoying comparative advantages in terms of raw materials and energy as well as a relatively good transport system. Part of the intermediates would be processed into fertilizers in countries with adequate consumption justifying production. Countries that do not fall in either category would have to rely on bulk imports of fertilizers for local mixing or finished fertilizers for direct use.

As most African countries will have to continue to import fertilizers from outside the region until local production units are established, they should organize central purchasing/procurement agencies serving groups of countries similar to those suggested for pharmaceuticals in Chapter 8. The agencies could serve their members better if they could review and reduce the number of fertilizer specifications used.

As for locating fertilizer bagging or blending plants, it may be advisable to locate them in areas with similar soil and ecological conditions. This approach would cater to the specific needs of the area, reduce cost of transporting bulky materials (as the unit would be close to the farmers), and decentralize industries to the rural area, thereby contributing to the much-needed dispersal of industries in the rural area. In a study on economic implications of fertilizer specifications, fertilizers with ordinary formula, such as 15-15-15 from bulk blending units in West Africa, have been found to be about 9 percent cheaper than those imported. The corresponding figure for specific formula, such as 12-22-12+5+1, was about 20 percent (*Proceedings of the Second Annual Meeting of the African Fertilizer Trade ...* ). It is clear that a combination of local blending and central purchasing could significantly reduce the prices of imported fertilizers.

The countries hosting intermediate producing units may not have all the inputs required. They would resource such inputs from member states, thus providing means for cooperation at the stage of resourcing raw materials.

The studies related to cooperation in the development of the fertilizer industry in SADC carried out by the World Bank could be cited as a good beginning for cooperation in the fertilizer industry. The studies have come out with a plan of action for the development of the fertilizer industry in SADC which now includes South Africa. Based on the fertilizer supply options model, the Bank suggested the following actions:

• SADC and South Africa to fully interact resulting in considerable savings in supply costs in constrained cases;

• Move to lower-cost straight fertilizers resulting in considerable savings in supply costs;

• Improve transport and handling resulting in considerable savings in supply costs;

• Construct a 500,000 ton per year ammonia-urea plant near Maputo, resulting in savings and capacity utilization;

• Keep NCZ plant operating to capacity; and
• Construct a potash plant in Botswana, feasible at 163,000 tons per year, resulting in saving to SADC (The World Bank/SADC, *SADC Fertilizer ...*).

As noted earlier, the continent does not produce potash fertilizers and is therefore completely dependent on import. Economic potash deposits in Africa, and for that matter in the world, are limited; they are mainly in developed countries. Congo, Ethiopia, and Botswana are the only African countries with deposits of economic significance (see Chapter 4). Some years back it was reported that the Holle potash mine in the Congo which was closed because of flooding and mining difficulty (irregular nature of the deposit) was going to be revived. The fate of the project was not known to the author up to the time of the publication of this book.

In respect of the Ethiopian potash in Dallol, a market study commissioned by ECA was undertaken in 1981. The study whose objective was to identify and quantify the potential markets for Ethiopian potash, particularly in Asia, the largest potash importing region in the world concluded that Ethiopia " *can secure at least about 25 percent share of the total consumption in the region [Asia] by 1990 and 35 percent by 2000 AD*" (The Fertilizer [Planning & Development] India Limited/ECA). It was followed, in 1984, by undertaking Phase 1A Report (by PEC Engineering of France) which reviewed available geological data and possible mining methods based on recalculated ore reserves and made recommendations on further test work to be carried out in phase 1B. The Phase 1A Report was reviewed by a Canadian company which advised the government on follow-up activities to be undertaken (Kilborn Engineering, *Ethiopian Dallol Potash Project*). These reports were intended to provide information required to prepare a feasibility study. The latter apparently was not conducted, since it was not possible for security reasons until 1991 to undertake field work as the site was in the area where the liberation movements were active. Now that peace has prevailed in the whole country, activities related to the project could be resumed.

Potassium sulfate, a potash source preferred to potassium chloride for some applications because of its sulfur content, constitutes part of the effluents from the Sua Pan soda ash production in Botswana. A positive outcome of the pilot plant that was in operation at the beginning of this decade could lead to the extraction of potassium sulfate at the rate of 21,000 tons per year and/or a larger unit based on the unlimited reserves of brine (The World Bank/SADCC, *An Action Plan ...*).

Preinvestment studies on potash fertilizer production should be carried out, followed by promotion and implementation of viable projects in the shortest time possible, if the continent is to reduce its complete dependency on imports of such strategic agricultural inputs that are essential to the development of the agricultural sector, the number one priority sector of the region.

There have been and continue to be improvements in fertilizer processing in many parts of the world. Downsizing plants is of special significance to Africa. Ammonia mini-plants are a case in point. From the number of such plants constructed and under construction mostly in developing countries, it appears that one of the major constraints in the development of nitrogenous fertilizer industry is being eased. Ammonia plants of 100 to 300 tons-per-day capacities can be economical, provided inexpensive raw materials and transport can offset the high cost of small units (Parish 1985). Such units and others based on low-cost electricity for the simpler electrolytic process could be considered among options for remote areas.

African countries planning fertilizer projects would be advised to review developments in the fertilizer area. These includes scrutinizing experiences of developing countries which have adopted technologies to suit their conditions and needs. In  phosphate processing, for example, Tunisia has something to offer. SIAPE, a fertilizer manufacturing firm, has developed a simple reactor for making phosphoric acid with a number of advantages compared with the conventional process. The advantages include its capability to treat low-quality phosphate rock with a good conversion rate, the use of concentrated sulfuric acid, the low energy consumption, the mechanical destruction of foam, and the lower investment costs. SIAPE has also developed a simple process for making triple superphosphate using the wet-process route. Its processes are being used in many countries, such as Turkey, Romania, Bulgaria, and Syria (Aboulhassen 1992).

Partial acidulation of phosphate rock is another process that should be considered as an alternative to phosphate fertilizer making. This process tolerates impurities better and  yields a relatively low cost product with $P_2O_5$ content higher than the completely acidulated version. In this connection, experience of the International Fertilizer Development Centre (IFDC) in Togo and Zimbabwe would be relevant (ECA, ECA/NRD/MRU/TP/3/94).

Generally, raw materials determine the technology to be used. In ammonia production, with the availability of natural gas in a number of countries, it is unlikely that African countries will resort to the more expensive coal or electricity as a source of hydrogen when making ammonia. The local unavailability of sulfur is a major problem facing phosphate fertilizer manufacture in Africa. Import of sulfur should be minimized by maximizing the use of sulfur from pyrites, non-ferrous metal smelter operations, recovery from the processing of hydrocarbons and gypsum, if viable. As African natural gases are generally sweet, sulfur recovery from them cannot be that significant. Under the circumstances, it may be worthwhile for countries with adequate and inexpensive electricity to consider basing their phosphate fertilizer industry on electricity rather than on sulfur.

With respect to potash, Africa could and should go for both potassium chloride (the most popular) and potassium sulfate to meet the agronomic requirement for potash. The world potash market has been, however, characterized by high competition because of excess capacities. African countries with potash resources should undertake activities and studies to establish the viabilities of exploiting their deposits and have all the necessary preinvestment studies and strategies ready for implementing potash projects as soon as conditions permit, i.e., as soon as cyclical indications of closing world supply/demand gaps are visible. It would be difficult, if not impossible, to penetrate the world market if a strategy of this kind is not adopted and plans of action are not readily available for implementation.

The inadequacy of information on soil conditions was referred to earlier. In many countries whatever research was undertaken in the past does not seem to have been put to full use. There is an urgent need to do so now. Each and every country should have soil maps of the major food producing areas prepared in the shortest time possible. Soils need to be classified by type; their nutrient contents determined; and their correlation with crops and fertilizers use established through field trials. These together with use of improved and high-yield seeds and recommended application of fertilizers, improved farming methods (including crop rotation, intercropping, planting legumes for replacing nitrogen), water management, judicious use of pesticides and herbicides and mechanization will, in the long run, result in the optimum use of resources and optimum yield of food.

For want of resources and capacity at the country level, many of the activities suggested above are better done at multi-country level. There is, fortunately, an organization, the Fertilizer Advisory Development and Information Network for Asia and the Pacific (FADINAP) that could be emulated and that could provide assistance. ECA and UNIDO were in the process of promoting the establishment of a similar organization with wider scope, the African Regional Network for Agricultural Chemicals and Machinery with national technical liaison offices (TLOs) linking the Network with the countries and serving as information centers at the country level (ECA/UNIDO, CAMI.12/6[b]). The network is intended to yield benefits to the vast majority of the rural population in the form of increased agricultural productivity and development, including benefits accruing from regional cooperation at the level of production. Although fertilizer production is supposed to be the focus of the network, there will, nevertheless, be major duplication of activities with other existing organizations. These include the African Centre for Fertilizer Development (ACFD) in Harare, Zimbabwe, and DFTMIN, a marketing and distribution network in Lome, Togo. At a time when attempts are being made to rationalize and harmonize subregional and regional institutions in Africa, there is a need to rationalize the activities of these organizations and those of the proposed network. In this connection, it should be noted that African countries have an aversion, and rightly so, to proliferating institutions, as they have not been able to finance those that already exist. For these reasons it would make economic sense to create a single organization that could combine the objectives of all three and yet require substantially less resources.

The potential role of biotechnology and genetic engineering not only in supplementing fertilizers but also in reducing the need for fertilizers should be recognized from the outset. Plant-beneficial micro-organisms produce and improve plant nutrition. The well-known micro-organisms that fix nitrogen from the air, for example, reduce the nitrogen requirement of plants and therefore the application of nitrogenous fertilizers. Maximizing the utilization of plant-beneficial micro-organisms, when practical, is likely to boost production with less use of fertilizers—hence the advisability of African countries to start research into and utilize beneficial micro-orgaisms. The same applies to increasing livestock production through embryo transfer, biosynthesis of growth hormones, enhanced animal feed production, and gene splicing and transfer.

Overuse of fertilizers has harmful effects on plants and the quality of soil and water and results in eutrophication. It is likely that the optimal use of fertilizers that will be attained with increasing application based on results of soil analysis will minimize some of these problems. In this connection, it should be noted that breakthroughs in other technological areas are likely to contribute to lesser application of fertilizers. The American farmer is already benefiting from "precision farming," using Global Positioning System network based on navigation satellites, which enables him to apply the exact amount of fertilizer or pesticides needed in each square meter of his farm.

## PESTICIDES

Flora and fauna are more diversified in humid tropical and semi-tropical countries than in the temperate climate. This, unfortunately, also applies to pests, pathogens (fungi, bacteria, viruses, protozoa, and mycoplasmas), and weeds which thrive in such conditions. In other words, agricultural losses are more serious in Africa, especially when outbreaks of locust and army worm occur. It calls for good agricultural practices and crop protection, both at pre-harvest and post-harvest stages. The FAO-sponsored Locust Control Programme, among the first measures taken by FAO to reduce agricultural losses in the Sahel and East Africa, has been in operation since 1952.

Pre-harvest and post-harvest losses up to consumption (harvesting, transportation, milling, processing, and storage) of over 40 percent (Abdurahman 1991) is one of the reasons why Africa is increasingly depending on food import. Dried and stored cereal grains, oil seeds and pulses lose 5 to 15 percent of total dry weight, 20 to 40 percent for roots and tubers. In Ethiopia, pests are responsible for the loses of 30 percent of standing crops and 10 percent of stored grain (*The Ethiopian Herald*, February 26, 1995). In Ghana, storage losses for all food crops have been estimated at 15 to 30 percent (FAO, *The State of Food and Agriculture 1994*). The above loss figures contrast with the average minimum of 10 percent for cereal grains and legumes and 20 percent for perishables and fish adopted for planning purposes in developing countries (National Academy of Sciences, *Post-harvest Food Losses in Developing Countries*). It is obvious that reducing losses could substantially raise the availability of and therefore self-sufficiency in food if not completely eliminate dependency in many countries. In other words, with the present level of fertilizer inputs, but better farm practices and storage aimed at sustainable crop protection, including the use of adequate pesticides and herbicides, there is a possibility of closing the gap. The benefits that can accrue from pest control can be illustrated by the $4 in return earned by the American farmer for every $1 he/she invests in pesticides (Microsoft, *Encarta 96 Encyclopedia*). It seems that both governments and donors in Africa have been focusing their attention on increasing productivity and production and practically neglecting reduction of food losses. This bias against the reduction of food losses was counter to the *"50 percent reduction in overall food losses by 1985"* goal of the United Nations General Assembly adopted in 1975 (National Academy of Sciences, *Post-harvest Food Losses in Developing Countries*).

Another factor contributing to the dependency on food import is vector-borne diseases. Malaria, river blindness (onchocerciasis) transmitted by blackfly, sleeping sickness (trypanosomiasis) in man and (nagana) in cattle by tsetse fly, bilharzia (schistosomiasis) by snails, elephantiasis (filariasis) by mosquitoes and rinderpest (possibly paramyxovirus) are the main vector-borne and animal diseases prevalent in Africa. About 7 million $km^2$ of the continent are infested by tsetse fly (Abdulrahman Abdulahi). Because of these diseases, the input of the farm labor force is effectively reduced and use of animal draught is minimal in tsetse-fl-infested areas, resulting in poor agricultural productivity. The N'Dama and West African Shorthorn are trypano-tolerant, i.e., less susceptible to the disease than other cattle breeds. In the absence of vaccine for trypanosomiasis, breeding trypano-tolerant cattle may be the solution. The program being undertaken to eradicate this disease will, it is hoped, be crowned with success. Eradication of river blindness by the year 2000 is being carried out with the assistance of the Carter Center. It has been reported that the World Bank will start the eradication of onchoceriasis in 1996 and the process is expected to take 10 years.

Following the ban on the broad spectrum organochlorine insecticides, DDT and BHC, except for public health purposes in malaria control and eradication, for instance, it seems that use of pesticides in Africa has been inhibited. Because of the huge variety of substitutes, mainly targeted at specific pests and weeds, and their high costs, African farmers find it increasingly difficult and expensive to use substitutes for DDT, BHC, PCBs, dieldrin, lindane, etc. It should be noted here that African agricultural products containing chlorinated pesticide residues, such as DDT and BHC, are prohibited entry into developed country market. Under the circumstances, African countries have no alternative but to comply with the requirements of the developed countries. This means that they have to resort to the use of the expensive variety of pesticides and herbicides. In this connection, it is difficult to predict the implication of the 1996 United States reauthorization of the Federal Insecticide, Fungicide and Rodenticide Act which allows a cancer risk level of one in a million cancer-causing pesticides instead of the previous virtually zero tolerance. Pesticides and herbicides, undoubtedly, will have to play a major role in reducing food losses. In view of the problems inherent in the use of pesticides, however, emphasis needs to be put on their optimal use and on integrated pest management, i.e., integrated crop protection and pesticide management. Integrated pest management is a system whereby the control of pests is optimized using various combinations of biological, chemical, and physical methods. It has been defined by FAO Panel of Experts on Integrated Pest Control, Rome, (ESCAP, Agro-pesticides) as *"A pest management system that, in the context of the associated environment and the population dynamics of the pest species, utilizes all suitable techniques and methods in as compatible a manner as possible and maintains the pest population at levels below those causing economic injury."* Natural control which is environmentally safe constitutes a crucial component of integrated pest management. It is achieved mainly through natural enemies (parasites, predators, and microorganisms) which feed on or cause harm to pests, thereby maintaining ecological balance. At present, parasites and pest-resistant plants are considered effective biological control techniques. Judicious use of chemical pesticides is important because of the harm they can do to the predators, thus resulting in disruption in the natural equilibrium. Integrated pest management reduces the use of pesticides.

Obsolete pesticides pose great hazards in developing countries. Banned or deteriorated pesticides in Africa have been estimated at 15,000-20,000 tonnes and more than 100,000 tonnes in all developing countries. The offer by the agro-chemical industry to cover about 30 percent of the cost of disposal should be welcome (FAO, *Agro-chemical Industry...Developing Countries*).

## Status of the Industry

Continental consumption of pesticides which is very low is mostly covered by the import of finished formulations as well as intermediates for local formulation. At current prices, the import bill of $435.2 million in 1978 fell to $418.6 million in 1979 (M.M.Suri.../ECA), probably partly due to a lack of foreign exchange. The major importers (importing more than $20 million in 1979) in descending order of magnitude were: Nigeria, Egypt, South Africa, Tanzania, Kenya, and the Sudan.

In 1989, the continent's share in world consumption was a mere 4 percent (Abdulrahman Abdulahi). In the early 1970s, annual Egyptian consumption of pesticides was reported to be at the 20,000 ton level (UNIDO, *Pesticides*). Based on FAO data, net imports of pesticides fell from $562.3 million in 1989 to $383.8 million in 1994 (see Annex 5.3).

Production of pesticide active principles is negligible in comparison to needs. Exceptions are DDT, 2,4-D, and zinc phosphide production in Egypt, pyrethrin extraction in Kenya, Tanzania, and Rwanda, and metal-based herbicides production in Zimbabwe and Zambia. Zimbabwe and Zambia produce copper-based fungicides (oxychloride and copper sulfate).A production unit was reported to exist in Algeria. In the 1970s, the three pyrethrin-producing countries accounted for about 90 percent of world production (ITC UNCTDA/GATT) which was about 200 tons at the beginning of the 1980s (M.M.Suri.../ECA).

Formulation units exist in some countries in Sub-Saharan Africa (Angola, Mozambique, Tanzania, Zambia, Zimbabwe, Senegal, and Mali). Some of them were reported to have closed down.

The production of pesticides, particularly those based on synthetic organic chemicals, is complex. Making traditional pesticides, for instance, requires the production of innumerable technical grade materials (chlorinated hydrocarbons, organophosphates, carbamates and synthetic pyrethroids), usually in relatively small quantities. This, coupled with numerous other chemicals that go into the making of formulations and product obsolescence, places it out of the reach of practically all African countries.

For the above reasons, production of pesticides in the region is practically limited to formulation of imported inputs and is practiced in only few countries. Part of the imports are in bulk and involve repackaging only. The rest are imported in the form of active ingredients or technical grades. Many countries import additives that form part of the formulations, i.e., inerts/carriers, solvents, surface active agents, and special additives, such as stabilizers and wetters. Some countries use locally available inerts/carriers (kaolin, diatomaceous earths, talc, pumice, corn cobs, etc., for dust formulations) and solvents (kerosene and benzene) from petroleum refineries.

## Priority Products

Most of the pesticides and herbicides are used on commercial crops: cotton, coffee, tea, sugar, and tobacco. A substantial quantity of insecticides are utilized for public health purposes. Use of pesticides and herbicides on food crops which are produced mainly by small farmers (generally un-aware of the benefits of pesticides and having no capacity to buy agricultural inputs) is minimal. There is therefore a huge untapped market.

Based on world sales ($26.4 billions) of pesticides in 1990, the percentage shares of their major components were as follows: herbicides (43.9), insecticides (29.2), fungicides (20.8) and plant growth regulators, and others (6.1) (UNIDO, *Industry and Development: Global Report 1992/93*). The ranking is insecticides, fungicides, and herbicides in the three countries in Table 9.5 in late 1970s. Unlike in developed countries, herbicides occupy third place, as most of the weeding is done manually. Nowadays, because of the large variety of pesticides in use, the quantity of individual pesticides applied is relatively small.

| TABLE 9.5 SHARE OF MAJOR PESTICIDES AND HERBICIDES IN TOTAL CONSUMPTION (%) | | | |
|---|---|---|---|
| | Insecticides | Fungicides | Herbicides |
| Ethiopia | 80 | 8 | 12 |
| Kenya | 42 | 42 | 16 |
| Congo K | 63 | 20 | 17 |
| Source: Compiled from M.M.Suri & Associates Pvt.Ltd/ECA, 1982, *Model Prefeasibility Study on Pesticide Formulation Units,* Addis Ababa. | | | |

A rough idea of the types and distribution of pesticides can be obtained from areas outside the continent with similar climatic conditions, the ASEAN countries. Although based on the number of registered products (not on tonnage), the ranking in the ASEAN countries, according to ESCAP/EU Database on Pesticides and the Environment, is insecticides, acaricides, herbicides, and fungicides (FADINAP, Vol..XVII, No.4). In terms of distribution by chemical groups, organophosphates accounted for 29 percent and pyrethroids for 14 percent, followed by carbamates and phenoxy. Of the total of 417 types of active ingredients used in the ASEAN countries, the most common in descending order were : 2,4-D, cypermethrin, monocrotophos, metamidophos, glyphosate, parathion-methyl, endosulfan, dimethoate, and paraquat dichloride

Insecticides commonly used for vector control in Ethiopia can also offer a rough indication of the types of insecticides used for such a purpose in Africa. They include chlorinated hydrocarbons (DDT for mosquitoes and dieldrin, toxaphene, aldrine, and lindane for ixodid tick); organophosphates (coumaphos, malathion, fenthion, and trichlorophon for ixodid tick); carbamates (CBM 8 for ixodid tick); pyrethroids (flumethrine, deltamethrine/SPOTON, and cypermethrine for tsetse fly) and copper sulfate for snails.

As pyrethrins are locally available and are broad spectrum, they should constitute among the priority insecticides in Africa. They are used for public health purposes in closed spaces. Unfortunately, because of their instability on exposure to light and air and therefore lack of persistence, their use in agriculture is limited to grain storage only.

Pesticides and herbicides are applied at varying levels of concentration and forms. The concentrations range between 5 and 30 percent of technical grade (thus making it virtually impossible, based on statistics in developing countries, to determine the actual quantity of active ingredients consumed). Based on information in the Congo, Ethiopia, Kenya, and Congo K at the beginning of the 1980s, water-dispersible powders, emulsifiable concentrates, followed by dust and granules were the most popular forms of formulations used at the time ( M.M.Suri.../ECA).

Biological control is one of the alternatives to chemical control. Although used, very little, if at all, in Africa, biological (living organisms and viruses) pesticides are likely to find their way into African agriculture sooner or later. In addition, parasites and predators have the potential of being used as pest-control agents. In view of the danger of ecological disequilibrium resulting from the continued use of chemical pesticides, the sooner the cautious use of biological control is introduced, the better things will be. As crop yields are positively correlated to the quantity of pesticides applied, there may be a tendency to intensify the use of pesticides in the future.

## Strategies for Development

As stated earlier, there is no escape from adopting intensive farming systems through progressively introducing intensive use of modern inputs, especially given the fact that per capita arable land is declining fast (according to FAO expected to decline from 0.80 hectares in 1997 to 0.38 hectares in 2020). This would mean worsening the damage to agricultural produce brought about by pests and weeds— thus necessitating the increasing use of pesticides and herbicides. The damage can, to some extent, be minimized by encouraging farmers and grain dealers to practice traditional pest control, such as smoking, using local herbs, and mixing grains with ash.

It is, at the time of writing, difficult, if not impossible, to come out with a strategy for the development of the production of technical materials (active pesticides and herbicides). First, innumerable pesticides and herbicides are used in small quantities. Secondly, the number of pest species with resistance to pesticides is growing fast.[2] Thirdly, because of environmental protection, there are likely to be more restrictions on their use. Fourthly, emerging technologies resulting from R&D worldwide may come up with better and cheaper pesticides and herbicides or other means of controlling pests, viruses, fungi, and weeds. Fifthly, the manufacture of technical materials requires a well-developed chemical industry which does not exist in practically most African countries. Thus, given the uncertainties regarding the choice of technology and the products to be used, there is not much that can be done except to wait: in other words, delay entry into technical material making in order to take advantage of more up-to-date technology and acceptable products and/or other means resulting from on-going R&D elsewhere.

As for pesticides for public health purposes, recent advances in the developed countries seem to focus on new formulations, a number of which are based on or incorporate natural pyrethrin. Being an environmentally friendly insecticide, natural pyrethrin should be a candidate for formulation R&D in Africa. Besides, because of the tendency toward the use of natural materials, pyrethrin formulations are likely to find a niche in the world market.

In the meantime, because of the high inert content (70 to 95 % of formulated pesticides and herbicides) ([M.M.Suri.../ECA) some of which are or could be made locally available in many countries and the high cost of transport of formulated products, it would be worthwhile developing formulation units wherever justified. As economies of scale are not significant for formulation plants, most countries should consider setting up one or more units, taking into account the use of multipurpose equipment and machinery. Furthermore, ways and means could be investigated (by those concerned with the application of pesticides) of optimizing their use and minimizing their waste and harmful impact, including reducing the pesticidal poisoning of persons and animals, arising mainly from misuse and mishandling in both agriculture and public health. In this connection, it should be noted that a number of insecticides are used for both purposes. Vector-borne diseases (some of them affecting livestock) which are controlled by pesticides are malaria, onchocerciasis, schistosomiasis, trypanosomiasis, and filariasis.

As stated above, indiscriminate use of chemical pesticides is not in the long-term interest of farmers because of the eventual ecological disequilibrium that would follow. African countries should take measures to introduce and encourage farmers to practice integrated pest management systems. As most farmers use little fertilizers or none at all, it should be relatively easy to improve their pest control capabilities by introducing integrated pest management while introducing good farming practice and the use of inputs.

In view of the importance of integrated pest management, the need for R&D cannot be overemphasized. Both preventive and curative R&D should be undertaken, so that those who make decisions will have broader options from which to choose. Because of its capability to manipulate genes and thereby modify organisms (pathogens and parasites) to serve different purposes, genetic engineering appears to deserve special focus in the R&D. African countries should not only follow developments abroad but also conduct their own R&D in biotechnology and genetic engineering, with a view to optimizing benefits suited to African conditions and needs. In this regard, optimum use of the International Centre of Insect Physiology and Ecology (ICIPE) in Kenya should be made.

The results of R&D should, of course, be translated into commercial pesticides. The pathogens and parasites isolated and mass produced should be introduced to the farmers by extension service agents as soon as the pesticides are ready. It should be noted here that developing biopesticides is likely to involve less expense and time as compared with chemical pesticides.

It is worth referring here to the small-scale processing of microbial pesticides. According to FAO (FAO, *Small-scale Microbial Pesticides*), the small-scale production of microbial insecticides in the tropics can compete with large-scale production in moderate climates because of the substantially lower amounts of energy needed to maintain cultivation temperatures in the process based on sterilization and fermentation. This, coupled with fewer long-term storage problems, makes it worthwhile for some African countries to venture into R&D and production, including formulation, without delay.

Crop-related research is another area worth entering into that would involve the development of pest- and disease-resistant crops, and any successes in that area would mean less use of pesticides.

Experiences and R&D results in other developing countries with similar climatic and other conditions would be worth tapping. The use of the nim seeds as insecticide for both crop protection and stored grain in India is a case in point. The chemical compounds in the seed were found capable of controlling over 200 species of pests and do not, apparently, have negative impact on mammals and birds (FAO, *Dimensions of Need*).

## BIBLIOGRAPHY

Abdel Monem Ahmed Akeel, *Experience in Utilization of Natural Gas in the Production of Basic Chemicals,* Cairo.

Abdurahman Abdulahi, 1991, *Assessment of Trends in Technological Innovations in the Production and Use of Pesticides in Africa,* Addis Ababa.

Aboulhassen Charfi, 1991, *Experience Tunisienne dans le Domaine de la Production d'Engrais*, Tunis.

ACFD, *Brochure on African Centre for Fertilizer Development*, Harare.

Ahmed El-Deeb, 1992, *Fertilizer Production and Consumption in Egypt*, Cairo.

Boudiaf S., *L'Expérience Algerienne dans l'Utilisation des Unites Existantes et de la Coopération dans le Domaine des Engrais Chimiques*, Alger.

ECA, 1994, *Les Matières Premières Minérales des Fertilisants de l'Afrique Subsaharienne (Période 1980-1989)*, (ECA/NRD/MRU/TP/3/94), Addis Ababa.

ECA, 1996, *Africa in the 1990s and Beyond: ECA-Revised Long-Term Development Perspectives Study* (ECA/SERPD/TP/96/3), Addis Ababa.

ECA/UNIDO, 1995, *Report on the Possibility for the Establishment of an African Regional Network for Agricultural Chemicals and Machinery* (CAMI.12/6[b]), Addis Ababa.

ESCAP, 1991, *Agro-pesticides: Properties and Functions in Integrated Crop Protection*, Bangkok.

FADINAP, 1994, "Pesticides and the Environment in Asean Countries," *Agro-chemicals News in Brief*, Vol. XVII, No. 4, October- December 1994, Bangkok.

FAO, 1992, "Small-scale Processing of Microbial Pesticides," *FAO Agricultural Services Bulletin 96*, Rome.

FAO, 1994, *FAO Trade Yearbook 1994*, Rome.

FAO, 1994, *The State of Food and Agriculture 1994*, Rome.

FAO, 1995, *Dimensions of Need*, Rome.

FAO, 1998, "Agro-chemical Industry to Pay Some of Clean-up Costs for Obsolete Pesticides in Developing Countries," Africa News Online (www.africanews.org), February 11, 1998.

ITC UNCTDA/GATT, 1976, *Pyrethrum, a Natural Insecticide with Growth Potential*, Geneva.

Khennas, Smail, ed,. 1992, *Industrialization, Mineral Resources and Energy in Africa*, CODESRIA, CODESRIA Book Series, Anthony Rowe, Oxford.

Kilborn Engineering/ECA, 1985, *Ethiopian Dallol Potash Project: Phase 1A Report Critique*, Toronto.

M. M. Suri & Associates Pvt. Ltd/ECA, 1982, *Model Prefeasiblity Study on Pesticide Formulation Units*, ECA, Addis Ababa.

Microsoft, 1996, *Encarta 96 Encyclopedia*, Redmond.

National Academy of Sciences, 1978, *Post-harvest Food Losses in Developing Countries*, Washington, D. C.

Osama El Ganiny, 1993, *The Changing Fertilizers Situation in Egypt*, Cairo.

Parish, Dennis H., 1985, "Appropriate Fertilizer Technology for Sub-Saharan Africa," Proceedings of *Fertilizer Efficiency Research and Technology Transfer Workshop for Africa South of the Sahara*, January 21-25, 1985, Douala.

_____. 1989, "Economic Implications of Fertilizer Specifications," *Proceedings of the Second Annual Meeting of the African Fertilizer Trade and Marketing Information Network*, November 15-17, 1989, Lome.

Samuelson, Robert J., 1995, "Surviving the Guillotine," *Newsweek*, November 20, 1995.

The British Sulphur Corporation Limited, 1985, *Fertilizer International*, N0.213, October 17, 1985, London.

The British Sulphur Corporation Limited, *1985, Phosphorous and Potassium*, No. 139, September- October 1985, London.

The Economist, 1996, *Feeding the World*, November 16, 1996.

The Ethiopian Herald, 1995, "Pesticide Production Plant under Construction," February 26, 1995, Addis Ababa.

The Fertilizer (Planning & Development) India Limited/ECA, 1981, *Market Feasibility Study for Ethiopian Potash,* Addis Ababa.

UNIDO, 1973, *Pesticides: Report of a Workshop,* May 28 - June 1, 1973, Vienna.

UNIDO, 1992, *Industry and Development: Global Report 1992/93,* Vienna.

World Bank/SADCC, 1991, *An Action Plan for the Development of the Fertilizer Industry* (Main Report, working draft), Washington, D.C.

World Bank/SADC, 1993, *SADC Fertilizer Supply Options Model,* Washington, D.C.

World Bank, 1996, *World Resources 1996-97,* Oxford University Press, New York.

## NOTES

1. African countries have the possibilities to choose and adopt new seed varieties from agricultural research conducted worldwide. The rice varieties with potential yields exceeding the current 10 tons per hectare developed by the Consultative Group on International Agricultural Research is a good indication of the potential awaiting African countries. Others include the higher yielding varieties of maize tolerant to acid and drought conditions and those for lowland and tropical environments developed by the Centro Internacional de Mejoramiento de Maiz y Trigo in Mexico (World Bank, *World Resources 1996-97*). It is apparent that most of these developments are of particular relevance to African conditions.

2. According to FAO, 520 insects and mites, 150 plant diseases, and 113 weeds have built up resistance to pesticides worldwide.

## CHAPTER 10

# AGRICULTURAL EQUIPMENT AND MACHINERY

It is quite common to hear and read that labor is abundant in Africa. This holds generally true for urban areas. In the rural area of Sub-Saharan Africa, where agriculture relies mainly on human and animal power, human labor accounts for about 80 percent of the energy used in agriculture (FAO, *Atlas of African Agriculture*). Although present labor shortages are mainly seasonal (during weeding), it is very likely that labor shortage in the rural area will become more serious as migration to urban areas continues and the rural population becomes increasingly old. During the period 1970-1980, the rural population increased by 24 percent to 325 million while the urban population grew by 72 percent to 121 million (FAO, *African Agriculture: the next 25 Years, Annex III*). In the future, unless substantive change takes place in agricultural practices, expansion of areas for cultivation will be constrained by a shortage of labor, especially in areas where animal draught is either not available or is not part of the cultural tradition or limited because of animal diseases. This will be exacerbated by women having to spend more time fetching fire-wood and water from increasingly longer distances, in addition to farming and doing all the house chores. The contribution of women farmers, who constitute the majority of food crop farmers in most countries, especially those heading farming households, should be taken into account when improving agricultural mechanization in Africa.

The majority of African farmers use obsolete and unproductive tools and therefore very labor-intensive methods. As a consequence, labor productivity is very low, limiting the capacity of a household to the cultivation of 1.5 to 2 hectares. Animal traction raises labor productivity five to ten fold.

Only state, cooperative, and large private farms (the third mainly engaged in cash crop production) resort to modern agricultural mechanization. The cash crops commonly cultivated include: cotton, coffee, tea, cocoa, groundnut, sugar, oil palm, and rice.

From the outset, it should be noted here that statistical information on agricultural equipment and machinery in Africa is hard to obtain. Information used in this chapter is thus based on estimates made in selected studies and reports (ECA, ECA/IHSD/IDPS/ENG/010/92).

As is the case with most industrial products, consumption is substantially lower than demand. Demand is restrained by a number of factors, the most important being very low purchasing power and a lack of foreign exchange to import industrial inputs.

In view of the low productivity and the decline in food self-sufficiency, there is no alternative to intensifying agriculture and expanding land under cultivation. Agricultural mechanization, which is in use on about 20 percent of the cultivated land, together with agricultural chemicals (dealt with in Chapter 9) is one of the means of intensifying food production. The question here is how fast and at what level.

Most African agriculture is based on rainfall. This dependence on rainfall is particularly critical in arid and semi-arid zones which are vulnerable to recurrent droughts. FAO distinguishes the following three categories of countries requiring irrigation:

• Countries with a growing period of 180 days and exceeding their population carrying capacity (Botswana, Burkina Faso, Kenya, Mali, Mauritania, Niger, Senegal, and Somalia)

• Countries with a growing period of less than 120 days on more than a quarter of their territory (Chad, Ethiopia, Sudan, and Tanzania);

• Countries having less than a quarter of their area in the semi-arid zone (Angola, Benin, Cameroon, Gambia, Guinea-Bisau, Lesotho, Madagascar, Mozambique, Nigeria, and Zambia).

As witnessed during the past 20 years, crop failures are becoming more frequent and are occuring in an increasing number of countries. Under the circumstances, the development of irrigation is essential. There is good potential for developing irrigation in Sub-Saharan Africa, where the irrigable area is estimated at 33.6 million hectares, of which about five million hectares were in use in 1982 (FAO, *Irrigation ... Sahara*). For the region as a whole, irrigated land as a percentage of cropland increased from 6 percent in 1981-83 to 7 percent in 1991-93, the corresponding figures for the world being 15 and 17. Africa's share in world's total irrigated land is about 5 percent (World Bank, *World Resources 1996-97*). According to the Director-General of FAO, *"the solution to the food problem on this continent necessarily implies the acceleration and improvement of its irrigation programmes and schemes."* He noted that only 11 million hectares (7% of arable land) was under irrigation in Africa in the mid-1990s.

Table 10.1 shows areas under irrigation in Africa in 1982 and projections to 2010. North Africa with a share of 62.5 percent, leads the other groupings in terms of irrigation. A breakdown by country shows the following ranking: Egypt (29.9%), Sudan (17.9%), Madagascar (10.1%), Nigeria (8.9%) and Morocco (8.4%). Country ranking within regions (presented in the last column under existing areas of the table) indicates the concentration of irrigation in a limited number of countries. Rice, wheat, cotton, sugarcane, and sugarbeet are the main crops grown in medium- and large-scale irrigation schemes.

TABLE 10.1
EXISTING AND PROJECTED IRRIGATED AREAS IN AFRICA
(1000 hectares)

| | Existing area (1982) | | | | Additional area (2010) | | |
|---|---|---|---|---|---|---|---|
| | Modern | Tradi-tional/small-scale | Total | Country ranking within region [a] | Modern | Tradi-tional/small-scale | Total |
| North Africa | 3409 | 780 | 4189 | Egypt (65.9%), Morocco (19.1%) | | | |
| Sudano-Sahelian Africa | 1917 | 340 | 2257 | Sudan (77.5%) | | | |
| Humid and sub-humid West Africa | 144 | 1190 | 1334 | Nigeria (63.6%) | | | |
| Humid central Africa | 18 | 60 | 78 | | | | |
| Sub-humid and mountainous east Africa | 282 | 910 | 1192 | Madagascar (80.5%) | | | |
| Sub-humid and semi-arid southern Africa | 308 | 150 | 458 | Tanzania (30.4), Zimbabwe (28.4) | | | |
| Total Africa | 6078 | 3430 | 9508 | | 1276 | 3708 | 4984 |

Source: FAO, 1986, *African Agriculture: the next 25 Years, Annex IV, Irrigation and Water Control*, Rome.
  a  Computed

Assuming adequate changes are made in favor of the development of irrigation and external assistance is forthcoming, irrigation areas could, during the period 1985-2010, increase at the following average annual rates in hectares: 50,000 modern scheme and 150,000 traditional and small-scale irrigation and existing schemes, rehabilitated at the rates up to 25,000 (FAO, *African Agriculture: the next 25 Years, Annex IV*). The additions work out to 5 million hectares, comprising 1.3 and 3.7 million hectares of modern and traditional/small-scale irrigation, respectively. Most of the increase  (73.5%) in the modern component is expected to come from Sub-Saharan countries. In terms of cereal production, the portion coming from irrigation is expected to increase from 4.55 million tons in 1982 to 15.1 million tons in 2010 in Sub-Saharan Africa. The corresponding figures for North Africa, excluding Sudan, are 9.0 and 13.7 million tons, respectively. The 1998 FAO initiative to promote irrigation related technology transfer and make R&D results available to farmers and decision-makers in developing countries could enhance and facilitate irrigated agriculture.

In view of the scarcity of financial resources for large-scale modern schemes and the relatively long time needed to plan and implement such schemes, the weight given to traditional/small-scale irrigation makes sense. This would mean focusing, in the short to medium term, on the development of small-scale irrigation schemes, including improved traditional irrigation and introducing low-cost technologies—porous jars, drip and sprinkler systems and  human-powered (treadle) and small motor pumps—while planning large-scale schemes. The plan (under implementation) to build 500 micro-dams in only one region in Ethiopia in 10 years gives an indication of what can be done in countries that depend on erratic rainfall. Such countries should supplement the water they need for rainfed agriculture by conserving rain water, including the seasonal storage of runoff water and run-of-river diversion, as well as ground water. Ground water accounts for 20 percent of the total water resources in Africa (*FAO, African Agriculture: the next 25 Years, Annex IV*). Double-cropping in some areas in these countries should contribute to a further increase in production. According to FAO *"irrigated land is twice as productive as rainfed land"* and in developing countries *"irrigation increases yields of most crops by 100 to 400 percent.* In some situations, after minimizing leaks during transmission, maximizing reuse of waste water, etc., have been exhausted, desalination of salty water may be the only means of or the last resort to providing water, especially in countries with hydrocarbon resources. Cost of desalination have been declining. The improved desalination technology that was being developed by an American/Israei consortium was expected to produce water at less than \$0.5 per $m^3$ compared to \$1 per $m^3$ in the Canary Islands (The Economist, April 4, 1998).

Agricultural equipment and machinery perform the following functions: breaking ground, planting, weeding, fertilizing, combating pests, and harvesting. They could be classified in a number of ways. For the sake of convenience, they are divided here into three categories: tools, implements and machinery, and powered machinery. This categorization roughly corresponds to the levels of agricultural mechanization in many African countries. Many peasant farmers rely on the first category; relatively well to-do-farmers on the second; and large farms and plantations on the third. There are, of course, overlaps, peasants using some implements from the second category and the well-to-do farmers some machinery from the third category, including hiring machinery. Under certain conditions, such as the availability of cheap labor, large farms and plantations may resort to the use, in part, of implements and machinery in the second category.

## AGRICULTURAL TOOLS

Traditional agricultural tools in use in Africa include: hoes, knives, pick-axes, spades, shovels, rakes, forks, walking-stick planters, hatchets, machetes, and sickles. They are the mechanical inputs most commonly used by peasant farmers, mainly farming less than two hectares. They are used on 45 to 50 percent of the cultivated area in Sub-Saharan Africa (ECA/IHSD/IDPS/ENG/010/92). In Eastern and Southern Africa, this is reported to be about 70 to 75 percent (ECA/HMT). In addition to the tools, some peasant farmers, depending on conditions and needs in their respective countries, may have access to one or more simple animal-drawn implements and manual seed and fertilizer drills, hand cultivators, dusters, knapsack sprayers, groundnut lifters, paddy threshers, and maize and groundnut shellers.

### Status of the Industry
As shown in Table 10.2, all African subregions produce agricultural tools. This is also true for practically all countries. Annex 10.1 provides details on agricultural tool manufacturing establishments in West Africa. Most of the tool production is carried out by blacksmiths (5,000 in Benin alone producing hand tools and objets

d'art). As may be appreciated, the qualities of the blacksmiths' products leave much to be desired; they are, however, relatively cheap and accessible to the peasant farmers.

The balance of production is carried out by relatively modern establishments in many countries. In Eastern and Southern Africa, for example, Zimbabwe, Kenya, Tanzania, Zambia, and Malawi have such establishments. However, capacity utilization of most of them is very low. In West Africa, for instance, in the 1980s it ranged from 10 percent in Liberia at Agro Machines Ltd. to 85 percent in Cote d'Ivoire at ABI. The figure for the other plants hovered around 50 percent.

From Table 10.2, it is apparent that total production covered less than half of the 1992 total consumption of developing Africa. Total projected demand is expected to be 2.7-fold of the 1992 production by the year 2000. As in 1992, North Africa will account for the lion's share of the projected demand. Much lower projections for animal drawn implements for the region as a whole are provided by ECA—1.4 (historical scenario) and 1.7 (normative scenario) million tons, respectively, in the year 2008, compared with 1.0 million tons in 1993 (ECA, *Africa in the 1990s and Beyond: ..*).

| TABLE 10.2 PRODUCTION, CONSUMPTION, CONSUMPTION/PRODUCTION GAP AND PROJECTED DEMAND OF AGRICULTURAL EQUIPMENT AND MACHINERY IN AFRICA [a] (1000 units) | | | | | | |
|---|---|---|---|---|---|---|
| Subregion | Type of products | Pro-duc-tion | Con-sump-tion | Production/ consump-tion gap | Projected demand | |
| | | 1992 | 1992 | 1992 | 1995 | 2000 |
| North Africa | Hand tools | 22000 | 40000 | 18000 | 50000 | 60000 |
| | Animal drawn implements | 165 | 300 | 135 | 300 | 400 |
| | Powered implements | 55 | 100 | 45 | 100 | 100 |
| Eastern and Southern Africa (excl. South Africa) | Hand tools | 3283 | 7074 | 3791 | 7400 | 7800 |
| | Animal drawn implements | 360 | 1100 | 740 | 1150 | 1200 |
| | Powered implements | 14 | 50 | 36 | 53 | 55 |
| West Africa | Hand tools | 4800 | 10116 | 5316 | 12000 | 12600 |
| | Animal drawn implements | 310 | 1930 | 1620 | 2000 | 2100 |
| | Powered implements | 15 | 103 | 87 | 110 | 116 |
| Central Africa | Hand tools | 1760 | 3708 | 1948 | 4400 | 4620 |
| | Animal drawm implements | 210 | 1500 | 1290 | 1150 | 1200 |
| | Powered implements | 10 | 82 | 72 | 64 | 68 |
| Total Africa | Hand tools | 31843 | 60898 | 29055 | 73800 | 85020 |
| | Animal drawn implements | 1045 | 4830 | 3785 | 4600 | 4900 |
| | Powered implements | 94 | 334 | 240 | 327 | 339 |

Source: ECA, 1993, *Guidelines on the Manufacture of Agricultural Tools, Implements and Low-cost Transport Equipment by Small-scale Engineering Industries in the Context of the Second Industrial Development Decade* for Africa, ECA/IHSD/IDPS/ENG/010/92, Addis Ababa.

   a Excluding tractors

Agricultural tools account for about 75 percent of the cultivation in the West African subregion. The capacity for the manufacture of the tools was reported to be adequate to meet demand in the late 1980s. The demand/supply gaps shown in Tables 10.2 and 10.3 resulted mainly from the lack of foreign currency to import raw materials and spare parts required for manufacturing.

## Priority Products

From the above, the need for agricultural mechanization is apparent At the peasant farmer level, the agricultural tools listed above (namely, hoes, knives, pickaxes, spades, shovels, rakes, forks, walking-stick planters, machetes, sickles, etc.) are used in different combinations. Hoes, walking-sticks and knives are the most rudimentary tools in use in some areas in a number of countries, the first for tilling, the second for planting, and the third for harvesting. These tools will continue to be used even though some of them will likely be replaced gradually up to a certain level by implements, particularly in areas (the Sahel and Eastern and Southern Africa) where switching over to animal draught is practical. The switchover can be achieved through graduation from one level to the next. Farmers using knives may switch over to sickles; those using hoes to animal traction and associated implements, provided the farming area is free from tse-tse fly; and those using animal traction to tractors and associated implements. This trend, however, does not mean that there will not be a jump over to the next level. It is possible that farmers could, for example, be organized in a relatively short time to use powered equipment and machinery.

## Strategy for Development

Given of the primitive nature of the traditional tools used by peasant farmers, improving the quality and design of such tools will certainly boost agricultural productivity and production. In addition there is a need to adopt and adapt farming methods that, among other things, can conserve soil and water as well as reduce labor requirements. For example, the difficulty of breaking ground with tools can be lessened by running duck's-foot tines through the soil and harvesting can be eased by using diesel-powered reapers carried on the back (ECA, ECA/SDA/IRD/89/1.1[i][b]).

Existing production units at the artisanal blacksmith level, mainly based on scrap, are considered adequate. They, however, need assistance in training; obtaining improved designs and drawings; and procuring improved working tools, equipment, and inputs to enhance their productivity and product quality. Reduction of drudgery in farming should be one of the factors to be taken into account when designing or improving the design of tools. Undertaking R &D and disseminating their results to tool manufacturers should be pursued.

At the factory level, although the technology for making tools was said to have been mastered, capacity utilization as noted earlier was low, partly due to lack of adequate imported inputs resulting from lack of foreign exchange. It was around 50 percent in some countries in West and Eastern and Southern Africa. In West Africa, in the late 1980s, it ranged from 10 percent in Liberia at Agro Machines Ltd. to 85 percent in Cote d'Ivoire at ABI. From this, it is apparent that tool production could be increased substantially through higher utilization of existing capacity, including increased number of shifts; as well as upgrading, expansion and/or diversification of same.

At the blacksmith level, anvil, hammer, chisel, hack-saw, and hand-operated blowers and grinding wheels are the basic equipment used to manufacture hand tools. Hand forging with heat treatment is the main operation for shaping and imparting some characteristics to the products. The requirements of a factory are more sophisticated. They include power-operated hammers, forges, presses, and welding sets. The local content of machinery and equipment for making agricultural tools should be optimized.

## Agricultural Implements

Agricultural implements in use in Africa comprise animal-drawn as well as powered implements. The former, which accounts for about 20 to 25 percent of cultivation in developing Africa (ECA/IHSD/IDPS/ENG/010/92) includes: ploughs, harrows, ridgers, cultivators, seed drills, planters as well as manually operated maize shellers, groundnut threshers, and paddy threshers. The latter comprise disc ploughs, mold board plows, chisel plows, disc harrows, ridgers, cultivators, seed drills, planters, fertilizer distributors, sprayers, groundnut lifters, harvesters, pumps, and irrigation equipment (including using animal power). At the post-harvest level, machines such as paddy threshers, maize shellers, and groundnut threshers seem to be gaining ground.

Generally, animal traction is used in farms covering less than five hectares and mostly for land preparation (ECA/IND/ENG/009/88). In Sub-Saharan Africa, it is extensively used in Ethiopia by an estimated 7.5 million households and is gaining ground in Nigeria and Zimbabwe. Although the potential in other countries, especially in areas free of tsetse fly, should be quite high, only 5 to 10 percent of the cultivated land is reported to make use of animal traction (ECA, ECA/SDA/IRD/89/1.1[ii][b]).

### Status of the Industry
According to Table 10.2 above, demand for animal drawn implements is projected to decrease from 4.8 million units in 1992 to 4.6 in 1995 and then increase to 4.9 in 2000. The corresponding figures for powered implements are 334,000, 327,000, and 339,000. Ratios of animal-drawn to powered implements work out to 11.1 and 14.5 for production and demand, respectively, indicating a much higher production and wider use of animal-drawn implements. In 1992, the consumption/production gaps were 3.8 million units of animal-drawn implements and 240,000 units of powered implements. As the demand projections for 1995 and the year 2000 show, these gaps are likely to grow unless new production units are added in time.

The number of countries involved in the manufacture of agricultural implements are far less than those producing agricultural tools. In 1992, their combined production were estimated at over just one million units of animal-drawn implements and 94,000 units of powered implements.

Annex 10.1, on West African agricultural implements and food processing equipment manufacturing facilities, could serve as an indication of the likely situation pertaining in the other subregions. As indicated in the annex, some of the units work one shift a day while others are known to work under capacity. This seems to confirm the conclusion arrived at in other sources that existing capacities for animal-drawn implements are adequate and that what is required is to diversify and expand their operations. In other words, the 3.8 million consumption/production gap in 1992 could have been substantially lower had the production units been operated at higher levels of capacity utilization, including operating a higher number of shifts.

Table 10.3 shows demand, supply, and demand/supply gap projections for a number of agricultural tools, implements, and tractors in the West African subregion. From the table, it is apparent that there were demand/supply gaps in agricultural tools ( machetes, hoes, rakes, etc.) of over 1.9 million units as well as in disc ploughs and disc harrows in 1990. The opposite held in the case of animal-rawn implements (ploughs, cultivators, planters, and harrows), implying the availability of excess capacity. It should be noted here that only about 10 to 15 percent of the cultivation in the subregion is carried out using animal-drawn implements.

TABLE 10.3

DEMAND, SUPPLY AND DEMAND/SUPPLY GAP PROJECTIONS FOR AGRICULTURAL TOOLS, IMPLEMENTS AND TRACTORS IN THE WEST AFRICAN SUBREGION (1000 units)

|  | Year | Ma-chetes | Hoe | Rakes | Culti-vators | Plan-ters | Ploughs | Disc ploughs | Har-rows | Disc har-rows | Trac-tors |
|---|---|---|---|---|---|---|---|---|---|---|---|
| Demand projections | 1985 | 5624.9 | 4362 | 116.8 | ... | ... | 56 | ... | ... | 40.7 | 16.1 |
|  | 1990 | 6749.9 | 5233.6 | 133.2 | ... | ... | 58.7 | ... | ... | 42.8 | 16.9 |
|  | 2000 | 6965.1 | 5495.3 | 139.6 | ... | ... | 61.7 | ... | ... | 44.9 | 17.7 |
| Supply * | 1990 | 6061.6 | 3693.3 | 131 | 90.2 | 25.4 | 162 | 10 | 30.6 | 5 | 6.1 |
| Demand/ supply gap | 1990 | -502.1 | -1363.9 | -31.6 | 10.1 | 7.8 | 105.4 | -23.7 | 2.5 | -14.1 | 10.8 |

Source: Compiled from ECA, 1988, *Manufacture of Agricultural Tools, Implements and Machinery in the West African Subregion*, Addis Ababa.

* The supply figures do not include figures for Mauritania, the Gambia, Guinea Bissau and Cape Verde and hence the discrepancies in demand/supply gaps.

The general situation regarding demand/supply gaps and the level of technology in use in the subregions are not likely to be very different from that of West Africa. Countries producing a mix of animal-drawn and powered implements include: Algeria, Morocco, Tunisia, Egypt, Benin, Burkina Faso, Cote d'Ivoire, Ghana, Niger, Nigeria, Senegal, Tanzania, and Zimbabwe.

Imports, exports and net imports of tractors are given in Annex 5.3 for the period 1989-1994.

## Priority Products

Considering the stage of agricultural development in Africa and the predominance of animal drawn- implements in some countries, such implements are likely to remain important for some time for the peasant farmer in areas not adversely affected by animal health, particularly trypanosmiasis. Seeders, fertilizer distributors, manual sprayers, and irrigation equipment, including water-lifting devices, will probably take the lead in the group. Use of post-harvest machines is likely to increase with the growing use of pre-harvest implements. The mix of agricultural implements and machinery to be manufactured will be determined by local conditions and needs.

In view of the unreliability of rain-fed agriculture, it would be advisable to accord special emphasis to irrigation and drainage equipment. Hydraulic rams, pumps (including treadle and chain- and -washer pumps), pipes, and accessories (fittings, couplings, valves, pressure regulators, water meters, hydrants, gates, baffles, weirs, siphons, and strainers) constitute the main equipment. Irrigation projects would do well to consider the hydraflo irrigation pump as an alternative. The pump does not require fuel or electric energy to drive it. It utilizes a fluid power transmission system and is reported to be relatively economical to install and operate. In view of dwindling availability of water to be expected, irrigation systems that optimize the use of water should be encouraged.

There are other products that could be included in the priority group identified above. Barbed-wire, wire mesh, fencing, poles and trailers, sluice gates, guides, and valves for irrigation systems would be required as farming develops.

## Strategies for Development

Some of the existing factories may need to be expanded, taking account of the demand of the host country as well as of neighboring countries that may not be able to develop their own production units. Countries without production units may either make supply arrangements with neighboring countries with production units or establish their own units, incorporating multi-purpose machines, whenever practical, that can produce different implements on a campaign basis.

Cooperation among producers would contribute to enhancing the capability of the region to meet its needs in locally made agricultural implements. Cooperation could include: standardization; exchange of designs, drawings, and field trial results; sourcing raw materials and intermediates in the region before resorting to overseas suppliers; central purchasing of imported inputs; setting up unit(s) to produce special parts and components requiring economies of scale; and joint efforts to replace imported inputs by local materials. Efforts would need to be intensified to undertake research and development so as to improve implements for African conditions and optimize local content and backward integration. In this regard it would be imperative to disseminate the results of such efforts and relevant developments achieved elsewhere, such as proven designs and field-tested prototypes, to manufacturers of agricultural equipment and machinery in the region. In this connection, results achieved by the Regional Network for Agricultural Machinery (RNAM) in Asia are worth looking into.

Given the apparent excess capacity for animal-drawn implements in many countries, increasing the number of shifts and upgrading, expanding, and diversifying existing facilities may be adequate to meet future requirement. New units, if and when needed, should be planned with optimal use of plant machinery and equipment that can produce groups of similar implements (and even agricultural tools) based on the same or closely related technologies, whenever practical. The production facility should include multipurpose machinery and equipment required for the purpose. Such arrangements would enable countries to minimize problems associated with economies of scale, especially in the smaller countries. This approach would be more relevant in the development of tractor-drawn implements whose local production, unlike animal-drawn implements, is far less than demand. In West Africa, for instance, additional production capacity of over 43,000 units was needed to meet the demand in the late 1980s (ECA, ECA/IND/ENG/ 007/88).

291

The design and operation of animal-drawn implements can be improved and supplemented by works done elsewhere. In this connection, the NIKART project that was being developed in the 1980s near Hydrabad, India, seems relevant. The objective of the project was to develop a simple and low-cost animal-drawn machine with accessories, including a simple fertilizer drill [Parish 1985).

The equipment and machinery required to manufacture agricultural implements and machinery is, obviously, at a higher level than that for agricultural tools. In addition to the power operated equipment and machinery for a tool factory, it requires some conventional machine tools, bending machines, gigs, fixtures, furnaces, and paint sprayers. The local manufacture of as many of these would ensure a measure of self-sufficiency in the production of agricultural implements and selected machinery. Combining the manufacture of agricultural equipment and machinery with those for a tool factory would reduce both investment and production costs.

As most African soils are fragile, farming practices that could minimize soil erosion should be introduced and popularized. This would require the innovation of agricultural implements and machinery, including those that would be within the reach of small farmers. No-tillage, minimum tillage, alley-cropping, and drip irrigation farming are among such innovations. Implements to perform these functions and machinery and equipment for their manufacture need to be developed.

The negative consequences of irrigation should be taken into account when planning the development of irrigation. Accretion of silt in dams, salinization, waterlogging, damage to the environment, and the risk of introducing health problems, such as bilharzia, are among the undesirable consequences.

## POWERED AGRICULTURAL MACHINERY

Powered agricultural mechanization, that is, use of tractors and other powered machinery (pumps, sprinkler irrigation systems, combine harvesters, threshers, shellers, etc.) in developing Africa, is limited and is commonly used on farms of more than ten hectares (ECA/IND/ENG/009/88). In West and Eastern and Southern Africa, for instance, only 5 to 10 percent of the cultivated area is estimated to benefit from powered machinery. Expensive machinery, costly maintenance due to lack of spare parts and skills, and the high cost of fuels are among the reasons for this state of affairs.

Information on powered agricultural machinery is hard to obtain. Presentation of this group is therefore limited to references to some subregional situations.

### Status of the Industry

Table 10.4 gives the number of tractors and harvesters-threshers in use in the continent. The declining trend during the period 1991-1993 is apparent. Also apparent is the high share of South Africa. In 1993, South Africa accounted for 23.8 percent of the tractors and 30.3 percent of the harvesters-threshers.

| TABLE 10.4 TRACTORS AND HARVESTER-THRESHERS IN USE IN THE CONTINENT (numbers) | | | | | | | |
|---|---|---|---|---|---|---|---|
| | Tractors, agricultural | | | | Harvesters-threshers | | |
| | 1979-1981 | 1991 | 1992 | 1993 | 1979-1981 | 1991 | 1992 | 1993 |
| Africa | 441287 | 521575 | 518052 | 508026 | 47662 | 42201 | 40607 | 39598 |
| South Africa | 174081 | 140000 | 131000 | 121000 | 29397 | 15000 | 13000 | 12000 |
| Developing Africa | 267206 | 381575 | 387052 | 387026 | 18265 | 27201 | 27607 | 27598 |
| Source: FAO, 1994, *FAO Production Yearbook*, Rome. | | | | | | | |

Based on FAO data (*FAO Trade Yearbook*, 1994) African imports of tractors averaged 32,533 units in 1989-1991 and fell to 26,067 in 1992-1994. As export averaged only about 600 per year these figures represent practically net imports. Table 10.5 gives imports and estimates of consumption and capacities of some powered agricultural machinery assembly units/plants in Eastern and Southern Africa, North Africa, and West Africa. In the first, during a ten year period (1976-1985), import of tractors peaked at 10,213 and averaged 8,264 between 1981 and 1985. The 1987 production of assembled tractors (1,562) and 1987/88 estimated consumption imply that about 10,558 tractors were imported in 1987. According to another source (UNIDO, *Appropriate ... Implements*), tractor requirements in Sub-Saharan Africa were estimated to increase from 22,000 in 1965 to 56,000 in 1985. The same source had estimated 1985 tractor supply rate of 12,000, of which 9,000 were for replacement. According to ECA projections based on FAO estimates, the continental annual demand will increase from 52,000 in 1993 to 73,000 (historical scenario) and 225,000 (normative scenario) by 2008, the last expected to result in production/supply gap of 76,500 (ECA, *Africa in the 1990s and Beyond: ...*).

There are tractor plants in North Africa (Algeria, Tunisia, Libya, and Egypt), with total capacity of over 14,000 units per year. Their combined annual output in the late 1980s was in excess of 10,000 units. The one in Libya is an assembly unit.

The capacities of other machineries in North Africa are shown in the table. The major producers are Algeria, Egypt, and Tunisia.

In West Africa, where annual demand in the year 2000 is projected at about 18,000 units, Nigeria, Burkina Fasso, and Ghana have tractor assembly plants. The Nigerian capacity is over 6,000 units per year.

| TABLE 10.5 IMPORTS, ESTIMATED DEMAND AND CAPACITIES OF POWERED AGRICULTURAL MACHINERY ASSEMBLY/PLANTS IN EASTERN AND SOUTHERN AFRICA AND NORTH AFRICA (units) | | | | | | | |
|---|---|---|---|---|---|---|---|
| Powered agricultural machinery | Imports | | | | Estimated demand | | Assembly capacity |
| | 1976 | 1980 | 1985 | 1990 | 1987/88 | 1991/92 | 1991/92 |
| Tractors | | | | | | | |
| Eastern and Southern Africa | 5687 | 10213 | 8789 | | 12120 | 16100 | 1,800[a] |
| North Africa | | | | | | | 14300 |
| Cote d'Ivoire | | | | | | | >6,060 |
| Harvesters - North Africa | | | | | | | 6,500 |
| Threshers - North Africa | | | | | | | 4400 |
| Irrigation pumps - North Africa | | | | | | | 2000 |

Source: - ECA/HMT,1988, *Engineering Industry Development Programme for Selected Eastern and Southern African Countries of Preferential Trade Area (Model Pre-feasibility Report — Agricultural Machinery, Equipment and Tractors)*, Addis Ababa.
   - ECA, 1993, *Guidelines on the Manufacture of Agricultural Tools, Implements and Low-cost Transport Equipment by Small-scale Engineering Industries in the Context of the Second Industrial Development Decade for Africa*, Addis Ababa.
   - ECA, 1988, *Manufacture of Agricultural Tools, Implements and Machinery in the West African Subregion*, Addis Ababa.
   a Does not include the capacities of the three units in Zimbabwe.

Table 10.6 presents some information on capacities and production of some agricultural equipment manufacturing units in the North African subregion. In spite of the limited information, the table is useful in that it gives an indication of the existence of such units.

| | No. | Type of operation | Capacity | | Production | | Products/remarks |
|---|---|---|---|---|---|---|---|
| | | | Year | t/y | Year | t/y | |

TABLE 10.6
CAPACITY AND PRODUCTION OFSOME AGRICULTURAL EQUIPMENT IN THE NORTH AFRICAN SUBREGION

| | No. | Type of operation | Capacity Year | Capacity t/y | Production Year | Production t/y | Products/remarks |
|---|---|---|---|---|---|---|---|
| **Pumps and valves** | | | | | | | |
| Algeria | ... | ... | ... | ... | ... | ... | Centrifugal and high pressure pumps, valves. |
| Egyp | ... | ... | ... | ... | ... | ... | Irrigation pump sets, taps, valves, pumps and catings. |
| Morocco | ... | ... | ... | ... | ... | 1750 | Pumps |
| Tunisia | ... | ... | ... | ... | ... | 4000 | Pumps |
| **Diesel engines** | | | | | | | |
| Algeria | 1 | Manufacturing | ... | 10000 | ... | ... | Engines for tractors, trucks and stationary equipment. |
| Egypt | 2 | Manufacturing | ... | ... | ... | ... | Engines for irrigation pumps, welding and standby generators. |
| Morocco | 2 | Assembling | ... | ... | ... | ... | Based on CKD kits. |
| Tunisia | 2 | Assembling | ... | ... | ... | ... | CKD engines for dumper trucks and pumps. |
| **Agricultural tractors** | | | | | | | |
| Algeria | 1 | Manufacturing | ... | 10000 | 1982 | 4500 | |
| Egypt | 1 | Manufacturing /assembling | ... | 5000 | ... | ... | |
| Libya | 1 | Assembling | ... | 5000 | ... | ... | |
| Morocco | 1 | Assembling | ... | 3000 | ... | ... | |
| Tunisia | 1 | Assembling | ... | 6000 | ... | ... | |
| Sudan | 1 | Assembling | ... | 3000 | ... | ... | |

Source: Compiled from UNIDO, 1987, *Strategies and Policies for the Development of the Capital Goods Sector in the Arab World*, Vienna.

The development of powered agricultural machinery in the region is at its initial stage. Most of the production units are assemblies, mainly based on imported SKD/CKD packs (engines, transmission systems, hydraulic systems, steering mechanisms, etc.), some of them with very little local content. As the assembled or imported machineries were not designed for African conditions, they usually require extensive maintenance and more frequent change of parts.

The assembly plants are located in Algeria, Libya, Tunisia, Egypt, Ethiopia, Tanzania, Zimbabwe, Nigeria, Burkina Faso, and Ghana. The three units in Zimbabwe are reported to operate only whenever barter deal, aid, etc., arrangements are made.

## Priority Products
Of the powered agricultural machinery, tractors constitute by far the most useful and widely used, both at pre- and post-harvest levels. In addition to their contribution on the farm proper, they provide services in transporting agricultural inputs and outputs.

Use of other machinery, such as combine harvesters, sprayers, and mowers, is likely to increase appreciably with time as mechanized and irrigation farming develops. Pumping water constitutes a high-cost element in irrigation. In view of the urgent need to substantially increase the production of food and therefore productivity, the role to be played by tractors and other machines would be increasingly critical.

## Strategies for Development

Unlike agricultural implements, powered agricultural machineries are complex to manufacture. This, coupled with small and fragmented national markets in practically all African countries and proliferation of makes and models, makes it difficult, if not impossible, to successfully operate production units at national level in most African countries.

Cooperation among groups of member states is the only practical solution if manufacturing of tractors and other powered machinery is to be developed in the region. As suggested in ECA/HMT, joint production units should be established to serve their needs. The units should be integrated, that is, central units manufacturing basic components for assembly plants (existing and new ones to be established) in the member states. This strategy is obviously based on pooling markets and resources of the member states concerned. In addition, arrangements could be made for production units within the country and within the subregions to have access to complementary use of support facilities in member countries. Foundries are good examples of such facilities. There is no need to duplicate costly facilities if access to existing ones can be arranged.

There are a number of conditions that need to be met for this strategy to work. The first is to rationalize and standardize the products to be locally made. This would mean selecting and determining the number of types and makes of simple and robust designs adapted to African conditions and taking into account the multipurpose role (farming and transporting) the tractors are expected to play. The second is for member states concerned to agree on the locations of the central units intended to make the critical sub-assemblies (engines, transmission systems, hydraulic systems, steering mechanisms, etc.) and the assembly plants as well as ancillary units specialized in the manufacture of certain critical parts and components, taking into account, as much as practical, fair distribution of production units among member states. In this connection, it should be noted that the engineering industry offers possibilities for fair distribution of manufacturing industries in the region.

As for other machinery, their manufacture could be taken up at a later stage. Experience gained in establishing and operating tractors would enhance their development.

The strategies suggested above will not be of much use unless they are complemented by proper maintenance system. It is therefore imperative that such a system be introduced and strictly applied with a view to increasing the service life of tractors and other agricultural machinery. This applies to all industries and services making use of engineering products.

Making capital goods (equipment and machinery) for manufacturing powered agricultural machinery is highly specialized and complex, comprising the manufacture of engines, transmission systems, hydraulic systems, steering mechanisms, etc., and support services, including foundries, die casting, and forges. It uses conventional and special-purpose machine tools, jigs, tools, fixtures, etc. and lots of parts and components, such as electrical components, instruments, gauges, tires, sheet glass, paint, etc., from ancillary industries, usually based on subcontracting arrangements. As it is unlikely that, under African conditions, all parts and components can be contracted or procured, the factories and assembling units will have to manufacture more parts and components than is common in the industrialized countries or NICs. In this connection, the development of ancillary industries should be promoted concurrently.

The early development of the capital goods under consideration would enable member states to achieve the production of powered agricultural machinery and reap the benefits resulting from standardization. In view of this, comprehensive studies should be carried out in the shortest time possible with a view to identifying, estimating demand for, and standardizing powered agricultural machinery as suggested above.

The study would be followed by other sets of studies whose objectives would be to determine (a) the viability of developing the local manufacture of powered agricultural machinery and (b) the capital goods industry for making that powered agricultural machinery. In other words, studies, including activities related to both industries, will have to be carried out in parallel. This approach would save both time and money and enhance early introduction of standardization and use of the capital goods manufacturing facilities.

In developing powered agricultural machinery, or for that matter any agricultural equipment, there is no need to reinvent the wheel. Many developing countries, particularly the NICs, with similar agro-climatic conditions, have adapted equipment and machinery from industrialized countries to suit their needs and conditions. It would be easier, quicker, and less expensive to adapt, if necessary, already adapted equipment and machinery for local manufacture. Drip irrigation is, for instance, a technology that African countries, particularly those with limited water resources, should adopt and try to manufacture locally the parts and components required therein.

The small market constraint to the local manufacture of tractors could be minimized by taking appropriate measures. Some of the measures relate to encouraging and supporting tractor hire, service and hire-purchase schemes. Another is the provision of maintenance and repair services within reasonable distances. Last but not least is to design and promote the use of a multipurpose tractor that, in addition to providing locomotion, can furnish power to tractor-drawn machines and drive equipment, such as pumps, grinders, and electric generators.

## BIBLIOGRAPHY

ECA, 1988, *Technical Publication of the Agricultural Equipment Maintenance Capacity on an Identified National, Subregional or Regional Institution for Maintenance of Agricultural Equipment,* ECA/IND/ENG/009/88, Addis Ababa.

ECA, 1988, *Workshop on the Manufacture of Agricultural Tools, Implements and Machinery in the West African Subregion* (ECA/IND/ENG/007/88), Addis Ababa.

ECA, 1989, *Role of Technology in Small Farmers' Productivity in Africa* (ECA/SDA/IRD/89/1.1(ii)(b)), Addis Ababa.

ECA, 1993, *Guidelines on the Manufacture of Agricultural Tools, Implements and Low-cost Transport Equipment by Small-scale Engineering Industries in the Context of the Second Industrial Development Decade for Africa,* ECA/IHSD/IDPS/010/92, Addis Ababa.

ECA, 1996, *Africa in the 1990s and Beyond: ECA-Revised Long-Term Development Perspectives Study* (ECA/SERPD/TP/96/3), Addis Ababa.

ECA/HMT, 1988, *Engineering Industry Development Programme for Selected Eastern and Southern African Countries of Preferential Trade Area (Model Pre-feasibility Report —Agricultural Machinery, Equipment and Tractors),* Addis Ababa.

FAO, 1986, *African Agriculture: the next 25 Years,* annex III, Rome.

FAO, 1986, *African Agriculture: the next 25 Years,* Annex IV, Rome.

FAO, 1986, *Atlas of African Agriculture* (African agriculture: the next 25 years), Rome.

FAO, 1994, *FAO Trade Yearbook,* Rome.

FAO, 1986, *Irrigation in Africa South of the Sahara,* Rome.

Parish, Dennis H., 1985, "Appropriate Fertilizer Technology for Sub-Saharan Africa," *Proceeding of Fertilizer Efficiency Research and Technology Transfer Workshop for Africa South of the Sahara,* January 21-25, Douala.

The Economist, 1998, "Squeezing Water from the Sea," April 4, 1998.

UNIDO, 1979, *Appropriate Industrial Technology for Agricultural Machinery and Implements,* Monographs on Appropriate Industrial Technology, No. 4, UN, New York.

World Bank, 1996, *World Resources 1996-97,* Oxford University Press, New York.

CHAPTER 11

# EQUIPMENT AND MACHINERY FOR PROCESSING AGRICULTURAL PRODUCTS

Agro-industral development is based on the processing of agricultural products. Agricultural processing is required to preserve products and to convert them into usable forms with reasonable shelf lives. Losses during processing are significant. Estimates by the American National Academy of Sciences (*Post-harvest Food Losses in Developing Countries*), for instance, show that losses in rice processing in Southeast Asia were 1 to 5 percent for drying, 2 to 10 percent for milling, and greater than 2 percent for washing prior to cooking. Examples of agricultural materials processing at small-scale level are given in Annex 11.1. The list includes agricultural materials relevant to African needs and conditions.

Many foodstuffs characterized by high moisture content (fruits, vegetables, cassava, potato, plantain, etc.) are perishable due to physical, physiological, and pathological damage. A substantial part of the food produced is lost for want of proper handling and storage at the farm, village, and urban levels. Post-harvest food losses, between and including threshing/shelling and storage, have been estimated at 20 to 40 percent, of which 5 percentage points are attributed to storage alone. In Nigeria, food losses during storage were 10 percent for coarse grains, 15 percent for major roots and tubers and fruits and vegetables, 10 to 20 percent for legumes, and 25 percent for fish (UNIDO, Appropriate ... Processing).

## FOOD PRESERVATION AND PROCESSING

Large amounts of food, especially seasonal produce are wasted for lack of preservation and inadequate processing technology and packaging, thus contributing to the growing shortage of food in Africa. Improvements in food preservation and processing could significantly improve self-sufficiency in food as well as minimize price fluctuations between post-harvest gluts and pre-harvest shortages. Drying, salt-pickling, and smoking are the traditional preservation methods practiced in Africa.

In most African countries, the food industry is the lead industry. Its contribution to manufacturing is high in 1985. It stood at 62 percent in Burkina Faso and 77 percent in Rwanda (UN, *Survey...in Africa*, 1987-1988).

The traditional method of food processing in developing countries is a tedious and time-consuming daily activity for the women. It is rather wasteful and its products have restricted shelf-lives. Unlike in developed countries, practically all food is prepared from basic raw materials at every home, at least in the rural and semi-urban areas. These inefficient and inconvenient means of processing include: shelling, husking, grating, drying, pounding, grinding, and cooking using inefficient and inconvenient means of processing and cooking.

The traditional processing equipment encompass the wooden mortar and pestle for pounding grain, stone grinders, cassava peelers and graters, and oil presses. These are giving way to hand- or pedal-operated mills and/or small custom grain mills (milling for a fee), improved cassava peelers/graters, and oil-expellers.

## Consumption/Production Gaps

In Africa, most of the food-processing equipment and machinery is imported. In a limited number of countries some of the equipment is made locally. Equipment manufactured in Africa includes: gari processors, palm kernel processors, and sugar cane crushers. As for traditional and mini-scale processing units, most are manufactured locally, mainly using imported raw materials. The supply/demand gap cannot be quantified and the potential for the local manufacture of food processing equipment and machinery cannot be determined.

## Priority Products

When considering priorities, the main concern is the need to reduce the time that women need to complete their daily routine (processing and preparing food and taking care of children as well as farming, fetching water, and collecting fuel wood). Their plight is worsening because of increasing distance to sources of water and wood. This calls for better technologies and equipment. Women should have at their disposal improved equipment for decorticating, dehusking, grinding, oil extracting, baking, cooking, and preserving. Fuel-efficient stoves would reduce both fuel collection time and deforestation. Some of the equipment could be solar- or wind- or water-powered.

At the industrial level, priority should be given to equipment and machinery for milling grain, processing roots and tubers, extracting oil, refrigeration/freezing, pasteurization, drying/dehydration, canning, making bread and confectionery.

## Current Stage of Development

As noted above, in most African households, food is processed at home. The traditional methods of processing are usually laborious and inefficient (wasteful and time-consuming); by-products are not used effectively. A trend towards processed food, particularly partially processed food, is becoming apparent in urban areas.

Better and more efficient equipment is being introduced as Africans' R&D gets under way. They include hand-held shellers, manual husking devices, and hand-operated grinders. Hammer mills are most commonly used, although plate mills are popular in parts of West Africa.

R&D into the small-scale industrial processing of non-wheat cereals and cassava has been carried out in some countries in Africa. The Food Research Centre (FRC) in the Sudan focuses on sorghum, the Institut de Technologie Alimentaire (ITA) in Senegal on millet, and the Société Ivoirienne de Technologie Tropicale in Cote d'Ivoire on cassava.

Cereal milling equipment has undergone modifications in a number of countries. The Botswana dehuller in Botswana, the Ndume hammer mills in Kenya, the Arusha hammer mills in Tanzania, the ABI dehuller in Cote d'Ivoire, the Simar hammer mill and dehuller and the Noflaye mill in Senegal are examples of successful adaptation. Some of the equipment is multi-purpose and can grind all types of cereals as well as roots and tubers.

Hand peeling was invariably the method used throughout Africa to process roots and tubers. A breakthrough, "Broyage différentiel," was achieved by the Société Ivoirienne de Technologie Tropicale (I2T) in Cote d'Ivoire in 1981-1983. Mechanical peeling of cassava became more efficient than hand peeling. Adaptations and innovations in regard to other cassava-related technologies include the ITDG pedal-operated cassava grater in Nigeria, the TAEC vertical drum grater in Sierra Leone, the TCC parallel board press in Ghana, and the AGRICO roaster and rotating drum sieve in Ghana. The Rural Agro-Industry Development Scheme (RAIDS) in Nigeria enjoyed great success with its gari-making equipment, with 1,500 village gari production units in operation (ECA, ECA/IHSD/AGR/010/91).

In the field of oil extraction, the traditional method is characterized by about 40 percent extraction efficiency. At industry level, the method commonly used is mechanical pressing. Use of solvent extraction is limited. Refining facilities are normally located in or near major consumption centers. The Nigerian Institute for Oil Palm Research (NIFOR) achieved a major breakthrough with its small-scale palm oil processing equipment, whose performance is claimed to be as good as or even better than industrial oil mills. It was being mass produced and supplied to small-scale oil palm growers. Extraction rates are as high as 97 percent. RAIDS has come with its version of a mini palm oil mill for village-level palm oil processing. More than 300 of these mills are in operation in Nigeria. Other adaptations and innovations include the AGRICO palm kernel nut roaster and TCC press in Ghana.

Other food-processing equipment manufactured in some countries includes a millet mill that can mill wet grain in Senegal, and groundnut shellers, rice hulling machines, coal pots, flour mixers, corn mills, power-presses and refrigerators in Ghana.

The following are among African manufacturers supplying equipment for processing cereals and cassava (ECA, ECA/IHSD/AGR/010/91) and (UNIFEM/ITDG, *Cereal Processing*):

- Ndume Hand Grinding Mill (maize) in Kenya;
- Ndume Hammer Muill (maize, sorghum, millet) in Kenya;
- Manghula Mechanical and Machine Tools Co. (cereals) in Tanzania;
- Mwanza Engineering Works (cereals) in Tanzania;
- Mike Motors, Auto Engines (cereals) in Tanzania;
- D&M Inventors (cereals) in Tanzania;
- Manik Engineers, Manufacturers of Maize Mills, in Tanzania;
- MGM Hammer Mill (maize, sorghum, millet) in Tanzania;
- PRL/RIIC (dehuller/hammer mill combination for sorghum) in Botswana;
- Chitetze Maize Sheller, in Malawi;
- Agricultural Engineers Ltd (cassava), in Ghana;
- Project Development Institute (cassava) in Nigeria; and
- Société Ivoirienne de Technologie Tropicale (cassava flour, gari and attieke) in Cote d'Ivoire.

## Strategies for Development

Traditional techniques for storing food include burying, coating with mud, wetting and placing under water. At both the farm and village levels, traditional storage facilities made from local materials (bins, cribs, barns) need to be improved, including redesigning and modifying existing structures, as well as popularizing plastic sacks and metal drums, bins, and tanks. In urban centers, godowns for storage in bags are common and relatively cheap compared with modern silos. These and other forms, such as silos and bins, as well as cryogenic-based storage facilities, should be developed to meet the needs dictated by climatic conditions. It should be noted that, in addition to conservation, storage is required in many African countries to hold buffer stocks for use during drought and to minimize supply fluctuations. Storage needs will increase in relation to growth in food production that will come about with the introduction of modern farming methods.

Under African conditions, food processing can be considered at three levels: household/village, small-scale, and medium-scale/large-scale. Most of the food consumed in rural, semi-urban, and a greater part of the urban areas is processed at home. Mini-scale food processing is slowly penetrating these areas, mainly in the area of flour milling, roots and tubers processing, and oil extraction. Generally, small-scale and medium-scale food-processing methods dominate the scene in large urban areas while large-scale food processing appears to be limited to relatively rich and large economies.

Given the warm and humid ambient conditions prevailing in most parts of the continent, agricultural produce, particularly those items with a high moisture content, are more exposed to micro-organisms and fungus and therefore degrade faster than in a temperate climate. They have to be kept at appropriate moisture levels so as to minimize attack by micro-organisms. In addition to providing proper storage, this means applying preservation methods relevant to specific products. Dehydration/drying (sun), salting, smoking and fermentation are among the traditional methods of preservation and processing.

Traditional and modern (imported) technologies and their combinations are in use. All these technologies, no doubt, require improvements and better adaptation. Upgrading traditional and indigenous products and developing and popularizing indigenous low-cost products would be among the desirable improvements and changes. Care, however, should be taken to ensure that such measures will not result in large-scale displacement of labor. It will, of necessity, take time. R&D will have to continue in order to reduce the drudgery of the women folk, improve efficiency, reduce waste, and improve hygiene in food processing and preparation at home and cottage levels.

Many unit operations and processes are used in food preserving and processing. They include the following:

• Cereal processing—threshing, shelling/decorticating, husking/dehulling, drying, milling/grinding, baking, fermenting (drinks);

• Roots and tubers processing—peeling, grating, pounding, pressing, sieving, fermenting, frying/roasting, drying, grinding/milling, curing;

• Vegetable oil processing—shelling/decorticating, drying, crushing, expelling, solvent extracting, refining;

• Fruit processing—dehulling, drying, pulping/extracting, filtering/straining, mixing (with other ingredients), heat treating/pasteurising, freezing, canning, fermenting (drinks);
  • Vegetable processing—drying, salting, pickling, sauce-making, fermenting;
  • Dairy industry—chilling, skimming, concentrating, drying;
  • Meat processing—drying, smoking, freezing, refrigerating, canning; and
  • Fish preservation—drying, smoking, salting, freezing, refrigerating, fermenting, canning.

Some of the unit operations and processes are common to more than one category of food materials. Drying is the most common. Exposure to sunlight and, to some extent, hot air based on wood and/or crop waste burning is extensively used in rural area. Because of its negligible running costs, use of solar energy could be significant in the future. Plastic sheeting cover can be used to improve hygienic drying. Research into solar energy should, therefore, be carried out to maximize the utilization of this huge potential in Africa. Related to this is the need to improve thermal efficiency in the food processing industry as a whole, as fuel economy could well determine the success of many food-processing ventures, existing and projected.

Cereal processing comprises primary and secondary processing. The former includes all activities from threshing to milling, while the latter deals with the production of food products for direct consumption (bread) or intermediates requiring final preparations (pasta).

Existing technologies for milling cereals (other than manual grinding and pounding) are based mainly on wheat. Because of the differences in characteristics between wheat and African staple cereals (maize, sorghum, and millet), the wheat-based technology needs to be adapted or completely new technologies introduced. With respect to maize, the situation is a little different. Maize farmers use rice dehullers, which have been successfully adapted to dehull maize  The small one-pass Japanese rubber roller mills with higher rice recovery are worth mentioning here for possible adoption and adaptation.

In the long run, small-scale mills are likely to face competition from large mills. Custom mills provide services that large mills do not. With custom mills, the customer can have grain milled at his/her convenience and in quantities commensurate with needs. This means the customer does not have to hold a large stock of flour and expose himself/herself to loss. In view of this and their contributions to rural industrialization, small-scale mills should be encouraged and protected.

It appears that there are no adequate storage systems for roots and tubers. Unlike many other crops, cassava can grow in dry and nutrient-deficient soils (UNIFEM/ITDG, *Root Crop Processing*) and can be harvested throughout the year (UNIDO, *Food-Processing Industry*). It can keep intact in the field for some months and is harvested in small quantity for use within 48 hours (UNIDO, *Appropriate ... Processing*). Traditional cassava processing involves detoxification through the release of hydrogen cyanide. Production of gari, one of cassava's products, entails peeling, grating, fermenting, and roasting. This technique has been translated into commercial operations in Brazil and Nigeria. In Nigeria, for instance, many gari plants designed and commercialized by the Federal Institute of Industrial Research (FIIR) are in operation. This is a good example of what can and should be done in upgrading traditional technologies.

The traditional village processing of oleaginous crops (oil-bearing seeds and fruits), which accounts for a greater part of demand, leaves much to be desired. Less than half of the oil (40% for oil seeds and 20-30% for palm fruit) (UNIFEM/ ITDG, *Oil Extraction*) is extracted; even the most perfect expellers leave at least six percent of oil in the cake (ILO, *Small-scale Oil Extraction ...*). Cakes rich in oil are not fit for use as animal feed.

High energy input is required to expel oil from oil-seeds. Better yields may be achieved either by using powered equipment or new innovation that does not require pressing, the latter being the ideal situation for oil extraction in rural areas without electricity.

The Technology Consultancy Centre in Ghana (UNIFEM/ITDG, *Oil Extraction*) has designed and constructed a hand-operated mini oil mill comprising a boiling tank, a pounding machine, a screw press, a clarifying tank, and a storage tank. About 30 mills were reported operating by mid-1980s. With an average capacity of 500 kg of oil per day and working 180 days per year, these mills produce about 2,700 tons of oil per year, a significant contribution to the reduction of palm oil imports.

At the industry level, oil processing is done mainly by powered screw expellers. Some relatively large oil mills use solvent extraction. The latter could collect cakes, if practical, from traditional and small mills and extract as much as possible the oil remaining in the cakes. Alternatively, solvent extraction units could be established to process oil seeds as well as cakes produced by other oil mills. With the exception of oils from large oil mills, which incorporate refining (neutralization, decolorization, filtration, and deoderization), practically all oils are consumed raw as produced. Generally, small-scale mills incorporate filtering. Here simple and inexpensive techniques are needed that could remove part of the impurities not removed by filtration. The same applies to increasing the extraction rate of small expellers.

As living standards improve, the market for refined oil will increase. Oil refining units, integrated oil mills, and/or oil refineries based on crude oil from small-scale oil mills will have to be set up near the major consumption centers.

Unlike cereals and, to some extent, some roots and tubers, fruits, vegetables, meat, dairy products, and fish deteriorate very rapidly and thus require immediate preservation and processing. Some of them, fruits and vegetables, are usually seasonal. Their shelf-lives should be increased if their use is to be optimized for an extended period of time and if their profitability is to be ensured.

Generally, fresh fruits are acidic and therefore do not provide good media for growth of dangerous micro-organisms. They can be preserved in the forms of syrups, juices, squashes, pickles, jams, marmalades, wines, and vinegar. Under African conditions, especially in rural areas, improved drying appears to be the most practical. As jams and pickles are produced by boiling whole fruit and other ingredients, there is no reason why they (with some acceptable quality) cannot be made in villages provided the other ingredients (sugar and vinegar) are available at affordable prices. Making deep-fried potato chips is another example of food processing that can be carried out at the village level.

Other processes use more relatively complex equipment for pulping, extracting juice, filtering, straining, mixing, heat treating (including pasteurizing), and fermenting. Because of these processes and the use of some chemicals and pH-adjustments, coupled with the precision requirement for some of the processes and very limited market, it is unlikely that processes other than drying are practical at the household level. One way to circumvent some of these constraints is to follow the example of Agrolab in Saint Vincent (UNIFEM/ITDG, *Fruit and Vegetable Processing*). Agrolab uses a van that goes from village to village, purchases fruit, squeezes the fruit on the spot, adds preservatives, and takes the juice back to the plant for further processing.

There is every potential for canning and bottling some of the exotic tropical fruits for export. As for vegetable preservation, drying is the simplest and cheapest method practiced at the household and cottage-scale levels. Other processes include salting, pickling, sauce-making, and fermenting. Freezing ( involving refrigerated stores and transport) and canning are used at the industrial level, as they require higher levels of technology and capital.

Irradiation is a process with apparent potential in Africa. According to a WHO statement in 1994, *"food irradiation is safe and effective,"* provided good manufacturing practices are followed. It would thus be worthwhile to promote its use. The same applies to dehydration.

Given the potential for African fruit and vegetable exports, particularly during winter in the northern hemisphere, there is no option but to use the latest state of the art of technology for the basic part of the operation if Africa is to compete successfully. This calls for the indigenous development of capabilities and capacities for manufacturing freezing and canning equipment and machinery as well as manufacturing cans and other packaging materials, in addition to equipment for cottage and small-scale processing units.

With respect to meat, meat products, and fish, the same applies as for fruits and vegetables, albeit to a lesser extent. A substantial part of the slaughtering is done at home or at the cottage level. Modern slaughterhouses are located solely in major urban centers. Most of their by-products and wastes are discarded, as the small quantities produced do not justify economies of scale.

Given the unfavorable climate, the prevalence of animal diseases, and poor animal husbandry practices, coupled with low lactation yields (200-300 kg per cow per year for marketing) (FAO, *African Agriculture: the next 25 Years, Annex III*), the dairy industry in Africa is in a sorry state. As a result, the region is dependent on imports of dairy products. Owing to its scarcity and unaffordable price, milk is a luxury food. Under these circumstances, the improvement of animal husbandry should obviously precede the development of manufacturing capability of dairy equipment.

Most poultry production is based on the traditional systems, with chickens being essentially left to feed themselves through scavenging. The annual egg production per chicken is of the order of 20 to 30. This output could be doubled by improving the traditional system (supplementary feed, vaccination, care of chicks, etc.) while improved breeds could increase productivity six-fold. Modern hatchery systems, incorporating integrated husbandry, could achieve similar results as in temperate climates (FAO, *African Agriculture: the next 25 Years, Annex III*). Given these possibilities and the relative simplicity of hatchery equipment, the local private sector could manufacture such equipment.

About 10 percent of world fish catch is lost up to and during distribution. This can rise to 40 percent in the case of small-scale fish processing (UNIFEM/ITDG,

Fish Processing). According to another source (ILO, *Small-scale Processing of Fish*), 25 percent of a catch of fish may be lost before consumption. If fish loss and spoilage were reduced, more protein would be available to offset protein-defficient diet of many Africans. Improvement in fish curing, including drying, salting and smoking, the traditional fish preservation methods, could also increase yield and thereby contribute to an increased protein intake. Certain advances are reflected in the Cote d'Ivoire kiln, an improved traditional method of smoking made from inexpensive materials (ILO, *Small-scale Processing of Fish*) and the Ghanaian Chorkor smoker characterized by low construction costs which has been introduced in Guinea and Togo [UNIFEM/ITDG, *Fish Processing*]. Other preservation methods, apparently not practiced in Africa, are boiling and fermentation. Boiling followed by drying could yield products that can keep for months [ILO, *Small-scale Processing of Fish*]. Fermentation, which inhibits spoilage by increasing the acidity within the fish (hydrolysis of proteins), is another fish preservation method. Fermented fish products range from those which retain substantially their original form to paste and liquid forms [ILO, *Small-scale Processing of Fish*]. Since both methods have not been tried extensively in Africa, it may be worthwhile to build on the experience of South East Asia. A more stable fish preparation can be made by comminuting fresh fish with cereals and roots and tubers.

Canning (thermal processing) is the ultimate method of preserving fish. It is beyond the capacity and capability of individual fishermen and processors unless they form cooperatives comprising fishermen, processors, and marketing people and organizations. Countries endowed with abundance of fish whose current rate of exploitation is far below the so-called maximum sustainable yield should consider optimal exploitation of this resource on an industrial scale. In many cases and in the initial stages this would mean canning mainly for export. In this connection, the replacement of cans by foil/plastic laminated pouches should be considered as an alternative to metal cans. The Cote d'Ivoire experience in tuna canning is a case in point.

Production and use of fish meal and fish oil do not appear to have taken root in Africa. Their use needs to be popularized, as their production can be integrated with other fish-processing activities, thereby offering economies of scale.

Improvements in fish curing will, however, need to be supplemented by providing fishermen with ice to minimize spoilage before curing. The ideal solution would be to establish networks of cold storage facilities supported by refrigerated transport accessible to fishermen. Some countries with adequate fish resources may consider manufacturing fishing nets and gears as well as processing machinery and equipment. Improved storage and packaging systems would complement their fishing and processing needs.

The fishery industry has a waste-disposal problem. In many tropical fisheries, catches often include more than 30 species (ILO, *Small-scale Processing of Fish*). A part of the catch may be rejected on account of tastes, preferences, or taboos. Given the differing preservation requirements for so many species, it may be impractical to cure the whole catch properly. This adds to the natural spoilage due to lack of adequate preservation before and during processing. Appropriate ways and means will have to be found to optimize the utilization of these wastes and use of offal, heads, and trimmings as manure/fertilizer and/or fish silage (animal feed).

At the industrial level, the African experience has been that many industries based on the processing of agricultural commodities failed for want of commodities of the right quality and quantity at the time required. It would, therefore, make sense to bring the cultivation and processing of food raw materials under the same ownership or work-out arrangements between growers, preferably cooperatives, and processors. The growers cooperative approach has some merit as it benefits the local farmers and therefore creates mutual vested interest in the success of the agro-industry project.

All food-processing industries invariably produce waste as well as by-products. In general, such wastes and by-products are discarded, as the small quantities generated by individual units cannot be converted into useful products because of economies of scale. This inability to utilize by-products and wastes contributes to low productivity in the agricultural processing activities. That notwithstanding, recycling and conversion into useful products should be encouraged and practiced. Conversion of coir from coconut processing into ropes, mats, bags, and brushes are examples of what can be done with wastes and by-products. One possible approach would be to set up central animal-feed units designed to process by-products and waste generated (oil cake, fish-meal, slaughterhouse meals, molasses, cereal bran, etc.) from food-processing units within a certain radius of the unit. They could also produce glue, gelatin, etc., from slaughterhouse by-products and waste or generate on-site energy through biogas fermentation. In short, all possible avenues for the utilization of by-products and wastes should be explored when planning food and other agricultural processing industries. Where applicable, existing industries should be reviewed to find out how their wastes can be utilized.

As is well known, starch constitutes the basic staple food for the majority of Africans; as a result most African diets are deficient in protein. There is, therefore, a need to improve the nutritional value. In addition to supplementing starch with high-protein foodstuffs, such as soybeans and groundnut, and increasing the protein content of staple crops, starch could be enriched with protein during processing. Protein from soybeans and fish protein concentrate (edible but not eaten) could be used for this purpose. This, of course, means that R&D has to be carried out.

Convenient foods and snacks are being introduced in major cities in many African countries. Demand is likely to increase with the fast-growing urbanization and labor force. Conventional convenience foods and snacks are based on wheat and other ingredients that may not be available locally. Because of this and the fact that they are too expensive for most workers, R&D should be carried out in convenience foods and snacks based on dietary staples.

At the industrial level, imported technologies should be adapted to local conditions. As shown above, there are Africans, in some countries at least, who have mastered adequate knowledge and experience to modify existing technologies and innovate technologies that meet African conditions and needs. Based on adapted and innovative technologies, including modern intermediate processing technologies, industrialists need to translate the results of that R&D into equipment and machinery for processing food and making the same available to food processors. Some kind of organization will be required to coordinate all these tasks and facilitate the commercialization of R&D results. In other words, indigenous capabilities and capacities need to be built into local R&D and the manufacture of processing machinery and equipment.

In conclusion, more food-processing equipment, both in terms of numbers and variety, needs to be adapted and innovated. They would include equipment for shelling, dehulling, decorticating, dehusking, peeling, grating, drying, roasting, milling, sieving, pressing (extracting), fermenting, baking, refrigerating, canning, and other means of preserving food and packaging. To this should be added extrusion equipment for the production of enriched flours for weaning foods. Technologies adapted or innovated in other developing countries could hasten their acceptance in Africa. The double-drum and Japanese drum threshers and mechanical threshing, drying, and milling that have proved viable in Asia could be, with perhaps small adaptations, adopted at the cottage level.

Some countries in Africa have been undertaking R&D activities with a view to formulating weaning foods based on local food substances. Many of them, however, failed because their products were too expensive. Following such failures, formulas and processing techniques were devised and put into practice in Benin and Sierra Leone. The weaning food made comprised a mixture of 60 percent cereals (rice, maize and sorghum), 15 percent pulses (pigeon peas or cowpeas) and 25 percent oilseeds (groundnuts or sesame). Roasting, cereal-and-bean mixture milling, oilseed milling, and mixing the milled components constitute the main processes used (UNIFEM/ITDG, *Cereal Processing*). CEREVAP, a weaning food based on local materials in Congo K, is among the successful variants. In Ethiopia, weaning food named "fafa" has been in use for over three decades. A mixture of 70 percent maize and 30 percent soybeans has been reported to have won acceptance in Tanzania.

Food for the majority of people will continue to be processed for a long time to come in the informal/traditional sector using the tedious and laborious traditional methods. The focus in food processing equipment should thus be on improving traditional and village level equipment and introducing innovative and time- and labor-saving techniques and devices. Simple manually operated equipment that can be made and maintained by village blacksmiths, needs to be improved, developed, and popularized for household use. This approach would, it is hoped, contribute to delaying and minimizing the negative impact, the loss of jobs that could result from modernizing the food-processing industry. In this connection, those involved in such activities should consult the UNIFEM/ITDG Food Cycle Technology Source Book series listed under "BIBLIOGRAPHY" on this chapter.

As most people will not, for a long time to come, be able to afford such means as refrigerators to keep food unspoiled, increasing the shelf-lives of foods is crucial. R&D in this area is of utmost importance to the rural people and the low-income urban dwellers. Non-African institutions, such as the Intermediate Technology Development Group (ITDG) of the United Kingdom, which have contributed to the improvement and development of food processing technologies and equipment, could heighten their contribution by redeploying their facilities to Africa and working under African environmental conditions.

Energy is one of the constraints in rural industrialization. Use of water for generating mechanical power is worth considering in areas endowed with streams that can be relatively easily harnessed. This approach is particularly applicable to flour and oil mills.

In many cases, success in food processing in rural areas may depend on pooling material, financial, and human resources. This could be done by establishing cooperatives, preferably comprising producers of food raw materials and individuals and marketing organizations. Because of the likelihood of more benefits accruing to rural areas, this approach should be considered when planning food-processing industries in those areas.

As is well known, domestic animals in Africa depend on grass and crop residues for their food. The lignin content in such feed is difficult to degrade. Research being carried out in the world includes addition of chemical additives to the feed and genetic manipulation of the microbes that degrade fibrous roughage. As the latter process offers great potential under African conditions, undertaking local R&D in this field would be worthwhile.

In the developed countries which supply African countries with the industrial machinery and equipment they require, the trend is toward sophisticated and complex (automated and computerized) food technology. R&D is currently geared towards meeting the changing life style of the people in developed countries, particularly eating away from home, thereby increasing reliance on convenience foods. The food technologies designed to meet such needs will not be relevant to African countries for a long time to come — hence the need to develop, as soon as possible, capabilities and capacities in the manufacture of traditional food processing and packaging machinery and equipment, packaging being an essential component of reducing loss and spoilage.

## TEXTILE MILLS

Africans have been weaving and, to a decreasing extent, will continue to weave along traditional lines; in some areas local wooden handlooms have been and continue to be improved. As they are among the first units to be established in developing countries, modern textile mills have been on the African scene for quite some time.

### Consumption/Production Gaps

Practically every country in Africa has at least one textile mill; most, however, are almost completely dependent on imported machinery and equipment. In other words, there are practically no industries manufacturing such equipment and machinery.

### Priority Products

The existing textile mills are mainly based on cotton. As cotton is likely to remain the major fiber for making textiles, cotton ginning, spinning, weaving, and finishing equipment and machinery would constitute the priorities in this industry. Use of hand spinning, hand looms, and finishing, such as tie-and-die, will continue for some time to come. Equipment and machinery for these processes need to be improved.

### Current Stage of Development

The absence of textile equipment manufacturing facilities in Africa is referred to above. It appears that there are no known plans for developing such industries.

## Strategies for Development

Textile mills have access to a wide range of techniques and technologies. According to UNIDO (*Appropriate...Textiles*), the alternatives for the major processes, excluding pre-spinning operations, include:

- Spinning—ring spinning frame, open-end spinning machine;
- Weaving—power looms, non-automatic looms, conventional automatic looms, high-speed automatic looms, shuttleless looms; and
- Printing—roller printing, flatbed screen printing, rotary screen printing.

These alternatives and their variations offer African countries a wide range of possibilities for combining technologies to meet their specific needs and choosing between capital-saving and labor-saving. In this connection, it should be noted that the general trend is towards greater automation.

The fact that there are a growing number of textile mills in the region points to the need to take measures to develop the textile equipment and machinery manufacturing industry. As with transport vehicles, this will involve rationalization and standardization, taking into account existing equipment and machinery. In view of the diversity of the equipment and machinery to be produced, the development of this industry would provide member states with opportunity to share production facilities fairly.

Measures, including negotiations, leading to the establishment of rationalized and standardized textile equipment and machinery manufacturing units will take time. In the mean time, existing mills should be rehabilitated and modernized, including balancing the equipment's productive capacity; and a start could be made by putting up factories to make critical and common parts and components for the existing mills, taking into account the future development of textile equipment manufacture.

As for traditional textiles, there is a need for improved equipment: hand spinning, hand weaving, and finishing techniques. Increased labor productivity and product quality should be the main objectives of the improvement. This could be achieved by R&D institutions (already established and to be established).

## MEDICINAL PLANTS PROCESSING

Processing fauna and flora, particularly medicinal plants, containing disease-preventing or curing substances, requires relatively simple technology and equipment. A good part of the equipment can be made in countries with advanced engineering industries.

### Consumption/Production Gaps

Production of medicines from plants is limited to some laboratories. There is virtually no information on production to warrant generalization. Under such circumstances, it may not be far from the truth to assume that production of equipment and machinery for processing medicinal plants in the region is practically nil.

### Priority Products

Equipment for processing medicinal plants can be divided into four functional categories: extraction of crude extract, isolation of active ingredient, conversion into active ingredient, and formulation. The need for and practicality of any one or a combination of this equipment will depend mainly on the size of the market.

## Current Stage of Development

As noted above, information on the local manufacture of medicinal plant processing equipment in the region, if any, is not available.

## Strategies for Development.

Capabilities for the manufacture of medicinal plant processing equipment, at least some parts and components, could be developed in some countries. A start could be made with manufacturing extraction equipment in line with chapter 8, which concluded that practically all African countries could and should go into the making of crude extracts. This could be followed by manufacturing equipment that can perform the other functions discussed in the same Chapter. As many formulation facilities already exist and more are likely to be established, earlier entry into the manufacture of certain parts and components for formulation could be justified.

## BIBLIOGRAPHY

ECA, 1991, *Technological Publication: Compendium of Selected Technologies and Equipment for Processing Maize, Tubers and Palm Oil* (ECA/IHSD/AGR/010/91), Addis Ababa.

FAO, 1986, *African Agriculture: the next 25 Years, Annex III, Raising Productivity*, Rome.

ILO, 1982, *Small-scale Processing of Fish*, Technical Memorandum No. 3, Geneva.

ILO, 1983, *Small-scale Oil Extraction from Groundnuts and Copra*, Technical Memorandum No. 5, Geneva.

National Academy of Sciences, 1978, *Post-harvest Food Losses in Developing Countries*, Washington, D. C.

UN, 1990, *Survey of Economic and Social Conditions in Africa, 1987-1988*, New York.

UNIDO, 1969, *Food Processing Industry*, Industrialization of Developing Countries: Problems and Prospects, UNIDO Monographs on Industrial Development, No. 9, UN, New York.

UNIDO, 1979, *Appropriate Industrial Technology for Food Storage and Processing*, Monographs on Appropriate Industrial Technology, No. 7, New York.

UNIDO, 1979, *Appropriate Industrial Technology for Textiles*, Monographs on Appropriate Industrial Technology, No. 6, New York.

UNIFEM/ITDG, 1987, *Oil Extraction*, 1 Food Cycle Technology Source Book, New York.

UNIFEM/ITDG, 1988, *Cereal Processing*, 3 Food Cycle Technology Source Book, New York.

UNIFEM/ITDG, 1988, *Fish Processing*, 4 Food Cycle Technology Source Book, New York.

UNIFEM/ITDG, 1988, *Fruit and Vegetable Processing*, 2 Food Cycle Technology Source Book, New York.

UNIFEM/ITDG, 1989, *Root Crop Processing*, 5 Food Cycle Technology Source Book, New York.

## CHAPTER 12

# EQUIPMENT AND MACHINERY FOR TRANSPORTING AGRICUTLURAL INPUTS AND OUTPUTS

In Africa, roads are the most common channels of transport that are used to convey both goods and passengers within a country and between neighboring countries. Since the advent of independence, more roads have been built than railways. Despite this, road density in Africa, which averages 0.05 km/km², is perhaps the lowest in the world and road networks are relatively poor.

In some countries many farmers are beyond the reach of the nearest road. For want of feeder roads some rural areas have limited or no access to the nearest towns where they can sell their produce or buy their needs, including agricultural inputs. The use of pack animals is not that significant in a number of countries. Vehicles in use are imported or assembled locally from imported components in semi-knocked-down ( SKD) or completely-kocked-down ( CKD) forms.

Road vehicles relevant to agriculture may be divided into two categories: large and small vehicles. The former are used to transport agricultural inputs from ports and local factories as well as other products to trading centers in the rural areas and agricultural products from such centers to consumption centers and ports for export. The latter render similar services between the farms and the trading centers or are used on the farm or the farmer's homestead.

## HEAVY AND LIGHT DUTY COMMERCIAL VEHICLES

Heavy-duty vehicles comprise trucks and lorries, with or without trailers. They include a wide variety of makes and models, thus contributing to the high cost of spare parts arising from the need to stock large inventories for each make and model.

### Status of the Industry

The production of transport equipment at five year intervals over a 15-year period is given in Annex 5.6. Among the six categories of vehicles, only trailers and semi-trailers showed steady increases throughout that period. All the other fluctuated, although in the case of lorries and trucks this occurred to a lesser extent.

The total number of commercial vehicles (all categories) in use in the private sector in 1983 in Africa was estimated at close to 4.38 million. This increased to 4.6 million in 1988 (ECA, *Guidelines... Africa*). In terms of vehicles per 1000 inhabitants, the ratio was 8.89 in 1983 and decreased to 8.27 in 1988. If the situation in Eastern and Southern Africa over the same period is any indication, 60 percent of the total figure represents light commercial vehicles. Demand for trucks (imported and locally assembled) in Eastern and Southern Africa in 1990 was estimated at 12,540 (ECA/HMT, *Model ... Vehicles*).

Locally assembled vehicles depend greatly on imported sub-assemblies, components, and parts. This, coupled with the import of vehicles and related parts and accessories, makes transport vehicles the group of imports with the highest drain on foreign exchange. During the second half of the 1980s, total imports at current FOB prices in that group increased from $6.7 billion in 1986 to close to $8 billion in 1990 (UNECE, *Bulletin ... Products*).

Table 12.1 gives some indication of trend and demand projections up to the year 2000 for commercial vehicles in Africa. It is apparent from the table that the density of commercial vehicles per 1000 inhabitants fell steadily over the years 1983, 1987, and 1992 in all subregions. The decreasing trend is evidently expected to continue up to the end of the century. This is in line with the deteriorating economic situation in the continent. In other words, things will likely get worse before they get better.

| TABLE 12.1 TOTAL FLEET OF AND DEMAND PROJECTIONS FOR COMMERCIAL VEHICLES IN AFRICA | | | | | | |
|---|---|---|---|---|---|---|
| Subregion | Population (1000 inhabitants) | Total fleet (units/1000 inhabitants) | | | | Demand (units/1000 inhabitants) |
| | 1987 | 1983 | 1987 | 1992 | 2000 | 2000 |
| North Africa | 135042 | 19.98 | 19.37 | 18.61 | 17.08 | 2.5 |
| West Africa | 186840 | 5.78 | 5.69 | 5.6 | 5.4 | 0.75 |
| Central Africa | 68492 | 4.42 | 4.17 | 3.86 | 3.24 | 0.45 |
| Eastern and Southern Africa | 183582 | 5.35 | 5.13 | 4.86 | 4.32 | 0.56 |
| Total developing Africa | 573962 | 8.89 | 8.27 | | | |
| Source: - United Nations, 1988 and 1990, *Survey of Economic and Social Conditions in Africa, 1986-1987 and 1987-1988, New York.*      - ECA estimates. | | | | | | |

Table 12.2 provides more details on the capacities and production of trucks and passenger cars in the North African subregion in early 1980s. Most of the units were based on assembling imported parts and components. They are generally small and some are below minimum economic size. Worse still, as can be observed from one case where both capacity and production figures are given, some of them have been reported as operating below capacity. Being preponderantly assembly units, the local content of parts and components utilized is necessarily relatively low.

| | | | | | | | |
|---|---|---|---|---|---|---|---|
| TABLE 12.2 CAPACITY AND PRODUCTION OF TRUCKS AND PASSENGER CARS IN THE NORTH AFRICAN SUBREGION | | | | | | | |
| Country | No. | Type of operation | Capacity | | Production | | Products/remarks |
| | | | Year | t/y | Year | t/y | |
| Trucks | | | | | | | |
| Algeria | 1 | Manufacturing | 1982 | 8000 | 1982 | 5540 | 7200 commercial vehicles produced in 1983. |
| Egypt | 1 | Manufacturing/ assembling | 1983 | 3000 | 1983 | 3000 | 8300 commercial vehicles produced in 1983. |
| | 1 | Assembling | 1983 | 7100 | ... | ... | |
| | 3 | Assembling | | 31500 | | | Reported being built or studied in 1987. |
| Libya | 1 | Assembling | ... | 3900 | ... | ... | |
| Morocco | 3 | Assembling | ... | ... | 1983 | 5760 | 1700 commercial vehicles produced in 1981. |
| Tunisia | 2 | Assembling | ... | >1000 | ... | ... | 9900 commercial vehicles produced in 1984. |
| Passenger cars | | | | | | | |
| Egypt | ... | Assembling | ... | ... | 1983 | 23700 | |
| Morocco | ... | Assembling | ... | ... | 1981 | 16000 | |
| Tunisia | ... | Assembling | ... | ... | 1984 | 2300 | |
| Source: Compiled from UNIDO, 1987, *Strategies and Policies for the Development of the Capital Goods ector in the Arab World,* Vienna. | | | | | | | |

Table 12.3 gives some information on truck and bus assembly plants in Eastern and Southern Africa. The plants in Kenya and Zimbabwe also assemble pick-ups and passenger cars. As may be noted in the table, capacity utilization ranges between 25 percent and 65 percent.

| TABLE 12.3 TRUCK AND BUS ASSEMBLY PLANTS IN THE EASTERN AND SOUTHERN AFRICAN SUBREGION IN THE 1980s | | | | |
|---|---|---|---|---|
| Country | Capacity (units) | Average capacity utilization (%) | Makes assembled | Payload capacity (t) |
| Angol | ... | ... | Scannia, Volvo | |
| Ethiopia | 900 | 50 | Iveco (Fiat) | |
| Kenya | 4000 | 65 | Leyland, Bedford, Isuzu, Nissan | 7, 8 and 10 |
| Tanzania | 1600 | 25 | Leyland, Scannia | 8, 19 and 12 |
| Zambia | 800 | 45 | Leyland, Tata | 7 to 10 |
| Zimbabwe | 2250 | 40 | Leyland | 7 to 10 |
| | | | DAF | 7 to 55 |

Source: ECA/HMT, 1988, *Engineering Industry Development Programme for Selected Eastern and Southern African Countries of Preferential Trade Area (Model Pre-feasibility Report — Low-cost Engine Driven Road Transport Vehicles)*, Addis Ababa.

Some of the assembly plants fabricate some parts and components such as radiators, silencers, batteries, exhaust pipes, seats, and fuel filters. Some of them procure these and other components, including tires, inner tubes, springs, paints, fan belts, gaskets, nuts and bolts, cable and wire, fuel tanks, brake lining, and flat and curved glass from local industries. The range of vehicle parts and components made in some countries (vide Zimbabwe) is wide and in some cases complex.

In addition to fabricating parts and components and assembling vehicles, some of the assembly units provide maintenance services. This should help to make their overall operations more viable.

## Priority Products

In view of the wide use of trucks and lorries, no other means of transport can compete with them. It is therefore very likely that they will continue to play the dominant role in the transport system of the continent. Because of increasing use of containerization, however, part of the vehicle population should be of sizes that can accommodate standard containers.

## Strategies for Development

The development of the transport vehicle manufacturing industry in Africa is complex and difficult. Small and fragmented national markets and a proliferation of vehicle makes and models are the major constraints. Pooling national markets and standardizing the vehicles to be manufactured are therefore prerequisites for the effective development of manufacturing capabilities.

This means that groups of member states, preferably at subregional level (ideally at regional level), should agree to pool their markets and the local manufacture of vehicles. This would involve selecting a limited number of trucks and determining their makes and models. Because of the foreign companies' vested interests in exporting vehicles to Africa as well as the interests of individuals in African countries (including some government officials) involved in related business activities, achieving the badly needed agreement will be both difficult and time consuming. Nevertheless, a start needs to be made without delay, if Africa is to make headway in this crucial area.

The basic design of the conventional vehicle engine has been practically unchanged during the past decades. The development and use of alternative motive power continues. Some models of some makes of cars (Mercedes, Volvo, Saab) already use turbo engines. The electric vehicle is making its debut. A prototype compressed-air engine (MDI-EC3) was reportedly being tested during the last quarter of 1996 in Europe. The engine, with separate compression and expansion cylinders, can be made to run on compressed air. It is light; it generates power at every second stroke; it is 50 percent more efficient than the four-stroke engine; it produces much less pollution; and it is much quieter than the conventional engine (*The Economist*, October 26, 1996). If and when any such engines, including a prototype with liquid piston, prove practical, especially the compressed-air version, these would, obviously, be the motive powers that African countries should adopt.

## LOW-COST VEHICLES

Low-cost vehicles comprise motorized and non-motorized vehicles. The former refer to 50 to 200 cc, 2-stroke engine vehicles (two- and three-wheelers) and the latter to animal-drawn carts, handcarts, and pedal-driven vehicles (bicycles, tricycles, and bicycle-drawn trailers). While animal-drawn carts, where they exist, are mainly limited to rural areas, all other vehicles would serve both urban and rural areas.

Motorized vehicles are relatively cheap, both in terms of initial investment and running expenses, as they are fuel-efficient and simpler to maintain; they are thus relatively more within the reach of more people. The three-wheeler, highly economical compared to light commercial vehicles, can be used as a private vehicle and as a taxi and a van. Its goods-transporting versions could have a payload capacity of up to 500 kg. In Nairobi, Kenya, it sells for as low as Ksh 100,000 (about $1,500 at March 1999 exchange rate); travels 25 km per liter of petrol; and charges 20 to 25 percent the taxi rate for a distance of 4.5 km. A battery-driven three-wheeler has been developed in Thailand with the help of UNDP. It is reported to use long-life batteries (*African Business*, September 1997).

### Status of the Industry
It is unlikely that low-cost transport equipment, other than wheelbarrows, handcarts, animal-drawn carts, and bicycles are produced in Africa. If any, their numbers would not be that significant. Alternative modes of transportation in rural areas are relatively limited, human porterage followed by pack animals being the most common means in rural areas where roads do not exist. It appears

that lack of appropriate government policies and support as well as inadequate infrastructure were the major reasons for this state of affairs.

Table 12.4 presents estimates of existing fleet of and demand for low-cost vehicles in developing Africa, with details on some countries in Eastern and Southern African countries in 1992-1993. By that time demand was supposed to have attained 225,000 in the case of two-wheelers and 47,000 of three-wheelers.

| TABLE 12..4 ESTIMATE OF FLEET OF AND DEMAND FOR LOW COST VEHICLES IN AFRICA 1992-1993 | | | | |
|---|---|---|---|---|
| Subregion/country | Existing fleet (units/1000 inhabitants) | | Demand (units) | |
| | Two-wheelers | Three-wheelers | Two-wheelers | Three-wheelers |
| Angola | 15.68 | 2.45 | 5000 | 1000 |
| Botswana | 14.7 | 2.3 | 1000 | 150 |
| Ethiopia | 4.33 | 0.68 | 8000 | 2000 |
| Kenya | 9.07 | 1.42 | 8000 | 2000 |
| Malawi | 5.6 | 0.87 | 1500 | 250 |
| Mozambique | 5.39 | 0.84 | 2500 | 400 |
| Tanzania | 8.13 | 1.27 | 10000 | 2000 |
| Zambia | 11.61 | 1.81 | 6000 | 1700 |
| Zimbabwe | 16.61 | 2.5 | 8000 | 2000 |
| Other countries | 10.16 | 1.59 | 22000 | 3500 |
| - Total Eastern and Southern Africa | | | 72000 | 15000 |
| - North Africa | | | 53040 | 11050 |
| - West Africa | | | 73354 | 15282 |
| - Central Africa | | | 26859 | 5596 |
| - Total Africa | | | 225253 | 46928 |

Source: - ECA/HMT,1985, *Engineering Industry Development Programme for Selected Eastern and Southern African Countries of Preferential Trade Area (Model Pre-feasibility Report — Low-cost Engine Driven Road Transport Vehicles)*, Addis Ababa.

 - ECA, 1993, *Guidelines on the Manufacture of Agricultural Tools, Implements and Low-cost Transport Equipment by Small-scale Engineering Industries in the Context of the Second Industrial Development Decade for Africa,*, Addis Ababa.

As noted above, practically no motorized low-cost vehicles are produced in the region. Countries such as Ethiopia and Tanzania had, at one time or another, plans to develop a low-cost vehicle industry in their respective countries. According to the latest information, a three-wheeler assembly project is among the projects submitted by investors and approved by the Ethiopian government.

## Priority Products
Where oxen, donkeys, horses, and mules are available, peasant farmers may opt for animal-drawn carts. This is particularly the case where feeder roads do not exist or are difficult to use. They also use wheelbarrows, handcarts, bicycles (with or without trailers), and tricycles.

For those with bigger farms and more funds or those who for climatic reasons cannot avail themselves of animal power, motorized vehicles may be the answer. Two-wheelers (mopeds, scooters, motorcycles, and motorized bicycles) and three-wheelers (passenger vehicles, pick-up vans, delivery vans) are the options. Others are multipurpose vehicles, such as dual-purpose tractors with trailers (see Chapter 10) and possibly modified conventional vehicles.

## Strategies for Development
The African rural area is characterized by a low level of development, subsistence agriculture based on human and, where available, animal power, and low rural income. Under the circumstances, it is neither possible nor realistic to modernize the on-farm and off-farm transport needs of the farmers all at once. It should be done step by step and by category of farmers. For the majority of the small subsistence farmers, pack animals, improved wheelbarrows, handcarts, and animal-drawn carts may meet immediate needs. Their transport needs will, however, change significantly as they use more agricultural inputs and increase production.

In view of its versatility as a means of conveying both passengers and loads, the bicycle could be accepted by farmers. It could be redesigned to suit rural conditions and needs. It should be rugged, simple, and easy to manufacture and maintain. Trailers with a capacity of 200 kg that could also be used as handcarts could be attached to the bicycles (UNIDO, *Appropriate Industrial... Areas*). The possibility of fitting some bicycles with small petrol engines should not be overlooked.

On relatively large farms, farmers may require motorized low-cost vehicles. The type and sophistication of the vehicles will depend upon the size and nature of the farm. Although some of their needs may be met by low-cost vehicles, large farms may have to resort to larger and more expensive conventional vehicles. Unlike heavy- and light-duty vehicles, low-cost vehicles offer great developmental potential in both rural and urban areas. The constraints that emanate from vested interest groups, if any, would be relatively small. One constraint would be initial resistance from potential customers who are suspicious of new products. This situation could be minimized by importing and introducing the same type of vehicles well in advance of their local production.

Because of economies of scale, some sub-assembly will have to be carried out in a limited number of central units. This will include the engines and related parts as well as pressed parts, that require expensive heavy duty presses and dies. These central units will supply assembly plants with the sub-assemblies. The assembly plants, which may be set up in as many countries as economies of scale justify, would manufacture some parts and components, including chassis. They would buy the balance of their requirement from other producers in their own country and from production units in other member states. With this strategy, based on specialization and exchange of parts and components, coupled with an optimization of existing vehicle parts and components manufacturing facilities referred to under heavy duty commercial vehicle, it is expected that close to 100 percent local content could be attained in a relatively short time.

The above integrated approach would need to be supplemented by measures enhancing the viability of the production and assembly plants. These would include: sourcing inputs from the subregion and region, buying inputs from abroad through central purchasing organs, and implementing commercialization strategy for the sale of products through marketing arrangements.

In planning and developing low-cost vehicles, a thorough assessment should be carried out of the experience in other developing countries. These include motorcycles and attachments (trailers, side-cars, etc.), multipurpose motorized farm vehicles (light conventional tractors, two-wheel tractors used in China, and single-axle tractors developed in the Philippines), and modifications of conventional vehicle designs (modified jeeps or the Asian Utility Vehicles produced and used in South-Asian countries) (UNIDO, *Appropriate Industrial ... Areas*).

UNIDO *(Industrial Development ... Cooperation)* advises against specialization in the development of certain engineering industries characterized by a rapid rate of product modification and redesign as well as product creation. This caution holds true for transport equipment and scientific apparatus. In the case of transport equipment, that note of caution seems to run against the approach suggested in this book. It is apparent that the warning does not apply as long as the developing countries develop vehicles suited to their local needs and conditions. They cannot afford the luxury of changing makes and models at the rate of an industrialized country—hence the caution seems unwarranted, at least for the low-cost vehicles.

## BIBLIOGRAPHY

African Business, 1997, "Taxi Tension Simmer," September 1997.

ECA, 1993, *Guidelines on the Manufacture of Agricultural Tools, Implements and Low-cost Transport Equipment by Small-scale Engineering Industries in the Context of the Second Industrial Development Decade for Africa*, Addis Ababa.

ECA/HMT, 1988, *Model Pre-feasibility Report—Low-cost Engine Driven Road Transport Vehicles, Engineering Industry Development Programme for Selected Eastern and Southern African Countries of Preferential Trade Area*, Addis Ababa.

The Economist, 1996, "Car Engines: Not All Hot Air," October 26, 1996.

UNECE, 1986-1990, *Bulletin of Statistics on World Trade in Engineering Products*, Geneva

UNIDO, 1979, *Appropriate Industrial Technology for Low-cost Transport for Rural Areas*, Monographs on Appropriate Industrial Technology, No. 2, Vienna.

UNIDO, 1984, *Industrial Development and South-South Cooperation*, Vienna.

## CHAPTER 13

# EQUIPMENT AND MACHINERY FOR ENERGY GENERATION AND TRANSMISSION

Although not usually included in the list of basic needs, there can be no doubt that life cannot exist without energy. The sun, directly or indirectly, is the ultimate source of most of the energy that the world uses. The food we eat, the clothes we wear, and the other basic needs require energy at different stages of production, processing/manufacturing, transportation, storage, and final preparation.

Power in whatever form (provided by human, animal, or machine) is an input without which no industrial operation can be performed. Most crafts and artisanal industries in Africa are based on human power. Animal power is mainly used in agriculture and services, thus indirectly contributing to industrial production. With the exception of some small-scale industries, industries use energy to provide process heat and to operate equipment and machinery in industrial establishments.

## ENERGY IN AFRICA

In almost all African countries, industries are concentrated in urban areas, particularly big cities. The availability of commercial energy, electricity in particular, is one of the major reasons for this state of affairs. Rural areas lack commercial energy. If modern industries are to be fairly distributed regionally, this can only be done by making commercial energy available in semi-urban and rural areas—hence the need to develop and exploit sources of energy and widen their availability.

In general, the limited availability of energy is among the factors constraining development in Africa. In some countries, supplies are inadequate, erratic, and unreliable. As a result, some industries have generating units to supplement their requirements and/or have them on standby to be used during breakdown.

As shown in Chapter 4, the continent is endowed with energy resources in the form of fossil fuels (petroleum, natural gas, coal), hydraulic energy, and geothermal energy. It has a huge potential in renewable sources of energy, particularly solar energy. Currently only a small part of the conventional energy potential is exploited. Biomass (wood and plant, animal and human wastes) can be converted into various sources or forms of energy (charcoal, methane gas, alcohol, and electricity). Fast-growing trees, such as eucalyptus and ipilpil or laucaena leucocephela (grown in even relatively bad soils in the Philippines) and others (hibiscus shrubs and rapier grass) are sources of biomass that could be hydrolyzed and fermented to alcohol for use as motor fuel (Omo-Fadaka 1981). It should be noted here that the utilization of biomass fuels does not raise the level of carbon dioxide in the air as the latter is recycled and used up by the plants, the source of the biomass. Unlike other natural resources whose comparative advantages for Africa have been eroding, it is likely that energy resources, when properly tapped, will ensure African industries some advantage over industries elsewhere.

In most households in Africa only 5 to 10 percent of the heat produced by burning wood to prepare food is utilized. In other words, 90 to 95 percent of the thermal energy is wasted because of inefficient combustion. Reducing this wastage would reduce the use of wood and dung and lessen the adverse ecological impact, such as depletion of forests, water run-off, soil erosion, desertification, and drought. The magnitude of the positive impact can be imagined from the fact that wood contributes 80 to 90 percent of the energy consumption of most African countries. In recognition of this reality, R&D has been and continues to be carried out in many African countries with a view to improving the thermal efficiency of burning wood for cooking purposes. Many prototypes of stoves based on local materials have been made and are being popularized. According to the users of one such stove in Ethiopia, the stove can save up to 85 percent of fuelwood (*The Ethiopian Herald*, January 21, 1995). The ideal stove should be such that (i) it is made from materials obtainable in the immediate area of the user; (ii) it can be made and repaired by the user; and (iii) the user can afford it.

Except for biomass that is used directly in such applications as cooking, most of the original energy used is converted into mechanical shaft power. This power is either used directly to drive machinery or converted into electricity. Energy source converters therefore constitute an important part of the equipment and machinery for the energy industry; they include furnaces, boilers, biogenerators, fermentors, steam engines, turbines, and generators.

Outside the household, wood is used to process agricultural products. It is used to dry crops, fruits, vegetables, tobacco, and fish; and to smoke fish and rubber. Other users include the brick, tile, lime, and leather-making industries. Wood is used in some industries to generate hot water and raise steam for process industries. The thermal efficiency of wood utilization in such industries needs to be greatly improved. In some countries some certain industries have switched over to commercial energy.

Transport and industry are the major consumers of commercial energy. While the former is generally limited to the use of petroleum products, the latter can and does use a mix of alternative sources of energy in addition to electricity, which itself is, in part, derived from fossil fuels. Although relatively small at present, the energy requirement for agricultural production and processing, mainly in the form of thermal energy, will grow as cultivation intensifies following the increasing use of irrigation, high-yield crops, fertilizers, and other inputs.

Petroleum products, kerosene and diesel oil in particular, are the most important commercial sources of energy in rural areas. This situation will have to change as greater use is made of renewable sources, including ethyl alcohol, particularly in those countries where molasses from sugar mills is available. In remote and isolated parts of a country, there may be no option but to resort to using biogas, solar, and wind energy. Any one or a combination of these resources as well as diesel generators could, for instance, be the only way to store medicines requiring refrigeration or air conditioning or for students to follow education via radio or TV in such areas. Other possible uses, particularly in remote and dry areas, are water heating, space heating and cooling, pumping water, drying, cooking, distillation, and telecommunication.

Research being carried out to run conventional diesel engines on sugar-based fuel mixtures (including sugar from grass, stalks, farm by-products, etc.) show that per unit cost of energy, the sugar route can be 30 percent to 50 percent lower than that of ethyl alcohol (ethanol). Following the success of the research which "*showed that a diesel fuel composed of nearly 15 percent water, 20 to 30 percent methanol or ethanol and 50 to 75 percent syrup—water and sugar—is an attractive recipe for the fuel.*" Patent application was reported pending (*AIChExtra*, May 1997).

For countries that are endowed with natural gas, especially those whose associated gas is being flared off or burned in the field, there appears to be an opportunity to convert the gas to liquid fuels (gasoline, diesel fuel, etc.). The Syntroleum Corp. (Tulsa) technology, one of the processes developed or being developed, is suitable for small gas fields with capacity as low as 5,000 barrels of liquid fuel per day. Plants based on this technology were expected to be operational as early as 1998 (McWilliams, *Business Week*, May 19, 1997).

## DEVELOPMENT OF GENERATION ENERGY

According to UNIDO (*Appropriate ...Requirements*), wood fuel accounted for 56.8 percent of total energy consumption in Africa in 1973. This was followed by commercial energy (32.3%) and agricultural waste (10.9%). The commercial energy part of the consumption translates into a per capita consumption of 0.19 tons of coal equivalent which compares with 0.23 and 1.0 for the Far East and Latin America, respectively.

Production, trade, and consumption of selected energy resources in Africa, including South Africa, are given in Annex 4.5 for the period 1970-1990. As the figures are expressed in different units, it is not possible to have an idea of the proportion of the different sources of energy consumed. Petroleum products and electricity are the major forms of commercial energy used in most countries in Africa.

Electricity, the most important form of energy used in industry, is generated from hydropower and thermal power. In Africa, as shown in statistics, production of electricity from hydropower takes the lead.

A start at utilizing some of the renewable sources of energy (geothermal, biogas, solar, wind) has been made. Exploitation of geothermal energy is still at the initial stage, Kenya with 45 mw installed capacity being the only African country generating geothermal electricity (Fridleifsson, *Renewable Energy*, May-August 1996). Based on current work being carried out in this field, Ethiopia is likely to be the next country.

In Africa, where the majority of people live in rural areas far from the national grids, solar and wind energies could be the most practical sources of energy. The former is the most feasible for less than five houses (Maldonado et. al., *Renewable Energy*, September-December 1996). Kenya is among African countries exploiting the use of solar energy. It boasts 20,000 to 40,000 photovoltaic systems in operation. The CILSS-project aimed at installing photovoltaic systems in the Sahel countries started in 1991 is financed by the Commission of the European Community. On completion in 1995, the project was supposed to have installed photovoltaic systems with a peak power of 1,252 kw$_p$ (Aulich, *Renewable Energy*, May-August 1996). Using photovoltaic modules to serve as roofing materials for buildings is an innovation that may find acceptability in Africa. Most of the photovltaic systems are based on the well-proven crystalline silicon technologies.

With increasing cell efficiency and better design since the 1950s and declining price per peak watt from $40 in 1970 to $5 in 1993 (Acker al., *Energy Policy*), the development of solar energy is likely to accelerate in Africa. By 1997, the cost of rooftop panels has gone down to 10 percent of what it was two decades earlier [Meyer, *The Washington Times*, August 29,1997). South Africa, Egypt, Kenya, Algeria, Zimbabwe, and Tunisia assemble or manufacture photovoltaic systems, some of them making locally practically all the components (solar panels, batteries, charge regulators, inventors, lamps, wire).

In spite of technological maturity and falling costs (currently, 1998, half of that of 1990), the development and utilization of wind energy in Africa is far behind that of solar energy. Exploitation of this resource is perhaps most advanced in South Africa, where wind energy has been proved to be more cost-effective than solar energy. According to Mays, wind-generated electricity (6.8 ECU Cents/kwh) in Europe is cheaper than nuclear energy; it becomes even cheaper than coal-generated power if impacts on the environment as well as potential disasters are taken into account. By the year 2000, wind (at 7.5 m/s) is expected to be the cheapest source of energy in Europe (Mays, *Renewable Energy*, May-August 1996). It is apparent that Africa needs to maximize the exploitation of this source of energy.

## STRATEGIES FOR DEVELOPING ENERGY-RELATED EQUIPMENT AND MACHINERY

As indicated in Chapter 4, the per capita consumption of energy needs to increase to a minimum of 300 to 400 kgce for basic needs (food and shelter) and to rise thereafter to a socially acceptable level of 900-1000 kgce. There is a huge gap between the demand for and supply of energy; this holds particularly true for electricity at the national level. There is a need to narrow the gap in the supply of electricity between urban and rural areas. There is a need to bring industry to the rural area. All these needs can only be met through huge investments which African countries cannot afford.

There are, fortunately, alternative sources of energy which can be harnessed. Depending on the resource endowments, a country can and should utilize its indigenous resources, particularly if it imports petroleum and/or petroleum products. The technological alternatives for exploiting energy resources are usually site-specific. Hydraulic energy for generating electric power or mechanical power is a good example. Others are geothermal, wind, and biomass. However, as there are currently no adequate alternative fuels for vehicles (excepting ethyl alcohol, whose raw material production may have to compete with other crops), petroleum-importing countries have no choice but to continue to import crude petroleum and/or petroleum products for this purpose. This situation may change for some counties in the long run. Research on converting biomass into fuel for engines are being carried out in institutions in developed countries. The University of Kansas in the USA, for instance, has succeeded in converting biomass (grass, stalks, trash, farm by-products, and maize stover—maize stalks without the ears) into sugar and using a solution of the sugar in conventional diesel engines (*Chemical Engineering Progress*, March 1997).

There are two systems of electrification. The first is the conventional system based on central generating stations-cum-national power grid. It is highly capital-intensive, characterized by high transmission losses and inequities because of geographic and other limitations. The second is based on a decentralized system —generally, diesel engines. It could and should, however, combine harnessing alternative renewable energy sources, such as flowing water, solar, wind, and biomass or a combination thereof. Depending upon the magnitude of electric energy required, it could comprise an integrated system consisting of production units based on different renewable sources available in the same or adjacent areas. In those areas where hydraulic energy is available, a mini- or small-scale hydroelectric plant could serve as nucleus. In this connection, it should be noted that in their resolution on the promotion of energy resources development and utilization in Africa, the First Regional Conference of Ministers responsible for the development and utilization of mineral resources and energy (1995) called upon African countries to initiate the local manufacture of turbines and generators for mini hydropower plants and equipment for exploiting renewable energy resources (ECA, *Report of the First Regional Conference ...* ).

So far, the conventional system has not succeeded in bringing electricity to rural areas in Africa. It is not likely to succeed in the foreseeable future either. Under these circumstances, the second alternative might be the answer in the short and medium term.

The exploitation of energy resources requires capacity and capability building in the manufacture of equipment and machinery for converting, transmitting, distributing and utilizing energy obtained from alternative sources of energy. These capital goods should be as simple and as low-cost as possible if they are to find acceptance, particularly in the rural areas where they are most needed.

Equipment and machinery utilize energy for different purposes. Wood and other solid fuels are burnt to generate heat for cooking and producing hot water and steam. Stoves, furnaces, and boilers constitute the main equipment for this purpose. Gas is used in cookers and fuel oil in furnaces and boilers.

All solid, liquid, and gaseous fuels can be and are used to generate electricity. The fuels are burnt in boilers which produce steam. The steam drives a turbine which is coupled with an electric generator which generates electricity. A diesel engine which combines the functions of a boiler and a turbine drives an electric generator and thus serves as an alternative to producing electric power using liquid fuels. In the case of geothermal energy, steam drives a turbine which in turn drives a generator.

In the case of hydropower, water replaces steam in driving the turbine. Unlike steam and hot water which are used captively at the place of production, electricity has to be transported to its users. This requires switchgears, transformers, cables, and towers.

In most instances, conversion of energy into electricity involves two steps: mechanical power followed by electrical power. The rotational power of turbines (water, steam, gas), water wheels and windmills can be used directly to drive mechanical equipment or machinery or drive electric generators. Flour mills are examples of the mechanical use of power generated by water wheels, or windmills.

From the above, it is clear that there is a whole gamut of equipment and machinery which needs to be made locally if some progress is to be made in the generation, supply, and use of energy. Making capital goods for fabricating stoves and cookers should present no difficulty, as some capability and capacity already exists. All that would be needed is to build on that capability. It would be worthwhile undertaking R&D on biogas and solar cookers concurrently. As for boilers, capability and capacity for manufacturing metal containers could be upgraded to make boilers.

With respect to diesel engines, capital goods for their manufacture could be incorporated with those for low-cost transport vehicles. An alternative would be to set up independent facilities which could include the production of engines for other uses.

As for turbines and generators, a start could be made by making capital goods for the manufacture of small units for small hydroelectric stations in existing electrical and mechanical equipment production facilities or workshops. The manufacture of water-wheels and hydraulic rams could be undertaken in the same facilities or workshops. The experience gained would be useful at a later stage when making larger units.

Because of some common factors, such as the use of copper, the making of wires and cables may be combined with that of transformers. This approach may be extended to the design and manufacture of capital goods for making such products. The manufacture of towers could be incorporated with facilities for fabricating metal structures.

Machinery and equipment for the production of biogas anaerobic digesters, solar energy-based cookers, water heaters and electric generators, and wind-based mechanical and electric power generators are needed to exploit renewable sources of energy. As most of the technologies for the manufacture of such equipment and machinery are fairly simple and proven, capital goods for their manufacture could be taken up with relative ease. Solar cookers, for instance, can be fabricated using cardboard, iron sheet, aluminum foil, glass, and vegetable residues for insulation. For a typical family of four in El Salvador, the daily cost of cooking food of $0.017 contrasts with $0.77 for wood burning (de Escobar, *Renewable Energy*, September-December 1996).

In order to achieve a measure of self-sufficiency in the local manufacture of some of the capital goods referred to above, a step-by-step approach should be adopted. This would include identifying appropriate technologies, adapting available technologies, innovating new technology, and developing prototypes for both capital and consumer goods related to energy exploitation and utilization. As far as possible, these technologies should be based on the exploitation of locally available energy and the use of raw materials for the manufacture of capital goods required for such exploitation. In view of the R&D carried and being carried out worldwide in this field, money and time would be saved by keeping track of developments elsewhere.

Taking African reality into account, where most people live at subsistence and sub-subsistence levels, it would, in the short and medium term, be rather difficult, if not impossible, to meet their energy needs. Under these circumstances, optimum use of available energy resources should be made; animal power is one such resource. In those parts of Africa where oxen, horses, mules, donkeys, and camels thrive, they could be used more efficiently and for more functions. In addition to ploughing, they could draw carts, thresh grain, lift water, and provide motive power to village industries, such as grinding and oil extraction. The optimum application of animal power to perform these tasks would require that farmers have access to improved devices and equipment. The use of animal power could be phased out as the peasant farmers' living standards improve.

Planners of power-generating projects should bear in mind the co-generation concept whereby waste heat from the electric generating unit is used to produce process steam or hot water. This saves costs and generally reduces pollution, depending upon the type of fuel used.

## BIBLIOGRAPHY

Acker, Richard H. and Daniel M. Kammen, 1996, "The Quite (Energy) Revolution: Analyzing the Dissemination of Photovoltaic Power Systems in Kenya," *Energy Policy*, January 1996, Elsevier Science Ltd.

AIChExtra, 1997, "Member Provides a Sweet Alternative for Diesel Engines," A Supplement to Chemical Engineering Progress, May 1997.

Aulich, Hubert A., 1996, "Small Economical PV Power Generation Systems to Provide Lighting, Communication and Water Supply to Rural Areas," *Renewable Energy*, May-August 1996.

Chemical Engineering Progress, 1997, *"One Lump or Two? Sugar Proposed to Improve Diesel Fuel,"* March 1997.

de Escobar. E.M., 1996, "Low Budget Cookers: an Alternative to Diminish the Use of Wood as a Source of Fuel," *Renewable Energy*, September-December 1996.

ECA, 1995, *Report of the First Regional Conference of African Ministers Responsible for the Development and Utilization of Mineral Resources and Energy* (ECA/NRD/RC/DUMRE/MIN/6), Accra.

Fridleifsson, Ingvar B., 1996, "Present Status and Potential of Geothermal Energy in the World," *Renewable Energy*, May-August 1996.

Maldomado, Pedro and Miguel Marquez, 1996, "Renewable Energy: an Energy Option for Sustainable Development," *Renewable Energy*, September-December 1996.

Mays, Ian, 1996, "The Status and Prospects for Wind Energy," *Renewable Energy*, May-August 1996.

McWilliams, Gary, 1997, "Gas to Oil: a Gusher for the Millennium?," *Business Week*, May 1997.

Meyer, Cord, 1997, "Climate, Technology and Trepidation," *The Washington Times*, August 29, 1997.

Omo-Fadaka, Jimoh, 1981, *The Implications of Renewable and New Sources of Energy and the Promotion of the New International Economic Order*, Nairobi.

The Ethiopian Herald, 1995, "Smoke-free Stoves Prevent Tracoma, T*B,* " January 21, 1995, Addis Ababa.

UNIDO, 1979, *Appropriate Industrial Technology for Energy for Rural Requirements*, Monographs on Appropriate Industrial Technology, *No. 5*, New York.

## CHAPTER 14

# OPTIONS FOR IMPLEMENTING
# INDUSTRIAL PRIORITIES

The priority industries identified in the preceding chapters require a variety of inputs. Production for any one of them could start at any stage of processing or fabrication. One extreme starting stage would be from basic raw materials. Another extreme would be starting at the final stage of processing or fabrication. A third would be some intermediate stage using imported intermediates. This chapter concentrates on the first option which needs to be adopted if Africa is to make some headway in economic development in general and industrial development (and therefore agricultural development) in particular.

## IMPORT OF INDUSTRIAL INPUTS

Most of the non-resource-based industries in Africa fall in the second or third option; they are import-oriented. Their dependence on imports is so high that their continuing operation or existence hinges on the availability of foreign exchange. The 1980s and early 1990s witnessed very low capacity utilization and closure of plants mainly for want of foreign exchange.

In Africa, development means using more and more foreign exchange. With slow increase in or stagnating foreign exchange earnings and growing foreign exchange requirements for both current needs and new developments, the appetite for foreign exchange cannot be satisfied. Despite this constraint, because of good economic performance in recent years (see Chapter 3) and barring unforseen circumstances, Africa seems to be ready to forge ahead. This is an opportune time for it to start in earnest developing local resource-based industries, especially agro-industries that provide agricultural inputs and process agricultural outputs.

## LOCAL PRODUCTION OF INDUSTRIAL INPUTS

The so-called traditional industries fall under the first option. They are integrated in that they start with basic raw materials and generally end up with final products.

The physical plant comprises equipment and machinery, products of the engineering industry, made up from metals and chemical products which are obtained from basic raw materials, such as iron ore, bauxite, copper ore, petroleum, natural rubber, and sand. It operates using supplies, such as lubricants, greases, and hydraulic oils from the chemical process industry. In other words, to make equipment and machinery for the agro-industry and operate agro-industries requires the development of the metallurgical and chemical industries.

## Engineering Industry

Engineering industry as used here is the industrial subsector which comprises manufacture of metal (SITC 69), equipment and machinery (SITC 71-75), and metalworking industries (ISIC 381-385). In terms of end use it is divided into consumer goods and capital goods, the latter producing the means of production. It encompasses technology ranging from labor-intensive to capital-intensive and from simple to highly sophisticated and automated fabrication methods.

The importance of the engineering subsector cannot be overemphasized. As a carrier of technology it embodies technology and is therefore the major medium of technology transfer. Its development is obviously crucial not only to the development of industry but also to all socio-economic sectors — hence its crucial role in appropriate technology. In a broad sense, it comprises the production, repair, and maintenance of capital and consumer goods.

It is generally skill-intensive and characterized by market fragmentation with many models and makes. Employment in the engineering industry is small relative to its ubiquitous nature as shown by its share in total manufacturing in the countries most advanced in the engineering subsector in Sub-Saharan Africa. Based on figures in late 1970s, employment in the subsector was 9.8 percent in Cote d'Ivoire, 12.2 percent in Nigeria, 17.3 percent in Zambia, 19.3 percent in Zimbabwe, and 23.4 percent in Kenya.

In the majority of African countries, the engineering subsector is at an early stage of development. It mainly focuses on metal working (metal furniture, structural metal products, tanks, containers, farm implements, household goods, trailers, etc.) and repair and maintenance of imported machinery and equipment. The capital goods part, in particular, is at an embryonic stage. According to UNCTAD, in early 1980s, production of capital goods in developing countries accounted for 10 to 15 percent of total MVA in contrast to 30 to 35 percent in developed countries (UN, *The Capital Goods Sector in Developing Countries: ...* ). The contribution of engineering industry to GDP in 1973 in some African countries ranged between 0.17 percent in Chad and 2.8 percent in Algeria (UN, *Metalworking Industries in Developing Countries of Africa*). Assembling operations of imported inputs predominate in a number of countries. Product design and manufacturing capabilities leave much to be desired. Egypt, Zimbabwe, Algeria, and Kenya are among the countries that have made a beginning in capital goods manufacturing.

Annex 14.1 cites examples of small-scale and relatively simple metal-working industries for making equipment and machinery that can be developed in the majority of African countries. The concept of size is relative. The so-called small-scale units may be considered medium scale in the small and mini states.

As for equipment and machinery for medium- and relatively large-scale industries, an integrated approach at the subregional level is called for. Here, there is a need to investigate what is available in the form of fabrication facilities in the member states and to use that information as a basis for planning. In this connection, it should be noted that some member states have specialized not only in operating certain industries, but also in manufacturing some of the parts and components needed by those industries. In addition to the diversified engineering industry in Zimbabwe, examples include: sugar-making equipment in Mauritius, rollers for sugar mills in Ethiopia, and mining equipment in Zambia.

## Machinery and Equipment for Traditional Industries
### •Priority Products

The information on production and trade discussed below is based on ISIC 381-384 (capital goods) (UNIDO, UNIDO/IS.502). Since the data used, however, include consumer goods, the broader term "engineering goods" seems more appropriate and is used instead of capital goods.

Non-electrical machinery production accounted for 2.69 percent of the manufacturing value added in the engineering subsector of African countries in late 1970s. This compares with 4.66 percent in Western Asia, the next lowest in rank. In 1977, value added for eight African countries ranged from $16 million in Cameroon and Madagascar to $558 million in Nigeria. Table 14.1 gives some idea of the share in value-added by ISIC branches of the engineering industry in the same countries-excluding Cameroon for which information was not available. From the figures, it is apparent that metal products take the lead, followed by transport equipment and electrical machinery.

TABLE 14.1
SHARE OF ENGINEERING BRANCHES (ISIC) IN THE VALUE ADDED OF THE
ENGINEERING INDUSTRY SUBSECTOR (%)

|  | ISIC | Nigeria | Zimbabwe | Cote d'Ivoire | Ghana | Gabon | Kenya | Madagascar |
|---|---|---|---|---|---|---|---|---|
| Metal products | 381 | 48 | 65 | 49 | 48 | 39 | 36 | 47 |
| Non-electrical machinery | 382 | 20 |  |  |  | 5 | 2 |  |
| Electrical machinery | 383 | 8 | 16 |  | 15 | 23 | 23 | 14 |
| Transport equipment | 384 | 24 | 19 | 51 | 37 | 32 | 38 | 39 |

Source: UNIDO, 1984, *The Capital Goods Industry in Africa: A General Review and Developments for Further Analysis,* Sectoral Studies Series NO. 14, UNIDO/IS.502, Vienna.

As for trade, based on the same source and using data that are not strictly comparable (involving differing years covering the second half of the 1970s and SITC formats), engineering goods in 31 African countries accounted for 30 to 39 percent of total imports (ranging from 18.5% in the Gambia to 49.5% in Gabon). For most of these countries, the shares of imports by branches (based on SITC, Rev.1), in descending order, were non-electrical machinery, transport equipment, and electric machinery. On the basis of SITC Rev.2, which comprises ten branches and therefore offers a better breakdown of the engineering industry subsector, the import shares of the branches are shown in Table 14.2.

TABLE 14.2
SHARE OF ENGINEERING BRANCHES (SITC) IN THE IMPORT VALUE OF
ENGINEERING GOODS IN AFRICA

| | SITC | % | | SITC | % |
|---|---|---|---|---|---|
| Road vehicles | 78 | 28 | Transport equipment | 79 | 7 |
| Machines for special industry | 72 | 15 | Power generating equipment | 71 | 6 |
| General industrial machinery not elsewhere specified | 74 | 14 | Telecommunications and sound equipment | 76 | 5 |
| Metal manufacture not elsewhere specified | 69 | 13 | Office machines | 75 | 1 |
| Electrical machinery not elsewhere specified | 77 | 10 | Metal working machinery | 73 | 1 |

Source: UNIDO, 1984, *The Capital Goods Industry in Africa: A General Review and Developments for Further Analysis, Sectoral* Studies Series N0. 14, UNIDO/IS.502, Vienna.

Engineering goods exports are practically negligible. This is illustrated by the engineering goods exports/ engineering goods imports ratios. The highest national ratios attained were: Zimbabwe (0.28), Senegal (0.15), and Mauritius (0.10).

Under present and near-future African realities, including the priority given to agriculture, the following constitute priority areas in the engineering subsector: agricultural tools, implements, and machinery; equipment and machinery for agro-industry; low-cost transport equipment for rural and urban use; equipment and machinery for selected small-scale industries; and equipment and machinery for the so-called traditional industries. Most of these, except equipment and machinery for fertilizers, pesticides, and traditional (food, beverages, textiles, leather, wood, and cement) industries, have already been dealt with in Chapters 10, 11 and 12. The focus of this chapter is therefore on these exceptions. In addition, because of the critical roles they play in the development of the engineering industry and maintenance of equipment and machinery for all economic and social activities, machine tools and spare parts deserve high priority within the engineering subsector. It is for this reason that they are dealt with separately below.

Of the world consumption of fertilizer equipment estimated on the basis of fertilizer capacity, Africa's share was about 2.7 percent in nitrogen equipment and 13.3 percent in phosphate equipment in 1991. Africa hosted eight[1] (two each in Nigeria and Tunisia and one each in Algeria, Egypt, Libya, and Tanzania) of the world total of 608 companies manufacturing fertilizers. This figure rises to 15 if South Africa is included (UNIDO, *Industry and Development: Global Report 1993/94*). These figures indicate that the use of machinery and equipment to produce fertilizers is significant enough to warrant venturing into their manufacture, starting with simple parts and components and replacement equipment.

### •Current Stage of Development
The very low level of the development of the engineering industry in the majority of African countries is manifested by the relatively small tonnage of casts and

forges produced. Around mid-1995, the continent possessed annual combined capacities of 500,000 tons in the foundry and 140,000 tons in forge shops. Production amounted to 200,000 tons of casts and 85,000 tons of forges, respectively (ECA/UNIDO, CAMI.12/6[A]).

Production facilities for making equipment and machinery for the manufacture of agro-chemicals and products produced by traditional industries are practically non-existent or limited in the region. Their manufacture involves significant economies of scale that are beyond the national markets of the individual countries. At most, there may be some capacity and capability for making some parts and components.

Annex 14.2 gives capacities and production of selected engineering goods in the North African Subregion.

### •Strategies for Development

The engineering industry subsector is relatively labor-intensive compared to both the chemical and metallurgical subsectors, which generally involve continuous processing. Many engineering products, particularly metal works (structures, containers, etc.) and simple mechanical parts, components, and equipment can be manufactured on a relatively small scale. Once capabilities and capacities have been built at this level, graduation to successively higher levels becomes relatively easy. This possibility must be borne in mind when planning and designing engineering industry projects.

It will not, for some time to come, be feasible to make all the parts and components for all the priority industries. The strategy should be to start immediately with simple parts and components and gradually proceed in stages to more complex parts and components, including replacement equipment. The first stage may, for instance, include the manufacture of storages for solid and liquid intermediates and final products; parts and components for bulk handling, blending, and bagging equipment; sulfur smelters and burners; granulators; manually operated pesticide sprayers; and equipment for tannery and mechanical pulping of wood. Existing facilities should be upgraded and diversified to manufacture parts and components more complex than the ones being made.

Existing fertilizer, pesticide, and traditional plants have been procured from different countries and manufacturers and at different periods or time. This diversity of suppliers means that the lack of standardization will seriously hamper any development of capacity to manufacture equipment and machinery for these industries.

Under the circumstances, while spare parts could be produced as suggested below under the section on spare parts, a different approach will have to be adopted for new plants. This should be done in stages. First, demand for the plants needs to be projected for groups of countries, subregion or region, depending on the magnitude of the potential demand. Secondly, standardized small-medium-, and large-scale modules should be designed, taking account of African needs and conditions. This would give decision makers latitude in planning production facilities. Thirdly, fabricating facilities should be allocated among member states, taking into consideration maximum use of existing fabricating facilities and infrastructure as well as fair distribution.

The new multinational facilities should focus on manufacturing relatively complicated equipment and machinery. The simpler parts and components, such as those based on metal cutting, soldering, and welding could be left for national units, existing or to be created. This approach together with a wider use of sub-contracting among medium- and small-scale enterprises at both the national and multi-national levels would enhance and facilitate maximizing production linkages and therefore cooperation among member states. The central enterprises responsible for assembling equipment and machinery, such as machine tools and engines requiring various parts and components, should help and guide subcontractors to produce the parts and components that the enterprises need. In other words, mutually advantageous working relationships should be established between the enterprises and their contractors.

Annex 14.3 was compiled from a study on Arab countries, including those in North Africa. It was included here to illustrate the potential in engineering industries related to the development of agriculture and basic needs. As advocated in this book, it is based on the concept of supply/demand gap relative to minimum efficient scale of production—hence its apparent relevance. The ratio of the supply/demand gap to the minimum efficient scale indicates whether a project should be implemented at the national, multi-country, subregional, or regional level. The higher the ratio, the greater the likelihood that the project is suited to operation at the national level in the relatively larger and well-to-do countries. According to the ratios in the annex, certain machine tools, textile machinery, and dying and finishing machinery, are such candidates.

The potential linkages, practically unutilized at present, provide a good basis for cooperation between countries. The forward and backward linkages that are characteristic of diesel engine manufacture, for instance, would enable member states to share  fairly equitably the production of engines for vehicles, tractors, fork-lift trucks, and other capital goods industries.

Some of the products in the annex are currently produced in Africa, particularly in the North Africa subregion, mainly in assembly plants based on imported inputs. In these units, priority needs to be given to reducing the import content by developing the local production of parts and components. Part of the additional demand could be met through the expansion of existing units.

Many parts and components for engineering goods, particularly capital goods, require a combination of basic production facilities: foundry, forging, heat treatment, machine shop, tool room, fabrication, and metal coating. The first three are generally absent in most engineering establishments in Africa. The functions carried out in such establishments are generally limited to cutting operations (sawing, drilling, turning, planing, and milling). They depend on metal work pieces, such as profiles, sheets, plates, casts, and forges. An integrated engineering establishment manufacturing capital goods requires foundry, forging, and heat-treatment facilities. As such facilities may not, because of economies of scale, justify captive units, it is possible to establish central units serving a number of engineering establishments. It would therefore be worthwhile considering this approach when planning engineering industries.

As noted earlier, economies of scale in many engineering industries where discrete operations are the characteristic feature are not as significant as those in process industries. In general, the engineering subsector  is labor-intensive and relatively skill-intensive. It can, of course, be highly sophisticated and automated, involving the use of numerically controlled (NC) and computer-numerically-controlled (CNC) machines. The labor-intensive characteristics make the engineering industry amenable to decentralization and to operations at small-scale and specialized production levels. In short, the potential offered by these characteristics could and should be optimally exploited, particularly when it comes to industrial cooperation between member states.

As stated elsewhere, equipment, machinery, and other engineering products incorporating sophisticated and complicated parts are, generally, over-designed for African conditions and use. Where applicable, manufacturers and users could simplify a product by removing complicated parts and components, thereby reducing the costs of investment and manufacture of the simplified version. Decisions should be made after considering the impact of the trade-off between the resulting more appropriate product and the benefits forgone. The other option is to modify and standardize, through adaptive imitation, the product to embody features suited to local conditions and meeting local requirement.

Metals constitute by far the greatest inputs into the engineering industry. Success in the development of the latter will, therefore, depend upon backward integration via processing ores into metals. This is dealt with under metallurgical industry in this chapter.

## Machine Tools Industry

The engineering industry manufactures equipment and machinery using machine tools. It has, therefore, to produce machine tools first. Machine tools are also required in workshops for repair and maintenance. Repair and maintenance of equipment and machinery require spare parts. Lack of spare parts creates production bottlenecks, a critical factor in Africa.

It is apparent that the capacity to develop the manufacture of the tools, implements, equipment, and machinery for agriculture, industry, and transport identified in this book as priorities for agricultural development depends on the development of the machine tool and related industries (jigs, fixtures, molds, dies, tools, and machine tool accessories). Furthermore, the development of the machine tool industry is basic to the development of the engineering industry which by its very nature would enhance industrial growth and promote self-reliant and self-sustaining development.

### •Priority Products

Machine tools may be divided into two categories according to technological complexity of production. The first category, based on simple technology, includes saws, bench drills, and grinders and simple shearing and planing machines. Jigs and fixtures may be included in this category. The second category, involving moderate technology, comprises lathes as well as milling, boring, planing, and shaping machines.

A study (ECA/HM—*Machine Tools*) carried out in the 1980s in the Eastern and Southern African countries concluded that the demand for wood-working machine tools was too low to justify their manufacture and should therefore be reviewed in the future. Depletion of forest reserves and conservation measures were among the reasons given for the low demand.

As for metal-working machine tools for which demand in 1992 was estimated at $55.5 million at 1982 prices, the study proposed the manufacture of certain types of machine tools in some of the countries. They included metal cutting machines (center lathes, milling machines, pillar drilling machines, and power saws) which, according to the study, accounted for 77 percent of the consumption.

As the situation in the other subregions may not be very different from that of the Eastern and Southern African subregion, it can be assumed that the above conclusions hold true for the region as a whole.

### •Current Stage of Development

The consumption of machine tools in Africa is relatively small, $315 million in 1991 (see Table 14.3 ). It accounted for 0.8 percent of world consumption in 1991 (0.6% in 1985). Africa's 1991 self-sufficiency ratio for machine tools works out at only 8.5 percent. In other words, Africa is overly dependent on imports of the basic machinery for manufacturing engineering products and therefore all manufacturing. The Algerian imports of $75.6 millions in 1990 exceeded the combined imports of all the other countries in the table. Consumption averaged $33 million in 1965-1968 in developing Africa (UN, *The Machine Tool Industry*).

| TABLE 14.3 PRODUCTION AND CONSUMPTION OF MACHINE TOOLS IN AFRICA AND TRADE IN THE SAME IN SOME COUNTRIES ($ m) | | | | | | | | | | | | | | |
|---|---|---|---|---|---|---|---|---|---|---|---|---|---|---|
| | Production | | | | Consumption | | | | | | Imports | | Exports | |
| | Total | | World share (%) | | Total | | | World share (%) | | | Total | World share (%) | Total | World share (%) |
| | 1990 | 1991 | 1990 | 1991 | 1985 | 1990 | 1991 | 1985 | 1990 | 1991 | 1990 | 1990 | 1990 | 1990 |
| Africa | 25 | 27 | 0.1 | 0.1 | 125 | 277 | 315 | 0.6 | 0.6 | 0.8 | | | | |
| - Algeria | | | | | | | | | | | 75.6 | 0.4 | 0.1 | - |
| - Cameroon | | | | | | | | | | | 2.2 | 0 | - | - |
| - Cote d'Ivoire | | | | | | | | | | | 1.9 | 0 | - | - |
| - Gabon | | | | | | | | | | | 0 | - | 0.1 | - |
| - Ghana | | | | | | | | | | | 7.3 | 0 | - | - |
| - Liberia | | | | | | | | | | | 0.4 | - | - | - |
| - Libya | | | | | | | | | | | 11.3 | 0.1 | 0.6 | - |
| - Morocco | | | | | | | | | | | 13.2 | 0.1 | 0.2 | - |
| - Nigeria | | | | | | | | | | | 11.7 | 0.1 | - | - |
| - Tunisia | | | | | | | | | | | 10.9 | 0.1 | 0.2 | - |
| - Congo K | | | | | | | | | | | 7.3 | 0 | - | - |

Source: Compiled from UNIDO, 1991,1992, *Industry and Development : Global Report 1 1991/92, 992/93.* Vienna.

In Sub-Saharan Africa, except in Tanzania, Zimbabwe, and Nigeria (Nigerian Machine Tools), the machine tool industry is non-existent. The Kilimanjaro Machine Tool Manufacturing Company in Tanzania has been in operation since 1983. It manufactures a range of metal-cutting and wood-working machines. In Zimbabwe, there are two facilities producing pillar drills, press brakes, and guillotines. One of them, Garba Industries of Norton, was reported to be exporting machine tools to neighboring Zambia.

As for North Africa, the machine tool industry seems to be better developed. Common standard types of machine tools are made in the majority of member states. As information on the type of operation is absent in Table 14.4, it is not possible to know which units assemble or manufacture or combine both operations.

| | Production | | Products/remarks |
|---|---|---|---|
| | Year | t/y | |
| Algeria | 1981 | 700 | Lathes, milling machines and drills. |
| Egypt | 1981 | 1000 | Lathes, milling, shaping and grinding machines and presses |
| Morocco | ... | ... | Lathes and milling machines, to have been completed in 1983 |
| Tunisia | 1980 | 1500 | Metal folders and cutters |

TABLE 14.4
PRODUCTION OF MACHINE TOOLS IN THE NORTH AFRICAN SUBREGION

Source: Compiled from UNIDO, 1987, *Strategies and Policies for the Development of the Capital Goods Sector in the Arab World,* Vienna.

In the 1980s, there were plans for developing machine tool industries in some countries, including Ethiopia, Kenya, Zambia, and Zimbabwe.

### •Strategies for Development

Machine tools can be produced at different levels of sophistication. The sophistication ranges from general purpose to precision machines and numerically controlled (NC) and computer-numerically-controlled (CNC) machines. It would be advisable to start with the production of selected general-purpose machine tools, such as standardized basic machine tools, and move steadily towards the more sophisticated versions. A wide range of application and versatility should be among the criteria used when deciding the product mix and the initial level of sophistication, using batch manufacturing technology. Some production characteristics of machine tools are given under the section on engineering in this chapter.

Unlike in industrialized countries, the machine-tool producing industries in Africa will have to make a much larger proportion of the parts and components they need. They could and should maximize the use of existing facilities, including foundries and forges, within the country as well as the subregion. They could make subcontracting arrangements with such facilities whereby the latter would undertake to make parts and components for the machine tool industry. They could also encourage and assist entrepreneurs to establish ancillary industries to produce parts and components for the machine tool industry.

During the construction of the machine tool establishments, the owners of the establishments would familiarize the market with the machines they plan to produce by importing exactly the same machines from foreign manufacturers who will collaborate with them in building up the local industry. Arrangements would also be made with the collaborators to supply the establishment with parts and components until these can be made captively and/or locally. With respect to critical and high precision parts and components, these arrangements will have to be phased over a longer period of time.

The ECA/HMT study has proposed a 230-unit-per-year capacity (48% of the 1992 estimated demand) at the national level in the large countries of Eastern and Southern Africa. The composition of the initial machine tools to be manufactured is: center lathes (100), milling machines (30), pillar drills (60), and power saws (40). The final capacity and product mix should, of course, be determined by undertaking full-fledged feasibility studies for each of the countries concerned in the region.

The country approach may be feasible in a limited number of countries. This not withstanding the markets and resources of groups of countries need to be pooled to justify the development of the machine tool industry. Depending on their capacities and specializations, certain countries would concentrate on the production of parts and components for assembly plants within their area. The national machine tool plants referred to above would play an important role in an integrated development system of this kind.

Countries which could not justify the development of machine tool industries would do well to start by making production aids, such as fasteners, jigs, fixtures, and dies or metal-cutting (saws, etc.) and forming (bending, etc.) machines.

The trend in machine tool production and consumption is towards numerically controlled (NC) manufacture. The share of NC machine tools production in the major producing countries in the world increased from 39 percent in 1987 to 48 percent in 1991. The corresponding 1991 shares at group level were: metal cutting (59%), machining centers (100%), lathes (76%), drilling and boring machines (49%), milling machines (72%), grinding machines (43%), and metal-forming machines (18%). The share of consumption in the same countries is even higher (UNIDO, *Industry and Development: Global Report 1993/94*). This implies that there may come a time when conventional machine tools may no longer be available in the world market and hence Africa needs to take timely action.

## Spare Parts Industry

Because of the absence or inadequacy of preventive and routine maintenance, the normal wear and tear of equipment and machinery in Africa is substantially higher than in industrialized countries. Discarding useful equipment for want of proper maintenance, including the reconditioning of worn-out parts, is not uncommon. Hence, parts and components require more frequent replacement. This incurs additional costs, both investment and operating costs, as well as a loss of production arising from frequent downtime.

An idea of the importance of spare parts can be gained from imports. During the period 1980-1985, the import of spare parts into Eastern and Southern Africa was conservatively estimated at $6 billion (ECA/HMT, *Spare Parts*), that is an average of $1 billion a year. For Africa as a whole, the 1981 imports of $4.1 billion was expected to accumulate to $26 billion during the period 1980-1985 (ECA, *Local Manufacture ... in Africa*).

Since the late 1970s, the lack or inadequate availability of spare parts, arising mainly from dwindling foreign exchange earnings, has hampered the proper functioning of African mining, energy, agriculture, industry and transport, and communications activities. This constraint was so critical that production units were forced to operate at capacities as low as 3 percent; some even had to close down.

The above state of affairs was compounded by spiraling prices demanded for imported spare parts and the expenses incurred in maintaining large stock of parts and components to ensure the uninterrupted functioning of the production units and services. If high stock levels were not maintained, production and services would have to be shut down until parts were procured, a lengthy process; and that could spell disaster. In some cases, equipment had to be cannibalized in order to compensate for the lack of parts and components. It is apparent that African industries cannot operate properly and be competitive unless the spare parts constraint is removed or, at least, minimized.

### •Priority Products

The number of spare parts required by the productive, service, and social sectors is alarmingly huge, owing, in part, to a lack of standardization and to market fragmentation. Under the circumstances, it is out of question to produce spare parts locally for all needs, given the numbers and investment required.

In view of the large variety of makes and models involved and the need to rationalize and standardize in the transport sector suggested in Chapter 10, the manufacture of spare parts for this sector, except for common and easily modifiable parts, will have to await the outcome of the rationalization and standardization measures. Of the remaining sectors, agriculture and industry appear to offer better possibilities.

In a study carried out on Eastern and Southern Africa (ECA/HMT, *Spare Parts*), it was suggested that priority should be given to the manufacture of spare parts for traditional industries (food, beverage, textile, cement) that abound in most African countries, as well as those related to stone crushing, glass production, and metal fabrication. The food and beverage industries so identified were grain milling, meat processing, edible oil processing, sugar mill, and brewery. The study also identified 1,116 types of spare parts and proposed an annual local production of 138,366 parts at the national level for the group of industries under consideration. It is not unlikely that similar studies would arrive at similar proposals, for other subregions, particularly West Africa.

### •Current Stage of Development

Spare parts manufacture is still at an initial stage in most countries; it is mostly based on imported inputs. A number of countries do make some parts and components for mining, agricultural, industrial, and transport equipment and machinery. They include: spares and components for agricultural hand tools and implements; batteries, fuel tanks, gaskets, radiators, exhaust systems, filters, leaf-springs, tires, bolts, nuts, and studs for transport mechanical spares and components for industry.

Although many countries have workshops that manufacture specific spare parts for captive uses, only a few countries have capacities for making a variety of spare parts for other users. These include South Africa, Zimbabwe, Egypt, Algeria, Tanzania, Uganda, and Ethiopia. Tanzania Engineering and Design Manufacturing Organization (TEMDO) in Tanzania, UGMA Engineering Corporation in Uganda, and Akaki Spare Parts & Hand Tools Factory in Ethiopia are among the enterprises that manufacture spare parts for other users. The last one, a centralized integrated complex, is oriented towards industrial parts and components. It was planned to produce 3,600 types mostly for the textile, sugar, cement, metals, etc. industries and the transport sector. It includes departments for producing castings and forged, machined, and fabricated parts and components; it also provides chrome plating, phosphating, wax dipping, heat treatment, and laboratory services. Its current and potential contribution to industrialization cannot be overemphasized.

Some countries have taken measures to encourage the local production of spare parts. Kenya, for instance, has banned the import of a number of auto parts and components that are now being supplied by local manufacturers.

### •Strategies for Development

Optimizing the useful lives of machinery and equipment should be the goal of the technical management of a plant. This can be done through organized preventive maintenance schemes, making maximum use of locally made spare parts. To this end, each country needs to carry out a study and identify local industries, particularly the so-called traditional industries, for which the manufacture of spare parts seems to offer some possibilities. This would be supplemented by identifying parts and components that could be made at the national and subregional levels followed by undertaking market research.

The above would then be followed by pre-investment and investment activities. At the national level, mechanical parts and components of relatively simple types, based on copying imported models, may be appropriate for most countries in the initial stage. These may include shafts, bushes, gears, pins, levers, and bearing housings. Others would include simple fabricated parts, some types of castings required for captive use and by other local industries as well as toolroom products (jigs, fixtures, molds, and dies). These could be followed by the manufacture of more complicated standard equipment, such as boilers, electric motors, and pumps. An integrated plant for the manufacture of these items, particularly those based on adaptive imitation, would comprise a fabrication shop, machine shop, tool room, forge shop, foundry, heat treatment, electro-plating, testing, and quality control. Some of these facilities, particularly the foundry, electro-plating, and heat treatment, could, if necessary, be planned to cater to the needs of other industries. Alternatively, central ancillary industries for the manufacture of parts and components, including facilities, such as casting and forging, could be developed to render similar services. It would be advisable to look into the possibility of converting or using part of the facilities of existing large workshops, including railway workshops, before deciding on green field sites. Investment requirement would be relatively low because of existing infrastructures and facilities.

As for complex parts and components, their manufacture, unlike those suggested for national plants, requires highly specialized precision equipment and machinery, which are highly capital-intensive. They are therefore beyond the reach of most countries. The countries thus need to pool their markets and resources. The parts and components identified above should be categorized into groups using the same or similar technologies. This would serve as a basis for deciding on the number of plants to plan for. Decision on their location would take account of fair distribution in addition to the usual techno-economic justifications, when and if practical.

Many spare parts that need to be manufactured may not have the drawings or specifications required for their manufacture. In such cases, resort will be made to "reverse engineering design" whereby a detailed study and analysis of the samples of the spare parts to be made is carried out and the necessary process know-how for their manufacture developed. Obviously, this requires a well organized product design department.

## Metallurgical Industry

Metallurgical and chemical industries provide the main inputs to the engineering industry. Their development is critical to the development of both industry and transport, which, in turn, are critical to the development of agriculture. Sustainable industrial development and therefore agriculture cannot be attained unless industrial development is integrated with the processing of minerals to metals that are needed by the engineering industry, the carrier of technology.

### •Priority Products

Iron and steel, aluminum and copper constitute the most important basic metal inputs to the engineering industry. Requirements for other metals in terms of tonnage compared to the basic metals are so small that they are either available locally within the region or can be imported from abroad. These include nickel, lead, zinc, tin, cobalt, and chromium.

In terms of tonnage, demand for iron and steel is by far, higher than the combined demand for aluminum and copper. Annex 14.4 shows imports, production, consumption, and projected demand for steel in Africa. Comparison of data in this table with those in Table 14.5 shows that projected demand in the latter, particularly for the year 2000, is significantly higher than those in the former. It should be noted that the production/demand gap in Annex 14.4 was obtained by adding imports to supply/demand gap in order to reflect the total (real) gap. According to the International Institute of Iron and Steel (1990), the apparent consumption of steel in Africa of 13 million tons in 1990 was expected to stagnate at that level or increase marginally to 14 million tons in 1995.

Table 14.5 shows projected demand for and capacities of iron and steel by subregion and region. According to the table, demand in the year 2000 is expected to increase to 62.9 million tons per year, more than double that of 1990, for the region as a whole. The projections, which seem to be on the high side were based on a normative scenario and average and increasing steel intensity of use (IU=kgs of steel/ $ million GDP) for North Africa; on a trend scenario and average steel intensities for West and Central Africa; and on a normative scenario for Eastern and Southern Africa. By comparison, steel demand for India was expected to rise to 43 million tons in the year 2000 (UNIDO, *Appropriate ... Industries*). According to ECA projections based on data from ECE, International Iron and Steel Institute Report 1987, continental demand for steel in 2008 is 124.5 million tons compared with 29.0 million tons in 1993. Computations using data in the same source show that, as in 1993, North Africa will have the lion's share of 56.3 percent followed by Eastern and Southern Africa (22.4%) and West Africa (20.7%). In the normative-scenario based-projection, there will be a production/consumption gap of 85.6 million tons (ECA, *Africa in the 1990s and Beyond: ...* ).

TABLE 14.5
PROJECTED CRUDE STEEL DEMAND AND CRUDE STEEL CAPACITIES
PROPOSED TO BE INSTALLED IN AFRICA

| Subreion/region | Population (millions) | Projected crude steel demand (mt/y) | | Crude steel capacities proposed to be installed (mt/y) | | |
|---|---|---|---|---|---|---|
| | | | | Crude steel | | Flats |
| | 1985 | 1990 | 2000 | 1990 | 2000 | 2000 |
| North Africa | 107.7 | 16.6 | 40.4 | 8.4 | 19.9 | 7.9 |
| West Africa | 168.8 | 5.1 | 10.9 | 3.6 | 7.7 | 3.1 |
| Central Africa | 61.5 | 1.5 | 3.2 | 0.8 | 1.7 | 0.7 |
| Eastern and Southern Africa | 167.1 | 3.5 | 8.4 | 2.4 | 5.6 | 2.3 |
| Total Africa | 505.1 | 26.7 | 62.9 | 15.2 | 34.9 | 13.9 |

Source: Compiled from ECA, 1987, *Technological Options for Small-scale Integrated Iron and Steel Plants based on Direct Reduction in ECA Member States, ECA/IND/MET/008/87,* Addis Ababa, Ethiopia.

The demand projections comprise both direct and indirect steels, the latter being steels incorporated in equipment and machinery that are imported. The projections of crude steel capacities to be installed were arrived at assuming that 80 percent of the direct steel and 20 percent of the indirect crude steel demands could, in the long run, be produced locally. The share of flats for the year 2000 was assumed to be 40 percent of the total crude steel to be produced. In view of the projection methodolgies used and the assumptions made, the figures in the table may be taken as indications of rough orders of magnitude.

A general idea of the composition by major groups of direct steel imports could be obtained from the 234,000 tons imported into Eastern and Southern Africa in 1988 (UNECE, *Statistics...*). Flat products accounted for 81.4 percent, followed by tubes (9.8%) and long products (8%).

During 1987-1989, the Eastern and Southern African subregion produced about 700,000 tons of steel and imported about 500,000 tons of direct and indirect steel (UNIDO, *Survey...PTA Region*). These resulted in an apparent consumption of 900,000 tonnes, after deducting exports from Zimbabwe to markets outside the subregion.

Table 14.6 presents production, trade, and consumption of the major non-ferrous metals. Overall, consumption of aluminum increased by 40 percent during the first half of the 1980s. The increase rose to 65 percent by 1991. The picture in regard to copper was the opposite, consumption of 29,900 tons in 1991 being lower than that of 1980. According to another source (Roskill Information Services Limited, *The Economics of Aluminum*), production of alumna increased from 535,000 tons in 1984 to 642,000 tons in 1990 and that of primary aluminum from 413,000 tons in 1984 to 614,000 tons in 1992, which apparently include figures for South Africa. Latest estimates show that Zambia produced 320,000 tons of copper in 1995/96 while Congo K, 50,000 tons in 1996 (ADB, *African Development Report 1997*).

| TABLE 14.6 PRODUCTION, TRADE AND CONSUMPTION OF ALUMINA, ALUMINUM AND COPPER IN AFRICA (1000 t) | | | | | | | | | | | | |
|---|---|---|---|---|---|---|---|---|---|---|---|---|
| | 1980 | 1981 | 1982 | 1983 | 1984 | 1985 | 1986 | 1987 | 1988 | 1989 | 1990 | 1991 |
| **Alumina** | | | | | | | | | | | | |
| - Production (Guinea) | 354 | 339.5 | 289 | 282 | 267.5 | 282.5 | 288 | 271 | 296.5 | 313.5 | 321 | 325.5 |
| - Exports | | | | | | | 287.3 | 273.5 | 297.7 | 313 | 320 | 325 |
| - Imports | | | | | | | 390.8 | 423.8 | 445.5 | 454.2 | 439.1 | 449.4 |
| - Apparent consumption | | | | | | | 184.5 | 120.7 | 148.7 | 172.3 | 201.9 | 201.1 |
| **Aluminum** | | | | | | | | | | | | |
| - Production | 120 | 142 | 141 | 140.2 | 172.5 | 178.5 | 176.9 | 179.2 | 181.3 | 179.5 | 179.6 | 177.9 |
| - Exports | | | | | | | 259 | 286 | 256.4 | 287.7 | 305.8 | 290 |
| - Imports | | | | | | | 13.2 | 24.7 | 18.2 | 19.4 | 34.9 | 23.3 |
| - Consumption | 100 | 110 | 115 | 130 | 140 | 140 | 130 | 150 | 150 | 150 | 150 | 165 |
| **Copper, refined** | | | | | | | | | | | | |
| - Production | 760.2 | 734 | 790.1 | 830.1 | 854.8 | 844.4 | 826.2 | 838.9 | 771.3 | 683 | 645 | 537.8 |
| - Export | | | | | | | 710.9 | 704.7 | 637.6 | 670 | 612.5 | 522.7 |
| - Imports | | | | | | | 2.3 | 2.9 | 1.2 | 4.4 | 2.5 | 1.7 |
| - Consumption | 31.5 | 25 | 24.6 | 24.7 | 24.5 | 21.5 | 29.2 | 28 | 29.7 | 29.3 | 28 | 29.9 |

Source: Compiled from United Nations, 1993, *UNCTAD Commodity Yearbook 1993*, New York. ª Computed

Demand for copper in 1990 was expected to be about 213,500 tons per year (ECA, ECA/NRD/TRCDUMRA/7). This was, apparently, too high compared with the 28,000 tons actual consumption shown in Table 14.7. In view of the combined capacity of over 1.4 million tons per year, availability for use in Africa will not be a problem unless total production is exported to earn foreign exchange.

The same conclusion applies to aluminum. Existing capacity (700,000 tons per year) could easily meet regional demand for aluminum which was estimated at 100,000 tons per year in late 1980s. Actual consumption was 165,000 tons in 1991 (see Table 14.7). In fact, the positive gap is likely to widen if projects, including that of Gencor, a South African company, reported to be considering building an aluminum smelter in Maputo (*The Economist*, May 25, 1996) would be implemented. At the present stage of development, aluminum is consumed mainly in the form of cables, electric conductors, utensils, containers, and construction materials (door and window frames).

Annex 14.5 gives IU and per capita consumption of copper in Africa and the world. Africa's IU increased while the world's IU decreased. Developing Africa's IU as a percentage of that of the world's IU has dramatically increased from 6.0 percent in 1965-1969 to 47.7 percent in 1990-1991. The decrease in world IU was partly due to substitution, economic recession, and miniaturization of machinery and equipment in developed countries, and the increase in Africa was a reflection of a faster growth in consumption relative to GDP growth rate. As for per capita consumption as a percentage of world per capita consumption, this rose from nil in the 1960s to 12.0 percent in 1990-1992. The major outlets for copper in Africa include wires, cables, profiles, tubes, fittings, and craft articles.

Continental consumption of lead and zinc, which had been rising during the second half of the 1980s, fell in 1990 to 111,000 tons and 157,000 tons, respectively. South Africa accounted for close to 60 percent of the former and 54 percent of the latter.

### •Current Stage of Development

Annex 5.5 presents details of the production of selected metals in the whole of Africa at five-year intervals for the period 1970-1990. According to the annex, the production of pig iron for steel making increased from 4.60 million tons in 1970 to 9.16 million tons in 1985 and fell to 8.69 million tons in 1990. The corresponding figures for crude steel ingots were: 5.15, 11.38 and 12.59; copper refined, unwrought, 0.95, 0.87, and 0.78; and aluminum, unwrought, 0.17, 0.43, and 0.57. As South Africa's production is relatively high in many of the metals, the share of developing Africa is significantly lower than the above figures. According to UNECE (*The Steel Market in 1988*) and (*The Importance... Member Countries*), Africa's steel production in 1988 was about 4.6 million tons, less than 0.6 percent of world production. In 1993, it was 6 million tons (excluding 8.6 million tons in South Africa) out of 10.5 million tons capacity (ECA/UNIDO, CAMI.12/6[A]). Some other metals and intermediates are produced by one or two countries. These include ferro-chromium and nickel (South Africa and Zimbabwe), manganese (Gabon and Ghana), and alumina (Guinea).

Annex 14.6 compares African major developing countries' production of selected ores and their metals with those of all principal developing countries. It should be noted that the aluminum produced in Cameroon does not figure in the table. This is apparent from the higher production figures from another source (UNIDO, *Industry and Development, Global Report 1992/93*): 401,000, 435,000, and 442,000 tons, respectively, in 1987, 1989, and 1990, compared with the totals for Ghana and Egypt. The corresponding figures for consumption were: 129,000, 132,000 and 130,000. Combined capacity was 450,000 tons in 1985 and 467,000 tons in 1991 and accounted for 10.1 percent of world capacity in 1990. Capacity utilization rate increased form 68 percent in 1985 to 92 percent in 1990. Capacity was expected to increase by 220,000 tons by 1995 based on a plan in Algeria.

Table 14.7 presents production of these major basic metals, namely steel, aluminum and copper. During the 12-year period, production of basic metals virtually stagnated.

| TABLE 14.7 PRODUCTION OF BASIC METALS IN AFRICA | | | | | | | | | | | | |
|---|---|---|---|---|---|---|---|---|---|---|---|---|
| | 1981 | 1982 | 1983 | 1984 | 1985 | 1986 | 1987 | 1988 | 1989 | 1990 | 1991 | 1992 |
| Pig iron | 2.7 | 2.7 | 2.5 | 2.8 | 3.2 | 3.2 | 3.3 | 3.1 | 3.1 | 3.1 | 3 | 2.7 |
| Crude steel | 2.7 | 2.9 | 3 | 2.9 | 3.7 | 3.5 | 4 | 4.4 | 4.1 | 2.8 | 2.8 | 4.4 |
| Alumina | 339.5 | 289 | 282 | 267.5 | 282.5 | 286 | 271 | 2965 | 313.5 | 321 | 325.5 | 301.5 |
| Aluminum | 397.9 | 394.1 | 260.1 | 245.6 | 308.6 | 382.6 | 401 | 424.8 | 435.4 | 441.3 | 438.7 | 440.2 |
| Copper, refined | 734 | 790.1 | 830.1 | 854.8 | 844.4 | 826.2 | 838.9 | 771.3 | 683 | 845 | 542.7 | 555.6 |
| Source: UNCTAD, 1994, *UNCTAD Commodity Yearbook 1994*, New York. | | | | | | | | | | | | |

Annex 14.8 is a compilation of the available information on pig iron, direct-reduced iron, and steel in Africa and the world. From the table, it is apparent that South Africa's share in the production of pig iron in 1987-1989 was double that of developing Africa. It is also apparent that South Africa dominates in production of steel, over 1.3 times the combined production of all other countries. Although the difference was marginal, the situation was the reverse in the case of the production of steel making via the direct reduction route, with developing Africa producing one million tons as against 900,000 tons for South Africa in

1989. As for steel, it is unfortunate that the production figures for developing Africa have been aggregated with other countries and therefore could not be shown in the table.

A number of African countries have re-rolling mills working on imported billets and rolling mills-cum- mini-steel plants. The latter are based on steel scrap and imported billets. In 1989, of the 4 million tons scrap used, 200,000 tons were imported.

Many countries are in the crude steel making business, mainly based on electric-arc-furnace using scrap. Those making pig iron were limited in number. Integrated facilities are unevenly distributed; the majority of them are in North Africa (Algeria, Egypt, and Tunisia), Nigeria, and Zimbabwe. Algeria and Egypt each contributed 40 percent to the 1991 output of 3.0 million tons. Despite its integrated steel works, Nigeria does not figure in the source from which the table was compiled.

Table 14.8 summarizes information on integrated iron and steel plants and projects under implementation and planned in the region. More details are provided in Annex 14.9 where, because of certain changes made on the original source of data, such as rearrangement of presentation and using net additions to existing capacities instead of total capacities, the figures in some cases may and do appear different. The combined integrated capacity of operating plants and those under implementation amounts to about 11 million tons per year. This is expected to increase to 39.2 million tons once the planned projects are implemented. This total excludes crude steel made in semi-integrated plants whose combined capacity in Eastern and Southern Africa alone is about 1.1 million tons per year (UNIDO, *Atlas...*). According to another source (ECA,CAMI.11/4), the total crude steel capacity of all plants is about 10.5 million tons per year. This is equivalent to 8.5 million tons of pig iron.

| | TABLE 14.8 SUMMARY OF INTEGRATED IRON AND STEEL CAPACITIES IN AFRICA (m t/y) | | | | |
|---|---|---|---|---|---|
| | Existing and under implementation | | | Project | Grand total |
| Subregion/region | In operation | Under implementation | Total | | |
| North Africa | 5.4 | 2 | 7.4 | 24.3 | 31.7 |
| West Africa | 1 | 1.3 | 2.3 | 3.9 | 6.2 |
| Central Africa | - | - | - | - | - |
| Eastern and Southern Africa | 0.8 | 0.6 | 1.3 | - | 1.3 |
| Africa, integrated plants | 7.2 | 3.9 | 11 | 28.2 | 39.2 |
| Source: Summarized from annex 12.2 | | | | | |

In addition to the integrated plants, there are 29 mini-plants (semi-integrated) and 32 long product, 11 tube, and 2 flat rolling mills. Their respective capacities in thousand tons are: 1,426, 3,984, 27, and 147. Some of these plants and mills were reported to have been under rehabilitation during the first half of the 1990s. Their combined additional steel capacities together with those planned works out to 7.4 million tons per year. This raises the 39.2-million-ton iron and steel capacity to 46.6 million tons.

The steel plants are mainly geared to produce non flat products, especially structural steels for the building and construction sector. Those in Algeria, Egypt, and Kenya (the last based on imported coils) which also produce flat products are exceptions. Tubes are produced in Algeria, Libya, Morocco, Kenya, and Zimbabwe.

There are about 45 rolling mills in 22 countries. Their annual capacities range between 12,000 and about 200,000 tons.

Assuming that all the projects are implemented by the year 2000, the combined capacity (existing and projected) will satisfy about 59.5 percent of the projected demand. This is very optimistic. First, in view of the economic and social difficulties that the countries had to endure during the 1980s and early 1990s, it is unlikely that much progress will be made on the projects. Secondly, it is possible that some of the projects have since been dropped. Thirdly, the above assumption implicitly assumes that the plants will operate at full capacity, which is not practical. Fourthly, the delays and long gestation periods associated with steel plants in Africa as exemplified by the Ajaokuta Steel Company in Nigeria will very likely have a negative impact on the volume of steel production. In short, the region's dependency on iron and steel imports can be expected to worsen with the passage of time—hence the need to take immediate measures to minimize such dependency. Recent plans for two direct reduction plants in Mozambique, if implemented, could substantially reduce the dependency.

As for non-ferrous metals, Table 14.9 below presents figures for the production of and capacities for copper, alumina, and aluminum in the continent. According to the projections in the table, there will not be increased alumina capacity. With the enormous reserves of high quality bauxite, hydroelectric potential, and doubling of aluminum capacity, it seems reasonable to assume that more alumina will be made in Africa during the 15-year period (1990-2005) than projected. The projections for aluminum production do not seem to take account of the 466,000-ton-per-year aluminum smelter which entered production in 1995 in South Africa nor that of the 180,000-ton-per-year unit which was expected to be operational in 1996 in Nigeria (Europa, *Africa South of the Sahara 1996*).

TABLE 14.9
COPPER, ALUMINA AND ALUMINUM: PRODUCTION AND CAPACITY IN THE CONTINENT (1000 t)

| | Production | | | | | | Capacity | | | |
| | Actual | | | Projected | | | Actual | Projected | | |
| | 1969-71 | 1979-81 | 1988 | 1995 | 2000 | 2005 | 1989 | 1995 | 2000 | 2005 |
|---|---|---|---|---|---|---|---|---|---|---|
| Copper refined | 871 | 872 | 822 | 773 | 800 | 796 | ... | | | |
| Alumina | ... | ... | ... | | | | 700 | 700 | 700 | 700 |
| Aluminum, primary | 172 | 440 | 597 | 632 | 665 | 824 | 636 | 636 | 766 | 1096 |

Source : World Bank, 1991, *Price Prospects for Major Primary Commodities, 1990-2005,* Volume I, Summary Energy, Metals and Minerals, Washington, D.C. (Actual figures mainly from World Bureau of Metal Statistics, Metal Statistics,Engineering and Mining Journal, and Metallgesellschaft).

Annex 14.10 gives some indications of the production and capacities of copper, alumina and aluminum by country in 1980 and 1986 and beyond for copper. The major producers are: Zambia and Congo K for copper, Guinea for alumina and Ghana, Egypt, Southern Africa and Cameroon for aluminum. It should be noted that while aluminum is produced in more than one country, alumina production is limited to one country, Guinea, whose output is converted into aluminum in Cameroon. Projects do, however, exist in Ghana and Cameroon.

The producers of primary copper by country and company are presented in Annex 14.11. In 1982, for which production figures are given in the annex, Eastern and Southern Africa accounted for 98.2 percent and 99.4 percent of mine and refinery production respectively. The major producers in descending order are Zambia Consolidated Copper Mines (ZCCM) of Zambia, La Générale des Carrières et de Mines (GECAMINES) of Congo K, and the production unit in South Africa. It was reported that in both Zambia and Congo K work was being carried out to increase production.

About 25 percent of the refined copper is locally fabricated into semi-manufactures and alloy products (brass and bronze). South Africa takes the lead in both tonnage and diversity of products. Products made by the other countries include: rods, rounds, bars, sheets, wires, cables, tubes, plumbing fittings, household goods, craft articles, and alloys. There is a large potential for increased production and diversification in this area in copper producing countries, particularly in wires and cables for electric power generation and transmission, telecommunications and electric transformers and motors as well as plates, sheets, and strips. Aluminum plays essentially similar and substitutive roles in many applications in aluminum-producing countries. In countries which produce none of the two, aluminum has an edge over copper in certain applications because of its light weight. Optical fibers and plastics (PVC) are among the substitute materials.

The integrated production of copper involves a number of unit operations and processes. In the conventional pyrometallurgical process, for instance, these include: mining, beneficiation, smelting to matte, blowing to blister, and electrorefining to cathode. This integration could be extended to fabrication and marketing.

From Annex 14.12 both mine and refined production in Africa show falling trends. This trend is also reflected in a decreasing share in world production. Mine production share fell from 19.7 percent in 1973 to 9.9 percent in 1993. Refined production which averaged 9.6 percent in 1980-1982 declined to 6.4 percent in 1990-1992. According to UNIDO ( *Industry and Development: Global Report 1993/94*) Africa accounted for 7.66 percent of world production. From the table, it is apparent that about half of the mine production is refined locally, the balance being exported for refining abroad.

Table 14.10 gives a more detailed and, probably, a more accurate picture of the copper industry in Africa. As can be observed from the table, only a part of the production was refined locally in 1988. The figures in the last two columns show the additional/expanded smelting and refining capacities that would be required if all the concentrate (matte) capacities under the column titled "mining" were to be converted into blister (smelting) and then to refined—hence a potential for investing.

TABLE 14.10
MAJOR MINING, SMELTING AND REFINING CAPACITIES OF COPPER IN
AFRICA IN 1988 (1000 t)

| Region/country | Existing capacity | | | Capacity gap | |
|---|---|---|---|---|---|
| | Mining | Smelting | Refining | Smelting | Refining |
| Total, developing Africa | 1535 | 1108 | 911 | 428 | 275 |
| - South Africa | 196 | 256 | 163 | - | - |
| Total Africa | 1731 | 1364 | 1074 | 428 | 275 |

Source: Compiled from UNIDO, 1990, *Industry and Development Report 1990/91*, Vienna., which was in turn obtained from N.Brown and B. McKern, 1987, *Aluminium, and Steel in Developing Countries*, Paris.

Annex 14.13 summarizes information related to the production, capacity, trade, and consumption of aluminum in Africa. It is apparent from the 1987 and 1990 figures that Africa's share in world production, trade and consumption stagnated. The major producers, in descending order, were Ghana, Egypt, and Cameroon. Capacity was to have increased by 220,000 tons (accounted for solely by an Algerian unit) to 687,000 tons by 1995 thus raising African contribution to world capacity to 3.1 percent (compared to 2.5 percent in 1990). Because of its potential in the generation of relatively cheap electric power, it is likely that Africa could in the future further increase its share in world aluminum capacity.

Production of primary aluminum has been steadily rising since mid-1980s and achieved capacity utilization of over 96 percent in 1992. Production and capacities of alumina and aluminum in the continent are presented in Annex 14.14. Guinea is the sole producer of alumina. Annual production level is approaching the 700,000-ton capacity, which represents 1.6 percent of world capacity. About 160,000 tons of its production is processed into primary aluminum by the Cameroonian company (ALUCAM) in Cameroon, the balance being exported outside the continent. Implementation of the planned capacities will more than quadruple the existing alumina capacity.

A new unit in Nigeria and expansions in Egypt and South Africa, reportedly under construction in 1994, were expected to more than double the 1992 African capacity of 637,000 tons to over 1.3 million tons by the second half of the 1990s. Other plans abound. They include those (capacities in tons/year) in Algeria (220,000), Cameroon (80,000 and 250,000), Congo K (210,000), Guinea (150,000), Libya (120,000), and Mozambique (250,000). Most of them seem to be experiencing difficulties in mobilizing financial resources. The Guinean integrated project, which may be financed by Société Guinea-Arabe d'Alumine et d'Aluminium as well as the Mozambican unit may prove to be among the exceptions.

Production of alumina in Guinea steadily increased to 700,000 tons in 1986 from 185,000 tons in 1960 ( Khennas 1992) and fell to 650,000 tons in 1991. The Friguia alumina plant, according to UNIDO, was expected to upgrade to 670,000 tons in 1993. With its huge bauxite reserves (7 billion tons) and hydro-electric power potential (6 gigawatts), Guinea has, so far, not been successful in integrating its alumina production with smelting. Its attempts at such development did not, apparently, coincide with the interest of those of the transnational corporations engaged in aluminum production and trade. This is probably why the Société Guineenne d'Alumine was established in 1976 with Arab partners to produce 2.0 million tons of alumina per year. The status of the project was not known at the time of writing, although the country was reported to have access to Russian technical and financial assistance for the project.

Trends in prices for copper, aluminum, and steel and with forecasts for 1995, 2000, and 2005 are shown in Annex 14.15. As may be observed, trends have been generally downwards for copper and aluminum. During the 1960-1989 period, the former attained its peak, $4,696, in 1966 and its trough, $1,165, in 1986. The corresponding figures for aluminum were $1,850 in 1988 and $1,023 in 1982. As for steel, the World Bank steel index shows that the composite steel price index reached its highest level in 1989 during 1980-1989. The prices forecasted for both copper and aluminum are lower than the 1989 prices. The opposite is the case for steel.

Lead, zinc, nickel, tin, cobalt, and chromium are other non-ferrous metals of relative importance to African countries. Production of their ores are shown in Annex 4.4. Production of lead, zinc, nickel, and tin are given in Annex 5.5. Capacities of lead and zinc refineries in 1984 by country and subregion are presented in Annex 14.16. The continent's share in world primary lead smelting and zinc refining were 5.5 percent and 4.6 percent respectively. South Africa accounted for 82.1 percent of African secondary lead smelting and 37.1 percent of primary zinc refining capacities.

As shown in Annex 14.17, the continent produced lead and zinc in excess of its consumption in the 1980s. The major producers were: Morocco, Namibia, and South Africa for lead and South Africa, Congo K, and Algeria for zinc slab. Morocco leads in the production of lead concentrates (about 150,000 tons).

### •Strategies for Development

The metallurgical industry is highly sensitive to economies of scale; it is capital- and skilled-labor-intensive. For these and other reasons, including the non availability of all the raw material and energy inputs within the borders of a country, it is out of the reach of the majority of African countries. It is for these very reasons that many national iron and steel projects have not moved beyond the drawing board for three decades in countries such as Liberia and Mauritania. One of the alternative approaches to developing the production of basic metals, therefore, is through cooperation between groups of member states.

Fortunately, the past three decades have witnessed technological breakthroughs in iron and steel making and their commercialization in the world. The share of electric arc furnace steel in world steel production, for instance, increased steadily from 8 percent in 1955 to 25.5 percent in 1989 (ECA, ECA/NRD/FRCDUMRA/ 3). The direct reduction-elecrtic arc furnace (DR-EAF) route which has been gaining popularity is viable at a much lower capacity as well as lower investment per unit of capacity compared with the conventional blast furnace-basic oxygen furnace (BF-BOF). The minimum economic size capacity of the BF-BOF is probably around five million tons per year while that of DR-EAF, which requires a shorter gestation period compared with the experiences in Egypt and Nigeria (up to 20 years) with the BF-BOF route, is, at most, in the hundreds of thousands. It has been reported that the DR-EAF route could go as low as 30,000 tons of direct reduced iron (DRI) per year for a plant based on solid reductant. Plants with 20,000 to 40,000 tons per year capacities were operating in India, Burma, and South Africa in mid-1980s (ECA, ECA/IND/MET/008/87). It should be noted here that, despite operating levels being less than expected in some countries, the direct reduction route seems to be here to stay in many developing countries.

The DR-EAF route does not require coking coal, one of the inputs that has been a major problem besetting projects based on BF-BOF. It can use a solid reductant, such as non-coking coal or a gas reductant such as natural gas, thus widening the material input options at the national level. In short, DR-EAF has brought iron and steel making within the reach of more developing countries. As a result of this breakthrough, many countries have shifted and are shifting their approach to DR-EAF.

The intermediate product of DR-EAF, DRI, or sponge iron, is a better one than scrap steel, the raw material used by the mini steel plants based on EAF in many countries. Another advantage of the DR-EAF route is that it provides a substitute for scrap steel or imported billets. It should be noted here that, because of the low generation of scrap steel in Africa, EAF plants have to import billets to supplement steel scrap. The importance of scrap worldwide is indicated by its increasing share in the production of steel, currently accounting for about one-third of steel output (UN, *Potentials and Policy Implications of Energy ...* ).

As for ferrous metals, it is apparent from Table 14.4 that African countries have adopted and are in the process of adopting the DR-EAF route to develop their iron and steel industry. As existing rolling mills are mainly geared to produce non-flat products, future projects should be planned to meet the growing demand for flat products. Because of the advantages inherent in continuous casting (CC) into billets, blooms, and slabs, its use should be taken into account when planning iron and steel as well as copper plants. In addition, the possibility of continuous steel making which combines DRI making, continuous casting and direct rolling should be explored. This approach would be more economical, as it could save energy as well as produce greater quantities of better quality steel, thus contributing to the viability of the plant.

Raw materials, reductants, and other inputs ( iron ore, coal, natural gas, electricity, etc.) for DR abound in the region (see Chaper 4). A lot of field work, however, needs to be undertaken to ascertain the size and qualities of reserves and their suitability for DR as well as the availability of adequate and inexpensive electricity. Availability of scrap steel also needs to be investigated, as it plays a role in determining the size of the DR plant. It would be advisable to carry out these activities, including ascertaining the supply of some of the inputs from other member states, after a positive outcome of a market study on DRI. The subregional Metallurgical Technology Centre in Zimbabwe and similar institutions could carry out some of these activities. This approach will avoid waste of resources and time.

Rehabilitation, upgrading, expansion, and diversification of existing metal production capacities should be part and parcel of the development of the metallurgical industry. The development of some ancillary industries is something that should be undertaken concomitantly with that of the metal industry. A good case in point is the production of refractories.

A charcoal-based blast furnaces is an alternative worth considering in countries endowed with renewable forest resources. This process for producing foundry steel as well as foundry pig iron is reported to be viable at scales in the hundreds of thousands. It could be of special interest to countries devoid of coal, hydrocarbon, and electricity resources.

As for non-ferrous metals, existing capacities are likely to be more than adequate to cover the needs of the engineering industry. As they are among the major foreign exchange earners, however, their production should continue to increase as long as there are markets for them outside the region. Both copper and aluminum are energy-intensive industries. Energy constitutes a major expense in refining the metals. This holds particularly true for intermediate alumina, which is usually transported to locations with abundant and inexpensive energy resources for refining. African energy resources, particularly hydropower, should be harnessed not only to refine African metals, but also to refine metals from outside the region. Inexpensive energy together with integration (bauxite mining, beneficiation, alumina and aluminum making, fabrication, and marketing) would, ultimately give African producers some competitive edge over such countries as the Commonwealth of Independent States, which have recently contributed to the surplus supply of aluminum in the world. The integrated approach could also be adopted for copper, as is already the case in South Africa, Zambia, Congo K, and Zimbabwe, where, to a large extent, mining, concentration, smelting, electrorefining, and, to a certain extent, fabrication are integrated within those countries.

The development of the metal industry has to be planned with a view to catering to the optimum needs of the engineering industry. The current production of metals, particularly steel, is limited to few standard qualities, mostly for the building and construction sector. Engineering quality steels are almost non-existent in most of the countries producing steels. Many such quality steels as well as other metals could be produced in existing metallurgical industries. All that is needed is to incorporate units for making them. As regards new metallurgical units, manufacture of special-quality metals should, whenever justified, be incorporated in the projects.

Although the focus in this book is on the development of the metallurgical industry to supply the needs of the engineering industry for manufacturing capital goods for agriculture and industries satisfying basic needs, it would not make economic sense to ignore the need for metals in other industries and export markets. The development of the metallurgical industry in Africa will, therefore, have to fulfill two major objectives. The first is to minimize the gap between mine production and the part of mine production converted into metals locally, i.e., maximize conversion of mine production into metals. As is well known, the major part of the iron ore and bauxite mined is exported. According to Annex 4.3, 32.5 million tons of the former and 19.4 million tons of the latter were produced in 1990. Take aluminum to illustrate what closing the gap means and entails. In addition to the 800,000-ton alumina unit in Guinea (see Table 14.10) , a combined capacity of 7.7 million tons of alumina would have been required to process all of the bauxite produced into alumina in 1990. Conversion of this into aluminum metal would have required an aluminum-smelting capacity of over 4.0 million tons in addition to and over the combined capacity of 700,000 tons in Cameroon, Ghana, and Egypt.

The second objective is to establish new mining and processing facilities, both for African use and for export outside the continent. In both cases, the development of the metallurgical industry is likely to yield better possibilities if it is planned to cater to local as well as foreign markets.

Processing ores into metals before export reduces weight and therefore freight cost. This advantage could, however, be negated by both discriminatory freight rates and tariffs that escalate with the degree of processing of the minerals that the developed countries import. In the 1960s, for instance, aluminum-related tariffs in force in the European Economic Community were: bauxite (0 %), alumina (5.6 %), aluminum unwrought (5.8%), and aluminum wrought (16.0%) (UNIDO, *Mineral Processing...*). Depending upon a favorable balance between these positive and negative factors and the high cost incurred in relation to environmental protection in industrialized countries, there may be cases that could give African countries a competitive edge in mineral processing for export, including minerals of strategic importance. In this connection, it should be noted that although the social cost of pollution is relatively low in developing countries, African countries would be advised to assess carefully the environmental implications of projects and obtain concessions from foreign collaborators that could minimize the cost of pollution control.

In recent years, the metallurgical industry has witnessed technological changes which make it possible to produce some metals in relatively small units, thereby minimizing the constraint arising from economies of scale. A good example of this is direct reduction of iron ore into sponge iron that can be converted into steel in an electric arc furnace, already referred to above. Other technological changes have to do with higher recovery rates and reduced production costs. Leaching-solvent extraction-electro-winning is an alternative to the conventional processing of copper ores. This technique can use poorer oxide ores and tailings from previous conventional operations to produce cathode copper at relatively low cost. These and other developments, including small-scale extraction from sulfide ores, should be taken into consideration when planning metallurgical projects.

## Chemical Industry

According to AIChExtra (January 1997) there are more than 15 million unique chemical substances. As a consequence, the chemical industry is a very diversified industrial subsector. Fortunately, a relatively small number of chemicals, which can be grouped into basic chemicals, soaps and detergents, pharmaceuticals, perfumes and cosmetics, paints, agricultural chemicals, plastics, synthetic rubbers and fibers, etc., are of significance for African needs and conditions. Some of these groups are basic needs, while others contribute to basic needs indirectly.

### •Priority Products

It is virtually impossible for a country to produce within its borders all the chemicals it needs. This holds particularly true for developing countries, where demand for most chemicals is generally very low. In African countries, agricultural chemicals (fertilizers and pesticides), pharmaceuticals, and basic chemicals constitute priority chemical groups or branches. As the first and second have already been dealt with in Chapters 9 and 8, respectively, and as most of the basic chemicals are produced in conjunction with fertilizer plants, this section on chemical industry offers a cursory review of basic chemicals.

Basic chemicals mainly comprise acids and bases. Under African conditions, sulfuric, nitric, phosphoric and hydrochloric acids are considered priority acids and caustic soda and soda ash, priority bases. To these, chlorine should be added.

**•Current Stage of Development**

In countries which host fertilizers plants, sulfuric and phosphoric acids and/or nitric acid are part and parcel of the fertilizer complexes. Generally, the acid units, including sulfuric acid associated with smelting, were planned for captive uses and therefore do not usually cater to the needs of other large industries. The same, more or less, applies to caustic soda and chlorine, which are usually produced captively in pulp and paper mills. Soda ash is extracted in Kenya, Botswana, and Ethiopia.

**•Strategies for Development**

As the name implies, basic chemicals are the building blocks of the chemical industry. Their development is, therefore, crucial not only to the development of the chemical industry but also to industry in general.

As in the past, their development should and will continue to be in association with industries that are their main consumers. Expansion of existing units and new projects should, however, take into consideration demand for other outlets when deciding on the capacities to be expanded or installed.

The chain of processing from basic raw materials through successive intermediates to final products is characteristic of the chemical industry. This, coupled with the lessening importance of economies of scale with successive downstream processing, makes the chemical industry amenable to dispersion. The development of basic chemical-based industries and services should be planned to maximize the use of such chemicals and take account of the fair regional distribution of production facilities.

## BIBLIOGRAPHY

ADB, 1997, *African Development Report 1997,* Oxford University Press Inc., New York.

AIChExtra, 1997, "Speak Out—the News about Chemistry, Health, and You," January 1997.

ECA, 1988, *Regional Survey of and Aluminium Fabricating Facilities and Prospects for Intra-African Manufacture and Trade in and Aluminium-based Products (ECA/NRD/TRCDUMRA/7)*, Addis Ababa.

ECA, 1984, *Local Manufacture of Selected Spare Parts for Engineering Industries in Africa*, Addis Ababa.

ECA, 1987, *Technological Options for Small-scale Integrated Iron and Steel Plants based on Direct Reduction in ECA Member Countries* (ECA/IND/MET/008/87), Addis Ababa.

ECA, 1991, *L'Industrie du Fer en Afrique durant la Periode 1980-1989* (ECA/NRD/FRCDUMRA/3), Addis Ababa.

ECA, 1993, *Report of the Eleventh Meeting of the Conference of African Ministers of Industry on Problems, Policies, Issues and Prospects by the Year 2000 of Africa's Basic Industries, namely: Chemical, Metal and Engineering Industries* (CAMI.11/4), Addis Ababa.

ECA, 1996, *Africa in the 1990s and Beyond: ECA-Revised Long-Term Development Perspectives Study* (ECA/SERPD/TP/96/3), Addis Ababa.

ECA/HMT, 1988, *Model Pre-feasibility Report—Machine Tools, Engineering Industry Development Programme for Selected Eastern and Southern African Countries of Preferential Trade Area*, Addis Ababa.

ECA/HMT, 1988, *Model Pre-feasibilty Report—Spare Parts, Engineering Industry Development Programme for Selected Eastern and Southern African Countries of Preferential Trade Area*, Addis Ababa.

ECA/UNIDO, 1995, *Report on Regional Strategy for Rational Location of Industries in the Context of the Abuja Treaty* (CAMI.12/6[A]), Addis Ababa.

Europa, 1996, *Africa South of the Sahara 1996*, Twenty-fifth Edition, Europa Publications Limited, London.

Khennas, Smail, ed., 1992, *Industrialization, Mineral Resources and Energy in Africa*, CODESRIA Book Series, Anthony Rowe, Oxford.

Roskill Information Services Limited, 1992, 1993, *The Economics of Aluminium*, London.

The Economist, 1996, "Mining in Africa: King Solomon's Mines," May 25, 1996.

UN, 1974, *The Machine Tool Industry*, New York.

UN, 1980, *Metalworking Industries in Developing Countries of Africa*, New York.

UN, 1985, *The Capital Goods Sector in Developing Countries: Technology Issues and Policy Options*, New York

UN, 1997, *Potentials and Policy Implications of Energy and Material Efficiency Improvement*, New York.

UNECE, 1988, *The Steel Market in 1988*, Geneva.

UNECE, 1989, *The Importance of the Iron and Steel Industry for the Economic Activity of ECE Member Countries*, Geneva.

UNECE,——,Statistics.

UNIDO, 1979, *Mineral Processing in Developing Countries*, Vienna.

UNIDO, 1981, *Appropriate Industrial Technology for Basic Industries*, Monographs on Appropriate Industrial Technology, No. 13, UN, New York.

UNIDO, 1984, *The Capital Goods Industry in Africa: A General Review and Developments for Further Analysis*, Sectoral Studies Series No. 14 (UNIDO/IS.502), Vienna.

UNIDO, 1986, *Survey on the Iron and Steel Industry in the PTA Region*, Vienna.

UNIDO, 1992, *Industry and Development, Global Report 1992/93*, Vienna.

UNIDO, 1993, *Industry and Development: Global Report 1993/94*, Vienna.

UNIDO, ——, Atlas ...

## NOTES

1. As shown in annexes 9.4 to 9.6, this figure seems to be, and in reality is, significantly low.

## CHAPTER 15

# STRATEGIES FOR INDUSTRIAL DEVELOPMENT

Financial and skilled manpower resources are limited in Africa. The judicious use of these resources is crucial. Because of these and other constraints discussed in Chapter 6 and elsewhere, industrial development requires some kind of government intervention at both the national and multinational levels. This approach was used in the form of central planning and state ownership of a good part of the means of production and services by most African countries in the past. In view of the failure of directive planning of the centrally-planned economies, however, indicative planning of the market economies has been and is being adopted by a number of countries. In mixed economies, which are most prevalent in Africa, indicative planning sets out policies and objectives to bring about the needed structural change. While the government may have a say in matters related to the public sector, its influence on the private sector should be through policies, incentives, and other promotional measures that guide and facilitate the development and activities of the private sector.

Industrial planning should be a continuous and iterative process; it should involve all relevant actors, including the private sector, who have to do with industrial development. The private sector involvement, mainly through manufacturers associations, chamber of industries and commerce, and professional associations, could from the outset include the policy-formulation stage. This will facilitate and enhance implementation, as some of the factors that may hamper and delay development will have already been taken care of. Inputs from the private sector will enable planners to improve the plan when and if required. The need for improvement is likely to surface because of, among other things, shortcomings in the data and information base used in the preparation of the plan. Industrial planning can be made more relevant and effective, and hence more likely to succeed, if it is drawn up on a rolling basis, being revised at the end of each year or every other year.

Industrial planning involves determining priorities and sequencing the activities to implement those priorities. A three-phase approach ( UNIDO, PPD.259 [SPEC]) based on experience in Eastern and Southern African subregion and characterized by overlapping activities is of some reference. The three phases, which include rationalization of existing industries as well as the creation of new industries, and which may take several years (in parentheses) to implement, are:

• Emergency phase, which includes the programs to complete the activities of the first level of priority (3);

• Consolidation phase, which mostly focuses on the programs of restructuring/rehabilitation/modernization as well as on the implementation of the necessary conditions for the next phase (3); and

• Expansion phase, which essentially deals with new industrial investments (4).

According to the source, *"productive investment increases exponentially as the environment improves,"* this indicates the significance and need for an enabling industrial environment. Considering the situation obtaining in the other subregions, the above approach and conclusion seem relevant to practically all subregions and the region as a whole.

It should be noted here that, individually and collectively, African countries as well as the international community have recognized the need to industrialize. Most African countries have taken and are taking measures and actions to restructure their economies and achieve diversification through sustainable and self-reliant industrialization. This chapter tries to indicate how the process of industrialization can be promoted and enhanced by focusing on developing integrated industries that provide inputs to agriculture and industries processing agricultural commodities.

## INDUSTRIALIZATION THROUGH MAXIMIZING INTEGRATION AT NATIONAL LEVEL

Depending on its stage of economic development, each African country has some industries. In the small and less endowed countries, the industries are generally of the small-scale category and perhaps more dependent on imported factor inputs. The picture in the larger and relatively well endowed countries is somewhat rosier. These countries possess a range of industries of all categories — small, medium, and large—with a good part of them based on indigenous resources. Most of the remaining countries fall somewhere in between.

Most of the industrial establishments operating in Africa, except those based on local resources, were planed and implemented with minimal integration, if at all. Small-scale and many of the medium-scale industries are generally engaged in processing/manufacturing intermediates into final products. In other words, both vertical integration (from basic raw materials to final products) and horizontal integration (involving an input/output relationship between industrial subsectors or among economic sectors), are minimal. The same applies to the industrial support services, such as consultancy, training, R&D, design, and field testing of prototypes, which were generally established to respond to limited needs. It is apparent that some of the services could and should be combined.

Failure to utilize potential linkages means a lost opportunity to stimulate manufacturing.

### Rationalization of Existing Facilities

As a result of the oil crises, particularly the crisis in 1979, and the multiple crises that followed, including the declining prices of Africa's export commodities, African countries found it increasingly difficult to operate their industries let alone establish new ones. At a time when they needed more foreign exchange, they found themselves forced to divert financial resources to import essential goods, such as fuels, food, and pharmaceuticals, at escalating prices and to repay growing debt.

There was practically very little, if any, foreign exchange available to import industrial inputs to keep industries running. Many of the industries had to work at very low capacity utilization or close down for want of foreign exchange to import spare parts, replacement equipment, and raw and intermediate materials.

By mid-1990s, the level of capacity utilization was 3 to 50 percent. According to a 1992 survey by the Manufacturers' Association of Nigeria, capacity utilization in Nigeria was 34.5 percent. It is obvious from this that, in the short-term, governments should place priority on raising capacity utilization to the maximum extent possible in both public and private enterprises engaged in production and related activities. Rationalizing measures for this purpose should be taken while at the same time planning and developing new projects.

### •Rehabilitation, Revitalization and Modernization of Existing Industries

Many of the industries in the region are old and dilapidated and need to be rehabilitated, upgraded, or replaced; some may even have to be closed down. The alternative to rehabilitation is the setting up of new ones. Given the poor economic conditions in most countries, it would be better to make the best use of existing facilities and thereby conserve scarce financial resources rather than going for new ones. Rehabilitation, including the revitalization of public enterprises and expansion, when justified, is likely to be more economical because existing infrastructure could be used and part of the equipment and machinery salvaged.

Most of the industries, many of which are based on second-hand machinery and equipment, are over 30 years old. Many of them use obsolete, uneconomical technology. Others may need to change some equipment and machinery, including equipment for balancing processing or fabrication, to make the production unit more efficient and profitable. There may be a need to switch over to a different type of raw material and/or energy. These and other needs call for rehabilitation and modernization of existing facilities.

The decision whether to rehabilitate or modernize an ailing industry should be based on a diagnostic study. The terms of reference for the study should include the financial, commercial, and management aspects in addition to technical considerations. Experience has shown that usually all of these contribute to the poor performance of plants in terms of capacity utilization, productivity, consumption coefficients, cost-effectiveness, and profitability.

### •Expansion and Diversification of Existing Industries

There could be cases for diversification, i.e., increasing the product mix of the products made in the plant. In Africa, most industrial projects have been generally conceived, designed, and implemented without due regard to vertical or horizontal integration. Such units operate in isolation. Had enough thought been given to the production of related products within the facility at the inception of the project, the project could have possibly been planned with a capacity and capability to produce more than one product, an advantage under African conditions where markets are limited.

There could be cases where, because of economic crises over the past 20 years, there has been no expansion of capacities while production in existing capacities was declining. The resultant growing supply/demand gap offer investors an opportunity to invest in expanding capacities to produce products well established in the market. Since the technologies used have proven appropriate or can be modified to take account of improvements made in the interim period, the risks would be minimal.

On the contrary, it is quite possible that after years of operation, the market may be saturated, tastes may have changed, or competition may have become crucial, partly as a result of substitutes, thus making it necessary to close or modify the plant.

## New Production Units
The scope for optimizing existing production facilities should be fully exhausted before venturing into new units. This approach is based on the premise that rehabilitation, modernization, or diversification or any combination thereof requires less investment and time than a new project.

### •Resource-based Import Substitution
As African countries are and will continue to be highly dependent on the import of industrial inputs, be they in technology, equipment, machinery, and raw or intermediate products, they will have to opt increasingly for resource-based industries, if they are to make headway in sustained industrial development. With the exhaustion of simple import substitution industries producing consumer goods, this means going into the processing and manufacture of intermediates from basic raw materials for further local processing and manufacture as well as for export. Production of local intermediates could broaden the industrial base and supply some of the inputs for import substitution consumer goods, thereby reducing dependency on imported inputs.

The logical starting point is increasing the local content of existing industries. Nigeria is among the countries that have been replacing imported inputs by local ones. Textile mills, breweries and motor assembling units are examples of industries that have shown a substantial shift to local raw materials and manufacturing of parts and components. According to UNIDO, the share of local raw materials increased from 30 percent in 1986 to 50 percent in 1990 and local sourcing accounted for 46 percent of the inputs of the motor assembly industry (UNIDO, *Industry and Development : Global Report 1991/92*). This trend will, unfortunately, be restrained by the requirement for abolishing local content requirements and trade balancing tests in 5 to 7 years as well as the anti-subsidy provisions imposed by the Uruguay Round agreements.

In general, when starting from basic raw materials, economies of scale become important. As evidenced by the number of the so-called traditional industries for which there were adequate markets, economies of scale in these industries were apparently not that crucial. Economies of scale are, however, serious constraining factors in processing basic raw materials into metals and chemical intermediates.

Developing basic (metals and chemical intermediates) industries to meet national demand would not be feasible for most African countries because of the small and fragmented national markets and the sensitivity of such industries to economies of scale. Such countries could only consider basic industries as a group.

### •Export-led Industrialization
Any African country can export to the world market, both within and without Africa, provided its product or service is competitive . As the exchange of goods and services is the basis for cooperation and integration, the focus of this section is on export to the rest of the world market.

As noted elsewhere, Africa has benefited little from the export of industrial products in the past. It is unlikely that it will do so in the near future. Low productivity, an increasingly competitive global economy (particularly competition with well-established exporters in other regions), the marginalization of Africa in the world economy through regional economic blocs, growing protectionist sentiments, and changing technologies (making the continuation of the deployment of such labor-intensive industries as clothing, footwear, toys, electronics, etc., to developed countries unlikely) are some of the reasons for this pessimistic view.

A country will have to find niches in the world market in order to succeed in export-oriented industries. This is not going to be that easy. A country with an adequate national market for a particular product could, however, establish a production unit with part of the output being for export. If worst comes to worst, resort could be made to marginal pricing in regard to the part of production targeted for export, i.e., provided an export market, including non-traditional markets[1] (fast growing Asian markets) is accessible. If, however, the unit cannot penetrate outside market by itself, the most sensible thing to do would be to go into joint venture arrangements with an overseas partner engaged in marketing. The arrangement could be in marketing or in both production and marketing.

Processed agricultural commodities, particularly tropical produce, offer increasing export possibilities in the global market. Preserved fruits and vegetables, provided they meet the health and phytosanitary standards for food in developed countries, could find markets in the affluent developed countries. This applies to the export of fresh vegetables not grown in developed countries during the cold seasons as well as to other horticultural exports. Processed fish (frozen, canned), coffee (extracts, essences, concentrates), cocoa (powder, butter, paste, oil, chocolate), tea, cotton, hides and skins (leather and leather goods), and wood (veneer, plywood, chipboard, knocked down-furniture kits) are other products that might find niches in the world market. It is in the interest of the world at large to let African countries specialize in tropical agro-industries so that they can earn the foreign currency to buy the capital and intermediate goods they need from the rest of the world. This could be done by redeploying industries processing tropical products in developed countries to African countries which export the raw materials or, at least, stop expanding such industries in developed countries.

Although the prospects for export of non-agricultural processed products may not be as good as those for agricultural products, there are nevertheless likely to be export possibilities for a number of them. Copper products (wires and cables), aluminum, and marble are examples in this group.

### •Optimization of Integration

Integration of and interdependence between African industries are limited. Many of the industries were developed independently and haphazardly, without taking account of their relationship with other industries. The opportunities lost to both the industries and the countries as a whole were enormous. Much therefore remains to be done in this area in both existing and new industries.

In each country, governments and existing industries would be well advised to review the state of their industrial sector with a view to identifying missing inter-industry linkages, including complementary projects. This should lead to planning and implementing measures and projects that could maximize advantages accruing from inter-dependence and the rationalization of production.

The same would apply to new industries. Investors would do well to maximize integration, both vertical and horizontal, with a view to contributing to the rationalization of the emerging production structures. Vertical integration from basic raw materials to final products may be automatic in the case of resource-based industrial projects. This may not be the case for those projects whose objectives are to produce and sell intermediates to other industries for further processing or fabrication. In either case, investors should explore all openings for broadening and deepening the impact of their projects, subject, of course, to maximizing their profits. This would, in the case of agro-industry, include contracting farmers to supply the agricultural commodity inputs or supplement the industry's own plantation.

As for integration, all or part of the intermediates at different stages of processing/fabricating could be passed on or subcontracted to other industries for further processing/fabricating into intermediate products. This process could be repeated a number of times until the final products reach the end-users. This implies the need for identifying the intermediate users (during market studies) well in advance and even involve them directly and/or indirectly in the project preparation and implementation, including ownership in the business, if possible. The vested interest thus created will pay dividends in the long-run.

Recycling and economic utilization of co- and by-products as well as industrial waste may be considered part of the integration process. Given the small size of most plants, and consequently the small quantities of co- and by-products and industrial wastes generated, coupled with lack of adequate markets, most African industries had no options but to discard and continue to discard such materials instead of converting them into useful products. Examples in the agro-industry include: straw, husk, bran, peels, and many other wastes from grain milling; oil cake from vegetable oil extraction; bagasse and molasses from sugar mills; and animal products from slaughter houses.

All products and wastes discarded from a production facility are potential pollutants. There will eventually come a time when those who produce them may be required to control pollution arising from their facilities. Under these circumstances, some of the facilities may resort to recycling and converting at least part of the pollutants into salable products. It would, of course, be advisable, to go for technologies that minimize wastes right from the start and/or arrange with other industries that could utilize as raw materials the by-products and wastes that would be generated.

Existing production units and projects would do well to maximize the benefits that can accrue from integration. Linkages with related industries and services, including subcontracting arrangements, could go a long way to ensuring the success of the project. New projects that may not be viable as sole units could prove more viable through integration and diversification, preferably involving sub-contracting for some of the production and service activities. The following provide examples of integration which may not necessarily be physically integrated:

• Cereals: dehusking, milling, baking;
• Oil seeds: extraction of oil, followed by making animal feed, soap;

• Forestry: logging and sawing followed by making veneer, particle board, furniture, pulp, viscose rayon, paper, etc.;

• Animal husbandry: tanning of hides and skins followed by making leather, shoes, other leather goods, products from slaughter house by-products;

• Natural fibers: spinning cotton yarn followed by making fabrics, garments, bandages, gauzes;

• Fishery: fishing integrated with refrigeration, canning, fish meal preparation, fish oil extraction,

• Clay: bricks, tiles, pipes, ceramics;

• Metal fabrication: containers, tanks, kitchenware, safes, structural (doors, windows, frames, grilles, etc.), furniture, fixtures;

• Steel wire-based products: nails, rivets, hoops, screens, fencing materials;

• Tools and implements: hand tools ( hammers, saws, etc. ), agricultural tools ( hoes, pick-axes, etc.), agricultural implements (ploughs, cultivators, etc.); and

• Central support facilities: castings provided by a foundry, forged items by a forging unit, heat treatment by heat treatment unit, etc. through subcontracting arrangements.

From the above it can be seen that a lot needs to be done. Governments will have to motivate the private and public sectors. Drawing the attention of investors to integration potentials related to their specific projects and advising them on how to go about it would be among the roles that governments will have to play in promoting integration. Others would include giving special incentives to those who, by the very nature of the integration process involved, including the optimization of substitution of local materials for imported inputs, need government assistance in order to coax them into accepting the desired integration under consideration.

It is possible that a gap in production and/or services may manifest itself in an integration process. In such a situation, if filling the gap in production required to complement or optimize the integration process is justified, the government may have to coax the investors concerned to include the necessary production unit(s). Similar coaxing may be required in the event that a government decides to bring industrial development to disadvantaged areas. In both situations, it should let the enterprises operate as autonomous enterprises, if they are public enterprises. The government should, in recognition of the opportunity cost of such investments, whether private or public, subsidize and/or give concessions to the enterprises to enable them earn adequate profit margins until they become profitable (at least self-supporting in the case of public enterprises). This approach should apply to all situations that impose conditions and additional cost implications on enterprises. Included in this are essential and strategic industries that provide crucial inputs and services to other industries and economic activities, thereby rendering them viable and beneficial to the country. A good example of this is the Akaki Spare Parts & Hand Tools Factory in Ethiopia (see Chapter 14).

## Adoption of Flexible Production/Fabrication Methods

As indicated elsewhere, economies of scale is one of the factors constraining industrial development in Africa. This is compounded by the fact that the technologies and industrial plants that developing countries use are those designed and made to serve the needs prevailing in industrialized countries. In other words, many of the industries operating in Africa could have been less costly in both investment and production cost and experienced less failure had they been designed to process African raw materials under African conditions. A number of approaches could be used to minimize this constraint.

### •Adaptation of Imported Plant to Local Conditions

At the project stage, in addition to identifying the peculiarities of conditions on the project site and making the necessary changes in the technologies to fit local conditions, the technology should be disaggregated with a view to determining which equipment and machinery can be manufactured locally in existing facilities. Structures and handling and packaging equipment are examples of possibilities that come to mind. The type of local manufacture and extent to which it can be involved will, of course, depend upon the level of development of the country concerned.

The haphazard manner in which technologies were previously adopted has harmed African development and heightened its dependence on outside manufacturers and or suppliers. Technologies for the same process and product are acquired from different suppliers. This makes it difficult for the acquiring country to adapt the technologies for use in new production units.

### •Designing Appropriate Equipment and Machinery

This approach differs from the foregoing in that the plant would be designed from the outset to meet African needs and conditions. It will, obviously, require the cooperation of and assistance from manufacturers and suppliers of industrial equipment and machinery. At the country level, governments will have to encourage and give assistance to those who innovate technologies. It should, in fact, organize groups with responsibilities to adopt, adapt, and innovate technologies for industries of prime interest to the country.

Many of the products, both consumer and capital goods, available from industrialized countries are not appropriate to African needs and conditions. Many of the consumer goods are too sophisticated and incorporate a host of functions only a fraction of which are used by the majority of consumers. In other words, they are targeted at the high-income, high-quality end of the market. TVs, videos, and cars are examples in this category. The consumer is forced to pay dearly for gadgets he does not even know how to operate. In the case of cars, for instance, what most people require are affordable cars stripped to their minimum and mechanically sound, i.e., good old cars but based on current technology.

As for capital goods, they are becoming increasingly sophisticated, automated, and computerized mainly to save high labor cost in industrialized countries. This trend, in general, is not in the interest of developing countries, where unemployment is high and on the increase. In Africa, a limited number of such industries may only be used, if needed, to produce export goods that have to meet stringent quality standards. For the majority of products, especially those intended for local use, at this stage of industrialization, traditional equipment and machinery incorporating improved technologies will suffice. As the manufacture of such capital goods is being phased-out in developed countries, developing countries will have to build the capability and capacity to manufacture the capital goods and spare parts themselves.

362

**•Production of Several Product Lines**

It is well known that many products can be made in a single plant. This fact should be borne in mind when planning projects, both new ones and expansions of existing ones. In this connection, the concept of multi-purpose equipment and machinery is significant in economies characterized by narrow and fragmented national markets, as is the case in the majority of African countries. It is meant to cut down on the underutilization of capacity that is rampant in Africa.

In a plant equipped with multi-purpose equipment and machinery, the equipment and machinery is designed for maximum conditions of temperature, pressure, etc. and has extra parts and components to accommodate the changing needs of the products to be made. It operates on a campaign basis. It involves thorough cleaning and adjustment of the equipment and machinery involved in each switch-over to another product line. This includes changing parts and components, when needed, and has to be done in the shortest time possible to minimize downtime. There is a need to design the multi-purpose equipment and machinery with a view to facilitating these operations.

The multi-purpose plant approach is flexible. Production can be switched over to another product line as soon as the market demands. It is suited to subcontracting arrangements. For these and the above reasons Africa would be well advised to encourage the multi-purpose approach.

It would be appropriate to refer here to other strategies that could increase the diversification of production. These include industrial estates, industrial free zones, business incubators or technology parks, and clusters of small firms. The first is common and exists in a number of African countries. The second is limited to few countries (Mauritius, Egypt, Tunisia, Senegal, Madagascar, Liberia, Togo, and Congo K). The Mauritian industrial free zone established in 1970 has, so far, been practically the most successful model in Africa. The fates of the export processing zones for which agreements were signed in 1993 in Egypt and Tunisia remain to be seen. Industrial free zones are usually planned to maximize the global benefit to the investor, including the use of factor inputs from production elsewhere or through the procurement of inputs from the cheapest source, and hence are imported-input oriented. In view of this, arrangements should be made for the local procurement of some of the inputs and future development of backward linkages when negotiating with interested investors.

As regards the practice of a "business incubator," it is virtually unknown in the continent. According to one source (ECA, *Focus on African Industry*, Volume VI, No.1), an incubator can be defined as *"a micro facility with a small management staff that provides the physical workspace, shared facilities and access to technical and business support services in one integrated and affordable package."* It is a means of instilling and fostering entrepreneurial culture with a view to increasing the number of indigenous entrepreneurs. It is usually associated with universities or R&D institutions, to benefit from their advisory services and/or commercialize their research results. In Africa, where the opportunity for translating research results is limited, universities and R&D institutions should be encouraged to involve themselves in industrial incubators.

The last comprises clusters of small-scale industries in industrial districts working through inter-firm cooperation and specialization. This approach enables small firms to minimize constraints arising from economies of scale. It has been very successful in Italy in the clothing, shoe, furniture, and food-processing industries. With government support it could work under African conditions where individual firms find it increasingly difficult to operate and compete in isolation.

## INDUSTRIALIZATION THROUGH SUBREGIONAL/REGIONAL INTEGRATION

Subregional or regional integration brings to mind first and foremost market integration, i.e., the exchange of goods and services across borders. This concept is more applicable to developed countries than to developing countries. In the latter, the goods and services to be exchanged do not exist or are, at best, limited to the same limited range of high cost products which are hampered by high transport and other costs. It is not likely that regional integration will work unless agricultural and industrial production are incorporated in the process of market integration. In the case of the industrial sector, diversification into the production of intermediates and capital goods is a crucial pre-condition for generating tradable goods. This approach seems to be the only option that could minimize constraints hampering trade between African countries and thereby enhance the integration process. In other words, regional integration will have to take account of increasingly diversified agricultural and industrial production based on indigenous raw material and energy resources which, fortunately, abound in the continent. The West African Gas Pipeline Project from Nigeria to Benin, Togo, and Ghana (for power generation and commercial and industrial use) whose construction is expected to start in 1999—involving the governments of the four countries and private enterprises—(Panafrican News Agency, October 1, 1998) could serve as an example of economic integration that is badly needed.

For the reasons referred to above and elsewhere, the development of certain industries, basic industries in particular, at the national level in the majority of the countries will be out of question for a long time to come. Industrial integration based on pooling markets and resources is the only option, if a measure of collective self-reliant and self-sustainable agricultural and industrial and, for that matter, economic and social development is to be achieved in the region.

There have been some attempts at industrial cooperation. Examples of joint or multinational industrial enterprises include: Ciments de l'Afrique de l'ouest (CIMAO) between Togo, Ghana, and Cote d'Ivoire (closed in 1984); Société des Ciments d'Onigbolo (SCO) between Benin, Nigeria, and F. L. Smith & Co. of Denmark; Industries Chimiques de Sénégal (ICS) between Senegal, Cameroon, Cote d'Ivoire, Nigeria, and India; Iron Pellet Plant between Mauritania, Algeria and Libya; and Soda Ash Botswana (SAB) between Botswana and AECI of South Africa. The Hand Tools Company in Tunisia, the Arab Machine Tools Manufacturing Company in Morocco, the Misr Iranian Textile Company (MIRATEX), and SOFOMECA in Tunisia are examples of joint ventures involving North African and Middle Eastern countries and financial institutions, i.e., in countries outside the continent. SAB and MIRATEX seem to be the only relatively successful companies in the group. An attempt has been made to summarize in Annex 15.1 two categories of constraints (project conception and design and problems in plant operations) that the enterprises had to face.

CIMAO and SCO failed for a number of reasons. Some of these were: inadequate project preparation (including wrong assumptions about market and prices), weakness in project and operational management, difficulties in mobilizing finance, failure of member states to honor agreements, delays in financing restructuring, and (in the case of CIMAO), conflicts of interests between managing agents, consulting engineers, and clinker grinding mills in Togo, Ghana, and Cote d'Ivoire. ICS, which faced similar constraints, survived because the host country assumed the burden of the huge financial restructuring (CFAF35.9 billion) required to continue operating the plants, thus increasing its equity from 20 percent to 53 percent. The constraints against individual multinational enterprises shown in Annex 15.1 are those that were specifically referred to in the source. The major constraints generally applicable to most of the enterprises dealt with and supplemented by others are summarized below under three headings: government ownership; reliance on foreign expertise; and mobilizing finance.

*Difficulties associated with government ownership*: inadequate project planning, management, monitoring, and follow-up; failure of member states to honor agreements, including delays in parliamentary ratifications/approvals resulting in cost escalation; inadequate information base; inadequate terms of reference for undertaking studies and advisory, supervision, and management services; lack of indigenous monitoring of work done by consultants, engineering firms, and management agencies; difficulty of taking timely decisions by board meetings which are virtually impossible to hold because of difficulties of bringing together board members comprising ministers and high-ranking government officials who are generally political appointees as well as unfamiliar with the complexities of enterprise management; appointment of civil servants to enterprise managerial posts who end up managing the enterprise as if it were a ministry or other government institution.[2]

*Excessive reliance (because of inadequate technical and managerial capabilities) on foreign consultants, engineering firms and management agencies*: some with conflicts of interest because of their association with manufacturers of plants and producers and distributors of products; some not familiar with local conditions and therefore recommending inappropriate technologies; wrong assumptions about market and prices, usually resulting in capacities much larger than demand, higher capital investment, and consequently high overhead costs, and declining market and prices; weaknesses and mistakes in plant designs, resulting in cost overruns, poor performance, and closure of plants; exorbitant remuneration accounting for a high proportion of cost of production.

*Difficulty in planning and mobilizing finance*: difficulty in organizing and coordinating many financial resources; soaring investment costs during project preparation, mainly due to delays in project planning and implementation; delays or failure in bringing about financial restructuring; and low equity/capital ratio resulting in increasing borrowing and therefore in increasing overhead cost.

In recognition of the above reality and based on the Lagos Plan of Action and the Final Act of Lagos, the General Assembly of the United Nations proclaimed the 1980s as the Industrial Development Decade for Africa (IDDA). The overall objective of the IDDA was to focus attention on African industrial development and was based on the concept of self-reliance and self-sustainment. Unfortunately, due to unfavorable world economic conditions in the 1980s as well as inadequate support from the African governments themselves, partly as a result of said conditions and the multiple crises they had to face, the IDDA was a failure. The second IDDA, covering the period 1993-2002, was therefore proclaimed with practically the same objectives as the first. It has to deal with practically all the constraints that IDDA I had to contend with. In fact, some of the constraints, such as debt and foreign capital investment, have worsened.

The two IDDAs did, however, differ in some  aspects, three of which are referred to here. The first is in the way the IDDA program was prepared. Whereas the first was prepared with limited inputs from the subregional organizations and the countries themselves, the second started at the grass-roots level; it involved all actors concerned. Both individual countries and their subregional economic cooperation organizations drafted their respective programs. At subregional meetings, the subregional programs were finalized and due account was taken of the national programs. The subregional programs formed the basis for the regional program.

The second difference had to do with a requirement that was not part of the first IDDA. During the deteriorating economic conditions in the 1980s, African industries, mainly for want of foreign exchange to import industrial inputs (particularly, spare parts and replacement equipment), suffered deterioration. In other words, these industries needed to be rehabilitated. The second IDDA is, therefore, expected to deal with both the rehabilitation of existing industries and the development of new industries. Under the circumstances, African countries could gainfully start their industrial cooperation and integration by converting existing underutilized or spare national industrial capacities into multinational ones. Generally, because of the economies of scale and small national markets, spare capacities are rampant in many industrial establishments. Petroleum refineries characterized by product mixes that do not correspond to local market needs are examples of industries that could be rationalized to serve the needs of neighboring countries. Candidate establishments could be expanded and rationalized and their scope of production diversified to take advantage of expanded market. The process of planning and negotiating new industries could be carried out concurrently.

The third difference is the realization by African countries of the driving role of the private sector in industrial development and therefore the emphasis on the involvement of that sector in IDDA II. In IDDA I, practically everything revolved around governments. Programs and projects were conceptualized and were intended to be promoted and implemented by governments. This was one of the reasons why IDDA I failed to materialize.

For new projects, one approach that seems to deserve consideration is to approach development at the subsector level. This approach could best be illustrated by the engineering subsector, as the latter is amenable to disaggregating production. Equipment and machinery comprise parts and components that are not necessarily made within the same establishment. In fact, most of them are made by hundreds of manufacturers, mostly small ones, specializing in certain products, thus making fair distribution of production facilities relatively possible. This subsector is likely to help minimize the polarization of industries that is bound to take place if industries are to, as they should, be located with a view to maximizing profit, i.e., based on natural resource endowment and other comparative advantages.

The difficulties experienced in and lessons learned from attempts at developing multinational industries referred to above (CIMAO, SCO,  ICS, etc.) could be useful in improved planning and promotion of future multinational industries. Projects would be planned better. Mistakes and omissions of equipment and infrastructures would be minimized. The difficulties arising from government ownership will be minimal as industrial cooperation will be mostly based at the private sector level. The same is likely to apply to many of the other difficulties once the initiative is left to the private sector and the institutions to be created (see section on modalities of cooperation and implementation). These coupled with the cumulative process of learning-by-doing could show substantial improvement in the planning, promotion, development and performance of multinational industries.

## Resource-Based Import Substitution

Most African countries depend on imports of agricultural inputs. Tools, implements, equipment, machinery, fertilizers, and pesticides are among such inputs. This dependency applies across the board to all factor inputs to other economic sectors as well as to many final consumption goods. Any industry that produces locally, a capital or consumer good, to replace an imported item falls in the import-substitution category.

Based on their raw material inputs, import substitution industries may be classified into (i) imported- input-oriented and (ii) resource-based. The first, which usually involves the final stage of processing or assembly, is characterized by small value-added. It imports bulk products or intermediates requiring minimum processing to final product and packaging; CKD and/or SKD parts and components and sub-assemblies for assembling into final equipment or machinery. Local content in imported input-oriented products is, therefore, negligible in most cases. Such industries, for obvious reasons, have become more liabilities than their resource-based counterparts, as they require yearly foreign exchange in addition to that needed by all industries for spare parts, replacement equipment, and supplies.

Provided certain conditions are fulfilled, imported input-oriented import-substitution industries can be integrated backwards through successive switches to intermediates within a given time period. This would mean importing the intermediate which is the raw material for the intermediate currently in use and repeating the process until use of the basic intermediate is finally attained. In the meantime, projects could be developed for the eventual production of the basic intermediate from basic raw materials. If properly planned and executed, this approach offers good possibilities for substituting an imported input.

Resource-based import-substitution industries offer a rosier picture, as they do not involve the yearly drain of foreign exchange for the import of raw materials. In general, they are larger in size and weather difficult times better. Resource-based industries offer member states better possibilities to significantly increase trade among themselves.

Industrial integration and cooperation can only be achieved if the multinational industries to be developed are competitive. This means locating those industries with a view to optimizing total costs, such as ex-factory price, transport cost and import tariffs *vis-a-vis* imports of the same products. This is particularly significant, as the exchange of intermediates and capital goods will necessarily form the bulk of trade between African countries. Being sensitive to economies of scale, such goods are beyond the reach of most countries and can therefore only be viable if they enjoy access to multinational markets and are competitive.

## Export-Led Industrialization

Export-led industrialization is an alternative to import-substitution industrialization. Comparative advantages derive from relative factor endowments or technology. At the current stage of African development and in the near future, technology is not likely to contribute significantly to comparative advantage. As for factor endowments, if a country is to succeed in the export market it has to have some real comparative advantages in terms of resources that would enable it to compete in the world market. In the past, having raw materials and cheap labor were among such advantages. This may no longer be the case because of the increasing importance of technological know-how, including fast-changing production processes and techniques derived from the application of informatics, new and substitute materials, and biotechnology, including genetic engineering. Technologies that could perform labor-intensive operations, market intelligence, and capacity to adapt to new situations in developed and newly industrializing countries are among developments that do not augur well for Africa's future. Infrastructure, including transport and communications, are among the other determinant factors. The increasingly crucial role of skilled manpower, particularly highly qualified technical and managerial personnel, is apparent under such unfolding circumstances. It is to be noted here that countries such as South Korea owe their miraculous development mainly to human resource development and competence.

From the above, plus the fact that Africa is a late-comer to the industrial products export market, it would appear that the opportunities for export-led industrialization may be limited. This does not, however, mean that countries should give up this route to industrialization. They should explore all avenues to find niches for tradable goods in the world market, including making arrangements with foreign companies engaged in activities related to the apparent comparative advantages the former may have. Canned tropical fruits, chocolate, leather goods, knocked-down furniture, and cotton cloth are examples of products that countries should consider for export development. It should be noted here that comparative advantage is not static. Newly discovered resources, developing skill and labor force, specializing in specific technologies, etc., could bring about new comparative advantages.

Despite the negative picture painted above, there may still be opportunities to exploit natural resource and manpower related advantages. Relatively cheap manpower will continue to exist in Africa. Comparison of extreme situations in term of labor costs in the world in 1990 shows that Tanzanian wage per employee was a mere 0.53 percent and gross output per person engaged was 2.1 percent of that of his German counterpart. Unit cost of production of labor per $100 of output was $6.32 for the former and $24.98 for the latter. In other words, the Tanzanian cost of labor was a quarter of that of the German (UNIDO, *Industry and Development: Global Report 1993/94*).

The price of a product to the consumer is determined by the cost of production, distribution, marketing, and profit margins of those involved in producing and selling the product. In recent years, distribution and marketing costs have become major cost items determining the price of goods. This state of affairs is likely to deter investors in production facilities unless they combine distribution and marketing with production. As regards transnational corporations, they want to and do optimize their activities and profits by integrating globally their sourcing of inputs, production, distribution, marketing, data processing, and R&D facilities.

Each country or group of countries should assess the world market for products that can be made using local resources with apparent comparative advantages. In other words, they should focus on processing minerals and agricultural commodities to higher levels of value-added that the world market can absorb. They should try to penetrate the world market by, among other things, associating with foreign companies engaged in marketing and related activities.

## Establishing and Strengthening Institutions

As national economies do not allow African countries to establish all the institutions they require for development, the only viable and least costly alternative they can resort to is to establish and operate institutions at the multi-country level. It is in recognition of this reality that African countries created a network of institutions at the subregional and regional levels, as shown in Annex 4.9. Most of the planning, training, technological, financial, and natural resources development institutions were designed to serve countries at multi-national, subregional and regional levels. Most of the institutions were initiated by the Economic Commission for Africa (ECA), Africa's regional economic and social think-tank, established as a regional office of the United Nations in 1958 in Addis Ababa, Ethiopia.

The institutions are financed by contributions from member states. Some of them, at one time or another, particularly in their formative years, received assistance from aid donors. In the 1980s, because of the multiple crises that African countries had to face, many member countries failed to meet their obligations. As a result of those defaults which still linger on, the institutions suffered and continue to suffer a lack of resources and consequently they have not been able to render the services to the extent that was expected of them. The African Development Bank (ADB) is an exception. Other institutions that, so far, seem to have fared relatively better include the African Institute for Economic Development and Planning (IDEP in French) and the Regional Institute for Population Studies (RIPS).

From the above, it is apparent that the existing institutions need to be rehabilitated. They should be strengthened by upgrading them and providing them with state-of-the-art technological and other inputs required for their respective operations. It is quite obvious that the number of institutions in Annex 4.6 is far from adequate for a region as vast as Africa. This, coupled with the fact that the region lacks many specialized institutions, means that much more needs to be done in addition to rehabilitating and strengthening existing institutions. These measures, it is hoped, will help African countries to reduce the rate of the widening development gap between them and the rest of the world.

## MODALITIES OF COOPERATION AND IMPLEMENTATION OF MULTINATIONAL PROJECTS

It is apparent from past experience that a piecemeal approach to industrialization cannot optimize the utilization of resources. Many of the industrial establishments were characterized by problems and failures. Industrial projects were conceived and developed in isolation. Their linkages within industry itself and with other sectors were either inadequately covered or not taken into account at all. Many of the projects were not properly evaluated before investment decisions were made.

## National Level

At the national level, industrial projects were conceived, developed, and implemented by the public and private sectors, the last including those with vested interest in the manufacture and sale of machinery and equipment or plant vendors whose objective was merely to sell machinery and equipment. Generally, the former had multiple and sometimes conflicting objectives, including improving income distribution, creating employment, and achieving measures of self-sufficiency. Naturally, the latter had one objective, making a quick profit. Some, if not many of the failed plants were initiated by unscrupulous plant vendors. In the 1960s and possibly 1970s, when most African countries were completely at the mercy of foreign experts, advisors, and consultants, vendors went from country to country offering seemingly viable projects tailor-made (based on models that were worked out using some data pertaining to the country in question) for the countries being visited. Many of them convinced, usually bribed, government officials to accept and implement the projects. Generally, such hoax projects were characterized by inappropriate machinery and equipment, second-hand plant sold as brand new, incomplete configuration of machinery and equipment, and insufficiently tested new processes. Some of them did not even reach the commissioning stage. Small nitrogenous plants that were bought but were never implemented in Kenya and Gabon are examples of vendor-promoted projects. In the 1960s, in one African country, a government official refused the author to have a look at a project submitted by an outsider initiative on the pretext that it was confidential. The plant that was subsequently established turned out to be one of the ailing public enterprises in the country.

As happened in other countries (Japan and the NICs), African countries tried to develop public enterprises for reasons similar to those experienced elsewhere, such as market imperfections, multiple constraints that the private sector could not handle, and projects that the private sector shuns. The main difference was that the African countries had to cope with additional constraints arising from non-indigenous ownership of the means of production and services that were the legacy of colonialism. This obviously compounded the difficulties associated with the process of development in African countries.

The multiplicity of objectives (social, political, and economic) compared to that of profitability for private enterprises is, no wonder, one of the reasons for the poor performance of public enterprises. Others reasons lay in inadequate preparation of projects, politically motivated decisions on projects and their locations, rigid government policies, excessive involvement and interference by public authorities, poor management (government bureaucrats lacking business acumen and loyal to the regime turned managers), inadequate resources at the disposal of management, price controls, overstaffing (management with limited power to hire and fire employees), poor remuneration of management, and corruption.

Public enterprises pass through different stages of decentralization over time. One source gives five stages characterized by increasing management decentralization (Meier 1989). At present, most African public enterprises are at the first stage (infancy) where governments play the ownership, strategic, and operating roles. Enterprises that, in recent years, were given autonomy fall under the second stage (growth). In view of the trend towards improving the performance of public enterprises, many of the enterprises that, for some reasons, would be retained by governments are likely to be accorded managerial autonomy and accountability and will therefore move to the second stage in the not too distant future. This means governments will play the lead strategic role while the reverse will be the case in regard to the operating role.

Following recognition of such shortcomings by some governments themselves and pressure by donors and international financial institutions, particularly the Word Bank and IMF, many African countries are in the process of reforming, restructuring, and rehabilitating their public enterprises. Ghana, Zambia and Ethiopia are among African countries that have taken measures to enable public enterprises to operate relatively independently. As a result, in 1987, 56 percent of 32 manufacturing firms surveyed in Ghana increased production over 1986 with only 15 percent registering lowered production (Meier 1989).

In Ethiopia, industrial establishments that were managed under 10 public corporations under the Ministry of Industry were reorganized into 98 public enterprises, each granted management autonomy accountable to its board of directors (*Negarit Gazeta*, November 10, 1992). Practically all of them were making losses before the change and some were on the verge of closing down. Following the reorganization and changes related to personnel, supply of inputs, foreign exchange availability, marketing, and distribution, all of them, except a few, increased their capacity utilization which had been reported to be about 43 percent (as low as 20 to 30% according to other sources) in 1991/1992 (Ministry of Planning ..., *Survey of Current Economic* ... Volume III, No.1) to 75 to 80 percent in 1994/95 (*The Ethiopian Herald*, May 25, 1995) and made profits following the reorganization and change. Most of them gave 5 to 10 percent rises in salary and bonuses equivalent to one or two months of wages and salaries. These enterprises are now competing with the private sector and some of them are advertising their goods and services, which was never the case before. Many of them (textile mills and a caustic soda plant, for example) were, unfortunately, in 1997, feeling the pinch from globalization.

As for rehabilitation, a review of the industrial subsectors, including their linkages with other industries and sectors (particularly agriculture) relevant to the country should be carried out. The review will serve as a basis for selecting and prioritizing the enterprises to be rehabilitated. This should be followed by diagnostic studies on each plant, covering the technical, managerial, structural, financial, marketing, and human resource aspects and other factors specific to the plant. The physical condition of the production unit, requirements for its rehabilitation/upgrading, the net worth of the enterprise, its continuing viability, and implications of its closure on other production and service units to which it is linked are among the factors that need to be considered in the study. Decisions on divestiture should only be made after thorough evaluation of the study by an independent body. Because of the urgency to resume normal production and avoid exposure of the physical facilities to further deterioration, it would be necessary to implement swiftly the recommendations emanating from the diagnostic exercises.

Final decisions on what to do with the diagnosed plants (rehabilitation and maintaining ownership or privatizing before or after rehabilitation, liquidation, etc.) should be done using criteria that take into account the economic and social conditions prevailing in the country, the insufficient number and capability of nationals to take over the enterprises, as well as the need to transfer such national wealth to as many citizens as possible with a view to effecting fair income redistribution. A number of options for privatization and developing industrial culture in nationals (investing in production activities) can be practiced. These include: management contracts, leases and divestiture. The last comprises different options, including partial government ownership and complete private ownership, with management-employee buyouts as a version of either option.

A number of modalities can be devised in favor of transferring part of the national assets to the local private sector. One is through "mass privatization", as was done relatively successfully in the Czech Republic, by which vouchers or coupons are given free to citizens to be redeemed for shares in any of the privatized enterprises. This approach may be difficult to implement in developing countries and poor governments may not afford it. Another is through public offerings of shares which, under African conditions, require facilitating purchases of shares by citizens. Shareholding, however, presupposes the existence or the establishment of capital markets, especially stock exchanges. Although the establishment of capital markets, which would be the case in most countries where such institutions do not exist, will delay privatization, it would be worth initiating it. This golden opportunity of widening the ownership of the means of production and services—spreading the wealth of a country to its people—should not be missed in view of the fact that most investments in Africa are already in foreign hands. In South Korea, transferring ownership of businesses to foreigners was not allowed until recently. Under the IMF pressure, following the 1997/98 financial crisis, it was reported that the ceiling on foreign ownership was going to rise from 26 percent to 55 percent (*The Wall Street Journal*, April 10, 1998). It would be appropriate to note here that the International Finance Corporation (IFC) was in mid-1990s fostering the development of stock markets in poor countries.

Another is to encourage and organize tradespeople engaged in activities related to the enterprises to be privatized. This could be done by identifying them, holding seminars, and providing them with the guidance and support they need to organize themselves. Still another would be for employees, both government and private, to borrow at attractive low interest rates and invest in their choice of privatized and/or to-be-privatized enterprises. In such a case the employees concerned would agree to the government and the private sector automatically effecting monthly loan repayments through paycheck deductions from the monthly payroll of the employees to the lending financial institutions. Farmers may be involved through their cooperatives. Funds owned by traditional savings and loan associations, cooperatives, insurance companies, and pension funds could be tapped.

In most cases involving transfer to local investors, it would be advisable to divest plants after they have been rehabilitated and are in good working conditions. Obviously, this will require a well-staffed privatization agency capable of doing this with help of consultants of doing this.

As regards foreign investors, it would be mutually beneficial to the investors and the host countries if the former could concentrate, preferably in joint ventures with local entrepreneurs, on the privatization of industries requiring new and improved technology, injection of large amounts of foreign currency, relatively complex management, and expansion and penetration of foreign markets. These requirements are also among the factors foreign investors should look into when contemplating investment in new industries in African countries.

Decision on closure, which, apparently, has been the fate of some public enterprises in some African countries, should be made only after exhausting all alternative solutions. One alternative is to diversify the product mix by making other products that can, with some modifications and additions of equipment, be produced in the facility. Another is to convert the facility to produce entirely different products that can optimally use the existing infrastructure, such as utilities, buildings, and storages, as well as some of the employees of the former enterprise. A good example of this approach is the Addis Metal Pressing Enterprise in Ethiopia, a former ammunition plant that was converted to produce civilian goods. The plant now produces engraving and pressing tools, rollers for textile mills and carbon printing work, spare parts, and electroplated and chrome-coated products, and also reconditions worn out parts.

The modalities of privatization in Ethiopia could serve as illustration of options that are worth considering. The process of privatizing industrial, agricultural, and service enterprises was started in January 1995 by the Ethiopian Privatization Agency following the successful operation of most industrial enterprises. Based on auction notices on privatization issued by the Agency, there are three modalities of privatization. The first is outright sale to investors, involving complete government divestiture (particularly wholesale and retail trade to local investors). This includes management-employee buy-outs of the enterprises. The second is partial divestment, whereby the state retains minority shareholding (25 to 49 percent); the private investors are required to submit project proposals or investment plans for the expansion/improvement of the establishment to be financed by their contributions. The third invites investment partners and international hotel operators to submit proposals for equity participation or management contract or lease agreement. The last two alternatives of the third approach (management contracts and lease agreements) could be considered when attracting private capital becomes difficult within a given time. In this connection, it may be worth considering making provision whereby those who contract or lease would be given the option to buy the enterprise within a given period of time. This is likely to induce some of the investors to eventually take over the enterprises they operate at some later date.

Privatization can and does entail social costs of which the negative impact on employees, is the most serious. In the privatization process in Ethiopia, employees of enterprises to be retrenched were given the following three choices: leave the enterprise for good with compensation; continue to work with the new owner; or opt for a management-employee buy-out of the enterprise taking advantage of a safety net program. The third choice involves taking over assets of public enterprise(s), usually enterprise(s) being privatized in which those who take over have operational knowledge and experience.

The transport sector was the first to implement privatization of part of its assets. Employees opting for the third choice became shareholders by investing their severance payments in three dry cargo transport enterprises in 1995, i.e., the former National Transport Corporation employees and some from the Retail Trade

Corporation own and operate the enterprises. The new enterprises were given access to low interest rate loans (at 5%, repayable in five years) from a revolving fund to buy the assets they acquired. The number was subsequently raised to four with the addition of one engaged in both freight and public transport. It appeared that most of them were not doing well in 1997 by the fact that they have not been able to meet their loan obligations. Apparently, old age of the vehicles and lack of adequate system of operation were among the factors contributing to this state of affairs. More government support during their formative years could have mitigated some of the problems facing the enterprises.

By 1997, 120 retail shops and magazines, 13 hotels and restaurants, and 22 industrial establishments were privatized to nationals. Unlike the transport companies, the majority of these were reported successful. The process of privatization was at different stages for a cigarette/tobaco factory, four tanneries, a textile mill, a package of agro-industries, two gold mines, a tantalum mining project, and a number of state farms. The next group slated for privatization and comprising larger and more diverse firms will be open to foreign participation (*The Ethiopian Privatization Agency Profile*).

There is no reason why the above Ghanaian and Ethiopian (both formerly socialist-oriented economies) and Zimbabwean (sale of a state marketing agency to nationals in 1996) experiences in managing public enterprises cannot be repeated elsewhere, provided dedicated leadership can be had and management is supervised by a board. On behalf of the government, the enterprise board would, in accordance with government policies and guidelines, formulate the overall objectives of the enterprise, appoint and dismiss the enterprise manager and approve annual accounts and dividend payments. The board should comprise the right mix of professions specific to the enterprise concerned and a minimum number of civil servants. Experience in many countries shows that it is very difficult to organize board meetings because government official members just do not have the time. There have been many cases when enterprises suffered because timely decisions could not be taken on urgent matters. Part of the remuneration of the board and the manager of the enterprise could be set as a percentage of the net profit as incentive.

From the constraints related to management dealt with in Chapter 6, it may seem that there had been no well managed and well performing public enterprises in the continent. A number of countries had such enterprises before the crises in the 1980s, while some of them still have them. National or central banks are good examples of well managed enterprises. Algeria, Botswana, Egypt, Ethiopia, and Zimbabwe are among the countries with relatively well-performing public enterprises. Examples of specific enterprises include Office Cherifien des Phosphates (OCP) in Morocco, SONELGAS in Algeria, SIAPE in Tunisia, and Ethiopian Airlines in Ethiopia. The World Bank had this to say in regard to the management of public enterprises: *"Nevertheless some countries, such as Ethiopia, have succeeded in building competent management"* (World Bank, *Sub-Saharan Africa ...*). This is an indication that, given the right conditions, there is no reason why other African managers of public enterprises cannot perform as well, if not better. What is needed is autonomous management operated by competent managers with all the power vested on the management of private companies, including hiring and firing. Enterprise should not be headed by bureaucrats (political appointees) who tend to run businesses as they do with government institutions. If public enterprises can be revitalized and made to operate profitably as autonomous enterprises, there does not appear to be a need to privatize them, at least some of them, especially in view of the fact that privatization has, in many African countries, proved intractably difficult and time consuming. Potential buyers are limited; and those who are interested, particularly foreign companies, want to buy them at giveaway prices as scrap metal and with special concessions that would enable them to recoup their investment in an extremely short period. The lease of a steel mill in Togo is an example of a financial loss that governments can incur in divesting their enterprises. The lease agreement stipulated tax exemption on raw materials and 41 percent protection rate in return for an annual payment of $175,000. The payment covered only a fraction of the interest the government had to continue to pay on the original large investment (Meier 1989). It would appear not advisable for African governments to transfer the meagre public wealth under such conditions. If they have to, they should hand them over to nationals. This could, among other things, contain the additional drain of foreign exchange resulting from the involvement of foreign investors in the operation of the production and service facilities.

For various reasons (strategic importance, production of goods and services that should be provided at minimum price, or industries that do not attract venture capital, or the private sector shies away, etc.) governments may want to retain certain enterprises or establish new ones or participate in equity in private enterprises. Infrastructure (roads, utilities, R&D institutions, etc.), for instance, falls into this category. Others may include enterprises producing essential and basic goods, such as pharmaceuticals and fertilizers, which are too expensive and for which pricing through market forces may be detrimental to the consumers and users. Public pharmaceutical companies could, for instance, make generic drugs from imported bulk drugs available at a relatively low cost in the world market; maximize the use of locally available ingredients; and maintain prices at lower rates of escalation than would be the case if left to the whims of the private sector. In short, bearing in mind the low level or absence of a developed entrepreneurial class and strong private sector as well as scarcity of capital and technical and managerial skills, the complete disengagement of the public sector may not be advisable at present nor in the foreseeable future.

Privatization has been a slow process in most countries, including developed countries. It requires four stages (setting up of a mechanism, selecting targets for privatizing, transferring assets, and monitoring the end results) which are time consuming. In Europe, in the past 15 years to 1995, privatization hovered around $1 billion per year during the first three years. It reached about $22 billion in 1987; peaked at $32.5 billion in 1994; and dropped to $25 billion in 1995. The United Kingdom and France accounted for most of the sales. There still remain salable assets worth about $250 billion in state hands. Loss of jobs, potential strikes, and the difficulty of pricing of firms for sale are among the causes of the slow process of privatization (*The Economist*, November 3, 1996). Despite the above relative success, privatization in Europe has been reported to be unpopular. In the United Kingdom, the conservative government is *"ambivalent about future privatizations ... it is too scared to promise full privatization of the Post Office."* According to polls conducted two years earlier, a fifth of the population wants more privatization, while a third wants more nationalization (*The Economist*, February 22, 1997). The Labor government, in 1998, was reported to be in favor of public-private partnership (*The Economist*, June 13, 1998).

In Africa, privatization has produced mixed results. In Sub-Saharan Africa, it was reported by World Bank researchers that the annual average rate of privatization was about three companies per country. Benin, Ghana, Guinea, Mozambique, Nigeria, Senegal, Tanzania, and Uganda were among the countries reported to have done relatively well. Thirty out of 80 enterprises slated for privatization were divested as of March 1996 in Uganda (ECA, ECA/IHSD/IPPIS/003/96). In Ghana, 63 (40%) public enterprises out of 158 targeted for divestment were divested during 1988-1991. According to another source (ILO, *World Labor Report 1995*) 86 enterprises were privatized or liquidated out of 300 in which government held a financial interest by the end of 1993. In Senegal, 23 percent of the public enterprises were privatized in 1980-1991 and only four enterprises in Cote d'Ivoire by 1991 (Husain 1994). Other relatively successful privatizations include the sale of 300 entities in Tunisia by the end of 1993 and $250 million in proceeds from sales of public enterprises in Morocco in 1993 (UNIDO, *Industrial Development: Global Report 1995*).

In Tanzania, only 15 enterprises out of 425 slated for privatization or liquidation were privatized by August 1993 (ECA, ECA/IHSD/IPPIS/035/93). By the beginning of 1995, thirty enterprises have been sold or leased and 117 were at various stages of preparation for privatization (*Foreign Report*, No. 2339); competition from cheap imports and depreciation of the shilling are reported to have contributed to the slow process of privatization. Attracting investors to purchase the Zambia Consolidated Copper Mines (ZCCM) was to be the main government preoccupation in 1995/96, with ZCCM Chambeshi mine already up for sale (*Africa Business*, March 1995). The process of privatizing ZCCM would have been completed before the end of 1998. In 1995, Nigeria was reported to be considering leasing public enterprises (oil refineries, steel mills, and fertilizer companies) after suspending a privatization program started in 1988. Privatization had been negligible until the early part of the 1990s. Low capacity utilization and deteriorating commercial and financial performance were reported to be among the reasons for that state of affairs.

Up to mid-1996, South Africa had been among the dwindling number of African countries that were not privatizing or not preparing for privatization. After his visit to Germany, President Mandela announced that privatization was the fundamental policy of his party, a complete reversal of the ANC policy which not so long ago was for nationalization (*The Economist*, June 1, 1996). Privatization in South Africa could hasten privatization in other African countries, particularly its neighbors.

The difficulty and complexity of privatization is not peculiar to Africa. Although to a much lesser extent, both the developed and the NIC countries go through a similar experience. For example, in 1993, the South Korean government approved a program to privatize half of 123 public enterprises by 1998. By the third quarter of 1996, only 16 were sold and six partly privatized. The government was reported to have had second thoughts. It was expected to sell small companies, keep the large ones, and retain large shareholdings in many of the partially privatized enterprises. Potential adverse political impact and the unwillingness to pass ownership to the local large dominating firms, the chaebol, were among the reasons for the change of the program (*The Economist*, November 2, 1996).

Public ownership *per se* is not the cause of the malaise besetting public enterprises. The problems that they encounter arise because they are not allowed to operate as commercial entities with managerial autonomy and on strictly commercial principles. Besides, they serve many masters. Public ownership of enterprises may perhaps be relatively high in Africa. According to Meier *"worldwide, public enterprises are responsible for about 10 percent of gross domestic product (GDP) on average in both developed and developing countries."* In regard to restructuring in Africa, he had this to say: *"With the proper mix of macroeconomic policies and internal management arrangements, African public enterprises can produce significant benefits for the country."* In other words, an appropriate mix between market forces and state intervention is what African countries require for some time to come, i.e., until the indigenous people are in a position to compete in local market, at least. Here it may be appropriate to refer to the roles the governments of the relatively material resource-poor small Asian NICs played, as both investors and facilitators, in achieving their economic miracles (see Chapter 7). From the developed world, the economies of the Scandinavian countries could be cited as examples of development, where a market-based economy is characterized by state involvement. Around mid-1970s, based on countries for which information is provided, percentage share in gross fixed capital formation of public enterprises ranged between 14.1 percent in Liberia and 49.7 percent in Zambia in Africa. The corresponding figures were 8.5 in Thailand and 39.6 in Myanmar in Asia, and 4.9 in the USA and 19.2 in Austria among industrialized countries and 13.4 in the world. Overall balances of public enterprises (percentage of GDP at market prices) were virtually negative for each and every country (Chang 1993). In France, Great Britain, and Italy, steamship and air transportation facilities are owned by governments (Microsoft, *Encarta 96 Encyclopedia*).

From the above, from the fact that the indigenous entrepreneurs and people with financial resources do not generally have the capability to run such relatively complex enterprises, and from the fact that capital is scarce, it would appear that governments who could successfully convert their loss-making enterprises into profit making enterprises would do well to retain such enterprises and operate them as autonomous entities until they are eventually taken over by local entrepreneurs. A similar approach was adopted in Tanzania where the government retains a stake in the enterprises which, in due course, will be sold to Tanzanians.

Governments should concentrate their efforts on assisting and encouraging the private sector, both local and foreign, to establish new production and service units where there is so much to be done. There is likely to be an investment gap following the pull-out of public investment. In this connection, it would be worthwhile here to refer to the "one-stop" or "one-window" approach being adopted by a number of African countries. This innovative approach, if efficiently managed, would simplify administrative procedures, thereby enabling investors to obtain in a relatively short time information and assistance and finalize formalities required to start construction activities through one office which coordinates activities related to information, government approval, company registration, land acquisition, industrial incentives, etc. It saves them from incurring unnecessary costs: bribing officials and an escalation in project costs and lost efficiency and competitiveness due to delays. In Ethiopia, investment certificate is given within 30 days after the investor fulfills requirements. African governments which have not adopted this incentive would do well to do so.

## Multinational Level
In view of the difficulties involved in developing industries at the national level, attempts were made by some countries to develop multinational industries. As noted earlier, most of these attempts ended in failure. The difficulties experienced at the country level also affect development at the multinational level. In fact, they are magnified, since national interests at the multinational level are more difficult to accommodate.

### •Modalities of Cooperation
Cooperation at multi-country, subregional, and regional levels offers African countries the possibility of mitigating constraints arising from small and fragmented national markets, economies of scale, and the lack or inadequacy of natural resources. Cooperation is likely to succeed if products made in multinational plants are competitive. The implication here is that multinational projects will have to be established in locations which yield optimum profits. This would, unfortunately, mean that industries will gravitate towards locations and countries with developed infrastructure and advanced industrial development. The result could be a widening gap in industrial development among member states; the exact opposite of what is intended.

An essential precondition to cooperation is the inclusion of multinational projects in national plans. Once a decision is made to locate an industrial establishment in a specific member country, the host country should take the responsibility for facilitating measures, including concessions, and carry out the activities required to implement the project. It should see to it that any unforeseen constraints are immediately removed as soon as they appear.

The polarization of industries mentioned above can be minimized because of comparative advantages arising from variation in relative factor endowments and through disaggregation of production facilities and by taking advantage of the so-called foot lose industries. The viability of basic industries, which would be the real basis for industrial cooperation, is generally strengthened if such industries are located at or near the source of raw materials and energy. Basic industries offer possibilities for downstream processing/manufacturing at locations away from the basic intermediate-making plants. For instance, chemical intermediates, such as ammonia made from natural gas, can be converted into fertilizers while metallurgical products, such as iron and steel made from ores, can be made into parts and components for equipment and machinery in member states that do not or cannot produce basic intermediates. All that is required is proper planning based on standardized equipment, machinery, and products to be made and the commitment of the member states concerned. It should be emphasized here that standardization of products, equipment, and machinery is crucial to industrial cooperation and integration.

If African countries are to develop (and they must as they do not have better options), ways and means must be found to mitigate the above constraints. Four modalities of cooperation are suggested here. The first is joint ownership of industries in which public and private companies and financial institutions in each member country become equity shareholders and therefore share in the benefits and risks of the industry in question. The second is to provide market access to products made in a member country. The third has to do with making available inputs, such as raw materials, intermediates, energy, and expertise, to a plant in another member country. The fourth is a combination of any of the three.

No matter what arrangements are made among member countries, the involvement of foreign collaborators and partners, both at the individual country and group-of-countries level, is something that is unavoidable, at least in the foreseeable future. The forms of involvement include turnkey, licensing, and joint venture arrangements. Given the lack of capabilities for selecting and disaggregating technologies and negotiating with suppliers of technology and plant, the first has been the most popular form of cooperation. For the same reasons, resort to the second has been minimal. In respect of the third, it seems to be the trend nowadays.

Cooperation in industrial development is not and should not be limited to African countries or their private sectors. Participation by foreign partners/investors is needed in practically all aspects of industrial development for a long time to come. In general and in view of the fact that economic activities are dominated by foreigners in most African countries, African governments seem to prefer joint venture arrangements, in which foreign investors combine their investment, technology, and marketing with those of local private and/or public sectors. From a survey of manufacturing executives (*The Economist*, April 11, 1998), it appears that about half of the respondents were pursuing strategies for global expansion in the form of joint venture and alliance in most countries. The joint venture approach as well as local stock ownership in foreign companies in the host country seem to be mutually advantageous to both the local and foreign investors and has the support of President Clinton whose administration *"will do its best to marry off some US corporations with African mates."* It provides the foreign investor with an additional guarantee in terms of investment security. In some African countries, upper limits have been set in regard to foreign investment. This was, for instance, the case with Nigeria, where the upper limit for foreign equity was set at 40 percent. Most foreign ownership limitations have, however, been removed in recent years. In Ethiopia, where foreign investment was completely barred, foreign ownership is now practically unrestricted.

Potential foreign partners should be involved as soon as specific projects are identified by local public and/or private sectors, following general agreement by African member states concerned to go ahead with the integrated development of particular subsectors and branches at multinational or subregional or regional levels. Here lies the end of government involvement and the beginning of the public and private sectors. Government participation in the board for specific establishments or branches would be nominal, for instance, one person representing all member states concerned, mainly to serve as a link with governments and advise the board on matters requiring government actions and interventions.

Potential foreign partners may be identified using different approaches. One is to organize investment promotion forums where investment portfolios/profiles are presented to invited potential investors. Another is to make use of UNIDO's network of investment-promotion services and facilities. Others are investment information services or agencies in developed countries established to encourage and support their enterprises to invest in developing countries (including providing insurance against political and financing risks). The Overseas Private Investment Corporation (OPIC)[3] of USA and Japan International Corporation Agency and Ministry of International Trade and Industry are examples of such agencies. In 1997, the president of OPIC announced that a $150 million (more than $750 million according to a more recent information) equity fund was allocated to Modern Africa Growth and Investment Company Fund to support new private-sector investment in 29 Sub-Saharan African countries beginning 1998. This is in addition to the $500-million fund for infrastructure investment in Sub-Saharan Africa. Most developed countries have investment information services of one kind or another. Examples of national and international institutions performing similar roles include: The Marek Enterprise, Inc., and its Africa Information Service in the United States, the International Financial Corporation (IFC), the Multinational Investment Guarantee Agency (MIGA), the Centre for the Development of Industry (CDI) of the EU, the International Trade Partners (ITP) and the International Trade Centre (ITC). Last but not least, countries can resort to financial institutions, such as the World Bank and the African Development Bank, as their intermediaries.

The involvement of all interested parties from the outset is likely to ensure the mobilization of funds needed to undertake pre-investment studies and activities. In the past, pre-feasibility or feasibility studies financed by governments or donors were presented to potential investors or partners. In those cases in which potential investors showed interest in specific projects they had to carry out their own studies before making decisions to invest. It is apparent that pre-investment studies and activities jointly undertaken by the African group (public and/or private) and potential foreign investors will substantially reduce the extra time and finance normally needed during the pre-investment stage and enhance investment decision making. It is not unusual for investment costs to increase inordinately because of slow progress in carrying out pre-investment activities, mobilizing investment and construction, and commissioning.

Other forms of cooperation that should be maximized include: undertaking joint activities and establishing related institutions, such as training and R&D; adaptation and development of technology; acquisition of technology; adoption of common standards and quality control; exchange of experts, experiences, information, and ideas; consultancy services; contractual and construction activities; mobilization of financial resources; purchase of machinery, equipment, raw and intermediate materials and other inputs; operating common repair and maintenance facilities for complex parts and components; and sales promotion and marketing. The advantages to be reaped from joint activities in these areas are obvious. Many of these areas constitute the major foreign exchange leakages in the continent.

### •Implementation Modalities or mechanisms

Institutional mechanisms will, of course, be needed to implement cooperation at the multinational level. Of all the mechanisms that could be thought of, a holding company appears to be the most practical, taking into account African conditions and needs. Public and private enterprises as well as governments would be share holders. The holding company which will operate on strictly business terms as if it were a transnational corporation will, following general policies and guidelines of its board representing governments and the private sector, operate as any private holding company. It would benefit from economies of scale not only in production but also in lowering the costs of financing, procurement, marketing, and R&D.

One holding company to deal with all kinds of industries at multi-country or subregional levels would be impractical. A number of them will therefore be needed. Holding companies specializing in industrial subsectors may be the answer. Holding companies could be established for each of the following subsectors: agricultural processing, metallurgy, chemical, and engineering. Industries producing products such as building materials are and could be included in one or more of the four holding companies suggested.

An alternative approach to developing the holding companies may be to start on a small scale. One simple and inexpensive way of starting would be to begin with one holding company undertaking activities related to all four subsectors. With the passage of time and increasing workload, each of the subsectors will start to operate independently.

At the subregional level, the holding company should, following the general guidance and priorities set by the member states concerned, operate as an autonomous body. It should have a close working relationship with the bodies set up under the IDDA II recommendations referred to in Chapter 7: industrial promotion coordinating committees and the Conference of African Ministers of Industry. It should conduct consultations with those bodies on a regular basis in addition to participating in their activities.

For each multinational or subregional project to be implemented, the roles of the host country, other member countries, and public and private investors (local and foreign) should be spelled out. These include: sources and arrangements for the supply of raw and intermediate materials and energy; marketing and access to national and export (outside member countries) markets for the products to be made; financing and equity share-holding; subcontracting, if needed; management of the enterprise; and linkages of the enterprise with corresponding national companies or corporations. The last aspect is a very important factor in industrial cooperation and integration. Multinational and subregional projects should be designed with a view to optimizing vertical and horizontal integration so as to distribute downstream production units fairly among the greatest number of countries without jeopardizing the viability of the projects.

## International Level

In this era it would be difficult, if not impossible, for a country, particularly a developing country, to develop by itself in isolation and catch up with the rest of the world. This would be tantamount to starting from scratch or reinventing the wheel.

If African countries are to achieve a measure of sustained and self-reliant industrial development in accordance with the approaches suggested in this book, assistance from the international community is crucial. It is true that the initiative and most of the resources needed will have to come from the African countries themselves. It is, however, obvious that the majority of them will need massive assistance if they are to improve the subsistence and sub-subsistence standards of living that most of their peoples endure. UNIDO plays a central role in providing assistance to and coordinating assistance provided by the United Nations system in the promotion of industrialization in the developing countries. Unlike other United Nations agencies, UNIDO is mandated to work directly with the private sector, including cooperatives. According to Mr. Mauricio de Maria y

Campos, the Director-General of UNIDO, the following will constitute the priority themes (narrower and more focused priority areas than those of the past) and basis for UNIDO work programs:
- Strategies, policies, and institution-building for global economic integration,
- Environment and energy;
- Small and medium enterprises—policies, networking, and basic technical support;
- Innovation, productivity, and quality for international competitiveness;
- Industrial information, investment, and technology promotion;
- Rural industrial development; and
- Africa and the least developed countries—linking agriculture with industry.

The last priority area confirms the need for Africa to industrialize; gives an indication of the strategy to be adopted; and supports the strategy advocated in this book. It is a reaffirmation of the high priority given to the industrialization of Africa (reflected in IDDA I and II, and many OAU, UN and UNIDO resolutions, declarations, and common African positions).

As industry cannot, in the real sense of the word, be developed without the development of other sectors, particularly infrastructure, agriculture, and mining, the concomitant development of these sectors is a necessary condition. In other words, although the focus in this book is on industry as an engine of growth and as a provider of inputs to agriculture and other economic activities, there is an obvious need to do something in regard to infrastructure (roads, railroads, electric power, etc.) which is and may continue to be a bottleneck to industrial development itself.

Assistance is required in all areas of industrialization. Because of the different stages of industrial development, factor endowments, and national priorities in individual African countries, assistance may range from project conception to plant operation and all the activities and inputs related thereto. The Federation of African Consultants (FECA), established with the support of ADB, could facilitate activities related to consultancy.

The role of information in all the above areas and other economic activities is apparent. Thanks to recent advances in information and communication technology, it is now relatively easy to establish information and data bases and gain access to world networks, such as INTERNET, provided resources are available. In an era characterized by exploding information, there is no option to developing Africa's information highway, linking its member countries with worldwide networks. The crucial role that such a regional highway could play in activities leading to the final stage of the African Economic Community cannot be overemphasized. The international community could assist in modernizing communications physical facilities in Africa and arranging working relationships with the major world networks.

Needless to say the above and other assistance would be futile unless it is associated with open markets for African products, particularly manufactured products, in developed countries. The current trend towards economic blocs seems to work against this need.

An attempt has been made in Annex 15.2 to list the types of assistance that may be required, together with the institutions that might provide the assistance. It should be noted that the list of institutions is by no means complete. At this stage, it is meant to give an indication of the types of institutions that would be involved. In due course and at the time of implementation, specific institutions would be selected to suit the requirements of the assistance in question. Examples of institutions that would be relevant include: Arthur D. Little in USA for consulting and R&D, the Intermediate Technology Development Group Ltd. in Great Britain for R&D, the German Appropriate Technology Exchange ( GATE/GTZ) in Germany, the Royal Tropical Institute in the Netherlands, the Groupe de Recherche et d'Echanges Technologiques in France, the Hindustan Machine Tools (International) Limited in India for consulting, and Battel Institute in Germany for consulting.

Theoretically there are thousands of institutions in the industrialized and the newly industrializing countries (NICs) falling in the categories listed in annex 15.2. Assuming that a fraction of these institutions would be willing to assist African countries, arrangements can be worked out through twinning whereby each African institution would be sponsored by/associated with one or more institution(s) in the aid-giving countries. With respect to assistance other than those having to do with institutional capacity strengthening and building, that is, those requiring mostly consulting firm inputs, arrangements would of course, be made on an ad-hoc basis when the need arises.

One source of assistance that African countries have not tapped is their nationals and/or former nationals living abroad. With their knowledge of and vested interest in the development of their mother countries, such experts could contribute immensely. Many of them would be willing and motivated to render services at relatively low cost (limited to covering their travel and hotel accommodation). This form of assistance can be accessed through a United Nations arrangement known as TOKTEN (transfer of knowledge through expatriate nationals).

Discussions between the European Union and the ACP (Lome Convention) countries starting in February 1995 ended in May the same year with an agreement on $17.3 billion funding for the eighth European Development Fund covering the period 1995-1999. With respect to the United States, congressional conservatives have reduced the 1996 development aid to Sub-Saharan Africa comprising 48 countries by 15 percent from $802 million in 1995 (*Africa Policy Information Center*, April 1995). More recent information shows that American aid to the same countries dwindled from its highest level of $840 million in 1992 to $700 million in 1998 and $711 million in 1999. This aid is insignificant compared with the over $3 billion and $2 billion given annually to Israel and Egypt, respectively and the annual French aid to Africa of about $3 billion.

There are voices who think that cutting assistance is against the interest of the United States. The Business Alliance for International Economic Development is one of them. In its White Paper, "Foreign Assistance: What's in it for America?" (SID, *Development Connections*, August-September 1996), it cited that South Korea *"annually consumes US exports worth three times the US assistance provided in the decade after the Korean War ... foreign assistance ... would be foolhardy to ignore."*

Mr. Brian Atwood, the USAID Administrator is another. In 1995, he stated that aid given to Africa is investment, not welfare. He cited Latin America to illustrate his argument. The investment of $30.7 billion made over four decades to 1993 had resulted in growing US exports to Latin America, $78 billion in 1993 (*The Ethiopian Herald*, June 7, 1995). In a paper announcing the forthcoming

(October 1995) Second Annual International Workshop on Trade and Business between Africa and the United States, he was quoted as saying that the African market was significant and has been growing. Based on past growth of seven percent per year imports, he expects imports will increase to $480 billion ($267 billion in today's dollars) in 2025. This would mean hundreds of thousands of jobs for Americans. Besides, the consequences of not acting now would mean bearing the major burden of humanitarian operations (endless famines, internal displaced persons, refugees, etc.), continuing the spread of political disorder, and confronting the environmental damage that will surely deteriorate with worsening living conditions in Africa. Prevention through development now will be much less costly than endless massive aid.

In recent years, there seems to be a change in the attitude of the United States towards assistance for Africa. According to Mr. David Lipton, Assistant Treasury Secretary for International Affairs, the government was reported to be in the process of initiating the mobilization of international efforts to help Africa economically (Stevenson 1997). In addition, the administration's 1998 $19.5-billion budget request for international affairs shows an increase of 7 percent over that of 1997, the increase including provisions for agricultural and food aid for Africa and for the African Development Foundation (SID, *Development Connections*, February- March 1997).

At a special meeting of foreign ministers of the Security Council of the United Nations in September 1997 focusing on Africa and launching a new partnership between the UN and the OAU, the meeting noted the significant progress made in Africa *"towards democratization, economic reform, and respect for and protection of human rights."* US Secretary of State Madeline Albright, noting that 48 Sub-Saharan countries have held democratic elections, expressed America's commitment to support African aspirations.

Ms. Carol Peasely, the Acting USAID Assistant Administrator for Africa, is among those with optimistic views about Africa's future. At the US-Africa Roundtable on Trade and Investment (October, 1997), she was encouraged by recent progress made in Africa, noting that the number of Sub-Saharan African countries registering positive per capita income growth has risen from 13 in 1992 to 28 in 1996. The need to support new leadership in Africa is among several needs identified in the USAID Report to the Senate Appropriations Committee.

## FINANCIAL RESOURCES

African countries are first and foremost responsible for their development and therefore for financing their development. Their capacity to mobilize internal financial resources is, however, limited. As may be appreciated, any additional income is absorbed by personal consumption in countries with low real per capita GDP. Chronic deficits in balances of payments, servicing heavy and growing debts and subsidies given to public enterprises, are other reasons for low domestic savings. This is true for many African countries, as attested by their very low rates of domestic savings and investment. For Africa gross domestic saving to GDP ratio (in %) at a 10-year interval peaked at 21.6 in 1980 and fell to 15.0 in 1991, a level less than the 15.6 in 1970 (UNCTAD, *UNCTAD Statistical Pocket Book*). According to UNIDO, it increased from 15.4 percent in 1993 to 19.1

percent in 1995 (UNIDO, *Industrial Africa*). The ratio in Sub-Saharan Africa fell from 17.8 in 1972 to 15.3 in 1981 and 12.6 in 1987 (World Bank, *Sub-Saharan Africa...* ). Average annual rates of domestic savings and investment in the 1980s, a period characterized by all sorts of crises, fell by 2.6 percent and 3.5 percent, respectively, while GDP grew at 1.8 percent in Sub-Saharan Africa (UNDP/World Bank, *African Development Indicators*). The proportion of investment in GDP in Africa plummeted from a record level of 27 percent in mid-1970s to 15 percent in mid-1990s (UNIDO, *Industrial Africa*).

The cumulative effect of economic reforms, particularly those related to the structural adjustment programs (SAPs) that continue to be adopted and implemented in most countries, is expected to increase domestic savings and therefore investment capacity over time. Government recurrent expenditures relative to revenues are likely to be reduced. Revitalization and privatization of public enterprises mean increased government revenue. Banks could become more development-oriented and play a more active role in mobilizing finance. Tapping the resources of financial instruments and services, such as insurance companies and pension funds as well as traditional savings associations, and developing capital and money markets that are absent in most countries are likely to boost domestic savings. Access to private individual savings could be encouraged, as was done in recent years in Ethiopia, through high interest rates on deposits. Employee share-ownership in business could be another means of increasing savings.

The numbers of operating stockmarkets are limited but increasing. Table 15.1 shows market capitalization and number of companies listed in the countries with stock markets (Versi, *African Business*). Malawi, Seychelles, Tanzania, Uganda, and Zambia were among the countries that were expected to open stock exchanges in 1995.

| TABLE 15.1 CAPITAL AND MONEY MARKETS IN SOME AFRICAN COUNTRIES | | | | | |
|---|---|---|---|---|---|
| Country | Market capitalization ($ b) | Number of listed companies | Country | Market capitalization ($ b) | Number of listed companies |
| Egypt | 7 | 23 | Kenya | 1.9 | 52 |
| Morocco | 5 | 52 | Mauritius | 1.7 | 36 |
| Tunisia | 2.5 | 23 | Namibia | 0.2 | 13 |
| Cote d'Ivoire | 0.5 | 26 | South Africa | 240 | 645 |
| Ghana | 2 | 18 | Swaziland | 0.3 | 4 |
| Nigeria | 1.3 | 180 | Zambia | 0.6 | 7 |
| Botswana | 0.4 | 11 | Zimbabwe | 2 | 65 |
| Source: Compiled from Versi, Anver, 1995., Africa - Jewel in the Investment Crown?, African Business, December 1995. | | | | | |

It is apparent from the table that the stock market in South Africa, with its Johannesburg Stock Exchange as the tenth largest in the world, is the most developed, with those of Egypt and Morocco trailing far behind. The disadvantages arising from many of the markets being small could be minimized by building multinational or subregional markets. The experience to be gained when Cote d'Ivoire converts its bourse to a multinational entity in July 1996 (*The Economist*, March 9, 1996) could give some indications as to the practicality of such an approach. The entity, the West African Regional Stock Exchange (BRVM), was reported operational in 1999 with simultaneous transactions taking place at the national bourses in all its member countries.

In view of the above and other enormous constraints, and despite the increased domestic savings that may accrue, the countries will continue to encounter financial constraints, particularly those related to foreign debt and worsening terms-of-trade. In the meantime, they need massive support, including greater trade concessions, by the international community for some time to come. In this connection, it should be noted that, in April 1997, the United States introduced the Africa Growth and Opportunity Act which stresses trade and growth (Warsh, *The Boston Sunday Globe*, May 4, 1997), i.e., expanding business, trade, and investment.

During his visit to six African countries in 1998 intended to focus on a new partnership between the US and Africa, President Clinton said that he believed in African renaissance and reaffirmed the above initiative by emphasizing trade rather than aid and promoting interest in Africa among American investors. In his own words *"if we face the future together it will be a future that is better for Africa and better for America."* In their joint communiqué in Kampla, Uganda, Mr. Clinton and six African regional heads of state and government, affirmed that *"... greater market access for African goods must be complemented by efforts to increase African capacity to diversify economies and produce exportable goods."*

The above Act which was passed by the House of Representatives in 1998 but has been awaiting Senate approval would be welcomed provided it is not a substitute for aid and could result in increased private investment (both foreign and local), particularly in manufacturing; as well as complete market access for African exports in the United States, including doing away with price and freight escalations based on the degree of processing. Faire and appropriate prices for African commodities (in relation to prices of final products made from them) as well as manufactures could reduce the level of underwriting and eventually getting rid of foreign aid in many African countries.

The Africa: Seeds of Hope Act aimed at rural development and improving agricultural productivity passed by Congress in 1998 would be expected to allay some of the misgivings related to the emphasis on trade. The first US-Africa Ministerial on Partnership for the 21st Century was held in March 1999. In his address to the conference President Clinton declared the tools to be used are "aid, trade and investment." The package of debt relief he announced at the conference, if accepted by the G-7 and implemented, would go a long way to make a difference in facilitation the development of the region.

As for other external financial resources, African countries have been, unfortunately, finding it increasingly difficult to mobilize. During the 1985-1993 period, long-term aggregate net resource flows into the continent increased to $22.9 billion in 1990 and seemed to have stabilized at about 21.0 billion in 1991-1993. Whereas net private loans showed an upward trend up to 1988, it was characterized by negative outflows during 1990-1993, reaching $1.6 billion in 1992. As reported by ADB, Cote d'Ivoire, Morocco, and Nigeria suffered a combined capital flight of about $36 billion during 1975-1991 (ADB, *African Development Report 1994*).

Up to the present, the World Bank and the IMF had strictly ensured that their loans were repaid no matter how desperate the debtors were. It is hoped that the heavily indebted poor countries (HIPCs) debt initiative, a new debt-relief plan (both bilateral and multilateral)—which includes increase in debt forgiveness from 50 percent to 67 percent—worked out by the World Bank and the International Monetary Fund in 1996, will significantly lighten the debt burden of many African countries pursuing sound policies. Because of slow pace in implementation and the dependence of the second stage of the initiative on a track record requirement, however, it appears that only a few of the 33 African countries included in the initiative will fully benefit from the debt relief in time to make a difference in their sustained economic development that is urgently needed. Uganda was to be the first eligible country to benefit from this gesture—a 20 percent debt reduction (Stevenson, *The New York Times*, March 12, 1997). According to subsequent decisions, Uganda would receive a debt-relief of $650 million (Deveney, *The Wall Street Journal*, April 10, 1998) while Mozambique, $2.9 billion. Burkina Faso and Cote d'Ivoire had already qualified; Mali and Guinea Bissau were likely to qualify; and Chad, Ethiopia, Mauritania, and Togo were reported among those being considered. To-date (October 1998) Uganda was the only country in Africa that benefited from the initiative. It is gratifying to note here that Britain's export credits to HIPCs for two years starting in 1998 were planned to focus on productive expenditures only (Brown, *The Economist*, February 21, 1998).

Other debt-relief schemes relevant to Africa include debt rescheduling in the Paris Club, ODA debt cancellation and commercial debt buy-back arrangement.

As for foreign direct investment (FDI), its flow into developing Africa has been erratic. It declined from $2.9 billion in 1985, reached its peak of $4.8 billion in 1989, fell in subsequent years, and rose to $3.5 billion (estimate) in 1994. In terms of net transfer, the annual average FDI transfer improved from an outflow of $1.48 billion in 1981-1985 to an inflow of $664 million in 1986-1990 and $1.06 billion in 1991-1993 (UN, *Foreign Direct Investment in Africa*). Its share (percent) in total world stock increased from 19.8 in 1960-1970 to 21.2 in 1970-1980 and thereafter decreased to 16.0 in 1981-1985, 11.2 in 1986-1990, 11.4 in 1991, and 11.0 in 1992. Its average annual flow (percent) during the same periods and years followed the same trend (13.0, 15.3, 12.0, 7.9, and 5.1) (ILO, *World Employment 1995*). Its share in total flows to all developing countries consistently fell from 12.9 percent in 1981-1985 to 11.4 percent in 1986-1990, 7.0 percent in 1991, and 5.9 percent in 1992 (ECA/UNIDO, CAMI.12/8). It stagnated at around 4.1 percent in 1993 and 1994 (UN, *Foreign Direct Investment in Africa*). The marginalization of Africa on global FDI stocks and flows is, therefore, apparent. What is worse is the minimal flow of FDI toward manufacturing and services in which Africa plays an insignificant role. This is compounded by the fact that most of the FDI went to resource-based activities in a limited number of countries, particularly oil-exporting countries, leaving very little for the LDCs. FDI flows and stocks by groups of countries is presented in Table 15.2.

| TABLE 15.2 FDI STOCKS AND INFLOWS TO AFRICA BY GROUPS OF COUNTRIES ($ m) | | | | | | | | | | | | | |
|---|---|---|---|---|---|---|---|---|---|---|---|---|---|
| | Flows | | | | | | Stocks | | | | | | |
| | 1980-1984 | | 1985-1990 | | 1991-1995 | | 1980 | | 1985 | | 1990 | | 1995 | |
| | V | S | V | S | V | S | V | S | V | S | V | S | V | S |
| North Africa a | 415 | 30.1 | 1278 | 46.4 | 1584 | 41.7 | 4429 | 11.9 | 8988 | 23.7 | 16109 | 30.7 | 20557 | 30.3 |
| Southern Africa b | 255 | 18.5 | 5 | ... | 71 | 1.9 | 23831 | 63.8 | 16423 | 43.4 | 16367 | 31.2 | 16524 | 24.4 |
| Rest of Africa | 711 | 51.4 | 1485 | 53.6 | 2138 | 56.4 | 9074 | 24.3 | 12481 | 32.9 | 20029 | 38.1 | 30714 | 45.3 |
| Total Africa | 1381 | 100 | 2768 | 100 | 3793 | 100 | 37334 | 100 | 37892 | 100 | 52505 | 100 | 67795 | 100 |

Source: UN, 1996, World Investment Report 1996 (UNCTAD estimates based on UNCTAD-DTCI, 1996a).

a Algeria, Egypt, Libya, Morocco, and Tunisia.      V= Value   S=Share (%)
b Botswana, Lesotho, Mozambique, Namibia, South Africa, and Zimbabwe.

The picture with regard to portfolio equity flows was worse. There were no flows to Sub-Saharan Africa during the 1989-1991 period. The flow in subsequent years rose to $860 million in 1994, accounting for 2.5 percent of the flow to all developing countries (World Bank, *Debt Tables*, 1995).

Infrastructural financing by the IFC was practically insignificant in so far as Africa was concerned. Africa's share (excluding North Africa) in IFC worldwide approval worked out to 3.38 percent of the number of projects, 0.61 percent of project size, 1.81 percent of loan, and 0.37 percent of equity. The corresponding figures for commitment were: 4.95, 0.94, 2.75, and 0.56 (IFC, *Financing Private Infrastructure*).

It is likely that Africa's dwindling share in FDI will be reversed with time as incentives being introduced in many African countries are put into practice and as the process of economic cooperation and integration takes hold. A statement made by Mr. Harald Muller, Deputy Director of the Federation of German Industries, may be cited in support of the latter. Referring to the SADC area, at the annual conference of Zimbabwe business chiefs in July 1995, he said: *"German industry has clearly stated their interest in the region as a bloc ... German firms don't look at small economies any more but economic regions."* This is an indication that foreign investment would be forthcoming provided national markets are pooled into multi-country and subregional markets, which constitutes the major objective of the African Economic Community (AEC). This optimism is supported by Mr. John Legat, Fund Manager, while launching GT Management's New Africa Fund (Versi, *African Business*, December 1995). In his words, *"We believe that Africa is on the threshold of a new era and will provide excellent investment opportunities for professional and institutional investors."* GT believes that Africa is in a position to emulate the Asians and Latin Americans in development and growth.

There is already concrete evidence in support of the above conclusion on the future likely increase of FDI. The UK-based Africa Business and Investment encourages foreign investment in Africa. The US-based include the African Investment Fund and the Emerging Markets Manangement. Both were oversubscribed, the former from $60 million to $300 million and the second from $30 million to about $60 million (Annibale, *Selamta*). Such oversubscriptions may be taken as an indication of renewed interest in investing in Africa. At individual country level, Mozambique, where GDP was expected to grow by 7 to 8 percent annually during 1997-1998, is a good example of what could be expected as regards FDI. Projects on mining, energy, manufacturing, transport, farming, and tourism worth about $6 billions were reportedly under consideration by foreign investors in 1997 (*The Economist, Mozambique* ... , March 15, 1997). Egypt is another example. Its FDI flow was forecast to reach $2.1 billion in 1997 (*The Economist*, Egypt's ... , March 15, 1997).

Hitherto, FDI was associated with industrialized countries. Some of the NICs in Asia and Latin America have either shifted or are in the process of shifting part of their labor-intensive manufacturing to relatively lower-labor-cost countries in Asia and Latin America. The recent investments in South Africa made by Malaysian, Singaporean, and South Korean companies could be a harbinger of new sources of investment. African countries should explore and tap investment opportunities from NICs while continuing to attract FDI from the developed countries. Skilled manpower being the major factor in such shifting, they should focus on skilled manpower development. Crash training programs should be organized. If such measures are not taken, the history of "missing the boat" will repeat itself and African countries will once again forgo the opportunity to attract labor-intensive industries.

Criteria for financial assistance by donors have changed following the end of the Cold War and the accompanying decline of geopolitical interest in Africa. Respect for human rights, democratic system of governance, liberalized market system, and environmental concerns are among the factors that seem to determine access to financial assistance for development purposes. Measures taken in these areas (political stability, democratization process, structuring the economy, revitalizing industry) by the government of Ethiopia seem to have contributed to the relatively large assistance provided by donors to that country.[4]

In view of the above, there seems to be no alternative to increased financial assistance from the international community, both bilateral and multilateral. As suggested in Chapter 7 of this book, some kind of Marshall Plan or Colombo Plan is needed if Africa is to attain a threshold of sustained development. According to ECA (E/ECA/CM.21/5), 10 to 25 percent of gross domestic investment for capacity-building activities, including technology transfer, will have to be mobilized from external sources. Thanks to the end of the Cold War, it should be possible for developed countries to increase their financial assistance substantially, using a fraction of their savings in military spending, although this has not been the case so far. On their part, African countries should minimize their defense budgets. The international colloquium that was held in Addis Ababa in May 1998 which discussed the restructuring of the military to play a role in socio-economic development seems to augur well. In this connection, it would be opportune to refer to the recommendations made by the Secretary General of the United Nations, Mr. Kofi Annan, in his report on Africa to the Security Council in 1998. Those endorsed by the Council as well as by the African countries the Secretary General visited during the first half of 1998 include limiting arms purchases to less than 1.5 percent of GDP and zero-growth of defense budget of African countries.

Part of the financing could be available if donors could meet the United Nations global target of 0.7 percent of their respective GDPs. The Nordic countries and the Netherlands are the only countries that not only met but also exceeded the target in 1995. According to *The Economist* (June 29, 1996), the OECD contribution averaged only 0.3 percent. The United States' appropriation for international affairs at current prices dwindled from $21.2 billion in 1993 to $20.1 billion in 1995 and $19.2 billion (0.25% of GDP) proposed for 1997 (United States Government, *Budget Supplement*). These figures represent only 1 percent, and not 15 percent, of the budget that many Americans, apparently, think goes to foreign affairs (*The Boston Globe Magazine*, June 1, 1997). The share of international development and humanitarian assistance which worked out to about 42 percent of the 1 percent in both years, fell to 38.9 percent in the 1997 proposed appropriation.

In addition to mobilizing aid from the traditional donors, Africa should solicit assistance from institutions in both developed and developing countries that have hardly been tapped hitherto (universities, schools of technology, R&D institutions, consulting firms, etc., with whom twinning arrangements can be made). It is hoped that this approach will substantially increase the aid provided, in addition to ensuring successful implementation of projects and programs to be assisted.

Financial assistance from the international community through the United Nations has, in recent years, been dwindling because of the funding crisis arising from the non-payment of contributions by certain member states. In view of this, there are proposals for introducing a global tax system. Taxes on international air tickets and industrial products that pollute the environment and levies on all international currency transactions are among the sources of income that were considered at one time or another. In the meantime, it is hoped that the United Nations System-Wide Initiative on Africa to raise $25 billion for Africa will become a reality.

The World Bank in its *Sub-Saharan Africa: From Crisis to Sustainable Growth* gives quantitative indications of the financial resources needed to reorient investment in that area. The projections in Table 15.3 illustrating levels of projected sectoral investment were based on an annual rate of investment of 25 percent of GDP in order to achieve a 5 percent GDP growth rate per year. It should be noted here that the former is twice the gross domestic saving in 1987.

TABLE 15.3
PROJECTED SECTORAL INVESTMENT IN SUB-SAHARAN AFRICA

| Sector | Investment (% of GDP) | Annual growth rate (%) |
|---|---|---|
| Agriculture (including rural infrastructure) | 4 | 4 |
| Manufacturing | 3 | 5 |
| Mining and energy | 2.5 | 5 |
| Infrastructure (excluding rural) | 5.5 | |
| Human resource development | 3 | |
| Other sectors | 7 | |

Source: World Bank, 1989, *Sub-Saharan Africa: From Crisis to Sustainable Growth, a Long-term Perspective Study*, Washington, D.C.

All African countries have financial institutions of one sort or another. Their form and objectives may vary from country to country. In addition to commercial banks, most of them have development-oriented financial institutions. These include agricultural and industrial development banks. At the subregional and regional levels, the African Development Bank (ADB) is at the forefront. Others are shown in Annex 15.3. ADB itself has been instrumental in creating regional and subregional institutions. These include Africa-Re, Association of African Development Finance Institutions (AADFI), SIFIDA, and African Export-Import Bank. The last was reported to be at the stage of promotion toward the end of the 1980s.

In addition to domestic banks, African countries have access to foreign financial institutions. Annex 15.3 gives an indication of the financial institutions that African countries can access both in the form of outright grants and loans. The African Project Development Facility (APDF) is one of the institutions that perform an investment-facilitating function, including the preparation of feasibility studies for private sector projects whose investment is within the $0.5 to $5.0 million range. It is sponsored by the United Nations Development Program, the International Finance Corporation, and the African Development Bank, and its offices are located in Abidjan and Nairobi.

ADB and the World Bank and their respective groups provide similar services. ADB and the World Bank provide long-term development loans at relatively high interest rates. The terms and conditions for ADF and IDA loans are 3/4 of 1% service charge, a 10-year grace period, and a 30-year repayment period. About 50% of the IDA replenishment of $20.5 billion for the period July 1999-June 2002 has been reserved for Africa for investing in people, promoting good governance, promoting broad-based growth, and protecting the environment. Commitment to poverty reduction, economic reform, and sustainable, broad-based growth are the conditions that African countries must meet to benefit from the replenishment.

Although IFC is mostly concerned with equity participation, it does provide long-term loans. In respect of other sources of assistance and finance, it is possible to have some idea as to the type of services they render from their names and/or headings under which they are given in Annex 15.3. Those categorized under grants and technical assistance provide funds and expertise to carry out advisory services, train personnel, conduct pre-investment studies and activities, establish and operate institutions, and finance capital goods. The last is, generally, limited to institutions such as the European Development Fund (EDF) and the United Nations Capital Development Fund (UNCDF). Some of the bilateral and multilateral loans are tied to the procurement of goods and services from the countries providing the loans.

With a substantial amount of liquid funds reportedly available, South Africa should be a source of funds for African development. FDI from South Africa has already started to flow to some African countries. Examples include: breweries in most Southern African countries, gold mining in Ghana, hotels in Botswana and Malawi, and joint ventures with Air Tanzania and Uganda Airlines. In addition to investing its own resources, South Africa is likely to serve as a springboard into African countries by investors from developed countries.

Compared to other regions, the role of foreign private investment in Africa has not been significant, averaging only about 1 percent of the $200 billion invested in developing countries. As noted elsewhere, foreign investment has increasingly become scarce in Africa. Since the end of the Cold War it has been and continues to be diverted to Eastern Europe and the newly industrialized countries (NICs). African countries are making efforts to attract foreign investment as indicated in Chapter 6. It would indeed be tragic if the fledgling democracies, many of which came into existence through pressures by donor countries and institutions, are denied the investment that they so badly need. Several attempts have been made to attract investors by organizing investment forums, mostly by UNIDO. ECA in cooperation with other institutions was preparing to organize an international conference on private investment in Africa in November 1995 in Accra, Ghana (see Chapter 6).

American interest and investment in Africa has been limited to a few large businesses, especially mining concerns. In view of this, it was comforting to learn that the United States is committed to Africa. The late Commerce Secretary Ron Brown, at the Third African-African American "Roots" Summit in May 1995, in Dakar, Senegal, organized by the Reverend Sullevan, told the Summit that *"the United States no longer concedes Africa's markets to European suppliers."* He added that undertaking steps to reform economies will qualify a country for receiving assistance from the United States of America. More recently, the National Summit on Africa started, at the end of 1997, the process of sensitizing the American public to the changing perception of Africa. This is expected to eventually lead to formulation of a plan of action for public and private sector policy interests. The choice of the Reverend Jesse Jackson, in 1997, as President Clinton's special envoy for promoting democracy in Africa, augurs well in improved American policy towards and commitment to Africa.

In the past, many industrial establishments have been burdened by overinvestment which included investment in infrastructural support services, thereby making such establishments unviable. It is not unlikely that many projects were rejected for inadequate returns arising from investments that should not normally figure in an industrial project. Investments in transport and communication links, utilities, and social amenities may, in some cases, account for more than investment in the industrial establishment proper. Countries hosting multinational as well as national industries, particularly those to be located in green sites, would be advised to take measures to minimize the adverse impact of infrastructural investments.

## BIBLIOGRAPHY

ADB, 1994, *African Development Report 1994,* Abidjan.

Africa Business, 1995, "Limits to Patience," No. 197, March 1995.

Africa Policy Information Center, 1995, *Africa: Dispelling the Myths,* Background Paper 002, April 11, 1995, Washington, D.C.

Annibale, Robert A., 1994, *The Scramble for Africa's Equities* in Selamta, July-September 1994, Camerapix Magazines Ltd., Nairobi.

Brown, Gordon, 1998, "Debt and Development: Time to Act again," The *Economist,* February 21, 1998.

Chang, Ha-Joon and Ajit Singh, 1993, "Public Enterprises in Developing Countries and Economic Efficiency," *UNCTAD Review*, No. 4, Geneva.

Deveney, Paul J., 1998, "Uganda Awarded Debt-Relief Deal of $650 Million," The *Wall Street Journal,* April 10, 1998.

ECA, 1993, *Focus on African Industry*, Volume VI, No. 1., Addis Ababa.

ECA, 1993, *Study on the Identification of Industrial Priorities and Sub-regional Cooperation in the Context of the Second IDDA (the case of the Eastern and Southern Africa Subregion)* (ECA/IHSD/IPPIS/035/93), Addis Ababa.

ECA, 1995, *Progress Report on a Framework Agenda for Building and Utilizing Critical Capacities in Africa* (E/ECA/CM.21/5), Addis Ababa.

ECA, 1996, *Measures to Consolidate Privatization in the African Industrial Sector with Special Emphasis on the Programme of the Second Industrial Development Decade for Africa* (ECA/IHSD/IPPIS/003/96), Addis Ababa.

ECA/UNIDO, 1995, *Mobilization of Financial Resources for the Implementation of the Programme for the Second IDDA* (CAMI.12/8), Addis Ababa (obtained from UNCTAD and World Investment Report 1994).

Foreign Report, 1995, No. 2339.

Husain Ishrat and Rashid Faruque, eds, 1994, *Adjustment in Africa, Lessons from Country Case Studies*, Regional and Sectoral Studies, Washington, D.C.

IFC, 1996, *Financing Private Infrastructure,* Washington, D.C.

ILO, 1995, *World Employment 1995,* Geneva.

ILO, 1995, *World Labour Report 1995,* Geneva..

Meier, Gerald M. and William F. Steel, eds., 1989, *Industrial Adjustment in Sub-Saharan Africa,* EDI Series in Economic Development, Published for the World Bank, Oxford University Press, New York.

Microsoft, 1996, *Encarta 96 Encyclopedia*, Redmond.

Ministry of Planning and Economic Development, 1995, *Survey of Current Economic Conditions in Ethiopia*, Volume III, No. 1, June 1995, Addis Ababa,

Negarit Gazeta, 1992, "Industrial Public Enterprises Establishment : Council of Ministers Regulations," No. 9, November 10, 1992, Addis Ababa.

Panafrican News Agency, 1998, "West Africa Gas Pipeline Project Begins 1999," October 1, 1998.

SID, 1996, "White Paper Cites Foreign Assistance Benefits for US Business," *Development Connections,* August-September 1996.

SID, 1997, "Administration's Budget Calls for Increase in Foreign Affairs," *Development Connections,* February- March 1997, Washington D.C.

Stevenson, Richard W., 1997, "Global Banks, Offer a First: Forgiveness on Some Debt," *The New York Times,* March 12, 1997.

The Boston Globe Magazine, 1997, "The New Diplomacy," June 1, 1997.

The Economist, 1996, "A Case of the DT's and Survey: Business in Europe," November 3, 1996.

The Economist, 1996, "Africa's Stockmarkets: Sleepy," March 9, 1996.

The Economist, 1996, "Emerging - Market Indicators," June 29, 1996.

The Economist, 1996," South Africa: Which Road for the Economy?," June 1, 1996.

The Economist, 1996, "South Korean Industry: Opening up the State Coffers," November 2, 1996.

The Economist, 1997, "Egypt's Economy: Sinkhole no More," March 15, 1997.

The Economist, 1997, June 21, 1997.

The Economist, 1997, "Mozambique: Benefits of Peace," March 15, 1997.

The Economist, 1997, "Privatization: Badly Sold," February 22, 1997.

The Economist, 1998, "Emerging Market Indicators," April 11, 1998.

The Economist, 1998, "The End of Privatization?," June 13, 1998.

The Ethiopian Herald, 1995, "Whither Africa," June 7, 1995, Addis Ababa.

The Ethiopian Herald, *1995,* "Workshop Discusses Programme Implementation," May 25, 1995, Addis Ababa.

The Ethiopian Privatization Agency, undated, *Profile,* Addis Ababa.

The Wall Street Journal, 1998, *"IMF's Moves Are Expected to Force Open Markets for Products, Investors,"* April 10, 1998.

UN, 1995, *Foreign Direct Investment in Africa,* New York.

UNCTAD, 1994, *UNCTAD Statistical Pocket Book,* 1994, Geneva.

UNDP/World Bank, 1992, *African Development Indicators.*

UNIDO, 1991, *Industry and Development: Global Report 1991/92,* Vienna.

UNIDO, 1993, *Industry and Development: Global Report 1993/94,* Vienna.

UNIDO, 1993, *Implementation of the Subregional Programme for the Second IDDA for Eastern and Southern Africa* (PPD.259 [SPEC]), Vienna.

UNIDO, 1995, *Industrial Development: Global Report 1995,* Oxford University Press, Oxford.

UNIDO, 1997, "Africa Moves Up Front," *Industrial Africa,* December 1997, Vienna.

United States Government, 1997, *Budget Supplement, Budget of the United States Government, Fiscal Year 1997,* Washington, D.C.

Versi, Anver, 1995, "Africa-Jewel in the Investment Crown?," *African Business,* December 1995.

Warsh, David, 1997, "A New Recipe for Africa: Trade, not Aid," *The Boston Sunday Globe,* May 4, 1997.

World Bank, 1989, *Sub-Saharan Africa: From Crisis to Sustainable Growth, a Long-term Perspective Study,* Washington, D.C.

World Bank, 1995, *Debt Tables,* Washington, D.C.

## NOTES

1. The G-15 of developing nations, whose eighth summit took place in Cairo in 1998, should play a more vigorous role in promoting trade among developing countries.
2. After a sojourn of over a year abroad, the author returned to Ethiopia. On presenting documents of his previous motor vehicle insurance to his insurance company (a public enterprise) and evidence that he was insured and has had no accident during his absence abroad, he was told to submit an application. He got his insurance from a private company in no time.
3. In 1997, the Senate of the US Congress voted mandating OPIC to continue operation for two years. The House of Representatives' vote was being awaited.
4. In four years following the demise of the communist regime in 1991, the Transitional Government of Ethiopia obtained financial assistance from bilateral and multilateral donors of the order of Birr 14 billion (over $2.2 billion), of which Birr 8.6 billion was in the form of grants and the balance of Birr 5.4 in soft

## CHAPTER 16

# CONCLUSIONS AND RECOMMENDATIONS

In Chapter 6, many of the factors constraining African industrial development were identified and ways and means of minimizing their impact were suggested. Considering the multiple and series of difficulties African countries had to contend with, commendable progress has been made in these past three decades. Many of the constraints that were critical following independence are no longer so. Even so, much more remains to be done.

This chapter summarizes the conclusions and recommendations on crucial constraints that do not appear to have received adequate attention on the part of individual African governments, their intergovernmental organizations, and their development partners. Unless African countries, individually and in groups, take immediate measures to implement recommendations similar or related to those below, it is likely that most of them will find themselves in an even worse state of affairs, with the development gap between them and the rest of the developing world forever widening.

The recommendations are addressed to both the African countries and the world community. Because of the overwhelming difficulties and exigencies, the efforts to be made by the African countries will have to be supplemented by outside assistance if the region is to achieve some progress towards a self-sustainable development from which Africa in particular and the world in general would benefit not only economically but also ecologically, politically, and socially — hence, a better world to live in.

| Conclusions | Recommendations |
|---|---|
| **African Countries** | |
| 1. Use of goods based on different types of standards works against the development of intra-African trade and industrial cooperation. | 1. Products and services should be standardized at the regional level as soon as possible. |
| 2. Small and fragmented national markets do not permit the development of industries sensitive to economies of scale.<br><br>Duplication of manufacturing facilities for certain products sensitive to economies of scale result in capacity underutilization. | 2. African countries should pool their markets with a view to providing large enough outlets to justify the establishment of appropriately sized units.<br><br>African countries should jointly plan and implement industries that take account of comparative advantages and specialization as well as fair distribution of production units.<br><br>Whenever possible, multi-purpose/multi-product manufacturing systems should be used.<br><br>Projects should be designed to take account of the optimal usage of backward and forward linkages, including the use and conversion of waste and by-products into useful products. |
| 3. African industries suffer from the high cost of imported inputs, partly because of small bulk purchases from abroad. | 3. Central purchasing of imported inputs should be instituted. |
| 4. In many cases, technologies designed for developed countries are not suited to African countries. | 4. Technologies to be used should be carefully selected and adapted to local conditions. |
| 5. Investors seem to have been shying away from Africa in recent years. | 5. African countries should continue to improve the enabling environment (political stability, governance, investment codes, etc.) |
| **The World Community** | |
| 1. Africa continues to suffer from a widening balance-of-trade deficit as a result of falling export prices and spiraling import prices. | 1. Developed countries should increase and expand coverage of their compensation to African countries for losses sustained from fluctuating and falling exports prices and/or pay fair prices to African exports. |
| 2. Availability of foreign exchange for purchasing imported industrial inputs continues to dwindle. | 2. Donors could ease the burden on borrowers by writing off the latters' debts. |
| 3. Import tariffs in developed countries and freight rates that escalate with the degree of processing of African raw materials impede African industrial development. | 3. Developed countries could abandon protection and abolish import tariffs and freight rates that escalate with the deg ree of processing and encourage manufactured imports from Africa. |
| 4. In recent years, the net flow of investment funds has been dwindling followed by net capital flight, thereby exacerbating the paucity of financial resources. | 4. Developed countries could encourage, and provide incentives, to their investors to invest in Africa. |
| 5. Many of the technologies acquired by African countries are inappropriate to their conditions and needs. | 5. Developed countries could reorient and redeploy some of their technological development activities and facilities to African countries. |
| 6. Provision of industrial pollution abatement measures significantly raises the cost of investment and production. | 6 Developed countries could provide African countries with pollution control technologies and hardware at significantly lower prices. |

# ANNEXES

**CHAPTER 5**

**ANNEX 2.1**

ECONOMIC AND SOCIAL INDICATORS BEFORE AND AFTER THE FALL OF
THE COMMUNIST REGIME IN ETHIOPIA

The reader will notice that many references have been made to Ethiopia in this
book whenever desirable development examples and trends in the continent could
be illustrated by happenings in the country. The main reasons for this are that
Ethiopia (i) was among the most recent African countries to achieve a measure of
fast economic recovery in the first half of the 1990s[1]; (ii) offers relative accessibility (to the author) of up-to-date information in some areas; and (iii) pursuing a
rural- and peasantry-centered 1995/1996-1999/2000 program for peace, economic
development and democracy based on 7-10 percent GDP growth and an agricultural led industrialization strategy. The program which rightly focuses on the
rural sector seems implementable given the enabling environment created and
continues to be created, measures and preparatory activities undertaken during
the transitional period, and barring adverse weather and other unforseen conditions. According to the Resident World Bank Representative in Ethiopia the country
*"has, over the last two years enjoyed food self-sufficiency at the national level,
and is exporting food grains this year [early 1997]."* Such a success story was,
unfortunately, followed by drought and untimely rains and floods (attributed to El
Nino) in many areas in the country later in 1997. According to FAO estimates,
production of cereals during the main crop season in 1997/98 decreased by 26
percent over that of the previous year.

As the world knows, Ethiopia is one of the African countries that have gone
through the devastation of war, drought, famine, human-right abuses and highly
centralized command planning which stifled private entrepreneurial initiative
and encouraged rent-seeking. It is the country where the longest war was fought
during the second half of this century in Africa and which was probably the
hardest hit. Having emerged from such a situation, the country has, from the very
outset, shown exemplary trend towards democratic governance. The democratically elected government inaugurated on 22 August 1995 is based on a federal
government system with nine federal states (excluding Addis Ababa, the capital),
mainly ethnically based, led by a prime minister, with independent judiciary and
legislative bodies (Council of Peoples' Representatives and Council of Federation). The federal system is an experiment in unity in diversity which, if successful, could be emulated by other African countries. The process of coalescing of
smaller clan- or ethnic-based parties in four states that continues to take place is
among the indications that the system is working and consolidating.

The following figures from the table below illustrate the commendable recovery from a near collapsing economy in 1991/92 to 1992/93-1996/97 (average)
achieved thanks to the implementation of the New Economic Reform Policy during the four years of the transition period and subsequent years:

- GDP annual change: -3.7% to 7.2%;
- Agriculture annual change: -3.3% to 4.8%,
- Industry annual change: nil to 14.4%;
- Manufacturing annual change: -20.7% to 16.96%;
- Consumer price index (1963=100) annual change: 21.0% to 3.8% .

| SOME ECONOMIC AND SOCIAL INDICATORS BEFORE AND AFTER THE FALL OF THE COMMUNIST REGIME IN ETHIOPIA | | | | | | | | |
|---|---|---|---|---|---|---|---|---|
| | Communist administration | | Democratic administration | | | | | |
| | 1989/90 | 1990/91 | 1991/92 | 1992/93 | 1993/94 | 1994/95 | 1995/96 | 1996/97 [a] |
| GDP, growth rate at constant factor cost, % | 3.6 | -4.4 | -3.7 | 12.4 | 1.7 | 5.4 | 10.6 | 5.7 |
| - Agriculture | 5.5 | 5.2 | -3.3 | 6.1 | -3.6 | 3.3 | 14.6 | 3.4 |
| - Industry | 0 | -23.1 | 0 | 28.4 | 7 | 8.1 | 5.6 | 7.9 |
| - Manufacturing | -8.3 | -32.1 | -20.7 | 49 | 12.7 | 9.4 | 7.7 | 5.6 |
| - Distribution | 6.3 | -23.5 | 0 | 22.2 | 6.2 | 6.4 | 8.9 | 9.3 |
| - Other services | 4 | -3.8 | -4 | 14.8 | 9.2 | 7.6 | 5.8 | 6.9 |
| Gross domestic saving as % of GDP, at current market prices | ... | ... | ... | 5.6 | 5 | 6.7 | 6.6 | 8.3 |
| Gross domestic capital formation as % of GDP, at current market prices | ... | ... | ... | 14.2 | 15.2 | 16.4 | 19.1 | 19.1 |
| Government revenue, % of GDP at current market prices | 17.3 | 3.6 | 10.8 | 12 | 13.7 | 17 | 17.8 | 18.2 |
| Expenditure on education [b] | ... | ... | ... | 17.6 | 16.8 | 16.7 | 18.2 | 19.1 |
| Expenditure on health [b] | ... | ... | ... | 5.5 | 6.4 | 6.1 | 6.4 | 6.4 |
| Expenditure on defense, public order and security [b] | ... | ... | ... | 24.1 | 19.9 | 19 | 20 | 18.3 |
| Trade deficit, rate of increase (%) | -10.5 | 45.9 | -4.2 | 137.4 | 3.6 | 3.7 | 66.9 | -15.6 |
| Budget deficit, including grants [c] | 5.5 | 18.4 | -13.6 | 7.4 | 38.7 | -34.4 | 39.3 | -68.4 |
| Budget deficit, excluding grants | -12.2 | 14 | -7 | 1.5 | 55.5 | -22 | 21.6 | -29.8 |
| Foreign exchange reserve, in weeks | 1.3 | 4.5 | 10 | 14.7 | 28.3 | 41.7 | 33.1 | 22.6 |
| Exchange rate, Birr/USD | ... | ... | ... | 4.27 | 5.78 | 6.25 | 6.34 | 6.51 |
| Consumer price index, 1963=100 (Addis Ababa) | 5.2 | 20.9 | 21 | 10 | 1.2 | 13.4 | 0.9 | -6.4 |

Source: Compiled from Survey of Current Economic Conditions in Ethiopia, Volume III, No.1, Ministry of Planning and Economic Development, June 1995, Addis Ababa, and updated with the help of the staff of the Ministry.
    a  Estimate    b  Percent of total recurrent expenditure rate of increase (%)

Foreign exchange rate had, by 1998, practically closed the margin between the bank and the parallel rates and was hovering around Birr 7.2 for US$ 1.00 (Birr 2.07 before devaluation in 1992) following the introduction of foreign exchange auction in 1995. Foreign exchange reserves in 1994/95 was equivalent to 41.7 weeks of imports compared with 1.3 weeks in 1989/90. According to the World Bank, Ethiopia has, on the basis of most indicators, begun to make progress during the transition period. It made substantial progress in the government's reform program, including public expenditure, a significant start toward liberalizing the economy, and a significant progress in improving its external debt situation. The economic, social and other indicators supporting the Bank's conclusions include:

- Transferring significant autonomy and responsibility to regional administrations;
- Visible beneficial impact on the living conditions of the ordinary people;
- Increasing number of people moving above the poverty line;
- Improvement in investment in human resource development;
- Avoidance of widespread famine in 1994 through timely government action;
- Real GDP rise from 1.2 percent during pre-reform period to 6.6 percent in 1993-1996;
- Increase of investment to GDP ratio from 11 percent prior to reform to more than 19 per ent in 1996;
- Rise of the share of private investment in total investment from 17 percent prior to reform to 60 percent;

- Establishment of private domestic banks and insurance companies;
- Introduction of one-step investment offices;
- Change of real interest rates from negative to positive;
- Devaluation of the Birr (Birr 2.07 to the dollar in 1992) to 6.3 in 1996;
- Reduction of average annual inflation from more than 20 percent in 1990-1992 to 6.5 percent in 1993-1996;
- Decontrolling of prices, except petroleum, fertilizers and pharmaceuticals;
- Elimination of export taxes, except for coffee;
- Reduction of fiscal deficit after grants from an average of 9.6 percent of GDP in 1990-1992 to 5.5 percent in 1993-1996;
- Reduction of defense expenditure from 31 percent of the budget prior to reform to 7 percent in 1995, the latter representing about 2 percent of GDP compared with an average of 4.5 percent for Sub-Sharan Africa;
- Higher expenditure on basic social services, up from 16 percent of the budget prior to reform to 23 percent in 1995; and
- Reduction of debt service ratio from 82 percent in 1992 to 30 percent in 1995.

(World Bank, 1996, *Trends in Developing Economies*, Washington, D.C.).

By 1993, the country had already moved to 168th from 174th in 1992 in the United Nations human development index ranking for 174 developing countries.

In regard to industry, UNIDO Country Industrial Statistics show that significant structural changes have taken place during the period 1990-1995. This is manifested by the following industrial branch shares (%) in total MVA: paper and paper products (0.5-1.4), other chemicals (2.2-3.6), other non-metallic mineral products (2.7-6.4), iron and steel (1.1-4.1) and non-electrical machinery (0.0-0.1).

# NOTES

1. Many organizations and individuals have attested the success story of Ethiopia in recent years. According to a UNIDO/ECA document "Agro-related Industrial Development in Africa," Uganda and Ethiopia were in 1997 *"in their strong recovery phase."* Another UNIDO document (*Report of the Mid-term Evaluation*, IDDA II) asserted that *"Ethiopia has registered some successes in its rehabilitation efforts and consequently raised capacity utilization to an average level of 75% to 80%."* The Reverend H. Sullivan, Chairman and convener of the African-African American Summit, stated that *"Ethiopia has demonstrated one of the most successful program implementation in the world and I'm proud of this"* (*The Ethiopian Herald*, October 1, 1997). During his state visit to Ethiopia in 1997 the President of Italy was impressed by Ethiopia's *"difficult but rewarding path of building democratic institutions based upon the recognition and positive appreciation of differences."* At the end of their visit to Ethiopia in 1997, US. Congressmen Tom Campbell and Donald Paine said that *"the governance in Ethiopia is exemplary for the African continent"* (*The Ethiopian Herald*, December 1997). Another mission led by Congressman Charles B. Rangel said *"the on-going reform in Ethiopia could be exemplary to other African countries"* (*The Ethiopian Herald*, December 9, 1997). On completion of her visit to Ethiopia the US. Secretary of State Madeleine K. Albright stated that *"Today Ethiopia is again earning the world's admiration ... for reforming, rebuilding, and reuniting ... writing a new chapter in African history"* (*The Ethiopian Herald*, December 11, 1997).

## ANNEX 2.2
### POPULATION OF THE CONTINENT BY SUBREGION AND REGION AT FIVE YEARS INTERVAL.

| Year | Actual | | | | | | | | | Projection (medium variant) | | | | | |
|---|---|---|---|---|---|---|---|---|---|---|---|---|---|---|---|
| | 1950 | 1955 | 1960 | 1965 | 1970 | 1975 | 1980 | 1985 | 1990 | 1995 | 2000 | 2005 | 2010 | 2015 | 2020 |
| **Total Population (m)** [a] | | | | | | | | | | | | | | | |
| Africa, total | 224 | 250.4 | 281.4 | 320.5 | 364.2 | 414 | 475.7 | 548.8 | 632.7 | 728.1 | 831.6 | 945 | 1069 | 1204 | 1348 |
| Central Africa | 30.9 | 33.9 | 37.5 | 42 | 47.3 | 53.4 | 61.5 | 71.4 | 93 | 96.7 | 112 | 129 | 148.2 | 169.8 | 193.7 |
| Eastern and Southern Africa | 76.6 | 86 | 97.4 | 111.4 | 127.8 | 145.1 | 169.2 | 195.2 | 225.5 | 260.2 | 298.9 | 339.7 | 386.1 | 437.3 | 518.5 |
| North Africa | 53.3 | 59.7 | 67 | 75.5 | 85.4 | 96.4 | 110.1 | 126.1 | 143 | 160.6 | 178.4 | 196.8 | 215 | 234.5 | 250.5 |
| West Africa | 63.2 | 70.8 | 80.2 | 91.6 | 103.7 | 118.1 | 134.8 | 156.1 | 181.1 | 210.7 | 243.3 | 279.5 | 319.9 | 364.3 | 411.8 |
| Africa, urban (m) | 32.5 | 40.8 | 51.5 | 66 | 83.4 | 103.5 | 129.9 | 162.4 | 202.5 | 252.7 | 312.7 | 385.6 | 472.5 | 573.1 | 686.1 |
| **Urban Population (% of total population)** [b] | | | | | | | | | | | | | | | |
| Africa, total | 14.5 | 16.3 | 18.3 | 20.6 | 22.9 | 25 | 27.3 | 29.6 | 32 | 34.7 | 37.6 | 40.8 | 44.2 | 47.6 | 50.9 |
| Central Africa | 12.4 | 13.8 | 15.5 | 18.2 | 21.5 | 23.1 | 24.5 | 26.1 | 27.9 | 30.1 | 32.7 | 39.2 | 34.6 | 427 | 46.5 |
| Eastern and Southern Africa | 12.2 | 13.4 | 14.7 | 15.6 | 17.4 | 19.1 | 21.1 | 23 | 25.1 | 27.5 | 30.3 | 33.3 | 36.4 | 39.8 | 43 |
| North Africa | 24.5 | 27.1 | 30 | 33.6 | 36.2 | 38.4 | 40.2 | 42.1 | 43.8 | 45.9 | 48.4 | 51.3 | 54.4 | 57.6 | 60.7 |
| West Africa | 10.2 | 12.2 | 14.4 | 16.9 | 19.7 | 22.7 | 26 | 29.5 | 33.2 | 37 | 40.8 | 44.7 | 48.6 | 52.3 | 55.9 |
| **African Average Annual Rates of Change of Urban Population and Urbanization** [b] | | | | | | | | | | | | | | | |
| **Average annual rate of change (%)** | | | | | | | | | | | | | | | |
| - Total population | | 2.22 | 2.39 | 2.55 | 2.65 | 2.66 | 2.88 | 2.91 | 2.95 | 2.93 | 2.81 | 2.7 | 2.61 | 2.5 | 2.33 |
| - Rural population | | 1.8 | 1.91 | 1.98 | 2.07 | 2.09 | 2.27 | 2.26 | 2.26 | 2.13 | 1.88 | 1.65 | 1.44 | 1.25 | 1.02 |
| - Urban population | | 4.55 | 4.69 | 4.92 | 4.75 | 4.46 | 4.59 | 4.54 | 4.51 | 4.53 | 4.46 | 4.33 | 4.19 | 3.97 | 3.68 |
| **Average annual rate of change of percentage:** | | | | | | | | | | | | | | | |
| - Urbanization | | 2.32 | 2.3 | 2.37 | 2.1 | 1.8 | 1.71 | 1.63 | 1.56 | 1.6 | 1.65 | 1.63 | 1.58 | 1.48 | 1.35 |
| - Ruralization | | -0.42 | -0.48 | -0.57 | -0.58 | -0.57 | -0.61 | -0.65 | -0.69 | -0.8 | -0.93 | -1.05 | -1.17 | -1.25 | -1.31 |

Source: - [a] United Nations, 1994, World Population: The 1994 Revision ( Annex tables), New York.
- [b] United Nations, 1993, World Urbanization Prospects, New York.
Note: - Subregional total population and percentage of urban population for Central and Eastern and Southern Africa have been adjusted to conform with ECA subregional membership.
- The total population figures from which the percent of the urban population was derived (second source) were marginally different from the total population figures given in the first source.
- The figures in the third part of this annex are for quinquennial periods ending in the year under which the figures are shown.

## ANNEX 2.3
### INDICATORS OF THE STATE OF EDUCATION IN AFRICA

| | 1960 | 1965 | 1970 | 1975 | 1980 | 1985 | 1990 | 1991 | 1992 |
|---|---|---|---|---|---|---|---|---|---|
| **Estimated gross enrollment ratio by level of education (%)** | | | | | | | | | |
| First level | 43.5 | 51.6 | 56 | 64.6 | 79.2 | 75.8 | 72.9 | 74.4 | 74.3 |
| Second level | 5.2 | 8 | 11.2 | 14.6 | 21.8 | 27 | 27.8 | 29.3 | 29.8 |
| Third level | 0.7 | 1.1 | 1.5 | 2.5 | 3.5 | 4.3 | 4.7 | 5.1 | 5.3 |
| All levels | 20.2 | 24.9 | 28.3 | 33.1 | 42 | 42.9 | 41.9 | 43.1 | 43.2 |
| All levels (1000) | | | | | 2260 | 2778 | 3498 | 3704 | 3885 |
| Teaching staff (1000) | | | | | 72 | 95 | 128 | 132 | 138 |
| **Scientific and technical manpower estimates** | | | | | | | | | |
| Number (1000) | | | | 18.6 | 1052 | 1623 | | | |
| Number per million population | | | | 52 | 2593 | 3451 | | | |
| **R&D** | | | | | | | | | |
| Scientists and engineers per million population | | | | | 111 | 106 | 117 | | |
| Expenditure as % of GNP | | | | | 0.28 | 0.25 | 0.25 | | |
| **Other indicators** | | | | | | | | | |
| Number of book titles published per million inhabitants | | | | 22 | | 25 | | 20 | 20 |
| Number of radio receivers and receivers per 1000 inhabitants | | | | 51 | 69 | 103 | 152 | | 170 |
| Number of TV receivers and receivers per 1000 inhabitants | | | | 4.5 | 6.6 | 17 | 26 | | 38 |

Sources: UNESCO , 1985, 1993, 1994, Statistical Yearbook 1985, 1993 and 1994, Maxe'ville, France.

| ANNEX 2.4 | | |
|---|---|---|
| **BALANCE SHEET OF HUMAN DEVELOPMENT IN SUB-SAHARAN AFRICA** | | |
| Progress | | Deprivation |

### Health

| Progress | Deprivation |
|---|---|
| - Between 1960 and 1993 life expectancy at birth increased from 40 to 51 years.<br>- In the past decade the proportion of the population with access to safe water nearly doubled from 25% to 43%. | - There is only one doctor for every 18,000 people, compared with 6,000 in the developing world as a whole and 390 in the industrialized countries.<br>- More than 10 million people are infected with HIV, two-thirds of all those infected in the world. |

### Education

| Progress | Deprivation |
|---|---|
| - During the past two decades adult literacy more than doubled from 27% to 55%.<br>- Between 1960 and 1991 the net enrollment ratio at the primary level increased from 25% to 50%, and at the secondary level from 13% to 38%. | - Only about half of the entrants to grade 1 finish grade 5.<br>- At the primary and secondary levels more than 80 million boys and girls are still out of school. |

### Income and poverty

| Progress | Deprivation |
|---|---|
| - Over the period 1980-92 five countries — Botswana, Cape Verde, Lesotho, Mauritius and Swaziland — had an annual GDP growth rate of more than 5%. | - About 170 million people (nearly a third of the region's population) do not get enough to eat.<br>- During the past three decades the ratio of military to social spending increased from 29% in 1960 to 43% in 1991. |

### Women

| Progress | Deprivation |
|---|---|
| - Between 1960 and 1991 the female enrollment ratio at the secondary level quadrupled from 8% to 32%.<br>- Women hold 8% of parliamentary seats, nearly double their 5% share in South Asia. | - The region has the world's highest maternal mortality rate — 929 per 100,000 live births (compared with 33 in the OECD countries).<br>- There are six HIV-infected women for every four infected men. |

### Children

| Progress | Deprivation |
|---|---|
| - Over the past six decades the infant mortality rate dropped from 167 per thousand live births to 97. | - About 23 million children in the region are malnourished, and 16% of babies are underweight. |

### Environment

| Progress | Deprivation |
|---|---|
| At less than 1,000 hectares a year, combined logging in primary and secondary forests is the lowest in the developing world, far lower than the 2,500 hectares a year in Asia and Latin America. | - During the past 50 years desertification has claimed an average 1.3 million hectares of productive land a year. |

### Politics and conflicts

| Progress | Deprivation |
|---|---|
| - Since 1990, 27 multiparty presidential elections have been held in 21 cases for the first time.<br>- Since 1980 opposition parties have been legalized in 31 countries. | - In 1994 there were still 16 governments representing a single-party system or a military regime.<br>- At the end of 1994 nearly six million people — 1% of the population — were refugees. |

Source: UNDP, 1996, *Human Development Report 1966*, Oxford University Press, New York.

| ANNEX 3.1 POPULATION, GDP, AREA AND LAND USE BY COUNTRY, SUBREGION AND REGION IN AFRICA | | | | | | | | | |
|---|---|---|---|---|---|---|---|---|---|
| Region/ subregion/ country | Population (1992) [a] | | | 1992 GDP at 1990 prices ($) [b] | | Total area and land use [a] | | | |
| | Total (m) | Agri-cultural (m) | Econo-mica-lly active populat-ion in agricul-ture (%) | Total (m) | Per capita | Total area (1000 km $^2$) [c] | Arable and perma-nent crops (m ha) | Forest and woodland (m ha) | Irriga tion (1000 ha) |
| **Africa, excluding South Africa** | 640.4 | 397.4 | 62.6 [d] | 355401 | 555 | 28150 | 169.4 | 651.9 | 10132 |
| **Africa, including South Africa** | 680.2 | 403.2 | 61.9 | ... | ... | 29371 | 182.6 | 656.4 | 11272 |
| **Central Africa** | 78.5 | 53.6 | | 33763 | 430 | 5295 | 23.7 | 265.8 | 145 |
| Burundi | 5.8 | 5.3 | 90.9 | 1320 | 227 | 26 | 1.4 | 0.1 | 75 |
| Cameroon | 12.2 | 7.2 | 59.3 | 11089 | 900 | 465 | 7 | 8.3 | 35 |
| Central African Republic | 3.2 | 1.9 | 60.5 | 1254 | 396 | 623 | 2 | 35.8 | ... |
| Chad | 5.8 | 4.2 | 72.5 | 1437 | 245 | 1259 | 3.3 | - | 14 |
| Congo | 2.4 | 1.4 | 59 | 2934 | 1241 | 342 | 0.2 | 21.1 | 5 |
| Equatorial Guinea | 0.4 | 0.2 | 53.4 | 167 | 451 | 28 | 0.2 | 1.3 | ... |
| Gabon | 1.2 | 0.8 | 65.9 | 5770 | 4668 | 258 | 0.5 | 19.9 | ... |
| Rwanda | 7.5 | 6.8 | 90.9 | 2596 | 346 | 25 | 1.2 | 5.5 | 4 |
| Sao-Tome and Principe | 0.1 | ... | ... | 54 | 425 | 1 | - | - | ... |
| Congo K | 39.9 | 25.8 | 64.7 | 7142 | 179 | 2268 | 7.9 | 173.8 | 12 |
| **Eastern and Southern Africa** | 248 | 159.6 | | 59975 | 288 | 8685 | 63.1 | 252.5 | 3070 |
| Angola | 9.2 | 6.4 | 69.8 | 10956 | 1108 | 1247 | 3.5 | 51.9 | ... |
| Botswana | 1.3 | 0.8 | 61.5 | 3786 | 2888 | 567 | 1.2 | 10.9 | 2 |
| Comoros | 0.6 | 0.5 | 78.1 | 267 | 457 | 2 | 0.1 | - | ... |
| Djibouti | 0.5 | ... | ... | 477 | 1021 | 23 | - | - | ... |
| Eritrea [f] | | | | | | | | | |
| Ethiopia | 53 | 38.9 | 73.4 | 5366 | 101 | 1101 | 13.9 | 26.9 | 165 |
| Kenya | 25.2 | 19.2 | 76.1 | 8887 | 353 | 570 | 2.5 | 2.3 | 52 |
| Lesotho | 1.8 | 1.4 | 78 | 606 | 327 | 30 | 0.3 | 2 | ... |

| Madagascar | 12.8 | 9.7 | 75.6 | 2963 | 231 | 582 | 3.1 | 15.5 | 940 |
|---|---|---|---|---|---|---|---|---|---|
| Malawi | 10.4 | 7.6 | 73.3 | 1775 | 174 | 94 | 1.7 | 3.4 | 22 |
| Mauritius | 1.1 | 0.2 | 21.8 | 2818 | 2569 | 2 | 0.1 | 0.1 | 17 |
| Mozambique | 14.9 | 12 | 81 | 1277 | 85 | 784 | 3.2 | 14 | 120 |
| Namibia | 1.5 | 0.5 | 33.5 | 2308 | 1505 | 823 | 0.7 | 18 | 4 |
| Seychelles | 0.1 | ... | ... | 373 | 5041 | 0 | ... | ... | ... |
| Somalia | 9.2 | 6.4 | 69 | 539 | 58 | 627 | 1 | 9 | 120 |
| South Africa | 39.8 | 5.8 | 12.8 | 103863 | 2547 ᵉ | 1221 | 13.2 | 4.5 | 1140 |
| Swaziland | 0.8 | 0.5 | 64.6 | 881 | 1096 | 17 | 0.2 | 0.1 | 64 |
| Tanzania | 27.8 | 21.8 | 79.8 | 2631 | 95 | 886 | 3.5 | 40.7 | 155 |
| Uganda | 18.8 | 14.9 | 79.7 | 3939 | 211 | 200 | 6.8 | 5.5 | 9 |
| Zambia | 8.6 | 5.9 | 68 | 3609 | 419 | 743 | 5.3 | 28.7 | 35 |
| Zimbabwe | 10.6 | 7.1 | 67.2 | 6517 | 618 | 387 | 2.8 | 19 | 225 |
| **North Africa** | 147.4 | 54.7 | | 183721 | 1248 | 8114 | 40.4 | 57.4 | 6533.3 |
| Algeria | 26.3 | 6 | 23.3 | 55678 | 2115 | 2382 | 7.9 | 4 | 206.3 |
| Egypt | 54.8 | 21.7 | 39.5 | 48953 | 894 | 995 | 2.6 | ... | 2645 |
| Libya | 4.9 | 0.6 | 13.2 | 29354 | 6032 | 1760 | 2.2 | 0.7 | 250 |
| Morocco | 26.3 | 9.1 | 34.8 | 25577 | 973 | 446 | 9.8 | 7.9 | 1280 |
| Sudan | 26.7 | 15.4 | 57.8 | 10311 | 387 | 2376 | 13 | 44.2 | 1920 |
| Tunisia | 8.4 | 1.9 | 22.4 | 13848 | 1650 | 155 | 4.9 | 0.6 | 232 |
| **West Africa** | 206.3 | 135.3 | | 77942 | 378 | 6058 | 55.4 | 80.7 | 1524 |
| Benin | 4.9 | 2.9 | 59.5 | 2005 | 408 | 111 | 1.9 | 3.4 | 7 |
| Burkina Faso | 9.5 | 8 | 83.9 | 2868 | 302 | 274 | 3.6 | 6.5 | 25 |
| Cape Verde | 0.4 | 0.2 | 41.7 | 399 | 1039 | 4 | ... | ... | 2 |
| Cote d'Ivoire | 12.9 | 6.9 | 53.7 | 9784 | 757 | 318 | 3.7 | 7.1 | 68 |
| Gambia | 0.9 | 0.7 | 80.3 | 328 | 362 | 10 | 0.2 | 0.1 | 15 |
| Ghana | 16 | 7.8 | 48.7 | 6782 | 425 | 228 | 2.7 | 7.9 | 8 |
| Guinea | 6.1 | 4.4 | 72.6 | 2971 | 486 | 246 | 0.7 | 14.5 | 26 |
| Guinea-Bissau | 1 | 0.8 | 77.8 | 272 | 270 | 28 | 0.3 | 1.1 | ... |
| Liberia | 2.8 | 1.9 | 68.9 | 1800 | 655 | 97 | 0.4 | 1.7 | 2 |
| Mali | 9.8 | 7.8 | 79.8 | 2951 | 264 | 1220 | 2.2 | 6.9 | 210 |
| Mauritania | 2.1 | 1.4 | 63.6 | 967 | 452 | 1025 | 0.2 | 4.4 | 15 |
| Niger | 8.3 | 7.1 | 86.4 | 2721 | 330 | 1267 | 3.6 | 1.9 | 45 |
| Nigeria | 115.7 | 74.1 | 64.1 | 36288 | 314 | 911 | 32.4 | 11.3 | 880 |
| Senegal | 7.7 | 6 | 77.9 | 5919 | 766 | 193 | 2.3 | 10.5 | 180 |
| Sierra Leone | 4.4 | 2.7 | 60.8 | 816 | 187 | 72 | 0.5 | 2 | 34 |
| Togo | 3.8 | 2.6 | 68.9 | 1431 | 381 | 54 | 0.7 | 1.4 | 7 |

Source: - a  FAO, 1993, *FAO Production Yearbook*, Rome
- b  ECA, 1994, *Economic Report on Africa 1994*, E/ECA/CM.20/2, Addis Ababa.
- c  World Bank, 1995, *African Development Indicators 1994-95*, Washington, DC.
- d  Calculated    e  Excluding South Africa  f  Figures included in Ethiopia.    g   1993

409

ANNEX 3. 2
SELECTED ECONOMIC AND SOCIAL INDICATORS IN THE CONTINENT

| | Continent | | | | | | | | | | | Sub-Saharan Africa (excluding South Africa) | | | | | | | | | | |
|---|---|---|---|---|---|---|---|---|---|---|---|---|---|---|---|---|---|---|---|---|---|---|
| | 1980 | 1984 | 1985 | 1986 | 1987 | 1988 | 1989 | 1990 | 1991 | 1992 | 1993 | 1980 | 1984 | 1985 | 1986 | 1987 | 1988 | 1989 | 1990 | 1991 | 1992 | 1993 |
| Population (m) | 468.4 | 526.2 | 541.7 | 557.7 | 574.1 | 590.9 | 608.1 | 625.8 | 643.7 | 661.9 | 680.2 | 350.6 | 394.7 | 406.6 | 418.9 | 431.7 | 444.9 | 458.6 | 472.7 | 487 | 501.7 | 616.6 |
| Urban population (% of total population) | 27.4 | | | 30.1 | | | | 33 | | | | 21.3 | | | 24.4 | | | | | | 27.8 | |
| Percentage of population of all ages in the labor force | 42.3 | | 41.2 | | | | | 40 | | | | 43.6 | | 42.3 | | | | | 41 | | | |
| GDP (b $ at constant 1987 prices) | 348.4 | 367 | 375.7 | 380.2 | 384.2 | 395.9 | 409.1 | 413.7 | 419.2 | 420.4 | 421.8 | 137.3 | 139.4 | 144.5 | 149.6 | 151.8 | 157.5 | 163.3 | 166.2 | 168.8 | 170.2 | 171.6 |
| Sectoral value added (% of GDP at constant 1987 prices) [a] | | | | | | | | | | | | | | | | | | | | | | |
| Agriculture | 18.77 | 17.38 | 18.07 | 18.99 | 19.05 | 18.94 | 19.38 | 19.12 | 19.8 | 19.08 | ... | 31.25 | 30.06 | 29.76 | 30.68 | 30.5 | 30.29 | 30.37 | 30.26 | 30.27 | 29.96 | ... |
| Industry | 3137 | 31.91 | 31.81 | 31.61 | 31.1 | 30.99 | 30.58 | 30.48 | 3008 | 30.14 | 30.13 | 26.44 | 25.54 | 25.54 | 24.93 | 24.77 | 24.89 | 25.05 | 25.15 | 25.36 | 25.26 | ... |
| Services | 35.85 | 40.38 | 41.02 | 41.32 | 41.91 | 42.23 | 42.14 | 42.23 | 41.98 | 42.72 | 42.67 | 36.64 | 39.67 | 40.07 | 39.77 | 39.99 | 39.94 | 39.62 | 39.83 | 40.17 | 40.36 | ... |
| Gross domestic savings (% of GDP) | 27.6 | 19.6 | 20.2 | 19.5 | 20.2 | 19.2 | 19.2 | 19.6 | 18.2 | 16.3 | 16.2 | 22.3 | 12.9 | 13.8 | 13.5 | 14.7 | 13.4 | 14.3 | 16.4 | 13.7 | 12.1 | ... |
| Gross domestic investment (% of GDP) | 25 | 20.7 | 19.7 | 21.7 | 20.8 | 21 | 21 | 20.5 | 19.2 | 18.6 | 18.7 | 21.2 | 13 | 13.3 | 17.1 | 18 | 17.4 | 16.6 | 17 | 17.1 | 16.9 | ... |
| GDP growth (%) | 3.8 | 2.1 | 2.4 | 1.2 | 1 | 3 | 3.3 | 1.1 | 1.3 | 0.3 | 0.3 | 2.4 | -0.4 | 3.6 | 3.5 | 1.5 | 3.8 | 3.7 | 1.8 | 1.6 | 0.9 | 0.8 |
| GNP per capita ($, Atlas method) [a] | 860 | 715 | 673 | 628 | 638 | 632 | 622 | 664 | 629 | 632 | 615 | 584 | 461 | 437 | 365 | 332 | 344 | 338 | 353 | 341 | 321 | 306 |
| Consumer price index (1987=100) | 45.4 | 78.5 | 82.8 | 92.5 | 100 | 109.4 | 120.9 | 135 | 150.5 | 174.9 | 204 | 45.4 | 78.8 | 82.8 | 92.7 | 100 | 109.6 | 120.9 | 135.1 | 150,1 | 168.4 | 199.9 |
| Net foreign direct investment (m $, at current prices) | -666 | 1420 | 991 | 629 | 1425 | 1471 | 3082 | 1340 | 2456 | 2698 | 1979 | 55 | 895 | 1037 | 717 | 1504 | 1056 | 2616 | 920 | 1919 | 1543 | 752 |
| Net ODA per capita from all donors ($ at current prices) | 23 | 20 | 24 | 25 | 27 | 29 | 30 | 42 | 40 | 38 | ... | 21 | 19 | 23 | 25 | 28 | 31 | 32 | 36 | 35 | 36 | ... |
| Total imports ($ b), of which (%) [b]: | ... | 61.79 | 53.07 | 61.12 | 56.53 | 59.7 | 61.75 | | 68 | | | | | | | | | | | | | |
| - Food | ... | 10.35 | 8.74 | 9.76 | 8.65 | 9.42 | 9.72 | | 10.78 | | | | | | | | | | | | | |
| - Fuels | ... | 9.34 | 10.01 | 9.02 | 8.33 | 7.72 | 8.24 | | 8.63 | | | | | | | | | | | | | |
| - Manufactured goods | ... | 65.9 | 64.91 | 66.77 | 65.93 | 68.39 | 66.82 | | 67.46 | | | | | | | | | | | | | |
| Total exports ($ b), of which (%) [b]: | ... | 63.44 | 63.4 | 51.77 | 54.51 | 51.77 | 59 | | 66.2 | | | | | | | | | | | | | |
| - Food, beverages, tobacco | ... | 12.52 | 12 | 16.3 | 16.57 | 16.81 | 15.83 | | 14.86 | | | | | | | | | | | | | |
| - Raw materials (excl. fuels) | ... | 8.1 | 7.16 | 10.3 | 9.01 | 9.77 | 9.85 | | 9.61 | | | | | | | | | | | | | |
| - Fuels | ... | 67.04 | 66.58 | 63.84 | 53.37 | 49.74 | 51.32 | | 51.51 | | | | | | | | | | | | | |
| - Manufactured goods | ... | 9.6 | 8.86 | 8.69 | 18.47 | 21.54 | 21.75 | | 23.94 | | | | | | | | | | | | | |
| External debt outstanding, disbursed ($ b) | ... | 125.3 | 182.9 | ... | 23.68 | 212.8 | 295.5 | 271.5 | 281.6 | 278.8 | | | | | | | | | | | | |
| Debt service (% of exports, incl. non factor services) | .. | 25.48 | 26.8 | ... | 27.4 | ... | 33.08 | 27.71 | | | | | | | | | | | | | | |
| Labor force (%) in: | | | | | | | | | | | | | | | | | | 44 | | | | |
| - Agriculture | | | | | | | | | 63 | | | | | | | | | 66 | | | | |
| - Industry | 11 | | 12 | | | | 14 | 14 | 15 | | | | | | | | | 9 | | | | |
| - Services | | | | | | | | | 22 | | | | | | | | | 25 | | | | |
| Life expectancy at birth (years) | 49 | | 51 | | 53 | | | 53 | 54 | 54 | 54 | | | | | 50 | | | | | 51 | 51 |
| - Male | 48 | | 50 | | | | 52 | 52 | 52 | 52 | 53 | | | | | | | | | | | |
| - Female | 50 | | 52 | | | | 55 | 55 | 55 | 55 | 56 | | | | | | | | | | | |
| Infant mortality (per 1000) | 127 | | 114 | | | | 102 | 94 | 93 | 91 | 89 | | | | | 107 | | | | | 100 | 97 |
| Average daily kilocalorie intake per capita | 2308 | | 2280 | | | | 2308 | 2315 | 2320 | 2327 | 2337 | | | | | 2136 | | | | | 2062 | 2096 |
| Literacy rate (%) | ... | 45 | 47 | 50 | 52 | | | 52 | | | | | | | | | | 50 | | | 56 |
| Primary school gross enrollment ratio (%) | 78 | | | | 72 | | | 72 | | | | 77 | | | 66 | | | | 66 | | | 66 |
| Pupil/teacher ratio | 42 | | | | 39 | | | | 36 | | | 45 | | | 42 | | | | 40 | | | |
| Secondary school gross enrollment ratio (%) | 20 | | | | 27 | | | | 28 | | | 15 | | | 17 | | | | 18 | | | |
| Road density (km/km 2) ? | .. | 0.05 | 0.05 | 0.05 | 0.52 | 0.53 | 0.5 | | 0.54 | | | | | | | | | | | | | |
| Number of telephones per 100 inhabitants | .. | 0.8 | 0.71 | ... | 0.82 | 0.8 | 0.89 | | 1.19 | | | | | | | | | | | | 1 | |
| Private motor vehicles per 1000 inhabitants | .. | 8.78 | 8.81 | ... | 8.57 | 8.36 | 8.68 | | 14.1 | | | | | | | | | | | | | |

Source: Compiled from
- World Bank, 1995. *African Development Indicators 1994-95*, Washington, DC. (All information on both the continent and Sub-Saharan Africa)
- ECA, 1985-1986, 1986-1987, 1990-1991, *Survey of Economic and Social Conditions in Africa*, Addis Ababa.
- ADB, 1994 and 1996, *African Development Report 1994 and 1996*, Abidjan.
- UNDP, 1996, *Human Resource Development 1996*, Oxford University Press, New York.
a GNP per capita as calculated by the World Bank's Atlas methodology of converting data in national currency to US dollars. In this method, the conversion factor for any year is the average exchange rate of that year and the two preceding years, adjusted for differences in rates of inflation between the country and the G-5 countries. The inflation rate of the G-5 countries is represented by changes in the SDR deflators.
b Calculated

ANNEX 3.3

GNP, GDP, SECTORAL CONTRIBUTIONS TO GDP, GROSS DOMESTIC SAVINGS AND GROSS DOMESTIC INVESTMENT IN SUB-SAHARAN AFRICA, INCLUDING SOUTH AFRICA (1973-1993)

| | 1973 | 1974 | 1975 | 1976 | 1977 | 1978 | 1979 | 1980 | 1981 | 1982 | 1983 | 1984 | 1985 | 1986 | 1987 | 1988 | 1989 | 1990 | 1991 | 1992 | 1993 |
|---|---|---|---|---|---|---|---|---|---|---|---|---|---|---|---|---|---|---|---|---|---|
| GNP per capita ($) | 280 | 350 | 420 | 460 | 480 | 510 | 600 | 720 | 770 | 730 | 630 | 590 | 570 | 530 | 510 | 540 | 530 | 520 | 530 | 540 | 520 |
| Gross domestic investment per capita, at 1987$ | 150 | 180 | 180 | 180 | 170 | 150 | 140 | 160 | 170 | 140 | 110 | 110 | 100 | 100 | 90 | 90 | 90 | 80 | 80 | 80 | 80 |
| GDP, at constant 1987$ b | 174.1 | 187 | 190.5 | 201 | 207.2 | 210.1 | 216.3 | 224.5 | 230.3 | 232.8 | 229.6 | 233 | 237 | 242.5 | 245.6 | 255.2 | 264 | 266.4 | 268.8 | 270.4 | 271.3 |
| Contribution (%) to growth of GDP of: | | | | | | | | | | | | | | | | | | | | | |
| - Agriculture | -0.5 | 2.5 | -1 | 0.4 | 1.3 | 0.1 | -0.3 | 0.7 | -0.5 | 1.2 | -1.3 | -0.1 | 0.5 | 1.7 | 0.3 | 0.5 | 1.1 | 0.2 | 0.5 | -0.9 | 1 |
| - Industry | 1.5 | 2 | -0.4 | 2.2 | 0.3 | 0.5 | 2.6 | 1.7 | 0.5 | -0.3 | -1.1 | 1.1 | 0 | 0 | 0.2 | 1.4 | 1 | 0.1 | -0.1 | 0.2 | -0.1 |
| - Services | 2.2 | 1.9 | 3.3 | 2.9 | 1.5 | 0.8 | 0.7 | 1.4 | 2.6 | 0.2 | 1 | 0.5 | 1.2 | 0.6 | 0.8 | 1.9 | 1.3 | 0.6 | 0.5 | 1.3 | -0.6 |
| Gross domestic savings percentage of GDP | 22.9 | 25.6 | 20.7 | 22.9 | 24.6 | 21.5 | 23.6 | 26.7 | 20.9 | 18.1 | 17.1 | 17.3 | 17.3 | 17.4 | 18.3 | 17.5 | 18.8 | 19.5 | 17.3 | 15.3 | 15.3 |
| Gross domestic investment percentage of GDP | 22.7 | 24.2 | 26 | 27.3 | 24.8 | 23.6 | 23.5 | 23.5 | 26.1 | 23.1 | 19 | 16.9 | 14.8 | 17.3 | 17.7 | 18 | 18.2 | 17.3 | 17.2 | 16.3 | 16 |

Source: World Bank, 1995, *World Tables 1995*, The Johns Hopkins University Press, Baltimore.
Note: GNP per capita as calculated by the World Bank's Atlas methodology of converting data in national currency to US dollars. In this method, the conversion factor for any year is the average exchange rate of that year and the two preceding years, adjusted for differences in rates of inflation between the country and the G-5 countries. The inflation rate of the G-5 countries is represented by changes in the SDR deflators.

ANNEX 3.4
FREE MARKET PRICES AND PRICE INDICES OF SELECTED AFRICAN EXPORTS OF PRIMARY COMMODITIES

| Year | 1982 | 1983 | 1984 | 1985 | 1986 | 1987 | 1988 | 1989 | 1990 | 1991 | 1992 | 1993 |
|---|---|---|---|---|---|---|---|---|---|---|---|---|
| Prices ($/t) [a] | | | | | | | | | | | | |
| Sugar (Caribbean ports) | 185.3 | 186.6 | 114.7 | 89.5 | 133.4 | 149 | 224.7 | 282 | 276.7 | 197.7 | 199.8 | 221 |
| Coffee (composite indicator price) | 2755.6 | 2821.5 | 3112.7 | 2934.2 | 3768.3 | 2376.7 | 2556.5 | 2021 | 1577 | 1472.7 | 1176.2 | 1358.7 |
| Cocoa (New York/London) | 1741.8 | 2118.7 | 2395.7 | 2254.5 | 2068.1 | 1996.2 | 1589.3 | 1246.1 | 1271.4 | 1195.2 | 1097.6 | 1118.7 |
| Tea (London auction prices) | 1931.7 | 2324.6 | 3456.8 | 1983.6 | 1930.2 | 1705.2 | 1764.4 | 2010.6 | 2039.5 | 1853.8 | 2003.6 | 1905.9 |
| Tobacco (US farmers price) | 4036.6 | 4104.2 | 4093.2 | 4085.9 | 3621.1 | 3461.2 | 3521.8 | 3779.1 | 3861.7 | 4074.8 | 4080.3 | 4017.9 |
| Cotton (Egypt) | 2866.7 | 3178.5 | 3674 | 3593.8 | 3466.3 | 3591.5 | 5495.4 | 6379.1 | 6613.5 | 6143.3 | 4694.5 | 4423.9 |
| Sisal (East Africa) | 593.2 | 570.8 | 583.8 | 535.7 | 514.2 | 512.1 | 550.6 | 653.1 | 715 | 662.9 | 505.6 | 615.4 |
| Rubber | 844.4 | 1054.1 | 836.9 | 754.9 | 797.9 | 993.3 | 1159.2 | 949 | 861.7 | 817.8 | 861.3 | 842.1 |
| Hides and skins | 179.8 | 189.7 | 234.5 | 202.1 | 173.8 | 191.7 | 259.6 | 260.8 | 238.8 | 144.6 | 140 | 180.3 |
| Tropical logs (f.o.b Cameroon, $/cum) | 175.9 | 160.8 | 175.1 | 173.9 | 221.6 | 258.9 | 270.9 | 273.7 | 343.5 | 316.1 | 331.1 | 314.4 |
| Phosphate rock (70% BPL, f.a.s. Casablanca) | 40 | 31.5 | 33.3 | 33.5 | 34.8 | 31 | 36 | 40.5 | 40.5 | 42.5 | 42.5 | 38 |
| Iron ore (61% Fe, c.i.f. North Sea Ports) | 32.5 | 29 | 26.1 | 26.6 | 26.3 | 24.5 | 23.5 | 26.6 | 30.8 | 33.3 | 31.6 | 28.1 |
| Copper (high grade, LME) | 1480.3 | 1592.1 | 1377.9 | 1417.5 | 1373.8 | 1781.4 | 2600 | 2846.7 | 2660.8 | 2338.2 | 2282.1 | 1912.6 |
| Crude petroleum ($/b) | 31.4 | 28.4 | 28.3 | 27 | 13.8 | 17.8 | 14.2 | 17.2 | 22 | 18.3 | 18.2 | 16.1 |
| Indices (1985=100) [a] | | | | | | | | | | | | |
| Tropical beverages | 92 | 96 | 110 | 100 | 124 | 81 | 82 | 70 | 62 | 57 | 49 | 52 |
| Food | 131 | 138 | 116 | 100 | 110 | 117 | 152 | 161 | 151 | 141 | 138 | 139 |
| Agricultural raw materials | 101 | 108 | 109 | 100 | 101 | 117 | 128 | 126 | 135 | 127 | 124 | 120 |
| Minerals, ores and metals | 105 | 113 | 105 | 100 | 96 | 113 | 164 | 164 | 148 | 134 | 129 | 110 |

| Commodity price indices (1990=100) [b] | | | | | | | | | | | | |
|---|---|---|---|---|---|---|---|---|---|---|---|---|
| Year | | | | | 1991 | 1992 | 1993 | 1994 | 1995[c] | | | |
| Food | | | | | 99.1 | 101.3 | 100 | 105.1 | 110 | | | |

| | | | | | | | | |
|---|---|---|---|---|---|---|---|---|
| Beverages | 93.5 | 80.5 | 85.6 | 149.7 | 151.8 | | | |
| Agricultural raw materials | 96.4 | 99 | 115 | 126.6 | 135 | | | |
| Metals | 85.7 | 83.7 | 71.9 | 83.8 | 99.8 | | | |
| Fertilizers | 103.2 | 98 | 83 | 89.6 | 97.6 | | | |
| Aluminum (all origins, London) | 79.5 | 76.6 | 69.5 | 90 | 108.3 | | | |
| Cocoa beans (NY & London) | 94.1 | 86.7 | 87.6 | 110.1 | 113.3 | | | |
| Coffee (other milds, NY) | 95.4 | 71.4 | 78.5 | 166.6 | 170.8 | | | |
| Copper (London) | 87.9 | 85.9 | 72 | 86.6 | 112.3 | | | |
| Cotton (Liverpool index) | 93.2 | 70.2 | 70.3 | 96.6 | 126.4 | | | |
| Gasoline (US Gulf coast) | 89.3 | 80.8 | 71.5 | 67.3 | 77.5 | | | |
| Groundnuts (Nigeria, London) | 93.4 | 60.3 | 82.4 | 72 | 63.4 | | | |
| Hides (USA, Chicago) | 86.1 | 82.3 | 86.8 | 94.1 | 100.2 | | | |
| Iron ore (Brazil, North Sea ports) | 108 | 102.6 | 91.3 | 82.7 | 87.7 | | | |
| Newsprint (USA, NY) | 101.1 | 91.8 | 93.7 | 97.4 | 128.9 | | | |
| Palm oil (Malaysia, NW Europe) | 117 | 135.8 | 130.3 | 182.6 | 218.4 | | | |
| Petroleum, spot, average crude price | 83 | 82.6 | 73.2 | 70.2 | 77.1 | | | |
| Phosphate rock (Morocco. Casablanca) | 104.9 | 103.1 | 81.5 | 81.5 | 86.4 | | | |
| Potash (Canada, Vancouver) | 110.9 | 114.2 | 109.5 | 107.7 | 121.3 | | | |
| Pulp (Sweden, Swedish ports) | 84.4 | 71.1 | 54.5 | 61.5 | ... | | | |
| Rubber (all origins, NY) | 94.9 | 93 | 94.4 | 97.5 | ... | | | |
| Sugar (EU, import prices) | 105 | 107.6 | 106.2 | 106.6 | 120.4 | | | |
| Superphosphates (US Gulf ports) | 101 | 91.6 | 84.9 | 100.2 | 111.9 | | | |
| Tobacco (US , all markets) | 103.2 | 101.4 | 79.5 | 87.7 | 73.7 | | | |
| Wheat (US Gulf ports) | 94.9 | 111.5 | 103.5 | 110.5 | 125.4 | | | |
| Urea (any origin, Europe) | 109.6 | 89.4 | 68 | 94.2 | 114.6 | | | |

Source: a Compiled from UNCTAD, 1993, *1994, UNCTAD Commodity Yearbook*, New York.
    b Compiled from IMF, 1995, *International Financial Statistics*, August 1995, Washington, DC.
    c June 1995

## ANNEX 3.5
## TOTAL IMPORTS AND EXPORTS ($ m)

| | 1965 | 1970 | 1975 | 1980 | 1985 | 1990 | 1991 | 1992 | 1993 |
|---|---|---|---|---|---|---|---|---|---|
| | | | | Imports | | | | | |
| World | 199762 | 309118 | 849130 | 1973874 | 1929422 | 3566693 | 3345855 | 3804201 | 3722472 |
| Developing Africa | 7922 | 11049 | 37843 | 74855 | 52407 | 71715 | 69608 | 75904 | 74803 |
| South Africa | 2459 | 3937 | 7584 | 19700 | 11448 | 17665 | 17837 | 18714 | 19090 |
| Total Africa | 10381 | 14986 | 45427 | 94555 | 63855 | 89380 | 87445 | 94618 | 93893 |
| | | | | Exports | | | | | |
| World | 188906 | 313792 | 876065 | 2011382 | 1935209 | 3437400 | 3421117 | 3654821 | 3634614 |
| Developing Africa | 7656 | 12576 | 34965 | 91436 | 59919 | 76289 | 73127 | 71788 | 71360 |
| South Africa | 1483 | 2151 | 5490 | 25540 | 16340 | 22834 | 22288 | 23418 | 23339 |
| Total Africa | 9139 | 14727 | 40455 | 116976 | 76259 | 99123 | 95415 | 95206 | 94699 |
| | | | | Net exports | | | | | |
| Developing Africa | -266 | 1527 | -2878 | 16581 | 7512 | 4574 | 3519 | -4116 | -3443 |
| South Africa | -976 | -1786 | -2094 | 5840 | 4892 | 5169 | 4451 | 4704 | 4249 |
| Total Africa | -1242 | -259 | -4972 | 22421 | 12404 | 9743 | 7970 | 588 | 806 |
| | | | | Developing African share in world (%): | | | | | |
| Imports | 3.97 | 3.57 | 4.46 | 3.79 | 2.72 | 2.01 | 2.08 | 2 | 2.01 |
| Exports | 4.05 | 4.01 | 3.99 | 4.55 | 3.1 | 2.22 | 2.14 | 1.96 | 1.96 |

Source: Based on UN, 1983, 1988, 1991, 1993, *International Trade Statistics Yearbook*, Volume I, New York.

| ANNEX 3.6 STRUCTURE OF DEVELOPING AFRICA'S SHARE IN WORLD IMPORTS AND EXPORTS (%) | Imports | | | | | | Exports | | | | | |
|---|---|---|---|---|---|---|---|---|---|---|---|---|
| Year | 1970 | 1975 | 1980 | 1985 | 1990 | 1992 | 1970 | 1975 | 1980 | 1985 | 1990 | 1992 |
| Total all commodities | 3.8 | 4.7 | 4.2 | 3.3 | 2.4 | 2.2 | 3.9 | 3.9 | 4.7 | 3.1 | 2 | 1.9 |
| Food, live animals, beverages and tobacco | 3.5 | 5.3 | 6 | 6 | 3.8 | 3.5 | 7.3 | 5 | 4.7 | 4.2 | 2.8 | 2.7 |
| Crude materials, oils, and fats (exl. fuels) | 1.3 | 2.1 | 2.6 | 3.2 | 2.5 | 2.7 | 7.4 | 7.3 | 5 | 4.1 | 3.3 | 3.6 |
| Mineral fuels, lubricants and related materials | 1.6 | 1.8 | 1.6 | 1.7 | 2.2 | 1.5 | 14 | 12.2 | 14.9 | 11.5 | 11.5 | 12.9 |
| Chemicals | 4.1 | 4.7 | 4.7 | 3.6 | 2.4 | 2.3 | 0.6 | 0.6 | 0.6 | 0.8 | 0.8 | 0.8 |
| Machinery and transport equipment | 5 | 7 | 6.2 | 3.7 | 2.5 | 2.3 | 0.1 | 0.1 | 0.1 | 0.1 | 0.1 | 0.1 |
| Other manufactured goods | 3.7 | 4.7 | 4.3 | 3 | 2 | 1.9 | 2.6 | 1.3 | 1 | 0.8 | 0.9 | 0.9 |
| Source: UN, 1983, 1988, 1991, *1993, International Trade Statistics Yearbook*, Volume I, New York. | | | | | | | | | | | | |

| ANNEX 3.7 PRIMARY COMMODITIES: SHARE IN TOTAL EXPORTS AND IN WORLD TOTAL EXPORTS | Excluding fuels | | | | | | Including fuels | | | | | |
|---|---|---|---|---|---|---|---|---|---|---|---|---|
| | 1970 | 1975 | 1980 | 1985 | 1990 | 1991 | 1970 | 1975 | 1980 | 1985 | 1990 | 1991 |
| **Exports of primary commodities as percent of total exports** | | | | | | | | | | | | |
| Africa | 61.2 | 35.4 | 20.9 | 25.4 | 25.2 | 23.6 | 92.9 | 93 | 95.3 | ... | 83.2 | 83.3 |
| - Excluding major petroleum exporters | 88.6 | 80.7 | 67.8 | 67.4 | 55.3 | 51.9 | 90.8 | 86.8 | 85.2 | ... | 64.8 | 64 |
| North Africa | 31 | 19.4 | 7.6 | ... | 11.1 | 10.1 | 92.7 | 90.9 | 96.2 | ... | 78 | 76.1 |
| - Excluding major petroleum exporters | 77.9 | 65.8 | 40.1 | ... | 32.3 | 28.1 | 83 | 78.2 | 79.6 | ... | 46.1 | 40 |
| Sub-Saharan Africa | 81.4 | 48.2 | 33.4 | ... | 36.3 | 35.5 | 93.1 | 94.7 | 94.4 | ... | 87.3 | 89.6 |
| - Excluding major petroleum exporters | 91.8 | 87.2 | 79.9 | ... | 67.3 | 66.7 | 93.1 | 90.6 | 87.7 | ... | 74.5 | 78.9 |
| Developing countries | 49 | 25.7 | 19 | 20.9 | 18.2 | 17.1 | 80.1 | 83.2 | 79.4 | ... | 46.6 | 42.8 |
| - Excluding major petroleum and manufactures exporters | 79.1 | 69.2 | 60 | 31.2 | 43.3 | 39.4 | 84 | 81.4 | 77.1 | ... | 53 | 48.4 |
| World | 27.2 | 21.2 | 18.8 | 16.5 | 15.4 | 15.1 | 36.1 | 40.3 | 42.7 | ... | 26.1 | 24.8 |
| **Share in world total export primary commodity values (%)** | | | | | | | | | | | | |
| Africa | 9.1 | 6.8 | 5.3 | ... | 3.5 | 3.3 | 10.4 | 9.4 | 10.5 | ... | 6.9 | 7.1 |
| - Excluding major petroleum exporters | 7.8 | 6.2 | 4.9 | ... | 3.4 | 3.2 | 6 | 3.5 | 2.7 | ... | 2.3 | 2.4 |
| North Africa | 1.8 | 1.6 | 0.9 | ... | 0.7 | 0.7 | 4.2 | 4.1 | 5.1 | ... | 2.8 | 3.1 |
| - Excluding major petroleum exporters | 1.6 | 1.5 | 0.9 | ... | 0.7 | 0.7 | 1.3 | 1 | 0.8 | ... | 0,6 | 0.6 |
| Sub-Saharan Africa | 7.3 | 5.2 | 4.3 | ... | 2.8 | 2.7 | 6.3 | 5.4 | 5.4 | ... | 4 | 4.1 |
| - Excluding major petroleum exporters | 6.3 | 4.6 | 4 | ... | 2.7 | 2.5 | 4.8 | 2.5 | 1.9 | ... | 1.8 | 1.8 |
| Developing countries | 33.1 | 29.7 | 28.9 | ... | 25.5 | 25.6 | 40.8 | 50.5 | 53.1 | ... | 38.5 | 38.9 |
| - Excluding major petroleum and manufactures exporters | 24.1 | 21 | 19.7 | ... | 16.1 | 15.8 | 19.3 | 13 | 11.1 | ... | 11.6 | 11.8 |
| World | 100 | 100 | 100 | 100 | 100 | 100 | 100 | 100 | 100 | 100 | 100 | 100 |
| Source: United Nations, 1993, *UNCTAD Commodity Yearbook 1993*, New York. | | | | | | | | | | | | |

| ANNEX 3.8 EXTERNAL FINANCE FOR SUB-SAHARAN AFRICAN COUNTRIES | | | | | | | | | | | |
|---|---|---|---|---|---|---|---|---|---|---|---|
| Year | 1970 | 1980 | 1986 | 1987 | 1988 | 1989 | 1990 | 1991 | 1992 | 1993 | 1994 [a] |
| **Summary debt data ($ b)** | | | | | | | | | | | |
| Total debt stocks (EDT) | ... | 84 | 138.5 | 165.8 | 166 | 173.4 | 192.2 | 196.3 | 195.4 | 200.4 | 210.7 |
| - Long-term debt (LDOD) | 5.7 | 58.7 | 103.9 | 130.1 | 131.6 | 137.7 | 157.7 | 155.2 | 151.7 | 150.9 | 159.7 |
| - Use of IMF credit | 0.1 | 3 | 7 | 7.6 | 7 | 6.4 | 6.6 | 6.6 | 6.3 | 6.2 | 6.3 |
| - Short-term debt | ... | 22.5 | 27.6 | 23.3 | 22.6 | 24.3 | 28.6 | 29 | 32.2 | 38.3 | 39.2 |
| Disbursements | 1.2 | 15.5 | 11.2 | 11.8 | 11.5 | 11.9 | 11.2 | 9.3 | 10 | 7.9 | 10.6 |
| Principal repayments | 0.4 | 3.3 | 7.9 | 6.7 | 7.4 | 6.1 | 7.7 | 6.4 | 6.7 | 6.7 | 4.2 |
| Interest payments (INT) | ... | 5.7 | 6.7 | 6 | 6.9 | 6.9 | 7.4 | 7.5 | 6.2 | 5.3 | 5.5 |
| Net transfers on debt | ... | 11.8 | -1.3 | -1.51 | -3.3 | -0.3 | -1.5 | -5.9 | -2 | -2 | 1.9 |
| Total debt service (TDS) | ... | 9 | 14.5 | 12.7 | 14.2 | 13.1 | 15.1 | 13.9 | 12.9 | 12 | 9.7 |
| Net resource flows | 1.6 | 15.1 | 11.2 | 14.6 | 14.3 | 18.1 | 16.6 | 16 | 17 | 15.7 | 21.9 |
| Foreign direct investment (net) | 0.4 | - | 0.7 | 1.4 | 1.1 | 2.5 | 0.9 | 1.9 | 1.8 | 1.8 | 2.2 |
| Grants (excl. technical cooperation) | 0.4 | 3.6 | 6.3 | 7.1 | 8.8 | 9.4 | 12 | 11.3 | 11.7 | 12.2 | 12.5 |
| Grants (technical cooperation) | 0.6 | 2.6 | 3.7 | 4 | 4.7 | 4.5 | 5.1 | 5.2 | 5.7 | 5.9 | 5.7 |
| Net transfers | 0.4 | 7.6 | 4.9 | 7.5 | 7.1 | 9 | 6.5 | 6.2 | 7.7 | 7.2 | 13 |
| **Major economic aggregates ($ b)** | | | | | | | | | | | |
| Gross national product (GNP) | 58.1 | 274.4 | 218.1 | 220.4 | 236.4 | 240.2 | 261.9 | 269.3 | 272.1 | 273.7 | 254.5 |
| Export of goods and services (XGS) | 13.4 | 92.2 | 58.3 | 65.5 | 68.4 | 73.7 | 83.5 | 81 | 81.7 | 79 | 82.8 |
| Imports of goods and services (MGS) | 15.5 | 92.6 | 65 | 75.2 | 83.2 | 84.9 | 94.6 | 96.3 | 99.1 | 93.3 | 87.7 |
| Current account balance | -1.8 | 1.4 | -2.4 | -4.8 | -9.2 | -4.5 | -4.4 | -8.6 | -10.2 | -7.9 | -10.6 |
| **Debt indicators (%)** | | | | | | | | | | | |
| EDT/XGS | ... | 91.5 | 237.4 | 253.1 | 242.8 | 235.3 | 232.3 | 242.3 | 239.2 | 253.6 | 254.5 |
| EDT/GNP | ... | 30.7 | 63.5 | 75.2 | 70.2 | 72..2 | 73.4 | 72.9 | 71.8 | 73.2 | 82.8 |
| TDS/XGS | ... | 9.8 | 24.9 | 19.4 | 20.8 | 17.8 | 18.1 | 17.2 | 15.8 | 15.2 | 11.8 |
| INT/XG | ... | 6.2 | 11.4 | 9.1 | 10 | 9.5 | 8.9 | 9.2 | 7.6 | 6.7 | 6.7 |
| Concesssional/EDT | ... | 18.6 | 23.8 | 25.1 | 26.5 | 27.4 | 29.2 | 31.1 | 32.7 | 33.7 | 35.9 |
| Grants/GNP [b] | 1.03 | 1.31 | 2.89 | 3.22 | 3.72 | 3.91 | 4.58 | 4.2 | 4.3 | 4.46 | 4.91 |
| **Other indicators** | | | | | | | | | | | |
| Share of Sub-Saharan Africa in FDI of all developing countries (%) [b] | 18.83 | - | 6.74 | 9.58 | 5.35 | 10.55 | 3.25 | 4.81 | 3.41 | 3.14 | |

Source: World Bank, 1993, 1994, *World Debt Tables*, 1993-1994, 1994-95, Volume 1, Washington, DC.
 [a] Projected , [b] Computed

| ANNEX 3.9 GDP, CONSUMER PRICES, EXTERNAL FINANCING, SAVINGS AND INVESTMENT IN AFRICA | | | | | | | | | | |
|---|---|---|---|---|---|---|---|---|---|---|
| | 1988 | 1989 | 1990 | 1991 | 1992 | 1993 | 1994 | 1995 | 1996 | 1997 |
| Real GDP (annual % change) | 4.1 | 3.4 | 1.8 | 1.8 | 0.8 | 0.9 | 2.9 | 3 | 5 | 5 |
| Consumer prices (annual % change) | 16.4 | 18.8 | 15.6 | 24.5 | 31.7 | 29.5 | 36.8 | 32.1 | 21.3 | 9.1 |
| Total, net external financing ($b) | 10.6 | 12.9 | 9.6 | 11.6 | 9.8 | 11.6 | 18.7 | 19.1 | 17.7 | 17.7 |
| Reserves ($b) | 10.9 | 12.8 | 17.6 | 21.4 | 18.7 | 19.7 | 24.6 | 26.6 | 28.1 | 30 |
| External debt ($b) | 213.3 | 220.8 | 236.4 | 243.8 | 241.8 | 254.2 | 268.2 | 283.4 | 282 | 284.3 |
| Debt-service payments (%b) | 23.9 | 27.8 | 29.7 | 30.6 | 29.2 | 24.7 | 22.9 | 33.3 | 34.7 | 36.4 |
| External debt/exports of goods and services (%) | 258.6 | 245.5 | 229 | 244 | 240.1 | 262.2 | 271.6 | 251.9 | 234 | 224.5 |
| Debt-service payments (% of exports of goods and services) | 28.9 | 31.3 | 28.8 | 30.6 | 29 | 25.5 | 23.2 | 29.6 | 28.8 | 28.7 |
| External debt/GDP ratio (%) | 61.1 | 63.6 | 61.4 | 65.5 | 63 | 68.3 | 74.8 | 66.7 | 62.8 | 66.3 |
| Interest payments (% of exports of goods and services) | 16.6 | 10.8 | 10.7 | 11.5 | 11 | 10.5 | 9.3 | 10.6 | 11.1 | 10.2 |
| Saving (% of GDP) | ... | ... | 18.2 | 18.5 | 17.4 | 15.4 | 17.1 | 19.1 | 18.6 | 19.9 |
| Investment (% of GDP) | ... | ... | 19.1 | 20.9 | 21 | 19.3 | 20.9 | 23 | 22.6 | 23.8 |

Source: IMF, 1996, *World Economic Outlook*, October 1996, Washington, DC.

| ANNEX 4.1 ||
| AFRICA'S MAJOR REGIONS BASED ON CLIMATE AND SOILS ||
|---|---|
| 1- Mediterranean and arid north Africa<br>Algeria, Egypt, Libya, Morocco, and Tunisia | No humid areas; 8% climatically suited to rainfed temperate crop production along the Mediterranean and Atlantic coasts; 92% of the region is arid mountains and deserts. |
| 2- Sudan-Sahelian Africa<br>Burkina Faso, Cape Verde, Chad, Djibouti, Gambia, Mali, Mauritania, Niger, Senegal, Somalia and Sudan | Predominantly desert and arid areas (32% and 36% respectively); potential for tropical rainfed annual crops in the moist sub-humid areas (7%); extensive grazing in the dry sub-humid (15%) and semi-arid (10%) parts of the region. |
| 3- Humid and sub-humid west Africa<br>Benin, Ghana, Guinea, Guinea-Bissau, Cote d'Ivoire, Liberia, Nigeria, Sierra Leone and Togo. | Dominated by moist sub-humid (47%) and humid conditions (35%); suited for a wide range of annual and perennial tropical crops; small areas with dry sub-humid (15%) and semi-arid conditions (3%). |
| 4- Humid central Africa<br>Cameroon, Central African Republic, Congo, Equatorial Guinea, Gabon, Sao Tome and Principe and Congo K. | Dominated by sub-humid (69%) and moist sub-humid (29%) conditions, suited for a limited number of annual and a wide range of perennial tropical crops; extensive areas under forest; small areas of dry sub-humid conditions (2%). |
| 5- Sub-humid and mountainous east Africa<br>Burundi, Comoros, Ethiopia, Kenya, Madagascar. Mauritius, Rwanda, Seychelles and Uganda. | This region encompasses the widest variety of environmental conditions, ranging from desert in the eastern lowlands to humid areas in the cool highlands; wide range of uses with potential for annual and perennial, temperate and tropical crop production; extensive grazing in the semi-arid parts of the region's desert, arid and semi-arid conditions account for 48% of area and dry sub-humid for 11%. Only 41% of area in humid and moist sub-humid zones. |
| 6- Sub-humid and semi-arid southern Africa<br>Angola, Botswana, Lesotho, Malawi, Mozambique, Namibia, Swaziland, Tanzania, Zambia and Zimbabwe. | Large extents of desert and arid (21%) and semi-arid (16%) conditions; more favorable environments in the dry sub-humid (19%), moist sub-humid (41%) and humid (3%) parts of the region; potentials for grazing and annual, mainly topical, but also important areas of temperate crop production. |
| Source: FAO, *African Agriculture: the next 25 Years*, Annex IV, Irrigation and Water Control, Rome. ||

| ANNEX 4.2 PRODUCTION OF MAJOR AGRICULTURAL COMMODITIES IN THE CONTINENT | | | | | | | | | | | |
|---|---|---|---|---|---|---|---|---|---|---|---|
| | 1961 | 1965 | 1970 | 1975 | 1980 | 1985 | 1990 | 1991 | 1992 | 1993 | 1994 | 1995 |
| CROPS (m t) | | | | | | | | | | | | |
| Cereals, total | 46.2 | 51.6 | 59.9 | 69.9 | 71.9 | 83.5 | 88.2 | 99.4 | 84 | 94.7 | 113.2 | 100.3 |
| Wheat | 5.1 | 6.7 | 8 | 9.5 | 9 | 10.4 | 13.7 | 17.7 | 13.2 | 13.3 | 15.7 | 14 |
| Rice | 4.3 | 5.5 | 7.3 | 8.1 | 8.6 | 9.5 | 12.5 | 13.7 | 14.2 | 14.8 | 14.2 | 14.9 |
| Coarse grains | 36.8 | 39.4 | 44.6 | 52.3 | 54.3 | 63.6 | 62 | 68 | 56.5 | 66.6 | 83.3 | 71.5 |
| Barley | 1.9 | 3.1 | 3.6 | 3.7 | 4.7 | 6 | 4.9 | 7.2 | 4.7 | 3.6 | 6.1 | 3.6 |
| Maize | 16.2 | 17 | 20 | 27.1 | 27.5 | 30.4 | 32.9 | 32.7 | 24.3 | 35.8 | 45.1 | 36.2 |
| Millets | 6.6 | 7 | 8 | 8.5 | 7.5 | 10.1 | 10.1 | 10.1 | 9.5 | 9.9 | 12 | 12.2 |
| Sorghum | 10.6 | 10.7 | 11.5 | 11.5 | 12.7 | 15.6 | 11.7 | 15.4 | 15.5 | 15.1 | 18.3 | 17.4 |
| Roots and tubers | 48.1 | 55.2 | 70 | 75.3 | 74.4 | 88.2 | 109.2 | 114 | 118.2 | 121 | 132.5 | 134.8 |
| Cassava | 31.6 | 35.3 | 40.5 | 46.5 | 48.5 | 59.1 | 70 | 71.8 | 73.4 | 74.8 | 82.1 | 82.8 |
| Yams | 7.6 | 10.3 | 16.8 | 13.7 | 10.6 | 10.7 | 19.9 | 22.2 | 25.5 | 26.8 | 31 | 31.6 |
| Pulses, total | 3.5 | 4.4 | 5 | 5.3 | 4.9 | 5.4 | 6.5 | 7.1 | 6.5 | 6.9 | 6.9 | 7.3 |
| Oilcr. (oil equiv.) | 4.1 | 4.5 | 4.6 | 5.1 | 4.7 | 4.7 | 5.6 | 5.8 | 5.6 | 5.9 | ... | ... |
| Palm oil | ... | .1 | 1.3 | 1.3 | 1.4 | 1.4 | 1.7 | ... | ... | 1.9 | 1.7 | 1.8 |
| Groundnuts, in shell | 4.9 | 5.8 | 5.3 | 5.7 | 4.3 | 3.8 | 4.5 | 4.6 | 4.7 | 5 | 5.8 | 5.9 |
| Sesame seed | 0.4 | 0.4 | 0.6 | 0.5 | 0.5 | 0.4 | 0.4 | 0.4 | 0.5 | 0.5 | 0.5 | 0.5 |
| Seed cotton | 2.2 | 3 | 3.8 | 3.1 | 3.1 | 3.6 | 3.5 | 3.6 | 3.4 | 3.7 | 3.6 | 3.9 |
| Cotton seed | 1.5 | 2 | 2.5 | 2.1 | 2 | 2.3 | 2.3 | 2.3 | 2.1 | 2.1 | 2.1 | 2.2 |
| Olives | 0.5 | 0.8 | 0.8 | 1.5 | 1.3 | 1.2 | 1.4 | 2.1 | 1.5 | 1.7 | 1.2 | 1.3 |
| Coconuts | 1.4 | 1.3 | 1.5 | 1.5 | 1.5 | 1.8 | 1.8 | 1.8 | 1.7 | 1.7 | 1.7 | 1.7 |
| Vegetables, total | 13.1 | 15.3 | 17.4 | 21.2 | 24 | 28.6 | 32.6 | 33 | 33.2 | 31.4 | 34.1 | 35 |
| Fruits, total | 25.5 | 27.6 | 35.5 | 40.1 | 39.3 | 44.7 | 49.8 | 50.8 | 51.3 | 52.4 | 53.5 | 52.2 |
| Bananas | 4.2 | 4.6 | 5.4 | 5.6 | 6 | 6.8 | 7.6 | 7 | 7 | 7.1 | 6.8 | 6.6 |
| Plantains | 9.2 | 9.3 | 15.1 | 18 | 14.9 | 17.7 | 19 | 19.8 | 19.9 | 20.5 | 21.8 | 22.2 |
| Oranges | 1.6 | 1.9 | 2.8 | 3 | 3.3 | 3.3 | 4 | 4.4 | 4.2 | 4.3 | 4.4 | 4 |
| Grapes | 3.1 | 3.6 | 2.4 | 2.2 | 2.4 | 2.6 | 2.8 | 2.8 | 3.1 | 2.8 | 2.9 | 2.9 |
| Dates | 0.8 | 0.8 | 0.7 | 1 | 1.1 | 1.1 | 1.2 | 1.3 | 1.3 | 1.3 | 1.4 | 1.4 |
| Mangos | 0.7 | 0.9 | 1 | 1.2 | 1.4 | 1.5 | 1.7 | 1.7 | 1.8 | 1.8 | 1.8 | 1.8 |
| Pineapples | 0.9 | 0.9 | 1.3 | 1.5 | 1.7 | 1.9 | 1.9 | 1.9 | 2 | 2 | 1.9 | 1.9 |
| Stimulants | | | | | | | | | | | | |
| Coffee | 0.9 | 1.1 | 1.3 | 1.3 | 1.2 | 1.2 | 1.3 | 1.2 | 1.1 | 1.1 | 1.1 | 1.2 |
| Cocoa beans | 0.8 | 0.9 | 1.1 | 1 | 1 | 1.1 | 1.4 | 1.3 | 1.3 | 1.3 | 1.4 | 1.5 |
| Tea | 0.1 | 0.1 | 0.1 | 0.2 | 0.2 | 0.3 | 0.3 | 0.3 | 0.3 | 0.3 | 0.3 | 0.4 |

| Tobacco leaves | 0.2 | 0.2 | 0.2 | 0.3 | 0.3 | 0.3 | 0.4 | 0.4 | 0.5 | 0.5 | 0.4 | 0.5 |
|---|---|---|---|---|---|---|---|---|---|---|---|---|
| Fiber crops | 1.2 | 1.5 | 1.8 | 1.5 | 1.5 | 1.5 | 1.5 | 1.6 | 1.5 | 1.6 | ... | ... |
| Sisal | 0.4 | 0.4 | 0.4 | 0.3 | 0.2 | 0.1 | 0.1 | 0.1 | 0.1 | 0.1 | 0.1 | 0.1 |
| Cotton lint | 0.7 | 1 | 1.3 | 1.1 | 1.2 | 1.3 | 1.4 | 1.4 | 1.3 | 1.4 | 1.4 | 1.3 |
| Other crops | | | | | | | | | | | | |
| Sugar cane | 28.1 | 32.6 | 44.2 | 51.3 | 57.2 | 69 | 71.9 | 75.5 | 67.1 | 63.2 | 70.7 | 73.7 |
| Sugar beets | - | 0.2 | 1.2 | 1.9 | 2.5 | 3.1 | 3.8 | 4.4 | 3.8 | 4.2 | 4.3 | 3.9 |
| Honey (1000 t) | 67.2 | 72.2 | 77.4 | 82.9 | 87.7 | 95.3 | 106.6 | 107.6 | 1105 | 113.8 | 131.2 | 131.7 |
| Rubber, natural | 0.1 | 0.2 | 0.2 | 0.2 | 0.2 | 0.2 | 0.3 | 0.3 | 0.3 | 0.3 | 0.3 | 0.3 |
| LIVESTOCK AND LIVESTOCK PRODUCTS ( m heads) | | | | | | | | | | | | |
| Cattle, stocks | 122.1 | 133.8 | 148.5 | 155.7 | 171.8 | 175.6 | 188.5 | 188.9 | 188 | 188.1 | 192.5 | 196.4 |
| Buffaloes, stocks | 1.5 | 1.6 | 2 | 2.2 | 2.3 | 2.4 | 2.9 | 3 | 3.2 | 3.5 | 3.2 | 3.3 |
| Sheep, stocks | 135.1 | 142.8 | 157.1 | 161.2 | 182.3 | 187.3 | 202.1 | 203 | 206.3 | 206.3 | 207.3 | 211.6 |
| Goats, stocks | 94.3 | 101 | 113.6 | 118.4 | 139 | 147.3 | 169.9 | 169.8 | 169.5 | 172 | 173.6 | 174.9 |
| 21.4 Pigs, stocks | 21.55.7 | 6.2 | 7.2 | 8.1 | 10.1 | 11.9 | 16.5 | 17.6 | 18.9 | 20.5 | 21.4 | 21.5 |
| Horses, stocks | 3.5 | 3.6 | 3.7 | 3.5 | 3.6 | 4.2 | 4.6 | 4.6 | 4.7 | 4.7 | 4.7 | 4.7 |
| Mules, stocks | 1.8 | 1.9 | 2.1 | 2.1 | 1.1 | 1.2 | 1.3 | 1.4 | 1.4 | 1.4 | 1.4 | 1.4 |
| Asses | 11 | 10.7 | 11 | 11.1 | 11.5 | 11.8 | 12.7 | 13.1 | 13.3 | 13.4 | 13.3 | 13.4 |
| Chickens, stocks | 274 | 316 | 394 | 465 | 562 | 711 | 895 | 918 | 932 | 962 | 978 | 1068 |
| Camels, stocks | 8.6 | 9.9 | 11.3 | 12.1 | 12.6 | 13.8 | 14.2 | 14.2 | 13.7 | 13.9 | 13.9 | 14.2 |
| Hen eggs, total (1000 t) | 397.6 | 480 | 594.4 | 765.6 | 947.8 | 1176.5 | 1548.9 | 1553.2 | 1579.1 | 1606.5 | 1768.4 | 1691.1 |
| Wool , greasy (1000 t) | 204.1 | 213.8 | 223.4 | 201.6 | 197.3 | 234.4 | 241.4 | 251.4 | 247.4 | 240.9 | 232.2 | 225.6 |

Source: - FAO, 1994, *FAOSTAT data*, Statistics Division, Rome
- FAO, 1969, 1972, 1977, 1986, 1991, 1993, *1995, FAO Production Yearbook*, Rome.

1. Agricultural production, import and export figures were rounded to the nearest 10,000 to conserve space. As a consequence, figures below 10,000 are indicated by (-). The symbol (...) means that data is not available.

2. Discrepancies in statistical figures that may arise are mainly due to different time references (calendar years), rounding of figures, revisions of preceding years figures and use of different classification of the same product by different countries.

3. Statistical data in many African countries are inadequate. Because of this and varying systems of recording, processing and reporting data, organizations, such as FAO, use conversion factors to convert data to comparable international level. They also fill in gaps of data whenever such gaps exist.

4. Some of the data were derived. These include cottonseed from ginned cotton production, wine from the quantity of grapes crushed at harvest time, eggs from total chicken numbers, hides and skins based on slaughtering, etc.

5. Some agricultural products (oil and cake/meal equivalent) are potential production figures that would have been produced had all the oil-bearing crops harvested been extracted.

6. Production figures of vegetables do not include those cultivated in small family gardens for household consumption. The same applies to fruits, including

those collected from wild plants. Trade in banana includes plantain. Production of nuts refer only to crops for sale.

7. Estimates of unrecorded trade in live animals are included in trade. Meat is in the ready-to-cook equivalent and includes meat from imported animals.

8. Production of veneer sheets is net of the sheets used captively in the production of plywood.

9. Fishery statistics are based on fishing inland, in shore, offshore and high sea areas. Imports include fish caught by foreign fishing craft while exports include fish caught by domestic fishing craft.

10. Trade in about 50 percent of African countries is based on general trade (total imports and total exports, including re-exports) and the rest on special trade.

ANNEX 4.3
IMPORTS, EXPORTS AND NET EXPORTS OF SELECTED AGRICULTURAL COMMODITIES IN THE CONTINENT

| Year | Imports | | | | | | | | Exports | | | | | | | | Net trade (+ = exports, - = imports) | | | | | | | |
|---|---|---|---|---|---|---|---|---|---|---|---|---|---|---|---|---|---|---|---|---|---|---|---|---|
| | 1965 | 1970 | 1975 | 1980 | 1985 | 1990 | 1993 | 1994 | 1965 | 1970 | 1975 | 1980 | 1985 | 1990 | 1993 | 1994 | 1965 | 1970 | 1975 | 1980 | 1985 | 1990 | 1993 | 1994 |
| **CROPS (m t)** | | | | | | | | | | | | | | | | | | | | | | | | |
| Cereals, total | 5.63 | 6.71 | 11.76 | 21.87 | 29.39 | 28.36 | 34.3 | 33.9 | 1.63 | 2.72 | 4.01 | 4.36 | 1.06 | 3.8 | 3.2 | 5.3 | -4 | -3.99 | -7.75 | -17.51 | -28.33 | -24.56 | -31.1 | -28.6 |
| Maize (corn) | 0.42 | 0.69 | 1.3 | 3.35 | 4.98 | 4.58 | 7.5 | 5.8 | 0.63 | 1.47 | 3.42 | 3.39 | 0.79 | 3.05 | 2.1 | 4.28 | 0.21 | 0.78 | 2.12 | 0.04 | -4.19 | -1.53 | -5.4 | -1.52 |
| Wheat | 4.09 | 4.28 | 9.24 | 15.51 | 19.87 | 19.02 | 20.5 | 22 | 0.22 | 0.16 | 0.06 | 0.17 | 0.12 | 0.47 | 0.3 | - | -3.87 | -4.12 | -9.18 | -15.34 | -19.75 | -18.55 | -20.2 | -22 |
| Rice, paddy | 0.82 | 0.83 | 0.72 | 2.38 | 3.03 | 3.05 | 3.8 | 3.7 | 0.35 | 0.74 | 0.12 | 0.12 | 0.02 | 0.09 | 0.2 | 0.3 | -0.47 | -0.09 | -0.6 | -2.26 | -3.01 | -2.96 | -3.6 | -3.4 |
| Barley | 0.05 | 0.2 | 0.22 | 0.39 | 0.97 | 1.28 | 2.1 | 1.8 | 0.02 | - | 0.01 | 0.04 | 0.04 | - | - | - | -0.03 | -0.2 | -0.21 | -0.35 | -0.93 | -1.28 | -2.1 | -1.8 |
| Malt | 0.08 | 0.14 | 0.31 | 0.4 | 0.5 | 0.32 | 0.3 | 0.3 | - | - | - | 0.01 | 0.01 | 0.01 | 0.01 | - | -0.08 | -0.14 | -0.31 | -0.39 | -0.49 | -0.31 | -0.29 | -0.3 |
| **Legumes an oil-bearing-crops** | | | | | | | | | | | | | | | | | | | | | | | | |
| Pulses, total | ... | ... | 0.26 | 0.29 | 0.31 | 0.34 | 0.57 | 0.91 | ... | ... | 0.32 | 0.19 | 0.07 | 0.23 | 0.17 | 0.15 | ... | ... | 0.06 | -0.1 | -0.24 | -0.11 | -0.4 | -0.76 |
| Groundnuts (in shell for production) | 0.01 | - | 0.02 | 0.02 | 0.04 | 0.06 | 0.06 | 0.06 | 1.16 | 0.74 | 0.45 | 0.17 | 0.08 | 1.01 | 0.06 | 0.12 | 1.15 | 0.74 | 0.43 | 0.15 | 0.04 | 0.95 | - | 0.06 |
| Cotton seed | - | - | - | - | - | - | 0.02 | 0.04 | 0.18 | 0.29 | 0.11 | 0.04 | 0.05 | 0.15 | 0.18 | 0.22 | 0.18 | 0.29 | 0.11 | 0.04 | 0.05 | 0.15 | 0.16 | 0.18 |
| Coconuts in shell | - | - | - | - | - | - | - | - | - | - | 0.02 | 0.01 | 0.02 | - | - | 0.01 | - | - | 0.02 | 0.01 | 0.02 | - | - | 0.01 |
| Sunflower seed | - | - | - | - | 0.02 | 0.02 | 0.02 | 0.2 | 0.01 | 0.02 | 0.02 | - | - | - | 0.02 | 0.02 | 0.01 | 0.02 | 0.02 | - | -0.02 | -0.02 | - | -0.18 |
| Soybeans | 0.01 | - | 0.01 | 0.03 | 0.03 | - | 0.02 | 0.02 | 0.02 | 0.01 | 0.01 | - | - | - | - | - | 0.01 | 0.01 | -0.01 | -0.03 | -0.03 | - | - | -0.02 |
| Sesame seed | - | 0.02 | 0.04 | 0.01 | 0.02 | 0.02 | 0.02 | 0.02 | 0.12 | 0.15 | 0.13 | 0.07 | 0.07 | 0.08 | 0.08 | 0.12 | 0.12 | 0.13 | 0.09 | 0.06 | 0.05 | 0.06 | 0.06 | 0.1 |
| Castor beans | - | - | - | - | - | - | - | - | 0.03 | 0.03 | - | - | - | - | - | - | 0.03 | 0.03 | - | - | - | - | - | - |
| **Fruits, excluding melons** | | | | | | | | | | | | | | | | | | | | | | | | |
| Bananas | 0.06 | 0.07 | 0.07 | 0.03 | 0.03 | 0.02 | 0.04 | 0.04 | 0.43 | 0.42 | 0.65 | 0.25 | 0.21 | 0.27 | 0.32 | 0.33 | 0.37 | 0.35 | 0.58 | 0.22 | 0.18 | 0.25 | 0.28 | 0.29 |
| Oranges | 0.01 | 0.01 | 0.02 | 0.01 | 0.01 | 0.02 | 0.02 | 0.02 | 0.94 | 1.13 | 1.07 | 1.3 | 1.09 | 1 | 0.96 | 1.02 | 0.93 | 1.12 | 1.05 | 1.29 | 1.08 | 0.98 | 0.94 | 1 |
| Grapes | - | - | - | - | - | - | - | - | 0.03 | 0.03 | 0.03 | 0.04 | 0.04 | 0.05 | 0.09 | 0.1 | 0.03 | 0.03 | 0.03 | 0.04 | 0.04 | 0.05 | 0.05 | 0.1 |
| Pineapples | ... | ... | - | - | - | - | - | - | ... | ... | ... | - | 0.11 | 0.18 | 0.15 | 0.15 | ... | ... | ... | 0.11 | 0.18 | 0.15 | 0.15 | 0.16 |
| Dates | 0.03 | 0.02 | 0.02 | 0.01 | 0.01 | 0.01 | 0.01 | - | 0.02 | 0.02 | 0.02 | - | 0.02 | 0.03 | 0.05 | 0.5 | -0.01 | 0 | 0 | -0.01 | 0.01 | 0.02 | 0.02 | 0.5 |
| **Spices** | | | | | | | | | | | | | | | | | | | | | | | | |
| Chilies and peppers, green | - | - | - | 0.01 | - | 0.01 | - | - | 0.01 | - | - | - | - | 0.01 | - | - | 0.01 | - | - | -0.01 | - | -0.1 | 0.01 | - |
| Vanilla (1000 t) | - | - | 0.01 | 0.03 | 0.02 | 0.03 | - | - | 1.21 | 1.39 | 1.42 | 0.43 | 0.83 | 0.96 | 0.8 | 1.1 | 1.21 | 1.39 | 1.41 | 0.4 | 0.81 | 0.93 | 0.8 | 1.1 |
| **Stimulants** | | | | | | | | | | | | | | | | | | | | | | | | |
| Coffee, green | 0.07 | 0.08 | 0.09 | 0.11 | 0.13 | 0.13 | 0.16 | 0.17 | 0.83 | 1 | 1.11 | 0.9 | 1 | 1.1 | 0.84 | 0.74 | 0.76 | 0.92 | 1.02 | 0.79 | 0.87 | 0.97 | 0.68 | 0.57 |
| Cocoa beans | - | - | 0.01 | - | - | - | - | - | 1.08 | 0.87 | 0.81 | 0.77 | 0.83 | 1.19 | 1.19 | 1.13 | 1.08 | 0.87 | 0.8 | 0.77 | 0.83 | 1.19 | 1.19 | 1.13 |
| Tea | 0.1 | 0.12 | 0.11 | 0.12 | 0.15 | 0.18 | 0.16 | 0.15 | 0.06 | 0.11 | 0.13 | 0.17 | 0.23 | 0.27 | 0.28 | 0.27 | -0.04 | -0.01 | 0.02 | 0.05 | 0.08 | 0.09 | 0.12 | 0.12 |
| Tobacco leaves | 0.05 | 0.06 | 0.09 | 0.09 | 0.11 | 0.11 | 0.11 | 0.18 | 0.17 | 0.09 | 0.14 | 0.18 | 0.18 | 0.23 | 0.31 | 0.34 | 0.12 | 0.03 | 0.05 | 0.09 | 0.07 | 0.12 | 0.2 | 0.16 |
| **Vegetable fibers** | | | | | | | | | | | | | | | | | | | | | | | | |
| Cotton lint | ... | 0.02 | 0.08 | 0.06 | 0.15 | 0.22 | 0.18 | 0.18 | ... | ... | 0.6 | 0.64 | 0.86 | 0.77 | 0.72 | 0.77 | ... | ... | 0.52 | 0.58 | 0.71 | 0.55 | 0.54 | 0.59 |
| Sisal | - | 0.02 | 0.02 | 0.02 | 0.01 | - | - | - | 0.36 | 0.37 | 0.21 | 0.12 | 0.06 | - | 0.04 | 0.04 | 0.36 | 0.35 | 0.19 | 0.1 | 0.05 | - | 0.04 | 0.04 |
| **Others** | | | | | | | | | | | | | | | | | | | | | | | | |
| Sugar, total, raw | .. | .. | .. | 3.19 | 3.58 | 3.7 | 4.17 | | .. | .. | .. | 2.69 | 2.52 | 1.4 | 1.75 | | .. | .. | .. | | 0.5 | 1.06 | -2.3 | -2.42 |
| Natural rubber | - | 0.05 | 0.07 | 0.08 | 0.06 | 0.09 | 0.09 | 0.98 | 0.15 | 0.19 | 0.18 | 0.14 | 0.19 | 0.28 | 0.26 | 0.24 | 0.15 | 0.14 | 0.11 | 0.06 | 0.13 | 0.19 | 0.17 | 0.74 |
| **LIVESTOCK (m head)** | | | | | | | | | | | | | | | | | | | | | | | | |
| Cattle | 0.22 | 0.93 | 1.04 | 1.3 | 0.98 | 0.6 | 0.92 | 1.11 | 0.41 | 1.04 | 1.08 | 1.27 | 1 | 0.84 | 0.82 | 0.83 | 0.19 | 0.11 | 0.04 | -0.03 | 0.02 | 0.24 | -0.1 | -0.28 |
| Pigs | - | - | - | - | - | 0.02 | 0.02 | 0.02 | - | - | - | 0.01 | - | - | - | - | - | - | - | 0.01 | - | -0.02 | -0.02 | -0.02 |
| Sheep and goats | 2.06 | 3.07 | 2.27 | 3.48 | 2.6 | 2.29 | 2.5 | 2.53 | - | 1.7 | 3.59 | 4.04 | 4.2 | 3.56 | 4.8 | 5.13 | -2.06 | -1.37 | 1.32 | 0.56 | 1.6 | 1.27 | 2.3 | 2.6 |
| **Livestock products (m t)** | | | | | | | | | | | | | | | | | | | | | | | | |
| Cowmilk, whole, fresh | ... | ... | 0.07 | 0.06 | 0.06 | 0.06 | 0.08 | 0.07 | ... | ... | 0.03 | - | - | - | - | - | ... | ... | -0.04 | -0.06 | -0.06 | -0.06 | -0.08 | -0.07 |
| Hen eggs | - | - | - | 0.05 | - | 0.01 | 0.01 | 0.01 | - | - | - | - | - | - | - | - | - | - | - | -0.05 | - | -0.01 | -0.01 | -0.01 |
| Wool, greasy | - | 0.02 | - | - | - | - | - | - | 0.11 | - | 0.07 | 0.05 | 0.04 | 0.05 | 0.03 | 0.03 | 0.11 | -0.02 | 0.07 | 0.05 | 0.04 | 0.05 | 0.03 | 0.03 |

Source: based on FAO, 1977, 1982, 1987, 1992, 1994, *FAO Trade Yearbook*, Rome.

| ANNEX 4.4 PRODUCTION OF SELECTED MINERAL ORES AND CONCENTRATES (ISIC 2301-2909) IN THE CONTINENT (1000 t) | | | | | | |
|---|---|---|---|---|---|---|
| Year | 1970 | 1975 | 1980 | 1985 | 1990 | 1992 |
| Iron-bearing ores (M) | 37491 | 34456 | 37760 | 34046 | 32014 | 34425 |
| Copper-bearing ores (M) | 1446 | 1608 | 1464 | 1370 | 1235 | 848 |
| Nickel-bearing ores (M) | 20.3 | 36.6 | 56.4 | 54.5 | 60.5 | 57.4 |
| Bauxite | 3284 | 9497 | 14887 | 15337 | 17983 | 17606 |
| Lead-bearing ores (M) | 219.1 | 166.2 | 278.7 | 275.3 | 164.5 | 176.9 |
| Zinc-bearing ores (M) | 265 | 291.4 | 247.9 | 258.1 | 225.4 | 193.9 |
| Tin-bearing area (M) | 20.4 | 15.9 | 11.4 | 9.6 | 5.6 | 3.5 |
| Manganese-bearing ores (M) | 2349 | 3924 | 3585 | 2756 | 3153 | 1934 |
| Chromium-bearing ores (M) | 881 | 968 | 1307 | 1263 | 1725 | 2089 |
| Rutile | ... | 10.4 | 95.6 | 135.6 | 208.3 | 233.3 |
| Tungsten (M) | 1 | 0.9 | 0.7 | 0.2 | 0.2 | 0.2 |
| Vanadium (M) | 6.9 | 11.2 | 14.9 | 14 | 17.1 | 15 |
| Antimony (M) | 19.5 | 17.7 | 13.8 | 8.4 | 5.1 | 4.4 |
| Cobalt-bearing ores (M) | 16.6 | 17.5 | 18.9 | 33.9 | 26.9 | 23.1 |
| Silver-bearing ores (M) | 0.3 | 0.3 | 0.5 | 0.5 | 0.6 | 0.5 |
| Uranium-bearing ores (M) | 3.6 | 4.6 | 15.3 | 12.7 | 9.5 | 6.7 |
| Gold-bearing ores (M) | 1 | 0.7 | 0.7 | 0.7 | 0.6 | 0.7 |
| Magnesite | 103.2 | 170.8 | 157 | 348.8 | 405.7 | 310.3 |
| Natural phosphate (P2O5) | ... | 8055 | 10373 | 10969 | 12253 | 11563 |
| Potash salts, crude (K2O) | 633 | 277 | - | - | - | - |
| Iron pyrites, unroasted (t) | 1091 | 1020 | 1666 | 1159 | 1372 | 1371 |
| Salt, unrefined | 2180 | 2339 | 2936 | 3279 | 3367 | 3182 |
| Diamonds, industrial (1000 carats) | 22055 | 22237 | 20357 | 29514 | 27499 | 23810 |
| Gypsum, crude | ... | 1367 | 2041 | 2319 | 2600 | 2693 |
| Graphite, natural | ... | 20.1 | 17.3 | 25.4 | 18.2 | 10.2 |
| Source: - United Nations, 1979, 1984, 1991, *Industrial Statistics Yearbook*, New York.<br>        - United Nations, 1992, *Industrial Commodity Statistics Yearbook*, New York.<br>M = Metal content | | | | | | |

| ANNEX 4.5 PRODUCTION AND CONSUMPTION OF PRIMARY ENERGY AND REFINERY CAPACITIES IN AFRICA | | | | | | | | | | | | | | |
|---|---|---|---|---|---|---|---|---|---|---|---|---|---|---|
| Year (19--) | Unit | 85 | 86 | 87 | 88 | 89 | 90 | '91 | 92 | 93 | 94 | 95 | % change 1995/ 1994 | 1995 share of world total (%) |
| **Primary energy** | | | | | | | | | | | | | | |
| - Consumption | mtpe | 181.9 | 186.3 | 191.5 | 204.6 | 206.3 | 212.6 | 212.1 | 213.3 | 218.7 | 227.2 | 237.6 | 4.6 | 2.9 |
| **Petroleum** | | | | | | | | | | | | | | |
| Refinery capacities | mb/ day | 2.56 | 2.55 | 2.63 | 2.81 | 2.81 | 2.86 | 2.86 | 2.79 | 2.82 | 2.86 | 2.86 | 0.1 | 3.7 |
| - Production | mt | 263.8 | 261.8 | 260.2 | 274.4 | 295.6 | 320.7 | 332.1 | 332.9 | 328.9 | 328.5 | 334.7 | 1.9 | 10.3 |
| - Consumption | mt | 82.4 | 80.9 | 84.7 | 88.7 | 92.3 | 95.4 | 95.2 | 97.6 | 98.2 | 100.2 | 102.7 | 2.6 | 3.2 |
| **Natural gas** | | | | | | | | | | | | | | |
| - Production | bm³ | 47.9 | 49.6 | 54.7 | 58.6 | 64.3 | 66.5 | 71.8 | 75 | 79 | 77.1 | 84.4 | 9.3 | 4 |
| - Consumption | bm³ | 24.6 | 27.6 | 27.9 | 30.5 | 32.5 | 33.4 | 34.7 | 36.8 | 38.8 | 41.4 | 42.1 | 1.7 | 2 |
| **Coal** | | | | | | | | | | | | | | |
| - Production | mtpe | ... | ... | ... | ... | 98 | 97.3 | 99.4 | 98.9 | 101.3 | 108.7 | 113.3 | 4.2 | 5.1 |
| - Consumption | mtpe | 70.9 | 72.6 | 74.6 | 80.1 | 75.7 | 78.8 | 76.8 | 74 | 77.5 | 81 | 87.8 | 8.4 | 3.9 |
| **Hydroelectricity** | | | | | | | | | | | | | | |
| -Consumption | mtpe | 5 | 5.5 | 5.3 | 5.6 | 5.9 | 5.9 | 6.3 | 6.3 | 6 | 6.2 | 6.3 | 1 | 2.9 |
| **Nuclear** | | | | | | | | | | | | | | |
| - Consumption | mtpe | ... | ... | ... | ... | ... | ... | ... | ... | ... | 2.6 | 3.1 | ... | ... |
| Source: *BP Statistical Review of World Energy 1996*, The British Petroleum Company p.l.c. 1996, Group Media and Publications. | | | | | | | | | | | | | | |

| ANNEX 4.6 PRIMARY ENERGY BALANCE IN AFRICA (% of total) | | | | | | |
|---|---|---|---|---|---|---|
| Commodity/subregion | Petroleum | Gas | Coal | Electricity | Traditional fuel | Consumption per capita (Gcal) |
| North Africa | 50.6 | 26.8 | 3.8 | 2.8 | 16 | 32 |
| West Africa | 31.6 | 0.7 | 0.5 | 2.4 | 64.8 | 4 |
| Central Africa | 27.4 | 0.8 | 0.2 | 4.3 | 67.3 | 7 |
| Eastern and Southern Africa (excluding South Africa) | 27.3 | 0.4 | 2.9 | 4.6 | 64.8 | 6 |
| Source: ECA estimates, 1994. | | | | | | |

| | | ANNEX 4.7 | | | | | | |
|---|---|---|---|---|---|---|---|---|
| | | PRODUCTION, TRADE AND CONSUMPTION OF SELECTED ENERGY RESOURCES IN | | | | | | |
| | Year | Produc-tion | Import | Export | Bunker | Change in stock | Consumption Total | Per capita |
| Solid fuels (m t of coal equivalent, per capita in Kg) 26.1% | 1970 | 53.5 | 2.2 | 2.4 | - | -0.2 | 53.5 | 150 |
| | 1975 | 62.3 | 2.5 | 2.9 | - | 0.5 | 61.5 | 150 |
| | 1980 | 98.4 | 2 | 24 | - | 3.9 | 80.3 | 169 |
| | 1985 | 136.4 | 3.3 | 44.6 | - | 0.3 | 94.9 | 170 |
| | 1990 | 139.5 | 4.6 | 42.9 | - | - | 101.2 | 157 |
| | 1992 | 140 | 42 | 43 | - | - | 101.2 | 149 |
| Hard coal (m t, per capita in Kg) 35.05% | 1970 | 59.9 | 1.8 | 2.5 | - | -0.2 | 59.3 | 166 |
| | 1975 | 75.3 | 2.2 | 3.3 | - | 0.5 | 73.8 | 180 |
| | 1980 | 121.7 | 1.7 | 29.7 | - | -4.8 | 98.4 | 207 |
| | 1985 | 178.5 | 3.1 | 44.5 | - | 0.3 | 136.9 | 246 |
| | 1990 | 182 | 4.4 | 42.7 | - | - | 143.7 | 214 |
| | 1992 | 182.3 | 4 | 42.8 | - | - | 143.5 | 210 |
| Coke (m t, per capita in Kg) 8.96% | 1970 | 4.5 | 0.6 | 0.2 | | ... | 4.9 | 10 |
| | 1975 | 5.5 | 0.5 | 0.1 | - | ... | 5.9 | 12 |
| | 980 | 2.7 | 0.3 | 0.1 | - | ... | 2.9 | 6 |
| | 1985 | 3.1 | 0.3 | 0.1 | - | - | 3.3 | 6 |
| | 1990 | 3.7 | 0.3 | 0.2 | - | ... | 3.8 | 6 |
| | 1992 | 3.9 | 0.3 | 0.1 | - | - | 4 | 6 |
| Fuelwood (m cubic meter) | 1970 | 292.7 | - | - | | | ... | ... |
| | 1975 | 336.3 | - | - | | | ... | ... |
| | 1980 | 392.1 | - | - | | | ... | ... |
| | 1985 | 409.6 | - | - | | | ... | ... |
| | 1990 | 455.6 | - | - | | | ... | ... |
| | 1992 | 480.4 | - | - | | | ... | ... |
| Crude petroleum (m t, per capita in Kg) 30.82% | 1970 | 292.3 | 21.7 | 283.7 | - | 2 | 28.3 | 79 |
| | 1975 | 241.2 | 33.4 | 224 | - | 1.3 | 49.3 | 120 |
| | 1980 | 298.5 | 32.4 | 244.2 | - | 14 | 72.7 | 153 |
| | 1985 | 242.5 | 30.9 | 174.1 | - | 2.3 | 96.9 | 174 |
| | 1990 | 294.3 | 31.7 | 213.7 | - | 2 | 110.7 | 172 |
| | 1992 | 306.4 | 32.9 | 229.8 | - | -2.1 | 111.6 | 164 |
| Motor gasoline (m t, per capita in Kg) | 1970 | 5.8 | 1.9 | 0.7 | - | 0.01 | 7 | 20 |
| | 1975 | 9.1 | 2.2 | 1.3 | - | - | 9.9 | 24 |
| | 1980 | 12.7 | 2.3 | 1.5 | - | -0.01 | 13.6 | 29 |
| | 1985 | 14.4 | 2.7 | 1.2 | - | - | 15.9 | 29 |
| | 1990 | 19.9 | 2.9 | 2.1 | - | - | 20.7 | 32 |
| | 1992 | 20.4 | 3.1 | 2.2 | - | - | 21.2 | 31 |

| | | | | | | | |
|---|---|---|---|---|---|---|---|
| Gas—diesel oils (m t, per capita in Kg) | 1970 | 7.1 | 4.8 | 0.9 | 1.4 | -0.1 | 9.8 | 27 |
| | 1975 | 13.1 | 3.8 | 1.3 | 1.5 | - | 14.1 | 34 |
| | 1980 | 20 | 4.3 | 2.9 | 1.5 | -0.2 | 20.1 | 42 |
| | 1985 | 24.4 | 4.9 | 5.6 | 1.8 | 0.1 | 21.7 | 39 |
| | 1990 | 29.9 | 4.5 | 7 | 1.2 | 0.1 | 26.1 | 41 |
| | 1992 | 30.3 | 4.6 | 6.7 | 1.1 | 0.1 | 26.9 | 40 |
| Residual fuel oil (m t, per capita in Kg) | 1970 | 11.1 | 5.2 | 1.8 | 5.8 | - | 8.7 | 24 |
| | 1975 | 18.9 | 3.1 | 4 | 4.2 | 0.2 | 13.5 | 33 |
| | 1980 | 24.7 | 3.6 | 6.7 | 5 | -0.3 | 16.9 | 36 |
| | 1985 | 29.7 | 2 | 8.3 | 4.7 | - | 18.8 | 34 |
| | 1990 | 34.2 | 2.5 | 12.8 | 2.8 | - | 212 | 33 |
| | 1992 | 34.3 | 3 | 12.5 | 2.4 | - | 22.4 | 33 |
| Natural gas ($10^{15}$ Joules, per capita in $10^9$ Joules) | 1970 | 76.7 | ... | 61.2 | - | - | 15.4 | 43 |
| | 1975 | 406.6 | ... | 272.2 | - | - | 134.4 | 327 |
| | 1980 | 101.4 | ... | 328.5 | - | - | 685.5 | 1440 |
| | 1985 | 1611.2 | 25.7 | 904.3 | - | ... | 732.7 | 1314 |
| | 1990 | 2701.6 | 39.2 | 1270.9 | - | ... | 1469.9 | 2288 |
| | 1992 | 2984.3 | 21.8 | 1439.8 | - | ... | 1566.3 | 2298 |
| Electricity ($10^9$ kwh, per capita in kwh) 22.34% | 1970 | 87.4 | 0.6 | 0.7 | | | 87.3 | 244 |
| | 1975 | 131.4 | 1.2 | 1.1 | | | 131.5 | 321 |
| | 1080 | 186 | 13.3 | 13.5 | | | 185.9 | 390 |
| | 1985 | 244.4 | 4.4 | 4.4 | | | 244.5 | 439 |
| | 1990 | 318.8 | 2.8 | 7.7 | | | 313.9 | 488 |
| | 1992 | 329.6 | 4.5 | 9.6 | | | 324.5 | 476 |

Source: UN, 1982, 1988, 1991, *1992, Statistics Yearbook,* New York.
% = Percent of world per capita consumption (computed).

## ANNEX 4.8

### INSTALLED CAPACITIES 0F REFINERIES AND NATURAL GAS LIQUID AND ELECTRIC GENERATING PLANTS IN THE CONTINENT

| Year | 1970 | 1975 | 1980 | 1985 | 1990 | 1991 | 1992 |
|---|---|---|---|---|---|---|---|
| Refineries (m t) | | | | | | | |
| Capacity, 3.8 % | 38.1 | 64.6 | 119 | 134.4 | 145.2 | 147.9 | 147.4 |
| Throughput | 29.2 | 50.6 | 72.6 | 96.1 | 110.2 | 110.8 | 111.9 |
| Output, 3.47% | 28 | 48.6 | 69.1 | 87.5 | 106.4 | 105.9 | 107.2 |
| Natural gas liquid plants ($10^9$ cubic meter) | | | | | | | |
| Capacity 5.43% | ... | ... | 80.2 | 84.3 | 87.9 | 87.9 | 94.1 |
| Total production (m t), 15% | 1 | 3.3 | 7.6 | 18.4 | 25.4 | 25.2 | 23.6 |
| Natural gas line | - | - | 0.6 | - | - | - | - |
| Condensate | 1 | 1.3 | 4.7 | 15 | 19.1 | 18.8 | 17.4 |
| LPG. | - | 0.7 | 0.8 | 2.9 | 5.4 | 5.3 | 5.2 |
| Other natural gas liquids | 1.3 | 1.5 | 1.8 | 0.5 | 1 | 1.1 | 1 |
| Electric generating plants (m kw) | | | | | | | |
| Total, 2.59% | 24.1 | 31.8 | 42.9 | 63.6 | 73 | 74.5 | 75 |
| Thermal, 2.87% | 16.8 | 22.3 | 29.7 | 44.6 | 53.1 | 54.7 | 54.9 |
| Hydro, 3.01% | 7.5 | 9.5 | 13.2 | 18 | 18.8 | 19.1 | 19.1 |
| Nuclear, 0.29 %, SA | ... | ... | ... | 1 | 1 | 1 | 1 |
| Geothermal, 0.85% | ... | ... | ... | - | 0.1 | 0.1 | 0.1 |

Source: UN, 1982, 1988, 1991, *1992, Statistics Yearbook*, New York.
   % = Percent of world 1990 capacity (computed)

| ANNEX 4.9 | | | | | |
|---|---|---|---|---|---|
| SUBREGIONAL, REGIONAL AND OTHER INSTITUTIONS PROVIDING SERVICES TO THE CONTINENT | | | | | |
| Name of institution | | Objectives (main) | Year est. | Country of location | Address of institution |
| A. ECA SPONSORED INSTITUTIONS | | | | | |
| United Nations Economic Commission for Africa (ECA) | | Promote and facilitate concerted action for the economic and social development of Africa. | 1958 | Ethiopia | P.O.Box 3001, Addis Ababa |
| **Earth Resources Service Group** | | | | | |
| 1- Eastern and Southern African Mineral Resources Development Center (ESAMRDC). | | Accelerate economic development of the subregion through increased exploitation of mineral resources. | 1976 | Tanzania | P.O.Box 1250, Dar-es Salaam |
| 2- Regional Center for Services in Surveying, Mapping and Remote Sensing (RCSSMRS). | | Promote services in surveying, mapping and remote sensing. | 1975 | Kenya | P.O.Box 18118, Nairobi |
| 3- Organization Africaine de Cartographie et de Teledetection (OACT) | | Promote the development of cartography and remote sensing, promote exploration and development of surveys. | 1988 | Algeria | B.P. 102. Algiers |
| 4- Centre Regional de Teledetection (CRTO) | | Facilitate and promote member states' use of remote sensing through: operation and maintenance of a receiving station. | 1977 | Burkina Faso | B.P. 1761. Ouagadougou |
| 5- Regional Centre for Training in Aerospace Surveys (RECTAS) | | Provide theoretical training in the fields of aerospace surveys, including photogrammetry, etc. | 1972 | Nigeria | P.M.B. 5545, Ile-Ife |
| 6- Central African Mineral Resources Development Centre (CAMRDC) | | Assist member states in the development of mineral resources, etc. | | Congo | P.O.Box 579, Brazzaville |
| 7- African Centre for Meteorological Applications and Development (ACMAD) | | Assist member states in the development of metrology and its applications. | 1987 | Niger | P.O.Box 13184, Niamey |
| **Financial and Banking Services Group** | | | | | |
| 1- Banque Africaine de Developpement (BAD) | | Contribute to the economic development and social progress of its members, individually and jointly. | 1963 | Cote d'Ivoire | B.P. 1387. Abidjan |
| 2- Association of African Central Banks (AACE) | | Promote cooperation in monetary, banking and financial matters in the African region. | 1968 | Senegal | P.O.Box 15, Dakar |
| 3- West African Clearing House (WACH) | | Provide a facility through which the participants in the system can use national currencies for imports originating within the West African subregion. | 1975 | Sierra Leone | PMB 218, Freetown |
| 4- Central African Clearing House (CACH) | | Provide a facility through which the participants in the system can use national currencies for imports originating within the Central Africa subregion. | | Congo K | B.P. 5513, Kinshasa |
| 5- PTA Clearing House | | | | Zimbabwe | Harare |
| 6- African Centre foe Monetary Studies (ACMS) | | Promote cooperation in monetary, banking and financial matters in the African region. | 1978 | Senegal | B.P. 1791, Dakar |
| 7- Association of African Tax Administration (AATA) | | Promote cooperation in the field of taxation policy, legislation and administration among African countries, study tax systems, policies and tax administration. | 1980 | Cameroon | P.O.Box 1325, Yaounde |

| | | | | |
|---|---|---|---|---|
| **Industrial Development Services Group** | | | | |
| 1. African Regional Centre for Engineering Design and Manufacturing (ARCEDEM) | Design ,develop and adapt machinery and equipment; develop and manufacture prototypes of machines and equipment. | 1980 | Nigeria | PMB 19, U.I. Post Office, Ibadan |
| 2. Centre Regional Africain de Technologie (CRAT) | Contribute to the development and use of technology in member states by assisting national centers in the development of indigenous technologies. | 1977 | Senegal | B.P. 2435, Dakar |
| 3. African Regional Organization for Standardization (ARSO) | Promote standardization activities in Africa; elaborate regional standards. | 1977 | Kenya | P.O.Box 57363, Nairobi |
| 4. African Institute for Higher Technical Training and Research (AIHTTR) | Develop technological manpower for Africa's development and assist member states in the development of natural resources, industry. | | Kenya | P.O.Box 53763, Nairobi |
| 5-African Regional Industrial Property Organization (ARIPO) | Modernize, harmonize and develop industrial property laws of member states. | 1976 | Zimbabwe | P.O.Box 4228, Harare |
| 6- Centre Regional Africain pour l'Energie Solaire (CRAES) | Promote the development and utilization of renewable sources of energy in general, and of solar, wind and biogas energy in particular. | 1982 | Burundi | P.O.Box 1950. Bujumbura |
| **Socio-economic Development Planning and Management Services Group** | | | | |
| 1- African Centre for Applied Research and Training in Social Development (ACARSTOD) | Contribute to the formulation of social development programs in Africa; undertake and coordinate research and training in the field of social development | 1977 | Libya | P.O.Box 80606, Tripoli |
| 2. Eastern and Southern African Management Institute (ESAMI) | Improve top managerial performance through management development programs, training, research and consultancy. | 1980 | Tanzania | P.O.Box 3030, Arusha |
| 3. Regional Institute for Population Studies (RIPS) | Provide intensive training and guided research in demography an d related field. | 1971 | Ghana | P.O.Box, Legon |
| 4. Institute de Formation et de Recherche Demographique (FORD) | Train demographers for member states; promote demographic research and population activities in member states. | 1972 | Cameroon | B P. 1556, Yaounde |
| 5- African Association for Public Administration and Management (AAPAM) | Provide senior officials with opportunities for exchanging ideas and experiences to foster public administration and management in Africa. | 1971 | Kenya | P.O.Box 61862, Nairobi |
| 6- United Nations African Institute for Economic Development and Planning (IDEP) | Offers practical training to African economic planners and senior officials of government agencies and institutions. | 1962 | Senegal | P.O.Box 3186, Dakar |
| 7- United Nations African Institute for the Prevention of Crime and the Treatment of Offenders | Assist in the formulation of policies and programs for crime prevention and criminal justice within the context of overall plans for national development. | 1989 | Uganda | P.O.Box 10590, Kampala |
| **Trade and Transport Services Group** | | | | |
| 1- Association des Organization Africaine de Promotion Commerciale (AOAPC) | Foster regular contact among African states in trade matters and assist in the harmonization of their commercial policies in order to promote intra-African trade. | 1974 | Morocco | B P. 23, Tangier |
| 2- Federation of African Chambers of Commerce (FACC) | Promote trade and investment cooperation among business operators in African countries. | 1983 | Ethiopia | P.O.Box 3001, Addis Ababa |
| 3- Port Management Association of Eastern and Southern Africa (PMAESA) | Seek improvement, coordination and standardization of Eastern/ Southern Africa port operations and equipment services. | 1973 | Kenya | P.O.Box 99209, Mombassa |
| 4- Port Management Association of West and Central Africa (PMAWCA) | Improve, coordinate and standardize African port operations. | 1972 | Nigeria | P.O.Box 1113 Apapa, Lagos |
| 5- Unions des Administrations Portuaires du Nord de l'Afrique (UAPNA) | Improve, coordinate and standardize African port operations. | 1975 | Tunisia | P.O.Box 52, Tunis |
| 6- Trans-East African Highway Authority (TEAHA) | Develop interstate road links to facilitate trade and travel; foster African economic integration. | 1981 | Ethiopia | P.O.Box 3001, Addis Ababa |

| | | | | |
|---|---|---|---|---|
| 7- Autorite de la Route Trans-Africaine Mombasa-Lagos (TAHA) | Promote the development of inter-state links in order to facilitate trade and movement of people. | 1981 | Ethiopia | P.O.Box 3001, Addis Ababa |
| **B. OAU SPONSORED INSTITUTIONS** | | | | |
| Organization of African Unity (OAU) | Promote the unity and solidarity of the Africa states, coordinate and harmonize members' economic, diplomatic, educational, health, defense, etc. policies. | 1963 | Ethiopia | P.O.Box 3243, Addis Ababa |
| 1. Inter-African Phytosanitary Council (IAPSC) | | | Cameroon | Yaounde, telex: 00-234 222528 |
| 2. Inter-African Bureau for Animal Resources (IBAR) | | | Kenya | Nairobi, fax: (00254-2) 330046 |
| 3. Scientific, Technical and Research Commission (STRC) | | | Nigeria | Lagos, fax: (00341) 636093 |
| 4. African Centre for Fertilizer Development (ACFD) | Stimulate the proper production and use of fertilizers in order to increase crop yields and farmers' incomes. | | Zimbabwe | P.O.Box A469, Harare |
| **C. GOVERNMENT SPONSORED REGIONAL AND SUBREGIONAL INSTITUTIONS** | | | | |
| **Regional** | | | | |
| African Economic Community (AEC) (incorporated in OAU) | Enhance and facilitate economic cooperation and integration of the African region | 1994 | Ethiopia | |
| African Development Bank (ADB) | Contribute to the economic development and social progress of its member countries, individually and jointly. | 1966 | Cote d'Ivoire | B.P. 1387, Abidjan |
| African Development Fund (AfDF) | Promote cooperation, increase international trade, etc. | 1973 | Cote d'Ivoire | B.P. 1387, Abidjan |
| African Export-import Bank (Afreximbank) | Extend credit to African exporters, importers of African goods and African businesses which want to import goods for conversion into exports. | 1994 | Egypt | Cairo |
| Société Internationale Financiere pour les Investissements et le Developpement en Afrique (SIFIDA) | Finance industrial projects in Africa and in independent developing countries | 1970 | Switzerland | P.B. 396, Geneva |
| African Project Development Facility (APDF) | Prepare feasibility studies and other project and loan documentation for private sector projects ($0.5-5.0 investment). | | Zimbabwe | Harare |
| Association of African Development Finance Institutions (AADFI) | Bring about cooperation in financing the economic development of Africa, accelerate economic integration. | 1975 | Cote d'Ivoire | B.P. 1387, Abidjan |
| African Groundnut Council (AGC) | Regulate supplies to the world market, etc. | 1964 | | |
| Cocoa Producers' Alliance (COPAL) | Exchange technical and scientific information; regulate cocoa supplies to the world market, etc. | 1962 | | |
| Intra-African Coffee Organization (IACO) | Stabilize coffee price in the world market; formulate common marketing policies; etc. | 1960 | | |
| African Timber Organization (ATO) | Coordinate disposal of timber and wood products in the world market; exchange information; etc. | 1975 | | |
| **Central Africa** | | | | |
| Economic Community of Central African States (ECCAS) | | | | |
| Union Douaniere et Economique de l'Afrique Centrale (UDEAC) | Harmonize policies on industry, agriculture, transport, resources, technology, etc. | 1964 | | |
| Economic Community of Great Lakes (CEPGL) | Promote cooperation in social, economic, political and cultural fields. | 1976 | | |
| Bank of Central African States (BEAC) | Maintain the common monetary unit and the pulling of foreign reserves in member countries. | 1973 | Cameroon | B.P. 1917, Yaounde |
| Subregional Institute for Statistics and Applied Economics (ISEA) | | | | |
| Multisectoral Institute of Applied Technology (ISTA) | Plan and evaluate projects in the UDEAC area. | | | |

426

| | | | | |
|---|---|---|---|---|
| Development Bank of the Great Lakes States (BDFGL) | | | | |
| Great Lakes Energy (EGL) | | | | |
| Agricultural and Stock-breading Research Institute (IRAZ) | | | | |
| Development Bank of Central African States (BDEAC) | Promote the economic and social development of the member states, etc. | 1975 | Congo | B.P. 1177 Brazzaville |
| **Eastern and Southern Africa** | | | | |
| Common Market for Eastern and Southern Africa (COMESA), former PTA | Break down trade barriers and boost interstate trade, initiatives related to economic integration, trade facilitation and development | 1994 | Zambia | P. O. Box 30051, Lusaka |
| Southern African Development Community (SADC) former SADCC | Seek to achieve collective self reliance , mutual interdependence and equitable economic integration. | 1992 | Botswana | Private Bag 0095, Gaborone |
| Indian Ocean Commission (IOC) | Develop trade and promote industrial cooperation | 1982 | | |
| PTA Trade and Development Bank | Stimulate trade in the PTA, now COMESA area. | | Burundi | Bujumbura |
| East African Development Bank (EADB) | Provide financial and technical assistance for the promotion of industrial, agricultural, etc, development | 1967 | Uganda | P.O.Box 7128, Kampala |
| Kagera Basin Authority (KBA) | Develop communications, energy, agriculture, etc. | 1977 | | |
| Inter-governmental Authority on Development (IGAD) (former IGADD) | Cooperate in political, economic, security, human and environmental areas. | 1996 | Djibouti | Djibouti |
| Desert Locust Control Organization of Eastern Africa (DLCOEA) | Promote the most effective control of the desert locust within the territories of member states. | 1962 | | |
| **North Africa** | | | | |
| Arab Maghreb Union (AMU) | Strengthen all forms of ties among member states and introduce free circulation of goods, services and factors of production. | 1989 | Morocco | 26-27 Rue Ogba, Rabat-Agdal |
| Maghreb Industrial Studies and Information Centres | | | | |
| Arab Industrial Development and Mining Organization | | | | |
| **West Africa** | | | | |
| Economic Community for West African States (ECOWAS) | Create an economic and monetary union.. | 1975 | Nigeria | P.M.B. 12745, Lagos |
| Fund for Cooperation, Compensation and Development (ECOWAS FUND) | Provides compensation to member states and guarantees in respect of foreign investment. | 1977 | Togo | B P. 2704 Lome |
| West African Economic Community (CEAO) | Promote the harmonized and balanced development of the economic activities of member states. | 1974 | Burkina Faso | B.P. 643, Ouagadougou |
| Mano River Union (MRU) | Expand trade and ensure a fair distribution of the benefits from economic cooperation.. | 1973 | Sierra Leone | P.M.Bag 133, Freetown |
| Council of the Entente | Promote economic development and integration of the region provide a guarantee fund. | 1959 | Cote d'Ivoire | B.P. 3734, Abidjan |
| Central Bank of West Africa States (BCEAO) | Promote the economic and social development of the member states, etc. (assumed to be the same as for BDEAC. | 1975 | Senegal | B.P. 3108 Dakar |
| West African Development Bank (BOAD) | Promote balanced development of the member states and bring about West African economic integration. | 1973 | Togo | B.P. 1172, Lome |
| West African Monetary Union | | | | |
| Liptako-Gourma Region Development Authority | Establish a preferential trade area and eventually a common market.. | 1970 | | |
| Niger Basin Authority (NBA) | Achieve most effective use of the water and other natural resources of the River Niger basin.. | 1964 | Niger | B.P. 729, Niamey |
| Organization of the Development of the Senegal River (OMVS) | Promote economic cooperation and trade; harness the resources of the Senegal River. | 1972 | | |

| West African Rice Development Association (WARDA) | Cooperate in rice research and training in rice farming | 1970 | | |
|---|---|---|---|---|
| Cattle and Meat Economic Community of the Council of the Entente States (CEBV) | Promote production, processing and marketing of cattle and meat at the national level, among member countries, and with third countries , etc. | 1970 | | |
| Interstate Permanent Committee for Drought Control in the Sahelian Zone (ICDCS) | Organize joint efforts to control drought and its effects in the Sudan-Sahel Zone | 1973 | | |
| West African Development Bank (WADB) | Promote balanced development of member states and achieve economic integration of West Africa | 1973 | | |
| Union Economique et Monetaire de lAfrique de l'Ouest (UEMOA) | Aims at promoting the free movement of people, goods and capital eventually leading to common market | 1995 | | |
| **Union Economique et Monetaire Ouest Afreaine (UEMOA) =** | **Promote economic and monetary union with single currency, the CFA Franc** | **1994** | | |
| **Inter-sub-regional** | | | | |
| African and Mauritian Common Organization (OCAM) | Strengthen cooperation and solidarity between African states and Mauritius to accelerate their economic, etc | 1964 | | |
| Lake Chad Basin Commission (LCBC) | Regulate and control the utilization of water and other natural resources in the basin. | 1964 | Chad | B.P. 727, N'Djamena |
| Commission du Bassin de la Riviere Kagera | Integrate the development of the Kagera River basin. | 1977 | | |
| African and Malagasy Sugar Agreement | Ensure regular outlets and supplies for sugar exporting and importing member countries. | 1966 | | |
| African and Malagasy Coffee Organization (OAMCAF) | Coordinate the interests of member countries within the International Coffee Organization. | 1960 | | |
| Joint Anti-locust and Anti-aviarian Organization (OCLALAV) | Destroy insect pests, in particular the desert locust and granivorous birds particularly the quela-quela. | 1965 | | |
| African and Malagasy Union of Development Banks (UAMBD) | Serves as center for collection and distribution of documentation, and for training and research. | 1962 | | |
| **D. OTHER INSTITUTIONS** | | | | |
| **International Institutions** | | | | |
| The World Bank (IBRD) | Help raise the standard of living in developing countries. | 1945 | USA | 1818 H Street, N.W., Washington, DC. 20433 |
| International Development Association (IDA) | The same as for the World Bank, but gives assistance on terms that bear less heavily on the balance of payments of the borrowing countries. | 1960 | USA | 1818 H Street, NW., Washington, DC., 20433 |
| International Finance Corporation (IFC) | Assist economic development in its less developed member countries by promoting the growth of the private sector of their economics. | 1956 | USA | 1818 H Street, NW., Washington, DC., 20433 |
| United Nations Capital Development Fund (UNCDF) | Assist developing countries in the development of their economies by supplementing the existing sources of capital assistance. | 1966 | USA | c/o UNDP, One United Nations Plaza, New York, NY. 10017 |
| European Investment Bank (EIB) | Finance investment promoting economic development in EU. Its activities have been extended to cover the ACP countries. | 1958 | Belgium | 100, Boulevard Konrad Adeauer, L 2950- Luxembourg |
| Nordic Development Fund (NDF) | Offer credits to the least developed low and lower middle income countries. | 1989 | Finland | P.O.Box 185, Helsinki |
| The OPEC Fund for International Development | Provide financial assistance to other developing countries on concessional terms. | 1976 | Austria | P.O.Box 995, Vienna |
| Abu Dhabi Fund for Development (ADFD) | Provide assistance to Arab, African and Asian countries for the development of their economies. | 1971 | United Arab Emirates | P.O.Box 814, Abu Dhabi |
| Arab African International Bank (AAIB) | Finance international trade and promote economic development in Arab and African countries. | 1964 | Egypt | P.O.Box 1143, Cairo |

428

| | | | | |
|---|---|---|---|---|
| Arab Authority for Agricultural Investment and Development (AAAID) | Function as a development agency specifically concerned with the improvement of agriculture and agro-industries in the Arab region.. | 1978 | Sudan | P.O.Box 2101, Khartoum |
| Arab Fund for Economic and Social Development (AFESD) | Contribute towards solving the food problem, attaining a greater degree of Arab economic integration. | 1971 | Kuwait | P.O.Box 21923, Safat 13080 |
| Arab International Bank | Undertake banking, financial and commercial transactions relating to economic development. | 1971 | Egypt | P.O.Box 1563, Cairo |
| Arab Investment Company SAA (TAIC) | Promote and invest in development projects in Arab countries. | 1974 | Saudi Arabia | P.O.Box 4009, Riyadh |
| Arab Mining Company (ARMICO) | Promote mineral development and mineral-related industries in Arab countries through equity investments | 1975 | Jordan | P.O.Box 20198, Amman |
| Arab Bank for Economic Development in Africa (BADEA) | Foster economic, financial and technical cooperation between Arab countries and countries in the Arab W World.. | 1975 | Sudan | P.O.Box 2640, Khartoum |
| Arab Monetary Fund (AMF) | Assist member countries in eliminating payments and trade restrictions, in developing capital markets. | 1977 | United Arab Emirates | P.O.Box 2818, Abu Dhabi |
| Kuwait Fund for Arab Economic Development | Provide assistance to developing countries in their efforts towards development. | 1961 | Kuwait | P.O.Box 2921. Safat 13030 |
| Arab Organization for Agricultural Development (AOAD) | Develop natural and human resources in the agricultural sector, increase agricultural productive efficiency. | 1972 | Sudan | P.O.Box 474, Khartoum |
| The Arab Planning Institute - Kuwait | Conduct training programs, develop research activities, and render advisory services. | 1966 | Kuwait | P.O.Box 5834, Safat 13059 |
| Arab Trade Financing Program (ATFP) | Develop and promote trade among Arab countries and enhance the competitive ability of Arab exporters. | 1989 | United Arab Emirates | P.O.Box 26799, Abu Dhabi |
| Saudi Fund for Development (SFD) | Finance development projects in developing countries by providing concessionary loans. | 1974 | Saudi Arabia | P.O.Box 50483, Riyadh |
| Islamic Development Bank (IDB) | Foster economic development and social progress of member countries and Muslim communities, in accordance with the principles of the Shari'ah. | 1975 | Saudi Arabia | P.O.Box 5925, Jeddah |
| Inter -Arab Investment Guarantee Cooperation (IAIGE) | Provides insurance coverage for inter-Arab investments and for export credits. | 1974 | Kuwait | P.O.Box 23568, Al Shuwaikih |
| League of Arab States | Seeks to promote closer ties among member states and coordinate their policies and their economic , cultural, and security plans, etc. | 1945 | Egypt | P.O.Box 11642. Cairo |
| International Livestock Research Institute (ILRI) | Improve animal agriculture throughout the developing world. | 1995 ? | Ethiopia and Kenya | Addis Ababa and Nairobi |

Source : - ª ECA, 1994, *Bulletin of ECA-Sponsored Institutions*, Addis Ababa, Ethiopia.
    - UNIDO, 1983, *Financial Resources for Industrial Projects in Developing Countries*, Third Edition, Volume 1, Vienna.
    - FAO, 1980, *Regional Food Plan for Africa*, Rome.
    - IMF, 1995, *Directory of Economic, Commodity, and Development Organizations 1995*, Washington, DC.
    - Others

429

## ANNEX 5.1

**MAIN TECHNOLOGIES IN USE FOR PROCESSING SELECTED AGRICULTURAL COMMODITIES AND INDICATIONS OF THE MAIN GROWING AREAS OF SUCH COMMODITIES IN THE CONTINENT.**

### Starch and Sugar Crops
- Rice: cleaning, hulling, pearling, polishing and grading
- Sorghum: grinding—Sudan, Egypt and the drier areas of Africa.
- Millet: grinding—drier areas of Africa.
- Maize: shelling, husking, debranning, degerming, grinding
- Wheat: cleaning, scouring, tempering, grinding, bolting
- Barley:—North Africa.
- Cassava: peeling, grating, pressing and drying—tropical and subtropical Africa.
- Yam: grinding
- Sugar cane: (raw sugar) shredding, crushing, clarifying, sedimenting, evaporating, crystallizing and centrifuging—Mauritius, Sudan, etc.

### Vegetable Fibers
- Cotton: ginning and baling—Egypt, Sudan, Nigeria, etc.
- Sisal: decorticating, drying, combing, grading and baling—Tanzania and other East African countries.
- Kenaf: decorticating—Nigeria, Egypt, South Africa, etc.

### Beverages
- Tea: withering, rolling, sifting, fermenting, firing or drying, dry sifting and packing—East Africa.
- Cacao: roasting, shelling, kernel grinding, expressing cacao butter, pulverizing cake—West Africa.
- Kola ( cola mitida): splitting pods, extracting seeds, sweating, washing and drying—West Africa and Sudan.
- Coffee: (wet process) depulping, fermenting, washing, drying, hulling, polishing and grading—Cote d'Ivoire, East Africa, etc.

### Vegetable Oils and Fats
- Oil palm: sterilizing, stripping, centrifuging or hydraulic pressing, purifying, separating nuts and pericap residue, drying and cracking nuts and separating kernels and shell fragments—West and other parts of Africa.
- Coconut: nut splitting, drying (to make copra), extracting oil and other operations for making other products, such as coconut coir fiber —East and West Africa.
- Cashew nut: roasting or solvent extracting (to remove poisonous oil) and kernel extracting—East Africa, Egypt and Nigeria.
- Sesame: reaping, binding and threshing—Sudan and East and West Africa.
- Sunflower: decorticating and oil extracting
- Melon seed: grinding into flour and oil extracting—Sudan.
- Castor seed: oil extracting—South Africa.
- Safflower: decorticating and oil extraction
- Shea butter: drying, dehusking and oil extraction—West and Central Africa.
- Groundnut: shelling and oil extracting—West, East and Central Africa, Sudan and Libya.

430

- Soybean: pressing (expeller) or solvent extracting
- Cotton seed: delinting, decorticating, separating meats, cooking, oil extracting
- Peanut:—East and West Africa.
- Niger seed:—Africa.
- Olive: pressing—North Africa and South Africa.

**Fruits**
- Banana:—Cameroon, Somalia and Cote d'Ivoire.
- Pineapple: canning (for distant export destination)— South Africa.
- Mango:—many countries in Africa.
- Avocado pear: oil extracting—South Africa.
- Papaya: latex straining and drying
- Date palm:—North Africa.

**Spices** (drying, grinding, special processing)
- Cloves: drying and distilling — Tanzania and Madagascar.
- Chilies: — East and West Africa.
- Vanilla fragrans: dipping in hot water, fermenting, drying and maturing—Seychelles Islands, Madagascar, Comoros islands and Reunion.
- Essential oils: distilling or expressing or solvent extracting —Algeria, Reunion, Egypt, East Africa, etc.

**Drugs and Insecticides**
- Cinchona tree: bark drying, grinding, extracting, neutralizing and recrystalizing to quinine sulfate—Congo.
- Senna: drying—Egypt
- Pyrethrum flowers: drying, sorting and extracting pyrethrin—Kenya, Tanzania and Congo K.
- Cola(nuts): extracting caffeine for making soft drinks, such as Coca Cola.
- Acacia (Senegal and sayal): bleaching in the sun— Sudan and other North African countries.
- Copals:—East and West Africa.

**Tans**
- Wattle (bark): drying and grinding followed by extracting—South Africa and East Africa.
- Mangrove (bark): extracting—East Africa.

**Others**
- Rubber (hevea): coagulating (latex), rolling, drying, curing and smoking—Liberia, Nigeria and  Congo.
- Tobacco: curing (flue- sun-, air- and fire-curing)—Zimbabwe, Malawi.

431

| ANNEX 5.2 PRODUCTION OF SELECTED PROCESSED AGRICULTURAL AND RELATED PRODUCTS IN THE CONTINENT | | | | | | | | | | |
|---|---|---|---|---|---|---|---|---|---|---|
| Year | 1961 | 1965 | 1970 | 1975 | 1980 | 1985 | 1990 | 1992 | 1993 | 1994 |
| Food, beverages and stimulants (mt) | | | | | | | | | | |
| Sugar centrifugal | 2.86 | 3.34 | 4.65 | 5.31 | 6.09 | 7.57 | 7.78 | 8 | 7.21 | 6.58 |
| Malt | ... | ... | 0.01 | 0.02 | 0.55 | 1.3 | 1.4 | | | |
| Olive oil | ... | 0.14 | 0.15 | 0.3 | 0.22 | 0.2 | 0.24 | 0.22 | 0.33 | 0.23 |
| Olive oil | 0.08 | 0.12 | 0.14 | 0.31 | 0.21 | 0.2 | 0.24 | 0.39 | 0.21 | 0.3 |
| Cocoa powder (1000 t) | ... | ... | 20.1 | 27.8 | 46.1 | 49.4 | 48.5 | ... | ... | ... |
| Cocoa butter (1000 t) | ... | ... | 42.6 | 53 | 36.2 | 42.3 | 46.4 | ... | ... | ... |
| Chocolate (1000 t) | ... | ... | 23.8 | 31.2 | 41.8 | 55.5 | 67.7 | ... | ... | ... |
| Slaughtered meat | 3.88 | 4.3 | 5.01 | 5.4 | 6.63 | 7.62 | 8.52 | 8.77 | 8.93 | 9 |
| Indig. cattle meat | 1.97 | 2.13 | 2.41 | 2.57 | 3.1 | 3.33 | 3.52 | 3.62 | 3.72 | 3.74 |
| Beef and veal | 1.88 | 2.07 | 2.35 | 2.46 | 3.03 | 3.26 | 3.34 | 3.47 | 3.53 | 3.51 |
| Buffalo meat | 0.08 | 0.09 | 0.09 | 0.11 | 0.12 | 0.14 | 0.14 | 0.15 | 0.15 | 0.16 |
| Mutton and lamb | 0.47 | 0.51 | 0.61 | 0.6 | 0.73 | 0.78 | 0.89 | 0.89 | 0.9 | 0.88 |
| Goat meat | 0.31 | 0.33 | 0.38 | 0.39 | 0.48 | 0.51 | 0.63 | 0.64 | 0.64 | 0.65 |
| Indig. sheep and goat meat | 0.79 | 0.86 | 1 | 1.01 | 1.22 | 1.31 | 1.54 | 1.55 | 1.56 | 1.55 |
| Pig meat | 0.19 | 0.21 | 0.26 | 0.3 | 0.34 | 0.43 | 0.6 | 0.63 | 0.68 | 0.69 |
| Poultry meat | 0.37 | 0.44 | 0.6 | 0.81 | 1.1 | 1.56 | 1.89 | 1.94 | 1.97 | 2.04 |
| Milk , total | 11.01 | 11.51 | 13.66 | 14.14 | 17.01 | 18.52 | 21.28 | 20.83 | 20.5 | 20.63 |
| Cow milk | 7.83 | 8.02 | 9.59 | 9.73 | 11.53 | 13.09 | 15.41 | 14.96 | 14.76 | 14.69 |
| Sheep milk | 0.55 | 0.61 | 0.71 | 0.78 | 1.29 | 1.3 | 1.4 | 1.37 | 1.3 | 1.32 |
| Goat milk | 1.31 | 1.42 | 1.5 | 1.55 | 1.87 | 1.8 | 2.01 | 1.96 | 1.92 | 1.95 |
| Dry whole milk (1000t) | 6.37 | 7.89 | 10.39 | 12.07 | 11.91 | 16.33 | 16.24 | 17.64 | 14.04 | 14.25 |
| Dry milk skimmed (1000t) | 4.59 | 5.62 | 13.72 | 19.63 | 21.46 | 24.03 | 25.54 | 30.52 | 20.57 | 27.99 |
| Milk evap./condensed (1000t) | 35.87 | 39.29 | 43.51 | 57.67 | 38.32 | 31.55 | 31.43 | 27.3 | 24.4 | 24.16 |
| Butter and ghee | 0.14 | 0.13 | 0.16 | 0.15 | 0.15 | 0.16 | 0.18 | 0.18 | 0.17 | 0.17 |
| Cheese, total | 0.25 | 0.27 | 0.3 | 0.33 | 0.37 | 0.41 | 0.47 | 0.48 | 0.48 | 0.48 |
| Ethyl alcohol for all purposes (m HL) | ... | ... | 0.44 | 0.64 | 0.61 | 0.33 | 0.32 | ... | ... | ... |
| Distilled alcohol beverages, excl. ethyl alcohol (m HL) | ... | ... | 0.26 | 0.57 | 0.6 | 1.11 | 1.02 | ... | ... | ... |
| Wine | 2.04 | 2.4 | 1.48 | 1.23 | 1.15 | 1.03 | 1.07 | 1.11 | 1.15 | 1.06 |
| Beer (m HL) | ... | ... | 17.8 | 28.7 | 35.1 | 46.8 | 57.3 | ... | ... | ... |
| Soft drinks (m HL) | ... | ... | 5.86 | 15 | 23.6 | 34.8 | 33.4 | ... | ... | ... |
| Mineral waters (m HL) | ... | ... | 0.8 | 1.8 | 2.9 | 3.2 | 3.6 | ... | ... | ... |
| Cigarettes (b units) | ... | ... | 84.3 | 121 | 150 | 178 | 185 | ... | ... | ... |
| Textiles | | | | | | | | | | |
| Wool. scoured (1000 t) | 96.7 | 102.4 | 120 | 104.4 | 95.9 | 118.7 | 119.8 | 123.3 | 121.7 | 118.3 |
| Wool yarn, pure and mixed (1000 t) | ... | ... | 25.5 | 29.5 | 28.4 | 31.9 | 28.9 | ... | ... | ... |
| Cotton yarn, pure and mixed (1000 t) | ... | ... | 282.2 | 329.4 | 417 | 416 | 448 | ... | ... | ... |
| Cotton woven fabrics (m m2) | ... | ... | 1952 | 2231 | 2270 | 1857 | 1515 | ... | ... | ... |
| Woolen woven fabrics (m m2 ) | ... | ... | 26 | 21 | 28.7 | 50.9 | 52.3 | ... | ... | ... |
| Linen fabrics (t) | ... | ... | ... | 2371 | 2343 | 4000 | 5100 | ... | ... | ... |
| Jute fabrics (1000 t) | ... | ... | 28.3 | 34.6 | 34.6 | 28.3 | 25.4 | ... | ... | ... |

| | | | | | | | | | | |
|---|---|---|---|---|---|---|---|---|---|---|
| Woven fabrics of cellulosic fibers  (m m2) | ... | ... | 187..9 | 103.2 | 34.1 | 26.5 | 26.5 | ... | ... | ... |
| Cordage, rope and twine (1000 t) | ... | ... | 46.1 | 45.6 | 54.2 | 34.6 | 38.3 | ... | ... | ... |
| Leather and leather goods | | | | | | | | | | |
| Cattle hides, fresh (1000 t) | 301.8 | 323.7 | 362.7 | 377.7 | 458.8 | 478.5 | 529 | 543.5 | 563.6 | 557.7 |
| Sheep skins (1000 t) | 83.7 | 86.8 | 109.1 | 110.9 | 132.1 | 144.5 | 158.8 | 160.5 | 162.9 | 161.9 |
| Goat skins  (1000 t) | 58.4 | 62.7 | 68.6 | 72.2 | 85.6 | 91.5 | 110.5 | 111.4 | 112.1 | 112.9 |
| Heavy leather (t) | ... | ... | ... | ... | ... | ... | ... | ... | ... | ... |
| Light leather (m m2) | ... | ... | 11.8 | 10.1 | 11.8 | 10.8 | 11.8 | ... | ... | ... |
| Footwear, total production, excl. rubber footwear (m pairs) | ... | ... | 126.7 | 158.7 | 204.4 | 199 | 198.5 | ... | ... | ... |
| Forest products | | | | | | | | | | |
| Roundwood (m cum) | ... | 260.9 | 294 | 327.1 | 431.4 | 447.9 | 513.9 | 526.2 | 539.7 | 553.1 |
| Sawnwood (m cum) | ... | 14.42 | 18.69 | 5.84 | 7.66 | 7.81 | 8.69 | 8.2 | 8.3 | 8.2 |
| Wood-based panels (m cum) | ... | 0.55 | 0.86 | 1.05 | 1.52 | 1.84 | 1.89 | 1.55 | 1.62 | 1.61 |
| Veneer sheets (m cum) | ... | 0.15 | 0.25 | 0.25 | 0.51 | 0.54 | 0.58 | 0.48 | 0.51 | 0.51 |
| Plywood (m cum) | ... | 0.24 | 0.31 | 0 | 0 | 0 | 0 | 0 | 0 | 0 |
| Particle board (m cum | ... | 0 | 0 | 0 | 0 | 0 | 0 | 0 | 0 | 0 |
| Fiberboard (m cum) | ... | 0.11 | 0.13 | 0.17 | 0.1 | 0.12 | 0.13 | 0.13 | 0.14 | 0.14 |
| Woodpulp, for pulp and paper m t) | ... | 0.71 | 0.84 | 1.18 | 1.43 | 1.64 | 2.28 | 2.31 | 2.8 | 2.63 |
| Chemical wood pulp (m t) | ... | 0.42 | 0.46 | 0.48 | 0.7 | 0.64 | 1.31 | 1.34 | 1.61 | 1.47 |
| Unbleached sulfate pulp (m t) | ... | 0.32 | 0.3 | 0.3 | 0.41 | 0.39 | 0.76 | 0.8 | 0.96 | 0.87 |
| Bleached sulfate pulp (m t) | ... | 0.1 | 0.17 | 0.16 | 0.24 | 0.19 | 0.45 | 0.44 | 0.53 | 0.48 |
| Paper and paperboard (m t) | ... | 0.6 | 0.9 | 1.17 | 1.71 | 2.14 | 2.74 | 2.69 | 2.64 | 2.34 |
| Newsprint (m t) | ... | 0.06 | 0.17 | 0.22 | 0.24 | 0.35 | 0.42 | 0.41 | 0.39 | 0.2 |
| Printing and writing paper (m t) | ... | 0.1 | 0.15 | 0.18 | 0.34 | 0.44 | 0.62 | 0.59 | 0.54 | 0.6 |
| Other paper and paperboard (m t) | ... | 0.44 | 0.59 | 0.77 | 1.13 | 1.35 | 1.7 | 1.7 | 1.72 | 1.54 |
| Wrapping and packing paper and board (m t) | ... | 0.25 | 0.37 | 0.12 | 0.87 | 1.16 | 1.47 | 1.47 | 1.5 | 1.34 |
| Fishery products (mt) | | | | | | | | | | |
| Fish, fresh, chilled or frozen | ... | ... | ... | ... | 0.2 | 0.4 | 0.38 | ... | ... | ... |
| Fish, dried, salted or smoked | ... | ... | ... | ... | 0.26 | 0.27 | 0.38 | ... | ... | ... |
| Crustaceans and molluscs, fresh, frozen, dried, salted, etc. | ... | ... | ... | ... | 0.04 | 0.11 | 0.13 | ... | ... | ... |
| Fish products and preparations | ... | ... | ... | ... | 0.1 | 0.13 | 0.21 | ... | ... | ... |
| Crustaceans and molluscs products and preparations | ... | ... | ... | ... | ... | ... | ... | ... | ... | ... |
| Oils and fats, crude or refined | ... | ... | ... | ... | 0.04 | 0.04 | 0.02 | ... | ... | ... |
| Meals, solubles and similar feedstuffs | ... | ... | ... | ... | 0.19 | 0.15 | 0.15 | ... | ... | ... |
| Agricultural equipment and machinery | | | | | | | | | | |
| Tractors in use (1000 units) | ... | 310 | 370 | 408 | 444 | 511 | 545 | ... | ... | ... |
| Harvesters-threshers in use (1000 units) | ... | ... | ... | ... | 42.6 | 49.3 | 70.9 | ... | ... | ... |

Source: - FAO, 1969, 1972, 1977, 1986, 1991, 1993, 1994, *FAO Production Yearbook,* Rome
  - FAO, , 1981, 1982, 1986, 1991, 1993, *FAO Yearbook of Forest Products*, Rome.
  - FAO , 1978, 1985, 1987, 1991, *FAO Yearbook of Fishery Statistics*, Rome.
  - FAO, 1994, *FAOSTATdata*, Statistics Division, Rome.
  - United Nations, 1978, 1984, 1991, *Industrial Statistics Yearbook*, New York.

ANNEX 5.3
TRADE OF SELECTED PROCESSED AGRICULTURAL AND RELATED PRODUCTS IN THE CONTINENT

| | Imports | | | | | | Exports | | | | | | Net trade (+ =exports, - = imports) | | | | | |
|---|---|---|---|---|---|---|---|---|---|---|---|---|---|---|---|---|---|---|
| Year | 1965 | 1970 | 1975 | 1980 | 1985 | 1990 | 1965 | 1970 | 1975 | 1980 | 1985 | 1990 | 1965 | 1970 | 1975 | 1980 | 1985 | 1990 |
| **Food and beverages (mt)** | | | | | | | | | | | | | | | | | | |
| Sugar, total, raw equivalent | 1.56 | 1.52 | 1.86 | 3.18 | 3.19 | 3.58 | 1.58 | 2.13 | 1.74 | 2.28 | 2.64 | 2.52 | 0.02 | 0.61 | -0.12 | -0.9 | -0.55 | -1.06 |
| Animal oil, fat and grease | 0.16 | 0.15 | 0.3 | 0.42 | 0.46 | 0.37 | - | - | 0.01 | - | 0.25 | 0.18 | -0.16 | -0.15 | -0.29 | -0.42 | -0.21 | -0.19 |
| Soybean oil | 0.09 | 0.12 | 0.19 | 0.37 | 0.34 | 0.29 | - | - | - | - | - | - | -0.09 | -0.12 | -0.19 | -0.37 | -0.34 | -0.29 |
| Cotton seed oil | 0.06 | 0.08 | 0.22 | 0.23 | 0.18 | 0.12 | 0.01 | 0.03 | 0.01 | - | - | - | -0.05 | -0.05 | -0.21 | -0.23 | -0.18 | -0.12 |
| Groundnut oil | 0.01 | 0.01 | - | - | - | - | 0.25 | 0.29 | 0.25 | 0.14 | 0.07 | 0.18 | 0.24 | 0.28 | 0.25 | 0.14 | 0.07 | 0.18 |
| Olive oil | - | 0.03 | 0.02 | 0.06 | 0.03 | - | 0.05 | 0.04 | 0.06 | 0.06 | 0.05 | 0.08 | - | 0.01 | 0.04 | 0 | -0.02 | -0.08 |
| Sunflower oil | 0.02 | 0.09 | 0.03 | 0.15 | 0.42 | 0.51 | - | - | - | 0.01 | 0.02 | 0.01 | -0.02 | -0.09 | -0.03 | -0.14 | -0.4 | -0.5 |
| Rape and mustard oils | 0.02 | 0.09 | 0.03 | 0.15 | 0.42 | 0.51 | - | - | - | 0.01 | 0.02 | 0.01 | -0.02 | -0.09 | -0.03 | -0.01 | -0.4 | -0.5 |
| Palm oil | 0.02 | 0.02 | 0.03 | 0.17 | 0.3 | 0.82 | 0.28 | 0.21 | 0.22 | 0.14 | 0.09 | 0.21 | 0.26 | 0.19 | 0.19 | -0.03 | -0.21 | -0.61 |
| Coconut oil | 0.02 | 0.03 | 0.03 | 0.03 | 0.02 | 0.02 | - | 0.01 | 0.01 | 0.02 | 0.04 | 0.04 | -0.02 | -0.02 | -0.02 | -0.01 | 0.02 | 0.02 |
| Oil cake, meal, veg. oil residue | 0.02 | 0.07 | 0.11 | 0.23 | 0.81 | 1.23 | 0.87 | 1.24 | 1.28 | 1.28 | 0.59 | 0.84 | 0.85 | 1.17 | 1.17 | 1.05 | -0.22 | -0.39 |
| Margarine, imitation lard, etc. | 0.02 | 0.02 | 0.01 | 0.03 | 0.03 | 0.07 | - | - | - | - | - | - | -0.02 | -0.02 | -0.01 | -0.03 | -0.03 | -0.07 |
| Poultry meat | - | - | 0.01 | 0.1 | 0.11 | 0.11 | - | - | - | 0.01 | - | - | - | - | -0.01 | -0.09 | -0.11 | -0.11 |
| Canned meat nes | 0.02 | 0.02 | 0.03 | 0.04 | 0.05 | 0.04 | 0.03 | 0.03 | 0.02 | 0.02 | 0.01 | - | 0.01 | 0.01 | -0.01 | -0.02 | -0.04 | -0.04 |
| Milk dry | 0.05 | 0.09 | 0.15 | 0.31 | 0.45 | 0.36 | ... | - | - | - | - | 0.01 | ... | -0.09 | -0.15 | -0.31 | -0.45 | -0.35 |
| Butter (incl ghee for prod) | 0.03 | 0.05 | 0.05 | 0.14 | 0.17 | 0.17 | - | - | - | - | - | - | -0.03 | -0.05 | -0.05 | -0.14 | -0.17 | -0.17 |
| Wine, vermouth & similar bev | ... | 0.22 | 0.18 | 0.16 | 0.19 | 0.12 | ... | 1.47 | 0.6.3 | 0.3 | 0.17 | 0.04 | ... | 1.25 | 0.45 | 0.14 | -0.02 | -0.08 |
| Beer | ... | 0.05 | 0.12 | 0.05 | 0.06 | 0.08 | ... | 0.02 | - | 0.02 | 0.02 | 0.04 | ... | -0.03 | -0.12 | -0.03 | -0.04 | -0.04 |
| **Forest products (mt)** | | | | | | | | | | | | | | | | | | |
| Roundwood | 0.57 | 0.62 | 0.56 | 0.79 | 1.01 | 0.71 | 6.15 | 7.34 | 5.25 | 6.37 | 4.63 | 4.97 | 5.58 | 6.72 | 4.69 | 5.58 | 3.62 | 4.26 |
| Sawnwood | 0.26 | 0.36 | 2.33 | 3.18 | 4.52 | 3.46 | 5.64 | 6.85 | 0.92 | 0.9 | 0.89 | 1.42 | 5.38 | 6.49 | -1.41 | -2.28 | -3.63 | -2.04 |
| Wood-based panels | 0.22 | 0.23 | 0.32 | 0.54 | 0.55 | 0.3 | 0.28 | 0.39 | 0.27 | 0.33 | 0.33 | 0.27 | 0.06 | 0.16 | -0.05 | -0.21 | -0.22 | -0.03 |
| Veneer sheets | 0.05 | 0.4 | 0.04 | 0.04 | 0.04 | 0.02 | 0.11 | 0.17 | 0.11 | 0.2 | 0.21 | 0.15 | 0.06 | -0.23 | 0.07 | 0.16 | 0.17 | 0.13 |
| Plywood | 0.09 | 0.1 | 0.17 | 0.27 | 0.45 | 0.26 | 0.11 | 0.13 | 0.1 | 0.09 | 0.11 | 0.05 | 0.02 | 0.03 | -0.07 | -0.18 | -0.34 | -0.21 |
| Particle board | 0.02 | 0.02 | 0.04 | 0.1 | 0.01 | 0.02 | - | - | - | - | - | - | 0.06 | -0.02 | -0.02 | -0.04 | -0.1 | -0.01 | 0.04 |
| Fiberboard | 0.05 | 0.08 | 0.07 | 0.14 | 0.04 | - | 0.05 | 0.07 | 0.06 | 0.03 | 0.01 | 0.02 | 0 | -0.01 | -0.01 | -0.11 | -0.03 | 0.02 |
| Wood pulp | 0.09 | 0.17 | 0.15 | 0.32 | 0.2 | 0.27 | 0.03 | 0.45 | 0.67 | 0.64 | 0.54 | 0.58 | -0.06 | 0.28 | 0.52 | 0.32 | 0.34 | 0.31 |
| Chemical wood pulp | 0.06 | 0.14 | 0.14 | 0.31 | 0.19 | 0.24 | 0.16 | 0.25 | 0.26 | 0.4 | 0.34 | 0.4 | 0.1 | 0.11 | 0.12 | 0.09 | 0.15 | 0.16 |
| Unbleached sulfate pulp | ... | 0.01 | 0.02 | 0.02 | 0.06 | 0.03 | ... | 0.07 | 0.14 | 0.33 | 0.27 | 0.31 | ... | 0.06 | 0.12 | 0.31 | 0.21 | 0.28 |
| Bleached sulfate pulp | ... | 0.05 | 0.06 | 0.21 | 0.09 | 0.17 | ... | 0.03 | 0.03 | 0.09 | 0.07 | 0.08 | ... | -0.02 | -0.03 | -0.12 | -0.02 | -0.09 |
| Paper and paperboard | 0.58 | 0.84 | 0.73 | 0.93 | 1.2 | 1.2 | 0.05 | 0.04 | 0.09 | 0.16 | 0.3 | 0.13 | -0.53 | -0.8 | -0.64 | -0.77 | -0.9 | -1.07 |
| Newsprint | 0.14 | 0.14 | 0.11 | 0.15 | 0.12 | 0.15 | - | - | 0.02 | 0.07 | 0.21 | 0.08 | -0.14 | -0.14 | -0.09 | -0.08 | 0.09 | -0.07 |
| Printing and writing paper | 0.14 | 0.24 | 0.21 | 0.28 | 0.37 | 0.39 | 0.02 | - | 0.01 | 0.02 | 0.06 | 0.02 | -0.12 | -0.24 | -0.2 | -0.26 | -0.31 | -0.37 |
| Other paper and paperboard | 0.3 | 0.47 | 0.41 | 0.5 | 0.71 | 0.68 | 0.03 | 0.03 | 0.06 | 0.07 | 0.04 | 0.03 | -0.27 | -0.44 | -0.35 | -0.43 | -0.67 | -0.65 |
| Wrapping, packing paper, board | ... | 0.17 | 0.09 | 0.29 | 0.53 | 0.26 | ... | 0.01 | 0.03 | 0.03 | 0.02 | ... | ... | -0.16 | -0.06 | -0.26 | -0.51 | ... |
| **Fishery products (mt)** | | | | | | | | | | | | | | | | | | |
| Fish, fresh, chilled or frozen | 0.07 | 0.12 | 0.26 | 0.86 | 0.83 | 1.16 | 0.04 | 0.04 | 0.1 | 0.15 | 0.24 | 0.32 | -0.03 | -0.08 | -0.16 | -0.71 | -0.59 | -0.84 |
| Crustaceans, molluscs, fresh, etc. | - | - | - | - | - | 0.01 | 0.01 | 0.01 | 0.04 | 0.04 | 0.14 | 0.16 | 0.01 | 0.01 | 0.04 | 0.04 | 0.14 | 0.15 |
| Fish products and preparations | 0.03 | 0.06 | 0.1 | 0.18 | 0.1 | 0.08 | 0.08 | 0.09 | 0.13 | 0.08 | 0.11 | 0.13 | 0.05 | 0.03 | 0.03 | -0.1 | 0.01 | 0.05 |
| Oils and fats, crude or refined | - | - | - | - | 0.02 | 0.03 | 0.06 | 0.07 | 0.02 | - | - | - | 0.06 | 0.07 | 0.02 | - | -0.02 | -0.03 |
| Meals, similar animal feedstuffs | 0.01 | 0.02 | 0.02 | 0.03 | 0.16 | 0.15 | 0.31 | 0.23 | 0.23 | 0.04 | 0.01 | 0.01 | 0.3 | 0.21 | 0.21 | 0.01 | -0.15 | -0.14 |

| **Agricultural inputs** * | | | | | | | | | | | | | | | | | | |
| | 1989 | 1990 | 1991 | 1992 | 1993 | 1994 | 1989 | 1990 | 1991 | 1992 | 1993 | 1994 | 1989 | 1990 | 1991 | 1992 | 1993 | 1994 |
| Pesticides ($ m) | 620 | 491 | 481 | 515 | 502 | 505 | 57.8 | 56.5 | 110 | 93.8 | 103 | 121 | 562 | 435 | 371 | 421 | 399 | 384 |
| Tractors (1000) | 31.9 | 32.5 | 33.2 | 25.7 | 24.6 | 27.9 | 0.6 | 0.6 | 0.5 | 0.7 | 0.6 | 0.6 | 31.3 | 31.9 | 32.7 | 25 | 24 | 27.3 |

Source: - FAO, 1972, 1976, 1977, 1982, 1987, 1992, 1994, *FAO Trade Yearbook*, Rome.
- FAO, 1975, 1981, 1982, 1986, 1991, *FAO Yearbook of Forest Products*, Rome.     a  See annex 9.1 for fertilizers.

### ANNEX 5.4
## PRODUCTION OF SELECTED CHEMICALS AND RELATED PRODUCTS (ISIC 3511—3559 AND 3610—3699) IN THE CONTINENT (1000 t)

| Year | 1970 | 1975 | 1980 | 1985 | 1990 |
|---|---|---|---|---|---|
| Sulfur, recovered as byproduct | 53 | 269 | 285 | 346 | 371 |
| Sulfur recovered from pyrites etc. | 384 | 364 | 563 | 723 | 576 |
| Acetylene, pure C2H2 | 2.9 | 9.1 | 10 | 6.4 | 5.5 |
| Ethylene ,pure C2H4 | - | 5 | 31 | 79.3 | 41 |
| Methanol, pure CH3OH | - | - | 42.9 | 89.4 | 93 |
| Glycerin | 4.9 | 5.2 | 6.2 | 9.6 | 12.2 |
| Chlorine | 7 | 9 | 23 | 27 | 33 |
| Hydrochloric acid (100% HCl) | 3.1 | 136.5 | 144.7 | 119.4 | 205 |
| Sulfuric acid (H2SO4) | 1520 | 1458 | 3007 | 3797 | 4773 |
| Nitric acid (100% HNO3) | - | 66 | 63 | 104 | 107 |
| Phosphoric acid (P2O5) | - | 102 | 824 | 1508 | 3229 |
| Ammonia ( 100% N) | - | 8 | 113 | 917 | 1133 |
| Caustic soda (NaOH) | 29 | 39 | 53 | 68 | 70 |
| Soda ash ( NaCO3) | 161 | 95 | 217 | 210 | 244 |
| Insecticides, fungicides, disinfectants etc. | 43.8 | 49.2 | 58.1 | 60.9 | 63.4 |
| Rubber, synthetic | 28.6 | 31.8 | 38.7 | 42.8 | 45.9 |
| Soap | 571 | 739 | 907 | 999 | 1151 |
| Washing powder and detergents | 87 | 115.2 | 275.5 | 302 | 455.5 |
| Carbon black | 26 | 40 | 45 | ... | ... |
| Explosives | 40.4 | 55.6 | 32.9 | 23.8 | 21.9 |
| Rubber inner tubes, for motor vehicles (1000 units) | 4890 | 5813 | 6144 | 5473 | 5342 |
| Tires for road motor vehicles (1000 units) | 5812 | 6638 | 8182 | 10016 | 14611 |
| Rubber footwear (million pairs) | 1 | 16.4 | 45.5 | 7.5 | 9.8 |
| Household ware of porcelain or china | 1.4 | 3 | 4.2 | 8.2 | 9.9 |
| Sanitary ceramic fittings (units) | 5094 | 6198 | 8688 | 18827 | 37936 |
| Glass bottles and containers (1000t) | 71 | 69 | 102 | 199 | 224 |
| Quicklime | 222 | 2363 | 3392 | 3359 | 3318 |
| Cement | 18204 | 23628 | 30900 | 41974 | 51790 |
| Ethyl alcohol for all purposes, 100% spirit | ... | 539 | 612 | 331 | 320 |

Source: United Nations, 1979, 1984, 1991, *Industrial Statistics Yearbook*, New York.

ANNEX 5.5
PRODUCTION OF BASIC METALS AND SELECTED RELATED PRODUCTS
( ISIC 3710—3720)  IN THE CONTINENT (1000t)

| | 1970 | 1975 | 1980 | 1985 | 1990 |
|---|---|---|---|---|---|
| Pig iron, foundry | 425 | 1440 | 1068 | 417 | 388 |
| Pig iron, steel-making | 4596 | 5888 | 8129 | 9156 | 8690 |
| Other ferro-alloys | 399 | 963 | 1602 | 1600 | 2128 |
| Ferro-chromium | ... | 500 | 978 | 867 | 1293 |
| Crude steel for castings | 270 | 353 | 276 | 273 | 332 |
| Crude steel ingots | 5149 | 7657 | 10975 | 11379 | 12593 |
| Angles, shapes and sections (total prod.) | 606 | 792 | 1812 | 460 | 567 |
| Plates (heavy), over 4.75 mm | 549 | 1213 | 1705 | 463 | 448 |
| Sheets under 3 mm, hot- rolled | 439 | 442 | 1187 | 1973 | 2781 |
| Sheets, galvanized | 285 | 319 | 509 | 55 | 81 |
| Wire, plain | 147 | 193 | 301 | 284 | 366 |
| Tube, welded | 174 | 467 | 734 | 688 | 685 |
| Steel castings in the rough state | 119 | 157 | 156 | 128 | 118 |
| Copper, blister and other unrefined | 1285.3 | 1344.3 | 1309.4 | 1267.1 | 1034.4 |
| Copper, refined, unwrought (total prod.) | 953.1 | 980.6 | 926.1 | 868.9 | 781.6 |
| Copper, primary, refined | 953.1 | 980.6 | 926.1 | 866.8 | 773.2 |
| Nickel unwrought | ... | 23 | 33.2 | 32.9 | 40.8 |
| Alumina, calcined equivalent | ... | 643 | 708 | 572 | 642 |
| Aluminum, unwrought (total prod.) | 165.4 | 272.5 | 432.4 | 430.8 | 572.6 |
| Aluminum, unwrought, primary | 165.4 | 272.5 | 432.4 | 430.8 | 569.2 |
| Aluminum plates, sheets, strips, foil | 5.4 | 9.5 | 18.5 | 16.5 | 45.1 |
| Lead, refined, unwrought (total prod.) | 143.5 | 98.4 | 117.4 | 113.7 | 107.1 |
| Zinc, unwrought (total prod.) | 117.2 | 117.4 | 104.5 | 122.6 | 63.7 |
| Tin, unwrought (total prod.) | 11.6 | 7.5 | 6.4 | 5 | 4.4 |
| Cadmium, unwrought | ... | 0.5 | 0.3 | 0.4 | 0.4 |

Source: United Nations, 1979, 1984, 1991, *Industrial Statistics Yearbook,* New York.

ANNEX 5.6
PRODUCTION OF SELECTED FABRICATED METAL PRODUCTS, MACHINERY AND EQUIPMENT
(ISIC 3811—3853) IN THE CONTINENT

| | Units | 1975 | 1980 | 1985 | 1990 | 1995* | 2000 |
|---|---|---|---|---|---|---|---|
| Metal products | | | | | | | |
| Locksmiths' wares, locks, padlocks, keys etc. | t | 1192 | 2094 | 1743 | 1743 | 2517 | 2555 |
| Hardware | t | ... | 491000 | 491000 | ... | 500000 | 530000 |
| Cables | 1000 t | 23.2 | 12.6 | 77.3 | 86.2 | 12 | 13 |
| Nails, screws, nuts, bolts, rivets, etc. | 1000 t | 869 | 155 | 160.6 | 130.4 | 147.8 | 154.6 |
| Non-electrical machinery | | | | | | | |
| Engines, diesel | units | 2437 | 7431 | 12035 | 8432 | 13800 | 18800 |
| Engines, internal combustion | 1000 units | 3 | 2 | 4 | 1 | 3 | 4 |
| Cultivators, scarifiers, weeders, hoes etc | units | 566 | 753 | 12480 | 138574 | 1200 | 1400 |
| Plows, animal- or tractor-operated | units | ... | 3978 | 1378 | 1379 | 230000 | 300000 |
| Seeders, planters | units | ... | 1429 | 1682 | ... | 1800 | 1900 |
| Combine harvesters | units | ... | 481 | 700 | ... | 1100 | 1300 |
| Mowers | units | ... | 2698 | 3431 | ... | 33000 | 36000 |
| Rakes | units | ... | 57016 | 744960 | ... | 800000 | 837000 |
| Fertilizer distributors | units | ... | 476 | 400 | ... | 500 | 550 |
| Threshing machines | units | ... | 48 | 48 | ... | 50 | 55 |
| Milling machines | units | ... | 10041 | 9682 | ... | 10000 | 10500 |
| Horticultural tractors | units | ... | 178742 | 112146 | ... | 150000 | 200000 |
| Tractors of 10 HP and over, other than industrial and road tractors | units | 4184 | 6668 | 12708 | 6132 | 10600 | 11000 |
| Drilling machines | units | ... | 34 | 209 | ... | 600 | 700 |
| Lathes | units | ... | 118 | 149 | ... | 178 | 200 |
| Milling machines | units | ... | 61 | 97 | ... | 200 | 250 |
| Other machine tools | units | ... | 38 | 240 | ... | 800 | 1100 |
| Concrete mixers | units | ... | 4687 | 4441 | ... | 4000 | 4500 |
| Stoves, ranges, cookers | 1000 units | 147 | 567 | 688 | 246 | 800 | 930 |
| Sewing machines | 1000 units | 66 | 61 | 34 | 15 | 25 | 30 |
| Pumps for liquids | 1000 units | 8 | 4 | 18 | 39 | 100 | 150 |
| Fork-lift trucks | units | ... | 1055 | 1055 | ... | 1080 | 1090 |
| Cranes | units | ... | 306 | 476 | ... | 650 | 750 |
| Refrigerators for household use | 1000 units | 437 | 558 | 892 | 988 | 1500 | 1700 |
| Washing machines for household use | 1000 units | 89 | 363 | 322 | 288 | 330 | 350 |
| Electrical equipment | | | | | | | |
| Motors, electric, of one HP and over | 1000 units | 571 | 384 | 315 | 843 | 950 | 1100 |
| Transformers of less than 5 KVA | 1000 units | ... | 139 | 244 | ... | 300 | 350 |
| Transformers of 5 KVA and over | units | 14542 | 14364 | 1584 | 798 | 14000 | 15000 |
| Television receivers | 1000 units | 543 | 1138 | 11330 | 5361 | 1250 | 13000 |
| Radio receivers | 1000 units | 1730 | 2096 | 1702 | 1395 | 1990 | 2150 |
| Telephones apparatus | 1000 units | 15 | 15 | 82 | 71 | 104 | 110 |

| | | | | | | | |
|---|---|---|---|---|---|---|---|
| Accumulators, electric, for motor vehicle | 1000 units | 2540 | 2966 | 3052 | 4004 | 4200 | 4600 |
| Lamps, electric | million units | 26 | 46 | 107 | 116 | 134 | 150 |
| Transport equipment | | | | | | | |
| Tankers | units | | 1 | - | | 1 | 2 |
| Other sea-going merchant vessels, launched | units | 19 | 8 | 7 | 9 | 3 | 6 |
| Goods wagons | units | | 175 | 175 | | 180 | 200 |
| Railway passenger carriages | units | 349 | 138 | 857 | 253 | 1100 | 1300 |
| Passenger cars, assembled from imported parts | 1000 units | 258 | 376 | 423 | 254 | 480 | 600 |
| Buses and motor coaches, assembled from imported parts | units | 14108 | 11779 | 10670 | 18940 | 25700 | 27400 |
| Lorries (trucks), incl. articulated vehicles, assembled from imported parts | units | 118.9 | 131.9 | 121.9 | 135 | 166800 | 181800 |
| Trailers and semi-trailers | units | 8286 | 25026 | 37314 | 42734 | 63500 | 75500 |
| Motor cycles, scooters etc. | 1000 units | 68 | 133 | 133 | 103 | 124 | 120 |
| Bicycles | 1000 units | 171 | 215 | 417 | 214 | 273 | 300 |
| Precision instruments | | | | | | | |
| Watches | 1000 units | 69 | 97 | 130 | ... | 114 | 120 |
| Clocks | 1000 units | ... | 149 | 130 | ... | 150 | 160 |

Source: - United Nations, 1984, 1991, *Industrial Statistics Yearbook,* Volume II, New York.
    - * ECA, 1993, *Report to the Eleventh Meeting of the Conference of African Ministers of Industry on Problems, Polices, Issues and Prospects by the Year 2000 of Africa's Basic Industries, namely: Chemical, Metal and Engineering Industries,* CAMl.11/4, Addis Ababa.

438

ANNEX 5.7
GROWTH RATES OF GDP, MVA AND TRADE OF SELECTED COUNTRY GROUPS AND AFRICA

Growth rates

| Year | Africa | | African LDCs | | Sub-Saharan Africa | | All developing countries | | | | |
|---|---|---|---|---|---|---|---|---|---|---|---|
| | 1975-1985 | 1985-1990 | 1975-1990 | 1985-1990 | 1975-1985 | 1985-1990 | 1975-1990 | 1985-1990 | | | |
| Growth of GDP, at constant 1980 prices (%) - total | 2.5 | 2.9 | 1.4 | 2.9 | 1.1 | 3.6 | 3.3 | 3.5 | | | |
| - Agriculture | 0.6 | 3.3 | 1.1 | 3.1 | 0.2 | 3.2 | 2.5 | 2.7 | | | |
| - Industry | 0.9 | 2.5 | 1.4 | 2.7 | -0.2 | 2.9 | 1.5 | 4.4 | | | |
| - Construction | 2.2 | 1 | 0 | 1.8 | -1.6 | 2.3 | 2 | 2.6 | | | |
| - Services | 4.4 | 3.5 | 1.8 | 2.8 | 2.7 | 3.9 | 4.4 | 3.4 | | | |
| Growth of MVA at constant 1980 prices (%) - total | 5.1 | 3.5 | 0.1 | 3.6 | 3.2 | 3.4 | 4.4 | 4.4 | | | |
| - Per capita | 2 | 0.4 | -2.8 | 0.4 | 0.1 | 0.1 | 1.9 | 2 | | | |
| Growth of exports, at current prices (%) - total | 5.5 | 2 | 2.9 | 2.6 | ... | ... | 7.8 | 10.1 | | | |
| -Food, beverages and tobacco | 3.6 | 1.5 | 3.8 | -1.7 | 4.3 | -0.3 | 5.8 | 7 | | | |
| - Crude materials, oils and fats | -0.2 | 3.5 | 1.1 | 3.9 | 0.7 | 8.9 | 5.5 | 7.5 | | | |
| - Mineral fuels | 7 | -0.9 | 13 | -14 | 6.9 | -0.6 | 4.7 | -1.1 | | | |
| - Non-ferrous metals | -2.2 | 10 | -3.5 | 8.6 | -3 | 10.8 | 5.7 | 11.6 | | | |
| - Manufactured goods | 8.3 | 19.7 | 12.6 | 6.3 | 6.5 | 10.9 | 16 | 20.6 | | | |
| Growth of imports, at current prices (%) - total | 3.4 | 7 | 2.9 | 8.3 | ... | ... | 7.8 | 11.9 | | | |
| - Food, beverages and tobacco | 5.4 | 2.8 | 5.3 | 2 | 4.3 | 3 | 5.4 | 9.4 | | | |
| - Crude materials, oils and fats | 8.9 | 4.2 | 6.8 | 8.5 | 7.6 | 3.5 | 9.9 | 9.5 | | | |
| - Mineral fuels | 6.2 | 6.3 | 2.2 | -5 | 3.7 | -2.9 | 9.5 | -1.3 | | | |
| - Non-ferrous metals | 2 | 11.3 | -3.9 | 12.7 | 0.4 | 11.7 | 8.4 | 14.9 | | | |
| - Manufactured goods | 2.2 | 8.4 | 2.1 | 11.3 | 2.1 | 8.5 | 7.5 | 14.9 | | | |

Growth of MVA at constant 1980 prices (index 1980=100)

| Year | 1980 | 1981 | 1982 | 1983 | 1984 | 1985 | 1986 | 1987 | 1988 | 1989 | 1990 |
|---|---|---|---|---|---|---|---|---|---|---|---|
| - Africa: total MVA | 100 | 106 | 113 | 115 | 116 | 122 | 127 | 133 | 140 | 141 | 148 |
| per capita MVA | 100 | 102 | 106 | 105 | 103 | 105 | 106 | 108 | 110 | 107 | 109 |
| -African LDCs: total MVA | 100 | 98 | 102 | 103 | 103 | 103 | 106 | 109 | 116 | 118 | 122 |
| per capita MVA | 100 | 95 | 96 | 95 | 93 | 90 | 90 | 89 | 92 | 90 | 90 |

Index numbers of manufacturing production (1985=100)

| Year | 1970 | 1975 | 1980 | 1989 | 1990 | 1991 | 1992 | 1993 | 1994 | | |
|---|---|---|---|---|---|---|---|---|---|---|---|
| - Africa | 47 | 60 | 85 | 117 | 124 | 134 | 127 | 122 | 144 | | |

Source : Compiled from  -  UNIDO, 1991, *1993, African Industry in Figures 1990 and 1993,* Vienna.
-  UNIDO, 1988, *Africa in Figures, 1988,* Vienna.
-  UNIDO, 1995, *International Yearbook of Industrial Statistics 1995,* Vienna.
-  ADB, 1996, *African Development Report 1996,* Abidjan.

439

| ANNEX 5.8 SHARE AND GROWTH OF MVA IN SELECTED COUNTRY GROUPS IN AFRICA | | | | | | | | | | |
|---|---|---|---|---|---|---|---|---|---|---|
| Year | 1970 | 1975 | 1980 | 1981 | 1982 | 1983 | 1984 | 1985 | 1986 | 1987 |
| Share of MVA (%, at constant 1980 prices) | | | | | | | | | | |
| - North Africa, excl. Sudan | 35.5 | 38.5 | 42.5 | 42.6 | 43.7 | 46.4 | 49.3 | 49.7 | 50 | 50.9 |
| - Sub-Saharan Africa, incl. Sudan | 64.5 | 61.5 | 57.1 | 57.4 | 56.3 | 53.6 | 50.7 | 50.3 | 50 | 49.1 |
| - West Africa, ECOWAS | 21.3 | 23.6 | 26.2 | 26.4 | 25 | 22.4 | 18.8 | 18.5 | 18.2 | 17.3 |
| - African LDCs | 25.4 | 19.8 | 13.9 | 12.9 | 12.6 | 12.5 | 12.4 | 11.7 | 11.6 | 11.8 |
| Share of MVA in GDP (%, at constant 1980 prices) | | | | | | | | | | |
| - North Africa, excl. Sudan | 6.1 | 8.9 | 9.1 | ... | ... | ... | ... | 11.1 | ... | ... |
| - Sub-Saharan Africa, incl. Sudan | 6.7 | 6.8 | 7.5 | ... | ... | ... | ... | 8 | ... | ... |
| - West Africa, ECOWAS | 4.2 | 4.7 | 6 | ... | ... | ... | ... | 5.8 | ... | ... |
| - African LDCs | 8.7 | 8 | 7.2 | ... | ... | ... | ... | 6.9 | ... | .. |
| Growth of MVA (index 1980=100) | | | | | | | | | | |
| - North Africa, excl. Sudan | ... | ... | 100 | 105 | 115 | 124 | 134 | 142 | 148 | 151 |
| - Sub-Saharan Africa, incl. Sudan | ... | ... | 100 | 106 | 111 | 108 | 103 | 108 | 111 | 109 |
| - West Africa, ECOWAS | ... | ... | 100 | 106 | 107 | 98 | 83 | 86 | 88 | 84 |
| - African LDCs | ... | ... | 100 | 98 | 102 | 103 | 103 | 103 | 106 | 108 |
| Source: Compiled from UNIDO, 1991, *African Industry in Figures 1990*, Vienna. | | | | | | | | | | |

There is a large disparity in the level of manufacturing attained at both the country and subregional levels. Annex 5.8 gives some indications of the situation in as far as groups of countries are concerned. North Africa and Sub-Saharan Africa constitute the main groups. In 1970, the ratio of Sub-Saharan Africa/North Africa MVA was 1:2. This steadily changed to 1:1 in 1984 and remained at this level up to 1987. In other words, by the second half of the 1980s, North African manufacturing output was equal to that of the rest of Africa. The MVA share of African LDCs drastically dropped from 25.4 percent in 1970 to 11.8 percent in 1987.

| ANNEX 5.9 SHARE, STRUCTURE AND GROWTH OF MANUFACTURED GOODS (EXCLUDING NON-FERROUS METALS) IN SELECTED COUNTRY GROUPS IN AFRICA | | | | | | | | | | | | | | |
|---|---|---|---|---|---|---|---|---|---|---|---|---|---|---|
| | Share in | | | | Structure of | | | | Growth of | | | | Net export ratios | |
| | Exports | | Imports | | Exports | | Imports | | Exports | | Imports | | | |
| Year | 1970 | 1988 | 1970 | 1988 | 1970 | 1988 | 1970 | 1988 | 1970 | 1988 | 1970 | 1988 | 1970 | 1988 |
| Africa | 100 | 100 | 100 | 100 | ... | ... | ... | ... | ... | ... | ... | ... | ... | ... |
| - North Africa, excl. Sudan | 40.9 | 61.3 | 31 | 57 | 7.4 | 22.8 | 68.2 | 64.4 | 17.2 | 16.7 | 23.2 | 5.2 | -74.6 | -66.1 |
| -Sub-Saharan Africa, incl. Sudan | 59.1 | 38.7 | 69 | 43 | 6.5 | 13.1 | 72.7 | 70.5 | 18.6 | 3.7 | 18.9 | -4 | -82.7 | -70.9 |
| - West Africa, ECOWAS | 13.6 | 9.9 | 26.3 | 15.6 | 4 | 6.8 | 74.8 | 67.6 | 19.7 | 3.8 | 23.6 | -9.2 | -89.2 | -78.6 |
| - African LDCs | 14 | ... | 20.6 | .. | 6.7 | ... | 70.9 | ... | 21.9 | ... | 15.4 | ... | -86 | ... |
| Source: Compiled from UNIDO, 1991, *African Industry in Figures 1990*, Vienna. | | | | | | | | | | | | | | |

The share, structure and growth of manufactured goods (excluding non-ferrous metals) in selected groups of African countries for the years 1970 and 1988 are given in annex 5.9. According to the annex, North Africa dominates in the share of both exports and imports in 1988. In regard to the structure of trade, the share of export of manufactured goods in total exports significantly increased while the share of imports slightly decreased in both North Africa and Sub-Saharan Africa. In the case of growth in trade of manufactured goods, although both groups of countries showed declining trend, the Sub-Saharan import growth rate dropped to -4.0 percent in 1988 from 18.9 percent in 1970. The net export ratios, ranging between -66.1 and -82.7 reveal the extremely high trade deficit in manufactured goods in developing Africa. It is even worse in West Africa and African LDCs.

ANNEX 5.10
AVERAGE ANNUAL GROWTH RATES AND SHARES OF MVA OF 28
INDUSTRIES IN SUB-SAHARAN AFRICAN COUNTRIES

| | | Growth rates (%) | | | Share in total MVA | |
|---|---|---|---|---|---|---|
| ISIC | Product group | 1970-1980 | 1980-1990 | 1990-1992 | Sub-Saharan Africa, 1990 | World 1993 |
| 311 | Food | 5.1 | 1.8 | 2.8 | 19.1 | 0.6 |
| 313 | Beverages | 5.5 | 2.6 | 0.1 | 14.7 | 1.9 |
| 314 | Tobacco manufactures | 2.7 | 0.3 | -0.8 | 4.1 | 0.7 |
| 321 | Textiles | 4.2 | -0.2 | 3 | 9 | 0.7 |
| 322 | Wearing apparel | 2.4 | 4.5 | 2.8 | 2.9 | 0.4 |
| 323 | Leather and fur products | 9.2 | 4.4 | 3.1 | 1 | 0.9 |
| 324 | Footwear, excluding rubber or plastic | 4.9 | 3.6 | -0.8 | 1.5 | 1 |
| 331 | Wood and cork products | 6.7 | -3.7 | 0.7 | 2.4 | ... |
| 332 | Furniture and fixtures | 8.6 | -2.5 | 1.7 | 1.2 | ... |
| 341 | Paper and paper products | 8.3 | 3.2 | 5.5 | 2.4 | ... |
| 342 | Printing and publishing | 7 | -0.8 | 1.4 | 2.3 | ... |
| 351 | Industrial chemicals | 4.5 | 1.8 | -0.2 | 2.3 | ... |
| 352 | Other chemical products | 10.7 | 2.1 | 1.7 | 6.4 | ... |
| 353 | Petroleum refineries | 1.9 | 2.3 | 1.2 | 4.8 | ... |
| 354 | Miscellaneous petroleum and coal products | 9.1 | -1.2 | -3.3 | 0.1 | ... |
| 355 | Rubber products | 2.4 | 1.3 | -1.4 | 1.2 | ... |
| 356 | Plastic products n.e.c. | 18.1 | -0.5 | 3.9 | 1.6 | ... |
| 361 | Pottery, china and earthenware | 7.1 | 3.3 | -17.9 | 0.2 | ... |
| 362 | Glass and glass products | 9.9 | -1.9 | 1.7 | 0.4 | ... |
| 369 | Other non-metallic mineral products | 3.9 | 4.4 | 1.6 | 4 | ... |
| 471 | Iron and steel | 9.6 | 2.4 | 0.5 | 2.6 | ... |
| 372 | Non-ferrous metals | 1.5 | 4.8 | 8 | 1.6 | ... |
| 381 | Metal products, excluding machinery | 6.1 | 0.1 | 0.4 | 4.7 | ... |
| 382 | Non-electrical machinery | 8.8 | 0.6 | 3.9 | 1.1 | ... |
| 383 | Electrical machinery | 9.7 | 0.5 | 3.2 | 1.8 | ... |
| 384 | Transport equipment | 18.7 | -3.6 | 4.9 | 5.5 | ... |
| 385 | Professional and scientific goods | 15.5 | 10.8 | 4.6 | 0.1 | ... |
| 390 | Other manufactures | 6.6 | -0.3 | 0.2 | 1 | ... |
| | Total | 6.2 | 1.1 | 1.9 | 100 | ... |

Source: UNIDO, 1993, *Industry and Development: Global Report 1993/94*, Vienna.

Annex 5.10 presents growth rates of MVA of 28 industries by ISIC classification and their 1990 shares in Sub-Saharan Africa. The overall growth rates given at the end of the annex show downward trend from 6.2 percent in 1970-1980, although an upswing was evident from the 1990-1992 rate.

| ANNEX 5.11 | | | | | | | | | | |
|---|---|---|---|---|---|---|---|---|---|---|
| STATISTICAL INDICATORS FOR NON-ENGINEERING INDUSTRIES IN SUB-SAHARAN AFRICA IN 1963,1965, 1970 AND 1979. | | | | | | | | | | |
| | Petroleum refining (353) | Petroleum and coal products (354) | Rubber (355) | Paper (341) | Industrial chemicals (351) | Other chemicals (352) | Glass (362) | Non-metallic mineral (369) | Non-ferrous metals (312) | Metal products (381) |
| Value added at constant 1975 prices ($m) | | | | | | | | | | |
| - 1963 | ... | ... | ... | 58 | 85 | 138 | 18 | 99 | 93 | 135 |
| - 1970 | ... | ... | ... | 115 | 127 | 214 | 31 | 189 | 108 | 280 |
| - 1979 | ... | ... | ... | 205 | 212 | 433 | 58 | 242 | 163 | 437 |
| Growth rates of value added at constant prices 1963-1979 | 5.81 | 2.43 | 6.81 | 7.45 | 5.99 | 14.04 | 6.8 | 4.77 | 5.98 | 11.14 |
| Share in world value added (%) | | | | | | | | | | |
| - 1965 | 0.8 | 0.1 | 1.3 | 1.6 | 2.3 | 3.8 | 0.5 | 2.7 | 2.5 | 3.7 |
| - 1970 | 2.6 | 1.1 | 1.6 | 1.8 | 2 | 3.4 | 0.5 | 3 | 1.7 | 4.5 |
| - 1979 | 2.7 | 1.1 | 2 | 2.4 | 2.4 | 5 | 0.7 | 2.8 | 1.9 | 5 |
| Shares of production in apparent consumption | | | | | | | | | | |
| - 1963 | ... | ... | ... | 0.6 | 0.51 | 0.63 | 0.46 | 0.77 | - | 0.57 |
| - 1970 | ... | ... | ... | 0.55 | 0.5 | 0.69 | 0.46 | 0.67 | - | 0.62 |
| - 1979 | ... | ... | ... | 0.49 | 0.46 | 0.7 | 0.3 | 0.52 | - | 0.51 |
| Employment per $1,000 value added at constant 1975 prices | | | | | | | | | | |
| - 1963 | 87 | - | 287 | 102 | 1157 | 84 | 107 | 264 | 99 | 194 |
| - 1970 | 23 | - | 172 | 144 | 337 | 108 | 119 | 208 | 39 | 211 |
| - 1979 | 40 | - | 119 | 136 | 218 | 118 | 160 | 244 | 33 | 168 |
| Source: Compiled from UNIDO, 1984, *Industrial Development and South-South Cooperation*, Vienna. | | | | | | | | | | |

Although lower than the overall growth rates achieved by other southern developing countries, Sub-Saharan Africa registered MVA growth rates higher than world averages in seven of the 10 industrial branches. In two of them, metal products (11.14%) and other chemicals (14.04%), the rates were more than double the world averages (annex 5.11). This phenomenon could be, in part, explained by the small industrial base of African countries.

Based on 1970, 1975 and 1977 figures, contribution of production to apparent consumption declined in all branches except other chemicals.

ANNEX 5.12
STATISTICAL INDICATORS FOR ENGINEERING (CAPITAL GOODS) INDUSTRIES IN
SUB-SAHARAN AFRICA IN 1963, 1967, 1970, 1975, 1977 AND 1979.

| | Non electrical machinery (382) | Electrical machinery (383) | Transport equipment (384) | Professional and scientific equipment (385) | Other machinery/ capital goods (390) | Total |
|---|---|---|---|---|---|---|
| **Value added ($m at 1975 prices)** | | | | | | |
| - 1963 | 30 | 55 | 122 | 1 | 46 | 254 |
| - 1967 | 44 | 75 | 133 | 1 | 66 | 319 |
| - 1970 | 57 | 104 | 182 | 2 | 93 | 438 |
| - 1975 | 82 | 142 | 271 | 3 | 154 | 652 |
| -1977 | 67 | 154 | 524 | 2 | 84 | 831 |
| - 1979 | 67 | 176 | 206 | 2 | 80 | 531 |
| **Growth rate of real value added (%)** | | | | | | |
| 1963-79 | 5.5 | 8.06 | 3.55 | 4.73 | 3.76 | 5.04 |
| 1970-77 | 2.73 | 6.76 | 19.27 | 0 | -1.68 | 11.26 |
| **Share in value added of Southern developing countries (%)** | | | | | | |
| - 1963 | 2 | 3 | 4 | ... | ... | 3 |
| - 1970 | 2 | 2 | 3 | ... | ... | 3 |
| - 1975 | 1 | 2 | 3 | ... | ... | 2 |
| - 1977 | 1 | 2 | 5 | ... | ... | 3 |
| - 1979 | 1 | 1 | 2 | ... | ... | 1 |
| **Share in value added of total manufacturing (ratio)** | | | | | | |
| - 1963 | 0.82 | 1.5 | 3.33 | 0.03 | 1.26 | 6.93 |
| - 1967 | 0.91 | 1.55 | 2.75 | 0.02 | 1.36 | 6.59 |
| - 1970 | 0.92 | 1.67 | 2.92 | 0.03 | 1.49 | 7.03 |
| - 1975 | 1.04 | 1.8 | 3.44 | 0.04 | 1.95 | 8.27 |
| - 1977 | 0.77 | 1.77 | 6.01 | 0.02 | 0.96 | 9.53 |
| - 1979 | 0.77 | 2.02 | 2.36 | 0.02 | 0.92 | 6.09 |
| **Share of production in apparent consumption (%)** | | | | | | |
| - 1970 | 0.1 | 0.29 | 0.1 | 0.11 | ... | 0.15 |
| - 1975 | 0.1 | 0.26 | 0.08 | 0.13 | ... | 0.13 |
| - 1977 | 0.11 | 0.29 | 0.21 | 0.11 | ... | 0.21 |
| **Share of employment in total manufacturing employment (%)** | | | | | | |
| - 1963 | 0.22 | 1.06 | 7.37 | 0.42 | 0.81 | 9.88 |
| - 1967 | 0.24 | 1.4 | 4.89 | 0.34 | 0.97 | 7.82 |
| - 1970 | 0.19 | 1.54 | 4.06 | 0.3 | 0.83 | 6.93 |
| - 1975 | 0.15 | 1.77 | 3.66 | 0.29 | 0.83 | 6.7 |
| - 1977 | 0.14 | 1.73 | 3.56 | 0.36 | 0.89 | 6.68 |
| - 1979 | 0.13 | 1.77 | 3.56 | 0.24 | 0.67 | 6.37 |

Source: Compiled from UNIDO, 1984, *Industrial Development and South-South Cooperation*, Vienna.

Annex 5.12 provides statistical information on the engineering subsector. Except for transport equipment, the growth rates for branches of the subsector are substantially lower than the world averages. In view of the general trend in value added in the annex, the high rate of growth of 19.3 percent for transport equipment in 1970-1977, based as it is on abrupt increase and therefore questionable 1977 value added figure, may not be taken as a representative figure. By the same token, the growth rate of 11.3 percent for all engineering industry which is 1.7 times the word average, does not seem realistic. From the share of Sub-Saharan Africa in the value added of southern developing counties it is apparent that the engineering industry is the least developed in this part of Africa. The total share stood at a mere one percent in 1979, having declined from 3 percent in 1963.

The contribution of the engineering subsector to manufacturing was low. During the 1963-1979 period, it was within the range of 6.1-9.5 percent, contrasting with 11.8-18.9 percent for Southern developing countries as a group and 28.5-34.1 percent for the world. Transport equipment and electric machinery accounted for the major part of the contribution. The same was true in respect of employment. The share of production in apparent consumption reveals the over dependence of African countries on import of engineering goods, particularly capital goods. Although the production/apparent consumption ratio had increased from 0.15 in 1970 to 0.21 in 1977, it was only about 37 percent of that of the south developing countries.

| ANNEX 5.13 | | | | | | | | | |
|---|---|---|---|---|---|---|---|---|---|
| ANNUAL GROWTH RATES AND SHARE OF MVA OF SUB-SAHARAN AND NORTH AFRICAN COUNTRIES (%) | | | | | | | | | |
| | Average annual growth rates | | Annual growth rates | | | | | | Share in total MVA |
| | 1970-1980 | 1980-1990 | 1990 | 1991 | 1992 | 1993 | 1994 | 1995 | 1994 |
| Sub-Saharan Africa | ... | ... | 3 | 2.7 | -0.1 | -1.1 | 2.9 | 3.8 | 100 |
| Benin | 0.4 | 1.3 | 2.7 | 0.5 | 5 | 2.6 | 3.3 | 3.1 | 1.1 |
| Botswana | 9.6 | 8.8 | ... | ... | ... | 5 | 11 | 18.8 | 1.2 |
| Burkina Faso | 4 | 1.1 | 3.8 | 5.4 | 3 | -3.1 | 9.6 | 6.7 | 1.8 |
| Burundi | 6.5 | 9.7 | 3.7 | 3 | 1 | -3.1 | 9.6 | 6.7 | 1.3 |
| Cameroon | 4.5 | 10 | -4 | 0.6 | -4.8 | -5.4 | -3.7 | -1.9 | 9.4 |
| Cape Verde | ... | ... | ... | ... | 6.5 | 6.4 | 6.5 | 6.5 | |
| Central African Republic | -1.9 | 2.8 | 1.5 | 2.1 | 1.9 | 0.4 | 3.1 | 2.7 | 0.6 |
| Chad | ... | ... | 2.9 | 2.9 | 2.6 | -3 | 3.9 | 2.7 | |
| Comoros | ... | ... | 0.6 | 2.7 | ... | ... | ... | ... | ... |
| Congo | 2.2 | 5 | 2.8 | 0.6 | 8.7 | -2.8 | -3.1 | -0.7 | 1.2 |
| Cote d'Ivoire | 6.3 | -1.1 | -5.7 | 0.3 | 2 | 0.3 | 2.5 | -1.1 | 7.3 |

| | | | | | | | | | |
|---|---|---|---|---|---|---|---|---|---|
| Djibouti | ... | ... | -5.2 | 4.4 | 4 | 2.4 | 2.8 | 2.4 | ... |
| Equatorial Guinea | .. | ... | 4.6 | 0.4 | -4.9 | 10 | - | 5.5 | ... |
| Ethiopia and Eritrea | 3.9 | 3.7 | 5.6 | -3.7 | -3.7 | 21.9 | 3.6 | 4.1 | 2.5 |
| Gabon | 10 | -1.6 | ... | ... | ... | 1.1 | 11.9 | 5.3 | 4.4 |
| Gambia | ... | .. | 0.9 | 6.9 | 4.9 | 2.8 | 4.9 | 5 | ... |
| Ghana | -1.8 | 0.7 | 4.9 | 6.9 | 5.8 | 2.3 | 9.6 | 9.6 | 3.8 |
| Guinea | ... | ... | 3.7 | 2.9 | 2.5 | 5 | 6 | 6.5 | ... |
| Guinea-Bissau | ... | ... | 0.9 | -0.3 | -0.1 | -1.4 | -1.4 | -1.4 | .. |
| Kenya | 10 | 4.8 | 6 | 5.8 | 2.5 | 1.8 | 4 | 4.9 | 5.8 |
| Lesotho | 9.7 | 12.2 | ... | .. | ... | 5 | 9.8 | 9.7 | 0.6 |
| Liberia | ... | .. | -1.8 | 5.9 | 0.3 | 2 | 0.8 | -1.6 | ... |
| Madagascar | 1.9 | -1.6 | 3.9 | 3.2 | -5.3 | 3.1 | -2.3 | -0.5 | 1.6 |
| Malawi | 9.4 | 3.7 | 8.6 | 5.2 | 1.2 | -1 | 11.1 | 7.3 | 2 |
| Mali | 4 | 8.6 | 2.4 | 0.7 | 3.3 | 6.5 | 9.2 | 7.5 | 1.6 |
| Mauritius | 6.6 | 9.6 | 10.3 | 7.5 | 8.8 | 10 | 9.4 | 7.4 | 4.1 |
| Mozambique | ... | ... | 5.9 | 4.3 | -0.2 | 21.7 | 27.3 | 22.4 | ... |
| Namibia | ... | ... | . | ... | ... | -2.8 | 2.1 | -2.6 | ... |
| Niger | -2.2 | 6.5 | 0.1 | 1.5 | 1.3 | 3.7 | 3.8 | 3.7 | 1.1 |
| Nigeria | 12.9 | 1.5 | 5.7 | 6.1 | 5.7 | -10.2 | -6 | -1 | 9.9 |
| Reunion | ... | ... | 2.4 | 4.4 | 4.1 | 3.9 | 4.4 | 4 | ... |
| Rwanda | 6.1 | 1.4 | ... | ... | ... | ... | -15 | 1.8 | 2 |
| Sao Tome and Principe | ... | ... | 3.6 | 1.2 | 1.3 | 11.5 | 2.2 | 1.2 | ... |
| Senegal | 2.8 | 4.6 | 5.8 | 5.4 | 3.1 | -1.4 | 4.4 | 3.8 | 4.7 |
| Seychelles | ... | ... | 8.4 | 8.2 | 7.9 | 12.4 | 9.9 | 10.5 | ... |
| Sierra Leone | ... | ... | 1.8 | 1.3 | 0.8 | 8.2 | 6.6 | 3.5 | ... |
| Somalia | ... | ... | ... | ... | ... | -5 | 5 | 5.2 | ... |
| Swaziland | 11.4 | 6.2 | 4.9 | 6.1 | 6 | 6.1 | 7 | 7.6 | 2 |
| Togo | ... | .. | 2.2 | -1.9 | -0.9 | -40.8 | -21.8 | -0.6 | ... |
| Tanzania | 3.5 | -1.4 | 4.5 | 1.2 | 2.9 | 7.4 | 5.3 | 6.1 | 0.7 |
| Uganda | -9.9 | 5.3 | 4.1 | 2.8 | 5.7 | 3.7 | 3.9 | 3.4 | 1.3 |
| Congo K | 1.5 | 4.1 | -1.6 | -1.9 | -8.4 | -11.5 | -4.2 | -3.2 | 5.7 |
| Zambia | 4.6 | 3.4 | -0.7 | -7.5 | -2.6 | 5.8 | 3.4 | 3.9 | 9.4 |
| Zimbabwe | 4.6 | 3.4 | 5.8 | 5 | -10.1 | -8.9 | 6.6 | 6 | 9.4 |
| North Africa | ... | ... | 5.6 | 3.1 | 4.1 | -0.4 | 2.9 | 2.7 | 100 |
| Algeria | 9.1 | 5.7 | 6.5 | 0 | -2.2 | -2.9 | 0.5 | -4.2 | 22.5 |
| Egypt | 4.2 | 10.4 | 3 | 2.2 | 6 | -3.1 | 1.9 | 3.9 | 24 |
| Libya | 13.5 | 9.8 | 13.4 | 9.1 | 9.7 | 9.6 | 9.7 | 9.6 | 12.6 |
| Mauritania | 3.3 | 6.7 | ?6.6 | 6.6 | 6.3 | 6.2 | 6.5 | 6.4 | 0.7 |
| Morocco | 5.6 | 4.3 | 4.8 | 4.1 | 4.4 | -2 | 1.5 | 4.2 | 21.3 |
| Sudan | 2.4 | -1.7 | -4.7 | 0.5 | 1 | 1.5 | 1.6 | -0.6 | 9.2 |
| Tunisia | 12.3 | 5.9 | 11.1 | 6.7 | ... | 3 | 6.9 | 6.3 | 9.7 |

Source: UNIDO, 1993, *Industry and Development: Global Report 1991/92, 1992/93,1993/94 and 1995*, Vienna.

Annex 5.13 gives indications of the development of manufacturing during the 1970s, 1980s and subsequent years in Sub-Saharan and North African countries. The MVA growth rate varied by wide margins from country to country and from year to year within the same country. During the first half of the 1990s, the rate of increase of MVA in Sub-Saharan Africa decelerated from 3.0 percent in 1990, reached a trough of -1.1 percent in 1993 and was expected to rise to 3.8 percent in 1995. The corresponding rates for North Africa were: 5.6, -0.4 and 2.7. Nigeria, Cameroon, Zimbabwe and Cote d'Ivoire accounted for 36 percent of the total MVA in Sub-Saharan Africa while Egypt, Algeria and Morocco for 67.8 percent of that of North Africa.

445

ANNEX 5.14
CONTINENTAL GDP AT CURRENT FACTOR COST AND SHARE OF
INDUSTRY AND MANUFACTURING IN GDP, 1992

| Region/country | GDP | | Industry total | Manufacturing |
|---|---|---|---|---|
| | $ m | % of region | % of GDP | % of GDP |
| North Africa | 209506 | 44.1 | 35.4 | 12.6 |
| - Algeria | 68207[a] | 14.4[a] | 52.1 | 11.8 |
| - Egypt | 33091 | 7 | 31.3 | 11.7 |
| - Morocco | ... | ... | 34.2 | 17.7 |
| West Africa | 70642 | 14.9 | 22.3 | 8.9 |
| - Nigeria | 38927 | 8.2 | 29 | 10.2 |
| - Ghana | 5827 | 1.3 | 16.6 | 11.2 |
| - Cote d'Ivoire | ... | ... | 21.6 | 13.6 |
| Central Africa | 24844 | 5.2 | 24.6 | 8.3 |
| - Cameroon | 11254 | 2.4 | 33 | 13.8 |
| - Congo K | 2404 | 0.5 | 31.3 | 1.4 |
| - Gabon | | | 50.3 | 7.4 |
| Eastern Africa | 38285 | 8 | 19 | 9.9 |
| - Mozambique | 9777 | 2 | 42.8 | 24.7 |
| - Mauritius | ... | ... | 33.5 | 23.5 |
| - Kenya | 7204 | 1.5 | 21.7 | 11.7 |
| Southern Africa | 131528 | 27.8 | 40 | 18 |
| - South Africa | 103724 | 21.8 | 34.5 | 24.9 |
| - Zimbabwe | 7960 | 1.7 | 41.8 | 28.8 |
| - Zambia | ... | ... | 51.2 | 38.2 |
| Total (10 countries) | 389673 | 60.8 | ... | ... |
| Africa total | 474805 | 100 | ... | ... |

Source: Compiled from ECA/UNIDO, 1995, *Report on Regional Strategy for Rational Location of Industries in the Context of the Abuja Treaty* (CAMI.12/6(A), Addis Ababa.
    a  1990

Annex 5.14 gives some indications of industry and manufacturing in selected countries in relation to GDP. Ten of the countries of the 15 account for 60.8 percent of the African GDP with South Africa taking the lion's share of 21.8 percent followed by Algeria (14.4%), Nigeria (8.2%) and Egypt (7.0%). The share of manufacturing in GDP range between 8.3 percent in Central Africa and 18.0 percent in Southern Africa in 1992. At the individual country level the range was 1.4 percent in Congo K and 38.2 percent in Zambia. The dominance of mining explains, in part, the low level of manufacturing share in GDP in the former.

| ANNEX 5.15<br>PERCENTAGE COMPOSITION OF MVA BY INCOME GROUPS IN DEVELOPING AFRICA, ASIA AND THE WORLD [a] | | | | | | | | | | | |
|---|---|---|---|---|---|---|---|---|---|---|---|
| | Africa [b] | | Low-income<br>Africa | | Low-income<br>Asia | | Middle-income<br>Africa | | Middle-income<br>Asia | | World | |
| | 1980 | 1991 | 1973 | 1984 | 1973 | 1984 | 1973 | 1984 | 1973 | 1984 | 1973 | 1984 |
| 1. Food, beverages and tobacco | 40.9 | 42.2 | 37.1 | 35 | 12.5 | 12.7 | 32.6 | 27.5 | 20.3 | 12.3 | 12.4 | 11.2 |
| 2. Textiles, apparel and leather | 35.9 | 35.1 | 22.3 | 15.9 | 24.2 | 14.7 | 13.2 | 9.9 | 22.6 | 28 | 10.2 | 8.4 |
| 3. Wood and wood products | 8.9 | 9.9 | 5.9 | 3.4 | 2.2 | 2 | 3.7 | 6.1 | 4.1 | 1.4 | 4.1 | 3.2 |
| 4. Paper and paper products | 6.5 | 5.2 | 4.9 | 5 | 4.4 | 3.5 | 4.8 | 6.5 | 5 | 4.6 | 6.3 | 8.1 |
| 5. Chemicals, petroleum and products | 22.4 | 20.5 | 11.7 | 28.5 | 14.5 | 19.7 | 16.2 | 14.2 | 18.9 | 14.4 | 14 | 17.7 |
| 6. Non-metallic mineral products | 15.5 | 17.6 | 4.1 | 2.8 | 4.7 | 4.9 | 4.5 | 5.3 | 4.2 | 2.2 | 5.3 | 4.7 |
| 7. Basic metals | 10 | 9 | 2.9 | 1.5 | 9.5 | 17 | 11.8 | 5.2 | 5 | 4.9 | 8.7 | 8.1 |
| 8. Metal products, machinery and equipment | 19.5 | 13.7 | 9.8 | 7.5 | 24.8 | 22.8 | 12.5 | 21.7 | 18.3 | 29.9 | 37.1 | 38.9 |
| 9. Other manufactures | ... | ... | 0.6 | 0.3 | 3.2 | 2.6 | 0.8 | 3.5 | 1.6 | 2.2 | 1.8 | 1.8 |
| Total manufacturing | ... | ... | 100 | 100 | 100 | 100 | 100 | 100 | 100 | 100 | 100 | 100 |
| Traditional industries (1-3) | ... | ... | 65.9 | 54.3 | 38.9 | 29.4 | 49.5 | 43.5 | 47 | 41.7 | 26.7 | 22.8 |
| Non-traditional industries (4-9) | ... | ... | 34.1 | 45.7 | 61.1 | 70.6 | 50.5 | 56.5 | 53 | 58.3 | 73.3 | 77.2 |
| Consumer goods industries (1, 2, 9) | ... | ... | 60.6 | 51.2 | 39.9 | 30 | 46.6 | 40.9 | 44.5 | 42.5 | 24.4 | 21.4 |
| Intermediate goods industries (3-7) | ... | ... | 29.6 | 41.3 | 35.3 | 47.1 | 40.9 | 37.4 | 37.2 | 27.6 | 38.5 | 39.7 |
| Capital goods industries (8) | ... | ... | 9.8 | 7.5 | 24.8 | 22.8 | 12.5 | 21.7 | 18.3 | 29.9 | 37.1 | 38.9 |

Source: - [a] Riddell, Roger C. et al, 1990, *Manufacturing Africa*, James Currey, London (originally from WB, check and update).
- [b] UNIDO, 1995, *International Yearbook of Industrial Statistics 1995*, Vienna.

Annex 5.15 gives details and comparison of the structure of manufacturing during 1973 and 1984 by income groups in developing Africa, Asia and the world. In general, in both low-income and middle-income Africa as in the rest of the world, the share of traditional industries (agro-industries, excluding paper and paper products) in MVA decreased. It fell from 65.3 percent in 1973 to 54.3 percent in 1984 in low-income Africa with the corresponding figures of 49.5 percent to 43.5 percent for middle-income Africa compared with 26.7 percent to 22.8 percent of world MVA. Production of consumer goods dominated, accounting for 40.9 to 51.2 percent of MVA in 1992. Intermediate goods increased while capital goods decreased in low-income Africa. The opposite was the case in regard to middle-income Africa. The contribution of capital goods to industrial goods production in low-income Asia was three times that of low-income Africa in 1984 (2.5 times in 1973) indicating how far Africa was being left behind in industrial development.

Production of food and beverage accounted for up to 70 percent of production in some countries. This increased to over 75 percent for combined agro-based production.

ANNEX 5.16
PERCENTAGE SHARE OF AFRICAN LEADING COUNTRY PRODUCERS IN WORLD PRODUCTION OF SELECTED MANUFACTURING BRANCHES (ISIC)

| | Year | Food (311/2) | Textiles (321) | Wearing apparel (322) | Leather and fur (323) | Foot-wear (324) | Other chemicals (352) | Iron and steel (371) | Non ferrous metals (372) | Metals products (381) | Non electric. machinery (382) |
|---|---|---|---|---|---|---|---|---|---|---|---|
| Morocco | 1980 | 1.5 | | | | 1.2 | | | | | |
| | 1992 | | 1.8 | 1.1 | 1.3 | 1.7 | | | | | |
| Algeria | 1980 | | | 1.6 | 2.2 | 1.6 | | | | | |
| | 1992 | | | 2 | 1.6 | 2.1 | | | | | |
| Egypt | 1980 | | 2.5 | | | | | 0.9 | 2 | | |
| | 1992 | | 2.4 | | | | | 1 | 2.1 | | 0.6 |
| Nigeria | 1980 | | | | | | 3 | | | 1.4 | |
| Ghana | 1980 | | | | | | | | 1.4 | | |
| | 1992 | | | | | | | | 0.7 | | |
| Zimbabwe | 1980 | | | | | | | 1.1 | | | |
| | 1992 | | | | | | | 1 | | | |
| Total (six countries) [a] | 1980 | 1.5 | 2.5 | 1.6 | 2.2 | 2.8 | 3 | 2 | 3.4 | 1.4 | |
| | 1992 | | 4.2 | 1.3 | 2.9 | 3.8 | | 2 | 2.8 | | 0.6 |

Source: UNIDO, 1995, *International Yearbook of Industrial Statistics*, Vienna.   a   Calculated

Annex 5.16 gives indications of the leading African country producers in selected branches. African share (total of the six countries) in world production based on the table ranges between 0.6 percent for non-electrical machinery and 4.2 percent for textiles. As the six countries are among the most advanced it is obvious that traditional resource-based industries dominate the manufacturing industry.

| ANNEX 5.17 MANUFACTURING INDUSTRY INDICATORS IN SUB-SAHARAN AFRICA IN 1963,1970, 1975, 1977 AND 1979. | | | | | | |
|---|---|---|---|---|---|---|
| Subsector | Food process-ing | Light industry | Basic products | Coal and petroleum products | Capital goods | Manufac-turing total |
| Share in MVA of southern developing countries (%) | | | | | | |
| - 1963 | 8.3 | 5.1 | 4.2 | 0.4 | 2.9 | 4.9 |
| - 1970 | 8.8 | 6.5 | 4 | 1.8 | 2.7 | 5.4 |
| - 1979 | 7.9 | 6 | 3.2 | 1.9 | 1.4 | 4.5 |
| Growth rates of MVA 1970-1977 (%) | 3.7 | 5.9 | 7.7 | 4.8 | 11.3 | 5.8 |
| Structural change ($) | | | | | | |
| - 1963 | 44.5 | 32 | 15.6 | 0.9 | 6.9 | 100 |
| - 1970 | 39 | 34.7 | 15.5 | 3.7 | 7 | 100 |
| - 1979 | 36.7 | 35.5 | 17.9 | 3.7 | 6.1 | 100 |
| Employment per $1m MVA at 1975 prices) | | | | | | |
| - 1963 | 129 | 239 | 260 | 87 | 287 | 203 |
| - 1970 | 180 | 242 | 157 | 24 | 182 | 192 |
| - 1979 | 170 | 205 | 185 | 40 | 139 | 172 |
| Employment in manufacturing (m) | | | | | | |
| - 1963 | 103 | 172 | 114 | 2 | 43 | 434 |
| - 1970 | 199 | 334 | 102 | 2 | 47 | 684 |
| - 1979 | 299 | 522 | 162 | 5 | 67 | 1054 |
| Share of sectoral employment in total manufacturing employment (%) | | | | | | |
| - 1963 | 23.6 | 39.7 | 26.3 | 0.4 | 9.9 | 100 |
| - 1970 | 20.1 | 48.8 | 14.9 | 0.5 | 6.9 | 100 |
| - 1979 | 28.3 | 49.5 | 15.3 | 0.5 | 6.4 | 100 |
| Gross production ($m at 1975 prices) | | | | | | |
| -1970 | 8.6 | 5.5 | 2.8 | ... | 1.2 | ... |
| - 1975 | 9.2 | 7.3 | 4.2 | ... | 1.9 | ... |
| - 1977 | 10.1 | 5.2 | 3.8 | ... | 1.7 | ... |
| Apparent consumption ($m at 1975 prices) | | | | | | |
| - 1970 | 8.6 | 7.3 | 0.9 | ... | 6.4 | ... |
| - 1975 | 9.4 | 9.8 | 5.7 | ... | 12.7 | ... |
| - 1977 | 11.4 | 7.9 | 5.7 | ... | 15.3 | ... |
| Share of gross production in apparent consumption | | | | | | |
| - 1970 | 1 | 0.8 | 0.3 | ... | 0.2 | ... |
| -1 975 | 1 | 0.7 | 0.7 | ... | 0.2 | ... |
| - 1977 | 0.9 | 0.7 | 0.7 | ... | 0.1 | ... |
| Source: Compiled from UINDO, 1984, *Industrial Development and South-South Cooperation*, Vienna. | | | | | | |

Annex 5.17 gives some idea of the manufacturing industry in Sub-Saharan Africa for some years in the 1960s and 1970s. The information was compiled from a number of tables providing figures by subsector and groups of southern developing countries (Latin America, Tropical Africa, North Africa- Middle East, South Asia and East Asia).

Comparisons of Sub-Saharan Africa with those of the other groups shows that the former lagged far behind the latter in practically all the indicators in the table. Its share in total MVA increased to 5.4 percent in 1970 and declined to 4.5 percent in 1979. At the subsectoral level the shares of the food and light industries were above whereas those of the remaining subsectors were below the average of the Southern developing country groups. This is a reflection of the structural change that was taking place as evidenced by the decline of the share of food processing in total MVA, 44.5 percent in 1963, 39.0 percent in 1970 and 36.7 percent in 1979. These falls were reflected as increases in the other subsectors, particularly coal and petroleum products, except in capital goods.

In regard to employment in manufacturing, the labor force in Sub-Saharan Africa increased from 434 million in 1963 to 1.05 million in 1979. Food processing and light industries accounted for about 71.2 percent of the labor force in 1979. Employment per unit ($1 million MVA at 1975 prices) declined to 172 persons in 1979 from 203 in 1963. This trend, more or less, applied to all subsectors, except food processing. The explanation for this, in part, may lie in improved labor productivity and structural changes towards more capital-intensive industries.

Among the Southern developing country groups, Sub-Saharan Africa registered the lowest gross production figures. The same applied to apparent consumption. Contribution of gross production to apparent consumption showed declining trend in all subsectors, except basic products, shown in the table. Food processing, for instance, dipped from 1.000 in 1970 to 0.892 in 1977. The corresponding figures for capital goods were : 0.194 and 0.109, implying high and increasing dependency on import of capital goods and therefore a potential for import substitution.

**ANNEX 5.18**
**SHARE AND STRUCTURE OF MVA, EXPORTS AND IMPORTS OF MANUFACTURES IN AFRICA**

| | 1970 | 1975 | 1980 | 1981 | 1982 | 1983 | 1984 | 1985 | 1986 | 1987 | 1988 | 1989 | 1990 |
|---|---|---|---|---|---|---|---|---|---|---|---|---|---|
| Share of MVA in GDP (%, at constant 1980 prices) | | | | | | | | | | | | | |
| - Africa | ... | 7.5 | 8.1 | 8.8 | 9.1 | 9 | 9.1 | 9.4 | 9.6 | 9.9 | 9.9 | 9.6 | 9.7 |
| - North Africa | ... | 9 | 8.8 | 9.8 | 9.8 | 10.3 | 10.4 | 10.9 | 11.1 | 11.7 | 11.8 | 11.3 | 11.7 |
| - Central Africa | ... | 6.5 | 7.1 | 7.9 | 9.1 | 9.4 | 9.8 | 10.1 | ... | ... | ... | ... | ... |
| - West Africa | ... | 4.6 | 5.9 | 6.3 | 6.4 | 6.2 | 5.7 | 5.7 | ... | ... | ... | ... | ... |
| - Eastern and Southern Africa | ... | 11.1 | 10.7 | 10.8 | 10.4 | 10.3 | 10.2 | 10.2 | ... | ... | ... | ... | ... |
| Sub-Saharan Africa | ... | 6.9 | 77 | 8.2 | 8.6 | 8 | 8.1 | 8.3 | 8.4 | 8.5 | 8.6 | 8.3 | 8.3 |
| - African LDCs | ... | 9.4 | 8.5 | 8.5 | 8.3 | 8.3 | 8.4 | 8.4 | 8.4 | 8.3 | 8.6 | 8.5 | 8.7 |
| - All developing countries | ... | 16.9 | 18.1 | 18.1 | 18.2 | 18.5 | 19.2 | 19.4 | 19.9 | 20.4 | 20.3 | 20.3 | 20.2 |
| Share in world MVA (%) | | | | | | | | | | | | | |
| - Africa | 0.8 | 0.8 | 0.9 | 0.9 | 1 | 0.9 | 0.9 | 1 | 1 | 1 | 1 | 0.9 | 1 |
| - African LDCs | 0.2 | 0.2 | 0.2 | 0.2 | 0.2 | 0.2 | 0.1 | 0.1 | 0.1 | 0.1 | 0.1 | 0.1 | 0.1 |
| **Share in developing countries MVA** | ... | 6.5 | 6.4 | ... | ... | ... | ... | 6.8 | ... | ... | ... | ... | 6.4 |
| Share of industry groups in total MVA, at constant 1980 prices (%) | | | | | | | | | | | | | |
| - By-end use | | | | | | | | | | | | | |
| . Consumer non-durables | ... | ... | 58.4 | ... | ... | ... | ... | 59.6 | | 58.9 | ... | ... | 58.4 |
| . Industrial intermediates | ... | ... | 23.5 | ... | ... | ... | ... | 24.1 | | 25 | ... | ... | 26.6 |
| . Capital goods, incl. consumer durables | ... | ... | 18.1 | ... | ... | ... | ... | 16.3 | | 16.1 | ... | ... | 15 |
| - By factor intensity | | | | | | | | | | | | | |
| . Labor-intensive industries | ... | ... | 24.3 | ... | ... | ... | ... | 24 | | 22.9 | ... | ... | 22.5 |
| . Capital-intensive industries | ... | ... | 43.5 | ... | ... | ... | ... | 40.8 | | 40.6 | ... | ... | 42.2 |
| . Resource-based industries | ... | ... | 26.9 | ... | ... | ... | ... | 28.7 | | 30.1 | ... | ... | 29.5 |
| . Technology-intensive industries | ... | ... | 5.3 | ... | ... | ... | ... | 6.6 | | 6.4 | ... | ... | 6.8 |
| Country group distribution of MVA, at 1980 constant prices (%) | | | | | | | | | | | | | |
| - North Africa (excluding Sudan) | 39.7 | 39.7 | 43.3 | 43.2 | 43.6 | 47.9 | 49.6 | 49.7 | 49.9 | 50.3 | 50.2 | 49.9 | 50.1 |
| - Central Africa | 8.6 | 7.9 | 7.4 | 8.2 | 9.4 | 9.8 | 10.7 | 10.9 | ... | ... | ... | ... | ... |
| - West Africa | 21.3 | 23.7 | 26.8 | 26.6 | 25.7 | 23 | 20.1 | 19.9 | ... | ... | ... | ... | ... |
| - Eastern and Southern Africa | 30.4 | 27.9 | 21.9 | 21.4 | 20.4 | 20 | 20.1 | 2010 | ... | ... | ... | ... | ... |
| - Sub-Saharan Africa | ... | 60.3 | 56.7 | 56.8 | 56.4 | 52.1 | 50.4 | 50.3 | 50.1 | 49.7 | 49.8 | 50.1 | 49.9 |
| - African LDCs | 25.5 | 24 | 17.7 | 16.9 | 15.6 | 16 | 15.5 | 14.8 | 14.5 | 14.5 | 14.7 | 14.8 | 14.6 |
| Share in world total exports (%, at current prices) | | | | | | | | | | | | | |
| - Africa | 4.1 | 4.1 | 4.7 | ... | ... | ... | ... | 3.2 | ... | ... | 1.9 | 1.8 | 2 |

| | | | | | | | | | | | | | |
|---|---|---|---|---|---|---|---|---|---|---|---|---|---|
| - African LDCs | 0.6 | 0.6 | 0.5 | ... | ... | ... | ... | 0.4 | ... | ... | 0.2 | 0.3 | 0.2 |
| **Share in world total imports (%), at current prices)** | | | | | | | | | | | | | |
| - Africa | 3.4 | 4.2 | 3.6 | ... | ... | ... | ... | 2.7 | ... | ... | 2.6 | 2 | 2.1 |
| - African LDCs | 0.7 | 0.9 | 0.7 | ... | ... | ... | ... | 0.5 | ... | ... | 0.4 | 0.4 | 0.4 |
| **Share in world exports, at current prices (%)** | | | | | | | | | | | | | |
| - Food, beverages and tobacco | ... | 5.2 | ... | ... | ... | ... | ... | ... | ... | ... | ... | ... | 2.8 |
| - Crude materials, oils and fats | ... | 7.7 | ... | ... | ... | ... | ... | ... | ... | ... | ... | ... | 3.4 |
| - Mineral fuels | ... | 12.9 | ... | ... | ... | ... | ... | ... | ... | ... | ... | ... | 11.8 |
| - Non-ferrous metals | ... | 8.1 | ... | ... | ... | ... | ... | ... | ... | ... | ... | ... | 2.9 |
| - Manufactured goods | ... | 0.4 | ... | ... | ... | ... | ... | ... | ... | ... | ... | ... | 0.4 |
| **Share in world imports, at current prices (%)** | | | | | | | | | | | | | |
| - Food, beverages and tobacco | ... | 4.9 | ... | ... | ... | ... | ... | ... | ... | ... | ... | ... | 3.3 |
| - Crude materials, oils and fats | ... | 2 | ... | ... | ... | ... | ... | ... | ... | ... | ... | ... | 2.2 |
| - Mineral fuels | ... | 1.6 | ... | ... | ... | ... | ... | ... | ... | ... | ... | ... | 2 |
| - Non-ferrous metals | ... | 1.5 | ... | ... | ... | ... | ... | ... | ... | ... | ... | ... | 0.8 |
| - Manufactured goods | ... | 5.4 | ... | ... | ... | ... | ... | ... | ... | ... | ... | ... | 2.1 |
| Share of Africa in exports of all developing countries by commodity group (%, at current prices) - total | 22.1 | 16.7 | 16.5 | ... | ... | ... | ... | 13.4 | 11.1 | 10.6 | 9.5 | | 9.2 |
| - Food, beverages and tobacco | 23.2 | 17.4 | 15.5 | ... | ... | ... | ... | 14.1 | 14.4 | 14.2 | 13.6 | | 10.8 |
| - Crude materials, oils, fats | 24.7 | 26.2 | 16.6 | ... | ... | ... | ... | 15 | 15.5 | 13.9 | 12.5 | | 12.4 |
| - Mineral fuels | 22.9 | 18 | 20.4 | ... | ... | ... | ... | 22.3 | 19.7 | 21.2 | 20.5 | | 22.5 |
| - Non-ferrous metals | 45.2 | 30.5 | 20.1 | ... | ... | ... | ... | 14.1 | 18.3 | 21.4 | 19.4 | | 13.1 |
| - Manufactured goods (excluding non-ferrous metals) | 8.3 | 5.2 | 3.4 | ... | ... | ... | ... | 2.6 | 2.9 | 2.9 | 2.9 | | 2.5 |
| Share of Africa in imports of all developing countries by commodity group (%, at current prices) - total | ... | 19.7 | 15.8 | ... | ... | ... | ... | 13 | ... | ... | ... | | 10.4 |
| - Food, beverages and tobacco | ... | 23.7 | 21.3 | ... | ... | ... | ... | 23.5 | ... | ... | ... | ... | 17.2 |
| - Crude materials, oils, fats | ... | 14 | 11.2 | ... | ... | ... | ... | 12.9 | ... | ... | ... | ... | 10 |
| - Mineral fuels | ... | 10.5 | 8.1 | ... | ... | ... | ... | 7.7 | ... | ... | ... | ... | 11.2 |
| - Non-ferrous metals | ... | 11.7 | 9.3 | ... | ... | ... | ... | 6.4 | ... | ... | ... | ... | 5.5 |
| - Manufactured goods (excluding non-ferrous metals) | ... | 22.1 | 17.7 | ... | ... | ... | ... | 13.3 | ... | ... | ... | ... | 9.9 |
| **Structure of exports, at current prices (%)** | | | | | | | | | | | | | |
| - Food, beverages and tobacco | ... | 15.2 | ... | ... | ... | ... | ... | ... | ... | ... | ... | ... | 12.3 |
| - Crude materials, oils and fats | ... | 14.2 | ... | ... | ... | ... | ... | ... | ... | ... | ... | ... | 8.7 |
| - Mineral fuels | ... | 60.8 | ... | ... | ... | ... | ... | ... | ... | ... | ... | ... | 60.3 |
| - Non-ferrous metals | ... | 4.3 | ... | ... | ... | ... | ... | ... | ... | ... | ... | ... | 2.9 |
| - Manufactured goods | ... | 5.3 | ... | ... | ... | ... | ... | ... | ... | ... | ... | ... | 15.1 |
| **Structure of imports, at current prices (%)** | | | | | | | | | | | | | |
| - Food, beverages and tobacco | ... | 13.8 | ... | ... | ... | ... | ... | ... | ... | ... | ... | ... | 13.7 |
| - Crude materials, oils and fats | ... | 3.6 | ... | ... | ... | ... | ... | ... | ... | ... | ... | ... | 5.3 |
| - Mineral fuels | ... | 7.5 | ... | ... | ... | ... | ... | ... | ... | ... | ... | ... | 9.5 |
| - Non-ferrous metals | ... | 0.7 | ... | ... | ... | ... | ... | ... | ... | ... | ... | ... | 0.8 |
| - Manufactured goods | ... | 73 | ... | ... | ... | ... | ... | ... | ... | ... | ... | ... | 69.3 |
| **Share in trade of all developing countries (%)** | | | | | | | | | | | | | |

| | | | | | | | | | | | | | |
|---|---|---|---|---|---|---|---|---|---|---|---|---|---|
| - Exports | ... | 16.7 | 16.5 | ... | ... | ... | ... | 13.4 | ... | ... | ... | ... | 9.2 |
| . Food, beverages and tobacco | ... | 17.4 | 15.5 | ... | ... | ... | ... | 14.1 | ... | ... | ... | ... | 10.8 |
| . Crude materials, oils and fats | ... | 26.2 | 16.6 | ... | ... | ... | ... | 15 | ... | ... | ... | ... | 12.4 |
| . Mineral fuels | ... | 18 | 20.9 | ... | ... | ... | ... | 22.3 | ... | ... | ... | ... | 22.5 |
| . Non-ferrous metals | ... | 30.5 | 20.1 | ... | ... | ... | ... | 14.1 | ... | ... | ... | ... | 13.1 |
| . Manufactured goods | ... | 5.2 | 3.4 | ... | ... | ... | ... | 2.6 | ... | ... | ... | ... | 2.5 |
| - Imports | ... | 19.7 | 15.8 | ... | ... | ... | ... | 13 | ... | ... | ... | ... | 10.4 |
| . Food, beverages and tobacco | ... | 23.7 | 21.3 | ... | ... | ... | ... | 23.5 | ... | ... | ... | ... | 17.2 |
| . Crude materials, oils and fats | ... | 14 | 11.2 | ... | ... | ... | ... | 12.9 | ... | ... | ... | ... | 10 |
| . Mineral fuels | ... | 10.5 | 8.1 | ... | ... | ... | ... | 7.7 | ... | ... | ... | ... | 11.2 |
| . Non-ferrous metals | ... | 11.7 | 9.3 | ... | ... | ... | ... | 6.4 | ... | ... | ... | ... | 5.5 |
| . Manufactured goods | ... | 22.1 | 17.7 | ... | ... | ... | ... | 13.3 | ... | ... | ... | ... | 9.9 |
| Net-exports ratios, at current prices (net exports/exports+imports) - total | ... | -3.4 | ... | ... | ... | ... | ... | .. | .. | ... | ... | ... | -5.2 |
| . Food, beverages and tobacco | ... | 1.4 | ... | ... | ... | ... | ... | ... | ... | ... | ... | ... | -10.5 |
| . Crude materials, oils and fats | ... | 57.2 | ... | ... | ... | ... | ... | ... | ... | ... | ... | ... | 19.2 |
| . Mineral fuels | ... | 76.7 | ... | ... | ... | ... | ... | ... | ... | ... | ... | ... | 70.3 |
| . Non-ferrous metals | ... | 68.7 | ... | ... | ... | ... | ... | ... | ... | ... | ... | ... | 53.9 |
| . Manufactured goods | ... | -87.4 | ... | ... | ... | ... | ... | ... | ... | ... | ... | ... | -67.1 |

Source:: compiled from  - UNIDO, 1991, *1993, African Industry in Figures 1990 and 1993*, Vienna.
 - UNIDO, 1988, *Africa in Figures, 1988*, Vienna.
 - UNIDO, 1995, *International Yearbook of Industrial Statistics 1995*, Vienna.

ANNEX 5.19
AFRICAN MVA: STRUCTURE, SHARE OF AFRICA IN WORLD MVA AND SHARE OF SELECTED COUNTRY GROUPS IN AFRICAN MVA (% at constant 1980 prices)

| Industrial branches | ISIC code | Structure of MVA | | | | Share of Africa in world MVA | | | | | Share of selected country groups in MVA of Africa | | | | | |
|---|---|---|---|---|---|---|---|---|---|---|---|---|---|---|---|---|
| | | | | | | | | | | | North Africa | | | African LDCs | | |
| | | 1970 | 1975 | 1980 | 1984 | 1970 | 1975 | 1980 | 1985 | 1990 | 1980 | 1985 | 1990 | 1980 | 1985 | 1990 |
| Food products | 311/2 | 25.9 | 18.6 | 18.7 | 20.9 | 2.4 | 1.8 | 1.8 | 2 | 1.9 | 41.1 | 45.7 | 42.8 | 26.3 | 23.7 | 26.6 |
| Beverages | 313 | 5.4 | 7.2 | 7.6 | 7.2 | 2.3 | 2.9 | 3 | 3.4 | 3.2 | 16.9 | 15 | 13.1 | 24.7 | 24.3 | 27.7 |
| Tobacco | 314 | 4.9 | 5.6 | 4.6 | 4.4 | 4.4 | 5.1 | 4.7 | 4.9 | 5.4 | 41.6 | 45.1 | 39.9 | 19.1 | 23.4 | 23.4 |
| Textiles | 321 | 16 | 17.6 | 14.3 | 14 | 2.5 | 2.8 | 2.4 | 2.6 | 2.7 | 45.7 | 55.8 | ... | 21.5 | 19 | ... |
| Wearing apparel | 322 | 3.1 | 3.1 | 3 | 3 | 0.9 | 1 | 1 | 1.1 | 1.1 | ... | ... | ... | ... | ... | ... |
| Leather and fur products | 323 | 0.8 | 0.9 | 0.8 | 0.9 | 1.2 | 1.5 | 1.5 | 1.6 | 1.5 | 54.6 | 61.2 | ... | 17.5 | 18.4 | ... |
| Footwear | 324 | 1.8 | 1.6 | 1.7 | 1.7 | 1.6 | 1.6 | 1.9 | 2 | 2 | 50.5 | 67.4 | ... | 17.2 | 14.2 | ... |
| Wood and cork products | 331 | 4.1 | 3.8 | 3 | 3.1 | 1.6 | 1.6 | 1.3 | 1.4 | 1.4 | 38.4 | 45.8 | 45.2 | 17.9 | 17.8 | 15.5 |
| Furniture, fixtures excluding metal | 332 | 1.5 | 1.5 | 1.4 | 1.5 | 0.8 | 0.8 | 0.7 | 0.9 | 0.8 | ... | ... | ... | ... | ... | ... |
| Paper | 341 | 1.7 | 1.7 | 2 | 1.8 | 0.6 | 0.7 | 0.7 | 0.7 | 0.6 | 51.1 | 49.3 | 53.4 | 12.7 | 12.7 | 14.3 |
| Printing and publishing | 342 | 1.9 | 2.1 | 2.4 | 2.1 | .. | ... | ... | ... | ... | ... | ... | ... | ... | ... | ... |
| Industrial chemicals | 351 | 1.4 | 1.7 | 1.7 | 2 | 0.4 | 0.4 | 0.4 | 0.4 | 0.4 | 43.1 | 55.2 | 50.5 | 19.8 | 15.7 | 15.4 |
| Other chemicals | 352 | 5.3 | 5.7 | 6.2 | 5.7 | 1.6 | 1.7 | 1.6 | 1.4 | 1.3 | 38.1 | 48.9 | ... | 11 | 10.3 | ... |
| Petroleum refineries | 353 | 2.1 | 3.3 | 4.7 | 5.7 | 0.8 | 1.2 | 1.6 | 2.3 | 2.3 | 71 | 79.5 | 82.2 | 17.2 | 12.9 | 10.1 |
| Products of petroleum and coal | 354 | 1.5 | 1.1 | 1.4 | 1.4 | ... | ... | ... | ... | ... | ... | ... | ... | ... | ... | ... |
| Rubber products | 355 | 1.2 | 1.2 | 1.2 | 1.1 | 0.9 | 0.8 | 0.8 | 0.8 | 1 | 42.5 | 43.1 | ... | 17.5 | 15.2 | ... |
| Plastic products | 356 | 0.8 | 1 | 1.1 | 1 | ... | ... | ... | ... | ... | ... | ... | ... | ... | ... | ... |
| Pottery, china, earthenware | 361 | 0.2 | 0.3 | 0.3 | 0.3 | 0.7 | 0.7 | 0.6 | 0.7 | 0.8 | 30.9 | 35.3 | 42.6 | 35.1 | 29.3 | 29.6 |
| Glass | 362 | 0.6 | 0.6 | 0.5 | 0.5 | 0.7 | 0.7 | 0.6 | 0.6 | 0.7 | ... | ... | ... | ... | ... | ... |
| Other non-metallic mineral products | 369 | 4.9 | 4.5 | 4.2 | 4.2 | 1.5 | 1.4 | 1.2 | 1.5 | 1.7 | 56.8 | 57.3 | 60.9 | 16.6 | 12.1 | 12 |
| Iron and steel | 371 | 2.5 | 2.4 | 2.5 | 2.5 | 0.4 | 0.4 | 0.4 | 0.5 | 0.5 | 50.4 | 57.5 | 59.2 | 8.3 | 8.2 | 6.1 |
| Non-ferrous metals | 372 | 2.3 | 1.6 | 1.5 | 1.4 | 1 | 0.7 | 0.6 | 0.6 | 0.7 | 35.4 | 47.1 | ... | 13.9 | 16.6 | ... |
| Metal products | 381 | 4 | 5.2 | 4.8 | 4.7 | 0.7 | 0.9 | 0.8 | 0.8 | 0.8 | ... | ... | ... | ... | ... | ... |
| Non-electrical machinery | 382 | 1.1 | 1.4 | 1.5 | 1.5 | 0.1 | 0.1 | 0.1 | 0.1 | 0.1 | 56.3 | 69.3 | ... | 12.4 | 10.3 | ... |
| Electrical machinery | 383 | 1.2 | 1.4 | 2 | 2.7 | 0.2 | 0.2 | 0.2 | 0.3 | 0.2 | 50.8 | 75.2 | 73.1 | 8.2 | 5.1 | 4.8 |
| Transport equipment | 384 | 2.9 | 3.8 | 5.9 | 3.9 | 0.3 | 0.4 | 0.6 | 0.4 | ... | 23.3 | 43.2 | ... | 6.6 | 10.1 | ... |
| Professional, scientific equipment | 385 | 0.1 | 0.1 | 0.1 | 0.1 | ... | ... | ... | ... | ... | ... | ... | ... | ... | ... | ... |
| Other manufactures | 390 | 0.8 | 1.1 | 0.9 | 0.7 | ... | ... | ... | ... | ... | ... | ... | ... | ... | ... | ... |
| Total manufacturing | 3 | 100 | 100 | 100 | 100 | ... | ... | ... | ... | ... | ... | ... | ... | ... | ... | ... |

Source: Compiled from  UNIDO, 1988,1993. *African Industry in Figures 1988 and 1993*, Vienna.

Annex 5.19 provides MVA based information for selected manufacturing branches. As may be observed from the structure of MVA, although the contribution of food products has substantially declined to 20.9 percent in 1984 from 25.9 percent in 1970, it still holds the lead. It is followed by textiles (14.0%), beverages (7.2%), other chemicals (5.7%), petroleum refineries (5.7%), metal products (4.7%), tobacco (4.4%) and other non-metal mineral products (4.2%). The trend has been towards a rising share in beverages, paper, industrial chemicals, petroleum refineries, electrical machinery and transport equipment, and a falling share in textiles, glass and non-ferrous metals.

In regard to Africa's share in world MVA, tobacco occupied the leading position, accounting for 5.4 percent of world MVA in 1990. Beverages, textiles, petroleum refineries, footwears and food products, in that order of importance, constitute branches whose shares fell between 1.9 and 5.4 percent. Beverages, leather and fur products, footwear, petroleum refineries and other non-metallic mineral products showed positive increases during the 1970-1990 period.

| | ANNEX 5.20 LABOR PRODUCTIVITY AND WAGE PER WORKER IN TROPICAL AFRICAN AND NORTH AFRICAN AND ASIAN COUNTRIES AS PERCENTAGE OF NORTH AMERICAN LEVEL | | | | | | | | | | | |
|---|---|---|---|---|---|---|---|---|---|---|---|---|
| Industry | Tropical Africa (29 countries) | | | | | | North Africa and Western Asia (18 countries) | | | | | |
| | Labor productivity | | | Wage per worker | | | Labor productivity | | | Wage per worker | | |
| | 1970 | 1980 | 1990 | 1970 | 1980 | 1990 | 1970 | 1980 | 1990 | 1070 | 1980 | 1990 |
| Food products | 13.02 | 9.59 | 9.77 | 10.39 | 9.71 | 10 | 22.63 | 17.49 | 13.8 | 20.05 | 22.76 | 19.21 |
| Beverages | 27.22 | 19.14 | 12.24 | 13.94 | 10.16 | 9.63 | 27.65 | 19.89 | 13.13 | 21.57 | 24.77 | 19.62 |
| Tobacco products | 16.19 | 8.9 | 4.06 | 17.44 | 9.87 | 8.9 | 30.37 | 10.43 | 9.61 | 27.28 | 20.97 | 14.72 |
| Textiles | 18.2 | 13.61 | 9.27 | 11.26 | 10.25 | 8.55 | 23.32 | 25.68 | 20.06 | 19.7 | 27.37 | 23.11 |
| Wearing apparel | 17.1 | 13.86 | 9.33 | 14.73 | 13.63 | 11.2 | 40 | 31.1 | 22.61 | 35.48 | 33.22 | 24.9 |
| Leather and fur products | 17.27 | 19.34 | 12.26 | 13.02 | 12.63 | 1.79 | 40.55 | 40.49 | 35.72 | 22.41 | 30.51 | 23.76 |
| Footwear, excl. rubber or plastic footwear | 21.85 | 18.63 | 15.48 | 15.27 | 17.2 | 14.92 | 62.96 | 35.83 | 36.17 | 29.02 | 37.69 | 36.94 |
| Wood and cork products | 9.44 | 9.52 | 10.13 | 9.98 | 8 | 8.28 | 34.89 | 29.5 | 29.15 | 21.22 | 31.18 | 31.28 |
| Furniture and fixtures | 11.5 | 12.19 | 10 | 11.2 | 11.19 | 9.16 | 29.74 | 32.7 | 30.66 | 22.43 | 25.15 | 26.87 |
| Paper and paper products | 18.8 | 12.61 | 7.23 | 13.37 | 10.65 | 8.9 | 24.3 | 20.94 | 15.93 | 19.14 | 27.69 | 21.45 |
| Printing and publishing | 13.41 | 11.71 | 7.85 | 13.63 | 10.72 | 8.59 | 23.25 | 19.8 | 21.86 | 20.52 | 25.75 | 24.05 |
| Industrial chemicals | 13.27 | 8.27 | 5.96 | 14.34 | 13.35 | 12.77 | 18.68 | 14.59 | 13.37 | 23.61 | 20.32 | 16.1 |
| Other chemical products | 11.7 | 10.61 | 6.18 | 10.99 | 10.34 | 10.83 | 15.64 | 14.98 | 15.37 | 15.46 | 24.13 | 20.95 |
| Petroleum refineries | 60.01 | 14.4 | 10.96 | 29.74 | 15.68 | 12.37 | 65.65 | 57.21 | 99.26 | 33.61 | 38.49 | 37.12 |
| Miscellaneous petroleum and coal products | 85.24 | 32.19 | 12.02 | 15.05 | 19.88 | 15.91 | 33.27 | 32.82 | 23.3 | 20.43 | 16.31 | 16.87 |
| Rubber products | 12.39 | 11.58 | 15.29 | 8.78 | 9.8 | 13.46 | 26.24 | 32.41 | 23.27 | 19.79 | 30.53 | 28.93 |
| Plastic products n.e.c. | 16.17 | 11.69 | 11.77 | 10.74 | 11.4 | 11.7 | 61.92 | 49.02 | 47.08 | 18.29 | 32.47 | 21.12 |
| Pottery, china and earthenware | 13.08 | 13.3 | 20.57 | 9.22 | 12.28 | 16.5 | 29.45 | 25.96 | 27.89 | 17.54 | 25.6 | 18.6 |
| Glass and glass products | 12.1 | 15.73 | 7.9 | 10.01 | 11.88 | 8.32 | 20.7 | 20.82 | 20.8 | 16.05 | 24.42 | 20.34 |
| Other non-metallic mineral products | 14.4 | 10.24 | 12.9 | 9.99 | 8 | 9.53 | 29.53 | 26.52 | 27.67 | 21.05 | 27.63 | 26.69 |
| Iron and steel | 17.64 | 19.96 | 8.78 | 14.7 | 14.15 | 11.08 | 35.15 | 21.29 | 20.37 | 20.67 | 21.93 | 17.83 |
| Non-ferrous metals | 52.95 | 20.81 | 29.27 | 21.36 | 11.26 | 12.39 | 21.26 | 15.19 | 33.82 | 14.86 | 17.26 | 19.03 |
| Metal products | 13.23 | 11.67 | 12.88 | 10.69 | 10.83 | 10.35 | 28.16 | 23.31 | 28.43 | 19.83 | 25.11 | 23.89 |
| Non-electrical machinery | 14.11 | 11.12 | 10.81 | 13.29 | 11.96 | 11.06 | 23.51 | 21.41 | 21.71 | 16.93 | 22.38 | 21.7 |
| Electrical machinery | 15.63 | 12.04 | 10.59 | 12.82 | 11.2 | 10.52 | 39.91 | 28.42 | 22.37 | 22.48 | 30.4 | 19.35 |
| Transport machinery | 10.92 | 23.58 | 9.73 | 9.22 | 6.77 | 7.02 | 32.37 | 19.58 | 15.85 | 18.92 | 24.89 | 14.81 |
| Professional and scientific goods | 10.97 | 6.46 | 9 | 13.38 | 5.83 | 7.17 | 22.13 | 21.57 | 12.83 | 25.22 | 33.61 | 16.84 |
| Other manufactures | 23.23 | 17.53 | 11.22 | 15.65 | 13.75 | 13.92 | 21.18 | 27.02 | 26.27 | 13.26 | 22.69 | 22.41 |
| Total | 15.7 | 12.57 | 10 | 10.5 | 9.2 | 8.68 | 32.33 | 24.85 | 18.65 | 24.15 | 19.98 | 19.98 |

Source: UNIDO, 1993, *Industry and Development: Global Report 1992/93*, Vienna.

ANNEX 6.1

A HIGHLY SIMPLIFIED SUMMARY OF DETAILS OF SOME OF THE COMMON FEATURES OF INVESTMENT CODES OF SIX AFRICAN COUNTRIES

| Legislation component | Tunisia | Morocco | Cote d'Ivoire | Mozambique | Ghana | Ethiopia |
|---|---|---|---|---|---|---|
| Title of relevant code | Investment code | Industrial investment code | Investment code | Investment code | Investment code | Encouragement, expansion and coordination of investment |
| Year of promulgation | 1969 | 1982 | 1984 | 1984 | 1985 | 1992 |
| Relevant organization, other than the ministry responsible for industry | Investment Promotion Agency (for industry) | Office of Industrial Development | Independent Service for Industrial Promotion and Documentation | Office for the Promotion of Foreign Investment | Ghana Investment Center | Office of Investment (plus regional/state counterparts) |
| Priority industries in which foreign investors can operate | | No priorities indicated, can own anything except farmland | - Agricultural processing - Manufacture of wide consumption goods | All economic sectors except those reserved for government (not identified) | | All industries except defense industries |
| Foreign ownership and/or participation | 100% for export industries, rest negotiable | Up to 100% equity | No restriction but usually 25% national shareholding | | Practically all industries jointly with Ghanaians | Up to 100% equity in new investment ($500,000 min) |
| Guaranteed transfer | - Capital and proceeds, profits and earnings | - Capital, dividends (tax free) | - Income, capital gain (18% tax on dividends) | - Profits, not exceeding capital imported, dividend - Expatriates salaries (35-50) | - capital, net profits, dividends, capital gain - Expatriate salaries for family maintenance, etc. | - Profits, dividends, foreign loans, interest - Expatriate salaries and other payments |
| Technology transfer and restrictive business practices | Patents valid for 5,10,15, 20 and trademarks 15 y | Patents and trade marks valid for 20 y | Patents and trade marks valid for 20 y | | Patents (16 years), trade marks (14 y) | Provision for technology agreement |
| Fiscal incentives and taxation - Customs duties exemptions - Corporate tax rate and exemption - Accelerated depreciation - Turn over tax | - 5-100%, equipment, raw materials, etc. for 20 y - 38%, 20 y for export industries - For replacement of equipment - Local purchases | - capital goods for certain zones, raw materials - 40%, partial or total (5-10 y) for certain zones - Accepted in certain sectors - 15% (average) | - Machinery, equipment, materials - 40%, business profits (5-7 y) - Plants with useful life> 5 years - 20-25%, normal rate | - Equipment, 50-100%, raw materials for export goods - 3-9 y | - Plant, machinery, etc. 45% Reduced rate (up to 5 y possible) 40% in investment year 20% in subsequent years | - Capital goods, materials for production for export provided not locally available - 40%, profit tax (3-8 y) depending on type of owner ship and location |
| Free zones with exemptions | All in ports on the Mediterranean Sea | Available | Warehousing and bonding facilities | | In Tema | |
| Investment guarantees | Agreement for the protection of investments in the member states of the Islamic Conference | Against nationalization and expropriation | Against war or revolution, nationalization, expropriation and non-convertibility of currency | Nationalization, expropriation (if needed, compensation) | Expropriation (if needed, adequate compensation will be paid) | No assets may be nationalized ( if needed, with payment of adequate compensation) |
| Settlements of disputes | Arbitration and conciliation (signatory to ICSID) | International arbitration | Convention on the Settlement of Investment Disputes | Arbitration | Arbitration, conciliation | International dispute settlement procedures (signatory to MIGA) |

Source:: - Compiled from UNCTC, 1988, *National Legislation and Regulations Relating to Transnational Corporations*. Volume VI and VII, New York.
- Investment Office of Ethiopia, undated, *Ethiopia: A Guide to Investment*, Addis Ababa, Ethiopia.
- Negarit Gazeta, 1992, *A Proclamation to Provide for the Encouragement, Expansion and Coordination of Investment*. No. 15/1992, Addis Ababa, Ethiopia.

ANNEX 7.1
COMPARATIVE ASSESSMENT OF POTENTIAL FOR INDUSTRIAL DEVELOPMENT IN 25 AFRICAN COUNTRIES

| No. | Countries ranked by established industries | Share of manufacturing in GDP (%) | Electricity production Gwh/y/energy consumption (Gcal/head) | Existing transport infrastructure (railways, roads, ports, etc.) | Population, (million/% in industry) | Land area, (1000 km²) | GDP per head ($) | Ores, minerals, fuels, agro, fish, forest, livestock, etc. | Water reserves | Combined potential for industrial development |
|---|---|---|---|---|---|---|---|---|---|---|
| 1 | South Africa | Zambia, 38 | South Africa 150/370 | South Africa | Nigeria, 116/13 | Sudan, 2506 | Algeria, 6107 | South Africa | Moderate | South Africa |
| 2 | Algeria | Zimbabwe, 29 | Egypt, 36/20 | Algeria | Egypt, 55/22 | Algeria, 2382 | Seychelles, 5306 | Nigeria | Huge | Algeria |
| 3 | Egypt | South Africa, 25 | Libya, 16/105 | Egypt | Ethiopia, 52/10 | Congo K, 2350 | Libya, 4456 | Zimbabwe | Large | Egypt |
| 4 | Nigeria | Swaziland, 25 | Algeria, 14/36 | Morocco | South Africa, 39/10 | Libya, 1760 | Gabon, 3432 | Algeria | Very limited | Nigeria |
| 5 | Libya | Mauritius, 24 | Nigeria, 10/5 | Zimbabwe | Congo K, 38/15 | Chad, 1284 | South Africa, 3202 | Mozambique | Large | Libya |
| 6 | Zimbabwe | Mozambique, 24 | Morocco, 9/10 | Nigeria | Tanzania, 30/5 | Niger, 1267 | Botswana, 3005 | Congo K | Huge | Zimbabwe |
| 7 | Tunisia | Senegal, 19 | Zambia, 9/7 | Congo K | Morocco, 27/29 | Angola, 1247 | Mauritius, 2728 | Libya | Very limited | Congo K |
| 8 | Morocco | Tunisia, 18 | Zimbabwe, 8/21 | Angola | Sudan, 27/10 | Mali, 1240 | Sudan, 2267 | Madagascar | Large | Morocco |
| 9 | Kenya | Morocco, 18 | Congo K, 6/2 | Kenya | Algeria, 26/30 | Ethiopia, 1222 | Tunisia, 1708 | Tanzania | Large | Angola |
| 10 | Ghana | Burkina Faso, 17 | Tunisia, 5/21 | Tunisia | Kenya, 26/8 | South Africa, 1221 | Namibia, 1320 | Egypt | Large | Tunisia |
| 11 | Cameroon | Lesotho, 15 | Ghana, 5/3 | Liberia | Uganda, 20/5 | Mauritania, 1031 | Congo, 1212 | Angola | Huge | Tanzania |
| 12 | Cote d'Ivoire | Cameroon, 14 | Kenya, 3/3 | Sudan | Mozambique, 17/8 | Egypt, 1001 | Swaziland, 1080 | Cote d'Ivoire | Large | Cameroon |
| 13 | Angloa | Algeria, 12 | Cameroon, 3/8 | Cameroon | Ghana, 16/20 | Tanzania, 945 | Cameroon, 1031 | Congo | Huge | Mozambique |
| 14 | Zambia | Egypt, 12 | Cote d'Ivoire, 2/6 | Tanzania | Cote d'Ivoire, 13/10 | Nigeria, 924 | Zimbabwe, 825 | Zambia | Large | Cote d'Ivoire |
| 15 | Congo K | Nigeria, 10 | Angola, 2/3 | Mauritania | Cameroon, 13/12 | Namibia, 824 | Angola, 811 | Gabon | Large | Kenya |
| 16 | Mauritius | Congo, 9 | Sudan, 1/2 | Mozambique | Madagascar, 13/10 | Mozambique, 802 | Egypt, 792 | Morocco | Limited | Sudan |
| 17 | Mozambique | Libya, 8 | Gabon, 1/34 | Cote d'Ivoire | Angola, 11/10 | Zambia, 753 | Morocco, 746 | Botswana | Very limited | Madagascar |
| 18 | Madagascar | Gabon, 7 | Tanzania, 1/1 | Benin | Zimbabwe, 10/10 | Somalia, 638 | Zambia, 665 | Liberia | Large | Ghana |
| 19 | Mauritania | Cape Verde, 7 | Liberia, 1/5 | Guinea | Mali, 10/3 | C.A.R., 623 | Mozambique, 634 | Tunisia | Limited | Zambia |
| 20 | Sudan | Mauritania, 7 | Ethiopia, 1/1 | Zambia | Burkina Faso, 10/5 | Madagascar, 587 | Cote d'Ivoire, 587 | Cameroon | Large | Uganda |
| 21 | Liberia | Togo, 7 | Senegal, 1/4 | Madagascar | Zambia, 9/11 | Kenya, 583 | Guinea, 572 | Senegal | Large | Gabon |
| 22 | Togo | Guinea, 5 | Mauritius, 1/12 | Congo | Malawi, 10/8 | Botswana, 582 | Togo, 522 | Ghana | Huge | Botswana |
| 23 | Senegal | Botswana, 5 | Uganda, 1/1 | Gabon | Tunisia, 9/41 | Cameroon, 475 | Senegal, 463 | Mauritania | Limited | Senegal |
| 24 | Guinea | Namibia, 4 | Malawi, 1/1 | Ghana | Niger, 8/3 | Morocco, 447 | Mauritania, 457 | Swaziland | Limited | Congo |
| 25 | Sierra Leone | Congo K, 2 | Madagascar, 1/2 | Ethiopia | Somalia, 8/10 | Zimbabwe, 391 | Madagascar, 405 | Kenya | Large | Mauritania |

Source: ECA/UNIDO, 1995, Report on Regional Strategy for Rational Location of Industries in the Context of the Abuja Treaty (CAMI.12/6(A), Gaborone.
Note: Some of the figures in the fourth and sixth columns were rounded.

| ANNEX 7.2<br>INDUSTRIAL PROJECTS INCLUDED IN IDDA II PROGRAM FOR THE CENTRAL AFRICAN SUBREGION | | | |
|---|---|---|---|
| **Industrial projects** | | | |
| Subsector/project | Host country/sponsor | Subsector/project | Host country/sponsor |
| **Agro- and agro-related industries** | | | |
| 1. Sugar, reconversion of Bon Jesus mills | Angola | 2. Phosphate fertilizers | Burundi |
| 2. Ethyl alcohol, distillery | Burundi | 3. Pharmaceuticals | Burundi |
| 3. Dairy products | Congo K | 4. Pharmaceuticals, laboratory | Central African Republic |
| 4. Cassava products | Central African Republic | 5. Potash, upgrading for the manufacture of chemicals | Congo |
| 5. Fish products | CEPGL | 6. Calcium carbide | Rwanda |
| 6. Forest products, integrated | CEPGL | 7. Active ingredients for pesticides | Rwanda |
| 7. Sugar, rehabilitation and expansion | Angola | 8. Petrochemicals for plastics | Gabon |
| 8. Ethyl alcohol, distillery | Sao Tome and Principe | 9. Petroleum products, improvement of efficiency and product quality | Congo |
| 9. Wood products, incl. particle board | Cameroon/UDEAC | 10. Human vaccines | Cameroon |
| 10. Children's food | Cameroon | 11. Insecticides for domestic use | Cameroon |
| 11. Leather | Chad | 12. Ammonia and urea from gas | Cameroon |
| 12. Cattle and fish resources | UDEAC | 13. Pesticides | UDEAC |
| **Building materials industries** | | **Metallurgical industries** | |
| 1. Cement, reactivation of Katana cement plant | Congo K | 1. Aluminum, integrated | Cameroon/UDEAC/ ECCAS |
| 2. Glass, expansion and diversification | Congo | 2. Iron and steel, integrated | ECCAS |
| 3. Ceramics | Chad | 3. Tin, expansion | Rwanda |
| 4. Flat glass | Cameroon | 4. Iron and steel, integrated | Cameroon/UDEAC |
| 5. Ceramics | Cameroon | 5. Products of rolling mill | Congo |
| **Chemical industries** | | **Engineering industries** | |
| 1. Methane gas from Lac Kivu | Congo K/Rwanda | 1. Agricultural machinery | |
| **Support projects** | | | |
| Project | | | Host country/sponsor |
| 1. Assistance to the Central African Customs and Economic Union (UDEAC) | | | UDEAC |
| 2. Assistance to the Central African Republic in the development of an integrated meat processing industry | | | Central African Republic |
| 3. Assistance to the Economic Community of the Great Lakes Countries (CEPGL) | | | CEPGL |
| 4. Development of peat resources | | | CEPGL |
| 5. Feasibility study on the manufacture of railway equipment in the Central African Republic | | | Central African Republic |
| 6. Assistance to the Economic Community of Central Africa States (ECCAS) | | | ECCAS |
| 7. Assistance to the subregional Higher Institute of Appropriate Technology (ISTA) | | | ISTA |
| 8. Assistance to the African Intellectual Property Organization (AIPO) | | | AIPO |
| 9. Multi-sectoral assistance to the Economic Community of the Great Lakes countries (CEPGL) | | | CEPGL |
| 10. Promotion of small-scale agro-food technologies | | | Burundi |
| 11. Assistance to the Higher National School for Agro-industries | | | Cameroon |
| 12. Establishment of a school for geological and mining studies | | | Cameroon |
| Source: - Compiled from United Nations, 1992, *Regional Cooperation: Second Industrial Development Decade for Africa Addendum Program for the Second Industrial Development Decade for Africa (1991-2000).* Volume II, Subregional and regional programs, New York. | | | |

ANNEX 7.3
INDUSTRIAL PROJECTS INCLUDED IN IDDA II PROGRAM FOR THE EASTERN AND SOUTHERN AFRICAN SUBREGION

Industrial Projects

| Subsector/project | Host country/sponsor | Status | Subsector/project | Host country/sponsor | Status |
|---|---|---|---|---|---|
| Agro- and agro-related industries | | | 12. Copper oxichloride, rehab. | Zambia | O, B |
| 1. Edible oil | Lesotho | P, B | 13. Copper oxichloride, rehab. | Zimbabwe | O, B |
| 2. Blanket | Lesotho | O | 14. Chrome tanning salts | Zimbabwe | O, B |
| 3. Vaccine, Botswana Vaccine | Botswana | O | 15. Pharmaceuticals, expansion | Lesotho/PTA | O, B |
| 4. Tannery | Botswana | O | 16. Essential oils, extraction | | O |
| 5. Bbandages | Botswana | O | Metallurgical industries | | |
| 6. Wood products | Mozambique | O, B | 1. Iron and steel, rationalization and upgrading | PTA | P |
| Building materials industries | | | | | |
| 1. Cement, blending and packaging | Lesotho | P, B | 2. Iron and steel, upgrading and diversification of ZISCOSTEEL | Zimbabwe | O, B |
| 2. Cement, rehabilitation and rationalization (second phase) | PTA | P, C | 3. Iron and steel, integrated | Madagascar | O, B |
| 3. Cement | Madagascar/OC | O, B | 4. Sponge iron | Moz/Tan/Uga/Zam | O, B |
| 4. Cement, rehabilitation (second phase) | PTA | P, C | 5. Iron and steel plant/rolling mills, rationalization and upgrading | PTA | P |
| Chemical industries | | | Engineering industries | | |
| 1. Phosphate fertilizers | Uganda | P, B | 1. Electric motors | Zambia | P, B |
| 2. Caustic soda | Kenya/India | p, b | 2. CAD/CAM, initiating demonstration network | PTA | P, B |
| 3. Chlor-alkali and PVC | Zimbabwe | P, C | 3. Low cost vehicles | Ethiopia | O, C |
| 4. Sheet glass | Tanzania | P, C | 4. Fabricate metals, for the building industry | | O |
| 5. Potash | Ethiopia/Libya | O, B | 5. Machine tools, feasibility study | | O |
| 6. Phosphate fertilizers | Burundi | O, B | 6. Automotives, feasibility study | | O |
| 7. Sheet glass | Madagascar | O, B | 7. Diesel engines for tractors, trucks, lorries and buses | Zimbabwe | P, B |
| 8. Salt, refining and packing | Somalia | O, C | 8. Pumps for irrigation and rural water supply | Swaziland/Zimbabwe | P, B |
| 9. Salt, rehabilitation | Mozambique | P, B | 9. Bicycles assembling, joint venture | Swaziland/Mozambique | O, B |
| 10. Urea fertilizers, rehabilitation | Somalia | O, B | 10. Spare parts | Keny/Tanzania/Zimbabwe | O, C |
| 11. Carbon black | Kenya | O, C | 11. Electronic, transformers | Zambia | P, B |

Support projects

| Project | Host/sponsor | Status |
|---|---|---|
| 1. Assistance to the African Regional Organization for Standardization (ARSO) and the African Institute for Higher Technical Training Research (AIHTTR) | ARSO, AIHTTR/ECA, OAU, UNIDO | P, C |
| 2. Upgrading of Kenya Textile Training Institute (KTTI) into a subregional training center | Kenya | P, C |
| 3. Tanzania Institute of Leather Technology | Tanzania | P, C |

458

| | | |
|---|---|---|
| 4. Consolidation of the Institute of Cement Technology | Tanzania | P, C |
| 5. Establishment of a pilot and demonstration physical manufacturing facilities | Tanzania | P, C |
| 6. Expansion of an existing marine resources training and research center | IOC/subregion | P, C |
| 7. Establishment of the Leather and Leather Products Institute (LLPI) | PTA/Ethiopia | P, C |
| 8. Pilot unit for small-scale industrial water treatment | PTA | P |
| 9. Establishment of the PTA Metallurgical Technology Centre (MTC) | PTA | P |
| 10. Sugar industry training center | PTA/Mauritius | P, C |
| 11. Upgrading of Ethiopian Management Institute into a subregional center | Ethiopia | O, C |
| 12. Upgrading of Management Training and Advisory Centre (MTAC) into a subregional center | Uganda | O, C |
| 13. Establishment of a cement institute at the Mugher cement plant | Ethiopia | C, O |
| 14. Engineering design and tools center | Ethiopia | P, A |
| 15. Upgrading the Mogadishu Industrial Vocational Training Centre (IVC) into a subregional center | Somalia | O, C |
| 16. Support of SADCC Industry and Trade Cooperation Division | SADCC | O, A |
| 17. Establishment of information exchange center | SADCC | O, A |
| 18. Exchange of information and strengthening of co-ordination facilities | IOC | O, B |
| 19. Inventory of subregional training facilities | SADCC | P, C |
| 20. Managerial and technical personnel training | SADCC | P, C |
| 21. Development of local entrepreneurship (directory of small-scale industrial project profiles) | ECA/UNIDO/OAU | P, C |
| 22. Proram for standardization, quality control and metrology in IOC countries | IOC | P |
| 23. Reassessment and updating of a feasibility study on the establishment of copper products plant for the PTA market | PTA | P |
| 24. PTA program for the production of spare parts | PTA/Eth/Mad/Mau/Som/ Tan/Uga/Zam/Zim | P |
| 25. Development of capabilities in industrial Project identification, formulation appraisal, monitoring and evaluation | PTA Zimbabwe | P, C |
| 26. Training of trainers in testing and quality control in food processing | PTA/Mauritius | O, C |
| 27. Training and curriculum development of an integrated production technology management system for the textile industry | PTA/Kenya | P, C |
| 28. Development of human resources for the petroleum industry | PTA | P |
| 29. Assistance to PTA member states in the promotion of standardization and quality control systems | Les/Swa/Rwa | P |
| 30 Subregional cooperation in small- and medium-scale industry promotion | Som/DJI/cOM | P |
| 31. PTA industrial information system | PTA | P |
| 32. PTA capacity for long-term integrated industrial development programming | PTA | P |
| 33. Promotion of industrial investment projects through investment fora | PTA | P |
| 34. Rationalization and harmonization of investment codes | PTA | P |
| 35. Railway rolling stock, list equipment, hydromechanic and metalo-mechanic products | Mozambique | P, A |
| 36. Leathers, training | Djibouti | P, B |
| 37. Standardization and quality control | SADCC | O, A |
| 38. Engineering design and product procurement | SADCC | O, A |
| 39. Development of small-scale industries, study/workshop | SADCC | O, B |
| 40. Research and development, study | SADCC | O, A |
| 41. Management and skills development | SADCC | O, B |
| 42. Study on the improvement of the investment climate | SADCC | O, B |
| 43. A system of direct trade measures, including bilateral trade agreements | SADCC | O, B |
| 44. General system of preferences study | SADCC | O, A |
| 45. Trade directory | SADCC | O, B |
| 46. Participation of SADCC firms in SADCC projects | SADCC | O, C |
| 47. Improvement and development of the cement industry | SADCC | O, C |
| 48. Survey of raw materials for the establishment of a refractory industry | | O |
| 49. Improvement and development of the cement industry | SADCC | C, O |

Source: Compiled from UNIDO, 1993, *Implementation of the Sub-regional Program for the Second IDDA for Eastern and Southern Africa* (PPD.259(SPEC)), Vienna.
P = priority   O = optional   A, B and C indicate stages of development of the project, C being the most advanced stage.

**ANNEX 7.4**
**INDUSTRIAL PROJECTS INCLUDED IN IDDA II PROGRAM FOR THE NORTH AFRICAN SUBREGION**

Industrial projects

| Subsector/project | Host country/sponsor | | Subsector/project | Host country/sponsor |
|---|---|---|---|---|
| Agro- and agro-related industries | | | | |
| 1. Sugar | Sudan | | 7. Sheet glass | Algeria/Maghreb |
| 2. Food | Libya/Morocco | | Engineering industries | |
| 3. Vegetable oil | Sud/Tun/Alg/Mor | | 1. Tractors | Sudan/Egypt |
| 4. Fish | Mauritania/Algeria | | 2. Diesel engines, expansion | Tunisia/Egypt |
| 5. Meat | Mauritania | | 3. Household washing machines | Algeria/Libya |
| 6. Paper | Sudan | | 4. Passenger cars and utility vehicles | Algeria/Libya |
| 7. Yarn, spinning | Tunisia/Libya | | | |
| 8. Cotton yarn | Sud/AIDMO/Tun/Mor/Alg | | 5. Gear boxes for automobiles | Algeria/Libya |
| Building materials industries | | | 6. High grade diesel engines for tractors and trucks | Algeria/Libya |
| 1. Cement | Sudan | | 8. Aluminum, electrolytic process | Algeria/Libya |
| 2. Marble tiles | Sudan/Egypt | | 9. Lorries | Libya/Tunisia |
| 3. Bricks | Algeria/Tunisia | | 10. High tension electrical transformers | Algeria/Tunisia |
| 4. Cement, rehabilitation | Morocco/Algeria | | 11. Machinery for sheet metal work | Algeria/Tunisia |
| Chemical industries | | | 12. Textile machinery | Algeria/Tunisia |
| 1. Pharmaceuticals | Libya/Morocco | | 13. Machinery for processing plastics | Algeri/Tunisia |
| 2. Urea and nitrate fertilizers | Liby/Tunisia | | 14. Thermostats, evaporate sheets, heat exchangers, cooking stoves, micromotors, cathode tubes, TVs, and printed circuits | Algeria/Tunisia |
| 3. Phosphate fertilizers | Sudan/Tunisia | | 15. Pistons, gudgeon pins, casings, sleeve bearings and transmission chains | Algeria/Tunisia |
| 4. Nitro-phosphate fertilizers | Algeria/Tunisia | | 16. Graphite electrodes | AIDMO/Algeria |
| 5. Chemical products | Algeria/Tunisia | | 17. Electric control panels | Algeria/Libya |
| 6. Petrochemicals | Algeria/Tunisia | | 18. Refrigerator compressors | AIDMO |

Support projects

| Project | Host country/sponsor |
|---|---|
| 1. Development of local entrepreneurship (directory of small-scale industrial project profiles) | Subregion |
| 2. Promotion of the food processing industry in North Africa | Subregion |
| 3. African regional centre for genetic engineering | Subregion |
| 4. Joint Tunisian/Libyan company for industrial maintenance and assembly | Tunisia/Libya |
| 5. Study on the promotion of capital goods manufacture in North Africa | Subregion |
| 6. Technical studies on the promotion of subregional cooperation in the fish processing industry | Subregion |
| 7. Technical studies on promotion of a subregional marine repair and maintenance industry | Subregion |
| 8. Technical studies related to industrial pollution | Subregion |
| 9. Subregional consultations on specific sectors | Subregion |

Source: Compiled from United Nations, 1992, *Regional Cooperation: Second Industrial Development Decade for Africa— Addendum— Program for the Second Industrial Development Decade for Africa (1991-2000)*. Volume II, Subregional and regional programs, New York.

| | | | | ANNEX 7.5 | | |
|---|---|---|---|---|---|---|
| | | | INDUSTRIAL PROJECTS INCLUDED IN IDDA II PROGRAM FOR THE WEST AFRICAN SUBREGION | | | |
| | | | Industrial projects | | | |
| Subsector/project | Host country/sponsor | Status | | Subsector/project | Host country/sponsor | Status |
| Agro- and related industries | | | | Metallurgical industries | | |
| 1. Poultry, integrated | Liberia | ST | | 1. Sponge iron | | LT |
| 2. Millet and sorghum products | Niger/Nigeria | ST | | 2. Steel, electric arc furnaces | | LT |
| 3. Food processing | Guinea | ST | | 3. Rerolled products, expansion and installation | | LT |
| 4. Manou Agro-industrial Co., rehabilitation and expansion | Guinea | ST | | 4. Iron and steel, flat and tubular, integrated | | LT |
| 5. Kinkelibah and other similar plants, processing | Senegal | ST | | 5. Iron ore, exploitation of Nimba mountains | | ST |
| 6. Exo-pulp (frozen fruit) | Guinea | MT | | 6. Alumina | Ghana | MT |
| 7. Pulp and paperboard | Cote d'Ivoire | MT | | Engineering industries | | |
| 8. Pulp and paper in MRU | Sierra Leone | MT | | 1. Agricultural tools and implements | Sierra Leone | ST |
| 9. Cotton wool, dressings and sanitary products | Senegal | ST | | 2. Agricultural implements and equipment | Nigeria | LT |
| Building materials industries | | | | 3. Palm oil mini mills, mobile | MRU | ST |
| 1. Cement, subregional | Liptako-Gourma region | ST | | 4. Village mills for millet and sorghum | Niger and Nigeria | ST |
| 2. Ceramic | Togo | ST | | 5. Four-wheel tractors | Senegal | MT |
| Chemical industries | | | | 6. Diesel engines for irrigation pumps and generators | Guinea | MT |
| 1. Phosphoric acid | Togo | ST | | 7. Irrigation pumps | Senegal | MT |
| 2. Ammonia and urea | Cote d'Ivoire | LT | | 8. Railway wagons | Burkina Faso/Senegal | MT |
| 3. Phosphate fertilizers, subregional | Liptako-Gourma region | ST | | 9. Pressed parts | Nigeria | ST |
| 4. Phosphoric acid and fertilizers, extension and rehabilitation | Senegal | ST | | 10. Diesel engines for tractors, trucks, lorries and buses | Nigeria | LT |
| 5. Pharmaceuticals, reactivation of Matoto plant | Guinea | ST | | 11. Diesel engine mounted-chassis for lorries, trucks and buses | Nigeria | ST |
| 6. Pharmaceuticals, rehabilitation of Seredu station | Guinea | ST | | 12. Hurricane lamps | Senegal | ST |
| 7. Pharmaceuticals | Nigeria | ST | | 13. Aluminum conductors and cables | Ghana | LT |
| 8. Salt, Tidekelt project | Manno River Union | ST | | 14. Steel towers | Nigeria | LT |
| 9. Salt and soda, expansion | Mano River Union (MRU) | ST | | | | |
| 10. Glass containers | Liberia | ST | | | | |
| 11. Glass containers | CEAO MEMBER STATES | MT | | | | |
| 12. Glass, Massou glassworks | Guinea | LT | | | | |
| Support projects | | | | | | |
| Project | | | | | Host country/sponsor | |
| 1. Assistance to ARCEDEM | | | | | ARCEDEM | |
| 2. Assistance to ARCT | | | | | ARCT | |
| 3. Assistance to CEAO | | | | | CEAO | |
| 4. Assistance to ECOWAS | | | | | ECOWAS | |
| 5. Assistance to ECOWAS in the development of an industrial training program | | | | | ECOWAS | |

| 6. Development of industrial consultancy and management capabilities | ECOWAS |
| 7. Assistance in the promotion of an integrated industrial development plan for the Liptak-Gourma region | Liptako-Gourma region |
| 8. Establishment of an industrial and technology fair serving the member states of the Mano River Union | MRU |
| 9. Establishment of a Mano River Union financing institute | MRU |
| 10. Processing of fish and other sea foods | |
| 11. Subregional development center for hides, skins, leather and leather products, Leather Research Institute | Nigeria |
| 12. Assistance to Niger/Nigeria Joint Commission (NNJC) | NNJC |
| 13. Assistance to OMVS | OMVS |
| 14. Togolese National Centre for Technology Development | Togo |
| 15. Industrial maintenance center | Benin |
| 16. Guinea pilot center | Guinea |
| 17. Use of plant materials in the building sector | Guinea |

Source: Compiled from United Nations, 1992, *Regional Cooperation: Second Industrial Development Decade for Africa : Addendum Program for the Second Industrial Development Decade for Africa (1991-2000)*, Volume II. Subregional and Regional Programs , New York.

SH = short-term, MT = medium-term, LT = long-term

## ANNEX 7.6

## CRITERIA FOR MULTINATIONAL/SUBREGIONAL CORE PROJECT IDENTIFICATION AND SELECTION

For a project to qualify for inclusion in a subregional program, it should:

1. Provide inputs to the priority sectors spelled out in the Lagos Plan of Action and the Final Act of Lagos, including food, transport and communications and energy;

2. Provide effective integration and linkages with other industrial and economic activities and infrastructures in the subregion;

3. Utilize and upgrade, to the maximum extent possible, African natural resources (raw materials and energy) so as to benefit, first, the subregion, second, other African countries and third, non-African countries;

4. Produce intermediates for further processing or fabricating in established or planned industries or produce engineering goods, particularly those related to food production and processing, building materials, textiles, energy, transport and mining;

5. Cater, first and foremost, directly or indirectly, to the basic needs of the peoples of the subregion and, if required, of other Africa countries;

6. Involve (a) economies of scale, (b) complex or upgraded technology, (c) large investment and (d) market(s) beyond the reach of individual countries in the subregion;

7. Offer scope for cooperation, especially among the African countries, in long-term supply/purchase arrangements for raw materials, intermediates and final products; subcontracting; barter arrangements; equity share-holding, etc.;

8. Contribute to reducing the region's heavy reliance on external factor inputs;

9. Offer actual or potential comparative advantages(s) over a similar project(s) in other group of countries (African and non-African), particularly in respect of raw materials, energy and the infrastructure required;

10. Complement a related project(s) or an existing production unit(s) in the subregion;

11. Earn foreign exchange through the export of its products and include the upgrading of raw materials;

12. Result in rehabilitation and rationalization of an existing production unit(s); and

13. Replace, whenever practical, synthetic materials by natural materials, particularly those that are renewable.

Source: Regional Cooperation: *Second Industrial Development Decade for Africa—Note by the Secretary-General—Addendum: Program for the Second Industrial Development Decade for Africa (1992-2000)*, E/1992/14/ Add.1 (Part II), New York.

| ANNEX 7.7 | | | | | |
|---|---|---|---|---|---|
| RANKING OF 44 AFRICAN COUNTRIES ACCORDING TO LEVELS OF FOOD SECURITY, AGRICULTURAL PRODUCTIVITY AND SHARE OF FDI IN GNP | | | | | |
| Increasing level of food security, 1994 | | Levels of agricultural productivity, percentage, 1993-1995 | | Share of FDI in GNP, percentage, 1993-1995 | |
| Country | Calorie per capita [a] | Country | Productivity indicator [b] | Country | FDI/GNP |
| Somalia | 48 | Angola | 38 | Botswana | -2.23 |
| Ethiopia/Eritrea | 51 | Niger | 43 | Gabon | -0.84 |
| Central African Republic | 54 | Mozambique | 51 | Central African Republic | -0.09 |
| Mozambique | 54 | Mauritania | 53 | Sudan | 0 |
| Sierra Leone | 54 | Botswana | 54 | Congo K | 0.01 |
| Malawi | 58 | Mali | 57 | Senegal | 0.02 |
| Rwanda | 58 | Somalia | 59 | Algeria | 0.03 |
| Angola | 59 | Senegal | 62 | Burkina Faso | 0.05 |
| Namibia | 62 | Tunisia | 63 | Togo | 0.07 |
| Zambia | 62 | Chad | 66 | Niger | 0.11 |
| Burundi | 62 | Gambia | 72 | Ethiopia/Eritrea | 0.11 |
| Cameroon | 63 | Sudan | 75 | Burundi | 0.11 |
| Zimbabwe | 64 | Algeria | 82 | Congo | 0.11 |
| Chad | 64 | Central African Republic | 88 | Uganda | 0.13 |
| Tanzania | 65 | Congo K | 89 | Malawi | 0.13 |
| Kenya | 66 | Burkina Faso | 90 | Somalia | 0.13 |
| Congo K | 66 | Ghana | 91 | Kenya | 0.13 |
| Madagascar | 68 | Malawi | 92 | Rwanda | 0.29 |
| Nigeria | 68 | Zimbabwe | 92 | Benin | 0.36 |
| Uganda | 69 | Sierra Leone | 93 | Guinea | 0.58 |
| Sudan | 70 | Cote d'Ivoire | 94 | Mauritius | 0.59 |
| Lesotho | 70 | Congo | 95 | Cote d'Ivoire | 0.62 |
| Ghana | 71 | Benin | 97 | Zimbabwe | 0.68 |
| Togo | 72 | Swaziland | 97 | Madagascar | 0.71 |
| Niger | 72 | Cameroon | 98 | Mali | 0.73 |
| Senegal | 72 | Togo | 101 | Mauritania | 0.79 |
| Botswana | 73 | Libya | 101 | Cameroon | 1.04 |
| Mali | 73 | Namibia | 103 | Tanzania | 1.07 |
| Congo | 74 | Rwanda | 103 | Chad | 1.08 |
| Swaziland | 75 | Guinea | 105 | Lesotho | 1.41 |
| Burkina Faso | 76 | Ethiopia/Eritrea | 107 | Morocco | 1.45 |
| Guinea | 76 | Lesotho | 108 | Tunisia | 1.49 |
| Gabon | 80 | Morocco | 109 | Zambia | 1.87 |
| Cote d'Ivoire | 80 | Zambia | 113 | Egypt | 2.17 |
| Benin | 81 | Kenya | 114 | Mozambique | 2.71 |
| Mauritius | 86 | Tanzania | 115 | Gambia | 2.77 |
| Mauritania | 86 | Nigeria | 117 | Sierra Leone | 3.28 |
| South Africa | 87 | Uganda | 117 | Angola | 3.51 |
| Algeria | 93 | Burundi | 119 | Ghana | 3.79 |
| Morocco | 95 | Gabon | 122 | Nigeria | 4.74 |
| Tunisia | 100 | Madagascar | 141 | Swaziland | 5.14 |
| Egypt | 100 | South Africa | 181 | Libya | - |
| Libya | 100 | Mauritius | 272 | Namibia | - |
| Gambia | - | Egypt | 425 | South Africa | - |

Source: UNIDO, 1997, *Agro-related Industrial Development in Africa, The* Thirteenth Meeting of the Conference of African Ministers of Industry (CAMI.13/12), Accra.
a Daily calorie supply per capita (index = 100)
b Average yield per hectare in cereals, roots and pulses, the African average being 100)

ANNEX 8.1
MAJOR TROPICAL AND OTHER HUMAN DISEASES PANDEMIC IN AFRICA

| Major diseases | | Causative agent | Mode of transmission | Major affected areas | Main therapeutic agents | | Remarks: R & D, eradication program |
|---|---|---|---|---|---|---|---|
| Common name | Scientific name | | | | Preventive | Curative | |
| Malaria | Malaria | Plasmodium vivax, P. falciparum, etc. | Anopheles mosquito | Between 20° N and 25 ° S | Chloroquine, pyremethamine | Chloroquine, quinine sulfate, mefloquine, fansidar | Several vaccines (sporozoite, asexual, altruistic) being developed and tested |
| Bilharzia | Schistosomiasis | S. haematobium and S. mansoni | Snail | Countries south of the Sahara and East and Central Africa | Lematoxin from "endod" (phytolacca dodencandra) | Biltricide, praziquantel, metrifonate, oxamniquine | Research on vaccines reported to be at a stage of recommending which antigen (s) to promote further |
| River blindness | Onchocerciasis | Onchocerca volvulus | Blackfly | Endemic in West Africa | | Ivermectin, diethyl-carbamazine, suramin | Onchocerciasis Control Program in West Africa since 1974 considered successful |
| Sleeping sickness | Trypansomiasis | Trypanosome gambiense, T. rhodesiense | Tsetse flies | Dry sub-humid to humid zones (10° N and 10°S) | Pentamidine isethio-nate, sterile insect technique being tried in Madagascar | Pentamidine isethionate, melarsoprol (Enflornithine found effective but expensive, $500 per patient) | Control program under implcmentation (a new insecticide, SPOTON, found effective in Ethiopia) |
| Elephantiasis | Filariasis | Microfilarac | Mosquitoes | Between 15° N and 20° S | Diethylcarbamazine | 5.6-benzo-a- pyrone ocouma rin reported promising in 1994 in China | 5.6-benzo-a- pyrone or coumarin reported promising in 1994 in China |
| Guinea worm | Drancontiasis | Dracunculus medinensis | Cyclops (crustacea) | Endemic to tropical Africa | | Thiabendazole, mebendazole, niridazole | Eradication program under implementation (sponsored by former US President Carter) |
| Cholera | Cholera | Vibro cholorae | Water (through fecal contamination) | Tropics | | ORS, doxycycline | |
| Diarrhoea (other than cholera) | Dysentery (other than cholera) | Protozoa (amoebic), bacillary (shigella) | Cyst passers | Tropics | | ORS, nalidixic acid, ciprofloxacine | |
| Food poisoning | Gastroenteritis botulism | Clostridium, botulinum toxins type A & B | Improperly preserved food | Worldwide | | Polyvalent botulinum antitoxin | |
| Typhus | Epidemic typhus | Rickctsia prowazeki | Body louse | | DDT spraying to climinate lousiness | Chloramphenicol , tetracycline | |
| Kala-azar | Leishmaniasis | Leishmania (flagellated protozoa) | Sand flies (phlebotmine type) | Tropics | DDT spraying to destroy sand flies | Pentostam | |
| Chronic hepatitis | Viral hepatitus | Virus A & B | Type "A" person to person, food, water; type "B" transfusion, acci-dental inoculation | Worldwide | Vaccine | | |
| Tuberculosis (pulmonary) | Mycobacterium tuberculosis | Tubercle bacilli | Airborne droplets, milk, infected food | Worldwide | Isoniazid (INH) | Isoniazid (INH) in combination with streptomycin ª, rifampcin | Resurgence in recent years |
| Broncho-pneumonia | Pneumococcal pneumonia | Streptococcus l'ore A virus or mycoplasma P | Droplets, dust, spitting, coughing | Developing countries | | Benzylpenicilin, amoxycillin, cotrimoxazole | |
| Lockjaw | Tetanus | Clostridium tetani | Through wounds | Areas lacking sanitation | Antitctanus serum (passive immunization) | Tetanus immune globulin, tetanus toxoid (active immunization) | Elimination of neonatal teta-nus is among the goals of the international community |
| Polio | Poliomyelitis | Polio verus types I, II and III | Food, water, droplets, flies | Developing countries | Monovalent or trivalent oral poliovirus vaccine | No specific therapy (solution is immunization) | Eradication program under implementation using "sabin" oral vaccine |
| German measles | Measles, rubella | Rubela virus | Droplets, contact | Worldwide | Live attenuated vaccine, immuno globulin | Solution is immunization | Eradication program under implementation in the world |
| Diphtheria | Diphtheria | Corynebacterium diphtcriae | Airborne, contact, contaminated milk | Developing countries | Diphtheria toxoid, diphtheria antitoxin plus penicillins | Solution is immunization | |
| Whooping cough | Pertussis | Bordetella pertussis | Airborne, contact with soiled articles | Worldwide | Triple (diphtheria, pertussis, tetanus toxoid) vaccine | Solution is immunization | |
| Whipworm (I.nematode) | Trichuriasis | Trichuris, Trichvra | Eggs ingestion | Tropics | | Menbendazole | |
| Ascaridisis (I.nematode) | Ascariasis | Ascaris lumbricoides | Eggs ingestion | Tropics | | Mebendazole, Piperazine, abendazole | |
| Hook worm (I.nematode) | | Ancylostoma d?vodonale | Flariform larvae | Tropics | | Pyrantel pamoate | |
| Strongy- losids | Strongy- loidiasis | S. stercoralis | Eggs ingestion | Tropics | | Thiabendazole | |

Sources: - Merck & Co. Inc., 1950, 1990, *The Merck Manual of Diagnosis and Therapy*, published by Merck & Co. Inc., Rahway, NJ.
- WHO, information obtained through correspondence with the WHO Regional Office for Africa, Brazzaville.
- WHO, 1993, *Technical Report Series*, No. 830, Geneva.
- UNDP/World Bank/ WHO, 1996, *Schistosomiasis Vaccine: an Update*, TDR News, June 1996.
- Berhe Scyoum, pharmacist
- Le-ake-Tsion G. Selassie, pharmacist, Addis Ababa.
a Streptomycin may be replaced by ethambutol, pyrazinamide in order to minimize injections. Drug resistance is associated with HIV/AID.

ANNEX 8.2
MAJOR VETERINARY DISEASES PANDEMIC IN AFRICA

| Major diseases | | Causative agent | Mode of transmission | Major affected areas | Main therapeutic agents | | Remarks: R & D, eradication program |
|---|---|---|---|---|---|---|---|
| Common name | Scientific name | | | | Preventive | Curative | |
| Rinderpest (cattle plague) | Morbillivirus | Morbillivirus | Contact | East Africa | Attenuated cell culture vaccine, vaccinia virus recombinant vaccine being tested | | Pan African Rinderpest Campaign under implementation |
| Contagious bovine pleuropneumonia | | Mycoplasma mycoides mycoides | Contact | West, north-east Africa, Congo K, Angola, Namibia | Attenuated vaccine (lyophilized T1/44) | Tylosin | Major breakdowns in control after successful curb in many countries |
| Foot-and-mouth disease | | Rhinovirus (types A, O, C, SAT 1,2 and 3 and Asia 1) | Direct contact between animals, airborne spread, milk | Types O, A, C north and south of the Equator, SAT 1,2,3 in southern Africa | Inactivated vaccine | No known cure | Major breakdowns in control after successful curb in many countries |
| Contagious caprine pleuro-pneumonia | | Mycoplasma mycoides capri, M. strain F38 , m. mycoides mycoides | Ineffective aerosol | | Attenuated and killed vaccine | Tylosin | |
| Lumpy skin disease | | Neethling pox virus | Contact infection | | Attenuated vaccine | Sulfonamides fro secondary infection | |
| Rift valley fever | | Phlebovirus | Mosquito-borne | | Vector control, inactivated vaccine | | |
| Sheep and goat pox | | Capripoxvirus | Contact transmission, air-borne | | Live attenuated vaccine | | |
| African horse sickness | | Orbivirus | Culicoides | | Inactivated and attenuated vaccines | | |
| Rabies | | Lyssavirus | Bite of rabid animal | | Inactivated , modified live vaccines | | |
| Newcasle disease | | Paramixovirus | Aerosol, contaminated food and water | | Live virus vaccine | | |
| Pesti des petitis ruminantis | | Morbillivirus | Contact transmission | West, central and east Africa | Rp cell culture vaccine | | |
| Bacterial diseases | | | | | | | |
| Anthrax | | Bacillus anthracis | Ingesting the spores, inhalation, wound contamination | Prevalenc higher in less developed tropical areas | Noncapsulated Sterne-strain vaccine (live) | Oxytetracycline, penicillin | |
| Backleg | | Clostridium chauvoei | Ingestion | | Inactivated bacterium containing C chauvoei and C septicum and penicillin | Penicillin | |
| Haemorragic septicemia | | Pasteurella multocida | Direct and indirect contact | | Oil-adjuvant vaccine | Sulfonamides, tetracycline, penicillin | |
| Dermato-philosis | | Dermatophilus congolensis | Contact and mechanical vectors | | Culling affected animals, controlling ectoparasites | Penicillin+strept omycine, long acting oxytetracycline, topical treatment | |
| Brucellosis | | Brucella abortus, B. melitensis | Direct and indirecr contact | | B abortus strain 19 vaccine, 45/20 bacterin in adjuvant, culling reactors | | |
| Protozoal and rickettisal | | | | | | | |
| Anapla-somsis | Anaplasma marginale. A. centrale | Ticks (Boohhilus, Dermacentor), flies (tahanus, stomoxys) | | Killing or repell-ing vectors, innoculation of blood containing A. centrale, use of virulent and attenuated A. marginale isolates | Tetracyclines | | |

| Babesiosis | | Babasia bovis, B. bigemina | Ticks of Boophilus spp, mechanically by biting flies | | Blood-derived vaccines of B. bovis and B. bigemia attenuated by passage through splenectomized calves, control tick vector with acaricides | Phenamidine isethionate, amicarbalide disethionate, diminazine aceturate, imidiocarb dipropionate | |
|---|---|---|---|---|---|---|---|
| Heart water | Cowdriosis | Cowdria ruminantium | Ticks of the genus Amblyomma | | Tick control, infected sheep blood is used as vaccine in combination with antibiotic at the time of infection | Tetracycline | |
| Nagana | Trypanoso-miasis | Trypanosoma congolense, T. vivax, T. brucei | Tsetse flies of the genus Glossina | Dry sub-humid to humid zones (10° N and 10° S) | Quinapyramine, isometamidium chloride | Diminazine aceturate, homidium chloride, isometamidium | Control program under implementation (a new insecticide, SPOTON, reported found effective in Ethiopia) |
| East Coast fever | Theileriases | Theileria parva, T. annulata | Ixodid tick (rhipicephalus appendiculatus) | East and central Africa | Immunization of cattle using an infection-and treatment procedure | Parvaquone, buparvaquone | |
| Helminth parasites | | | | | | | |
| Trimatode (liverfluke) | Fascioliasis | Fasciola hepatica, F. gigantica | Snail intermediate host | Area below 1,800 and above 2,000 meters above sea level | Mollucide, biological method | Oxyclozanide, diamphenethide, rafoxanide, nitroxynil, albendazol, closantel, triclabendazol, clorsulon | |
| Nematodes | | Haemonchus, trichostrongylus, ostertagia, chabertina, oesophagostomum, bunostomum, cooperia, nematodirus | Ingestion of ineffective larvae | | | Thianbendazole, albendazole, mebendazole, fenbendazole, oxfendazole, levamizole | |

Source: - Ristic, Miodrag and McIntyre, Ian (editors). 1981. *Diseases of Cattle in the Tropics*, Martinus Nijhoff Publishers, The Hague.
- Fraser, Clarence M. (editor), 1991. *The Merck Veterinary Manual*, Seventh Edition, Merck & Co., Inc., Rahway, NJ., USA.
- Abebe Wondimu, veterinary doctor, Addis Ababa.

| ANNEX 8.3 WHO'S MODEL LIST OF ESSENTIAL DRUGS | | |
|---|---|---|
| MAIN LIST | | COMPLEMENT ARY LIST |
| **1. Anaethetics** | | |
| 1.1 General anaethetics and oxygen | Ether, anaethetics, diazepam, halothane, ketamine, nitrous oxide, oxygen, thiopental | |
| 1.2 Local anaethetics | Bupivacaine, lidocaine | |
| 1.3 Preoperative medication | Atropine, chloral hydrate, diazepam, morphine, promethazine | |
| **2. Analgesics, Antipyretics, Nonsteroidal Antiinflammatory Drugs, and Drugs Used to Treat Gout** | | |
| 2.1 Non-opioids | Acetylsalicylic acid, allopurinol, ibuprofen, indometacin, paracetamol | Colchicine, probeneacid |
| 2.2 Opioid analgesics | Codeine, morphine | Pethidine |
| **3. Antiallergics and drugs used in anaphylaxis** | Chlorphenamine, dexamethasone, epinephrine, hydrocortisone, prednisolone | |
| **4. Antidotes and other substances used in poisonings** | | |
| 4.1 General | Charcoal (activated), ipecacuanha | |
| 4.2 Specific | Atropine, deferoxamine, dimercaprol, methionine, methylthioninium chloride, naloxone, penicililamine, sodium calcium edetate, sodium nitrite, sodium thiosulfate | |
| **5. Antiepileptics** | Carbamazepine, diazepam, ethosuximide, phenobarbitol, phenytoin, vaproic acid | |
| **6. Antiinfective drugs** | | |
| 6.1 Anthelminthic drugs | Mebendazole, niclosamide, piperazine, praziquantel, pyrantel, tiabendazole, diethylcarbamazine, suramin sodium, metrifonate, oxamniquine, praziquantel | Levamisole, ivermectin |
| 6.2 Antibacterials | Ampicillin, benzathine benzylpenicillin, benzylpenicillin, cloxacllin, phenoxymethylpenicillin, piperacillin, procaine benzylpencillin, chloramphenicol, erythromycin, gentamycin, metronidazole, spectinomycin, sulfadimidine, sulfamethoxazole +trimethoprim, tetracycline, clofazimine, dapsone, rifampicin, ethambutol, isonaizid, pyrazinamide, rifampicin, streptomycin, thioacetazone + isniazid | Doxycycline, nitrofurantoin, trimethoprim |
| 6.3 Antifungal drugs | Amphotericin, griseofulvin, ketoconazole, nystatin | Flucytosine |
| 6.4 Antiprotozoal drugs | Diloxanide, metronidazole, meglumine antimonaite, pentamidine, sodium stibogluconate, chloroquine, primaquine, quinine, proguanil, melarsoprol, pentamidine, surmin sodium, benznidazole, nifurtimox | Chloroquine, dehydro- emetine, mefloquine, sulfadoxine + pyri- methamine, tetracycline |
| **7. Antimigraine drugs** | Acetylsalicylic acid, ergotamine, paractamol | |
| **8. Antineoplastic and Immunosuppressive drugs** | | |
| 8.1 Immunosuppressive drugs | Azathioprine, | |
| 8.2 Cytotoxic drugs | Bleomycin, cisplatin, cyclophosphamide, cytarabine, dactinomycin, doxorubicin, etoposide, fluorouacil, mercaptopurine, methotrexate, procabazine, vinblstine vincristine | Calcium folinate |
| 8.3 Hormones and antihormones | Dexamethasone, ethinylestradiol, prednisolone, tamoxifen | |
| **9. Antiparkinsonism drugs** | Biperden, levedopa +carbidopa | |
| **10. Blood, drugs affecting the:** | | |

| 10.1 Antianaemia drugs | Ferrous salt, ferrous salt + folic acid, folic acid, hydroxocobalamine | Iron dextran |
|---|---|---|
| 10.2 Anticoagulants and antagonists | Heparin, phytomenadione, protamine sulfate, warfarin | |
| **11. Blood products and blood substitutes** | | |
| 11.1 Plasma substitutes | Dextran | |
| 11.2 Plasma fractions for specific uses | Albumin (human) | Factor VIII concentrates, factor IX complex |
| **12. Cardiovascular drugs** | | |
| 12.1 Antianginal drugs | Glyceryl trinitrate, isosorbide dinitrate, propranolol, nifedipine | |
| 12.2 Antidysrhythmic drugs | Lidocaine, propranolol, verapamil | Procainamide, quinidine |
| 12.3 Antihypertensive drugs | Hydralazine, hydrochlorothiazide, nifedipine, prpranolol | Methyldopa, reserpine, sodium nitropruside |
| 12.4 Cardiac glycosides | Digoxin | Digitoxin |
| 12.5 Drugs used in vascular shock | Dopamine | |
| **13. Dermatological drugs** | | |
| 13.1 Antifungul drugs | Benzoic acid + salisylic acid, miconazole, nystatin | |
| 13.2 Antiinfective drugs | Methylrosanilinium, neomycin + bacitracin, silver sulfadiazine | |
| 13.3 Antiinflammatory and antipruritic drugs | Betamethasone, calamine lotion, hydrocortisone | |
| 13.4 Astringent drugs | Aluminium diactate | |
| 13.5 Keratoplastic and keratolyctic agents | Coal tar, dithranol, podophyllum resin, salicylic acid | |
| 13.6 Scabicides and pediclicides | Benzyl benzoate, lindane | |
| **14. Diagnostic agents** | | |
| 14.1 Opthalmic drugs | Fluorescein, tropicamide | |
| 14.2 Radiocontrast media | Amidotriazoate, barium sulfate, iopanoic acid, propyliodone | Iohexol, iotroxate |
| **15. Disinfectants** | Chlorhxidine, iodine | |
| **16. Diuretics** | Amiloride, furosemide, hydrochlorothiazide | Mannitol, spironolactone |
| **17. Gastrointestinal drugs** | | |
| 17.1 Antiacids and other antiulcer drugs | Aluminum hydroxide, cimetidine, magnesium hydroxide, sodium citrate | |
| 17.2 Antiemetic drugs | Metoclopramide, promethazine | |
| 17.3 Antihaemorrhoidal drugs | Local anaesthetic, astrigent and antiinflammatory drug | |
| 17.4 Antiinflammatory drugs | Hydrocortisone, sulfasalazine | |
| 17.5 Antispasmodic drugs | Atropine | |
| 17.6 Cathartic drugs | Senna | |
| 17.7 Diarrhoea drugs | Oral rehydration salts, sodium chloride, trisodium citrate dihydrate, potassium chloride, glucose, codeine | |
| **18. Hormones, other endocrine drugs, and contraceptives** | | |

| | | |
|---|---|---|
| 18.1 Adrenal hormones and synthetic substitutes | Dexamethasone, hydrocortisone, prednisolone | Fludrocortisone |
| 18.2 Androgens | | Testosterone |
| 18.3 Contraceptives | Ethinylestradiol + levonorgestrel, ethinylestradiol + norethisterone, copper-containing device, condoms with or without spermicide, diaphragms with spermicide | Depot medroxy-progesterone acetate, norethisterone, norethisterone enantate |
| 18.4 Estrogens | Ethinylestradiol | |
| 18.5 Insulin and other diabetic agents | Insulin injection, intermediate-acting insulin, tolbutamide | |
| 18.6 Ovulation inducers | | Clomifene |
| 18.7 Prosgestogens | Norethisterone | |
| 18.8 Thyroid hormones and antithyroid drugs | Levothyroxine, potassium iodide, propylthiouacil | |
| 19. Immunologicals | | |
| 19.1 Diagnostic agents | Tuberculin, purified protein derivative (PPD) | |
| 19.2 Sera and immunoglobulins | Anti-D immunoglobulin (human), antirabies hyperimmune serum, antivenom sera, antiscorpion sera, diphtheria antitoxin, immunoglobulin ( human normal), tetanus antitoxin, tetanus antitoxin (human) | |
| 19.3 Vaccines | BCG vaccine, diphtheria-pertussis-tetanus vaccine, diphtheria-tetanus vaccine, measles vaccine, poliomyelitis vaccine (inactivated), poliomyelitis vaccine (live attenuated), tetanus vaccine, hepatitis B vaccine, influenza vaccine, meningococcal vaccine, rabies vaccine, rubella vaccine, typhoid vaccine, yellow fever vaccine | |
| 20. Muscle relaxants (peripherally acting) and cholinesterase inhibitors | Gallamine, neostigmine, suxamethonium | Pyridostigmine |
| 21 Ophthal mological preparations | | |
| 21.1 Antiinfective agents | Idoxuridine, silver nitrate, sulfacetamide, tetracycline | |
| 21.2 Antiinflammatory agents | Hydrocortisone | |
| 21.3 Local anaesthetics | Tetracaine | |
| 21.4 Miotcs and antiglaucoma drugs | Acetazolamide, pilocarpine, timolol | |
| 21.5 Mydriatics | Homatropine | Epinephrine |
| 22. Oxytocics and antioxytocics | | |
| 22.1 Oxytocics | Ergometrine, oxytocin | |
| 22.2 Antioxytocics | Salbutamol | |
| 23. Peritoneal dialysis solution | Intraperitoneal dialysis solution | |
| 24. Psychotherapeutic drugs | Amitriptyline, chlorpromazine, diazepam, fluphenazine, haloperidol, lithium carbonate | |
| 25. Respiratory tract, drugs, acting on the | | |
| 25.1 Antiasthmatic drugs | Aminophylline, epinephrine, salbutanol | Beclometasone, cromoglicic acid, ephedrine |
| 25.2 Antitussives | Codeine | |
| 26. Solutions correcting water, electrolyte, and acid-base disturbances | | |
| 26.1 For oral rehydration | Oral rehydration salts, potassium chloride | |
| 26.2 Parenteral | Compound solution of sodium lactate, glucose, glucose with sodium chloride, potassium chloride, sodium bicarbonate, sodium chloride | |
| 26.3 Miscellaneous | Water for injection | |
| 27. Vitamins and Minerals | Ergocalciferol, nicotinamide, pyridoxine, retinol, riboflavin, sodium floride, thiamine | Ascorbic acid, calcium gluconate |

Source: - Compiled from WHO, 1988, *The Use of Essential Drugs*, Technical Report Series 770, Geneva.

| ANNEX 8.4 | | | | | |
|---|---|---|---|---|---|
| A GUIDE TO SOME COMMONLY USED HERBS | | | | | |
| Common name | Source | Part used | Principal uses | AE | PS |
| Aloe | Aloe barbadensis | 1. Fresh gel<br>2. Dried juice | Wound healing, burns<br>Cathartic | X | X |
| Apricot pits<br>(Laetrile) | Prunus armeniaca | Seed kernels | Anticancer | X | X |
| Buther's broom | Ruscus aculeatus | Rhizome and root | Improve circulation | O | O |
| Calendula<br>(marigold) | Calendula officinalis | Flower parts | Facilitates wound healing | ? | X |
| Chamomiles and<br>yarrow | Matricaria recutita<br>Chamaemelum nobile<br>Achillea milefolium | Flower heads<br>Flower heads<br>Flowering herb | Anti-inflammatory, digestive aid,<br>antispasmodic, anti-infective | X | X |
| Comfrey | Symphytum officinale and<br>Symphytum x uplandicum | Rhizome and roots, leaves | General healing agent | X | O |
| Dandelion | Taraxacum officinale | 1. Rhizome and roots<br>2. Leaves | Digestive aid, laxative<br>Diuretic | ?<br>? | X<br>X |
| Dong quai | Angelica polymorpha,<br>sinensis variety | Root | Uterine tonic, antispasmodic, alterative | ? | O |
| Echinacea | Echinacea angustifolia and other<br>species | Rhizome and roots,<br>overground plant | Anti-infective, wound healing, immune<br>stimulant | X | X |
| Evening primrose | Oenothera biennis | Seed oil | Treatment of atopiceczema, mastalgia | ? | ? |
| Fennel | Foeniculum vulgare | Fruits (seeds) | Stomachic, digestive aid | X | X |
| Feverfew | Tanacetum parthenium | Leaves | Migraine preventive | X | X |
| Ginger | Zingiber officiale | Rhizome | Motion sickness preventive | X | X |
| Ginkgo | Ginkgo biloba | Leaf extract | Enhance cerebral blood flow | X | X |
| Goldenseal | Hydrastis canadensis | Rhizome and roots | Bitter tonic, digestive aid, treatment of<br>genitourinary disorders | ? to<br>X | X |

| Hawthorn | Crataegus laevigatas | Fruits (haws), leaves, flowers | Dilate blood vessels, strengthen heart, lower blood pressure | X | X |
|---|---|---|---|---|---|
| Jojoba oil | Simmondsia chinenis | Expressed fro seeds | 1. Anisebum shampoos<br>2. Emollient lotions, cosmetics | ?<br>? | X<br>X |
| Juniper | Juniperus communis | Fruits (berries) | Duretic | X | ? |
| Kelp | Laminaria, Marcocystis, Nereocystis, and Fucus species | Entire plant | 1. Bulk laxative, demulcent<br>2. Control obesity, atherosclerosis | X<br>O | ?<br>? |
| licorice | Glycyrrhiza glabra | Rhizome and roots | Expectorant, demulcent, flavor | X | X to O |
| Papaya | Carica papaya | Dried latex and leaves | Digestive aid, vermifuge | O | X |
| Red clover | Trifolium pratense | Flowers | Alterative, anticancer treatment | O | X |
| Rose hips | Rosa species | Fruits | Antiscorbutic | X | X |
| Rue | Ruta graveolens | Leaves | Antispasdomic, menstruation stimulant | O | O |
| Sassafras | Sassafras albidum | Root bark | 1. Stimulant, antispasdomic, sweat stimulant, antirheumatic, tonic<br>2. Flavor | O<br><br><br>X | O<br><br><br>O |
| Suna | Hebanthe paniculata | Root | Adaptogen, cure-all | O | ? |
| Valerian | Valeriana officinalis and related species | Rhizome and roots | Tranquilizer, sedative | X | X |
| Witch hazel | Hamamelis virginiana | Leaves, bark | Astrigent | X | X |
| Yucca | Yucca species | Leaves | Antiarthritic | O | X |

Source: The Boston Globe Magazine, 1997, "A Guide to Some Commonly Used Herbs," 13 July 1997 (originally from Commission of Germany's Federal Health Services).

AE  Apparent efficacy    PS   Probable safety

X  Effective, safe in normal individuals, when used appropriately    ?  Inconclusive    O  Ineffective, not safe

**ANNEX 9.1**
**FERTILIZERS: PRODUCTION, TRADE, CONSUMPTION AND PRODUCTION/CONSUMPTION GAPS**

|  | African continent (1000t) | | | | | | | World (m t) | | | | | | |
|---|---|---|---|---|---|---|---|---|---|---|---|---|---|---|
|  | 75/76 | 80/81 | 85/86 | 90/91 | 91/92 | 92/93 | 93/94 | 75/76 | 80/81 | 85/86 | 90/91 | 91/92 | 92/93 | 93/94 |
| Nitrogenous fertilizers (N) | | | | | | | | | | | | | | |
| Production | 595 | 1066 | 1667 | 2241 | 2410 | 2478 | 2624 | 43.9 | 62.8 | 73.1 | 81.9 | 80.5 | 79.9 | 79.5 |
| Imports | 701 | 857 | 879 | 751 | 684 | 726 | 696 | 8.1 | 13 | 16.6 | 19.8 | 20.3 | 21.2 | 21.4 |
| Exports | 38 | 82 | 470 | 821 | 900 | 1089 | 1040 | 7.1 | 13.2 | 15.3 | 19.1 | 19.7 | 20.8 | 19.6 |
| Net exports | -663 | -775 | -409 | 70 | 216 | 363 | 344 | -1 | 0.2 | -1.3 | -0.7 | -0.6 | -0.4 | -1.8 |
| Consumption | 1251 | 1757 | 1957 | 2097 | 2065 | 2144 | 2340 | 42.9 | 60.8 | 69.8 | 77.2 | 75.1 | 73.6 | 72.8 |
| Production/ consumption gap | -656 | -691 | -290 | 144 | 345 | 334 | 284 | 1 | 2 | 3.3 | 4.7 | 5.4 | 6.3 | 6.7 |
| Phosphate fertilizers (P$_{2O5}$) | | | | | | | | | | | | | | |
| Production | 882 | 1287 | 1799 | 2611 | 2396 | 2392 | 2499 | 26.2 | 34.5 | 34.6 | 39.9 | 37.9 | 34.8 | 31.7 |
| Imports | 174 | 337 | 484 | 323 | 323 | 408 | 378 | 3.9 | 6.6 | 8.3 | 10 | 10.7 | 10.5 | 10.6 |
| Exports | 176 | 474 | 1007 | 1876 | 1725 | 1619 | 1864 | 3.9 | 7.5 | 8 | 10.3 | 11.9 | 10.5 | 11.3 |
| Net exports | 2 | 137 | 523 | 1553 | 1402 | 1211 | 1486 | 0 | 0.9 | -0.3 | 0.3 | 1.2 | 0 | 0.7 |
| Consumption | 824 | 1092 | 1256 | 1105 | 1027 | 1135 | 1155 | 25.2 | 31.7 | 33.2 | 36.3 | 35.4 | 31.5 | 28.8 |

| | | | | | | | | | | | | | |
|---|---|---|---|---|---|---|---|---|---|---|---|---|---|
| Production/ consumption gap | 58 | 195 | 543 | 1506 | 1369 | 1257 | 1344 | 1 | 2.8 | 1.4 | 3.6 | 2.5 | 3.3 | 2.9 |

Potash fertilizers (K₂O)

| | | | | | | | | | | | | | |
|---|---|---|---|---|---|---|---|---|---|---|---|---|---|
| Production | 277 | - | - | - | - | - | - | 23.4 | 27.5 | 28.3 | 26.7 | 24.9 | 23.4 | 20.4 |
| Imports | 369 | 419 | 524 | 521 | 537 | 537 | 544 | 12.2 | 16.2 | 17 | 18.7 | 17.8 | 17.1 | 18.1 |
| Exports | - | - | - | - | - | - | - | 11.9 | 16.7 | 16.7 | 18.1 | 16.5 | 16.3 | 16.6 |
| Net exports | -369 | -419 | -524 | -521 | -537 | -537 | -554 | -0.3 | 0.5 | -0.3 | -0.6 | -1.3 | -0.8 | -1.5 |
| Consumption | 327 | 392 | 473 | 485 | 499 | 501 | 498 | 21.4 | 24.2 | 25.6 | 24.5 | 23.5 | 20.8 | 19.1 |
| Production/ consumption gap | -50 | -392 | -473 | -485 | -499 | -501 | -498 | 2 | 3.3 | 2.7 | 2.2 | 1.4 | 2.6 | 1.3 |

Total fertilizers (N+P2O5+K2O)

| | | | | | | | | | | | | | |
|---|---|---|---|---|---|---|---|---|---|---|---|---|---|
| Production | 1754 | 2353 | 3466 | 4853 | 4806 | 4871 | 5113 | 94.3 | 124.8 | 136 | 147.6 | 143.3 | 138.1 | 131.6 |
| Imports | 1232 | 1613 | 1887 | 1594 | 1544 | 1670 | 1618 | 24.3 | 35.9 | 41.9 | 48.6 | 48.8 | 48.8 | 50.1 |
| Exports | 214 | 556 | 1487 | 2697 | 2704 | 2708 | 2904 | 22.8 | 37.4 | 40 | 47.8 | 47.6 | 47.6 | 47.5 |
| Net exports | -1018 | -1057 | -400 | 1103 | 1160 | 1038 | 1276 | -1.5 | 1.5 | -1.9 | -0.8 | -1.2 | -1.2 | -2.6 |
| Consumption | 2358 | 3242 | 3687 | 3687 | 3590 | 3780 | 3495 | 90.4 | 116.7 | 128.6 | 138 | 134 | 126 | 120.7 |
| Production/ consumption gap | -604 | -889 | -221 | 1166 | 1216 | 1091 | 1130 | 3.9 | 8.1 | 7.4 | 9.6 | 9.3 | -12.2 | 10.9 |
| Consumption per hectar of arable land and permanent crops (kg) | 13.4 | 18.4 | 20.1 | ... | ... | ... | ... | 63.2 | 80.1 | 87.1 | ... | ... | ... | ... |

Rock phosphate (m t)

| | | | | | | | | | | | | | |
|---|---|---|---|---|---|---|---|---|---|---|---|---|---|
| Production | 27 | 33 | 35043 | 37937 | 34491 | 35245 | 33200 | 107.9 | 137.9 | 147.3 | 155.4 | 146.8 | 146.6 | 122.7 |
| Imports | 34 | 72 | 91 | 15 | 327 | 364 | 364 | 45.5 | 52.2 | 45.7 | 36.8 | 31.3 | 28.4 | 26.6 |
| Exports | 21 | 23 | 21280 | 18293 | 16081 | 15682 | 14661 | 44.4 | 50.4 | 45.9 | 37.2 | 31.6 | 29.5 | 26.8 |
| Net exports | -13 | -49 | 21189 | 18278 | 15754 | 15318 | 14297 | -1.1 | 1.8 | 0.2 | 0.4 | 0.3 | 1.1 | 0.2 |

Source: FAO, 1979,1981, 1992, 1993, *1994, FAO Fertilizer Yearbook*, Rome.
Notes: Consumption per hectar and natural phosphate rock figures refer to calendar years corresponding to the first part of the split year.

| 634ANNEX 9.2 TRADE IN AMMONIA AND PHOSPHORIC ACID IN THE AFRICAN CONTINENT (1000 t) | | | | | | | | | | | | |
|---|---|---|---|---|---|---|---|---|---|---|---|---|
| | 1980 | 1981 | 1982 | 1983 | 1984 | 1985 | 1986 | 1987 | 1988 | 1989 | 1990 | 1991 | 1992 |
| Ammonia (N) | | | | | | | | | | | | |
| Imports | 193.1 | 190.3 | 227.4 | 239.3 | 302.8 | 303.1 | 269.2 | 498.7 | 579.7 | 817.9 | 858.4 | 790.8 | 671.9 |
| Exports | 68.8 | 63 | 233 | 315.6 | 195.5 | 186.2 | 152.7 | 106.5 | 221.1 | 175.4 | 261.9 | 327 | 441.3 |
| Net exports | -124.3 | -127.3 | 5.6 | 76.3 | -107.3 | -116.9 | -116.5 | -392.2 | -358.6 | -642.5 | -596.5 | -463.8 | -230.6 |
| Phosphoric acid (P2O5) | | | | | | | | | | | | |
| Imports | - | 0.6 | - | 0.7 | - | - | - | - | - | - | - | - | 36.7 |
| Exports | 1088 | 1030 | 1249 | 1361 | 1626 | 1326 | 1085 | 1327 | 1865 | 1271 | 1272 | 2288 | 2444 |
| Net exports | 1088 | 1029 | 1249 | 1360 | 1626 | 1326 | 1085 | 1327 | 1865 | 1271 | 1272 | 2288 | 2407 |

Source: Obtained by adding trade figures given for individual countries in FAO, 1992, 1993, FAO Fertilizer Yearbook, Rome.

| ANNEX 9.3 DEVELOPING AFRICA'S SHARE IN WORLD FERTILIZER PRODUCTION AND TRADE (%) AND CONSUMPTION RATIO S | | | | | | | | |
|---|---|---|---|---|---|---|---|---|
| | 75/76 | 82/83 | 83/84 | 84/85 | 85/86 | 86/87 | 87/88 | 88/89 |
| Nitrogenous fertilizers (N) | | | | | | | | |
| Production | 0.3 | 0.4 | 0.4 | 0.4 | 0.5 | 0.6 | 0.7 | 1 |
| Consumption | 1 | 1 | 1 | 1 | 1.2 | 1.2 | 1.1 | 1 |
| Imports | 3.9 | 4.2 | 3.3 | 2.9 | 3.5 | 3.4 | 2.7 | 2.6 |
| Exports | 0.1 | 0.7 | 0.8 | 0.6 | 0.8 | 0.8 | 1.1 | 2.9 |
| Phosphate fertilizers (P2O5) | | | | | | | | |
| Production | 1.6 | 2.8 | 3.3 | 2.7 | 3.5 | 3.5 | 3.6 | 4.6 |
| Consumption | 1.4 | 1.5 | 1.6 | 1.6 | 2 | 1.8 | 1.7 | 1.5 |
| Imports | 3.8 | 3.7 | 4.4 | 3.5 | 4.7 | 4.3 | 4.1 | 3.1 |
| Exports | 3.8 | 9.4 | 11 | 7.1 | 11.3 | 9.8 | 11.4 | 14.2 |
| Potash fertilizers (K2O) | | | | | | | | |
| Production | 1.2 | - | - | - | - | - | - | - |
| Consumption | 0.9 | 1.1 | 1 | 1 | 1.2 | 1.1 | 1.1 | 1 |
| Imports | 1.7 | 1.6 | 1.7 | 1.6 | 2.1 | 1.7 | 1.7 | 1.7 |
| Exports | - | - | - | - | - | - | - | - |
| Consumption ratio (N:P2O5:K2O when N=1) | 0.82:0.44 | 0.77:0.40 | 0.80:0.40 | 0.78:0.37 | 0.79:0.38 | 0.74:0.35 | 0.76:0.39 | 0.71:0.35 |

Source: FAO, 1979, 1986, 1989, FAO Fertilizer Yearbook, Rome.

| ANNEX 9.4 AMMONIA PRODUCTION AND CAPACITIES IN AFRICA (N, 1000t/y) | | | | | | | |
|---|---|---|---|---|---|---|---|
| Subregion/country/ company | Location | Production | | Capacity | | Project/capacity | | Status of project |
| | | Tons | Year | Tons | Year | Tons | Year | |
| North Africa | | | | | | | | |
| Algeria | | | | | | | | |
| SONATRACH | Annaba | | | 900 [a] | | 272 | 84/85 | Status unknown |
| | Arzew | | | | | 272 | 83/84 | Status unknown |
| Libya | | | | | | | | |
| - Secretariat of Heavy Industry | Sirte | | | | | 365 | 87/88 | Status unknown |
| - Government | Mersa El Brega | | | | | 365 | 87/88 | Status unkown |
| Egypt | | | | | | | | |
| - Abu Kir Fertilizer Co. | Abu Kir | | | 1320 [b] | | 272 | 92 | Status unknown |
| - Egypt. Chem. Ind. Kima | Helwan | | | | | 272 | 93 | Status unknown |
| -SEMADCO? | Suez | | | | | 108 | 89 | Status unknown |
| Sudan | | | | | | | | |
| - Government | Port Sudan | | | | | 108 | 83/84 | Status unknwon |
| West Africa | | | | | | | | |
| Nigeria | | | | | | | | |
| - National Fertilizer Company of Nigeria Ltd. | Port Harcourt | 272 | 1990s | 330 | 1988 | | | |
| Senegal | | | | | | | | |
| -Fertisen | Cayar | | | | | 74 | 82/83 | Status unknown |
| Eastern and Southern Africa | | | | | | | | |
| Somalia | | | | | | | | |
| -Ministry of Industry | Mogadishu | | | 25 | | | | |
| Kenya | | | | | | | | |
| -Ken-Ren | Mombassa | | | | | 54 | 80/81 | Status unknown |
| Tanzania | | | | | | | | |
| -Kilwa Ammonia Co. | Kilwa Masoko | | | | | 330 | 87/88 | Status unknown |
| Zambia | | | | | | | | |
| -Nitrogen Chemical | Kafue | | | 55 | | | | |
| Zimbabwe | | | | | | | | |
| - Sable Chemical Industries Limited | | | | 65 | | | | |
| South Africa | | | | | | | | |
| - Fedmis | Sasolburg | | | | | 140 | 83/84 | Status unknown |
| Madagascar | | | | | | | | |
| - Ze-Ren | Tamatave | | | | | 74 | 87 | Status unknown |

Source: - FAO, 1981 to 1986, *FAO Fertilizer Yearbook*, Rome
- ECA, 1993, *Focus on African Industry*, Volume CI, No. 1, Addis Ababa, Ethiopia
- Many other publications
a  Total capacity for  Arzew and Annaba    b  Total capacity for the country

| Subregion/country/ company | Location | Capacity | | Extention/ capacity | | Project/ capacity | | Status of extention/ project |
|---|---|---|---|---|---|---|---|---|
| | | Tons | Year | Tons | Year | Tons | Year | |
| ANNEX 9.5 WET PHOSPHORIC ACID CAPACITIES IN AFRICA (P2O5, 1000 t/y) | | | | | | | | |
| North Africa | | | | | | | | |
| Algeria | | | | | | | | |
| - SONATRACH | Tebessa | | | | | 165 | 84/5 | Status unknown |
| | Annaba | | | | | 165 | 87/88 | |
| Morocco | | | | | | | | |
| - Maroc-Chimie | Safi | 320 | | | | | | In operation. |
| - Maroc-Phosphore I | Safi | 640 | | | | | | In operation. |
| - Maroc-Phospohre II | Safi | 475 | | | | | | In operation. |
| - Maroc-Phosphore III | Jorf Lasar | 640 | | | | | | In operation. |
| - Maroc-Phosphore IV | Jorf Lasar | 640 | | | | | | In operation. |
| - Maroc-Phosphore V | Nador | | | 640 | | | | Deadline 1995. |
| - Maroc-Phosphore VI | Laayoune | | | 640 | | | | Deadline 1995. |
| - Maroc-Phosphore VII | Essaouira | | | 640 | | | | Deadline 1995. |
| Tunisia | | | | | | | | |
| - Industries chimiques de Gafsa | Gafsa | | | | | 90 | 85/86 | Status unknown |
| - SIAPE | La Skhirra | | | | | 330 | 88 | Status unknown |
| - Industries chimiques Maghrebines | Gabes | | | | | 165 | 84/85 | Status unknown |
| Egypt | | | | | | | | |
| - Abu Zaabal Fent Chem | Abu Zaabal | | | | | 66 | 84/85 | Status unknown |
| West Africa | | | | | | | | |
| Senegal | | | | | | | | |
| - Société des Industries chmiques du Senegal | Darou-Kho udous | 476 | 1984 | | | 94 | 91 | Status unknown |
| Togo | | | | | | | | |
| - Ste. des Engrais | | | | | | 330 | 90 | Status unknown |
| Central Africa | | | | | | | | |
| Eastern and Southern Africa | | | | | | | | |
| Zimbabwe | | | | | | | | |
| - Zimbabwe Phosphate Industries | | 22.5 | | | | | | |

Source: - FAO, 1981 to 1986, *1989, FAO Fertilizer Yearbook*, Rome.
- " Khennas, Smail, 1992, *Industrialization, Mineral Resources and Energy in Africa*, CODESRIA, Antony Rowe, Oxford.
- Many other publications

ANNEX 9.6

CAPACITIES AND PRODUCTION OF FERTILIZER PLANTS IN AFRICA (1000 t, 1992/93 for capacity and 1991/91 for production)

| | H2SO4 (a) | H3PO4 (b) | HNO3 (c) | NH3 (d) | AN (e) | AS (f) | CAN (g) | Urea (h) | ON (i) | SSP (j) | TSP (k) | GRP (l) | OP2O5 5 (m) | DAP (N) (P2O5) | NPK (o) | N (p) | P2O5 (q) | K2O (r) | Total (s) | CU (%) (t) |
|---|---|---|---|---|---|---|---|---|---|---|---|---|---|---|---|---|---|---|---|---|
| **North Africa** | | | | | | | | | | | | | | | | | | | | |
| **Algeria** | | | | | | | | | | | | | | | | | | | | |
| -Capacity (fert. materials) | 495 | 165 | 660 | 990 | 825 | 325 | 250 | 132 | | | | | | | 550 | | | | : | |
| ( nutrients) | | | | | 272 | | 40 | 61 | | | | | | | 190 | 333 | | - | 523 | |
| - Production (nutrients) | | | | | 71 | | - | | 2 | | | | 24 | | 108 | 73 | 35 | - | 216 | 41.3 |
| **Egypt** | | | | | | | | | | | | | | | | | | | | |
| - Capacity (fert. materials) | | | 1122 | 1320 | 1320 | 325 | 250 | 1155 | | 1225 | 130 | | | | 1100 | | : | | : | |
| ( nutrients) | | | | | 458 | 70 | | 540 | | 245 | 50 | | | | | 1108 | 295 | - | 1403 | |
| - Production (nutrients) | | | | | 408 | | 14 | 402 | | 124 | 18 | 26 | 75 | | | 824 | 163 | - | 987 | 70.4 |
| **Libya** | | | | | | | | | | | | | | | | | | | | |
| - Capacity (fert. materials) | | | | | 175 | | | 720 | | | | | | | | | | | | |
| (nutrients) | | | | | 58 | | | 331 | | | | | | | | 389 | - | - | 389 | |
| - Production | | | | | | | | | | | | | | | | 173 | - | - | 173 | 44.5 |
| **Morocco** | | | | | | | | | | | | | | | | | | | | |
| - Capacity (fert. materials) | 5045 | 2800 | | | | 200 | | | | 150 | 1800 | | | 1300 | | | | | | |
| (nutrients) | | | | | | 42 | | | | 30 | 648 | | | 234 | 614 | 276 | 1292 | - | 1568 | |
| - Production (90/91) | | | | | | | | | 37 | 17 | 268 | | | 307 | 820 | 344 | 1180 | - | 1416 | 90.3 |
| **Tunisia** | | | | | | | | | | | | | | | | | | | | |
| - Capacity (fert. materials) | 4769 | 1422 | 270 | | | 88 | | | | 60 | 890 | | | | 495 | | | | | |
| ( nutrients) | | | | | | 29 | | | | 12 | 481 | | | 125 | 325 | 154 | 818 | - | 1222 | |
| - Production (nutrients) | | | | | | | | | 24 | 4 | 321 | 16 | | 104 | 266 | 209 | 631 | - | 841 | 68.8 |

**West Africa**

| | | | | | | | | | | |
|---|---|---|---|---|---|---|---|---|---|---|
| **Senegal** | | | | | | | | | | |
| - Capacity (fert. materials) | 627 | 476 | | | | | 254 | 120 | - | - |
| (nutrients) | | | | | | | 120 | - | … | 47 |
| - Production (nutrients) | | | | 27 | 9 | 38 | 27 | 47 | - | 73 |
| | | | | | | | | | | 60.8 |
| **Nigeria** | | | | | | | | | | |
| - Capacity (fert. materials) | 330 | 450 | 100 | | | | 300 | 380 | - | |
| (nutrients) | | 207 | 20 | | | | 153 | … | … | - |
| - Production (nutrients) | | 125 | 106 | 4 | 54 | | 231 | 58 | - | 289 |
| | | | | | | | | | | 76.1 |
| **Cote d'Ivoire** | | | | | | | | | | |
| - Capacity (fert. materials) | | | | | | | 120 | 60 | | |
| (nutrients) | | | | | | | 60 | … | … | - |
| - Production (nutrients) | | | | | | 3 | - | 3 | - | 3 |
| | | | | | | | | | | 5 |

**Eastern and Southern Africa**

| | | | | | | | | | | |
|---|---|---|---|---|---|---|---|---|---|---|
| **Madagascar** | | | | | | | | | | |
| - Capacity (fert. materials) | 60 | 90 | | | | | | | | |
| (nutrients) | | 41 | | | | | 41 | - | - | 41 |
| - Production (nutrients) | | | | | | | … | … | … | … |
| **Mauritius** | | | | | | | | | | |
| - Capacity (fert. materials) | 52 | 66 | | | | | 90 | | | 65 |
| (nutrients) | | 22 | | | | | 43 | … | - | - |
| - Production (nutrients) | | 1 | 11 | | | | 12 | 12 | - | 12 |
| | | | | | | | | | | 18.5 |
| **Mozambique** | | | | | | | | | | |
| - Capacity (fert. materials) | 50 | 60 | 10 | | | | | | | 14 |
| (nutrients) | | 12 | 2 | | | | 12 | 2 | - | |
| - Production (nutrients) | | | | | | | - | - | - | - |
| **Somalia** | | | | | | | | | | |

478

| | Capacity (fert. materials) | (nutrients) | Production (nutrients) |
|---|---|---|---|
| **Swaziland** | | | |
| - Capacity (fert. materials) | 30 · · 90 · 122 · · 50 · · · 23 | | |
| (nutrients) | 23 · 40 · · · 23 · 40 | | |
| - Production (nutrients) | · | · · | - - |
| **Tanzania** | | | |
| - Capacity (fert. materials) | 87 · 25 · · 40 · 79 | | 23 |
| (nutrients) | 9 · 43 · 43 · 52 | | |
| - Production (nutrients) | 2 · 1 · 2 - · 2 · 3 · 3 · 6 | | 11.5 |
| **Uganda** | | | |
| - Capacity (fert. materials) | | | |
| (nutrients) | | | |
| - Production (nutrients) | · · | · · · | - |
| **Zambia** | | | |
| - Capacity (fert. materials) | 60 · 130 · 96 · 140 · 50 | | 57 |
| (nutrients) | 46 · 11 · 57 · | | |
| - Production (nutrients) | 4 · 1 · 5 · 5 | | 8.8 |
| **Zimbabwe** | | | |
| - Capacity (fert. materials) | 125 · 21 · 165 · 60 · 215 · 360 · 70 | | 168 |
| (nutrients) | 71 · 72 · 3 · 25 · 71 · 97 · 128 | | |
| - Production (nutrients) | 32 · 3 · 1 · 41 · 83 · 45 · 5 | | 76.2 |

Source: Compiled from (a) country (papers, 1992, *Atelier Regional sur la Cooperation dans l'Utilisation Efficace des Unites Existantes de Production d'Engrais en Afrique, 23-27 Novembre 1992. Tanger* and (b) FCA mission reports.
(a)= sulfuric acid, (b)=phosphoric acid, (c)=nitric acid, (d)=ammonia, (e)=ammonium nitrate, (f)=ammonium sulfate, (g)=calcium ammonium nitrate, (h)=Urea, (i)=other nitrogen, (j)=single super phosphate, (k)=triple superphosphate, (l)=ground rock phosphate, (m)=other P2O5, (n)=N and P2O5 in DAP, (o)=complex fertilizers, (p)=total N, (q)=total P2O5, (r)=total K2O, (s)=total all fertilizers nutrients, (t)=capacity utilization.

| | ANNEX 9.7 | | | | | | | |
| --- | --- | --- | --- | --- | --- | --- | --- | --- |
| | INTEGRATED FERTILIZER PLANTS IN THE CONTINENT | | | | | | | |
| Country | Plant / product | Year est. | Location | Capacity (1000 t) | | Production (1000 t of nutrients) | | Remarks/capacity utilization |
| | | | | Inter-mediate | Final product | 1981/82 | 1992/93 | |
| | North Africa | | | | | | | |
| Algeria | | | | | | NPK46 | NPK122 | |
| | Ammonia I | 1969 | Arzev | | | N24 | N88 | |
| | - Ammonia | | | 330 | | P23 | P34 | 35% in 1973 |
| | - Nitric acid | | | | | K- | K- | |
| | - Ammonium nitrate | | | | 165 | | | 72% in 1971 |
| | - Urea | | | | 132 | | | |
| | Ammonia II | 1982 | Arzev | | | | | |
| | - Ammonia | | | 330 | | | | 71% in 1984 |
| | - Nitric acid | | | | | | | |
| | - Ammonium nitrate | | | | 330 | | | 32% in 1984 |
| | Ammonia / B | 1984 | Annaba | | | | | |
| | - Ammonia | | | 330 | | | | 51% in 1987 |
| | - Nitric acid | | | | | | | |
| | - Ammonium nitrate | | | | 330 | | | 57% in 1987 |
| | Phosphate fertilizer complex | 1972 | Annaba | | | | | |
| | - Sulfuric acid | | | | | | | |
| | - Phosphoric acid | | | | | | | |
| | - Triple super phosphate | | | | 200 | | | 62% in 1987 |
| | - Diammonium phosphate | | | | 125 | | | |
| | - NPK | | | | 150 | | | |
| | - PK | | | | 75 | | | |

480

| Egypt | | | | | | NPK600 | NPK1000 | |
|---|---|---|---|---|---|---|---|---|
| Société el Nasr d'Engrais et d'Industrie Chimique | 1951 | Suez | | | N482 | N825 | | Feedstock changed from refinery gas to natural gas in 1977. The old 230 t/d ammonia plant was reported to have been phased out follow-ing the commissioning of a new one of 400 t/d capacity |
| - Ammonia | | | 132 | | P117 | P175 | | |
| - Nitric acid | | | | | K- | K- | | |
| - Calcium nitrate (15.5%) | 1951 | | | 250 | | | | |
| - Ammonium sulfate (20.6%) | 1963 | | | 66 | | | | |
| The Egyptian Chemical Ind. Co. (Kima) | 1960 | Aswan | | | | | | Based on electrolytic hydrogen, expected to be replaced by natural gas-based plant. |
| - Ammonia | | | 132 | | | | | |
| - Nitric acid | | | 264 | | | | | |
| - Ammonium nitrate (?) | | | | 320 | | | | |
| El Nasr Company for Manufacturing of Coke and Chemicals | 1971 | Helwan | | | | | | Based on coke oven gas. |
| - Ammonia | | | | 56 | | | | |
| - Nitric acid | | | | | | | | |
| - Ammonium nitrate | | | | | | | | |
| - Calcium ammonium nitrate (20.5%) | 1971 | | | | | | | |

| Country | Item | Year | Location | | | NPK- | NPK286 | Notes |
|---|---|---|---|---|---|---|---|---|
| | - Calcium ammonium nitrate (33.5%) | 1973 | | | | | | |
| | El Nasr Fertilizers and Chemicals Company | 1975 | Talkha | | | | | An ammonia/urea complex with 360,000 ammonia capacity (estimated using natural gas/ammonia ratio of 1) was added in 1980. |
| | - Ammonia | | | 132 | | | | |
| | - Nitric acid | | | 264 | | | | |
| | - Calcium ammonium nitrate (26%) | 1975 | | | | | | |
| | - Ammonium nitrate (31%) | 1976 | | | 330 | | | |
| | - Ammonia | 1980 | | 360 | | | | |
| | - Urea (46%) | 1980 | | | | | | |
| | Abu Qir Fertilizers and Chemicals Industries Company | 1979 | Abu Qir | | | | | Based on natural gas. The 790,000 unit was commissioned in 1991 |
| | - Ammonia | 1979 | | 330 | | | | |
| | - Urea (46%) | 1979 | | | 465 | | | |
| | - Ammonia | 1991 | | 330 | | | | |
| | - Nitric acid | | | 600 | | | | |
| | - Ammonium nitrate, granulated (33.5% N) | 1991 | | | 790 | | | |
| | Société Financiere et Industrielle d'Egypte | 1936 | | | | | | |
| | - Single superphosphate (15%) | 1969 | Kafr el Zayat | | | | | |
| | - Single superphosphate | | Assiut | | | | | |
| | Abu Zaabal Fertilizer and Chemical Co. | 1948 | Abu Zaabal | | | | | |
| | - Sulfuric acid (98%) | | | 200 | | | | |
| | - Phosphoric acid (50%) | | | 66 | | | | |
| | - Single superphosphate (15%) | | | | | | | |
| | - Triple superphosphate (45%) | 1987 | | | 180 | | | |
| Libya | | | | | | NPK- | NPK286 | |
| | ? | | | | | N- | N286 | Source: not given |
| | - Ammonia | 1978 | | 396 | | P- | P- | |
| | - Urea | 1981 | | | 330 | K- | K- | |
| | -Ammonia | 1991 | | 330 | | | | |
| | - Urea | 1984 | | | 580 | | | |
| | - Ammonium nitrate (33%) | | | | 175 | | | |

| Morocco | | | | | | NPK225 | NPK1294 | |
|---|---|---|---|---|---|---|---|---|
| Maroc Chimie I | 1965 | Safi | | | | N26 | N297 | |
| - Phosphoric acid (P2O5) | | | 132 | | | P199 | P997 | |
| - Ttiple superphosphate (?) | | | | 600 | | K- | K- | |
| - NPK (?) | 1973 | | | 200 | | | | |
| Maroc Chimie II | 1976 | Safi | | | | | | |
| - Phosphoric acid ( P2O5) | | | 165 | | | | | |
| Maroc Phosphore I | 1976 | Safi | | | | | | |
| - Phosphoric acid ( P2O5) | | | 500 | | | | | |
| - Phosphoric acid (P2O5) | 1980 | Safi | 165 | | | | | |
| - Monoammonium phosphate (?) | | | | 400 | | | | |
| Maroc Phosphore II | 1981 | Safi | | | | | | |
| - Phosphoric acid (P2O5) | | | 500 | | | | | 475 acc. to Khennas |
| Maroc Phosphore III and IV | 1986 | Jorf Lasfar | | | | | | |
| - Phosphoric acid (P2O5) | | | 1320 | | | | | 1,280 acc. to Khennas |
| - Diammonium phosphate | | | | 1120 | | | | 1,000 acc. to Khennas |
| - Triple superphosphate | | | | 450 | | | | 40 acc. to Khennas |
| - Ammonium-sulfide phosphate (ASP) | | | | 225 | | | | 200 acc. to Khennas |
| Maroc Phosphore V | | Nador | 640 | | | | | Expected start in 1995 |
| Maroc Phosphore VI | | Laayoune | 640 | | | | | Expected start in 1995 |
| Maroc Phosphore VII | | Essaouira | 640 | | | | | Expected start in 1995 |

| Tunisia | | Year | Location | | | NPK543 | NPK889 | |
|---|---|---|---|---|---|---|---|---|
| | Usine de Sfax | 1952 | Sfax | | | N69 | N202 | |
| | - Sulfuric acid | 1952 | | 99 | | P474 | P687 | |
| | - Sulfuric acid | 1964 | | 248 | | K- | K- | |
| | - Phosphoric acid (P2O5) | | | 132 | | | | |
| | - Triple superphosphate (?) | | | | 330 | | | Two units |
| | Industries Chimiques Maghrebines | 1972 | Gabes | | | | | |
| | -Sulphuric acid | 1972 | | 297 | | | | |
| | - Phosphoric acid (P2O5) | 1972 | | 102 | | | | |
| | - Sulfuric acid | 1974 | | 495 | | | | |
| | - phosphoric acid (P2O5) | 1974 | | 132 | | | | |
| | - Sulfuric acid | 1982 | | 990 | | | | Two units |
| | - Phosphoric acid (P2O5) | 1982 | | 165 | | | | |
| | - Dicalcium phosphate | | | | 60 | | | |
| | - Sulfuric acid | | | ?000 | | | | Two units |
| | - Phosphoric acid (P2O5) | | | 330 | | | | Two units |
| | - Monoammonium phosphate (?) | | | | 100 | | | |
| | - Diammonium phosphate (?) | | | | 700 | | | |
| | - NPK | | | | 500 | | | |
| | Usine d'Ammonium nitrate | 1983 | Gabes | | | | | |
| | - Nitric acid (100%) | | | 260 | | | | |
| | - Ammonium nitrate, agricultural (?) | | | | 310 | | | |
| | - Ammonium nitrate, porous(?) | | | | 17 | | | |
| | Société Industrie d'Acide Phosphorique & d'Engrais | 1988 | La Skhira | | | | | |
| | - Sulfuric acid | | | 1150 | | | | Two units |
| | - Phosphoric acid (P2O5) | | | 400 | | | | Two units |
| | - Superphosphoric acid (P2O5) | | | 330 | | | | Concentrated form of above? |
| | Usine de M'dhilla | 1985 | M'dhilla | | | | | |
| | - Sulfuric acid | | | 500 | | | | |
| | - Phosphoric acid (P2O5) | | | 165 | | | | |
| | - Triple superphosphate | | | | 450 | | | Two units |
| | West Africa | | | | | | | |

484

| | | | | | | | | |
|---|---|---|---|---|---|---|---|---|
| Cote d'Ivoire | | | | | | NPK5 | NPK3 | |
| | | | | | | N2 | N- | |
| | - Granulated fertilizers (50%) | | | | 120 | P3 | P3 | |
| Nigeria | | | | | | NPK10 | NPK354 | |
| | - Sulfuric acid | | | | | N- | N271 | |
| | - Single superphosphate (20%) | | | | 100 | P10 | P83 | |
| | - Ammonia | | | | 330 | K- | K- | |
| | - Urea (46%) | | | | 450 | | · | |
| | - DAP/NPK | | | | 300 | | | |
| Senegal | | | | | | NPK30 | NPK58 | |
| | Industries Chimiques du Senegal | 1984 | | | | N5 | N25 | Based on imported sulfur and ammonia. |
| | - Sulfuric acid (100%) | | Taiba | 560 | | P25 | P33 | About 50% of the phosphoric acid exported to India. |
| | - Phosphoric acid (P2O5) | | Taiba | 220 | | K- | K- | |
| | - Triple superphsphate | | M'Bao | | 45 | | | |
| | - Diammonium phosphate | | M'Bao | | 165 | | | |
| Eastern and Southern Africa | | | | | | | | |
| Angola | Ammonia-based fertilizer project | | | | | | | Among projects considered for SADC. |
| | - Ammonia | | | 495 | | | | |
| Botswana | Potash project idea | | | 163 | | | | World Bank-based on brines. |
| Madagascar | | | | | | NPK- | NPK- | |
| | - Ammonia | | | | 60 | | | |
| | - Urea (46%) | | | | 90 | | | |
| Mauritius | | | | | | NPK8 | NPK15 | |
| | | | | | | N8 | N15 | |
| | - Nitric acid | | | | 52 | P- | P- | |
| | - Ammonium nitrate (33%) | | | | 66 | K- | K- | |
| | - NPK (48) | | | | 90 | | | |

| Country | Item | Year | Location | | | Cap. A | Cap. B | Code 1 | Code 2 | Notes |
|---|---|---|---|---|---|---|---|---|---|---|
| Mozambique | | | | | | | | NPK5 | NPK- | Stopped operation in |
| | Quimica General SARL | 1972 | Maputo | | | | | N3 | N- | |
| | - Sulfuric acid | | | | | 50 | | P2 | P- | |
| | - Single superphosphate (20%) | | | | | | 15 | K- | K- | |
| | - Ammonium sulfate (20%) | | | | | | 60 | | | |
| | - NPK | | | | | | 20 | | | |
| | Ammonia-based fertilizer project | | | | | | | | | Among projects considered for SADC. |
| | Ammonia | | | | | 360 | | | | |
| Somalia | | | | | | | | NPK- | NPK- | |
| | - Ammonia | | | | | 30 | | | | |
| | - Urea (46%) | | | | | | 50 | | | |
| Swaziland | | | | | | | | NPK3 | NPK- | |
| | Farm Chemicals | | | | | | | N3 | N- | Only blending accord.-ing to World Bank |
| | - Nitric acid | | | | | 90 | | | | |
| | - Ammonium nitrate (33%) | | | | | 122 | | | | |
| Tanzania | | | | | | | | NPK19 | NPK- | Plant ceased operation in 1991. Note nil production in adjacent column in 1992/93 |
| | Tanga Fertilizer Company | | Tanga | | | | | N8 | N- | |
| | -Sulfuric acid | | | | | 87 | | P11 | P- | |
| | - Phosphoric acid (P2O5) | | | | | 46 | | | | |
| | - Triple superphosphate (54%) | | | | | | 79 | | | |
| | - Ammonium sulfate (21%) | | | | | | 60 | | | |
| | - NPK/triple superphsphate | | | | | | 65 | | | |
| | Ammonia-based fertilizer project | | | | | | | | | Feasibility study based on Song-Songo Island natural gas. Among projects considered for SADC |
| | - Ammonia | | | | | 495 | | | | |
| | - Urea | | | | | | 580 | | | |

| Country | Company / Product | Year | Location | Cap. | Cap. | | | Notes |
|---|---|---|---|---|---|---|---|---|
| Zambia | | | | | | | NPK4 | Based on coal gasification. Rehabilitated. |
| | | | | | | NPK5 | | |
| | National Chemicals of Zambia | | | | | N5 | N4 | |
| | - Sulfuric acid | | | 60 | | | | |
| | - Ammonia | 1970 | | 100 | | | | |
| | - Nitric acid | 1970 | | | | | | |
| | - Ammonium sulfate (20%) | 1982 | | | 47 | | | |
| | - Ammonium nitrate (33%) | 1970 | | | 140 | | | |
| | - NPK | 1982 | | | ... | | | |
| Zimbabwe | Zimbabwe Phosphate Industries Limited (ZIMPHOS) | 1924 | Msasa, Harare | | | NPK110 | NPK97 | Originally based on bones. Sulfuric acid based on pyrites and imported sulfur. ZIMPHOS and Sable products and imports are converted into granular compounds by Zimbabwe Fertilizer Company (210,000 t) and Windmill (Pvt.) Limited (200,000 t) |
| | - Sulfuric acid (100%) | | | 145 | | N70 | N57 | |
| | - Phosphoric acid (P2O5) | | | 21 | | P40 | P41 | |
| | - Single superphosphate (P2O5) | | | | 360 | | | |
| | - Triple superphosphate (P2O5) | | | | 70 | | | |
| | Sable Chemical Industries Limited | 1972 | Kwe Kwe | | | | | |
| | - Ammonia | 1972 | | 70 | | | | Based on electrolysis |
| | - Nitric acid | 1969 | | 82 | | | | |
| | - Ammonium nitrate (33%) | 1969 | | | 225 | | | Explosive grade. |
| South Africa | | | | | | NPK957 | NPK750 | The capacity figures represent combined capacities of 10 major finished product units (The World Bank/SADCC, Main Report). |
| | LAN | | Johannesburg | | 140 | N447 | N410 | |
| | - Urea | | | | 226 | P510 | P340 | |
| | - Compounds (15-1716) | | | | 1630 | K- | K- | |
| | LAN | | Cape Town | | 180 | | | |
| | - Compounds (13-19-7) | | | | 268 | | | |
| | -DAP | | Durban | | 400 | | | |
| | - Compounds (18-10-19) | | | | 254 | | | |
| | Sasol I - ammonia | | Sasolburg | 220 | | | 200 | Likely plant capacities and production in 1995 (The World Bank/SADCC, Main Report). Four plants based on coal and one, on refinery off-gas. |
| | Sasol II -ammonia | | Secunda | 95 | | | 95 | |
| | Sasol III -ammonia | | Secunda | 110 | | | 104 | |
| | AECI -ammonia | | Modderfontein | 300 | | | 275 | |
| | Kynoch -ammonia | | Milnerton | 80 | | | 65 | |
| | Other small plants -ammonia | | | ... | | | 46 | |

Source: - Bondiaf S.,1992, *l'Experience Algerienne dans l'Utilisation des Unites Existance et dans la Cooperation dans le Domaine des Engrais Chimiques.* Alger.
- Ahmed El-Deeb, 1992, Fertilizer *Production and Consumption in Egypt*, Cairo.
- OCP, 1992, *Communication Presentee par Monsieur Kendili El Hadi, lors de L'atelier Regional sur la Cooperation dans l'Utilization des Engrais en Afrique*, Rabat.
- Abdel Monem Ahmed Akeel, undated, *Experience in Utilization of Natural Gas in the Production of Basic Chemicals*, Cairo.
- Yosry A. El Khayat, 1993, *Ammonium Nitrate Project Abu Qir II 1985-1991 Consolidated Case Study*, Cairo.
- Aboulhassen Charfi, 1992, *Experience Tunisienne dans le Domaine de la Production d'Dengrais*, Tunis.
- Kachere, M.S./UNIDO. 1992, *A Diagnostic Analysis of the Production Activity at Zimbabwe Phosphate Industries Limited*. Vienna.
- *The World Bank/SADCC. 1990, A Strategic Assessment of the Fertilizer Industry of the SADCC Countries, including Working Paper No. 3* Washington DC
- The World Bamk/SADCC.1991, *An Action Plan for the Development of the Fertilizer Industry*, Working Paper I and II, Washington DC.
- The World Bank/SADC, 1993, *SADC Fertilizer Supply Options Model*, Washington, DC.
- Khennas, Smail, ed., 1992, *Industrialization Mineral Resources and Energy in Africa*, CODESRIA, CODESRIA Book Series, Antony Rowe, Oxford.
- Brochures and booklets on Senegal.
- FAO, 1993, *FAO Fertilizer Yearbook*, Rome (for production figures).

| ANNEX 10.1 AGRICULTURAL IMPLEMENTS AND FOOD PROCESSING EQUIPMENT MANUFACTURING FACILITIES IN THE WEST AFRICAN SUBREGION IN LATE 1980s (units/y) | | | | |
|---|---|---|---|---|
| Country/manufacturing company | Implements produced | Capacity | Production | Remarks |
| Senegal -SISMAR | | | | Based on one 8 hours shift. Plan to diversify into irrigation equipment, etc. |
| | Plows and cultivators | 150000 | ... | |
| | Planters | 500 | ... | |
| Niger - AFMA | | | | |
| | Hand-pushed cultivators | 1000 | ... | |
| | Mouldboard ploughs | 4000 | ... | |
| | Ridgers | 4000 | ... | |
| | Rice threshers | 500 | ... | |
| | Carts, rakes and axes | 10000 | ... | |
| Mali - SMECMA | | | | Production refer to 1979. |
| | Animal drawn implements | ... | 23000 | |
| Cote d'Ivoire - ABI | | | | Production refer to 1986 |
| | Mouldboard ploughs | 2000 | 500 | |
| | Harrows | 2000 | 1500 | |
| | Planters | 1800 | 500 | |
| | Ridgers | 2500 | 2500 | |
| | Water pumps | 2000 | 2000 | |
| | Carts | 1000 | 1000 | |
| | Cassava graters | 150 | 30 | |

| | | | | |
|---|---|---|---|---|
| Nigeria | | | | |
| - Crocodile Machetes Ltd. | Pumps | | ... | |
| | Irrigation equipment | | ... | |
| | Parts for tractor assembly | ... | ... | |
| | Hot metal | 400 | ... | |
| - Steyr Nigeria Ltd | Machetes | 240000 | 216000 | |
| | 2-row ridgers | 5000 | ... | In addition to tractors the company also assembles trucks. |
| | 3-row disc ploughs | 5000 | ... | |
| | Planters, seeders and farm trailers | 10000 | ... | |
| - National Truck Manufacturers Ltd. | Tractors (45 HP and 60 HP) | 2000 | ... | |
| - John Holt Engineers Ltd. | Tractors (assembly) | 2000 | ... | |
| | Trucks (assembly) | 5000 | ... | |
| | Disc ploughs | 5000 | ... | |
| | Mould board ploughs | 3000 | ... | |
| | Ridgers | 2500 | ... | |
| | Tillers | 2500 | ... | |
| - Addis Engineering Ltd. | Irrigation pumps | 10000 | ... | Excess capacity for producing food processing equipment |
| | Grinders | 40000 | ... | |
| | Gari making plants | 5000 | ... | |
| | Rolling planters | 1000 | ... | |
| | Grinders | 500 | ... | |
| | Palm oil and palm kernel processing machines | 200 | ... | |

| | | | | | |
|---|---|---|---|---|---|
| Togo<br>- UPROMA | | | | | Based on one shift. |
| | Hand-pulled planters | 200 | ... | | |
| | Ploughs | 500 | ... | | |
| | Farm carts | 350 | ... | | |
| | Bicycle cars | 50 | ... | | |
| | Groundnut shellers | 50 | ... | | |
| | Hand pumps | 250 | ... | | |
| | Cow-pulled water containers | 150 | ... | | |
| Ghana<br>- Ghana Railway Shop | Hoes, cutlasses, shovels, rakes, farm carts and wheel barrows | ... | ... | | It also produces cocoa and coconut harvesting hooks, grain hopper, corn mill plates and fishing spears. |
| - Agricultural Engineers Ltd. | Harrows | 300 | ... | | |
| | Crop planters | 1000 | ... | | |
| - Farmers Technical Services and Technological Centre | Palm oil plants | 120 | ... | | |
| | Sugar cane crushers | 200 | ... | | |
| | Planters (maize) | 200 | ... | | |
| | Rice threshers | 120 | ... | | |
| | Metal parts for bullock carts | 100 | ... | | |
| | Oil expellers/mills | 50 | ... | | |
| | Soap making machine | 25 | ... | | |
| | Caustic soda plant | 25 | | | |
| Burkina Faso<br>- APICOMA | | | | | Work done on a job offer basis. |
| | Forks | 950 | ... | | |
| | Ploughs | 2000 | | | |
| - CHEA | Cultivators | 750 | ... | | |
| | Carts | 3700 | ... | | |
| | Ploughs | 4000 | | 4082 | Production refer to 1986. |
| - SOFITEX | Cultivators | 4300 | | 4416 | |
| | Hoes | 127 | | 127 | |
| | Carts | 2350 | | 348 | |
| | Tractors (28 HP) | 60 | | | |

| Guinea | | | | At closure the factory was operating below 10%. |
|---|---|---|---|---|
| | Machetes | 30,000 | ... | |
| | Pick axes, axes | 3000 | ... | |
| | Forks | 200 | ... | |
| | Shovels | 220000 | ... | |
| | Ploughs | 3000 | ... | |
| Benin<br>- COPEMAC | | | | Production refer to 1986. |
| | Mold board ploughs | 2000 | 751 | |
| | Ridgers | 1800 | 751 | |
| | Planters | 500 | 166 | |
| | Weeders | 500 | 101 | |
| | Harrows (spike tooth type) | ... | 20 | |
| | Carts | 600 | 400 | |
| Sierra Leone<br>- National Workshop | | | | |
| | Hoes | 5000 | ... | |
| | Machetes | 10000 | ... | |
| | Digging forks | 2000 | ... | |
| | Axes | 2000 | ... | |
| | Rakes | 2000 | ... | |
| Liberia<br>- Agro Machines Ltd. | | | | |
| | Cassava graters | 50 | ... | |
| | Palm oil expellers | 50 | ... | |
| | Sugar cane crushers | 15 | ... | |
| | Autoclave | 10 | ... | |

Source: Compiled from ECA, 1988, *Manufacture of Agricultural Tools, Implements and Machinery in the West African Subregion*, Addis Ababa.

| ANNEX 11.1 EXAMPLES OF AGRICULTURAL MATERIAL PROCESSING AT SMALL-SCALE LEVEL RELEVANT TO AFRICAN NEEDS AND CONDITIONS | | |
|---|---|---|
| **Food** | | **Wood and pulp** |
| - Sifted maize flour | - Tomato ketchup production | - Saw milling |
| - Maize degerming | - Fruit jam and sauce processing | - Briquetting of agricultural and forestry resdues |
| - Rice milling | - Tropical fruit juice processing | - Small-scale furniture production |
| - Sorghum processing | - Citronella oil distillation | - Bags and paper envelope manufacture |
| - Manioc chips processing | **Cotton textiles** | - Paper ruling |
| - Manioc pellets processing | - Small-scale weaving | - Tooth-picks and ruler manufacturing |
| - Gari production | - Gauze and bandage making | **Leather and leather goods** |
| - Concentrated vegetable protein flour preparation | **Medicinal plants** | - Tannery |
| - Biscuit making | - Extraction of essential oils | - Leather goods production |
| - Weaning food production | - Extraction of medicinal plants | - Shoe sole making |
| - Soya milk production | - Isolation of active ingredients | - Leather shoe making |
| - Vegetable dehydration | - Processing medicinal plants into dosage form | **Others** |
| - Vegetable oil extraction | - Preparation of tablets | - Laundry soap making |
| - Palm oil extraction | - Preparation of ointment | - Cocoa butter skin cream making |
| - Palm kernel oil extraction | - Preparation of liquid orals | - Small-scale brown sugar mill |
| - Canning | | - Alcohol from molasses |

| ANNEX 14.1 EXAMPLES OF SMALL-SCALE METAL WORKING INDUSTRIES FOR MAKING EQUIPMENT AND MACHINERY UNDER AFRICAN NEEDS AND CONDITIONS | | |
|---|---|---|
| **Agricultural tools, equipment and machinery** | **Other equipment and machinery** | |
| - Tools and implements | - Bolts and nuts | - Small containers/dust beans |
| - Hand shovels | - Machine screws and rivets | - Adjustable hospital beds |
| - Forks | - Hair pins | - Air conditioning duct |
| - Seed drills | - Hair brushes | - Mechanical toys |
| - Insecticide dusters, manual | - Wire brushes | - Springs |
| - Disc harrows | - Paper pins | - Hand making tools |
| - Pump, assembling | - Staplers and punching machines | - Automobile radiator cores |
| - Gabions (nets) | - Steel padlocks | - Automobile silencers |
| - Barbed wire | - Gate hooks | - Engine valves |
| **Food preservation and processing equipment and machinery** | - Wire nails | - Automobile handles and locks |
| - Grain dryers | - Cupboard and drawer locks | - Belt fasteners |
| - Can making | - Steel tables | - Spare parts |
| - Dairy equipment | - Tin trays | - Brick molds |
| **Household articles** | - Bread-baking trays | - Bins, tanks, etc. |
| - Utensils | | - Wheelbarrows |
| - Containers | | - Pipe fittings |
| - Buckets | | - Furniture, pallets, racks, ladders, etc. |
| - Kerosene stoves | | |

### ANNEX 14.2
### CAPACITIES AND PRODUCTION OF SELECTED ENGINEERING GOODS IN THE NORTH AFRICAN SUBREGION

| | No. | Type of operation | Capacity | | Production | | Products/remarks |
|---|---|---|---|---|---|---|---|
| | | | Year | t/y | Year | t/y | |
| Transformers | | | | | | | |
| Algeria | ... | ... | ... | 10300 | ... | ... | Small transformers. |
| Egypt | 1 | Assembling | ... | ... | ... | ... | Distribution transformers. |
| Libya | ... | Assembling | ... | ... | ... | ... | |
| Morocco | 2 | ... | ... | ... | ... | ... | Distribution transformers. |
| Tunisia | 1 | Assembling | ... | 3500 | ... | ... | |
| Hydraulic excavators | | | | | | | |
| Algeria | 1 | ... | ... | 900 | ... | ... | To have been completed in 1984. |
| Mobile cranes | | | | | | | |
| Algeria | | | ... | ... | 300 | ... | ... | Part of the above mobile crane unit. |

Source: Compiled from UNIDO, 1987, *Strategies and Policies for the Development of the Capital Goods Sector in the Arab World,* Vienna.

### ANNEX 14.3
### CHARACTERISTICS OF THE MANUFACTURE OF SOME ENGINEERING/CAPITAL GOODS RELEVANT TO AFRICAN CONDITIONS

| Product | Minimum efficient scale [a] | Ratio of supply-demand gap to minimum efficient scale | Invest-ment/sales ratio | Employ-ment/invest-ment ratio | Labor/sales ratio | Technol-ogical complexity of production | Potential forward/backward linkages |
|---|---|---|---|---|---|---|---|
| Bench drills, saws, bench grinders, simple shearing and planing machines | 0.9 | 499 | 2.2 | 25 | 55 | Simple | Low , backward |
| Lathes, milling and boring machines planing and shaping machines | 2.9 | 117 | 2 | 19 | 38 | Moderate | High , backward |
| Pumps and valves, low pressure and temperature | 20 | 31 | 3 | 8.3 | 25 | Moderate | Backward to motors, actuators |
| Diesel engines, high speed (1200-4000 rpm) | 120 | 3.3 | 0.3 | 84 | 21 | Moderate | Large forward and backward |
| Agricultural tractors | 155 | 5.3 | 0.5 | 50 | 26 | Moderate | Large backward |
| Spinning machines and looms | 10 | 41.5 | 2.3 | 9 | 30 | Complex | Backward to casting , infrastructure |
| Dyeing and finishing machinery | 3 | 130 | 2.3 | 19 | 43 | Complex | Backward to casting |
| Mineral crushing, grinding and sorting equipment | 45 | 9.3 | 0.9 | 24 | 22 | Simple | Backward to castings, diesel engines, etc. |
| Buses, lorries and trucks | 500 | 17 | 3.5 | 2.6 | 9 | Moderate | Backward to diesel engines, tires, electrical components |

Source: Compiled from UNIDO, 1987, *Strategies and Policies for the Development of the Capital Goods Sector in the Arab World,* Vienna.
[a] Millions of US $ at 1980 prices   [b] Employment in man-years and investment in millions of US $ at 1980 prices.

| ANNEX 14.4 AFRICAN IMPORTS, PRODUCTION, CONSUMPTION AND ESTIMATED DEMAND FOR STEEL (m t/y) | | | | | | | | | | |
|---|---|---|---|---|---|---|---|---|---|---|
| Year | 1960 | 1965 | 1970 | 1975 | 1980 | 1985 | 1990 | 1995 | 2000 |
| Imports | 2.5 | 3 | 3.5 | 5.7 | 6.8 | 5.9 | 3 | 6 | 9 |
| Local production | 0.5 | 0.6 | 0.7 | 1.2 | 2.4 | 3.7 | 4.5 | 6 | 9 |
| Apparent consumption | 3 | 3.6 | 4.2 | 6.9 | 9.2 | 9.6 | 7.5 | 12 | 18 |
| Imports as apparent consumption | 83 | 83 | 83 | 83 | 74 | 62 | 40 | 50 | 50 |
| Estimated demand | 3.5 | 4 | 5 | 7.6 | 10 | 15 | 20 | 30 | 40 |
| Production/demand gap | 0.5 | 0.4 | 0.8 | 0.6 | 0.8 | 5.4 | 12.5 | 18 | 22 |
| Production/demand gap, total gap | 3 | 3.4 | 4..3 | 6..3 | 7.6 | 11.3 | 15.5 | 24 | 31 |

Source: - - - -, ———, *The Steel Market, 1969-1991,*
- - - -, ———, *Statistics of World Trade in Steel, 1960-1991*

| ANNEX 14.5 INTENSITY OF USE AND PER CAPITA CONSUMPTION OF COPPER IN AFRICA AND THE WORLD | | | | | | | |
|---|---|---|---|---|---|---|---|
| | 1960-1964 | 1965-1969 | 1970-1974 | 1975-1979 | 1980-1984 | 1985-1989 | 1990-1991/2 |
| Intensity of use (IU), (kgs Cu/ $ m GDP) | | | | | | | |
| South Africa | 1236.2 | 967.4 | 1231.4 | 1290.2 | 1515.8 | 1250.8 | 1056.5 |
| Africa, developing | 107.8 | 62.6 | 136.6 | 353 | 374 | 355.4 | 390 |
| World | 1100.6 | 1049.4 | 1008.8 | 949.2 | 895.8 | 836.6 | 817 |
| Developing, Africa's IU as (%) of world IU | 9.8 | 6 | 13.5 | 37.2 | 41.8 | 42.5 | 47.7 |
| Per capita consumption (kgs Cu) | | | | | | | |
| South Africa | 1.6 | 1.5 | 2.1 | 2.2 | 2.7 | 2.1 | 1.6 |
| Africa, developing | 0 | 0 | 0.1 | 0.2 | 0.2 | 0.3 | 0.3 |
| World | 2.2 | 2.3 | 2.5 | 2.6 | 2.6 | 2.6 | 2.5 |
| Developing Africa's per capita consumption as % of world per capita consumption | | | 4 | 7.7 | 7.7 | 11.4 | 12 |

Source : Compiled and computed from ECA/UNIDO, 1995, *Prospects for the Increased Production of and Intra- African Trade in Metal and Based Products*, ECA/UNIDO/AFRICOP/TP/2/ 94, Addis Ababa (originally obtained from UNCTAD Secretariat and World Metal Statistics. July 1994.

### ANNEX 14.6
### PRIMARY PRODUCTION AND SUBSEQUENT PROCESSING OF SELECTED ORES IN MAJOR AFRICAN PRODUCERS AND PRINCIPAL DEVELOPING COUNTRIES (1000 t)

| Commodity/country | 1980-1982 | | | | 1989-1991 | | | |
|---|---|---|---|---|---|---|---|---|
| | Primary production | Processed output | | | Primary production | Processed output | | |
| | | 1st stage | 2nd stage | 3rd stage | | 1st stage | 2nd stage | 3rd stage |
| Aluminum (Al content) | Bauxite | Alumina | Aluminum refined | Refined Al consumption | Bauxite | Alumina | Aluminum refined | Refined Al consumption |
| Guinea | 2956.3 | 327.5 | | | 3987.5 | 320 | | |
| Ghana | 35.4 | | 184.1 | 6 | 81.6 | | 172.7 | 9.7 |
| Egypt | | | 134.3 | 49.3 | | | 179 | 79.2 |
| Developing countries | 9614.3 | 3264.7 | 1932.2 | 1564.5 | 11312.2 | 5280.8 | 3765.3 | 2799.4 |
| Copper (Cu content) | Copper ore | Unrefined copper | Refined copper | Refined Cu consumption | Copper ore | Unrefined copper | Refined copper | Refined Cu consumption |
| Zambia | 583.4 | 587.2 | 586 | 2.3 | 473 | 451.9 | 427.9 | 9.2 |
| Congo K | 489.1 | 453.4 | 156.8 | 2.6 | 348.6 | 343.5 | 165.9 | 2.2 |
| Developing countries | 3705.2 | 2769 | 2232.7 | 968.3 | 4117.3 | 34135 | 2999.1 | 1718.5 |
| Iron (Fe content) | Iron ore | Pig iron | Crude steel | | Iron ore | Pig iron | Crude steel | |
| Liberia | 11343.7 | | | | 3904 | | | |
| Mauritania | 5515.3 | | | 10 | 7012 | | 5 | |
| Developing countries | 134732.7 | 43862.7 | 66364.3 | ... | 182613.4 | 75677.6 | 115366 | ... |
| Nickel (Ni content) | Nickel ore | Refined nickel | Refined Ni consumption | | Nickel ore | Refined nickel | Refined Ni consumption | |
| Botswana | 17.2 | | | | 20.2 | | | |
| Zimbabwe | 14.3 | 14 | | | 12.6 | 18.7 | | |
| Developing countries | 247.6 | 106 | 35.6 | ... | 314.3 | 164 | 82.7 | ... |

Source: UNCTAD, 1994, *UNCTAD Commodity Yearbook 1994*, New York.

### ANNEX 14.7
### PRODUCTION OF BASIC METALS BY COUNTRY IN THE CONTINENT IN 1992 (1000 t)

| | Crude steel (1993) | Primary aluminum | Refined copper |
|---|---|---|---|
| Algeria | | | |
| Egypt | 2800 | 178 | 0.4 |
| Libya | 800 | | |
| Tunisia | 200 | | |
| Nigeria | 200 | | |
| Ghana | | 180 | |
| Cameroon | | 83 | |
| Congo K | | | 57 |
| Zambia | | | 472 |
| Zimbabwe | 600 | | 1.2 |
| South Africa | 8600 | 174 | 116 |
| Others | 300 | | |
| Total , continent | 15000 | 615 | 662 |

Source: UNECE, 1993, Production and Trade in Aluminum and Copper, *The Steel Market*, Geneva.

ANNEX 14.8
PRODUCTION OF PIG IRON, DIRECT REDUCED IRON AND STEEL IN AFRICA, 1987-1989

| | Production (mt) | | | | Share in world production (%) | | | | Capacity (1989) | | |
|---|---|---|---|---|---|---|---|---|---|---|---|
| | 1983 | 1987 | 1988 | 1989 | 1983 | 1987 | 1988 | 1989 | Total (1000t) | Utiliz- ation (%) | Share in world ca- pacity (%) |
| **Pig iron** | | | | | | | | | | | |
| World | | 502.1 | 530.6 | 476.4 | | 100 | 100 | 100 | | | |
| - Developing Africa | | 3 | 3 | 3 | | 0.6 | 0.6 | 0.8 | | | |
| - South Africa | | 6.3 | 6.1 | 6.5 | | 1.3 | 1.1 | 1.7 | | | |
| Total Africa | | 9.3 | 9.1 | 9.5 | | 1.9 | 1.7 | 2 | | | |
| **Steel making-grade direct-reduced iron** | | | | | | | | | | | |
| World | | | | 15.3 | | | | 100 | 24.3 | 63 | 100 |
| - Egypt | | | | 0.8 | | | | 5.4 | 0.7 | 113.9 | 3 |
| - Libya | | | | 0.1 | | | | 6 | 0.6 | 16.4 | 2.3 |
| -Nigeria | | | | 0.1 | | | | 0.8 | 1 | 12.7 | 4.2 |
| Total developing Africa | | | | 1 | | | | 6.5 | 1.4 | 71.4 | 5.8 |
| - South Africa | | | | 0.9 | | | | 5.8 | 1.4 | 65.4 | 5.8 |
| **Total Africa** | | | | 1.9 | | | | 12.3 | 2.8 | 67.9 | 11.6 |
| **Steel** | | | | | | | | | | | |
| World | 663.4 | | 779.9 | 782.5 | 100 | | 100 | 100 | | | |
| South Africa | 7.2 | | 8.8 | 9.4 | 1.2 | | 1.1 | 1.1 | | | |

Source : Compiled and computed from UNIDO, 1990, *Industry and Development Global Report 1990/91*, Vienna which was in turn obtained from International Iron and Steel Institute, 1989, Western *World Coke making Capacity*, Brussels.

ANNEX 14.9
EXISTING AND PLANNED IRON AND STEEL CAPACITIES IN AFRICA (m t/y)

| Subregion/region | Country | Plant/project | Location | Route | Capacity (m t/y) | Stage of implementation |
|---|---|---|---|---|---|---|
| Existing plants | | | | | | |
| North Africa | Algeria | SIDER | El Hadjar | BF-LD- rolling mill | 1.8 (pig iron) | In operation. |
| | Egypt | Egyptian Iron and Steel Works | Hadisolb | BF-LD-EAF- rolling mill | 1.5 | In operation |
| | | Alexandria National Iron and Steel Co. | El Dkheila | DR | 0.84 | Commissioned in 1986. |
| | Libya | Executive Board Iron and Steel Co. | Misurata | DR-EAF-CC - rolling mill | 1.1 (DRI) | Commissioned in 1989. |
| | Tunisia | Société Tunisienne de Sirerurgie | El-Fouladh | BF-BOF- rolling mill | 0.19 | In operation. |
| | | | | | 5.43 | |
| West Africa | Nigeria | Delta Steel Co. | Aladja | DR-EAF- rolling mill | 1 | In operation. |
| Eastern and Southern Africa | Zimbabwe | ZISCOSTEEL | Redcliff | BF-BOF- rolling mill | 0.75 (pig iron) | In operation |

| | | | | | | |
|---|---|---|---|---|---|---|
| Total (iron and steel) | | | | | | 7.18 | |

| | | | | | | |
|---|---|---|---|---|---|---|
| | | | | Projects under implementation | | | |
| North Africa | Algeria | | Jijele | DR-EAF-CC | 1 | Completion date : 1995 |
| | | SNS | Bellara | | 1 | Start up : early 1990s |
| Subtotal | | | | | 2 | |
| West Africa | Nigeria | Ajaokuta Steel Co. [a] | Ajaokuta | BF-BOF-rolling mill | 1.3 | Start up : 1991 |
| Eastern and Southern Africa | Zimbabwe | ZISCOSTEEL [a] | Redcliff | | 0.55 | Modernization and expansion to 1.3 mt/y |
| Total | | | | | 3.85 | |
| | | | | Planned projects | | | |
| North Africa | Algeria | La Matca Integrated Iron and Steel Plant | La-Matca | | 10 | Under consideration |
| | Egypt | | Sadat | | 1 | Feasibility study available |
| | | Egyptian Iron and Steel Co. [a] | Hadisolb | | 1 | Expansion to 2.5 mt/y under consideration |
| | | | 2 new plants | | 10 | Under consideration |
| | Libya | Executive Board Iron and Steel Co. [a] | Misurata | | 1.4 | Expansion to 2.5 mt/y |
| | Morocco | Société Sider | Nador | | 0.7 | Backward integration under consideration |
| | Tunisia | Société Tunisienne de Siderurgie [a] | El-Fouladh | | 0.21 | Expansion to 0.4 mt/y under consideration |
| | | | | | 24.31 | |
| West Africa | Nigeria | Ajaokuta Steel Co. [a] | Ajaokuta | | 3.9 | Plan for expansion to 5.2 mt/y |
| Total | | | | | 28.21 | |
| | | | | Other projects | | | |
| Eastern and Southern Africa | Angola | | | DR | 1.3 | Project. |
| | Kenya | Iron and steel plants | Mombassa | | 0.9 | Prefeasibility prepared in 1978. |
| | Madagascar | Steel plant | | DR | 0.1 | Project. |
| | | Ferro-chrome plant | | | 0.1 | Project. |
| | Mozambique | Integrated steel plant | Nacala | DR-EAF-CC | 0.4 | Project. |
| | Tanzania | Iron and steel plant | | DR | 0.28 | Feasibility. |
| West Africa | Guinea | | | DR | 0.8 | Project was under consideration in 1983. |
| | Liberia | | | DR | 1.5 | Prefeasibility prepared in 1977. |
| | Mali | Mini-steel plant | | DR | 0.03 | Prefeasibility study. |
| | Mauritania | | | DR | 0.6 | Project envisaged in 1977. |
| Central Africa | Congo K | Maluku Steel Plant | Maluku | DR-EAF-CC | ... | Project concept. |

Source: Compiled from ECA, 1992, "Survey of the Development of the Africa's Iron and Steel Industry and Perspectives for the Year 2000." *Focus on African Industry*, Volume V, No. 2, Addis Ababa.
    BF= blast furnace  LD=oxygen converter  BOF= basic oxygen furnace?  DR=direct reduction unit
    EAF=electric arc furnace  C=continous casting
  a  Capacities given as total capacities in the sources were corrected to reflect net additions.

ANNEX 14.10
COPPER, ALUMINA AND ALUMINUM CAPACITIES AND PRODUCTION IN AFRICA (1000 t/y)

| | Capacity | | | Production | | | | | | | | | |
|---|---|---|---|---|---|---|---|---|---|---|---|---|---|
| | Existing | Planned | Total | 1980 | 1986 | 1987 | 1988 | 1989 | 1990 | 1991 | 1992 | 1993ᵃ | 1994ᵇ |
| Copper (smelter) | | | | | | | | | | | | | |
| - Congo K | 480 | 100 | 580 | 2.3 | 528 | 516 | 496 | 466 | 373 | 251 | 144 | 80 | 50 |
| - Zambia | 695 | - | 695 | ... | 462 | 463 | 457 | 466 | 436 | 410 | 433 | 418 | 420 |
| - Others | 121 | - | 121 | ... | ... | ... | ... | ... | ... | ... | ... | ... | ... |
| Total | 1304 | 100 | 1404 | 1310 | 1195 | ... | ... | ... | ... | ... | ... | ... | ... |
| Alumina | | | | | | | | | | | | | |
| - Guinea | 700 | ... | 1300 | ... | 571 | ... | ... | ... | ... | ... | ... | ... | ... |
| - Ghana | - | 500 | 500 | - | - | - | - | - | - | - | - | - | - |
| - Cameroon | - | 800 | 800 | - | - | - | - | - | - | - | - | - | - |
| Total | 700 | 1300 | 2600 | ... | 571 | ... | ... | ... | ... | ... | ... | ... | ... |
| Aluminum | | | | | | | | | | | | | |
| - Egypt, Ghana, Cameroon | 700 | - | 700 | ... | 415 | ... | ... | ... | ... | ... | ... | ... | ... |
| - Cameroon | - | 80 | 80 | - | - | - | - | - | - | - | - | - | - |
| - Libya | - | 120 | 120 | - | - | - | - | - | - | - | - | - | - |
| - Congo K | - | 21 | 21 | - | - | - | - | - | - | - | - | - | - |
| Total | 700 | 221 | 921 | 387 | 415 | ... | ... | ... | ... | ... | ... | ... | ... |

Source: - UNIDO, 1987, *Financial Aspects of the and Aluminun Industry.D/WG.470/2*, Vienna.
- ECA, 1988, *Development of the African Mineral Sector during the Period 1985 to 1987 and Projected Prospects for the Period 1988 and Beyond*, ECA/NRD/TRCDUMRA, Addis Ababa, Ethiopia.
- ECA, 1988, *Regional Survey of and Aluminum Fabricating Facilities and Prospects for Intra-African Manufacture and Trade in and Aluminum-based Products*, ECA/NRD/TRCDUMRA/7, Addis Ababa.
- ECA, 1996, *Africa*
- The CRB Commodity Yearbook, 1995, Knight-Rider Financial/Commodity Research Bureau, John Wiley & Sons, Inc., New York.

a Preliminary   b Estimate   c Egypt (60,000 t/y), Nigeria (180,000 t/y), South Africa (466,00 t/y)

| ANNEX 14.11 SUMMARY OF PRIMARY COPPER PRODUCERS IN AFRICA (1000t) | | | | |
|---|---|---|---|---|
| Country | Producer | 1982 production | | Remarks |
| | | Mine | Refinery | |
| **Africa** | | 833.4 | 661.6 | |
| **North Africa** | | 15.4 | 4 | |
| Egypt | The Egyptian Copper Works | - | 4 | Produced from scrap |
| Morocco | Cie Minifere de Tourist | 1.5 | - | |
| | Cie Miniere de Guemassa | 0.5 | - | |
| | Ste de Dev. Cuivre de l'Anti-Atlas | 2.5 | - | |
| | Ste. Minierede Bougafer | 10.9 | - | |
| | Sub-total | 15.4 | - | |
| **Eastern and Southern Africa** | | 818 | 657.6 | |
| Botswana | BCL Ltd | 18.6 | - | copper/nickel matte refined in Zimbabwe |
| Namibia | Tsumeb Coprporation | 34.6 | - | Blister copper |
| South Africa | Black Mountain | 4 | - | Copper concentrate |
| | Impala Platinum | 4 | 4 | By-product of PGM production |
| | O'okiep Copper Co. | 23.3 | - | Copper concentrate and blister copper |
| | Palabora Mining Co. | 128.8 | 104.3 | Cathode and rod |
| | Phosphate Development Corporation | 12 | - | Concentrate smelted in Zimbabwe |
| | Rustenberg Platinum Mines | 6 | 6 | By-product of PGM production |
| | Sub-total | 180.1 | 116.3 | |
| Congo K | Gecomines | 130 | 57.2 | |
| | Ste de Dev. Ind. & Min. du Congo K | 14 | - | |
| | Sub-total | 144 | 57.2 | |
| Zambia | ZCCM | 432.6 | 472 | |
| Zimbabwe | Bindura Nickel Corp. | 1.1 | 1.1 | By-product of nickel production |
| | Mhanguru Copper Mine 7.0 | 7 | 11 | |
| | Sub-total | 8.1 | 12.1 | |

Source: ECA/UNIDO, 1995, *Prospects for the Increased Production of and Intra-African Trade in Copper Metal and Copper Based Products*, ECA/UNIDO/AFRICOP/TP/2/94, Addis Ababa.

| ANNEX 14.12 MINE AND REFINED PRODUCTION IN AFRICA AND THE WORLD (1000 t of metal) | | | | | | | | | |
|---|---|---|---|---|---|---|---|---|---|
| | Mine production | | | | | | | Refined production | |
| | 1973 | 1978 | 1983 | 1988 | 1993 | 1980-82 | 1990-92 | 1980-82 | 1990-92 |
| Africa, developing | 1302.1 | 1162.6 | 1214.1 | 1036.1 | 560 | 1184.7 | 777.9 | 761.4 | 563.3 |
| South Africa | 175.8 | 209.3 | 211.8 | 192.1 | 188.6 | 209.9 | 194.5 | 145.1 | 125.3 |
| Africa, total | 1477.9 | 1371.9 | 1425.9 | 1228.2 | 748.6 | 1394.6 | 972.4 | 906.5 | 688.6 |
| World, total | 7501.8 | 7854.2 | 8101 | 8778.6 | 7542.1 | 8063.9 | 9124.3 | 9443.2 | 10760 |
| Share of Africa total in world total (%) | 19.7 | 17.5 | 17.6 | 14 | 9.9 | 17.3 | 10.7 | 9.6 | 6.4 |

Source: Compiled and computed from *ECA/UNIDO, 1995, Prospects for the Increased Production of and Intra- African Trade in Metal and Based Products*, ECA/UNIDO/AFRICOP/TP/2/ 94, Addis Ababa (originally obtained from UNCTAD Secretariat and World Metal Statistics, July 1994.

| ANNEX 14. 13 PRODUCTION, CAPACITY, TRADE AND CONSUMPTION OF ALUMINUM IN AFRICA | | | | | | | | | | | |
|---|---|---|---|---|---|---|---|---|---|---|---|
| | Production, capacity, trade and consumption (1000t) | | | | Percentage change | | World share (%) | | Capacity utilization rate (%) | | Planned capacity |
| | 1985 | 1987 | 1989 | 1990 | 1989-90 | 1987-90 | 1987 | 1990 | 1985 | 1990 | 1995 |
| Production | 309 | 401 | 435 | 442 | 1.6 | 10.2 | 2.4 | 2.4 | | | |
| Export | | 121 | 164 | 154 | -6.1 | 27.3 | 2.1 | 2.1 | | | |
| Import | | - | - | - | - | - | - | - | | | |
| Consumption | | 129 | 132 | 130 | -1.5 | 0.8 | 0.7 | 0.7 | | | |
| Capacity | 457 | 450 | 462 | 467 | 1.1 a | 3.8 a | 2.5 a | 2.5 a | 68 | 95 | 687 b |
| - Algeria | | | | | | | | | | | 220 |
| - Cameroon | | 80 | 87 | 87 | | | | 1.9 c | | | 87 |
| - Egypt | | 170 | 175 | 180 | | | | 3.8 c | | | 180 |
| - Ghana | | 200 | 200 | 200 | | | | 4.4 c | | | 200 |

Source: Compiled from UNIDO, 1992, Industry and Development : Global Report 1992/93, Vienna.
a Computed  b Existing and new capacity  c Share in developing countries

| ANNEX 14.14 PRODUCTION AND CAPACITIES OF ALUMINA AND PRIMARY ALUMINUM IN THE AFRICAN CONTINENT (1000 t) | | | | | | | | | | |
|---|---|---|---|---|---|---|---|---|---|---|
| | Production | | | | | | Capacity | | | |
| | 1982 | 1984 | 1986 | 1988 | 1990 | 1992 | 1991 | 1992 | Planned 1995 | Planned |
| Alumina | | | | | | | | | | |
| Africa | 578 | 535 | 572 | 593 | 642 | | 700 | | | 2600 |
| Ghana | | | | | | | | | | 800 |
| Guinea | | | | | | | 700 | | | 1800 |
| Primary aluminum | | | | | | | | | | |
| Africa | 501 | 413 | 553 | 597 | 602 | 614 | | 637 | 1343 | |
| Cameroon | 79 | 73 | 81 | 80 | 88 | 83 | | 87 | 87 | |
| Egypt | 141 | 173 | 177 | 181 | 180 | 178 | | 180 | 240 | |
| Ghana | 174 | | 125 | 164 | 174 | 180 | | 200 | 200 | |
| Nigeria | | | | | | | | | 180 | |
| South Africa | 107 | 167 | 170 | 172 | 160 | 174 | | 170 | 636 | |

Source: Compiled from ECA/UNIDO, *Prospects for the Increased Production of and Intra-African Trade in Aluminum Commodities and Metal Products*, ECA/UNIDO/AFRIALUM/TP/1/94, Vienna ( originally from The Economics of Aluminium,1992, Roskill Information Services Limited, London, World Bureau of Metal Statistics)

| ANNEX 14.15 WORLD PRICES FOR COPPER, ALUMINA AND ALUMINUM | | | | | | | | | | |
|---|---|---|---|---|---|---|---|---|---|---|
| | Actual | | | | | | | Forecast | | |
| | 1960 | 1965 | 1970 | 1975 | 1980 | 1985 | 1989 | 1995 | 2000 | 2005 |
| Copper and aluminum | | | | | | | | | | |
| Copper (1985 constant $) | 2243 | 4099 | 3865 | 1877 | 2080 | 1417 | 2056 | 1099 | 1403 | 1292 |
| Primary aluminum (1985 constant $) [a] | 1657 | 1554 | 1477 | 1047 | 1649 | 1110 | 1412 | 1173 [b] | 1293 [b] | 1178 [b] |
| Steel (Current $/ t) | | | | | | | | | | |
| Cold-rolled sheets | | | | | 386.1 | 326.3 | 550.4 | 572.2 | 719.8 | 833.9 |
| Hot-rolled sheets | | | | | 323.3 | 245.8 | 441.9 | 451 | 563.4 | 647.9 |
| Galvanized sheets | | | | | 471 | 369.6 | 735 | 720.7 | 924.1 | 1091.5 |
| Merchant bars | | | | | 342.5 | 229.6 | 416.3 | 465.6 | 599.8 | 711.9 |
| Plates | | | | | 341.7 | 266.7 | 478.8 | 517.3 | 666.4 | 791 |
| Sections | | | | | 358.3 | 246.7 | 441.7 | 479.4 | 620.5 | 740.1 |
| Wire rod | | | | | 350.8 | 272.9 | 350.8 | 398.5 | 515.9 | 615.3 |
| Rebars | | | | | 330.8 | 225.4 | 341.7 | 387.7 | 494.8 | 581.6 |
| Steel (index 1985=100) | | | | | 131.1 | 100 | 1747 | 184.1 | 234.6 | 275.5 |

Source: World Bank, 1991, *Price Prospects for Major Primary Commodities, 1990-2005*, Volume I, Summary Energy,
 Metals and Minerals, Washington, DC.
  a  Deflated by manufacturing unit value (MUV) index.   b  London Metal Exchange (LME) cash.

| ANNEX 14.16 LEAD AND ZINC REFINERY CAPACITIES IN THE AFRICAN CONTINENT IN 1984 (1000 t) | | | | | | |
|---|---|---|---|---|---|---|
| Subregion/country | Lead smelting | | | | Zinc refining | |
| | Primary capacity | Main primary capacity | Secondary capacity | Number of secondary smelting companies | Primary capacity | Main primary capacities |
| North Africa | | | | | | |
| Algeria | - | - | 5 | 1 | 40 | S.Siderur (40) |
| Morocco | 45 | Sfplomb (45) | - | - | - | - |
| Tunisia | 30 | Tmtunisia (30) | - | - | - | - |
| Eastern and Southern Africa | | | | | | |
| Kenya | - | - | 2 | 1 | - | - |
| Namibia | 75 | Tsuneb (75) | - | - | - | - |
| South Africa | - | - | 46 | 3 | 105 | Zinc Co. (105) |
| Congo K | - | - | - | - | 68 | Gecamine (68) |
| Zambia | 30 | ZCCM (30) | 1 | 1 | 70 | ZCCM (70) |
| Zimbabwe | - | - | 2 | 1 | - | - |
| Africa and the world | | | | | | |
| Africa | 180 | 4 in number | 56 | 7 | 283 | 4 in number |
| World , excl. socialist countries | 3283 | 37 in number | 2842 | 160 | 6089 | 62 in number |
| African share (%) | 5.5 | - | 2 | | 4.6 | |

Source: ECA, 1991, *Development of Lead and Zinc Resources in Africa*, NRD/MRU/TP/1/91, Addis Ababa (originally from The Lead and Zinc Industries, World Bank Staff Commodity Working Paper No. 22, 1990)

ANNEX 14.17
PRODUCTION AND CONSUMPTION OF REFINED LEAD AND ZINC SLAB IN THE AFRICAN CONTINENT IN THE 1980S
(1000 t)

| | 1980 | 1981 | 1982 | 1983 | 1984 | 1985 | 1986 | 1987 | 1988 | 1989 | 1990 |
|---|---|---|---|---|---|---|---|---|---|---|---|
| Lead, refined | | | | | | | | | | | |
| Production | 157 | 156 | 167 | 148 | 126 | 155 | 144 | 160 | 169 | 162 | 150 |
| Exports | 53 | 65 | 100 | 94 | 63 | 74 | 73 | 85 | 50 | 63 | |
| Consumption | 102 | 94 | 100 | 95 | 84 | 98 | 104 | 109 | 111 | 116 | 111 |
| Zinc slab | | | | | | | | | | | |
| Production | 183 | 199 | 212 | 214 | 221 | 218 | 194 | 190 | 186 | 180 | 162 |
| Exports | 50 | 103 | 96 | 106 | 78 | 88 | 95 | 71 | 81 | 69 | 47 |
| Consumption | 144 | 156 | 165 | 146 | 151 | 142 | 146 | 147 | 155 | 167 | 157 |

Source: Based on ECA, 1991, *Development of Lead and Zinc Resources in Africa*, NRD/MRU/TP/1/91, Addis Ababa ( originally obtained from World Bureau of Metal Statistics).

ANNEX 15. 1
EXAMPLES OF CONSTRAINTS FACED BY MULTINATIONAL INDUSTRIAL PROJECTS IN AFRICA

| 1- Name of the enterprise /plant 2- Host country 3- Products made by the plant 4- Ownership of the enterprise/ plant | 1- Ciments de l'Afrique de l'Ouest (CIMAO) 2- Togo 3- Clinker 4- Togo, Cote d'Ivoire and Ghana | 1- Industries Chimiques du Senegal (ICS) 2- Senegal 3- Phosphoric acid and fertilizers 4- Senegal, Nigeria, Cameroon, Cote d'Ivoire and India | 1- Save Sugar Project (SSS) 2- Benin 3- Sugar | 1- Société des Ciments d' Onigbolo (SCO) 2- Benin 3- Cement 4- Benin (49%), , Nigeria (43%) and F. L. Smith & Co. of Denmark (6%) | 1- Misr Iranian Textile Company (MIRATEX 2- Egypt 3- Yarn 4- Egypt and Iran | 1- Kuwaiti-Egyptian Shoe Factory 2- Egypt 3- Shoes 4- Egypt and Kuwait (Bally Co. of Switzerland supplied plant on turnkey basis) |
|---|---|---|---|---|---|---|
| Project concept and design | | | | | | |
| Inadequate project preparation and conflict of interest | Engineering firm was producing and marketing cement in West Africa and involved in manufacturing cement equipment | | | Bottlenecks in infrastructure, no market arrangements with Nigeria | | Turnkey plant supplier (Bally Co. of Switzerland manufactures and exports shoes) |

| Wrong assumptions regarding market and prices | Market and price projection s proved optimistic. Clinker produced at $66 could not compete with $32 clinker from Europe | International demand and therefore prices of products fell from $600 to below $300 at start of operation . | Price of sugar fell from $600 to $270 when the plant started operation | | | |
|---|---|---|---|---|---|---|
| Wrong or incomplete designs and technical problems | Kiln designed on expensive fuel oil when European kilns were converting to coal, Frequent break downs and repairs | Nominal capacities halved mainly because of acid linkage and frequent boiler breakdown | Low productivity mainly attributed to types of soils and quality of sugar cane planted | Missing infra-structure limiting maximum capacity utilization to 33% | | |
| Weakness in foreign technical and project implementation supervision | Over design and design changes proposed by supplier involving 75% cost overruns implemented without the approval of board | | | | Did not require engineering and foreign managerial assistance | |
| Weakness on the part of partners | Difficulty in holding board meetings and lack of owner/operator monitoring | Difficulty in holding board meetings and lack of owner/operator monitoring | Difficulty in holding board meetings and lack of owner/operator monitoring | | | |
| Under capitalization (low equity ratio) | 20% equity capital | 25% equity capital | Less than 20% equity capital | Less than 20% equity capital | | |
| Problems of mobilization and coordinating multinational financing arrangements | Project preparation and financing took 8 years and implementation 4 years, resulting in doubling investment cost | Organizing and co- ordinating over 13 governments and financing institutions was complex and time consuming | | | | |
| Problems in plant operations | | | | | | |
| Reliance on foreign management | Poor financial records, no financial statements after 1980, conflict of interest, etc. | Engaged foreign managing agency | Engaged foreign managing agency | Engaged foreign managing agency | No problems experienced because of local managerial and technical capabilities | Failure attributed mainly to lack of managerial and technical capabilities of promoters |
| Marketing and pricing problems | Failed to realize competitive business spirits | Failed to realize competitive business spirits | Failed to realize competitive business spirits | Failed to realize competitive business spirits | | Failed to realize competitive business spirits |
| High cost of production | High depreciation and interest, expensive infrastructure, excessive management fees, shortage and expensive electric power, etc. | High depreciation and interest, expensive infrastructure, high labor cost, heavy management fees, expensive utilities, etc. | High depreciation and interest, expensive infrastructure, high management fees, no cost accounting undertaken, etc. | High depreciation and interest, expensive infrastructure, high management fees, etc. | | |
| Delays in financing restructuring | Inaccessibility to loans and delay in restructuring resulted in closing the plant | Restructuring by host country with assistance from ADB saved the plant from closing | Inaccessibility to loans and delay in restructuring resulted in closing the plant | | | |
| Failure of member states to honor agreements regard- ing the purchase of products | High prices of cement | Availability of products under commodity aid and soft loans | Imposition of custom duties and timely availability of foreign exchange | Imposition of custom duties and timely availability of foreign exchange | | |

Source: Compiled from ECA, *Sustainable Financing of Selected Industrial Development Decade Multinational Industrial Projects in African Subregions* (ECA/IHSD/IPPS/008/92), Addis Ababa.

| | | ANNEX 15.2 | | |
|---|---|---|---|---|
| | | TYPES OF ASSISTANCE AND MAJOR PROVIDERS | | |
| Areas requiring assistance | Specific areas of assistance | | | Assistance providers |
| | | Information | | |
| Data and information | Economical, technical, managerial, etc. | | | World networks, United Nations and its agencies, R&D institutions, firms, etc. |
| | | Project related activities | | |
| 1. Pre-investment studies and activities | 1.1 Preparation of pre-feasibility studies | | | 1.1 Consulting firms, UNDP, UNIDO |
| | 1.2 Preparation of support studies | | | 1.2 Consulting firms, UNDP, UNIDO |
| | 1.3 Preparation of feasibility studies | | | 1.3 Consulting firms, UNDP, UNIDO |
| | 1.4 Preparation of Engineering | | | 1.4 Consulting firms, UNDP, UNIDO |
| | 1.5 Undertaking field work related to raw materials, energy, transport, etc. | | | 1.5 Geological institution and consulting firms specialized in transport, etc. |
| 2. Industrial negotiation | 2.1 Technology | | | 2.1 Consulting firms, UNIDO |
| | 2.2 Commercial | | | 2.2 Consulting firms, UNCTC, UNIDO |
| | 2.3 Legal | | | 2.3 Consulting firms, UNCTC, UNIDO |
| 3. Bids/tenders | 3.1 Preparation | | | 3.1 Consulting firms, UNIDO |
| | 3.2 Evaluation | | | 3.2 Consulting firms, UNIDO |
| | | Plant related activities | | |
| 1. Procurement of plant and related inputs | 1.1 Identification of suppliers | | | 1.1 Consulting firms, UNIDO |
| | 1.2 Evaluation of goods to be procured | | | 1.2 Consulting firms, UNIDO |
| | 1.3 Inspection of goods before loading | | | 1.3 Consulting firms, UNIDO |
| 2. Commissioning and operating plants | 2.1 Undertaking activities related to plant start-up | | | 2.1 Consulting firms |
| | 2.2 Undertaking activities related to plant operation | | | 2.2 Consulting firms |
| 3. Maintenance | 3.1 Preparing planned maintenance system | | | 3.1 Consulting firms |
| | 3.2 Introducing planned maintenance system | | | 3.2 Consulting firms |
| | 3.3 Application of planned maintenance system | | | 3.3 Consulting firms |
| | 3.4 Introducing inventory system | | | 3.4 Consulting firms |
| 4. Assessment of plant operation | 4.1 Technical | | | 4.1 Consulting firms |
| | 4.2 Managerial | | | 4.2 Consulting firms |
| | 4.3 Commercial | | | 4.3 Consulting firms |
| | 4.4 Financial | | | 4.4 Consulting firms |
| 5. Diagnosis | 5.1 Establishing need for diagnosis | | | 5.1 Consulting firms |
| | 5.2 Undertaking diagnostic study | | | 5.2 Consulting firms |
| 6. Introducing changes | 6.1 Rehabilitation | | | 6.1 Consultant firms |
| | 6.2 Modernization | | | 6.2 Consultant firms |
| | 6.3 Diversification | | | 6.3 Consultant firms |
| | 6.4 Integration | | | 6.4 Consultant firms |
| | | Technology | | |
| 1. Acquisition | 1.1 Identification of sources of technology | | | 1.1 Consultant firms |
| | 1.2 Selection | | | 1.2 Consultant firms |
| | 1.3 Negotiation | | | 1.3 Consultant firms |

505

| ANNEX 15.3 SOME FINANCIAL INSTITUTIONS AND DONORS ACCESSIBLE TO AFRICAN COUNTRIES | |
|---|---|
| 1- National commercial and development banks, investmentcorporations, and subsidiary foreign commercial banks | |
| 2- Subregional sources of finance | . Caisse Francaise de Developpement (CFD) |
| . Banque Ouest-Africaine de Developpement (BOAD) | . CIDA of Canada |
| . Fonds de Solidarite et d'Intervantion pour le Developpement de la Communaute (FOSIDEC) | . KFW of Germany |
| . Fonds pour le Develeppoment de la Communaute (FCD) | . Swedfund for Industrial Cooperation |
| . ECOWAS Fund | . Danish Industrialization Fund |
| . East African Development Bank (EADB) | . FOM of Netherlands |
| . Inter-Arab Manufacturing Joint Venture (IAJV) | . NORAD |
| . PTA Bank | . Abu Dabbi Fund |
| . Banque de Develeppoment des Etats de l'Afrique Centrale (BDEAC) | . Kuwait Fund |
| . Banque de Developpement des Etats de Grands Lacs (BDEGL) | . Saudi Fund |
| . Banque Centrale des Etats de l'Afrique de l/Ouest (BCEAO) | . SBI of Belgium |
| . Ecobank | . Overseas Private Investment Corporation (OPIC) of USA |
| . Arab Fund for Economic and Social Development (AFESD) | . Mondimpresa of Italy |
| . Arab Industrial Investment Company (AIIC) | . CCCE of France |
| . Inter-Arab Manufacturing Joint Venture (IAMJV) | 6- International grants and technical assistance |
| 3- Regional sources of finance | . UNDP-IPF |
| . African Development Bank (ADB) and its group | . United Nations Capital Development Fund (UNCDF) |
| - African Development Fund (ADF) | . Other UN bodies and agencies: UNIDO, FAO, ILO, WHO, UNESCO, etc. |
| - Nigerian Trust Fund | 7- Multilateral grants and technical assistance |
| . Arab Bank for Economic Development in Africa (BADEA) | . European Development Fund (EDF) |
| . African Project Development Facility (APDF) | . Centre for the Development of Industry (CDI) of EU |
| | . European Investment Bank (EIB) |
| 4- Bilateral grants and technical assistance | . Rehabilitation Advisory Services (ARS) of EU and DEG |
| . CIDA of Canada | . Common Wealth Development Fund |
| . DANIDA of Denmark | 8- Loans from international institutions |
| . KFW of Germany | . International Bank for Reconstruction and Development (IBRD) and its affiliates |
| . ODA of United Kingdom | - International Development Association (IDA) |

| | |
|---|---|
| . AID of France | - International Finance Corporation (IFC) |
| . NORAD of Norway | . International Monetary Fund (IMF) |
| . FINIDA of Finland | . European Investment Bank (EIB) |
| . SIDA of Sweden | |
| . AID of Netherlands | . OPEC Fund |
| . USAID of USA | . Nordic Investment Bank |
| | . Islamic Development Bank |
| 5- Bilateral sources of loans | 9- Foreign direct private investment (FDPI) |
| . Common Wealth Development Corporation (CDC) of United Kingdom | 10- Suppliers/export credit, lease-purchase, debt equity swaps, etc. |
| | 11. Others: hire- or lease-purchase, floating bonds, stocks and shares, debt equity swaps, etc. |

Source: Compiled mainly from:
- ECA, 1992, *Sustainable Financing of Selected Second Industrial Development Decade Multinational Industrial Projects in African Subregions,* Addis Ababa.
- ECA, 1993, *Promotion of Investment in Industrial Projects in the Context of the Second Industrial Development Decade for Africa* (ECA/IHSD/IPPIS/029/93), Addis Ababa.

# INDEX

ACP 61

ADB 9, 29, 31, 36, 39, 41-44, 47, 55, 60, 62, 64, 67, 69, 71, 74-75, 95, 106, 109, 234, 247, 260

Adoption 18, 52, 61-62, 68-69, 232, 257

AEC 17, 32, 70, 71-72, 76-78

African Economic Community 66-68, 70, 76-77, 106, 210, 382, 388

African leaders 12, 14, 17, 19, 22-33, 136

African soils 87, 207, 263-264, 270, 292

Agricultural chemicals 208, 263-264, 270, 274, 281, 283, 352

agricultural equipment 1, 118, 208, 283, 286, 291, 292, 294, 297

Agricultural implements 122, 289-292, 296, 361

agricultural machinery 291-293, 295-298

agricultural processing 113, 299, 307, 381

Agricultural Tools 10, 85, 200, 207, 286, 288-292, 297-298, 320, 332, 361

Agro-industry 195, 211, 301, 307, 329, 332, 360

Algeria 4, 8-9, 12, 15, 20, 49, 94, 96-97, 101, 103, 121-122, 129, 162, 168, 171, 187, 203, 237-238, 246, 255, 257, 267, 269-270, 277, 290, 293, 295, 324, 330, 332, 339, 344-346, 348-349, 364, 374

alternative technologies 217

Aluminium 353, 354

AMU 55, 71

Angola 4, 9, 12, 16-17, 35, 37, 39, 60, 78, 91, 94, 96-99, 103

animal feed 228, 232-233, 274, 304, 306, 360

animal traction 48, 207, 283, 288-289

appropriate products 213, 215

appropriate technologies 163, 215, 221-222, 252, 326

Aquatic Resources 89

archaeological 7, 9, 10

artisanal blacksmith 288

ASEAN 75, 139, 278, 281

assembled 293, 295, 313, 314

assemblies 119, 215, 295-296, 314, 319, 367

assembly 66-67, 117-118, 122, 137, 148, 170-171, 186, 192-193, 202, 215, 275, 293, 295, 314-316, 319,-320, 334, 338, 358, 365-367

balance of payments 68

balkanization 14

basic chemicals 2, 109, 209, 280, 352-353

basic metals 2, 163, 209, 341, 344, 349

basic needs 1, 3, 60, 67, 155, 181-182, 186, 198, 201, 205, 208, 210, 213, 215, 225, 227, 258, 321, 325, 334, 351-352

battles 12, 33

bauxite 57, 94-96, 142, 329, 346, 348, 351-352

Benin 4, 9, 19, 60, 97, 101, 103, 149, 177, 191, 284, 286, 290, 308, 364, 376

beverages 47, 55, 117, 121, 125, 130, 162, 185, 210, 227, 259, 332

bioclimatic regions 81